CONGRESS: STRUCTURE AND POLICY

POLITICAL ECONOMY OF INSTITUTIONS AND DECISIONS

editors:
Professor James E. Alt, Washington University
Professor Douglass C. North, Washington University

CONGRESS: STRUCTURE AND POLICY

Edited by

MATHEW D. McCUBBINS
TERRY SULLIVAN

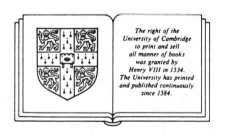

The right of the
University of Cambridge
to print and sell
all manner of books
was granted by
Henry VIII in 1534.
The University has printed
and published continuously
since 1584.

CAMBRIDGE UNIVERSITY PRESS

Cambridge

New York   New Rochelle   Melbourne   Sydney

Published by the Press Syndicate of the University of Cambridge
The Pitt Building, Trumpington Street, Cambridge CB2 1RP
32 East 57th Street, New York, NY 10022, USA
10 Stamford Road, Oakleigh, Melbourne 3166, Australia

First Published 1987
Reprinted 1988

Printed in the United States of America

Library of Congress Cataloging-in-Publication Data
Congress: structure and policy.
(Political economy of institutions and decisions)
Includes index.
1. United States. Congress. I. McCubbins, Mathew D.
(Mathew Daniel), 1956–   . II. Sullivan, Terry
(Terry O.) III. Series.
JK1061.C588   1987   328.73   86-28372

British Library Cataloguing in Publication Data
Congress: structure and policy.
(Political economy of institutions and
decisions)
1. United States – Congress
I. McCubbins, Mathew D. II. Sullivan,
Terry III. Series
328.73   JK1061

ISBN 0 521 33169 2 hard covers
ISBN 0 521 33750 X paperback

To H. W. and Gertrude McCubbins and
Elizabeth Doremus and Melissa Manning

Contents

Contents

Series editors' preface

The Cambridge Series on the Political Economy of Institutions and Decisions is built around attempts to answer two central questions: How do institutions evolve in response to individual incentives, strategies, and choices; and how do institutions affect the performance of political and economic systems? The scope of the series is comparative and historical rather than international or specifically American, and the focus is positive rather than normative.

The work collected in this volume demonstrates how economic and political outcomes reflect choices constrained by institutions while also explaining why and how, in view of the outcomes, such institutions should have developed. Institutions are taken broadly to include constraints on and prescriptions for individual actions, including both formal rules and procedures and informal norms. The particular institution studied is the American Congress, but much of the theoretical work applies to other legislatures as well. Thus, the concern with the impact of structure on strategy begins with representation, including both desire for reelection and interest in legislative policy content. It focuses particularly on the development of informal universalistic and reciprocal arrangements as well as election strategies, committee assignments and powers, party organization, and congressional and presidential leadership. Later chapters provide a theoretical understanding of the origins and institutional constraints on the choices of individual congressmen. These chapters detail the impact of broader institutional structure on the internal conduct of business and thus on agendas and outcomes. This theoretical structure permits systematic reasoning about legislative preferences for particular types of policy outcomes like the decision to regulate, choice of regulatory forms, actions by regulatory agencies, and budgeting and location decisions.

Thus, the political economy perspective of the papers in this volume offers a comprehensive and systematic view of the evolving relationships among public policy outcomes, the aspirations of legislators, and the procedures, norms, and formal structures of legislative institutions.

Preface

We began this book because we wished to describe an emerging paradigm in congressional studies. This paradigm has as its central focus the study of institutions and the way institutions shape the collective choices of government. The best way to describe this new paradigm is not to *talk* about what Congress scholars *ought* to do but rather to show what they have already *done* in this vein. We hope that the inclusion of this material in one place will make it obvious that there is indeed a collected and coherent body of work on Congress.

Of course, the development of "institutional" theories is not new in political science, nor is it a new idea in American thought. The saga of the American revolutions is a story of institutional theory and design at work. Its continuity with America's past and political science is one of the most alluring aspects of the work that we have brought together here.

Many people contributed to the development of this volume. We asked some of our colleagues for original works. We hoped that their contributions would bridge the gap between the completed research and ongoing efforts. At the same time, we wanted to insure that these contributors had every opportunity to receive the kinds of assistance in their writing that they would normally receive in the course of scholarly publication. With this in mind, we decided upon a commitment to blind peer review of all of the original material in the reader. Each of the original papers was submitted to the same rigors that articles receive when they have been submitted to a journal. We are convinced that these contributions received a much stronger evaluation through our process than they might have received had the authors actually submitted them to journals of their choosing (indeed, we rejected several articles), because in the process of preparing this volume we were aided by a wonderful crew of referees. We acknowledge their support and assistance first and foremost. They are Joel Aberbach, James Alt, Bruce Cain, Gary Cox, John Ferejohn, Rodney Fort, Thomas Hammond, Roderick Kiewiet,

Preface

Roger Noll, Douglass North, Peter Ordeshook, Benjamin Page, Kenneth Shepsle, Richard Smith, and Barry Weingast. We also owe a debt to two reviewers who gave us some excellent advice when we first began to explore this volume with publishers. They are David Mayhew and Gary Jacobson.

Several people assisted us along the way in the production of this reader. They are Kenneth Collier, Nancy Aurora, Betty McKuen, Michael Hargrove, Brenda Hollada, and Lisa Marguis at the University of Texas. At Carnegie-Mellon University, we received help from Alberta Ragan, Stephanie Stang, and Joy Lee. David Fallek assisted us at Stanford University. At Washington University, we were assisted by James Alt and Barry Weingast.

Over the three years that we took to prepare this volume, we also received institutional support from the University Research Institute, University of Texas at Austin; the Business School and Center in Political Economy, Washington University; and the Center for the Study of Public Policy, Graduate School of Industrial Administration, Carnegie-Mellon University. We are very grateful to all of these. We also would like to acknowledge the staff and editors of the Cambridge University Press. In particular, we greatly appreciate the support of the editors of the Series on the Political Economy of Institutions and Decisions, James Alt and Douglass North. Of course, the results of research published in this volume are not the responsibility of the individuals or organizations here acknowledged.

Research, like any other obsession, takes us away from home and families too often. Though it is customary to thank one's family, the thanks are no less sincere. For those who have worked with us through this and many other projects: Susan Quon McCubbins and Colin McCubbins and Elizabeth Doremus and Melissa Manning.

Mathew McCubbins
Terry Sullivan

Introduction:
institutional aspects of decision processes

To form a new Government requires infinite care and unbounded attention, for if the foundation is badly laid, the superstructure must be bad.... A matter of such moment cannot be the work of a day.

> George Washington to John Washington, May 31, 1776

The purpose of this book is to study decision making in an institutional context. All of the selections presented here have a common theme: they approach the study of congressional behavior from the standpoint that the "structure" of decision making matters. The selections, of course, focus on different aspects of congressional institutions. Some are concerned with how the broader constitutional structure of representation affects governmental decision making. Some are concerned with the influence that internal rules of procedure have on policy outcomes. Others choose to examine the organizational aspects of congressional activity and inquire as to why such organization is adopted and why it persists. Together, however, they form a comprehensive view of congressional politics.

In America the study of institutions has an impressive history and tradition. The political debates surrounding the American Revolution and the Constitutional Convention involved richly woven institutional theories about the appropriate forms of representation. These theories were embodied in the new state constitutions and the Articles of Confederation. The country's experience under the Articles, however, aroused further debate about the nature of institutional forms. Many feared that the original state constitutions in conjunction with the Articles were somehow not matched to the true nature of republican politics and, more importantly, of politicians. Indeed, popularly elected legislators passed laws that confiscated property arbitrarily, debased state currencies, suspended debts, undermined the credit of the governments, and otherwise impeded commerce between states. Moreover, the

1

legislatures changed so rapidly that few policies were ever stable. One legislator complained: "The revised laws have been altered – realtered – made better – made worse; and kept in such a fluctuating position, that persons in civil commission scarce know what is law."[1]

To the founding fathers, the solution to the ills of the "republican monarchy" established by the Articles was to create a new institutional structure. The ratification of the new U.S. Constitution, however, engendered further debate over the nature of institutions and the effects of structure on governmental decisions. *The Federalist* papers, of course, can be read as an elaborate theoretical defense of the Constitutional Convention's structural selections.

A SCIENCE OF POLITICS: INSTITUTIONAL DESIGN

The independence of America considered merely as a separation from England, would have been a matter but of little importance had it not been accompanied by a revolution in the principles and practise [sic] of governments.

Thomas Paine, *Rights of Man*

To what expedient, then, shall we finally resort, for maintaining in practice the necessary partition of power among the several departments as laid down in the Constitution? The only answer that can be given is...by so contriving the interior structure of the government as that its several constituent parts may, by their mutual relations, be the means of keeping each other in their proper places. Without presuming to undertake a full development of this important idea, I will hazard a few general observations which may perhaps place it in a clearer light, and enable us to form a more correct judgment of the principles and structure of the government planned by the convention.

James Madison, *Federalist*, no. 51

The Constitutional Convention was preceded by an era of intense debate, which formed a new conception of politics and political theory. The Constitution's founders conceived of an institutional system driven by the competition of individual ambitions. Institutional design in the Constitution was intended to channel these ambitions and enmesh them in a *system* of "checks and balances." Adhering to this constitutional "structuring principle," the founders created an institutional setting that induced cooperation by permitting no single branch of government to have enough of the tools necessary to carry out policy by itself. Within Congress, this principle was particularly important: Members of one house were required not only to share power with the executive but to share it with those of the "other body" as well. Eventually, individual ambitions fostered a set of procedural reforms intended to decentralize decision making, which did in fact further emphasize cooperation. The founders consciously designed an institutional structure that inescapably

2

linked together the branches of government, the internal procedures of those branches, the ambitions of the membership of those branches, and the policies that are their product.

This dynamic of individual ambitions and institutional checks and balances still functions today, long after the initial historical conditions that fostered them have receded. It is possible that the principle of checks and balances has been so enduring because it focused not so much on the nature of interests (although the most celebrated *Federalist* – number 10 – was partially concerned with just that issue) as on the nature of institutional settings and structures.

This book brings together literature from many different schools in political science. The study of institutional design has much to learn from each of them. The development of what Alexander Hamilton referred to as a science of politics (*Federalist*, no. 1) requires a synthesis of the various schools in political science. In particular, we explore two topics originating in the Constitutional Convention and of great importance today: the nature of representation, and the impact of organizations and procedures on political choice.

STRUCTURE OF THIS BOOK

The natural question to begin our inquiry and perhaps the most difficult to answer is: What are institutions? The difficulty is that institutions not only provide the structure for policy choices but are themselves in turn often amended by these very choices. It is difficult, then, to distinguish choices of policy, strategy, or behavior from choices of institutions. Though we may be able to agree on what constitutes an institution "when we see one," general definitions that meaningfully differentiate between routinized behavior and institutional structure are elusive. The definition we adopt, though it does not provide a sharp differentiation, is that institutions are the rules of the game that constrain individual choices and provide incentives for individual action. This definition provides us with some analytic leverage.

Part I is concerned with republican institutions and how these institutions affect the behavior of congressmen. In the context of our definition of institutions, we can say that different institutions lead to different patterns of individual behavior. The patterns of behavior that result from the particular form of geographical representation established by the Constitution are the topic of Part I.

Institutions, however, are not handed down on stone tablets; rather, they are choices made explicitly to govern the process of policy choice. The Constitution was created by the Constitutional Convention and ratified by the several states. Indeed, the Constitution was designed to

3

replace a previous institutional choice, the Articles of Confederation. But neither is institutional structure exclusively derived from the Constitution. The Constitution creates the superstructure of the legislature and its external setting of *inter*institutional relationships. Politicians are left to determine the details of the internal workings of the legislature. Part II presents a selection of articles that examine some institutional innovations and organizational arrangements that have evolved in response to incentives and constraints provided in the Constitution.

A new and exciting theoretical literature in political science suggests that choices in pure majority-rule situations are unstable. However, what we learn in studying congressional behavior is that there is a stability to the policies chosen and the organizations adopted: These choices are not continually overturned by ever-changing majority coalitions. We can conclude, then, that something about congressional institutions makes them different from pure majority rule. Part III considers how institutions may serve to constrain and channel collective choices, and how institutions may provide a stability to politics.

The Constitution created a system wherein power over policy making is shared by Congress and the executive. An important institutional innovation in response to this separation of powers has been the creation of a vast executive bureaucracy that not only administers and executes the laws passed by Congress but actually makes law on a wide variety of important issues. Congress, in delegating its lawmaking authority, designs institutional arrangements that enable it to influence and organize bureaucratic decision making. These institutional arrangements constitute an important set of structural choices by Congress. Part IV analyzes the structural choices involved in delegating authority – how these choices constrain and channel the behavior of bureaucrats, and how they ultimately affect policy choices.

THE NEW INSTITUTIONALISM

Politics is studied in a wide variety of ways. Since each scholar analyzes only a small part of the political process, and since the boundaries between these parts are not well defined, an overview of the discipline often looks like a patchwork quilt. The study of legislatures is a microcosm of this phenomenon. But we believe this work can be integrated and that the various subdisciplines can be woven into a uniform, if somewhat lumpy, piece of cloth. Though the authors of the articles in this book employ different technologies to address their problems, we can learn from each and integrate their lessons into a wider picture of politics. The remainder of this introduction outlines an approach to this integration.

Institutional aspects of decision processes

An approach to the study of institutional choice

The founding fathers analyzed the effect on behavior and policy of alternative institutional arrangements in order to choose among them. Modern scholars study the same topic in order fully to appreciate how our government functions. The debate and analysis surrounding many of the choices made at the Constitutional Convention are well documented. But most of the structure we observe in society was not chosen in an open forum or debated publicly in the newspaper. All but a few such institutional arrangements evolved through practice and slowly took on the form they have today.

Much of the theory of institutional choice and evolution has emerged in the last ten years, though its beginnings of course are much older. Many of the articles in this volume have their roots in the institutional analyses of Woodrow Wilson, George Brown, Robert Luce, Lauros McConachie, Paul Hasbrouck, and especially Alexander Hamilton, John Jay, and James Madison. The research approach of the "new institutionalism" has its origins in the pioneering work of Ronald Coase (1937). Coase recognized that an understanding of actions requires an appreciation of the institutional context in which such actions take place. Though his focus was limited to economic institutions, Coase raised a question fundamental to the study of institutions: Why do these organizations exist? In particular, why do economic agents coordinate their decisions via central authority rather than rely upon the automatic coordination provided by the market? These questions have parallels in the study of Congress: Why do committees exist? Why do members coordinate their decisions via a committee system rather than rely upon majority-rule voting on the floor of Congress?

Coase noticed that complex production processes involve numerous transactions (e.g., exchanges) among owners of land, labor, capital, and other specialized inputs, and that these transactions are costly. The owners of these inputs, in producing some product, will seek to minimize their costs. Coase argues that the costs of transacting can be reduced by shifting from the market-exchange relationships between input owners to a nonmarket arrangement that provides centralized planning and the hierarchical division of production. The driving force behind the emergence of the firm, then, is efficiency (i.e., the firm's ability to minimize the costs of production). Input owners substitute authority relations for market relations in order to reduce transactions costs and thereby promote their own goals more effectively.

A necessary condition for the emergence of firms in this view is the existence of transactions costs. The firm will expand its activities to the point where the costs of an additional transaction within the firm equal

5

the costs of the same transaction in the market. In equilibrium, some transactions will be internalized by firms whereas others will be external.

Although Coase focused on the firm, the approach he employed is useful in studying all institutions. Indeed, the common thread tying the analyses of congressional institutions in this volume to the larger study of institutions in general is the approach of studying how institutions enable members within them to pursue their goals effectively.

In another important study of institutions, Armen Alchian and Harold Demsetz (1972) define a particular type of transactions cost and argue that firms reduce these special transactions costs better than do markets. Input owners can produce more by cooperating than by producing separately and exchanging their produce in the market. Input owners, then, prefer to coordinate their actions. Coordinated or team production introduces many problems. Teams produce a single output. But, since coordination has been substituted for independent action, it is difficult within the team to determine the contribution of any individual to the team's output. Obviously, each individual's efforts will have some impact on the team's profits, but their individual rewards are only weakly related to their efforts; and although they individually bear the full costs of their own efforts they individually receive only a part of what their efforts produce. On the other hand, when individuals shirk (i.e., engage in any form of nonproductive activity) by reducing their effort, the savings in effort accrue only to them; the resulting losses in team production are borne largely by the other team members. It is, then, in each member's own interest to shirk.

Alchian and Demsetz notice that even though the team members may realize their actions are suboptimal they cannot by themselves solve the problem. They argue that the way to mitigate shirking is to monitor the efforts of team members. Teams could be made better off by hiring a monitor and giving the monitor the authority to adjust payments on the basis of information with respect to productivity. But, because the monitor will also have an incentive to shirk, the team will give him marketable title to the team's production and establish him as the central contacting agent. In other words, the team will organize itself into a firm.

Again, the particular institutions studied by Alchian and Demsetz are not as important as the approach they use and the types of problems they discuss. The approach of comparing institutions with respect to how well they enable members to pursue their goals is useful in studying both congressional committees and firms. Problems of monitoring and shirking are evident in legislatures as well as firms; transactions costs are incurred in building coalitions (e.g., contacting and bargaining with the members of the coalition take time, effort, and other resources).

Institutional aspects of decision processes

Though not of the Coase school, Morris Fiorina uses this approach in Part I to answer the question, "Why have the number of marginal congressional seats declined?" His approach is institutional: members of Congress adopt institutional arrangements that facilitate their reelection. In part, Fiorina argues that members have established the federal bureaucracy in order to increase their casework opportunities and decrease the likelihood of their sharing blame for policy choices.

In Part II, Barry Weingast uses this approach to study an institutional arrangement in Congress, the norm of universalism. Weingast argues that members prefer a rule requiring that money for projects be shared universally among the members to a system of pure majority-rule decision making.

Mathew McCubbins and Talbot Page, in Part IV, examine the consequences of information problems and conflict of interest for the delegation of legislative authority to the federal bureaucracy. They explore the structural devices Congress employs to control the bureaucratic choice of policy when faced with these consequences. In a related chapter, also in Part IV, Mathew McCubbins and Thomas Schwartz argue that in overseeing bureaucratic activity Congress will prefer a decentralized oversight system – what they term a fire-alarm system – to one that is more centralized. The key to their argument, like that of Coase and of Alchian and Demsetz, is that a fire-alarm system is more effective in reducing costs for members of Congress than a more centralized system.

Also in Part IV, John Ferejohn postulates a "structuring principle" for administrative agencies. The structuring principle he offers provides insight into how agencies structure their decision procedures in response to their political environment. Roger Noll takes a broad view of congressional-bureaucratic relations in examining the structure of administrative procedure. He argues that certain structural choices in promulgating regulatory policy are the result of incentives in the system of government created by the Constitution. The structure of the regulatory process will be a microcosm of the American national government; geographically based special interests will have their influence designed into the process; interests that are not usually represented in the electoral arena will not be enfranchised in the regulatory process.

How institutions work

In choosing a constitutional system, our founding fathers analyzed the effect of alternative institutional features on the behavior of individuals and then attempted to predict the form of the policies that would emerge

7

from alternative institutional systems. In part, such predictions depend upon an analysis of the types of rules and organizations members of Congress adopt in attempting to govern within the boundaries defined by the Constitution. The general theme of the works in this volume, like that of most modern studies of institutions, is that institutions are designed to enable members to pursue their goals effectively.

David Mayhew in Part I studies the effect of the constitutional requirement of frequent elections on the behavior and strategies of members of Congress. He further suggests that the election-seeking behavior of members leads to an overemphasis on distributive (i.e., pork barrel) policies by Congress. Richard Fenno, in Part II, examines how different committees induce divergent patterns of behavior. In addition, he argues that the collective choice processes of each committee lead to different strategies for proposing legislation on the floor of the House. In a related chapter in Part II, Charles Jones examines how the demands and constraints of party leadership in Congress shape the behavior of congressional leaders. More importantly, he analyzes two examples where members changed the rules and organization of Congress in order to maintain control of their leaders. Also in Part II, David Rohde and Kenneth Shepsle explore how the tugs and pulls of institutional requirements even affect the way members are assigned to committees.

The conclusions to be drawn from these articles are that members pursue reelection and that they structure the collective choice process in Congress to facilitate this goal. These in turn imply that members should be increasingly successful at competing for election. This is the point of Morris Fiorina's article in Part I. This argument further suggests that representative institutions become less representative over time as members better insulate themselves from competition. On the other hand, Gary Jacobson (Part I) argues that inventive challengers will find effective means of using these very structures to their advantage. He shows that even though members are winning reelection by larger margins, these larger margins carry with them less electoral safety than they previously did.

Institutions, and the behavior they instill in members, influence the policy choices of the legislature as well. Thomas Schwartz, Kenneth Shepsle, and Keith Krehbiel in Part III review three decades of research on the properties of majority-rule institutions and suggest how some common structural arrangements in legislatures impart stability to legislative choices. In Part IV, Randall Calvert, Mark Moran, and Barry Weingast, as well as Douglas Arnold analyze the influence of the committee system on bureaucratic decision making. They argue that, since committees play a central role in congressional decision making and Congress a similar role in controlling the bureaucracy, committees should play a central role in influencing bureaucratic decisions as well.

In a broader examination of the congressional system, Terry Sullivan, in Part II, examines the ability of the president to affect congressional policy choices. He suggests that the president's constitutionally defined powers to influence Congress are rather limited (constrained to the use of a qualified veto). He further argues that institutional evolution in Congress has left his informal powers impotent as well.

Institutional evolution

This revolution principle – that, the sovereign power residing in the people, they may change their constitution and government whenever they please – is not a principle of discord, rancor, or war: it is a principle of melioration, contentment, and peace.   James Wilson, *Lectures on Law*

If the theme of the "new institutionalism" is that basic institutions matter in politics, then how those institutions change over time is of fundamental importance. Theories about institutional evolution should be extensions of theories about how institutions work and theories of institutional choice. Yet, theories about institutional evolution are scarce indeed. Probably the best is contained in a paper by Alchian (1950). Alchian argues that because of uncertainty and costly information, institutions can be designed only imperfectly to serve desired ends. In part they evolve through trial and error: those better suited to the current environment survive and are imitated. Those that are not fit enough or those incapable of responding to changing environmental conditions fail. Thus, an observed uniformity among the surviving institutional arrangements is derived from "An evolutionary, adoptive, competitive system employing a criterion of survival" (p. 31). Alchian's approach posits a "natural selection" among institutional forms: Evolution takes place as institutional innovations, chosen in response to changing environmental conditions, compete for survival.

Three chapters in Part II of this volume deal with the evolution of institutional features in Congress. Nelson Polsby chronicles the changing institutional features of the House of Representatives and speculates on the conditions that led to these changes. David Brady, Joseph Cooper, and Patricia Hurley analyze the evolution of the party system in the House. David Brady and Mark Morgan explore the evolution of the appropriations process. In each of these chapters, institutional change is related to exogenous forces – changes in the environment – to which individuals in an institutional setting – the House of Representatives – must respond in order to survive as members.

Introduction

A FEW WORDS ABOUT THE ORGANIZATION OF THIS BOOK

This book is organized around the questions outlined in the beginning of this introduction. Part I is concerned with how institutions affect individual behavior. Part II examines the institutional innovations in Congress that organize the business of legislating. Part III studies the effect institutions have on policy choices. And Part IV considers the institutional choices made by Congress to control the execution of delegated authority.

Some of the chapters in Parts II and III contain technical materials. In each case we give a simplified discussion of the technical arguments in our introduction to the chapters; it is intended to aid the student in reading those selections. For the most technical part, Part III, which contains articles by Kenneth Shepsle and Keith Krehbiel, we commissioned Thomas Schwartz to write a basic introduction to the theory of social choice. He masterfully simplifies and integrates thirty years of technical results in political science, thereby providing an invaluable teaching aid on these topics.

At the end of the introduction to each part, there are bibliographic references to the citations in the introduction and a short list of suggested readings for the interested student. In these suggestions, we have attempted to span several different approaches to the study of Congress. Some readings are central to several different topics and, as a result, they are included in more than one list. The suggestions are arranged alphabetically, and we have indicated, with an asterisk (*), which we believe to be the most significant. We have tried to focus on books rather than journal articles since the former are more readily available to students. Unfortunately, some of the most significant literature on the Congress appears, at least initially, as journal articles. Of course, the reader should remember that these suggestions are an *editorial statement*. We encourage the reader to seek out other bibliographies on the Congress for further materials.

NOTE

1 "Address to the Council of Censors," February 14, 1786, Slade, ed. *Vermont State Papers*, p. 540. Cited in Wood 1969, p. 405.

REFERENCES AND SUGGESTED READINGS

Alchian, Armen A. 1950. "Uncertainty, Evolution, and Economic Theory." *Journal of Political Economy* 58, no. 3: 211–21.
Alchian, Armen A., and Harold Demsetz. 1972. "Production, Information Costs,

and Economic Organization." *American Economic Review* 62, no. 5: 777–95.

Axelrod, Robert. 1984. *The Evolution of Cooperation.* New York: Basic Books.

Brown, George. 1927. *The Leadership of Congress.* Indianapolis: Bobbs-Merrill.

Burke, Edmond. 1949. *Burke's Politics.* Edited by Ross Hoffman and Paul Levack. New York: Knopf.

Coase, Ronald H. 1937. "The Nature of the Firm." *Economica* 4.

*Davis, Lance E., and Douglass C. North. 1971. *Institutional Change and American Economic Growth.* Cambridge: Cambridge University Press.

*Fenno, Richard F., Jr. 1966. *The Power of the Purse: Appropriations Politics in Congress.* Boston: Little, Brown.

*Hamilton, Alexander, John Jay, and James Madison. [Any edition.] *The Federalist.*

Hasbrouck, Paul D. 1927. *Party Government in the House of Representatives.* New York: Macmillan.

*Madison, James. 1966. *Notes on Debates in the Federal Convention of 1787.* New York: Norton.

*Manne, Henry G. 1975. *The Economics of Legal Relationships: Readings in the Theory of Property Rights.* St. Paul: West.

McConachie, Lauros G. 1898. *Congressional Committees: A Study of the Origins and Developments of Our National and Local Legislative Methods.* New York: Crowell.

North, Douglass C. 1981. *Structure and Change in Economic History.* New York: Norton.

North, Douglass C., and Robert Paul Thomas. 1973. *The Rise of the Western World: A New Economic History.* Cambridge: Cambridge University Press.

Olson, Mancur. 1971. *The Logic of Collective Action: Public Goods and the Theory of Groups.* New York: Schocken Books.

Paine, Thomas. 1792. *Rights of Man.* London: H. D. Symonds.

Rieselbach, Leroy. 1973. *Congressional Politics.* New York: McGraw-Hill.

Riker, William. 1983. "Political Theory and the Art of Heresthetics." In *Political Science: The State of the Discipline,* ed. A. Finifter. Washington, D.C.: American Political Science Association.

Truman, David B. 1971. *The Governmental Process: Political Interests and Public Opinion.* 2nd ed. New York: Knopf.

Wilson, James. [1790–92] 1896. *Lectures on Law.* In *The Works of James Wilson,* ed. James DeWitt Andrews. Chicago: Callaghan.

*Wilson, Woodrow. [1885] 1973. *Congressional Government.* Gloucester, Mass.: Peter Smith.

Wood, Gordon. 1969. *The Creation of the American Republic, 1776–1787.* New York: Norton.

Young, James S. 1966. *The Washington Community, 1800–1828.* New York: Columbia University Press.

Representation

The genius of republican liberty seems to demand on one side not only that all power should be derived from the people, but that those intrusted with it should be kept in dependence on the people by a short duration of their appointments.
James Madison, *Federalist*, no. 37

Representation is the feet on which free government stands.
Moses Mather, *America's Appeal to an Impartial World*, 1775.
Cited in Wood 1969, p. 164

At the heart of our democracy is representation. The activities legislators engage in while representing their constituents color all legislative politics. The topics of Part I are: How do our electoral institutions affect the behavior of members? What patterns of behavior are derived from the incentives created by these electoral institutions? How does the behavior of members affect and change these electoral institutions?

Madison sought a republican form of government as a cure for factional politics. Factional politics (i.e., group or party politics) had led to injustice, instability, and a restriction of commerce under the Articles of Confederation. The key to preventing the emergence of "factionalism" was representation. According to Madison, representation serves to "refine and enlarge the public views, by passing them through the medium of a chosen body of citizens, whose wisdom may best discern the true interest of their country" (*Federalist*, no. 10).

A republican form of government with frequent elections has other consequences as well. In studying these aspects of representation, David Mayhew makes two simplifying assumptions about Congress and its members: that constituencies are homogeneous, and that members of the Congress are motivated by a desire to be reelected. From this simple model, Mayhew first concludes that members of Congress will spend the bulk of their time engaging in electoral activities. In Chapter 1 Mayhew suggests three kinds of activities members will engage in to further their electoral chances: "advertising," "credit claiming," and issue-specific "position taking." In addition, Mayhew concludes, members in selecting their strategies and institutional arrangements will favor reelection-related activities to the exclusion of the sorts of policy-oriented concerns normally associated with the legislature. He suggests that where the official responsibilities of representation require attention to a public policy issue – such as social security or national defense – the electoral connection motivates members to transform the issue into one on which "particularized" benefits are possible, that is, where the policy is transformable into small parcels that serve some electoral purpose. Thus, a debate on national defense is concerned not with defense strategy but rather with the location of bases and their accompanying payrolls. Social security becomes a matter of constituency casework rather than a debate over an appropriate insurance policy.

In a study not included in this volume, Richard Fenno, Jr. (1978) modifies Mayhew's basic model and includes a different assumption about constituencies: that members' districts are composed of a variety of groups, each with a somewhat different relationship with their representative. In this important extension of Mayhew's simple institutional analysis, Fenno, by assuming that the electoral process includes a primary as well as a general election, and by focusing on differences in constituents, finds a somewhat different pattern of predictions about the activities of congressmen. Fenno argues that some constituents insist the member take a position on certain issues, whereas others demand projects or general statements. Members will pursue strategies to satisfy as many of these demands as possible. Thus, in terms of representation, Fenno suggests that members will spend more time on nonissue, non-particularistic position taking than does Mayhew.

Both Mayhew and Fenno developed analyses of how members might go about securing the electoral support or "trust" of their constituents. The end result of adopting these various strategies for representation, it would seem, is a long-running successful career as a representative. Empirically, it seems that most members *do* enjoy a high level of constituency trust and support. In an article not included in this volume, John Ferejohn (1977) investigates this phenomenon of continuing (and in fact increasing) levels of reelection support. He considers several potential explanations:

- Because they can influence the shape of district boundaries, incumbents are able to secure for themselves an electoral advantage.
- Some basic shift has occurred in the way constituents decide for whom to vote that has had the effect of emphasizing incumbency over other candidate characteristics.

- Incumbents have become more adept at serving their constituents and, in this way, insulated themselves from the risks of policy decision making.

According to Ferejohn, the evidence suggests that the best-supported hypothesis is the middle one: some fundamental element in the voter's calculus had changed so as to afford the incumbent some basic advantage over potential challengers. Thus, the most interesting theories about strategies for representation may be those which emphasize the development of a different way of considering incumbents. That would surely suggest that Fenno's investigation of constituency home styles as a means of creating this evaluation of trust is a productive line of investigation. It also suggests that a theory is needed to explain the source of such changes in constituency evaluations over time.

In an article that is included here, Morris Fiorina (Chapter 2) examines a somewhat different aspect of representation. Fiorina is concerned with how members represent their constituents' interest in interactions with the bureaucracy. Fiorina adopts a model similar to Mayhew's, with the additional institutional assumption that the legislature shares policy-making authority with budget-maximizing bureaucrats in the executive branch. He concludes that members shun making often difficult policy decisions in favor of representing their constituents as ombudsmen in bureaucratic decision making. Fiorina suggests that members find casework a risk-free way to represent their constituents and that over time the expansion of congressional office staffs to do casework has helped the members to enjoy increasingly safe electoral seats.

All the chapters in this part suggest a wide variety of activities members will pursue in order to represent their constituents. Gary Jacobson (Chapter 3) provides a masterful summary of the literature in this area, relating some of the papers here to the body of knowledge on this topic. More importantly, Jacobson makes an important observation: that many of the activities members undertake to insure their electoral safety are also adopted, or at least countered, by challengers seeking office. By pointing out that challengers to legislative officeholders choose strategies that counteract the strategies members adopt to keep office, Jacobson offers an important extension to the models of Mayhew, Fenno, and Fiorina. Jacobson concludes that congressional seats are "unsafe at any margin" and that a new era of electoral competition may be coming.

REFERENCES AND SUGGESTED READINGS

Achen, Christopher. 1978. "Measuring Representation." *American Journal of Political Science* 20:475–501.

Part I

Arterton, F. Christopher, Gary Jacobson, Xandra Kayden, and Orren Gary. 1979. *An Analysis of the Impact of the Federal Election Campaign Act, 1972–1978*. Report to the Campaign Finance Study Group of the House Committee on House Administration.

Bauer, Raymond A., Ithiel de Sola Pool, and Lewis A. Dexter. 1963. *American Business and Public Policy*. New York: Atherton.

Buck, J. Vincent. 1972. "Presidential Coattails and Congressional Loyalty." *Midwest Journal of Political Science* 16, no. 3: 460–72.

Campbell, Angus, Phillip Converse, Warren E. Miller, and Donald Stokes. 1960. *The American Voter*. New York: Wiley.

Champagne, Anthony. 1984. *Congressman Sam Rayburn*. New Brunswick, N.J.: Rutgers University Press.

Cherryholmes, Cleo, and Michael Shapiro. 1969. *Representatives and Roll Calls: A Computer Simulation of Voting in the Eighty-eighth Congress*. Indianapolis: Bobbs-Merrill.

Clausen, Aage. 1973. *How Congressmen Decide: A Policy Focus*. New York: St. Martin's Press.

Clausen, Aage, and Carl E. Van Horn. 1977. "The Congressional Response to a Decade of Change, 1963–1972." *Journal of Politics* 39, no. 3: 632–54.

Dodd, Lawrence C. 1970. "Congress and the Quest for Power." In *Congress Reconsidered*, ed. Dodd and Bruce Oppenheimer. 1st ed. New York: Harcourt Brace & World.

*Fenno, Richard F., Jr. 1978. *Home Style: House Members in Their Districts*. Boston: Little, Brown.

Ferejohn, John. 1977. "On the Decline of Competition in Congressional Elections." *American Political Science Review* 71:166–76.

*Fiorina, Morris P. 1974. *Representatives, Roll Calls, and Constituencies*. Lexington, Mass: Lexington Books.

* 1977. *Congress: Keystone of the Washington Establishment*. New Haven: Yale University Press.

* 1981. *Retrospective Voting in American National Elections*. New Haven: Yale University Press.

*Hamilton, Alexander, John Jay, and James Madison. [Any edition.] *The Federalist*.

Jacobson, Gary C. 1980. *Money in Congressional Elections*. New Haven: Yale University Press.

* 1983. *The Politics of Congressional Elections*. Boston: Little, Brown.

Jacobson, Gary C., and Samuel Kernell. 1983. *Strategy and Choice in Congressional Elections*. New Haven: Yale University Press.

*Key, V. O., Jr. 1966. *The Responsible Electorate: Rationality in American Presidential Voting, 1936–1960*. Cambridge, Mass.: Harvard University Press.

*Kiewiet, D. Roderick. 1983. *Macroeconomics and Micropolitics*. Chicago: University of Chicago Press.

Kingdon, John. 1979. *Congressmen's Voting Decisions*. 2nd ed. New York: Harper & Row.

Maass, Arthur. 1983. *Congress and the Common Good*. New York: Basic Books.

MacRae, Duncan. 1958. *Dimensions of Congressional Voting*. Berkeley: University of California Press.

Mann, Thomas, and Raymond Wolfinger. 1980. "Candidates and Parties in

Congressional Elections." *American Political Science Review* 74:617–32.

*Mayhew, David. 1974. *Congress: The Electoral Connection*. New Haven: Yale University Press.

Miller, Warren, and Donald Stokes. 1963. "Constituency Influence in Congress." *American Political Science Review* 57:43–56.

Moos, Malcolm. 1952. *Politics, Presidents, and Coattails*. Baltimore: Johns Hopkins University Press.

Olson, Mancur. 1971. *The Logic of Collective Action: Public Goods and the Theory of Groups*. New York: Schocken Books.

Rae, Douglas. 1971. *The Political Consequences of Electoral Laws*. New Haven: Yale University Press.

Sullivan, John L., and Eric Uslaner. 1978. "Congressional Behavior and Electoral Marginality." *American Journal of Political Science* 22:536–53.

Tufte, Edward R. 1978. *Political Control of the Economy*. Princeton, N.J.: Princeton University Press.

Wood, Gordon. 1969. *The Creation of the American Republic, 1776–1787*. New York: Norton.

Wright, Gerald C., Jr. 1978. "Candidates' Policy Positions and Voting in U.S. Congressional Elections." *Legislative Studies Quarterly* 3:445–64.

1

The electoral connection and the Congress

DAVID R. MAYHEW

How to study legislative behavior is a question that does not yield a consensual answer among political scientists. An ethic of conceptual pluralism prevails in the field, and no doubt it should. If there is any consensus, it is on the point that scholarly treatments should offer explanations – that they should go beyond descriptive accounts of legislators and legislatures to supply general statements about why both of them do what they do. . . .

Mostly through personal experience on Capitol Hill, I have become convinced that scrutiny of purposive behavior offers the best route to an understanding of legislatures – or at least of the United States Congress. In the fashion of economics, I shall make a simple abstract assumption about human motivation and then speculate about the consequences of behavior based on that motivation. . . .

The discussion to come will hinge on the assumption that United States congressmen are interested in getting reelected – indeed, in their role here as abstractions, interested in nothing else. . . . Surely it is common for congressmen to seek other ends alongside the electoral one and not necessarily incompatible with it. Some try to get rich in office, a quest that may or may not interfere with reelection. Fenno assigns three prime goals to congressmen – getting reelected but also achieving influence within Congress and making "good public policy."[1] . . . Anyone can point to contemporary congressmen whose public activities are not obviously reducible to the electoral explanation; Senator J. William Fulbright (D., Ark.) comes to mind. Yet, . . . the electoral goal has an attractive universality to it. It has to be the *proximate* goal of everyone, the goal that must be achieved over and over if other ends are to be entertained. One former congressman writes, "All members of Congress have a primary interest in getting re-elected. Some members have no other interest."[2] Reelection underlies everything else, as indeed it should if we are to expect that the relation between politicians and public will be one of accountability.[3] What justifies a focus on the reelection goal is the juxtaposition of these two aspects of it – its putative empirical primacy and its importance as an accountability link. For analytic purposes, therefore, congressmen will be treated in the pages to come as if they were single-minded reelection seekers. Whatever else they may seek will be given passing attention, but the analysis will center on the electoral connection.

Yet another question arises. Even if congressmen are single-mindedly interested in reelection, are they in a position as individuals to do anything about it? If they are not, if they are inexorably shoved to and fro by forces in their political environments, then obviously it makes no sense to pay much attention to their individual activities. . . .

The actual impact of politicians' activities is more difficult to assess. The evidence on the point is soft and scattered. It is hard to find variance in activities undertaken, for there are no politicians who consciously try to lose. There is no doubt that the electorate's general awareness of what is going on in Congress is something less than robust.[4] Yet the argument here will be that congressmen's activities in fact do have electoral impact. Pieces of evidence will be brought in as the discussion proceeds.[5]

The next step here is to offer a brief conceptual treatment of the relation between congressmen and their electorates. . . . A congressman's attention must rather be devoted to what can be called an "expected incumbent differential." Let us define this "expected incumbent differential" as any difference perceived by a relevant political actor between what an incumbent congressman is likely to do if returned to office and what any possible challenger (in primary or general election) would be likely to do. And let us define "relevant political actor" here as anyone who has a resource that might be used in the election in question. At the ballot box the only usable resources are votes, but there are resources that can be translated into votes: money, the ability to make persuasive endorsements, organizational skills, and so on. By this definition a "relevant political actor" need not be a constituent; one of the most important resources, money, flows all over the country in congressional campaign years.[6]

It must be emphasized that the average voter has only the haziest awareness of what an incumbent congressman is actually doing in office. But an incumbent has to be concerned about actors who do form impressions about him, and especially about actors who can marshal resources other than their own votes. Senator Robert C. Byrd (D., W.Va.) has a "little list" of 2,545 West Virginians he regularly keeps in touch with.[7] ... Of campaign resources one of the most vital is money. An incumbent not only has to assure that his own election funds are adequate, he has to try to minimize the probability that actors will bankroll an expensive campaign against him.... Availability of money can affect strength of opposition candidacy in both primary and general elections.

A final conceptual point has to do with whether congressmen's behavior should be characterized as "maximizing" behavior. Does it make sense to visualize the congressman as a maximizer of vote percentage in elections – November or primary or, with some complex trade-off, both? For two reasons the answer is probably no. The first has to do with his goal itself, which is to stay in office rather than to win all the popular vote. More precisely his goal is to stay in office over a number of future elections, which does mean that "winning comfortably" in any one of them (except the last) is more desirable than winning by a narrow plurality. The logic here is that a narrow victory (in primary or general election) is a sign of weakness that can inspire hostile political actors to deploy resources intensively the next time around. By this reasoning the higher the election percentages the better. No doubt any congressman would engage in an act to raise his November figure from 80 percent to 90 percent if he could be absolutely sure that the act would accomplish the end (without affecting his primary percentage) and if it could be undertaken at low personal cost. But still, trying to "win comfortably" is not the same as trying to win all the popular vote. As the personal cost (e.g. expenditure of personal energy) of a hypothetical "sure gain" rises, the congressman at the 55 percent November level is more likely to be willing to pay it than his colleague at the 80 percent level.

The second and more decisive reason why a pure maximization model is inappropriate is that congressmen act in an environment of high uncertainty.... Behavior of an innovative sort can yield vote gains, but it can also bring disaster (as in Senator Goodell's case). For the most part it makes sense for congressmen to follow conservative strategies. Each member, after all, is a recent victor of two elections (primary and general), and it is only reasonable for him to believe that whatever it was that won for him the last time is good enough to win the next time. When a congressman has a contented primary electorate and a comfortable November percentage, it makes sense to sit tight, to try to keep the coalition together....

Whether they are safe or marginal, cautious or audacious, congressmen must constantly engage in activities related to reelection. There will be differences in emphasis, but all members share the root need to do things – indeed, to do things day in and day out during their terms. The next step here is to present a typology, a short list of the *kinds* of activities congressmen find it electorally useful to engage in. The case will be that there are three basic kinds of activities. It will be important to lay them out with some care, for [later] arguments will be built on them.

One activity is *advertising*, defined here as any effort to disseminate one's name among constituents in such a fashion as to create a favorable image but in messages having little or no issue content. A successful congressman builds what amounts to a brand name, which may have a generalized electoral value for other politicians in the same family. The personal qualities to emphasize are experience, knowledge, responsiveness, concern, sincerity, independence, and the like. Just getting one's name across is difficult enough; only about half the electorate, if asked, can supply their House members' names. It helps a congressman to be known. "In the main, recognition carries a positive valence; to be perceived at all is to be perceived favorably."[8] A vital advantage enjoyed by House incumbents is that they are much better known among voters than their November challengers. They are better known because they spend a great deal of time, energy, and money trying to make themselves better known.[9] There are standard routines – frequent visits to the constituency, nonpolitical speeches to home audiences,[10] the sending out of infant care booklets and letters of condolence and congratulation. Of 158 House members questioned in the mid-1960s, 121 said that they regularly sent newsletters to their constituents;[11] 48 wrote separate news or opinion columns for newspapers; 82 regularly reported to their constituencies by radio or television; 89 regularly sent out mail questionnaires.[12] ... Congressional advertising is done largely at public expense. Use of the franking privilege has mushroomed in recent years.... By far the heaviest mailroom traffic comes in Octobers of even-numbered years.[13] ... Advertising is a staple congressional activity, and there is no end to it. For each member there are always new voters to be apprised of his worthiness and old voters to be reminded of it.

A second activity may be called *credit claiming*, defined here as acting so as to generate a belief in a relevant political actor (or actors) that one is personally responsible for causing the government, or some unit thereof, to do something that the actor (or actors) considers desirable. The political logic of this, from the congressman's point of view, is that an actor who believes that a member can make pleasing things happen will no doubt wish to keep him in office so that he can make pleasing things happen in the future. The emphasis here is on individual accomplishment (rather than, say, party or governmental accomplishment) and on the congressman as doer (rather than as, say, expounder of constituency views). Credit claiming is highly important to congressmen, with the

21

consequence that much of congressional life is a relentless search for opportunities to engage in it.

Where can credit be found? If there were only one congressman rather than 535, the answer would in principle be simple enough. Credit (or blame) would attach in Downsian fashion to the doings of the government as a whole. But there are 535. Hence it becomes necessary for each congressman to try to peel off pieces of governmental accomplishment for which he can believably generate a sense of responsibility. For the average congressman the staple way of doing this is to traffic in what may be called "particularized benefits."[14] Particularized governmental benefits, as the term will be used here, have two properties: (1) Each benefit is given out to a specific individual, group, or geographical constituency, the recipient unit being of a scale that allows a single congressman to be recognized (by relevant political actors and other congressmen) as the claimant for the benefit (other congressmen being perceived as indifferent or hostile). (2) Each benefit is given out in apparently ad hoc fashion (unlike, say, social security checks) with a congressman apparently having a hand in the allocation. A particularized benefit can normally be regarded as a member of a class. That is, a benefit given out to an individual, group, or constituency can normally be looked upon by congressmen as one of a class of similar benefits given out to sizable numbers of individuals, groups, or constituencies. Hence the impression can arise that a congressman is getting "his share" of whatever it is the government is offering....

In sheer volume the bulk of particularized benefits come under the heading of "casework" – the thousands of favors congressional offices perform for supplicants in ways that normally do not require legislative action.... Each office has skilled professionals who can play the bureaucracy like an organ – pushing the right pedals to produce the desired effects. But many benefits require new legislation, or at least they require important allocative decisions on matters covered by existent legislation. Here the congressman fills the traditional role of supplier of goods to the home district. It is a believable role; when a member claims credit for a benefit on the order of a dam, he may well receive it. Shiny construction projects seem especially useful.[15]...

A final point here has to do with geography. The examples given so far are all of benefits conferred upon home constituencies or recipients therein. But the properties of particularized benefits were carefully specified so as not to exclude the possibility that some benefits may be given to recipients outside the home constituencies. Some probably are. Narrowly drawn tax loopholes qualify as particularized benefits, and some of them are probably conferred upon recipients outside the home districts.[16] (It is difficult to find solid evidence on the point.) Campaign contributions flow into districts from the outside, so it would not be surprising to find that benefits go where the resources are. . . .

So much for particularized benefits. But is credit available elsewhere? For governmental accomplishments beyond the scale of those already discussed? The general answer is that the prime mover role is a hard one to play on larger matters – at least before broad electorates. A claim, after all, has to be credible. If a congressman goes before an audience and says, "I am responsible for passing a bill to curb inflation," or "I am responsible for the highway program," hardly anyone will believe him. . . .

Yet there is an obvious and important qualification here. For many congressmen credit claiming on nonparticularized matters is possible in specialized subject areas because of the congressional division of labor. . . . Thus many congressmen can believably claim credit for blocking bills in subcommittee, adding on amendments in committee, and so on. The audience for transactions of this sort is usually small. But it may include important political actors (e.g. an interest group, the president, the *New York Times*, Ralph Nader) who are capable of both paying Capitol Hill information costs and deploying electoral resources. . . .

The third activity congressmen engage in may be called *position taking*, defined here as the public enunciation of a judgmental statement on anything likely to be of interest to political actors. The statement may take the form of a roll call vote. The most important classes of judgmental statements are those prescribing American governmental ends (a vote cast against the war; a statement that "the war should be ended immediately") or governmental means (a statement that "the way to end the war is to take it to the United Nations"). The judgments may be implicit rather than explicit, as in: "I will support the president on this matter." But judgments may range far beyond these classes to take in implicit or explicit statements on what almost anybody should do or how he should do it: "The great Polish scientist Copernicus has been unjustly neglected"; "The way for Israel to achieve peace is to give up the Sinai." The congressman as position taker is a speaker rather than a doer. The electoral requirement is not that he make pleasing things happen but that he make pleasing judgmental statements. The position itself is the political commodity. . . .

The ways in which positions can be registered are numerous and often imaginative. There are floor addresses ranging from weighty orations to mass-produced "nationality day statements." There are speeches before home groups, television appearances, letters, newsletters, press releases, ghostwritten books, *Playboy* articles, even interviews with political scientists. On occasion congressmen generate what amount to petitions;

whether or not to sign the 1956 Southern Manifesto defying school desegregation rulings was an important decision for southern members.[17] Outside the roll call process the congressman is usually able to tailor his positions to suit his audiences. A solid consensus in the constituency calls for ringing declarations.... Division or uncertainty in the constituency calls for waffling; in the late 1960s a congressman had to be a poor politician indeed not to be able to come up with an inoffensive statement on Vietnam ("We must have peace with honor at the earliest possible moment consistent with the national interest"). On a controversial issue a Capitol Hill office normally prepares two form letters to send out to constituent letter writers – one for the pros and one (not directly contradictory) for the antis.[18] ...

Yet it is on roll calls that the crunch comes; there is no way for a member to avoid making a record on hundreds of issues, some of which are controversial in the home constituencies. Of course, most roll call positions considered in isolation are not likely to cause much of a ripple at home. But broad voting patterns can and do; member "ratings" calculated by the Americans for Democratic Action, Americans for Constitutional Action, and other outfits are used as guidelines in the deploying of electoral resources....

These, then, are the three kinds of electorally oriented activities congressmen engage in – advertising, credit claiming, and position taking.... The organization of Congress meets remarkably well the electoral needs of its members. To put it another way, if a group of planners sat down and tried to design a pair of American national assemblies with the goal of serving members' electoral needs year in and year out, they would be hard pressed to improve on what exists. The second point is that satisfaction of electoral needs requires remarkably little zero-sum conflict among members. That is, one member's gain is not another member's loss; to a remarkable degree members can successfully engage in electorally useful activities without denying other members the opportunity successfully to engage in them....

A scrutiny of the basic structural units of Congress will yield evidence to support both these prefatory points. First, there are the 535 Capitol Hill *offices*, the small personal empires of the members.... The Hill office is a vitally important political unit, part campaign management firm and part political machine. The availability of its staff members for election work in and out of season gives it some of the properties of the former; its casework capabilities, some of the properties of the latter. And there is the franking privilege for use on office emanations. The dollar value of this array of resources in an election campaign is difficult to estimate.... In 1971 a House member put it at $100,000 (including a sum for general media exposure).[19] The value has certainly increased over the last decade. It should be said that the availability of these incumbency advantages causes little displeasure among members....

A final comment on congressional offices is perhaps the most important one: office resources are given to all members regardless of party, seniority, or any other qualification. They come with the job.

Second among the structural units are the *committees*, the twenty-one standing committees in the House and seventeen in the Senate – with a scattering of other special and joint bodies. Committee membership can be electorally useful in a number of different ways. Some committees supply good platforms for position taking. The best example over the years is probably the House Un-American Activities Committee... whose members have displayed hardly a trace of an interest in legislation.[20]... Some committees perhaps deserve to be designated "cause committees"; membership on them can confer an ostentatious identification with salient public causes....

Some committees traffic in particularized benefits. Just how benefits of this sort are likely to be distributed by governments has been the subject of theoretical speculation.... In giving out particularized benefits where the costs are diffuse (falling on taxpayer or consumer) and where in the long run to reward one congressman is not obviously to deprive others,[21] the members follow a policy of universalism.[22] That is, every member, regardless of party or seniority, has a right to his share of benefits. There is evidence of universalism in the distribution of projects on House Public Works,[23] projects on House Interior,[24] projects on Senate Interior,[25] project money on House Appropriations,[26] project money on Senate Appropriations,[27] tax benefits on House Ways and Means,[28] tax benefits on Senate Finance,[29] and... urban renewal projects on House Banking and Currency.[30]... House Public Works, writes Murphy, has a "norm of mutual advantage"; in the words of one of its members, "[We] have a rule on the Committee, it's not a rule of the Committee, it's not written down or anything, but it's just the way we do things. Any time any member of the Committee wants something, or wants to get a bill out, we get it out for him.... Makes no difference – Republican or Democrat. We are all Americans when it comes to that."[31]... An interesting aspect of particularistic politics is its special brand of "rules." There have to be allocation guidelines precise enough to admit judgments on benefit "soundness" (no member can have everything he wants), yet ambiguous enough to allow members to claim personal credit for what they get. Hence there are unending policy minuets; an example is the one in public works where the partners are the Corps of Army Engineers with its cost-benefit calculations and the congressmen with their ad hoc exceptions.[32]...

Finally, and very importantly, the committee system aids congressmen simply by allowing a division of labor among members. The parceling out of legislation among small groups of congressmen by subject area has two effects. First, it creates small voting bodies in which membership may be valuable. An attentive interest group will prize more highly the favorable issue positions of members of committees pondering its fortunes than the favorable positions of the general run of congressmen. Second, it creates specialized small-group settings in which individual congressmen can make things happen and be perceived to make things happen. "I put that bill through committee." "That was my amendment." "I talked them around on that." This is the language of credit claiming. It comes easily in the committee setting and also when "expert" committee members handle bills on the floor. To attentive audiences it can be believable....

The other basic structural units in Congress are the *parties*. The case here will be that the parties, like the offices and committees, are tailored to suit members' electoral needs. They are more useful for what they are not than for what they are. It is easy to conjure up visions of the sorts of zero-sum politics parties could import into a representative assembly. One possibility – in line with the analysis here – is that a majority party could deprive minority members of a share of particularized benefits, a share of committee influence, and a share of resources to advertise and make their positions known. Congressional majorities obviously do not shut out minorities in this fashion. It would make no sense to do so; the costs of cutting in minority members are very low, whereas the costs of losing majority control in a cutthroat partisan politics of this kind would be very high.... The general picture of the congressional party system is one of a system in slow decline – or, to put it another way, a system whose zero-sum edges have been eroded away by powerful norms of institutional universalism. In a good many ways the interesting division in congressional politics is not between Democrats and Republicans, but between politicians in and out of office. Looked at from one angle the cult of universalism has the appearance of a cross-party conspiracy among incumbents to keep their jobs.[33]

NOTES

1 Richard F. Fenno, Jr., *Congressman in Committees* (Boston: Little Brown 1973), p. 1.
2 Frank E. Smith, *Congressman from Mississippi* (New York: Random House, 1964), p. 127. It will not be necessary here to reach the question of whether it is possible to detect the goals of congressmen by asking them what they are, or indeed the question of whether there are unconscious motives lurking

behind conscious ones. In Lasswell's formulation "political types" are power seekers, with "private motives displaced on public objects rationalized in terms of public interest." Harold D. Lasswell, *Power and Personality* (New York: Viking, 1948), p. 38.

3 Of other kinds of relations we are entitled to be suspicious. "There can be no doubt, that if power is granted to a body of men, called Representatives, they, like any other men, will use their power, not for the advantage of the community, but for their own advantage, if they can. The only question is, therefore, how can they be prevented?" James Mill, "Government," in *Essays on Government, Jurisprudence, Liberty of the Press, and Law of Nations* (New York: Augustus M. Kelley, 1967), p. 18. Madison's view was that the United States House, by design the popular branch, "should have an immediate dependence on, and an intimate sympathy with, the people. Frequent elections are unquestionably the only policy by which this dependency and sympathy can be effectively secured." *The Federalist Papers*, selected and edited by Roy Fairfield (Garden City, N.Y.: Doubleday Anchor, 1961), no. 52, p. 165.

4 Donald E. Stokes and Warren E. Miller, "Party Government and the Saliency of Congress," ch. 11 in Angus Campbell et al., *Elections and the Political Order* (New York: Wiley, 1966), p. 199.

5 The most sophisticated treatment of this subject is in Warren E. Miller and Donald E. Stokes, "Constituency Influence in Congress," ch. 16 in Campbell et al., *Elections and the Political Order*, pp. 366–70. Note that a weird but important kind of accountability relationship would exist if congressmen thought their activities had impact even if in fact they had none at all.

6 To give an extreme example, in the North Dakota Senate campaign of 1970 an estimated 85 to 90 percent of the money spent by candidates of both parties came from out of state. Phillip M. Stern, *The Rape of the Taxpayer* (New York: Random House, 1973), p. 384.

7 Robert Sherrill, "The Embodiment of Poor White Power," *New York Times Magazine*, February 28, 1971, p. 51.

8 Stokes and Miller, "Party Government," p. 205. The same may not be true among, say, mayors.

9 In Clapp's interview study, "Conversations with more than fifty House members uncovered only one who seemed to place little emphasis on strategies designed to increase communications with the voter." Charles L. Clapp, *The Congressman: His Work as He Sees It* (Washington, D.C.: Brookings, 1963), p. 88. The exception was an innocent freshman.

10 A statement by one of Clapp's congressmen: "The best speech is a non-political speech. I think a commencement speech is the best of all. X says he has never lost a precinct in a town where he has made a commencement speech." *The Congressman*, p. 96.

11 These and the following figures on member activity are from Donald G. Tacheron and Morris K. Udall, *The Job of the Congressman* (Indianapolis: Bobbs-Merrill, 1966), pp. 281–88.

12 Another Clapp congressman: "I was looking at my TV film today – I have done one every week since I have been here – and who was behind me but Congressman X. I'll swear he had never done a TV show before in his life but he only won by a few hundred votes last time. Now he has a weekly television show. If he had done that before he wouldn't have had any trouble." *The Congressman*, p. 92.

13 Monthly data compiled by Albert Cover.
14 These have some of the properties of what Lowi calls "distributive" benefits. Theodore J. Lowi, "American Business, Public Policy, Case-Studies, and Political Theory," 16 *World Politics* 690 (1964).
15 "They've got to *see* something; it's the bread and butter issues that count – the dams, the post offices and the other public buildings, the highways. They want to know what you've been doing." A comment by a Democratic member of the House Public Works Committee. James T. Murphy, "Partisanship and the House Public Works Committee," paper presented to the annual convention of the American Political Science Association, 1968, p. 10.
16 For a discussion of the politics of tax loopholes see Stanley S. Surrey, "The Congress and the Tax Lobbyist – How Special Tax Provisions Get Enacted," 70 *Harvard Law Review* 1145–82 (1957).
17 Sometimes members of the Senate ostentatiously line up as "cosponsors" of measures – an activity that may attract more attention than roll call voting itself. Thus in early 1973, seventy-six senators backed a provision to block trade concessions to the U.S.S.R. until the Soviet government allowed Jews to emigrate without paying high exit fees. "'Why did so many people sign the amendment?' a Northern Senator asked rhetorically. 'Because there is no political advantage in not signing. If you do sign, you don't offend anyone. If you don't sign, you might offend some Jews in your state.'" David E. Rosenbaum, "Firm Congress Stand on Jews in Soviet Is Traced to Efforts by Those in U.S.," *New York Times*, April 6, 1973, p. 14.
18 Instructions on how to do this are given in Tacheron and Udall, *Job of the Congressman*, pp. 73–74.
19 Richard Harris, "Annals of Politics: A Fundamental Hoax," *New Yorker*, July 7, 1971, p. 48.
20 The best account of HUAC activities is in Walter Goodman, *The Committee* (New York: Farrar, Straus and Giroux, 1968).
21 There can be controversy, of course, over specific benefits. If only one federal office building is to be built in the Midwest it cannot simultaneously be put in Des Moines and Omaha. But over time office buildings are the sorts of goods that can be given out in fair shares. Another kind of problem arises with pre-1934 tariff bargaining, a game not all congressmen were in a position to play. But the evidence is that most of the time all who wanted to play were dealt in (e.g. Pennsylvania and Louisiana Democrats). Members who had no protectable products suffered no political deprivation, for they could fall back on militant antitariff position taking.
22 In Polsby's treatment of the House, this is one of the properties of an "institutionalized" organization. Nelson W. Polsby, "The Institutionalization of the U.S. House of Representatives," 62 *American Political Science Review* 145 (1968).
23 Murphy, "House Public Works Committee," pp. 3, 23, 39.
24 Fenno, *Congressmen in Committees*, p. 58.
25 Ibid., pp. 165–66.
26 Richard F. Fenno, Jr., *The Power of the Purse* (Boston: Little, Brown and Co., 1966), pp. 85–87.
27 Fenno, *Congressmen in Committees*, p. 160; Stephen Horn, *Unused Power: The Work of the Senate Committee on Appropriations* (Washington, D.C.: Brookings, 1970), p. 91.
28 John F. Manley, *The Politics of Finance: The House Committee on Ways and*

Means (Boston: Little, Brown, 1970), pp. 78–84; Surrey, "Congress and the Tax Lobbyist."

29 Fenno, *Congressmen in Committees*, pp. 156–59; Surrey, "Congress and the Tax Lobbyist."

30 Charles R. Plott, "Some Organizational Influences on Urban Renewal Decisions," 58 *American Economic Review* 306–11 (May 1968).

31 Murphy, "House Public Works Committee," p. 23.

32 See Murphy, "House Public Works Committee," pp. 39–47; and also Arthur Maass, *Muddy Waters: The Army Engineers and the Nation's Rivers* (Cambridge: Harvard University Press, 1951), ch. 1. In the late years of the congressional tariff there was a set of allocation guidelines based on differences between home and foreign production costs of individual products. The economics of all this was decidedly dubious, and the cost figures were virtually nonexistent. But the idea was politically serviceable. See E. E. Schattschneider, *Politics, Pressures, and the Tariff* (New York: Prentice-Hall, 1935), pp. 67–84.

33 One place where universalism prevails over party division is in House districting. Wherever congressmen have a say on line drawing, they seem to prefer cross-party deals among members of a state delegation assuring safe seats for all incumbents. For an account of the California districting of 1967 see Joseph W. Sullivan, "Massive Gerrymander Mapped in California by 38 Congressmen," *Wall Street Journal*, November 9, 1967, p. 1. For an account of the incumbency plan proposed by the Illinois delegation for 1972 see "Redistricting: Intervention of U.S. Court in Illinois," *Congressional Quarterly Weekly*, October 23, 1971, pp. 2180–85. "Most of the [Illinois] Republican incumbents preferred a map that cost the party a chance to win three seats but preserved their own districts virtually intact" (p. 2181). For a general discussion see David R. Mayhew, "Congressional Representation: Theory and Practice in Drawing the Districts," ch. 7 in Nelson W. Polsby (ed.), *Reapportionment in the 1970's* (Berkeley: University of California Press, 1971), pp. 274–84.

2

The case of the vanishing marginals: the bureaucracy did it

MORRIS P. FIORINA

INTRODUCTION

The ongoing Erikson-Mayhew-Tufte-Burnham-Ferejohn exchange illustrates once again that political events and processes are easier to describe than to explain. We now are aware of a clear political trend: the decline of competition for House seats. The significance of this trend becomes apparent when coupled with evidence that policy change in the Congress results more from the replacement of incumbents than from changes in their behavior.[1] Seemingly, the primary determinants of change in national policies will soon be individual deaths and retirements rather than elections.

But what are we to do? Any attempt to stimulate competition in congressional elections presupposes an understanding of the factors which foster and inhibit it. And here E-M-T-B-F come to a parting of the ways. Somewhat casually, Tufte suggests that institutional change, namely redistricting, has put marginal districts on the endangered list. Ferejohn rejects Tufte's suggestion, as does Bullock in another contribution.[2] Among other possibilities, Mayhew recalls the venerable Stokes-Miller dictum that "to be known at all is to be known favorably" and exhibits evidence that now, more than ever, congressmen follow the sage advice, "use the frank, use the frank, use the frank." But here too, Ferejohn raises questions. Neither in absolute nor in relative terms do the incumbents of today enjoy a greater informational advantage than those of yesteryear.

Having discarded two potential explanations Ferejohn next offers his own. Following Erikson and Burnham, Ferejohn argues that changes in

Reprinted from *American Political Science Review* 71, no. 2 (March 1977): 177–81. Without implicating any of them, I wish to thank Richard Fenno, John Kingdon, Charles Bullock, David Mayhew, Douglas Price, and Glenn Parker for their thoughtful comments and criticisms.

electoral behavior underlie the vanishing marginals. Perhaps many citizens use simple rules of thumb when voting in low information elections such as those for the House. According to proponents of the behavioral change view, party identification probably serves as the most common rule of thumb. But in recent years the citizenry has apparently become more informed, issue conscious, and ideological. And as this changing electorate monitored the divisive, highly charged politics of the 'sixties, increasing numbers of citizens grew suspicious of their traditional rule of thumb. Ferejohn and others suggest that incumbency voting has filled the void left by weakening party identification: for a significant number of citizens voting for the incumbent has replaced voting for their party.

The preceding argument has a curious ring to it. On the one hand we are to believe that party identification has declined in importance because citizens are increasingly aware and informed. But on the other hand we are to believe that these same citizens increasingly rely on the seemingly simpleminded rule of voting for incumbents. In a nutshell, voters are getting smarter, while voting behavior (other than presidential) is getting dumber. Moreover, consider the data analyzed by Arthur Miller.[3] With citizens increasingly dubious about government competence, intentions, and efficiency, is it plausible to argue that they increasingly support the objects of their cynicism?

Marginal districts are on the wane. Why? Some kind of incumbency effect exists, and apparently has come to exert an increasingly strong influence on congressional elections. But what is the nature of the incumbency effect, and why has it become more important over time? In this comment I propose another possible answer to the preceding questions. My thesis emerged during explorations of two congressional districts relatively alike in their demographic profiles but strikingly different in their electoral history. Basically, I will argue the following.

In the postwar period we have seen both the decline of the marginal district and the expansion of the federal role and its attendant bureaucracy. I believe that these two trends are more than statistically related, that they are in fact causally related. An institutional change – the growth of the bureaucracy – has encouraged behavioral change *among congressmen*, which in turn has encouraged behavioral change among some voters.

THE TWO DISTRICTS

The two congressional districts studied are reasonably similar in their demographic profiles. Both are in the same region of the country. Neither is metropolitan nor rural – each contains more than two counties, one medium-size city, and an important agricultural sector. Politically, however, the two districts present a striking contrast. District A is the quintessential marginal district. Since its creation in 1952 no election has produced a victory percentage as high as 58 per cent; the average winning percentage is 53. Both parties have won the seat with at least two different candidates during the 1952–1974 period. In contrast, the political history of district B illustrates Burnham's "triumph of incumbency."[4] Until 1964, Republicans won the district with margins around 55 per cent. But in 1964 a Democrat squeaked through, held on in 1966, and from the statistical record now appears safe.

Are there important differences between the two districts? Why did the Democrat who captured district A in 1964 not duplicate the feat of his counterpart in district B? Why has district A not experienced the triumph of incumbency on the Republican side? One explanation we can eliminate is redistricting. District A underwent no boundary change between 1952 and 1972, and then underwent a change amounting to less than 5 per cent of the district population. District B has remained unchanged since World War II. What then, explains the political differences between districts A and B?

Consider District A. During the 1950s both national and state races activated local ties, to Republican advantage in the former case and Democratic advantage in the latter. Congressmen rose and fell partially for reasons beyond their control. The Republican congressman who followed the Eisenhower era was a rural conservative, a crusty personality of unquestioned integrity, who took pride in his attendance record, perceived his job as the making (and obstructing) of national policy, and in general operated rather independently of his district. In 1964 he refused to separate himself from Goldwater and followed his leader into enforced retirement. Unlike the beneficiary of the Johnson landslide in district B, however, the Democrat in district A failed to retain his seat in 1966, losing it to the Republican he defeated two years earlier. In 1974, after more narrow victories, the conservative Republican retired. His party held the seat – by the narrowest of margins – but now Democrats and Republicans alike agree that after a year in office the freshman Republican successor is safe.

Why this turnabout, this triumph of incumbency? Several explanations are offered. The new Republican blankets his district with communications both greater in number and more "effective" than his predecessor's. District observers perceive that the freshman Republican's voting record is more closely attuned to his district than was his predecessor's conservative stands. "He throws a few votes our [opponents'] way now and then." And finally, the freshman Republican travels around his district from meeting to meeting saying, "I'm your man in Washington.

The case of the vanishing marginals

What are your problems? How can I help you?" While generally favorable to his successor, the former Republican disapproves of the amount of time his successor spends in the district: "How can he do his job in Washington when he's back here so much? People shouldn't expect a Congressman to be running back home all the time."

In summary, district A was influenced by broader political forces during the 1950s. During the 1960s it elected congressmen who did not make all-out efforts to maximize their vote. Now that someone is doing so, local observers and participants are betting that another marginal has vanished.

Now consider district B which is simply ten years ahead of district A. Until 1964 district B was marginally Republican. The Representative for most of this period was involved in controversial legislation such as Taft-Hartley and Landrum-Griffin. He had a personal problem, and probably more important, a political problem: declining Republican registration. In 1948 Republicans had a comfortable registration edge, by 1964 this edge has dwindled, and today the parties are dead even. Some district politicians believe that the registration shift has little significance for national elections, that it is felt mostly on the local level. But it seems prudent to bear in mind that the triumph of incumbency in district B may reflect the changing political allegiances of the district. A defeated Republican congressman is partial to this view.

Still, the Democrat who barely won in 1964 bucked the tide in 1966 and has won by margins of 40,000 votes at times since. District observers agree that his strength is bipartisan; a county chairman contends that in only one instance has any other national, state, or local candidate of either party run ahead of the Democratic congressman in the district, or in the relevant common subarea of it. Equal registration does not explain such electoral one-sidedness.

But here again we find a behavioral difference between the pre-1964 Republican and the post-1964 Democratic congressmen. Although district B is not located in prime Tuesday-to-Thursday club area, the Democratic incumbent belongs to the club nonetheless. By general agreement he is a pervasive presence in the district. He relies on no campaign organization other than the formal party structure. But he personally works the district at a feverish pace. A party chairman from a Republican area commented: "Congressman _____ comes to see people. _____ [former Republican congressman] didn't. The people know _____. He's the first Congressman to take an active interest in them."

The Democratic incumbent maintains well-staffed offices in district B. In these offices secretaries busily work on social security and veterans' affairs matters. Here too we find a difference between the Democratic incumbent and his Republican predecessor. The latter commented:

"When I was in office I had four staff members. Now they have a regiment. That's just not necessary. It's a waste of the taxpayer's money, a frivolous expense."

The matter of the congressional staff is especially interesting in that the retired Republican in district A spontaneously brought it up. In discussing examples of the "hypocrisy" of modern congressmen (one of which was the 1967 expansion of the staff) he said flatly: "No congressman could possibly use 16 staff members." The Democratic incumbent in district B is using them (ten in his district) and one can not dispute the results.

Clearly, the two districts show evidence that major changes in their congressional election patterns are associated with behavioral differences on the part of the congressmen they elected. What might produce such differences? Former Republican congressmen in the two districts lean toward the view that today's congressmen are not as good as the pre-1960 variety. Oversimplifying a bit, in olden days strong men walked the halls of the Capitol. They concentrated more heavily on affairs of state than do their successors. More than today's congressmen they believed that the public interest should take precedence over reelection.

Political scientists are justifiably skeptical of theories which postulate that human nature has changed for the worse, that yesterday's political giants have given way to today's political pigmies. Thus, I will not dwell on the notion that today's congressmen are more concerned with reelection than they were in the recent past. In all likelihood, since the New Deal era the average congressman's desire for reelection has remained constant. What has changed, however, is the set of resources he possesses to invest in his reelection effort. Today's congressmen have more productive reelection strategies than previously. And these strategies are an unforeseen by-product of the growth of an activist Federal government.

BETTER TO BE REELECTED AS AN ERRAND BOY THAN NOT TO BE REELECTED AT ALL

A plausible explanation of the differing political histories of the two cases I have studied would run something like this. The changing nature of congressional elections in these districts stems from the changing behavior of the congressmen who represented these districts. Both districts are heterogeneous in their socioeconomic characteristics, and in their political allegiances (e.g., registration). Thus, so long as these districts are represented by congressmen who function primarily as national policy makers (pre-1964 in district B, pre-1974 in district A) reasonably close congressional elections will naturally result. But given congres-

sional incumbents who place heavy emphasis on nonpartisan constituency service, the districts will shift out of the marginal category. Can
we expand this explanation, and use it to explain the vanishing marginals
nationally?

A basic fact of life in post-New Deal America is the growth of the
federal role and its instrument, the federal bureaucracy. Bureaucracy is
the characteristic mode of delivering public goods and services. Ceteris
paribus, the more the government attempts to do for people, the more
extensive a bureaucracy the government will require.

While not malevolent, bureaucracies make mistakes (of commission
and omission). Moreover, attempts at redress often meet with a characteristic unresponsiveness, inflexibility, and incorrigibility. Members of
the U.S. Congress, however, hold an almost unique position vis-à-vis the
bureaucracy: congressmen possess the power to expedite bureaucratic
activity. This capability flows directly from congressional control over
what bureaucrats value most – higher budgets and new program authorizations. In a very real sense congressmen are monopoly suppliers of
bureaucratic "unsticking" services.

As the scope of government expands, more and more citizens and
groups find themselves dealing with the federal bureaucracy. They may
be seeking positive benefits such as social security checks and government
grants or seeking to escape costs entailed by bureaucratic regulations. But
in either case their congressman is a source of succor. And the greater the
scope of government activity, the more often will his aid be requested.
Moreover, unlike private monopolists, congressmen can not curtail the
demand for their services by raising their price (at least legally). When the
demand for his services rises, the congressman has no real choice except
to meet that demand – to supply more – so long as he would rather be an
elected official under any circumstances, than an unelected one. This
vulnerability to constituency demands, however, is largely academic.
Congressmen probably do not resist the gradual transformation from
national legislator to errand person. They have not rushed to create a
national ombudsman, for example, nor to establish Congressman
Reuss's Administrative Counsel of the Congress. The nice thing about
casework is that it is mostly profit; one makes many more friends than
enemies. In fact, some congressmen undoubtedly stimulate the demand
for their bureaucratic fixit services. Recall that the new Republican in
district A says, "I'm your man in Washington. What are your problems?
How can I help you?" And in district B the demand for the
congressman's services presumably did not rise so much between 1962
and 1964 that a "regiment" of constituency staff become necessary.
Rather, possessing the regiment, the new Democrat did his damnedest to
create the demand to which he could apply his regiment.[5]

In addition to profitable casework let us remember too that the expansion of the federal role has also produced a larger pork barrel. The pork barreler need not limit himself to dams and post offices. There is LEAA money for the local police; urban renewal and housing money for local officials; and educational program grants for the local education bureaucracy. The congressman can stimulate applications for federal assistance, put in a good word during consideration, and announce favorable decisions amid great fanfare. Bureaucratic decisions bestow benefits as well as create costs. By affecting either kind of decision, the congressman can accrue electoral credit.

Let us turn now to the matter of the incumbency effect. If, over time, an increasing number of U.S. representatives are devoting increasing resources to constituency service, then at the district level we would expect that increasing numbers of voters think of their congressman less as a policymaker than as an ombudsman. If so, other implications are immediate. First, party identification will be less influential in determining the congressional vote, not just because of the unusual presidential politics of the late 1960s, but because *objectively* the congressman is no longer considered so important for policymaking as he once was.[6] In legislative matters he holds one paltry vote out of 435. But in bureaucratic matters he is a benevolent, nonpartisan power. And if more and more citizens come to think of their congressmen in this manner, then the basis of the incumbency effect is obvious. *Experience in Washington and congressional seniority count when dealing with the bureaucracy.* Thus, so long as the incumbent can elude a personal morality rap, and refrain from causing outlandish votes, he is naturally preferred over a newcomer. *This incumbency effect is not only understandable, it is rational.* And it would grow over time as increasing numbers of citizens come to regard their congressman as a troubleshooter in the Washington bureaucracies.

The preceding argument provides a critical insight into Ferejohn's critique of Mayhew. Ferejohn concludes that the incumbency effect is not explained by the information that incumbents shower on constituents, because the informational advantage incumbents possess has not increased between 1958 and 1970, while the incumbency advantage apparently *has* increased during that period. But what if the *content* of the information has changed over time? What if in 1958 voters who have "heard or read something" about the incumbent have heard or read about a policy stand, whereas in 1970 they have heard or read about the good job the incumbent is doing to get Vietnam veterans' checks in the mail? Some voters will agree with a policy stand, some will disagree. But everyone will applaud the congressman's efforts in behalf of the veterans. Thus, a constant informational advantage may be quite consistent with an increasing incumbency advantage if information about the incumbent has become increasingly noncontroversial in content. And, as suggested above, those voters who have "heard or read nothing" about either candidate act quite sensibly in voting for the incumbent to the extent that he is an ombudsman rather than a legislative giant.

For clarity's sake I have drawn the preceding argument in very bold strokes. Let me now fill in the picture a bit. In order to account for the vanishing marginals we do *not* need to argue that *all* congressmen have opted *exclusively* for an ombudsman role, and that *all* constituents now think of their congressmen in nonprogrammatic terms. The disappearance of a marginal requires only marginal change. To illustrate, if one deflates Mayhew's 1972 bimodal distribution by Erikson's 5 per cent estimated incumbency effect, the trough in the marginal range disappears. To explain the vanishing marginals one need only argue that over the past thirty years, expanded constituency service opportunities have given the marginal congressman the ability to capture 5–10 per cent of his district's voters who might otherwise oppose him on party or policy grounds.

One further question arises. The growth of the federal role has been continuous and reasonably gradual, although with definite jumps during the New Deal and World War II. The decline of congressional competition, however, has been more erratic. We would expect some lag between the onset of bureaucratic expansion and the decline of the marginals because congressmen presumably would not grasp the new opportunities immediately. But how would we explain the especially pronounced decline of congressional competition in the late sixties? It would be a bit much to contend that Great Society programs translated into casework and votes quite so quickly. One plausible explanation of the sixties decline lies in recent work by Richard Fenno.[7]

Fenno discusses the congressional "homestyle," a congressman's basic patterns of interaction with his district. According to Fenno, homestyles tend to persist once established. Now consider that between the 88th and 90th Congresses one-third the membership of the House changed. I think it is plausible to hypothesize that the homestyles of the new representatives placed relatively greater emphasis on constituency service than did the homestyles of the more senior congressmen they replaced.[8] The average freshman in 1965 for example, replaced a congressman elected in 1952 or 1954. Paradoxically, then, the electoral upheavals of the 1960s may have produced the electoral stability of the early 1970s. New congressmen chose homestyles best adapted to the changed congressional environment. Is it purely coincidence that these fresh Congresses raised staff allotments by almost 50 per cent (eleven to sixteen) between 1967 and 1973?

37

Morris P. Fiorina

CONCLUSION

Congressmen can earn electoral credit by taking positions on the issues, by bringing home the bacon, and by providing individual favors. The first option is inherently controversial. The latter two need not be. As the federal role has expanded, congressmen have shifted emphasis from the controversial to the noncontroversial, from the programmatic to the nonprogrammatic. Ferejohn no doubt is correct; electoral behavior has changed. But at least part of that change is endogenous to the system. Congressmen are not merely passive reactors to a changing electoral climate. In no small part they have helped to change that climate.[9]

NOTES

1 Herbert Asher and Herbert Weisberg, "Congressional Voting Change: A Longitudinal Study of Voting on Selected Issues," paper presented at the *American Political Science Association Meeting*, San Francisco, 1975.

2 Charles S. Bullock III, "Redistricting and Congressional Stability, 1962–1972," *Journal of Politics* 37 (May, 1975), 569–575.

3 Arthur H. Miller, "Political Issues and Trust in Government: 1964–1970," *American Political Science Review* 68 (September, 1974), 951–972.

4 Walter D. Burnham, "Party Systems and the Political Process," in *The American Party Systems*, ed. William Chambers and Walter Burnham, 2nd ed. (New York: Oxford, 1975), pp. 308–357.

5 The expansion of the congressional office cries out for further study. At the beginning of the 90th Congress in which the last major expansion took place *Congressional Staff Directory* listed 3,276 individuals of whom 26 per cent were in the districts. In 1974, 34 per cent of 5,109 were in the districts. What are these people doing?

6 Cf. Burnham, "Party Systems," p. 335. Burnham believes that the decline of party identification as an influence on congressional voting has increased the attractiveness of the ombudsman role. I am arguing that the causal influence is reciprocal if not the reverse.

7 Richard Fenno, "Congressmen in their Constituencies: An Exploration," forthcoming, *American Political Science Review*.

8 I should point out that the Democrat who won district A in 1964 and lost it in 1966 did *not* adopt an errand boy homestyle. According to local supporters he became totally engrossed in his Washington affairs.

9 Obviously, my argument suggests a variety of implications for the future operation of the American government. Space precludes me from entering upon such a discussion here. The interested reader should refer to my *Congress – Keystone of the Washington Establishment* (New Haven: Yale, 1977).

3

Running scared: elections and congressional politics in the 1980s

GARY C. JACOBSON

Being a member of Congress is a terrible job. The campaign ought to be reflective
of the job.   Bernadette Budde, BIPAC

The discovery that the electoral value of incumbency had increased
sharply during the 1960s (Erikson 1971; Mayhew 1974a) set the
congressional election research agenda for the subsequent decade. It
focused attention on the question of why House incumbents win
reelection so frequently and, more pointedly, why their electoral margins
became distinctly larger in the mid-1960s. Other important political
changes during the same period offered a variety of possible explanations
and suggested that the shift was part of a larger sea change in American
political life; this naturally intensified interest in the issue.

Meanwhile, members of Congress continued to act as if they felt
anything but safe; indeed, the pursuit of reelection seemed to absorb ever
more of their time and energy. Anyone observing the incessant scramble
for attention and credit, the constant shuttling between Washington and
the district, the vast outpouring of newsletters, pamphlets, questionnaires, booklets, letters, and other messages from the member to his
constituents, the increasingly hectic and undignified hustling of campaign
contributions, could hardly come away with the sense that incumbent
security is a major fact of political life. Yet, from the perspective of raw
statistics, it is.

This irony of present-day congressional election politics is my central
theme. I will argue that the same conditions that made it possible for
members of Congress to insulate themselves from the effects of partisan
tides, to turn a political franchise into a personal franchise, quickly bred
institutional innovations that have made electoral politics more pres-
sured, uncertain, and demanding. Political developments in the 1960s
offered new opportunities for members to control their own political
fates, but at, in the long run, a heavy price. New institutional players

39

with new campaign techniques attuned to the current electoral environment have, over time, cut into whatever advantage these developments may have given incumbents, so they find it necessary to run ever harder just to stay in the same place. Members of Congress accepted, willy-nilly, a kind of Faustian bargain: greater power over their own electoral fortunes, but at the price of being condemned to unrelenting entrepreneurial effort. The bargain has consequences far beyond the electoral arena, for the internal politics of Congress and its performance as an institution are deeply affected by how its members win and hold office. This is why it is important to understand what has happened.

EXPLAINING THE VANISHING MARGINALS

Scholars did not have to look far for potential explanations of the growing reelection margins incumbents experienced in the 1960s and the consequent decline in the number of marginal congressional seats (as conventionally defined).[1] Indeed, the problem was to determine which of several entirely plausible accounts was closest to the truth. One explanation was quickly tested and dismissed. Contrary to Tufte's (1973) hypothesis, incumbents were not made safer by favorable redistricting following the 1960 census and adjustments required by *Baker* v. *Carr* (Cover and Mayhew 1977; Ferejohn 1977).

All of the other ready alternatives – explanations based on declining partisanship among voters, proliferating government projects and programs, the sharp increase in official resources (staff, office, travel, and communications allowances) available to members of Congress, the development of new campaign technologies and the related rise in campaign costs – were supported by at least circumstantial evidence and found backers. Mayhew (1974a, 1974b) suggested that incumbents might be doing better because they were using greatly augmented communications resources to advertise themselves more widely and effectively. Ferejohn (1977) offered evidence that weakening party ties led voters to substitute the simple cue of incumbency for the simple cue of party. Fiorina (1977) argued that the proliferation of new government programs enacted by Congress increased the demand for casework; enlarged congressional staffs increased the supply; and the combination enabled members to entrench themselves by shifting from an emphasis on making national policy to delivering noncontroversial and nonpartisan local services. The new campaign technologies put individual candidates at the center of the campaign and diminished the role of parties, making it easier for incumbents to establish independent political identities that insulated them from external political trends (Crotty and Jacobson 1980).

Table 3.1. *House incumbents winning at least 60 percent, 1956–1982*

Year	Number of incumbents running in general election	Percentage reelected with at least 60% of the major-party vote
1956	403	59.1
1958	390	63.1
1960	400	58.9
1962	376	63.6
1964	388	58.5
1966	401	67.7
1968	397	72.2
1970	389	77.3
1972	373	77.8
1974	383	66.4
1976	381	71.9
1978	377	78.0
1980	392	72.9
1982	381	72.2

Sources: 1956–1980: Ornstein et al. 1982, Table 2-10; 1982: compiled by author.

No consensus has developed around any one explanation (see Born 1979; Collie 1981; Cover 1977; Cover and Mayhew 1977; Krehbiel and Wright 1983; Nelson 1978–79; Payne 1980); all of these changes were interconnected and mutually reinforcing, making it difficult, if not impossible, to untangle their separate effects. But together they surely amount to a transformation of electoral politics sufficient to account for larger incumbent vote margins. Thus, it is curious that many of these trends continued through the 1970s without adding a jot to the average incumbent's margin of victory or the number of supposedly "safe" incumbents.

To grasp this point it is useful to review some data. First, Table 3.1 reports one kind of evidence for the "vanishing marginals." It lists the percentage of House incumbents who won 60 percent or more of the vote in elections from 1956 through 1982. The sharp decrease in marginal seats around 1966 is unmistakable. In elections from 1956 through 1966, an average of 61.8 percent of the incumbents were reelected with more than 60 percent of the vote. From 1968 through 1982, the figure is 73.6 percent. But notice that there has been no further increase over this latter period – there are no more safe seats at the end of the period than there were at the beginning. Figures on reelection rates of incumbents tell an even more interesting story. The probability of *losing* was the same for incumbents in the 1970s as it had been two decades earlier. Only for the 1968, 1970, and 1972 elections do reelection rates suggest that incumbents had become any safer in the crucial sense that their

Gary C. Jacobson

Table 3.2. *Party-line voters, defectors, and independents in House elections, 1956–1982 (in percentages)*

Year	Party-line voters	Defectors	Pure independents
1956	82	9	9
1958	84	11	5
1960	80	12	8
1962	83	12	6
1964	79	15	5
1966	76	16	8
1968	74	19	7
1970	76	16	8
1972	75	17	8
1974	74	18	8
1976	72	19	9
1978	69	22	9
1980	69	23	8
1982	77	16	7

Sources: 1956–1978: Mann and Wolfinger 1980; 1980 and 1982: NES/CPS American National Election Studies.

likelihood of defeat had diminished. Subsequent elections have found them as vulnerable to defeat as their predecessors had been in the 1950s (Jacobson 1985c). I will say more about this later.

Now consider several other time series that have been used to exemplify changes thought to have contributed to the vanishing marginals. Table 3.2 shows the declining impact of party identification on voters in congressional elections from 1956 through 1980 (it remains to be seen whether 1982 indicates a reversal of this trend). Table 3.3 exhibits the growth in personal staffs of members of Congress since 1935, the increase in the share of staff based in distict offices since 1960, congressional mailings in election years from 1954 to 1982, and the growth in reimbursed trips back to the district from 1965 through 1977.

Accurate data on campaign spending do not exist prior to 1972, so we have only anecdotal evidence that it grew rapidly during the 1950s and 1960s. But Federal Election Commission data show that, adjusting for inflation, the average amount spent by House incumbents more than doubled between 1972 and 1982. Spending by challengers grew more slowly, so in both absolute and relative terms incumbents gained ground financially over this period (Jacobson 1984).

In every case, these data indicate that the trends supposedly responsible for the vanishing marginals continued, sometimes even accelerated, after the mid-1960s. But electoral advantages of incumbency did not grow at all. Nor do cross-sectional studies consistently turn up

Table 3.3. *Trends in congressional staff, mail, and travel allowances,*
1935–1982

Year	Personal staff employees	Percentage of staff in district	Pieces of mail (millions)	Paid trips to district
1935	870			
1947	1,440			
1954			43.5	
1957	2,441			
1958			65.4	
1960		14	108.0	
1962			110.1	3
1964			110.5	
1966			197.5	5
1967	4,055	26		
1968			178.2	12
1970			201.0	
1972	5,280	23	308.9	18
1975				26
1976	6,939	28	401.4	
1977	6,942	30		33
1978	6,944	33	430.2	unlimited[a]
1980	7,371	34	511.3	
1982	7,511	36	587.1	

Note: Mail data include both House and Senate; other data are for the House only.
[a] Since 1978, travel expenses have been included in an overall lump sum for offices, equipment, supplies, postage, communications, etc., which members may budget as they see fit.
Sources: Fiorina 1977, p. 61; Ornstein et al. 1982, Tables 5.2, 5.3, 5.12, and 6.6.

unambiguous evidence that what incumbents supposedly do to make their seats safe actually makes any difference in how well they do at the polls. Federal spending in the district does not seem to matter (Feldman and Jondrow 1984); time spent in the district has very limited effects (Parker and Parker 1982). It is even possible to argue that personal and district services do not influence voters (Johannes and McAdams 1981), although on this question there is a good deal of contrary evidence (Fiorina 1981; Jacobson 1981; Powell 1982; Yiannakis 1981). As for campaign spending, the more money incumbents raise and spend, the *worse* they do on election day (Jacobson 1980, 1985a).

This last example suggests what is actually going on. Incumbents do not really lose votes by spending money; rather, they spend more the more strongly they are challenged, and the more strongly they are challenged the smaller their vote. Similarly, the absence of a simple correlation between levels of district attention and reelection margins does not mean that district attention has no effect; members simply work the district harder the more insecure they are (Fiorina 1981). Their efforts are not necessarily ineffective; but the longitudinal data indicate that officeholders have had to work ever harder at reelection in order to maintain the same degree of electoral safety. The cost in time, money, and energy of holding onto a seat in Congress seems to have escalated. Why should this be so? The answer lies in the nature of present-day electoral politics – in the behavior of voters, in campaign institutions and practices, and in the way national electoral forces come to be expressed in candidate-centered elections.

VOTERS IN CONGRESSIONAL ELECTIONS

A generation of survey research has spawned a bewildering array of models of individual voting behavior, but most portray the voting decision as the result of some combination, simple or complex, of the voter's views of the parties, candidates, and issues involved in the election. However one looks at voting in congressional elections, it is clear that partisanship has become less important, candidates more important, over the time period covered by adequate surveys. The roles of issues, ideology, and related phenomona have been more difficult to ascertain, perhaps because they vary irregularly from district to district and election to election; again, I will say more about this later.

The diminishing importance of party and the growing focus on candidates are open to various explanations; an adequate review of them would take us too far afield (see Jacobson 1983*a* for a short account). Whatever dynamics are involved, however, there is little doubt that members of Congress used the general decline in party loyalty among voters as an opportunity for strengthening personal, as opposed to partisan, ties with their constituents and that this contributed significantly to increasing their vote margins (Fenno 1978; Ferejohn 1977; Krehbiel and Wright 1983). Whether incumbents reduced the significance of party by their own behavior or merely took advantage of a shift arising elsewhere, they clearly managed to benefit from it. But a less partisan electorate presents problems as well as opportunities.

It is, first of all, more volatile. This not only magnifies the usual anxiety excited by the uncertainties of electoral politics (Fenno 1978; Jacobson 1983*a*), it also means that *larger electoral margins are no guarantee of a reduced chance of defeat*. Consider a hypothetical example. Suppose the average incumbent wins with 55 percent of the vote and that the standard deviation of the interelection vote shift is 5 percentage points. This means that, other things equal, an incumbent with the average

Table 3.4. *Means and standard deviations of interelection vote swings for incumbent candidates for the U.S. House of Representatives, 1952–1982*

Year	Change in Democrat's vote from the previous election		
	Mean	Standard deviation	N
1952	−2.4	5.3	254
1954	4.0	4.6	289
1956	−2.2	4.9	301
1958	6.4	5.4	283
1960	−2.9	5.5	286
1962	−1.3	5.6	283
1964	5.2	6.1	318
1966	−6.7	6.6	323
1968	−0.7	6.8	317
1970	3.6	6.9	308
1972	−1.8	8.9	295
1974	6.4	9.1	290
1976	−1.9	8.4	329
1978	−2.0	8.4	307
1980	−3.4	9.0	302
1982	3.4	8.0	292
Averages			
1952–60	—	5.1	1413
1962–70	—	6.4	1549
1972–80	—	8.8	1523

Note: Includes only incumbents with major party opposition in both the current and previous election; the vote is computed as the percentage share of the two-party vote.
Source: Jacobson 1985c.

margin has about a .84 chance of winning in the next election (based on the normal distribution). Now suppose the average incumbent's vote increases to 60 percent. If the standard deviation of the interelection shift does not change, the average incumbent's probability of winning next time jumps to .98. But if the standard deviation increases to 10 percentage points, the incumbent's seat is just as much at risk as it was before. With this in mind, observe Table 3.4. It shows that the standard deviation of the interelection vote shift in House districts grew from an average of 5.1 in the 1950s to an average of 8.8 in the 1970s. This helps explain why the sharp reduction in marginal seats has not produced a significant increase in the proportion of incumbents actually reelected (Collie 1981). It suggests that incumbents are not entirely irrational in behaving as if their seats were less than secure. As a side note, these data also suggest that the criterion for marginality requires adjustment if comparisons are to be made across election years; a margin that was reasonably safe in the 1950s might no longer be so in the 1980s (Jacobson 1985c).

It is not hard to understand why the decline in partisanship should produce a more volatile electorate. Without the anchor of party identification, voters are more open to the influence of short-term political forces – new personalities, issues, persuasive messages. A shift in focus of attention from parties to individual candidates introduces a new element of stability but undermines it from another direction. One candidate – the incumbent – often remains the same over a series of elections; but the challenger normally changes from election to election, and the variation among challengers and their campaign resources is what accounts for most of the district-level interelection differences in election results (Jacobson 1983a).

A less partisan, more fickle electorate also demands more frequent and extensive attention. Fewer strong partisans mean fewer automatic votes *against* an incumbent – providing an opportunity to increase the margin of electoral safety – but fewer automatic votes *for* him as well. Support may be easy to lose as well as to win. A member's personal relationship with constituents can keep the district safely in his hands, but only through a continuously high level of personal attention. Mayhew was careful to remind us that to say "Congressman Smith is unbeatable" means only that he "is unbeatable as long as he continues to do the things he is doing" (1974b, p. 37). Fenno (1978) emphasized that the bonds of trust members sought to establish with constituents – the key, by his analysis, to a member's ability to hold his seat – took much time and effort to develop and could be maintained only through continual reinforcement. The legendary constituent's question has never been more pointed: "What have you done for me *lately*?"

The decline in partisanship among voters, then, opened the way for individual representatives to establish a personal political franchise that could insulate them from external partisan forces, but only as long as they are willing to invest the time and energy it takes to maintain it. If they are not willing to pay this price, they may be even more vulnerable to challengers than they were in the days when they could count on a larger core of party regulars for a reliable base of support.

Most of them are willing to pay the price, at least for a time; retirement or defeat awaits those who refuse. As a consequence, survey studies of individual voters in recent House elections show House members to be remarkably successful practitioners of candidate-centered electoral politics. How the focus on candidates works so strongly to the advantage of House incumbents has been fully realized only recently. The pioneering survey studies of congressional election voting had shown that, aside from party identification, the most important variable was whether a voter knew who the candidates were (Arsenau and Wolfinger 1973; Stokes and Miller 1966). Other things equal, voters were more likely to vote for candidates whose names they could recall than those whose names they could not.

This finding was the basis for suspecting that the growing victory margins enjoyed by incumbents in the 1960s were the result of expanded resources for self-promotion. But Ferejohn (1977) found the flaw in this argument: incumbents had a large advantage in name recall, all right, but it had not grown over the relevant period. Furthermore, voters were significantly more inclined to vote for incumbents even when they could not recall their names.

This curious discovery raised doubts about name recall as the measure of familiarity, and subsequent work showed that many more voters could recognize candidates' names on a list (as on a ballot) than could recall them directly (Mann 1977; Mann and Wolfinger 1980). By this and other measures, familiarity with congressional candidates is more general than scholars had supposed. But House incumbents still enjoy a large advantage, no matter how familiarity is measured. This is clear from the data in Table 3.5 from the 1982 American National Election Study survey;[2] they are typical of recent years.

The electoral advantage familiarity gives to incumbents is evident from Table 3.6, which lists the percentage of partisan voters defecting to the other party's candidate, depending on levels of familiarity with the two candidates. The more familiar voters are with a candidate, the more willing they are to vote for him, the effect also depending, symmetrically, on how well they know the other candidate. In 1982, only 2 percent of the voters defected to candidates less familiar than their own party's; 53 percent defected to candidates who were more familiar.

These data show why the greater familiarity among voters enjoyed by incumbents translates into an advantage at the polls. But there is more to the incumbency advantage than this. Incumbents are better liked as well as better known than their challengers. At any level of familiarity, 1982 voters who were asked if they liked or disliked anything about each candidate were significantly more inclined to mention something liked about the incumbent than about the challenger; they were also slightly more inclined to report disliking something about the challenger than about the incumbent.

On another affective measure, the "feeling thermometer" scale, which runs from 0 to 100, with 50 as neutral, the average rating of House incumbents was 66, that of challengers 53, and that of candidates for open seats 58. This is important because it is the voters' comparative evaluations of the candidates, rather than simple familiarity, that has the

Gary C. Jacobson

Table 3.5. *Incumbency status and voters' familiarity with House candidates, 1982 (in percentages)*

Incumbency status	Recalled name	Recognized name	Neither
Incumbents	54	94	6
Challengers	26	63	37
Open seat	29	77	23

Source: NES/CPS American National Election Study, 1982.

Table 3.6. *Familiarity with candidates and voting behavior in 1982 House elections (percentage of voters defecting)*

	Familiarity with own party's candidate		
	Recalled name	Recognized name	Neither
Familiarity with other party's candidate			
Recalled name	16	45	62
Recognized name	2	17	54
Neither	4	1	10

Source: NES/CPS American National Election Study, 1982.

strongest impact on the vote. The equations in Table 3.7 demonstrate this point.

The first equation considers the vote choice to be a function of party identification and incumbency. All three variables have a strong impact on the vote; the probability of voting Democratic in the 1982 House election shifts by .31 depending on whether the Democrat or the Republican is an incumbent. The second equation adds measures of candidate familiarity to the equation. This reduces the impact of incumbency, to below standard levels of statistical significance in the case of Republican incumbents. Part of the incumbents' advantage is evidently connected with greater familiarity. But the third equation indicates that familiarity and incumbency are both to a large extent surrogates for voters' evaluations of candidates. Each of the four evaluative variables, taken from responses to the likes/dislikes questions, has a strong impact on the vote, and their presence increases the explanatory power of the equation substantially (compare the R^2s). Voters are not impressed by incumbency per se, nor does the incumbency advantage in House elections arise merely from greater public awareness of incumbents. Of

Table 3.7. *Regression models of the voting decisions in the 1982 House elections*

	Regression coefficient	Standard error	R^2
Dependent variable			
Respondent's vote (N = 614)			
Independent variables (Eq.1)			
Intercept	.46		
Party identification	.30	.02	.48
Democrat is incumbent	.19	.04	
Republican is incumbent	−.13	.04	
Independent variables (Eq.2)			
Intercept	.48		
Party identification	.29	.02	
Democrat is incumbent	.13	.04	
Republican is incumbent	−.05	.04	.51
Familiarity with Democrat	.21	.04	
Familiarity with Republican	−.26	.04	
Independent variables (Eq. 3)			
Intercept	.52		
Party identification	.22	.01	
Democrat is incumbent	.07	.04	
Republican is incumbent	−.06	.04	
Familiarity with Democrat	.08	.04	.63
Familiarity with Republican	−.18	.04	
Likes something about Democrat	.26	.03	
Dislikes something about Democrat	−.12	.03	
Likes something about Republican	−.22	.03	
Dislikes something about Republican	.16	.03	

Note: Respondent's vote = 1 if Democratic, 0 if Republican; party identification = 1 if respondent is strong, weak, or independent Democrat, 0 if independent, −1 if strong, weak or independent Republican; incumbency variable = 1 if the candidate is an incumbent, 0 if not; familiarity = 1 if respondent recalls candidate's name, .5 if candidate's name is recognized but not recalled, 0 if name is neither recognized nor recalled; likes and dislikes = 1 if respondent likes (dislikes) something about the candidate, 0 if not.

Source: NES/CPS American National Election Study, 1982.

much greater importance are the very favorable public images voters have of them and the relatively negative images – if any – projected by their opponents. Comparable evidence from the 1978 and 1980 elections supports the same conclusion (Jacobson 1983a).[3]

Gary C. Jacobson

Table 3.8. *Voters' contacts with House candidates, 1982*
(in percentages)

Type of contact	Incumbent	Challenger	Open seat
Any	91	56	73
Met personally	22	9	12
Saw at meeting	17	7	6
Talked to staff	15	4	9
Received mail	75	27	40
Read about in newspaper	70	42	40
Heard on radio	40	20	25
Saw on TV	62	34	40
Family or friend had contact	37	16	27

Source: NES/CPS American National Election Study, 1982.

Why are House incumbents so familiar and agreeable to voters? The survey evidence suggests that all of the things they supposedly do to win relection have some payoff. The data in Table 3.8 show how much more successful they are in reaching voters than are their opponents. Ninety-one percent of the voters reported having some contact with the incumbent, compared to 56 percent for the challenger. The most common avenue of contact (75 percent) was through the mails, reflecting generous use of the frank. Newspaper and television contact with incumbents was also widely reported. Plainly, House incumbents know how to keep themselves in the public eye.

House members also win high marks from voters on various aspects of their job performance. This is evident from the data in Table 3.9, which are taken from responses to a number of general and specific questions about the incumbent's services to the district and accomplishments in Washington. The left-hand column lists the percentage of voters who offered a relevant response to each question. For example, 19 percent had asked the member for assistance or information, received a reply, and so were able to report their level of satisfaction with it. The distribution of responses to the question indicates that 55 percent of the voters in this group were very satisfied, and the right-hand column in the table shows that 96 percent of these very satisfied people voted for the incumbent.

Most voters could evaluate the incumbent's general job performance and express an opinion on how helpful he would be if asked for assistance with some problem. Fifty-seven percent were able to judge whether or not they generally agreed or disagreed with the way the incumbent voted. Fewer – from 15 to 36 percent – were able to respond more specifically to

Table 3.9. *Evaluations of the incumbent's performance and the vote
in the 1982 House elections (in percentages; N = 529)*

Relevant responses		Evaluation of performance	Distribution of responses	Voting for incumbent
76	General job performance	Approve	85	86
		Disapprove	15	12
	District services			
86	Expectations about	Very helpful	36	86
	incumbent's helpfulness	Somewhat helpful	50	74
	in solving voter's	Not very helpful	10	36
	problem	It depends	3	60
19	Level of satisfaction	Very satisfied	55	96
	with response to	Somewhat satisfied	30	87
	voter-initiated	Not very satisfied	9	44
	contact	Not at all satisfied	6	0
22	Level of friend's	Satisfied	70	90
	satisfaction	Somewhat satisfied	20	83
	with response	Somewhat dissatisfied	3	67
		Not satisfied	7	25
30	Could voter recall	Yes	30	83
	anything special	No	70	66
	incumbent did for			
	the district?			
	Voting and policy			
57	General agreement or	Agreed	42	94
	disagreement with	Agreed somewhat,		
	incumbent's votes	disagreed somewhat	50	67
		Disagreed	8	4
15	Agreed or disagreed	Agreed	55	95
	with vote on a	Disagreed	45	39
	a particular bill			
36	Which candidate would	Incumbent	70	93
	do a better job on	Challenger	30	4
	most important problem?			
27	Ideological proximity	Closer to incumbent	57	91
		Closer to challenger	43	23

Source: NES/CPS American National Election Study, 1982.

questions of service and performance; but a solid majority could respond in terms of at least one of the more specific questions.

Evaluations of House incumbents on all of these dimensions are consistently positive. Eighty-five percent of those having an opinion approve of the way their representative is handling his job generally; 86

percent think he would be very or somewhat helpful if asked for help in dealing with a constituent's problem. The level of satisfaction with responses to actual requests for help is also very high. Agreement is much more common than disagreement with the member's voting record; he is expected to do a better job handling the most important problem by a large majority of the voters who had an opinion one way or the other. Only on the vote for a particular bill and ideological proximity is the incumbent's advantage less than decisive. And here the proportion of respondents involved is relatively low.

The significance of such consistently positive evaluations is evident from their association with the vote. On every question, the more positive the response to the incumbent, the more likely the respondent is to vote for him. The sharpest differences are on the more specific questions about policy and ideology. These patterns are very similar to those found in the 1978 and 1980 surveys (Jacobson 1983*a*, pp. 106–109). Although responses to the questions naturally overlap, they have a clear cumulative effect as well. If responses are scored positive and negative and added up, the sum is strongly and monotonically related to the vote (Jacobson 1981).

By the survey evidence, then, present-day House members seem to be highly successful political entrepreneurs, expert practitioners of candidate-centered electoral politics. The fruits of assiduous cultivation of constituents are abundantly evident. But the evidence also suggests that one major source of their electoral strength is the overall weakness of their opponents. Challengers as a class are, by every measure, not only weaker than incumbents but also weaker than the other nonincumbent candidates running for open seats. Table 3.5 shows us that House challengers are comparatively obscure; they also enjoy a much less favorable ratio of likes to dislikes than other types of candidates; Table 3.8 reveals their inferior ability to reach voters. All of these findings appear in other election years as well (Abramowitz 1980; Jacobson 1983*a*; Mann and Wolfinger 1980).

With this in mind, it is instructive to observe how voters react in those races where incumbents *are* strongly challenged. The strongest challenges are, by definition, the successful ones. Table 3.10 shows the differences in voters' responses to selected questions about winning and losing challengers and incumbents in 1980 and 1982. Winning challengers are much better known than losing challengers and do not differ significantly from incumbents on this score; among incumbents, losers are better known than winners. Winning challengers are much more successful in making contact with voters in a variety of ways, greatly reducing their incumbent opponent's advantage here, too.

The most interesting data concern voters liking or disliking something

Table 3.10. *Voters' responses to winning and losing challengers and incumbents in the 1980 and 1982 House elections (in percentages)*

	1980 challenger		1982 challenger	
	Won	Lost	Won	Lost
Familiarity with candidates				
Recalled challenger's name	53	18	77	23
Recognized challenger's name	92	51	93	63
Neither	8	49	7	37
Recalled incumbent's name	75	43	61	53
Recognized incumbent's name	97	92	97	94
Neither	3	8	3	6
Contact with challenger				
Any	81	40	84	54
Met personally	9	4	23	9
Received mail from challenger	37	13	32	26
Read about challenger	59	24	61	25
Saw challenger on TV	51	21	61	33
Evaluations of candidates				
Likes something about challenger	39	13	58	22
Dislikes something about challenger	15	11	26	18
Likes something about incumbent	59	58	61	59
Dislikes something about incumbent	46	18	48	24
Policy most important problem				
Challenger would handle better	24	4	29	9
Incumbent would handle better	7	18	23	25
Neither	69	78	48	66

Sources: NES/CPS American National Election Studies, 1980 and 1982.

about the candidates. The data indicate that successful challengers accomplish two things. They make voters aware of their own virtues, and they make them aware of the incumbent's shortcomings. Voters are just as inclined to like something about losing incumbents as about winning incumbents. They are also just as likely to approve of their general job performance and to think they would be of assistance if asked, and they are even more likely to remember something specific they have done for the district (Jacobson 1983a). Incumbents do not lose by failing to elicit support on these grounds. They lose when challengers are able to project a positive image of their own and to persuade voters that the incumbents have liabilities that outweigh their usual assets. Issues are evidently part of this; winning incumbents have a large advantage on the question of who would handle the most important national problem better; but losing incumbents are at a disadvantage, one which was particularly large in 1980.

The surveys provide one bit of evidence, then, that the electoral success widely enjoyed by House incumbents is contingent on relatively feeble opposition. This implies several things: that the most effective reelection strategy is to discourage strong opposition, that most House members manage to do this, but that those who fail may be a good deal more vulnerable than the aggregate data on incumbent reelection margins and rates would suggest.

COMPETITION AND CAMPAIGN RESOURCES

Successful challenges are distinguished by another crucial feature: they are much better financed. In fact, the simplest and best measure of the strength of a challenge is how much money the challenger raises and spends. The kinds of candidates who make the best challengers – people with experience in elective office, notable political talents, attractive personal attributes – are also able to raise the most money; the availability of enough money for the campaign attracts superior challengers (Jacobson 1980; Jacobson and Kernell 1983). A strong, well-financed challenger is the chief threat to an incumbent's reelection.

This is plain from analyses of the effects of campaign spending in House elections. For every election since 1972, when accurate campaign finance data first began to be collected, the result is the same: other things equal, the more challengers spend on the campaign, the greater their share of the vote on election day. A strong, positive relationship between spending and votes for challengers remains no matter how the data are analyzed. For incumbents, it is quite the reverse. The simple relationship between their expenditures and vote share is negative; the more they spend, the worse they do. This is not because spending money loses them votes but rather because they spend more the more strongly they are challenged, and a strong challenge costs them votes. With challenger spending controlled, spending by incumbents is statistically unrelated to the vote (Jacobson 1980, 1985a).

Variation in the vote is determined by what the challenger spends, not by what the incumbent spends. The reason for this is that campaigning is subject to diminishing returns. House members are able to exploit the resources that come with office to conduct a perpetual campaign. Most evidently saturate the public with information about their virtues and accomplishments before the official campaign begins. Thus, the additional campaigning they do during the official election period has comparatively small payoffs, if any. Challengers, in contrast, usually begin the campaign in obscurity. If they remain there they are certain losers. Their only hope lies in gaining the attention and approbation of voters. This normally requires vigorous campaigning, and vigorous campaigning costs money. The more money the challenger spends, the more he is able to reduce the incumbent's advantage in familiarity and popular regard, and thus the more votes he is able to attract (Jacobson 1983a).

This raises the crucial question of what generates a vigorous, well-financed challenge. One obvious consideration is the apparent vulnerability of the incumbent. The best potential challengers – those with active political careers and progressive ambitions – avoid contests where the odds seem strongly stacked against them; losing does little to enhance a career (Jacobson and Kernell 1983). Thus, they are very reluctant to take on a member who has a firm grip on the district. Their knowledge that people who distribute campaign money prefer not to waste it on hopeless causes is another reason to stay out. An incumbent who convinces potential candidates and contributors that he is virtually invulnerable attracts the kind of weak opposition that guarantees invulnerability.

House incumbents are fully aware of this. Members work to maintain a strong presence in the district, not only to build support from constituents but also to impress on potential opponents how tough it would be to unseat them. They campaign hard for reelection even when weakly challenged in order to win by margins large enough to prevent them from becoming targets in the future (Fenno 1978). They accumulate large campaign treasuries independently of any manifest electoral threat in order to make the cost of taking them on appear too high. But insofar as safe electoral margins are won by discouraging serious opposition, security is illusory. It is based on a bluff, and when, for some reason, the bluff is called, winning reelection may be anything but automatic. Members are doubtless aware of this, which helps to explain the sense of insecurity apparent in their behavior. Worst-case possibilities give them much to be insecure about and reinforce the sense that they are "unsafe at any margin" (Mann 1977).

Indeed, if the behavior of incumbents is any measure, subjective electoral insecurity has clearly increased in the past decade. Some signs of this appear in Table 3.3. But the clearest evidence is found in their campaign finance practices. Journalists' accounts are rich with anecdotes detailing an increasingly frantic pursuit of campaign funds, particularly from political action committees (Drew 1982a, 1982b; Hunt 1982; *Time* 1982). More systematic data make the same point. House incumbents have always spent reactively; the more the challenger raises and spends, the more the incumbent raises and spends. The simplest way to see this is to regress incumbent expenditures on challenger expenditures (more complicated models, with various controls, support the same conclusion;

Table 3.11. *Incumbents' expenditures as a function of challengers'*
expenditures in House campaigns, 1972–1982

| | Regression coefficient | | |
| | Intercept | Challenger's expenditures | R^2 |
Year			
1972	80.9	.57	.35
N = 296		(12.56)	
1974	82.1	.63	.41
N = 319		(14.90)	
1976	106.2	.49	.36
N = 328		(13.66)	
1978	136.6	.49	.38
N = 308		(13.66)	
1980	135.9	.73	.39
N = 302		(13.78)	
1982	195.6	.57	.34
N = 292		(12.26)	
1984	223.2	.62	.41
N = 318		(14.84)	

Notes: Expenditures are in $1,000s, adjusted for inflation (1984 = 1.00); *T*-ratios of regression coefficients are in parentheses; all are significant beyond .001.
Source: Compiled by author.

see Jacobson 1980). Table 3.11 presents the results of these regressions for House elections from 1972 through 1984. The spending data have been adjusted for inflation (1984 = 1.00). Two things stand out in this table. First, the slope of the relationship between incumbent and challenger spending is very stable across these years; an *F*-test indicates that only for 1980 is it significantly different from the other years; incumbent spending is, by this evidence, consistently reactive. Second, the intercept has grown dramatically over the years. Incumbents, it seems, have been raising and spending more and more money independently of what their particular challengers have been doing. The typical incumbent would have spent $80,900 in 1972 if the challenger had spent nothing; by 1984, that figure had, in real dollars, nearly tripled, reaching $223,200.

There is something curious about these patterns, since all the statistical evidence from regressing votes on expenditures says that spending money on campaigns does incumbents no good. Obviously, they do not believe it. Nor should they, for the null results do not preclude the possibility that vigorous, expensive campaigning is necessary to hold off a stiff challenge (Jacobson 1985a, 1985d). And as long as there is any chance that it makes a difference, risk-averse congressional careerists are bound to spend heavily when threatened. Indeed, one possible reason for the null findings is that there are so few cases in which incumbents do *not* spend heavily when seriously challenged. The clearest situation in which incumbents might profit from additional campaigning is when changed conditions (or the points being scored by a skilled challenger) make it necessary to change the message. This was the case for Republican incumbents in 1982, as we shall see.

What explains the trend toward increased spending independent of the challenge? Considerations of both supply and demand are involved. The supply of funds available to House incumbents has grown with the proliferation of political action committees (PACs), most of which favor incumbents because their contributions are intended to buy access to the legislative process, if not more specific advantages (Jacobson 1980, 1984). The demand has grown because, despite typically large victory margins and reelection rates, members of Congress view electoral politics as increasingly difficult and uncertain.

And they have reasons. Congressional incumbents are not the only politicians who have learned to play entrepreneurial electoral politics. New organizations – PACs, renascent party committees, polling and direct-mail outfits – with new campaign skills have joined the game; potential opposition looks increasingly formidable. More money is available to challengers as well as to incumbents. House members' relative advantage in campaign spending has increased, to be sure, but far more important is the fact that absolute levels of spending by challengers have grown, and this is what really matters. Challengers are more likely to gather sufficient funds to make a serious contest out of it. They are also more likely to get help from well-organized single-issue groups like environmentalists or opponents of abortion who are skilled at raising highly emotional and divisive issues. The possibility of suddenly finding oneself targeted by a pack of PACs becomes more unsettling as it becomes less remote.

"Independent" PACs, whose expenditures cannot be limited by law, are another new and growing threat. Independent spending has gone primarily for campaigns attacking incumbents, often well before the challenger has even been nominated. The idea is to demolish the incumbent's political support. Since independent campaigns are not subject to normal electoral constraints (their perpetrators are not subject to punishment at the polls), it is easy for them to become very unpleasant. Indeed, they form part of the trend toward increasingly harsh personal attacks on politicians. There is a logic to this. If members of Congress win and hold office on the basis of personal attributes rather than party affiliation or policy positions, then the way to undermine their support is by attacking them personally. It should come as no surprise that shrewd opponents aim directly at the source of the incumbent's hold on the district. Negative ad hominem campaigning is a predictable component of candidate-centered electoral politics.

New campaign technologies are another reason for worry. For example, computerized direct-mail messages can now be targeted to almost any specified subgroup in the electorate. Guided by information on people's attitudes gathered by polls, requests for money, campaign charges and attacks, and other campaign messages can be tailored to selected audiences. Campaigning of this sort is scarcely public and so need not be moderated to appeal to a broad constituency. Direct-mail messages are most effective when they exploit strong emotions – outrage or fear or anger (Sabato 1981) – that, once aroused, are capable of stimulating surprising changes in behavior.

Members of Congress themselves have been quick to adopt direct-mail technology, but this does little to calm worries about what opponents might do with it. Consider a favorite tactic of desperate candidates in recent California elections: the last-minute hit piece, a pamphlet full of wild and often wildly inaccurate charges against the frontrunner that is timed to arrive in the mail on Monday before election day, too late for the victim to defend himself or counterattack. It is not difficult to imagine the anxiety the threat of such a hit piece excites in potential targets.

Democratic incumbents face yet another new source of insecurity. The effective direct-mail fundraising system developed by national-level Republican party committees generates enormous sums of money ($190 million in the 1981–82 election cycle, more than six times as much as Democratic committees were able to raise). Republican party officials have devised clever ways to funnel the money into campaigns legally despite the low ceiling on direct party contributions imposed by federal law. They have also learned how to distribute the money efficiently; the party maintains an extensive polling operation to help its strategists target those close races where party (and cooperative PAC) money would be spent most usefully. Republican officials also put a great deal of effort into recruiting and training promising challengers (Jacobson 1985b). It is hardly a surprise that incumbent Democrats suffer from a heightened sense of vulnerability or that they feel the need to be fully prepared with their own resources just in case the Republican party's formidable resources are suddenly mobilized against them.

The central point here is that the very same electoral conditions – diminished partisan loyalty, a more volatile electorate, new resources and techniques for reaching voters, the focus on candidates, new sources of campaign funds – that once allowed House incumbents to strengthen their personal grip on the district have, with the passage of time, inspired innovations that make the task of maintaining it more demanding and more uncertain. Nor, on the evidence of the most recent elections, have these developments insulated House incumbents from the effects of national political forces; national political conditions and issues still affect candidate-centered electoral politics, although in rather complicated and indirect ways.

NATIONAL POLITICS IN HOUSE ELECTIONS

One immediate implication of vanishing marginals was that more House incumbents would be safe from the effects of national political tides. Wider electoral margins should reduce the proportion of defeats produced by any general vote shift away from the incumbents' party. The "swing ratio" – the ratio of seat shifts to vote shifts in House elections – should decline. This would weaken the impact of changes in national political sentiments on the composition of Congress; it would be harder for voters to register discontent by throwing the rascals out. Mayhew called it the "blunting of a blunt instrument" (1974a, p. 314). The only problem with this argument is that the swing ratio has not, in fact, declined (Ferejohn and Calvert 1984). To understand how this could be so, recall the earlier demonstration that greater average electoral margins are no guarantee of a smaller chance of defeat.

Nor have recent elections given incumbents much reason to believe that they are immune to national forces. In 1974, the year of Watergate and recession, 36 Republican House members lost; in 1980, with Carter and inflation, 27 incumbent Democrats were defeated; 26 Republican incumbents were ousted in 1982 amid the highest levels of unemployment since the Depression. Still, there is a good deal of evidence that the *way* national conditions influence electoral politics has changed. One important trend is well documented: presidential coattails have shrunk. Studies employing a variety of methods have uniformly found a diminished connection between presidential and congressional voting in recent years (Burnham 1975; Calvert and Ferejohn 1983; Edwards 1980; Ferejohn and Calvert 1984; Jacobson 1983a). House members are certainly more insulated from the top of the ticket than they once were. Other links between national politics and district-level election results remain, however, though they have become more complicated, variable, and unpredictable.

National forces were once thought to have a rather simple, direct effect on congressional election results: The vote looked very much like a referendum on the current administration. Kramer (1971), Tufte (1975, 1978), Arcelus and Meltzer (1975), and Bloom and Price (1975) showed that the state of the economy, variously measured, and the popular standing of the president were strongly related to the national partisan vote shift in House elections. In aggregate, the House vote rewards or punishes a party for its administration's performance in office.

Individually, people were assumed to be casting House votes on the basis of their own economic experiences and evaluations of the president. But survey studies of individual voters turned up only weak and sporadic evidence that they did so. In some years the expected connections appeared; more often they did not. Even the most generous reading of the evidence suggests that individual analogs of national conditions influence individual voters much less strongly and systematically than the strong aggregate relationships would predict (Jacobson 1983a).

What then accounts for the apparent referendum? Fiorina (1978) and Kernell and I (1983) have proposed an explanation. Voters base their choice primarily on their knowledge and opinions of the specific candidates running in the district. Differences among challengers account for most of the variation here, and these differences are by no means random. Better electoral odds attract superior challengers – those with political skills, experience, and ambition – and more money to their campaigns. Hopeless races are left to inexperienced amateurs who are ignored by contributors.

One important consideration in estimating odds is whether it promises to be a good or bad year for the party. And this, it is widely believed, depends on national economic conditions and what the public thinks of the administration's performance. When things look bad for a party, its most promising potential challengers sit the election out and wait for a better day. Its contributors concentrate on trying to shore up threatened incumbents. The party thus fields a collection of unimpressive, under-financed challengers. Ambitious career politicians in the other party, sensing favorable electoral tides, enter the lists in larger numbers than usual. One inducement is that fundraising is easier because the party's contributors, too, see an unusual opportunity to go after the other party's seats. The party thought to be favored by national conditions therefore mounts an unusual proportion of formidable challenges.

As a consequence of these strategic decisions, the choice between pairs of candidates across districts varies systematically with national conditions; one party produces a much larger proportion of vigorous challenges than the other. Voters need only respond to the choices offered at the district level to reflect national forces in their collective behavior. It is not necessary for individuals to vote their economic experiences or feelings about the president directly or consciously, though some may do so. The intervening strategic decisions of congressional candidates and activists provide a mechanism sufficient to explain how national forces come to be expressed in midterm congressional election results.

If this explanation is correct, more than a little self-fulfilling prophecy is involved. Strategic decisions, guided by electoral expectations, help generate the very conditions that fulfill them. National forces must exert *some* direct influence on voting, or else (unless we assume that politicians are irrational or stupid) the process would decay. But their influence is multiplied by the strategic behavior of congressional elites. This means that the full effects of national forces do not appear automatically; they depend on what elites choose to do. If career and campaign finance decisions may serve to reinforce anticipated national trends, they may also serve to counteract them. The connection between national forces and election outcomes is therefore unstable, adding another element of unpredictability to congressional election politics. An analysis of the 1980 and 1982 House elections will illustrate the complex interactions among the variables at work here.

THE ELECTIONS OF 1980 AND 1982

The results of the 1980 House elections were certainly consistent with the idea that national conditions matter. Republicans took control of the Senate and picked up 33 House seats. It is easy to see this as a direct response by voters to the failings of the Carter administration, assigning Democrats in Congress a share of the blame for high inflation, high unemployment, and inept leadership. But a closer analysis of what happened in 1980 shows that individual candidates and campaigns were decisive in translating popular discontent into Republican gains.

The distribution of candidacies and campaign money in 1980 indicated that congressional elites responded strategically to expected national trends. Republicans mounted an unusually high proportion of strong challenges; Democrats did the opposite (Jacobson and Kernell 1983). And strong Republican challenges were essential to their electoral gains. The data in Table 3.12 demonstrate that successful Republican challengers did not simply ride into office on a favorable national tide. The table lists the percentage of winning Republican challengers according to two criteria: whether or not the Democratic seat was marginal (won by more or less than 60 percent of the vote last time), and whether or not the Republican candidate mounted a vigorous challenge (spending more than $100,000 on the campaign).

The vigor of the challenge is plainly the decisive variable. One-third of the strong challenges were successful, compared to 2.1 percent of the rest (and two of the three losing incumbents here were under indictment). Marginal Democrats predictably attracted more vigorous challenges (58

61

Table 3.12. *Winning Republican challengers, 1980 House elections (in percentages)*

	Democratic incumbent		
	Marginal	Nonmarginal	Total
Republican challenger			
Strong challenge	29 (38)[a]	48 (27)	37 (65)
Weak challenge	0 (27)	3 (117)	2 (144)
Total	17 (65)	11 (144)	13 (209)

Note: Marginal cases are those in which the Democratic incumbent won less than 60 percent of the two-party vote in 1978. Strong challenges are those in which the challenger spent at least $100,000.
[a] Number of cases from which percentages were calculated.
Source: Jacobson 1983a, Table 6.11.

percent, compared to 19 percent for nonmarginal Democrats). But strong Republican challengers actually had a higher rate of success in *nonmarginal* districts; and no Republican challenger who spent *less* than $100,000 took a marginal seat from a Democrat.

A surprising number of powerful senior Democrats were among the victims. Eight of the defeated Democratic incumbents had served nine or more terms in the house; one was majority whip, and five chaired committees. This reflected an important change in Republican strategy. Republicans had attempted to rebound in 1976 from the 1974 debacle by targeting freshmen Democrats who had just taken Republican seats; in 1978 they focused on open seats; neither approach was very fruitful. In 1980 they shifted attention to a number of more senior Democrats, hoping that they might be vulnerable because duties in Washington kept them away from home and linked them to the federal government's failures. As a result, some incumbents who, by the evidence of previous electoral margins, were quite safe turned out to be paper tigers once their bluff was called. This was a striking illustration of how contingent the value of incumbency is on the behavior of members and perceptions of potential opponents, and it did not go unremarked; it shocked surviving Democratic incumbents into activities that had a profound effect on the 1982 election.

Had the 1982 election followed the pattern of previous postwar midterms, the Republicans would have lost between 40 and 60 House seats. The economy was in its worst postwar recession, and the Republican president's job performance rating in the preelection Gallup poll (42 percent approving) was lower than that of any president since Truman in 1946. Under these conditions, different referendum models predicted Republican losses of varying magnitude (Hibbs 1982; Jacobson 1983*b*), but none came close to predicting accurately that Republicans would lose as few as 26 House seats. The difference in 1982 was that neither Republicans nor Democrats behaved in ways that consistently reinforced the expected effects of national forces.

Republicans avoided disaster by using money and organization to conduct what amounted to a countercyclical campaign. First, the national party's active recruitment drive produced a much stronger group of challengers than would have emerged spontaneously given election-year conditions. Party officials recruited vigorously in 1981, when the administration was riding high and a rosy Republican future could be envisioned. They worked successfully to hold on to most of those who had signed up, even as conditions turned bleak. As a result, Republicans fielded their most experienced group of challengers since 1972. One reason they managed to keep their recruits was that they could promise them well funded campaigns despite the contrary national trends, at least insofar as party money was concerned. Every Republican challenger showing any real possibility of winning could count on close to the maximum amount of help the national party could legally offer (upward of $50,000).

Largely in response to what the Republicans were doing, Democrats also departed from patterns expected in what promised to be a good Democratic year. One anticipated pattern did hold. After a slow start, Democrats had no trouble finding qualified challengers; the economy's precipitous decline inspired a large number of ambitious, experienced Democrats to attempt the move up to Congress. A postwar-record 42 percent of the Democratic House challengers had held elective office. Experienced Democrats were especially likely to challenge Republican freshmen, 60 percent of whom faced opponents with experience in elective office.

But money did not flow into the campaigns of Democatic challengers in nearly the proportion expected in a good Democratic year (Jacobson 1985*b*). The reason is that Democratic incumbents, stunned by what had happened to some of their colleagues in 1980 and fearful of the resources Republican challengers appeared to be mobilizing against them for 1982, went on a fundraising binge. "Panic is not too strong a word to describe it," said one Democratic campaign official. "Even people who were traditionally safe went out and really raised money in Washington and around the country in a way that they haven't before" (Clymer 1983*a*).

Much of this feverish fundraising activity took place in 1981 and in the first half of 1982, before the thrust of national conditions was fully evident. But by the time Democratic incumbents felt secure enough to relax their fundraising efforts, they had absorbed so much of the

Gary C. Jacobson

available money that many otherwise promising challengers were unable to finance their campaigns adequately. In the end, many incumbent Democrats accumulated much more money than they needed. But the party had no institutional means to redistribute any of the surplus into the campaigns of promising challengers. The Republicans, with greater central control over campaign assets, could respond strategically to changing circumstances; the Democrats could not.

This became crucial as economic conditions deteriorated. The October 8 announcement that unemployment had reached a postwar high of 10.1 percent had, in the words of Joseph Gaylord, political director of the National Republican Congressional Committee, "a devastating impact on Republican challengers. We saw people who in their survey research were within two or three points of a Democrat drop 15 or 18 points behind. . . . The same held true of a lot of incumbent areas, where we had members with 20- and 25-point leads who watched those evaporate down to six, seven, three" (Duncan 1983). According to his boss, Nancy Sinnott Dwight, "it was a disaster facing us, of major proportions – 55 to 60 seats" (Clymer 1983b).

They responded by rushing assistance to the newly endangered candidates. In every contest that seemed remotely close, Gaylord said, "we were on the phone asking 'What do you need? Is there anything we can do? Do you want to change the message?'" (Clymer 1983b). The committee spent $2.5 million in the last 18 days of the campaign, all of it in the most doubtful contests. It was a strategy aimed at minimizing losses; in the end, the party finally gave up on its challengers and concentrated instead on endangered incumbents and candidates for open seats who still had a chance.

The economy had given the Democrats an extraordinary opportunity, but they were organizationally incapable of exploiting it. National Democratic committees had little to contribute, and Democratic incumbents who suddenly found themselves home free and flush with cash could not be persuaded to part with it. "By late September it was pretty clear that Democrats were moving like mad. The incumbents were safe, and our challengers were moving up," said one Democratic fundraiser. "But our [spending] decisions were already made, and once the money is out there, you can't get it back" (Fialka and Farney 1983).

Republicans avoided disaster in 1982 because the national party committees worked to counter the effect of bad times to the collective benefit of their party. They fostered stronger challenges than would otherwise have emerged and thereby put Democrats on the defensive, inducing incumbents to soak up resources that could otherwise have helped an impressive group of Democratic challengers. They used centralized control over money and skill to focus their effort where it would be most effective, helping threatened incumbents and candidates for open seats in tight races during the final weeks of the campaign. Their intervention manifestly disrupted the usual connection between national conditions and the alternatives presented to voters in individual districts and so helped materially to avoid a disastrous party defeat.

NATIONAL ISSUES IN LOCAL CAMPAIGNS

Not only do national conditions affect strategic decisions about whether to run or contribute money, they also affect the substantive content of campaigns. This, in turn, determines the form in which national issues are presented to, and therefore influence, individual voters. The connections between national issues and individual voting decisions are shaped by the rhetoric of campaigns and so vary as the campaigns vary. Variation occurs both across districts in a single election and across election years. Variation across election years helps explain why survey findings about the determinants of the vote are so often inconsistent from one election to the next (Fiorina 1983; Kiewiet 1983).

Remember from the discussion of voting behavior that, to succeed, challengers must accomplish two basic tasks: building support for themselves and undermining that of their incumbent opponents. The former is insufficient without the latter. Adverse national conditions (for the incumbent's party) contribute to the first task by encouraging the best-qualified challengers to run and by inspiring contributors to support them when they do. They contribute to the second task by giving challengers an instrument for undermining the incumbent's support.

Incumbents are, as a class, remarkably adept at taking credit for the good things that the government does while avoiding responsibility for its failures. Under neutral or favorable conditions, a member who cultivates his district diligently and avoids personal scandal makes an extremely difficult target. But if people are sufficiently unhappy with an administration, if the economic situation is sufficiently dire, it may become a good deal more difficult to avoid guilt by association – *if* there is an energetic challenger continually reminding voters of the connection. This is crucial. A vigorous campaign is still essential to defeat an incumbent, no matter how bad the political conditions for his party. Someone has to tie him to his party and the administration and to offer voters an acceptable alternative. Someone has to turn national issues into local issues. But any challenger is helped enormously by having an issue to work with that is at the center of public attention and that can make the incumbent look bad.

None of this is news to congressional candidates. Democratic challengers zeroed in on the economy and the administration's "unfair"

65

policies in 1982, just as Republican challengers had used inflation, stagnation, and the Carter administration's incompetence to flay their opponents in 1980. Indeed, the ready availability of a powerful campaign theme as a weapon for attacking the incumbent may be another factor that attracts high-quality challengers and encourages people to finance and work for their campaigns.

What helps one party's challengers obviously also hurts the other party's challengers. Even good candidates with plenty of money have trouble finding an avenue of attack when incumbents enjoy "favorable" national conditions as well as the usual advantages of incumbency. They may accomplish the first task – convincing people that they are qualified to be members of Congress – but they have a much tougher time persuading voters that the current incumbent needs replacing. In 1982, a Republican challenger's best hope was to run the 1980 election over again: blame the Democratic incumbent for double-digit inflation and national decline under the Carter administration. The recession could then be explained as a necessary, if unfortunate, price that had to be paid for years of Democratic folly.

Incumbents' campaign strategies are also structured by national conditions. Incumbents of the party out of power in bad times have the best of both worlds, of course. They can campaign on their own record of district service and selective support for the president's more popular proposals, blaming the administration's errors for everything that has gone wrong. Any serious trouble they face is likely to be their own fault – lapses in sobriety or morality or extreme negligence in looking after the district.

Incumbents of the party afflicted by adverse political conditions face a more complicated set of options. One obvious strategy is to avoid responsibility for bad times by fashioning a political identity separate from the party and the administration. Incumbent Democrats running in 1980 were careful to avoid association with Carter and his policies; doing so was relatively easy because Carter had always kept aloof from the party and his fellow Democrats in Congress. Eluding responsibility for the general state of the nation was somewhat more difficult, because Democrats had controlled Congress for 25 years; this no doubt contributed to the defeats of some senior members who had let their district connections atrophy.

In 1982, a number of Republican incumbents – often on the advice of party officials – tried to distance themselves from the administration and its policies on at least a few issues. And of course they emphasized their own personal standing and record of service to the district. But not every incumbent took this tack, and not everyone who did managed to avoid association with the administration's troubles. Several things conspired

66

to make it more difficult than it has usually been in recent years for incumbents facing such problems to establish separate political identities. For one, Republicans in Congress *had* given virtually unanimous support to the president's most prominent domestic policies during the first year of his administration. Especially loyal were those first elected in 1980, "Reagan's Robots" to their opponents. Many had conducted campaigns that featured their support for Reagan and attributed at least some of their success to the party's national campaign urging people to "Vote Republican. For a Change." Both things made it harder for them to develop independent political identities, and, as freshmen, they had shorter records of service to constituents to fall back on.

This is no doubt part of the explanation for the unusually large number of first-term Republicans who were denied reelection (13 of 52 lost). In other recent elections, freshmen have been remarkably difficult to dislodge; for example, 72 of the 74 Democrats first elected in 1974 who sought reelection in 1976 were victorious; none of the House Democrats defeated in 1980 was a freshman. Indeed, the "sophomore surge" has been a primary measure of how the electoral value of incumbency has increased. The results of 1982 suggest that the sophomore surge is not an automatic consequence of incumbency but depends on how contests are framed by candidates and their campaigns. Freshmen who take office having featured national issues and who, as a consequence, identify themselves strongly with national policies should be more vulnerable to policy failures than are freshmen who pursue a personal franchise from the beginning.

The Republican party put on another national campaign in 1982, spending $14 million to urge voters to "Stay the Course." Insofar as the campaign was persuasive, it helped Republican candidates. But it made a strategy of detachment from the administration and party more difficult to pull off. It played into the hands of challengers working to tie Republican incumbents to the administration, injecting a national component into electoral situations where incumbents might have been happier running on their own performance. Once the economy became a major campaign issue, Republican incumbents could cope with it best by directing attention away from the present, toward the past (Democrats had created this mess) and future (Reaganomics would eventually bring prosperity without inflation). In this context, "Stay the Course" was a sensible theme.

National conditions, then, prescribe different campaign strategies in different electoral situations. Because campaign strategies differ, so does the substantive content of specific campaigns. The choices offered to voters are framed in different ways in different contests, so it is not surprising that the determinants of the vote decision also vary from year to year and from district to district. In 1978, for example, voters' ratings of Jimmy Carter had little effect on the House vote (Jacobson 1981). In 1982, on the other hand, assessments of Ronald Reagan's performance had a major influence on it. The reason is that Carter and his policies were not hot issues in local campaigns, whereas Reagan and his policies clearly were. If presidential performance *ever* matters to voters, it would in an election like 1982, when it was often a prominent focus of local campaigns.

Similarly, connections between economic conditions and the vote in 1982 were shaped by the terms in which the economic issue was thrashed out in campaigns. Voters' *personal* economic experiences – changes in income, employment status, federal benefits, tax payments – were unrelated to the vote. What mattered was whether voters thought that Reagan's economic programs would eventually help or hurt the economy and which party they thought would handle inflation or unemployment better (Jacobson 1983*b*). This is precisely the form in which economic issues were brought to the attention of voters by candidates and parties in the course of the campaign. The economic variables that best reflect the substantive content of the campaigns turn out to be the ones that matter for the individual vote.

Furthermore, voters' judgments about economic policy and performance influenced decisions differently depending on the party of the incumbent. In districts with Republican incumbents, the key question was whether the voter believed that Reaganomics would eventually help or hurt the economy; to a lesser degree, judgments about which party would handle unemployment better also mattered. In districts held by Democrats, the most important economic question concerned which party could deal with inflation more effectively (Jacobson 1983*b*).

These differences reflect the alternative campaign themes available to candidates in 1982. Democratic challengers worked to make political hay of the recession, with its double-digit unemployment, by blaming it on the administration and its Republican allies in Congress. In response, Republican incumbents could only argue that, although the economy was in bad shape now (mostly the Democrats' doing), Reagan's policies would eventually make things better. The economic question was whether or not to "stay the course." How voters answered it had a major influence on their decisions.

Republican challengers had little to gain, under the circumstances, from dwelling on the administration's economic programs. Times were bad, the future uncertain, and they shared no responsibility for what the administration had done. Most of their Democratic opponents had avoided records of unrelieved opposition to the administration (at least in districts where this might have hurt). Nor could Democrats be attacked for thwarting the president's programs, since his programs had not been thwarted. The best news Republican challengers had going for them was the dramatic drop in inflation that accompanied the recession, so it made good tactical sense to remind people as forcefully as possible of the double-digit inflation the Democrats (and, specifically, by association, the incumbent) had so recently bequeathed to the country.

Economic issues, then, exercise no simple mechanical influence over voting decisions. How they affect voters depends in good part on how they are presented by candidates and other activists during the course of the campaign. Competing campaigns naturally strive to cast the issues in the form that helps them most (or hurts them least). And it matters who prevails. In 1982, Republicans were able to make responsibility for inflation (in districts with Democratic incumbents) and the future success or failure of Reagan's programs (in districts with Republican incumbents) the determining economic questions. Considering the state of the economy, these were clearly their strongest suits. Of those voters with an opinion one way or the other, 53 percent thought Republicans would handle inflation better; only 19 percent thought they would handle unemployment better. Similarly, 65 percent thought the country was currently worse off because of Reaganomics; but 62 percent were persuaded that the administration's programs would, in the long run, help the economy (Jacobson 1983b). More often than not, Republican candidates won the battle to define what the contest was about, thereby limiting the damage inflicted by bad economic conditions. Money and superior organization evidently paid off.

Considering the problems faced by disadvantaged incumbents in situations like 1982, it is reasonable to suppose that campaign spending would help them. The campaign is more than simply an extension of the reelection work they have been doing all along. New messages may have to replace old ones. A member who has been celebrating his budget-cutting prowess suddenly has to show he has compassion, too. One who has made a point of his support for the administration finds it wise to separate himself from a few of its less popular policies; support for Ronald Reagan could be balanced by criticism of James Watt, for example. Money is useful in the battle to define what the contest is about, in casting it as a local rather than national event, or in making the future promise rather than the present performance of the economy the issue. The abundant funds available to Republican incumbents in 1982 could be put to good use.

This is not to argue that national conditions are open to unconstrained manipulation and are therefore, by themselves, unimportant. Quite the contrary. They force issues onto the electoral agenda and make competing arguments more or less persuasive. Republican campaigns were clearly damaged when unemployment hit double digits a month before election day. It was not so much a problem of losing the votes of the unemployed as of losing ground in the battle to define the economic issues. National conditions distribute real campaign advantages and disadvantages to individual candidates, and hence it is entirely rational for congressional elites to take them into account in their strategic thinking.

Still, the fact remains that the electoral impact of national conditions is strongly mediated by the decisions and strategies of congressional elites. The effects of national forces are neither simple nor direct nor automatic. It matters a great deal what candidates and activists choose to do with the opportunities or difficulties these forces present. This, again, gives incumbents a chance to exercise some control over their own fates by shaping the local definition of national issues. But the increasing organization and sophistication of opposing elites give them little reason to think that they can do so without a fight.

It is no accident that Republicans have been the chief innovators here. Greater security for incumbents works against the collective interest of the minority party (in becoming the majority party) even if it serves the individual interests of its incumbents. The 1974 disaster and the party's feeble comeback in 1976 drove Republican leaders to invent new political institutions and techniques adapted to the realities of contemporary electoral politics. Innovation has started to pay off, inspiring imitation by Democrats, who nonetheless remain far behind (Jacobson 1985b). Although energetic national party committees naturally offer plenty of help to incumbents, they promise to make elections more competitive because they generate stronger challenges, and the strength of the challenge determines the level of competition. Party committees are able to give nonincumbents some of the resources that incumbents have used to such advantage in pursuing entrepreneurial electoral politics.

SENATE ELECTIONS

So far I have focused on House elections. This is typical of congressional election scholarship. House elections have attracted particular attention for several reasons. Most of the theoretically interesting changes have been much more evident in House than in Senate contests; the data (particularly survey data) on them are better and more extensive; House elections are far more numerous and more obviously comparable; idiosyncratic factors seem to play a much more prominent role in Senate contests. But a brief look at Senate elections is useful and instructive, because they illustrate in a striking way some of the main points I have been trying to make.

At first it seemed that Senate seats, too, had become safer during the 1960s. Kostroski's (1973) study of Senate elections from 1946 through 1970 found evidence that the importance of party had declined sharply while that of incumbency had increased almost as sharply. Aggregated by decade, the average reelection rate of Senate incumbents in general elections remained very close to 75 percent from the 1920s through the 1950s; in the 1960s, it jumped to 90 percent. Since 1970, however, it has fallen back to its old level (78 percent). It has also shown a great deal of variation from year to year, hitting a postwar low of 55 percent in 1980, then rising to 93 percent in 1982. The proportion of seats won by incumbents with more than 60 percent of the vote has held steady over the entire period (Ornstein et al. 1982).

The weakening of party ties is just as evident in Senate as in House elections; the proportion of defecting partisans has grown identically in both. But Senate incumbents have not benefited from this development nearly as much. Defections currently favor House incumbents five to one, Senate incumbents only two to one (Jacobson 1983a). Whatever is supposed to have made House incumbents safer has not helped senators much. Why?

Certainly it is not because senators have been shy about increasing their own staff, office, communications, and travel allowances; the Senate has been as generous as the House in such matters (Ornstein et al. 1982). On the other hand, senators are not nearly so well situated as representatives to use these resources to develop strong personal ties with constituents. For most, the constituency is simply too large, too diverse. Even the most elaborate constituency service operation can reach only a small fraction of the voters. Hence, voters report fewer personal contacts with senators and their staffs. Contact is made primarily through the mass media, particularly television (Jacobson 1983a).

Indeed, Fenno (1982) identified the importance of mass media to senators as a crucial difference between the two houses. The media pay much more attention to senators; but this does not necessarily work to their benefit, because they do not control the message or the expectations reporters have about what senators are supposed to do. Activity in the Senate is more conspicuous, and senators are more likely to be associated with controversial and divisive issues. Senators could not devote themselves exclusively to nonpartisan and noncontroversial constituency services even if constituency size were no problem because the news media would not let them.

The news media pay more attention to senators for structural reasons. Not only are there fewer of them, but their "constituency" – the state – is

71

much more likely to match one or more media markets. This has another important consequence: it makes challenges to incumbent senators easier because the mass media can be used efficiently to reach voters. This is only one of a variety of factors that converge to make it much more likely that a Senate incumbent will be seriously challenged. And it is the much greater frequency of strong challenges that makes incumbent senators more vulnerable.

About two-thirds of the Senate challengers in recent elections have previously held elective office. Those who have not are often well known for other achievements: they were astronauts or basketball stars or ambassadors. Prominent challengers are attracted by the prestige and power of the Senate; so are campaign contributors, who are also attracted to prominent challengers. Contributors realize as well that the shift of a single Senate seat will make more difference than the shift of a single House seat; each senator is worth, from this perspective, 4.35 representatives. History also tells them that Senate challenges are more likely to succeed. It makes strategic sense for people who control campaign funds to focus on Senate seats, and that is what they do. The campaign finance laws also allow national party committees to spend much larger sums for Senate candidates; the party ceiling for California in 1982 was $1.4 million, for example (Jacobson 1985*b*). Thus, Senate challengers are much more likely to enjoy adequate campaign funds.

With adequate financing, Senate challengers are able to hire campaign professionals and to exploit the technological instruments of modern campaigns: polls, computers, direct mail, broadcast advertising, and so forth. They also enjoy far more free media coverage; Senate contests are bigger news than House contests because senators are bigger news than representatives (Fenno 1982). Small wonder that Senate challengers are typically so much more familiar to voters than are House challengers (Jacobson 1983*a*).

One other important difference should be mentioned. Senators, with six-year terms, do not have the pressure of a two-year election cycle to keep them attuned to the district. This not only makes it easier for them to lose touch with constituents but also makes it harder to maintain an illusion of invulnerability. The electoral margin last time is not regarded as a valid indicator of the incumbent's strength because circumstances and issues can change so much over a six-year period. An easy win in one election does not discourage a vigorous challenge in the next.

Senate incumbents do not always face strong challenges, of course; and when they do not, they win as easily as do House incumbents with feeble opposition (Westlye 1981). The difference is that weak challenges are much less the norm in Senate elections.

Senators, then, unlike representatives, have not been able to exploit the changing political environment to solidify their personal hold on the constituency. At the same time, they are more immediately threatened by the electoral innovations spawned by changing conditions: new information-gathering and communication techniques, PACs and national party committees with millions of dollars to spend, aggressively negative independent campaigns. House members may at least enjoy the benefits as well as the costs of more volatile, candidate-centered electoral politics *if* they are willing to invest the necessary entrepreneurial effort. Senators, by and large, do not even have that choice, because the means used by House members to preserve a strong personal grip on the district are not available to them. Thus, for senators the sources of incumbent *insecurity* in present-day electoral politics stand out starkly.

ELECTIONS AND THE POLITICS OF CONGRESS

The electoral politics of Congress deserve careful study for one simple reason: how Congress works, how well it performs as a governing institution, is inextricably bound to how its members win and hold office. This was the central theme of Mayhew's (1974*b*) classic account of the electoral connection. The Congress of the early 1970s seemed perfectly designed to serve the reelection needs of its members. Resources, structures, and rules provided countless opportunities for members to advertise themselves, to claim credit for delivering benefits to constituents, and to take popular positions on issues. The result was a decentralized legislature, its fragmented party coalitions guided by tolerant party leaders, that was best suited to trafficking in particularized benefits. A few institutional elements – the Appropriations and the Ways and Means committees in the House, for example – defended collective institutional interests by checking rampant distributive politics and rewarding (with influence and status) contributions to serious legislative work. But, structurally, the collective performance of Congress was clearly subordinate to the individual pursuit of reelection.

This produced a Congress that was inordinately responsive without being responsible. Individual members could be keenly sensitive and responsive to people and groups whose support or opposition mattered for reelection while avoiding responsibility for Congress's less than sparkling collective contribution to governing the country. Thus, popular contempt for Congress as an institution, or politicians as a class, did not preclude remarkably high regard for individual members or wide incumbent-reelection margins (Fenno 1975; Parker and Davidson 1979).

The evolution of electoral politics over the past decade has reinforced many of the institutional tendencies Mayhew identified. The close

73

reciprocal relationship between the external and internal politics of Congress means that changes in one inevitably produce changes in the other. Congressional life has been altered to accommodate an ever more frantic pursuit of electoral security, and other institutional changes have, in turn, helped make it more frantic. But countertrends are, as usual, also at work; so there is no reason to think that any new equilibrium has been reached.

Reinforcing trends are easy to find. The data in Table 3.3 show the continued growth in time, energy, and other resources devoted to electorally oriented activities. Changes in House rules in the early 1970s decentralized authority from committees to subcommittees, parceling out more, if smaller, chunks of legislative turf. The parallel movement to open up the process to outside scrutiny – recorded votes in the Committee of the Whole House, committee and subcommittee hearings open to the public – exposed members to a host of new outside pressures. PACs and other organized interest groups, dramatically expanding their own activity at this time, were there to take advantage of it. Simultaneously, the growing demand for campaign funds (see Table 3.11) and the prospect that burgeoning PAC resources might be mobilized against them sharpened members' sensitivity to organized interests.

The 1970s also saw a sharp increase in the number of voluntary retirements and so, despite high incumbent reelection rates, a high level of turnover in House membership. By 1981, members elected since Richard Nixon's resignation constituted a majority. This younger generation established new standards for district attention (Parker 1980), sensitivity to external demands, and, on the Democratic side, disloyalty to the party (Sinclair 1981). Its members, particularly on the Republican side, also practiced more aggressively ideological politics.

All of these things contributed to the decay of traditional congressional norms (Fenno 1973). Specialization and apprenticeship fell to competitive prospecting for hot issues and the compulsion to make an immediate splash in what had become a much more public forum. Seniority was subverted with the votes of the large contingent of younger members whose experience and career pursuits left them unwilling and unable to wait patiently for time and reelection to elevate them to positions of power. Reciprocity diminished along with specialization and the claims of expertise it justified. Courtesy, too, declined as the pursuit of public attention and the desire to score ideological points took precedence.

One consequence is that congressional life is less congenial and pleasant than it used to be; ironically, changes arising from a more vigorous pursuit of the prize – a seat in Congress – produce conditions that seem to diminish its value. More importantly, these changes have undermined Congress's institutional effectiveness. Legislative coalitions are harder to assemble, coherent policy decisions more difficult to reach. Part of the explanation is certainly the many baffling and divisive problems on Congress's current agenda; but developments in electoral politics share a major part of the blame.

It seemed at first that the vanishing marginals should produce a more insulated, ingrown Congress. But in fact the opposite has happened. The focus of congressional politics is far more external than it used to be. More time and attention is devoted to politics outside the institution; outside influences on internal politics are far stronger and more pervasive. Consider lobbying. Bauer, Pool, and Dexter's (1968) research in the 1950s revealed a process dominated by insiders. Lobbyists worked through friends and allies in Congress, supporting them with various kinds of assistance. This encouraged them to take on projects they were already inclined to pursue by making it easier and less costly of time and other resources. Lobbyists persuaded members to help them out by helping members to look good when they did. They ignored opponents, abjuring pressure tactics that might antagonize people they would need to work with later on something else. Members, not surprisingly, found lobbying to be basically helpful and benign.

Few members would take the same view today. Some insiders still lobby in the old way (see Drew 1983), but they have now been joined by a host of lobbyists whose influence comes from the outside – people able to mobilize extensive campaign resources and grass-roots constituencies. Dozens of groups now rate members' votes, compile lists of targets, stimulate mail and phone calls, and mobilize campaign volunteers, all in addition to raising and distributing campign money. And they have no compunction about threatening to withdraw support from, or to support the opponents of, members who oppose them; this is what they are in business for. Members certainly feel pressure now from lobbies working from the outside, and they resent it. But it is a fact of life, a direct consequence of the system of electoral politics they have helped to create and sustain.

Interest groups pursue outside strategies because they have found them to be effective; environmentalists, antiabortionists, used-car dealers, bankers, the health industry, and milk producers are among those who have played the game successfully in recent years. Effective outside demands contribute to the fragmentation of Congress and make the chore of assembling policy-making coalitions (except, perhaps, those which are purely distributive logrolls) more difficult. Congressional leaders are the quintessential insiders, and their traditional styles of leadership are most effective in the internal arenas of congressional politics. Even with a greatly strengthened office, House Speaker Tip

O'Neill had to work extraordinarily hard for limited success with Carter's legislative program (Sinclair 1981).

One strategy he used suggests, however, that inside leaders, too, can exploit the outside approach. On occasion, O'Neill worked through influential groups in the districts of members the party wanted to bring on board, getting local leaders to persuade the member to the party's position (Dodd and Sullivan 1980). The Reagan administration also recognized the potential in grass-roots lobbying and used it very effectively in its early battles to cut spending and taxes. Administration strategists used the nationwide network it had built up for the 1980 campaign to stimulate an avalanche of letters and telephone calls that helped convince a number of reluctant Democrats that they had no choice but to come along (Wehr 1981).

In this and in other ways, parties and party leaders have shown signs of learning how to cope with the challenges to leadership posed by the contemporary Congress and its electoral politics. If members are inordinately responsive to grass-roots pressures, work through local elites. If they seem worried about having campaign money and other resources available if a strong challenge should materialize, find ways to provide them. If elections are predominately candidate-centered, work to recruit and train the most promising candidates. If you want members committed to a national agenda, help them get elected by using national issues to advantage in the local campaign. The Republicans have been doing all of these things, and the Democrats have begun to do some of them. They represent trends running counter to the others discussed here, and they seem to be gathering strength. It is not, therefore, inevitable that the further evolution of electoral politics and institutions will bring only greater individual responsiveness and collective irresponsibility. If Madison was right, the genius of American political institutions has resided in their ability to harness individual self-interest to collective ends; national leaders may yet devise ways to exploit entrepreneurial electoral politics to achieve collective purposes.

NOTES

1 The definition of marginal seats is arbitrary; two favorite thresholds of marginality are 55 or 60 percent of the two-party vote; the proportion of marginal seats held by incumbents declined by both these definitions in the 1960s (Mayhew 1974*a*).

2 The data used in this section were made available by the Inter-University Consortium for Political and Social Research. The data for the 1982 American National Election Study were originally collected by the Center for Political Studies of the Institute for Social Research, the University of Michigan, under a grant from the National Science Foundation. Neither the original collectors of

the data nor the Consortium bear any responsibility for the analyses or interpretations presented here.

3 Because the dependent variable in these equations – the respondent's vote – is categorical, the error term cannot be normally distributed, so ordinary least squares is not, strictly speaking, an appropriate estimation technique. I employ it nonetheless because the OLS coefficients are so easily interpreted. I also estimated the equations using probit, the proper technique for a dichotomous dependent variable, and the results are listed below. Although the equations cannot be interpreted directly from estimated coefficients, the probit results clearly duplicate the OLS results reported in Table 3.11. The standard errors are in parentheses.

	1	2	3
Intercept	4.84	4.95	4.95
	(.16)	(.20)	(.24)
Party identification	1.01	1.02	1.01
	(0.7)	(.08)	(.10)
Democrat is incumbent	.76	.55	.40
	(.18)	(.20)	(.24)
Republican is incumbent	−.51	−.17	−.21
	(.18)	(.20)	(.24)
Familiarity with Democrat		.54	.37
		(.11)	(.14)
Familiarity with Republican		−.68	−.47
		(.12)	(.15)
Likes something about Democrat			1.38
			(.20)
Dislikes something about Democrat			−.92
			(.23)
Likes something about Republican			−1.35
			(.22)
Dislikes something about Republican			1.06
			(.24)

REFERENCES

Abramowitz, Alan I. 1980. A comparison of voting for U.S. Senator and Representative. *American Political Science Review* 74:633–640.
Arcelus, Francisco, and Allan H. Meltzer. 1975. The effects of aggregate economic variables on congressional elections. *American Political Science Review* 69:1232–1239.
Arseneau, Robert B., and Raymond E. Wolfinger. 1973. Voting behavior in congressional elections. Paper delivered at the annual meeting of the American Political Science Association, New Orleans, September 4–8.
Bauer, Raymond A., Ithiel de Sola Pool, and Lewis Anthony Dexter. 1968. *American Business and Public Policy*. New York: Atherton.
Bloom, Harold S., and H. Douglas Price. 1975. Voter response to short-run

economic conditions: the asymmetric effect of prosperity and recession. *American Political Science Review* 69:1240–1254.

Born, Richard. 1979. Generational replacement and the growth of incumbent reelection margins in the U.S. House. *American Political Science Review* 73:811–817.

Burnham, Walter Dean. 1975. Insulation and responsiveness in congressional elections. *Political Science Quarterly* 90:411–435.

Calvert, Randall L., and John A. Ferejohn. 1983. Coattail voting in recent presidential elections. *American Political Science Review* 77:407–419.

Clymer, Adam. 1983a. Campaign costs up sharply in 1982. *New York Times,* April 3, p. 14.

1983b. The economic basis for "throwing the bums out" in the 1980 and 1982 American elections. Paper delivered at the annual meeting of the American Political Science Association, Chicago, September 1–4.

Collie, Melissa P. 1981. Incumbency, electoral safety, and turnover in the House of Representatives, 1952–1976. *American Political Science Review* 75: 119–131.

Cover, Albert D. 1977. One good term deserves another: the advantage of incumbency in congressional elections. *American Journal of Political Science* 21:523–542.

Cover, Albert D., and David R. Mayhew. 1977. Congressional dynamics and the decline of competitive congressional elections. In *Congress Reconsidered,* ed. Lawrence C. Dodd and Bruce I. Oppenheimer. New York: Praeger.

Crotty, William J., and Gary C. Jacobson. 1980. *American Parties in Decline.* Boston: Little, Brown.

Dodd, Lawrence, and Terry Sullivan. 1980. House leadership success in the vote gathering process: a comparative analysis. Paper delivered at the annual meeting of the Midwest Political Science Association, Chicago, April 24–26.

Drew, Elizabeth. 1982a. Politics and money – I. *New Yorker,* December 6, pp. 54–149.

1982b. Politics and money – II. *New Yorker,* December 13, pp. 57–111.

1983. Charlie. In *Interest Group Politics,* ed. Allan J. Cigler and Burdett A. Loomis. Washington, D.C.: CQ Press.

Duncan, Phil. 1983. Wealthy and well-organized GOP panel eyes 1984 elections. *National Journal,* July 2, p. 1351.

Edwards, George C., III. 1980. *Presidential Influence in Congress.* San Francisco: W. H. Freeman.

Erikson, Robert S. 1971. The advantage of incumbency in congressional elections. *Polity* 3:395–405.

Feldman, Paul, and James Jondrow. 1984. Congressional elections and local federal spending. *American Journal of Political Science* 28:147–164.

Fenno, Richard F., Jr. 1973. The internal distribution of influence: the House. In *The Congress and America's Future,* ed. David B. Truman. 2nd ed. Englewood Cliffs, N. J.: Prentice-Hall.

1975. If, as Ralph Nader says, Congress is "the broken branch," how come we love our congressmen so much? In *Congress in Change,* ed. Norman J. Ornstein. New York: Praeger.

1978. *Home Style: House Members in Their Districts.* Boston: Little, Brown.

1982. *The United States Senate: A Bicameral Perspective.* Washington, D.C.: American Enterprise Institute for Public Policy Research.

Ferejohn, John A. 1977. On the decline of competition in congressional elections.

American Political Science Review 71:166–176.

Ferejohn, John A., and Randall Calvert. 1984. Presidential coattails in historical perspective. *American Journal of Political Science* 28:127–146.

Fialka, John J., and Dennis Farney. 1983. Democrats trail GOP in ability to direct cash to closest races. *Wall Street Journal*, November 7, p. 1.

Fiorina, Morris P. 1977. The case of the vanishing marginals: the bureaucracy did it. *American Political Science Review* 71:177–181.

1978. Economic retrospective voting in American national elections: a micro analysis. *American Journal of Political Science* 22:426–433.

1981. Some problems in studying the effects of resource allocation in congressional elections. *American Journal of Political Science* 25:543–567.

1983. Who is held responsible? Further evidence on the Hibbing-Alford thesis. *American Journal of Political Science* 27:158–164.

Hibbs, Douglas A., Jr. 1982. President Reagan's mandate from 1980 elections: a shift to the right? *American Politics Quarterly* 10:387–420.

Hunt, Albert. 1982. An inside look at politicians hustling PACs. *Wall Street Journal*, October 1, p. 1.

Jacobson, Gary C. 1980. *Money in Congressional Elections.* New Haven: Yale University Press.

1981. Incumbents' advantages in the 1978 congressional elections. *Legislative Studies Quarterly* 6:183–200.

1983a. *The Politics of Congressional Elections.* Boston: Little, Brown.

1983b. Reagan, Reaganomics, and strategic politics in 1982: a test of alternative theories of midterm congressional elections. Paper delivered at the annual meeting of the American Political Science Association, Chicago, September 1–4.

1984. Money in the 1980 and 1982 congressional elections. In *Campaign Finance in the 1980s*, ed. Michael J. Malbin. Washington, D.C.: American Enterprise Institute and Chatham House.

1985a. Money and votes reconsidered: congressional elections, 1972–1982. *Public Choice.*

1985b. Party organization and the efficient distribution of congressional campaign resources: Republicans and Democrats in 1982. *Political Science Quarterly.*

1985c. The marginals never vanished: incumbency and competition in elections to the U.S. House of Representatives, 1952–1982. Paper delivered at the annual meeting of the Midwest Political Science Association, Chicago, April 17–20.

1985d. Enough is too much: money and competition in House elections, 1972–1984. Paper delivered at the Thomas P. O'Neill, Jr., Symposium "Elections in America," Boston College, October 4–5.

Jacobson, Gary C., and Samuel Kernell. 1983. *Strategy and Choice in Congressional Elections.* 2nd ed. New Haven: Yale University Press.

Johannes, John R., and John C. McAdams. 1981. The congressional incumbency effect: Is it casework, policy compatibility, or something else? *American Journal of Political Science* 25:512–542.

Kiewiet, D. Roderick. 1983. *Macroeconomics & Micropolitics: The Electoral Effects of Economic Issues.* Chicago: University of Chicago Press.

Kostroski, Warren Lee. 1973. Party and incumbency in postwar Senate elections: trends, patterns, and models. *American Political Science Review* 67:1213–1234.

Kramer, Gerald H. 1971. Short-term fluctuations in U.S. voting behavior. *American Political Science Review* 65:131–143.

Krehbiel, Keith, and John R. Wright. 1983. The incumbency effect in congressional elections: a test of two explanations. *American Journal of Political Science* 27:140–157.

Mann, Thomas E. 1977. *Unsafe at Any Margin: Interpreting Congressional Elections.* Washington, D.C.: American Enterprise Institute for Public Policy Research.

Mann, Thomas E., and Raymond E. Wolfinger. 1980. Candidates and parties in congressional elections. *American Political Science Review* 74:617–632.

Mayhew, David R. 1974a. Congressional elections: the case of the vanishing marginals. *Polity* 6:295–317.

1974b. *Congress: The Electoral Connection.* New Haven: Yale University Press.

Nelson, Candice. 1978–79. The effects of incumbency on voting in congressional elections. *Political Science Quarterly* 93:665–678.

Ornstein, Norman J., Thomas E. Mann, Michael J. Malbin, and John F. Bibby. 1982. *Vital Statistics on Congress, 1982.* Washington, D.C.: American Enterprise Institute for Public Policy Research.

Parker, Glenn R. 1980. Sources of change in congressional district attentiveness. *American Journal of Political Science* 24:115–124.

Parker, Glenn R., and Roger H. Davidson. 1979. Why do Americans love their congressmen so much more than their Congress? *Legislative Studies Quarterly* 4:53–61.

Parker, Glenn R., and Suzanne L. Parker. 1982. The causes and consequences of congressional district attention. Paper delivered at the annual meeting of the American Political Science Association, Denver, September 2–5.

Payne, James L. 1980. The personal electoral advantage of House incumbents, 1936–1976. *American Politics Quarterly* 8:375–398.

Powell, Lynda W. 1982. Constituency service and electoral margin in Congress. Paper delivered at the annual meeting of the American Political Science Association, Denver, September 2–5.

Sabato, Larry J. 1981. *The Rise of the Political Consultants.* New York: Basic Books.

Sinclair, Barbara. 1981. Coping with uncertainty: building coalitions in the House and the Senate. In *The New Congress,* ed. Thomas E. Mann and Norman J. Ornstein. Washington, D.C.: American Enterprise Institute for Public Policy Research.

Stokes, Donald R., and Warren E. Miller. 1966. Party government and the saliency of Congress. In *Elections and the Political Order,* ed. Angus Campbell, Philip E. Converse, Warren E. Miller, and Donald R. Stokes. New York: John Wiley.

Time. 1982. Running with the PACS. October 25, pp. 18–26.

Tufte, Edward R. 1973. The relationship between seats and votes in two-party systems. *American Political Science Review* 67:540–554.

1975. Determinants of the outcomes of midterm congressional elections. *American Political Science Review* 69:812–826.

1978. *Political Control of the Economy.* Princeton, N.J.: Princeton University Press.

Wehr, Elizabeth. 1981. White House's lobbying apparatus produces impressive tax victory. *Congressional Quarterly Weekly Report*, August 1, pp. 1372–73.

Westlye, Mark C. 1981. Information and partisanship in Senate elections. Paper delivered at the annual meeting of the American Political Science Association, New York. September 3–6.

Yiannakis, Diana Evans. 1981. The grateful electorate: casework and congressional elections. *American Journal of Political Science* 25:568–580.

The shape of congressional institutions

Part II focuses on institutional choice. Institutions are not rigidly cast, nor are they predetermined by nature; they are made by men and can be changed by men. Congressional, like all institutional, choices are constrained and influenced by previous institutional choices; but to a great extent, they are made to satisfy members' desires.

In the Introduction we suggested that institutions provide an effective way for members to achieve their goals. Over time legislatures fine-tune their own internal structure in order to achieve greater effectiveness. Changes may be in response to changing environmental conditions. Alchian (1950) argued that the more effective institutional structures, those that allow members to pursue their goals with the least cost to themselves, are those that will endure. Effective institutional structures will replace ineffective ones.

A universal method for improving efficiency is to divide labors. Firms divide labor among the many inputs to production. This allows the firm to capture efficiency gains due to specialization. Legislatures divide labor for a similar reason.

In legislatures labor is usually divided in two ways, through the committee system and through the party system. Committee systems allow members to divide the various policy issues that face the legislature into distinct and separate jurisdictions, each delegated to a different committee. Committee members specialize in the aspects of their particular issues, and the legislature captures some gains in efficiency.

On the other hand, parties provide management and coordination. Parties fulfill many of the same functions that managers in firms fulfill. As we discussed in the Introduction, an important function of a manager is to reduce transactions costs within the firm. Parties reduce the transactions costs associated with building coalitions within the legislature. When there are enduring coalitions (i.e., the congressional parties) the process of building coalitions on any matter does not have to take place anew each time, and thus the costs of negotiating bargains and securing votes are saved.

In dividing labor, however, legislatures face many of the same problems as firms. The informational problems and the resulting problems with shirking, discussed by Alchian and Demsetz (1972), exist in legislatures as well. The rules and procedures that constrain the actions of committees, that sequence the flow of legislation, and that determine the rules for deciding issues provide the mechanisms in legislatures to overcome these problems. This part examines committees, parties, and party leaders, and the rules and procedures of the congressional system.

THE DEVELOPMENT OF INSTITUTIONAL ARRANGEMENTS

Nelson Polsby is widely recognized as having made a ground breaking analysis of the organizational development of the House. He suggests the ways in which the organizational structure of the House serves the interest of its members. Polsby argues that as an institution becomes more powerful its members become progressively more interested in the benefits that the organization can provide for them. As a result, the institution takes on certain characteristics in order to satisfy these individuals' goals. For example, the institution may become characterized by a common career pattern. This includes both a general career pattern, which differentiates the institution and its membership from the rest of society (what Polsby calls a "boundary"), and a more specific career pattern, which structures advancement within the organization (e.g., patterns of leadership recruitment and apprenticeship norms). Polsby also notices that a legislative institution develops clearly defined procedural structures that routinize decision making and conflict resoluting. Institutional evolution also leads to a pattern of decentralization that spreads authority in the institution among its members. These expectations about the development of the House appear to be borne out by empirical evidence, which Polsby also presents.

Barry Weingast extends Polsby's analysis by examining the rational choice basis for the "institutionalization" of the House. Specifically, Weingast offers an explanation for the emergence of a norm of universalism in Congress.[1] By a universalism norm, Weingast refers to a practice in Congress whereby members implicitly agree to distribute projects to all who may require them, thereby reducing competition over resources between members.

In Weingast's view, norms are institutional mechanisms that facilitate cooperation between legislators. Since there is no external enforcement mechanism for "deals" struck in a legislature, and since members may occasionally find it to their advantage to renege on such deals, agreements, such as norms, must be in the interest of the legislators who ultimately enforce them. Weingast shows why a norm of universalism is in the self-interest of legislators. His argument centers on the uncertain benefits associated with coalitional politics when funds are provided only to coalition members.

In distributing some fixed amount of project dollars by majority rule the unstable world of minimum-winning-coalition politics might easily prevail (a winning coalition in a majority-rule setting is any coalition that contains more than one-half of the members). In voting over the allocating of projects to congressional districts, a congressman may be a member of a winning coalition one time but not the next. An institutional system in which projects are divided among the members of a winning coalition, with none going to the losers, presents a great deal of uncertainty to congressmen. This uncertainty concerning their inclusion in winning coalitions, and thus about their ability to bring electorally important projects home to their districts, creates a situation in which members might prefer some specific, for-certain, sharing rule. For example, members can better achieve their reelection by developing and adhering to a norm of universalism in distributing projects, where everyone who wants one gets one, than they can by competing under pure majority rule for a somewhat larger share of the project dollars.

Imagine a three-person legislature where the membership must vote, by majority rule, to divide $100 for projects to their districts. Any two of the members can form a coalition, outvote the other member two to one, and split the $100 between them. Suppose for simplicity that they split it evenly. There are four possible coalitions that might form: member 1 with member 2, member 1 with member 3, member 2 with member 3, and a coalition of the whole. However, if a coalition of the whole forms, then one of the two-person coalitions can form from it and split the money between just the two of them, thereby increasing each of their shares at the expense of the member who is left out. Each of these two-person coalitions is referred to as a minimal winning coalition. Without a norm of universalism it is expected that the coalition that forms to split the project dollars will be minimal-winning.

Under pure majority rule each member would get $50 two-thirds of the time (being in two of the three minimal winning coalitions) and $0 one-third of the time. Under a norm of universalism, however, each member receives one-third of the total amount of project dollars for their district, that is, $33⅓. Though the systems have the same expected value to each member ($50 × ⅔ + $0 × ⅓ = $33⅓), the system wherein the project money is divided among the members by a norm of universalism has less risk. The members need not suffer through feast-and-famine cycles in their ability to bring home project money. Because over time the two methods yield the same amount of project dollars to their districts, members prefer the universalism norm as it reduces uncertainty and insures a steady supply of electorally important project dollars.

COMMITTEES

Richard Fenno, Jr., examines a different aspect of congressional organization: the impact on decision making of decentralization through a standing committee system. Decentralization allows the legislature to capture the efficiency gains that arise through specialization. Also, decentralization allows members to specialize in aspects of policy making that are best suited to the goals they pursue. Thus, members who are most concerned with reelection join committees whose jurisdiction focuses on what Mayhew in Chapter 1 referred to as particularistic legislation, like Public Works or Interior and Insular Affairs, which oversees the development of rivers and harbors projects and the disposal of western public lands. On the other hand, those more interested in power within the institution join committees that have jurisdiction over policies affecting all members, for example, the Committee on Ways and Means or Appropriations. Those who are most concerned with crafting good public policy join committees where position taking is central, for example, Education and Labor. Fenno argues that the difference in the goals of members of different committees leads to differences in the strategies adopted by the committees, the procedures for conflict resolution within the committees, and ultimately the ability of the committee to get its legislation passed through Congress. In this fashion, Fenno's comparative study of committees links the literature on the electoral connection with the models of procedural structure and with the literature on the policy outputs of committees.

Fenno argues that committees specialize by providing different types of forums for members to achieve their goals. Committees are structured to facilitate the pursuit of these goals. Membership on the right committee is important to members, but membership on particular committees is a scarce commodity. David Rohde and Kenneth Shepsle examine the mechanisms and procedures by which committee assignments are determined. They find that membership on committees is largely self-selected: most members get on committees of their choice. For senior members the property rights that accompany seniority guarantee this outcome. Rohde and Shepsle, however, go further and show that members' committee choices are related to the type of district they represent and that most members are granted some committee they requested.

A curious feature of the assignment process that has been pointed out by Barry Weingast is that it provides incentives to members to reveal truthfully their preferred committee choice, thus increasing efficiency in the assignment of members of committees. As Fenno points out, some committees are more prestigious and powerful than others and everyone would like to get membership on those. Only a few can get a membership, however. For any freshman the likelihood of getting a membership is small. If the system operates to award as many members as possible their first-choice committee, then requests for one of the premier committees reduce the likelihood of receiving a committee assignment that enables them to pursue their goals, since these other committees may also be filled on the first round. Thus, members request those committees that promise to enable them to serve their goals most effectively, not necessarily the premier committees.

Both the Fenno and the Rohde and Shepsle chapters examine the functioning of the Committee system. Further, these chapters suggest reasons why the peculiar committee system we see in Congress was adopted and survives. As environmental conditions change, however, the committee system changes. Also, as new institutional innovations are discovered that are perhaps more efficient than the existing institutions, they will replace the existing ones. David Brady and Mark Morgan examine a particular instance of institutional change, the evolution of the appropriations committees in Congress. Prior to the Civil War appropriations were within the jurisdiction of Ways and Means. During the four decades from 1880 to 1920 jurisdiction over appropriations was shared by authorizing committees and the appropriations committees. Only in two historical periods, 1865–80 and 1920 to the present, has jurisdiction over appropriations been centralized in the appropriations committees. Brady and Morgan suggest that the decision to centralize spending authority in the appropriations committees resulted from incentives to reduce budget deficits after the Civil War and World War I. Changes in environmental conditions, then, led to a greater demand by constituents and therefore by members for fiscal responsibility. Brady and Morgan argue that the institutional powers delegated the appropriations committees provide a method for achieving fiscal responsibility.

PARTIES

Many of the voting rules in legislatures provide the membership a way to constrain the actions of its committees. Other structures, possibly the appropriations committees as suggested by Brady and Morgan, provide mechanisms to enforce agreements among members and a method to oversee the activities of members. These institutional arrangements mitigate the informational and shirking problems that often result from collective action.

Another institutional feature frequently used in legislatures to provide oversight and manage coalition formation is the party. But as alternative institutional arrangements that facilitate coalition formation and oversight have emerged (such as the decentralized committee system in the twentieth-century Congress), the need for parties has dwindled. David Brady, Joseph Cooper, and Patricia Hurley detail the resulting decline in the power of parties in Congress. In particular, they show that the ability of parties to form coalitions declines from 1887 to 1968.

Parties do still provide a way to organize coalitions and monitor the actions of committees. Party leaders are given a wide range of powers to discipline and reward members and to direct the process of legislation. But House leaders are accountable to the members of their party. If they exercise "excessive leadership," the costs to the membership of these excesses may exceed the benefits from the institutional arrangement. In such cases the leader may be removed. In extreme cases, the House may attempt to reform the basic institutional arrangements to prevent such excesses. Charles Jones examines the limits of leadership and how institutional features in the House have evolved to prevent excessive leadership.

Finally, Terry Sullivan examines the impact of the constitutional division of powers between the president and Congress. The ability of the president to affect congressional decisions is founded in the Constitution, but much of the president's ability to influence congressional decisions arises from his ability to act as a leader in the legislative process. Sullivan analyzes the influence of the president and how congressional institutions channel and constrain his influence.

Sullivan's study provides an opportunity to test some of the notions suggested by the other authors in Part II. By examining a large data set about the coalition process – data on the initial positions of members and their commitments prior to voting – the model explicitly considers the desire for institutional power as a motivating force for members. It predicts that this motivation leads to differential patterns of conversion on issues important to the president. Sullivan assumes that the quest for power, however, is secondary to the more practical and immediate concern with reelection. Thus, it is expected that the institutional variables designed to test the power motive are not as effective in accounting for behavior as are the constituency variables. The evidence Sullivan offers supports this expectation, although it may also suggest that, in fact, institutional motivations play *no role* whatsoever in coalition formation.

NOTE

1 Norms are standards that prescribe acceptable and unacceptable behavior in an organization. They are informal rules that prescribe "how things are done here" (Hinckley 1971).

REFERENCES AND SUGGESTED READINGS

Alchian, Armen A. 1950. "Uncertainty, Evolution, and Economic Theory." *Journal of Political Economy* 58, no. 3: 211–21.

Alchian, Armen A., and Harold Demsetz. 1972. "Production, Information Costs, and Economic Organization." *American Economic Review* 62, no. 5: 777–95.

Buck, J. Vincent. 1972. "Presidential Coattails and Congressional Loyalty." *Midwest Journal of Political Science* 16, no. 3: 460–72.

Bullock, Charles. 1962. "House Careerists: Changing Patterns of Longevity and Attrition." *American Political Science Review* 67:1295–1300.

Burns, James MacGregor. 1978. *Leadership.* New York: Harper & Row.

Champagne, Anthony. 1984. *Congressman Sam Rayburn.* New Brunswick, N.J.: Rutgers University Press.

Cherryholmes, Cleo, and Michael Shapiro. 1969. *Representatives and Roll Calls: A Computer Simulation of Voting in the Eighty-eighth Congress.* Indianapolis: Bobbs-Merrill.

Clausen, Aage. 1973. *How Congressmen Decide: A Policy Focus.* New York: St. Martin's Press.

Cooper, Joseph. 1970. "The Origins of the Standing Committees and the Development of the Modern House." *Rice University Studies* 56; no. 3.

Cronin, Thomas, ed. 1982. *Rethinking the Presidency.* Boston: Little, Brown.

Cummings, Milton. 1966. *Congressmen and the Electorate.* New York: Free Press.

Dodd, Lawrence C. 1970. "Congress and the Quest for Power." In *Congress Reconsidered,* ed. Dodd and Bruce Oppenheimer. 1st ed. New York: Harcourt Brace & World.

Dodd, Lawrence C., and Terry Sullivan. 1979. *Partisan Vote-Gathering in the House: Concepts, Models, Measures, and Propositions.* APSA Convention paper, Washington, D.C.

Edwards, George III. 1980. *Presidential Influence in Congress.* San Francisco: Freeman.

Enelow, James. 1980. Legislative Amendments and a Theory of Optimal Compromise. Paper delivered at the Public Choice Society convention, San Francisco.

1981. "Saving Amendments, Killer Amendments, and an Expected Utility Theory of Sophisticated Voting." *Journal of Politics* 43:1063–89.

1984. "A New Theory of Congressional Compromise." *American Political Science Review* 28, no. 3:708–18.

Enelow, James, and David Koehler. 1980. "The Amendment in Legislative Strategy: Sophisticated Voting in the U.S. Congress." *Journal of Politics* 42:396–413.

*Fenno, Richard F., Jr. 1973. *Congressmen in Committees.* Boston: Little, Brown.

Follett, Mary P. 1896. *The Speaker of the House of Representatives.* New York: Longmans, Green.

Froman, Lewis, and Randall Ripley. 1965. "Conditions for Party Leadership: The Case of House Democrats." *American Political Science Review*, March, pp. 52–63.

Goodwin, George. 1970. *The Little Legislatures*. Amherst: University of Massachusetts Press.

*Hamilton, Alexander, John Jay, and James Madison. [Any edition.] *The Federalist*.

Hinckley, Barbara. 1971. *Stability and Change in Congress*. New York: Harper & Row.

*Kiewiet, D. Roderick. 1983. *Macroeconomics and Micropolitics*. Chicago: University of Chicago Press.

Kingdon, John. 1979. *Congressmen's Voting Decisions*. 2nd ed. New York: Harper & Row.

MacRae, Duncan. 1958. *Dimensions of Congressional Voting*. Berkeley: University of California Press.

Madison, James. 1966. *Notes on Debates in the Federal Convention of 1787*. New York: Norton.

Manley, John. 1970. *The Politics of Finance*. Boston: Little, Brown.

Matthews, Donald, and James Stimson. 1970. "Decision Making by U.S. Representatives." In *Political Decision Making*, ed. S. Sidney Ulmer. New York: Van Nostrand.

——— 1975. *Yeas and Nays: Normal Decision Making in the U.S. House of Representatives*. New York: Wiley.

*Mayhew, David R. 1966. *Party Loyalty among Congressmen*. Cambridge, Mass.: Harvard University Press.

——— 1974. *Congress: The Electoral Connection*. New Haven: Yale University Press.

Moos, Malcolm. 1952. *Politics, Presidents, and Coattails*. Baltimore: John Hopkins University Press.

Price, David. 1975. *The Commerce Committees: A Study of the House and Senate Commerce Committees*. New York: Grossman.

Redman, Eric. 1975. *The Dance of Legislation*. New York: Simon & Schuster.

Sinclair, Barbara. 1981. "The Speaker's Task Force in the Post-Reform House of Representatives." *American Political Science Review* 75, no. 1:397–410.

——— 1983. *Majority Party Leadership in the U.S. House*. Baltimore: John Hopkins University Press.

Smith, Steven, and Christopher Deering. 1984. *Committees in Congress*. Washington, D.C.: Congressional Quarterly.

Sullivan, Terry. 1984. *Procedural Structure: Success and Influence in Congress*. New York: Praeger.

Sundquist, James. 1969. *Politics and Policy*. Washington, D.C.: Brookings Institution.

Swanstrom, Roy. 1962. *The United States Senate, 1787–1801*. S. Doc. 64, 87th Congress, 1st session.

Wayne, Stephen J. 1978. *The Legislative Presidency*. New York: Harper & Row.

The development of institutional arrangements:

4

The institutionalization of the U.S. House of Representatives

NELSON W. POLSBY

Most people who study politics are in general agreement, it seems to me, on at least two propositions. First, we agree that for a political system to be viable, for it to succeed in performing tasks of authoritative resource allocation, problem solving, conflict settlement, and so on, in behalf of a population of any substantial size, it must be institutionalized. That is to say, organizations must be created and sustained that are specialized to political activity.[1] Otherwise, the political system is likely to be unstable, weak, and incapable of servicing the demands or protecting the interests of its constituent groups. Secondly, it is generally agreed that for a political system to be in some sense free and democratic, means must be found for institutionalizing representativeness with all the diversity that this implies, and for legitimizing yet at the same time containing political opposition within the system.[2]

Our growing interest in both of these propositions, and in the problems to which they point, can begin to suggest the importance of studying one of the very few extant examples of a highly specialized political institution which over the long run has succeeded in representing a large number of diverse constituents, and in legitimizing,

Reprinted from *American Political Science Review* 62, no. 2 (March 1968): 144–68. This paper was written while I was a Fellow at the Center for Advanced Study in the Behavioral Sciences. I want to thank the Center for its incomparable hospitality. In addition, the study of which this is a part has received support from The Rockefeller Foundation, the Social Science Research Council, Wesleyan University, and the Carnegie Corporation of New York, which granted funds to The American Political Science Association for the Study of Congress. H. Douglas Price has been a constant source of ideas, information, and criticism. I gratefully acknowledge also the assistance of Barry Rundquist, Edward Dreyfus, John Neff, Andrew Kleinfeld, and Miriam Gallaher, whose efforts contributed greatly to the assembly of a large number of the historical time series reported here. My colleague Paul Kay took time from his own work to suggest ways in which they could be presented. An earlier version was presented at the 1966 meetings of the American Political Science Association.

expressing, and containing political opposition within a complex political system – namely, the U.S. House of Representatives.

The focus of my attention here will be first of all descriptive, drawing together disparate strands – some of which already exist in the literature[3] – in an attempt to show in what sense we may regard the House as an institutionalized organ of government. Not all the necessary work has been done on this rather difficult descriptive problem, as I shall indicate. Secondly, I shall offer a number of speculative observations about causes, consequences, and possible lessons to be drawn from the institutionalization of the House.

The process of institutionalization is one of the grand themes in all of modern social science. It turns up in many guises and varieties: as Sir Henry Maine's discussion of the change from status to contract in the history of legal obligations,[4] as Ferdinand Tönnies' treatment of the shift from *Gemeinschaft* to *Gesellschaft*,[5] as Max Weber's discussion of the development of "rational-legal" modes of legitimization as an alternative to "traditional" and "charismatic" modes,[6] as Durkheim's distinction between "mechanical" and "organic" solidarity in his treatment of the consequences of the division of labor[7] and finally – dare we say finally? – as the central process at work in the unfolding of organizations that are held to obey Parkinson's Law.[8]

Such theoretical riches are bound to prove an embarrassment to the empirical researcher, since, unavoidably, in order to do his work, he must pick and choose among a host of possibilities – not those that initially may be the most stimulating, but those that seem most likely to be reflected in his data, which, perforce, are limited.[9] Thus the operational indices I am about to suggest which purport to measure empirically the extent to which the U.S. House of Representatives has become institutionalized may strike the knowledgeable reader as exceedingly crude; I invite the ingenuity of my colleagues to the task of suggesting improvements.

For the purposes of this study, let us say that an institutionalized organization has three major characteristics: 1) it is relatively well-bounded, that is to say, differentiated from its environment. Its members are easily identifiable, it is relatively difficult to become a member, and its leaders are recruited principally from within the organization. 2) The organization is relatively complex, that is, its functions are internally separated on some regular and explicit basis, its parts are not wholly interchangeable, and for at least some important purposes, its parts are interdependent. There is a division of labor in which roles are specified, and there are widely shared expectations about the performance of roles. There are regularized patterns of recruitment to roles, and of movement from role to role. 3) Finally, the organization tends to use universalistic

rather than particularistic criteria, and automatic rather than discretionary methods for conducting its internal business. Precedents and
rules are followed; merit systems replace favoritism and nepotism; and
impersonal codes supplant personal preferences as prescriptions for
behavior.

Since we are studying a single institution, the repeated use of words
like "relatively" and "tends" in the sentences above refers to a comparison of the House of Representatives with itself at different points
in time. The descriptive statement: "The House of Representatives has
become institutionalized over time" means then, that over the life span of
this institution, it has become perceptibly more bounded, more complex,
and more universalistic and automatic in its internal decision making.
But can we find measures which will capture enough of the meaning of
the term "institutionalization" to warrant their use in an investigation of
the process at work in the U.S. House of Representatives?

THE ESTABLISHMENT OF BOUNDARIES

One aspect of institutionalization is the differentiation of an organization
from its environment. The establishment of boundaries in a political
organization refers mostly to a channeling of career opportunities. In an
undifferentiated organization, entry to and exit from membership is easy
and frequent. Leaders emerge rapidly, lateral entry from outside to
positions of leadership is quite common, and persistence of leadership
over time is rare. As an organization institutionalizes, it stabilizes its
membership, entry is more difficult, and turnover is less frequent. Its
leadership professionalizes and persists. Recruitment to leadership is
more likely to occur from within, and the apprenticeship period
lengthens. Thus the organization establishes and "hardens" its outer
boundaries.

Such measures as are available for the House of Representatives
unmistakably show this process at work. In the 18th and 19th centuries,
the turnover of Representatives at each election was enormous.
Excluding the Congress of 1789, when of course everyone started new,
turnover of House members exceeded fifty per cent in fifteen elections –
the last of which was held in 1882. In the 20th century, the highest
incidence of turnover (37.2 per cent – almost double the twentieth
century median) occurred in the Roosevelt landslide of 1932 – a figure
exceeded forty-seven times – in other words almost all the time – in the
18th and 19th centuries. As Table 4.1 and Figure 4.1 make clear, there
has been a distinct decline in the rate at which new members are
introduced into the House. Table 4.2 and Figure 4.2 make a similar point
with data that are partially independent; they show that the overall

Table 4.1. *The establishment of boundaries: Decline in percentage of first term members, U.S. House of Representatives, 1789–1965*

Congress	Year of 1st term	% 1st term members	Congress	Year of 1st term	% 1st term members
1	1789	100.0	45	1877	46.6
2	1791	46.5	46	1879	42.3
3	1793	56.5	47	1881	31.8
4	1795	38.9	48	1883	51.5
5	1797	43.1	49	1885	38.0
6	1799	36.0	50	1887	35.6
7	1801	42.5	51	1889	38.1
8	1803	46.9	52	1891	43.8
9	1805	39.9	53	1893	38.1
10	1807	36.2	54	1895	48.6
11	1809	35.9	55	1897	37.9
12	1811	38.5	56	1899	30.1
13	1813	52.6	57	1901	24.4
14	1815	42.9	58	1903	31.3
15	1817	59.2	59	1905	21.0
16	1819	40.8	60	1907	22.5
17	1821	45.2	61	1909	19.9
18	1823	43.2	62	1911	30.5
19	1825	39.4	63	1913	34.4
20	1827	33.2	64	1915	27.2
21	1829	41.0	65	1917	16.0
22	1831	38.0	66	1919	22.7
23	1833	53.7	67	1921	23.6
24	1835	40.0	68	1923	27.1
25	1837	48.6	69	1925	16.3
26	1839	46.3	70	1927	13.3
27	1841	37.7	71	1929	17.7
28	1843	66.7	72	1931	19.0
29	1845	49.0	73	1933	37.2
30	1847	50.4	74	1935	23.4
31	1849	53.1	75	1937	22.7
32	1851	53.3	76	1939	25.5
33	1853	60.5	77	1941	17.0
34	1855	57.5	78	1943	22.9
35	1857	40.2	79	1945	15.8
36	1859	45.1	80	1947	24.1
37	1861	53.9	81	1949	22.3
38	1863	58.1	82	1951	14.9
39	1865	44.3	83	1953	19.5
40	1867	46.0	84	1955	11.7
41	1869	49.2	85	1957	9.9
42	1871	46.5	86	1959	18.2
43	1873	52.0	87	1961	12.6
44	1875	58.0	88	1963	15.2
			89	1965	20.9

Sources: Data for 1st through 68th Congresses are from Stuart A. Rice, *Quantitative Methods in Politics* (New York: Knopf, 1928), pp. 296–297. Data for 69th through 89th Congresses are calculated from *Congressional Directories*.

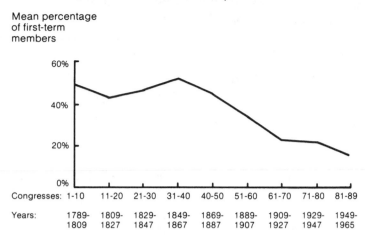

Figure 4.1. The establishment of boundaries: decline in percentage of first-term members, U.S. House of Representatives, 1789–1965. Data from Table 4.1.

stability of membership, as measured by the mean terms of members (total number of terms served divided by total number of Representatives) has been on the rise.

These two tables provide a fairly good indication of what has happened over the years to rank-and-file members of the House. Another method of investigating the extent to which an institution has established boundaries is to consider its leaders, how they are recruited, what happens to them, and most particularly the extent to which the institution permits lateral entry to and exit from positions of leadership.

The classic example of lateral movement – possibly the most impressive such record in American history – is of course contained in the kaleidoscopic career of Henry Clay, seventh Speaker of the House. Before his first election to the House, Clay had already served two terms in the Kentucky House of Representatives, and had been sent by the legislature to the U.S. Senate for two nonconsecutive short terms. Instead of returning to the Senate in 1811, he ran for the Lexington seat in the U.S. House and was elected. He took his seat on March 4, 1811, and eight months later was elected Speaker at the age of 34. Three years later, he resigned and was appointed a commissioner to negotiate the Treaty of Ghent with Great Britain. The next year, he returned to Congress, where he was again promptly elected Speaker. In 1820 he resigned once again and left public office for two years. But in 1823 he returned to the House, served as Speaker two more terms, and then resigned again, to become Secretary of State in John Quincy Adams' cabinet. In 1831, Clay became

Table 4.2. *The establishment of boundaries: increase in terms served by incumbent members of the U.S. House of Representatives, 1789–1963*

Congress	Beginning term	Mean terms of service*	Congress	Beginning term	Mean terms of service*
1	1789	1.00	45	1877	2.11
2	1791	1.54	46	1879	2.21
3	1793	1.64	47	1881	2.56
4	1795	2.00	48	1883	2.22
5	1797	2.03	49	1885	2.41
6	1799	2.23	50	1887	2.54
7	1801	2.25	51	1889	2.61
8	1803	2.14	52	1891	2.44
9	1805	2.36	53	1893	2.65
10	1807	2.54	54	1895	2.25
11	1809	2.71	55	1897	2.59
12	1811	2.83	56	1899	2.79
13	1813	2.31	57	1901	3.11
14	1815	2.48	58	1903	3.10
15	1817	1.93	59	1905	3.48
16	1819	2.15	60	1907	3.61
17	1821	2.23	61	1909	3.84
18	1823	2.29	62	1911	3.62
19	1825	2.42	63	1913	3.14
20	1827	2.68	64	1915	3.44
21	1829	2.55	65	1917	3.83
22	1831	2.59	66	1919	3.74
23	1833	2.15	67	1921	3.69
24	1835	2.23	68	1923	3.57
25	1837	2.13	69	1925	3.93
26	1839	2.17	70	1927	4.26
27	1841	2.30	71	1929	4.49
28	1843	1.76	72	1931	4.48
29	1845	1.90	73	1933	3.67
30	1847	2.00	74	1935	3.71
31	1849	1.92	75	1937	3.84
32	1851	1.84	76	1939	3.91
33	1853	1.69	77	1941	4.24
34	1855	1.81	78	1943	4.22
35	1857	2.04	79	1945	4.50
36	1859	2.02	80	1947	4.34
37	1861	1.83	81	1949	4.42
38	1863	1.75	82	1951	4.73
39	1865	2.00	83	1953	4.69
40	1867	2.12	84	1955	5.19
41	1869	2.04	85	1957	5.58
42	1871	2.11	86	1959	5.37
43	1873	2.07	87	1961	5.65
44	1875	1.92	88	1963	5.65

*Total number of terms served divided by total number of Representatives.

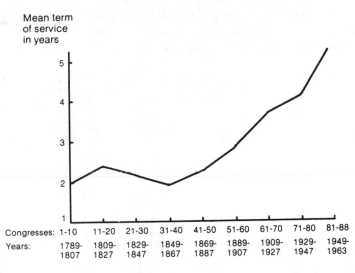

Figure 4.2 The establishment of boundaries: increase in terms served by incumbent members of the U.S. House of Representatives, 1789–1963. Data from Table 4.2.

a freshman Senator. He remained in the Senate until 1844, when he resigned his seat. Five years later he re-entered the Senate, this time remaining until his death in 1852. Three times (in 1824, 1832, 1844) he was a candidate for president.[10]

Clay's career was remarkable, no doubt, even in a day and age when the boundaries of the House of Representatives were only lightly guarded and leadership in the House was relatively open to lateral entry. But the point to be emphasized here is that Clay's swift rise to the Speakership is only slightly atypical for the period before the turn of the 20th century.

Table 4.3 demonstrates that there has been a change over time in the seniority of men selected for the Speakership. Before 1899, the mean years of service of members selected for the Speakership was six; after 1899, the mean rises steeply to twenty-six. Figure 4.3 and Table 4.4 summarize the gist of the finding in compact form.

Just as 19th-century Speakers arrived early at the pinnacle of House leadership, many left early as well and went on to other things; freshman Senators, state legislators, Cabinet members and judges in the state courts. One became President of the U.S., one a Justice of the Supreme Court, one a Minister to Russia, one the Mayor of Auburn, New York, and one the Receiver-General of the Pennsylvania land office. Indeed, of the first twenty-seven men to be Speaker, during the first eighty-six years of the Republic, *none* died while serving in the House of Representatives.

97

Table 4.3. *The establishment of boundaries: years served in Congress*
before first selection as Speaker

Date of selection	Speaker	Years	Date of selection	Speaker	Years
1789	Muhlenberg	1 or less	1861	Grow	10
1791	Trumbull	3	1863	Colfax	8
1795	Dayton	4	1869	Pomeroy	8
1799	Sedgwick	11	1869	Blaine	6
1801	Macon	10	1875	Kerr	8
1807	Varnum	12	1876	Randall	13
1811	Clay	1 or less	1881	Keifer	4
1814	Cheves	5	1883	Carlisle	6
1820	Taylor	7	1889	Reed	12
1821	Barbour	6	1891	Crisp	8
1827	Stephenson	6	1899	Henderson	16
1834	Bell	7	1903	Cannon	28
1835	Polk	10	1911	Clark	26
1839	Hunter	2	1919	Gillett	26
1841	White	6	1925	Longworth	22
1843	Jones	8	1931	Garner	26
1845	Davis	6	1933	Rainey	28
1847	Winthrop	8	1935	Byrns	25
1849	Cobb	6	1936	Bankhead	15
1851	Boyd	14	1940	Rayburn	27
1855	Banks	2	1946	Martin	22
1857	Orr	7	1962	McCormack	34
1859	Pennington	1 or less			

Mean Years of prior
service by Speakers

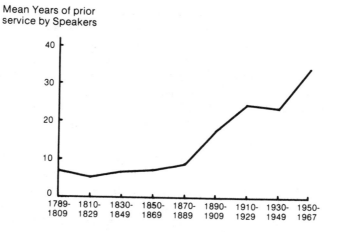

Figure 4.3 The establishment of boundaries: mean years served in Congress
before first becoming speaker, by 20-year intervals. Data from Table 4.3.

Table 4.4. *The establishment of boundaries: summary of years served in Congress before first selection as Speaker*

	Before 1899	1899 and after
8 years or less	25	0
9–14 years	8	0
15–20 years	0	2
21–28 years	0	10
	33 Speakers	12 Speakers

In contrast, of the last ten Speakers, six died while serving, and of course one other sits in the House today. Table 4.5 and Figure 4.4 give the relevant information for all Speakers.

The importance of this information about Speakers' careers is that it gives a strong indication of the development of the Speakership as a singular occupational specialty. In earlier times, the Speakership seems to have been regarded as a position of political leadership capable of being interchanged with other, comparable positions of public responsibility – and indeed a high incidence of this sort of interchange is recorded in the careers of 19th century Speakers. That this sort of interchange is most unusual today suggests – as do the other data presented in this section – that one important feature in the development of the U.S. House of Representatives has been its differentiation from other organizations in the political system, a stabilization of its membership, and a growing specialization of its leaders to leadership of the House as a separate career.[11]

The development of a specifically House leadership, the increase in the overall seniority of members, and the decrease in the influx of newcomers at any point in time have the effect not only of separating the House from other organizations in the political system, but also of facilitating the growth of stable ways of doing business within the institution, as we shall see shortly.

THE GROWTH OF INTERNAL COMPLEXITY

Simple operational indices of institutional complexity and universalistic-automated decision making are less easy to produce in neat and comparable time series. As for the growth of internal complexity, this is easy enough to establish impressionistically, but the most obvious quantitative measure presents a drastic problem of interpretation. The temptation is great to measure internal differentiation by simply counting

99

Table 4.5. *The establishment of boundaries: emergence of careers specialized to House leadership*

Speaker (term)	Elapsed years between last day of service as Representative and death	How Speakers finished their careers
1. Muhlenberg (1789–90, 1793–94)	6	Receiver-general of Pennsylvania Land Office
2. Trumbull (1791–92)	14	Governor of Connecticut
3. Dayton (1795–98)	25	Senator 1805; private life
4. Sedgwick (1799–1800)	12	Judge of Supreme Court of Massachusetts
5. Macon (1801–06)	17	Senate
6. Varnum (1807–10)	10	U.S. Senate and State Senate, Massachusetts
7. Clay (1811–13, 1815–19, 1823–24)	27	Senate
8. Cheves (1814)	42	President, Bank of U.S.; Chief Commissioner of Claims under Treaty of Ghent; private life
9. Taylor (1820, 1825–26)	21	State Senate, New York; private life
10. Barbour (1821–22)	11	Associate Justice, U.S. Supreme Court
11. Stevenson (1827–33)	23	Minister to Great Britain; Rector, University of Virginia
12. Bell (1834)	28	Senate; private life
13. Polk (1835–38)	10	President of U.S.
14. Hunter (1839–40)	40	State Treasurer, Virginia; Collector, Tappahannock, Virginia
15. White (1841–42)	1	Judge, 19th Judicial District, Virginia
16. Jones (1843–44)	3	Representative to Virginia State House of Delegates and Speaker
17. Davis (1845–46)	12	U.S. Commissioner to China, Governor of the Oregon Territory
18. Winthrop (1847–48)	44	Senator by appointment; unsuccessful candidate for Senate, Governor; private life
19. Cobb (1849–50)	11	Secretary of Treasury, Buchanan cabinet; Confederate major general; private life
20. Boyd (1851–54)	4	Lt. Governor of Kentucky
21. Banks (1855–56)	3	Served many nonconsecutive terms *after* Speakership; unsuccessful candidate; private life
22. Orr (1857–58)	14	Minister to Russia
23. Pennington (1859–60)	1	Failed of reelection; died soon after
24. Grow (1861–62)	4	Speaker in 37th; later private life; later still reelected to Congress; declined renomination; private life

25. Colfax (1863–68)	16	Private life; Vice-President
26. Pomeroy (1869)	36	Speaker 1 day; Mayor of Auburn, New York; private life
27. Blaine (1869–74)	17	Secretary of State; President, Pan-American Congress
28. Kerr (1875)	0	Speaker at his death, 1876
29. Randall (1876–80)	0	House of Representatives
30. Keifer (1881–82)	22	Not renominated to House after served as Speaker; Major General in Spanish American War; returned later to House; private life
31. Carlisle (1883–88)	20	Senate; Secretary of Treasury; private life
32. Reed (1889–90, 1895–98)	3	Private life; law practice
33. Crisp (1891–94)	0	U.S. House of Representatives (nominated for Senate at time of death)
34. Henderson (1899–1902)	3	Private life; retired, House of Representatives
35. Cannon (1903–10)	3	Retired, House of Representatives
36. Clark (1911–18)	0	House of Representatives
37. Gillett (1919–24)	10	Senate; private life
38. Longworth (1925–30)	0	House of Representatives
39. Garner (1931–32)	32+	Vice-President; private life
40. Rainey (1933–34)	0	House of Representatives, Speaker
41. Byrns (1935–36)	0	House of Representatives, Speaker
42. Bankhead (1936–39)	0	House of Representatives, Speaker
43. Rayburn 1940–45, 1947–52, 1955–61)	0	House of Representatives, Speaker
44. Martin (1946–47, 1953–54)	1+	Defeated for renomination, 1966, in his 82nd year and his 44th consecutive year of House service
45. McCormack (1962–67)	0+	House of Representatives, presently Speaker (1967)

the number of standing committees in each Congress. This would produce a curiously curvilinear result, because in 1946 the number of standing committees was reduced from 48 to 19, and the number has since crept up only as far as 20.[12]

But the "streamlining," as it was called,[13] of 1946 can hardly be said to have reduced the internal differentiation of the House. On the contrary, by explicitly delineating the legislative jurisdictions of the committees, by consolidating committees with parallel and overlapping functions, by assigning committees exclusive oversight responsibilities over agencies of the executive branch, and by providing committees with expanded staff aid, the 1946 reorganization contributed to, rather than detracted from, the reliance of the House upon committees in the

101

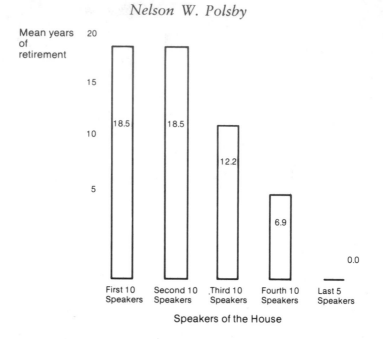

Figure 4.4 The establishment of boundaries: emergence of careers specialized to House leadership. Date from Table 4.5.

conduct of its business. Thus the mute testimony of the sheer numbers of committees cannot be accepted as an appropriate index of internal complexity. I shall therefore attempt a more anecdotal accounting procedure.

Briefly, the growth of internal complexity can be shown in three ways: in the growth in the autonomy and importance of committees, in the growth of specialized agencies of party leadership, and in the general increase in the provision of various emoluments and auxiliary aids to members in the form of office space, salaries, allowances, staff aid, and committee staffs.

A wholly satisfactory account of the historical development of the House committee system does not exist. But perhaps I can swiftly sketch in a number of plausible conclusions from the literature.

From the perspective of the present-day United States, the use of standing committees by Congress is scarcely a controversial issue.[14] Yet, in the beginning the House relied only very slightly upon standing committees. Instead of the present-day system, where bills are introduced in great profusion and automatically shunted to one or another of the committees whose jurisdictions are set forth in the rules, the practice in the first, and early Congresses was for subjects to be debated initially in the whole House and general principles settled upon, before they were parceled out for further action – fact-finding, detailed consideration or the proposal of a bill – to any one of four possible locations: an officer in the Executive Branch, a Committee of the Whole, a Select Committee formed *ad hoc* for the reception of a particular subject, or a standing committee. Generally, one of the alternatives to standing committees was used.

Of the First Congress, Harlow writes:

The outstanding feature of procedure in the House was the important part played by the Committee of the Whole. Much of the business in the House of Delegates of Virginia was transacted in that way, and the Virginians were influential enough to impose their methods upon the federal House.... It was in Committee of the Whole that Congress worked out the first tarriff bill, and also the main outlines of such important measures as the laws organizing the executive departments. After the general principles were once determined, select committees would be appointed to work out the details, and to frame bills in accordance with the decision already agreed upon in Committee of the Whole. Considerable work was done by these select committees, especially after the first session.[15]

And Alexander says:

In the early history of the House the select committee...was used exclusively for the consideration of bills, resolutions, and other legislative matters.[16] As business increased and kindred subjects became scattered, however, a tendency to concentrate inaugurated a system of standing committees. It rooted itself slowly. There was an evident distrust of the centralizing influence of permanent bodies. Besides, it took important business from the many and gave it to a few, one standing committee of three or five members often taking the place of half a dozen select committees.[17]

It is difficult to disentangle the early growth of the standing committee system from concurrent developments in the party system. For as Alexander Hamilton took control of the administration of George Washington, and extended his influence toward men of like mind in Congress, the third alternative to standing committees – reference to a member of the Executive Branch – became an important device of the Federalist majority in the House.

By the winter of 1790 [Harlow writes] Hamilton was attracting attention because of his influence over Congress.... His ready intelligence grasped the truth at once that Jefferson spent more than ten years learning: that not even the Constitution of the United States could keep apart two such inseparable factors in government as executive and legislature.[18]

In the first two Congresses Hamilton is said to have used the Federalist caucus to guide debate in the Committee of the Whole, and also to have arranged for key financial measures to be referred directly to himself for detailed drafting.[19] This practice led, in the Second Congress, to sharp clashes with followers of Jefferson, who

made it perfectly clear that if they should ever get the upper hand in Congress, they would make short work of Hamilton, and restore to the House what they considered to be its constitutional authority over finance.[20]

The Republicans did in fact gain the upper hand in the Third Congress (elected in 1792) and they restored detailed power over finances to the Committee of the Whole. This did not work satisfactorily, however, and in the Fourth Congress a Committee on Ways and Means was formed. Harlow says:

The appointment of...standing committees, particularly...Ways and Means, was in a way a manifestation of the Republican theory of government. From their point of view, the members of the House, as the direct representatives of the voters, ought to be the mainspring of the whole system. Hitherto, the Federalists had sold their birthright by permitting the executive to take a more active part in the government than was warranted by the Constitution. The Republicans now planned to bring about the proper balance between the different branches, by broadening at once the scope of the operations of the House, and restricting the executive. It was the better to enable the House to take its assigned part that the new type of organization was worked out. Just as the heads of departments were looked upon as agents of the executive, so the committees would be considered as the agents of the House.[21]

During the presidency of Thomas Jefferson, committees were constituted and employed as agents of the President's faction in Congress which was in most matters actively led by the President himself. Binkley says:

...When the House of Representatives had elected its Speaker and the committee chairmen had been appointed it was apparent to the discerning that lieutenants of the President had not appointed them, but his wishes, confidentially expressed, had determined them just as surely as if he had formally and publicly nominated them. Here was the fulfillment of Marshall's prediction that Jefferson would "embody himself in the House of Representatives."[22]

There is, however, some doubt as to Jefferson's absolute mastery over committee appointments, since it is also reported that Speaker Macon was extremely important in constituting the committees, and, in particular, in keeping John Randolph on as chairman of the Ways and Means Committee for some time after Randolph had repeatedly and violently broken with the Jefferson administration.[23]

Recently the suggestion has been made that the direct evidence is slight and contradictory that political parties in Congress went through rapid organization and differentiation in the earliest years of the Republic. This revisionist interpretation lays greater stress upon boarding house cliques, more or less sectional and more or less ideologically factional in their composition, as the heretofore neglected building blocks out of which the more conventionally partisan Congressional politics of the Jacksonian era eventually grew.[24]

But even revisionists concede to Jefferson a large influence over Congressional politics; the conventional accounts of the growth of the committee system are pretty much undisturbed by their critique. In essence, by the early years of the 19th century, the House committee system had passed through two distinct phases: the no-committee, Hamiltonian era, in which little or no internal differentiation within the institution was visible; and a Jeffersonian phase, in which factional alignments had begun to develop – these were exploited by the brilliant and incessant maneuverings of the President himself, who selected his lieutenants and confidants from the ranks of Congress *ad hoc*, as political requirements and opportunities dictated. During this period a small number of standing committees existed, but were not heavily relied upon. Their jurisdictions were not so securely fixed that the Speaker could not instead appoint select committees to deal with business that ought to have been sent to them.[25]

The advent of Henry Clay and the victory of the War Hawk faction in the elections of 1810 brought the committee system to its third phase. Clay for the first time used the Speaker's prerogative of appointment of members to committees independently of Presidential designs. There is some question whether Clay's appointment policies were calculated to further his policy preferences or merely his popularity (and hence his Presidential ambitions) within the factionally divided house,[26] but there seems no reason to doubt that Clay won for the Speakership a new measure of independence as a power base in the American political system. Under Clay five House committees were constituted to oversee expenditures in executive departments, the first major institutionalization of the Congressional function of oversight. William N. Chambers writes:

[By] 1814 the committee system had become the dominant force in the chamber. Thus effective power was exercised not by the President, as had been the case with Jefferson, but by factional Congressional leaders working through the speakership, the caucus, and the committees.[27]

For the next 100 years the committee system waxed and waned more or less according to the ways in which committees were employed by the party or faction that dominated the House and elected the Speaker. Figures from the latter decades of the 19th century testify amply to the leeway afforded Speakers – especially new ones – in constituting committees regardless of their prior composition.[28] In part, it was

Speaker Cannon's increasing use of this prerogative in an attempt to keep control of his fragmenting party that triggered the revolt against his Speakership in 1910–11, and that led to the establishment of the committee system as we know it today.[29]

Under the fourth, decentralized, phase of the committee system, committees have won solid institutionalized independence from party leaders both inside and outside Congress. Their jurisdictions are fixed in the rules; their composition is largely determined and their leadership entirely determined by the automatic operation of seniority. Their work is increasingly technical and specialized, and the way in which they organize internally to do their work is entirely at their own discretion. Committees nowadays have developed an independent sovereignty of their own, subject only to very infrequent reversals and modifications of their powers by House party leaders backed by large and insistent majorities.

To a degree, the development over the last sixty years of an increasingly complex machinery of party leadership within the House cross-cuts and attentuates the independent power of committees. Earlier, the leading faction in the House elected the Speaker and the Speaker in turn distributed the chairmanships of key committees to his principal allies and opponents. Thus the work of the House was centralized to the extent that the leading faction in the House was centralized. But differences of opinion are not uncommon among qualified observers. The Jeffersonian era, for example, is widely regarded as a high point of centralization during the 19th century. Harlow reports:

From 1801 to 1808 the floor leader was distinctly the lieutenant of the executive. William B. Giles, who was actually referred to as "the premier, or prime minister," Caesar A. Rodney, John Randolph of Roanoke, and Wilson Cary Nicholas all held that honorable position at one time or another. It was their duty to look after party interests in the House, and in particular to carry out the commands of the President. The status of these men was different from that of the floor leader of today.... They were presidential agents, appointed by the executive, and dismissed at his pleasure.[30]

But another observer, a Federalist congressman quoted by Noble Cunningham, suggests that the Jeffersonian group was not at all times well organized:

The ruling factions in the legislature have not yet been able to undrstand each other.... There evidently appears much rivalry and jealousy among the leaders. S[amuel] Smith thinks his experience and great address ought to give him a preponderance in all their measures, whilst Nicholson evidently looks upon these pretensions of his colleague with contempt, and Giles thinks the first representative of the Ancient Dominion ought certainly on all important occasions to take the lead, and Johnny Randolph is perfectly astonished that his great abilities

106

should be overlooked. There is likewise a great number of other persons who are impatient of control and disposed to revolt at any attempts at discipline.[31]

This certainly squares with the reports of Jefferson's own continued attempts, also revealed in his letters, to recruit men to the House with whom he could work.[32]

Despite Jefferson's difficulties, he was the most consistently successful of all the 19th century Presidents in "embodying himself in the House of Representatives." After Jefferson, the Speaker became a power in his own right; not infrequently he was a candidate for the Presidency himself, and the House was more or less organized around his, rather than the President's, political interests. There was no formal position of majority leader; the leading spokesman for the majority party on the floor was identified by personal qualities of leadership and by the favor of the Speaker (or in the Jeffersonian era, of the President) rather than by his institutional position.[33]

Later, however, the chairman of the Ways and Means Committee – a key post reserved for the chief lieutenant of the Speaker – became *de facto* floor leader, a natural consequence of his responsibilities in managing the tariff bills that were so important in 19th century congressional politics. Occasionally the chairman of the Committee on Appropriations was the *de facto* leader, especially during periods of war mobilization, when the power of the House in the political system was coextensive with the power of the purse.[34] In the last part of the 19th century, however, the Committee on Appropriations was temporarily dismantled, and the chairman of the Ways and Means Committee began to receive the formal designation as party leader.

The high point of the Ways and Means chairman's power came in the aftermath of the 1910 revolt against the Speaker. The power of committee appointments was for Democrats lodged in the Ways and Means Committee. Chairman Oscar Underwood, in cooperation with President Wilson, for a time (1911–1915) eclipsed the Speaker and the committee chairmen by operating the majority party by caucus.[35]

But Underwood's successor as Chairman of Ways and Means, Claude Kitchin (majority leader 1915–1919), disapproved of Wilson's war policies; this made it cumbersome and impractical for the leader of the majority on the floor and in caucus to hold this job by virtue of what was becoming an automatic succession through seniority to the chairmanship of Ways and Means. A separation of the two roles was effected after the Democrats became the minority in 1919.[36] Ever since then, the majority leader's job has existed as a full-time position; the incumbent now holds a nominal, junior committee post but he rarely attends committee meetings. At the same time, the majority leader has become less of a

President's man, and the caucus is now dormant as an instrument of party leadership – although it now sometimes becomes a vehicle, especially at the opening of Congress, for the expression of widespread dissatisfaction by rank-and-file House members. Thus, while binding votes on policy matters have not been put through the caucus by party leaders, the Republican caucus has three times in recent years deposed party leaders and the Democratic caucus has deprived three of its members of their committee seniority.

Formally designated party whips are, like the differentiated post of majority leaders, an innovation principally of the twentieth century. The first whips date back to just before the turn of the century. In the early years, the designation seems to have been quite informal, and it is only recently that an elaborate whip system, with numerous deputies, a small staff, and formal procedures for canvassing members, has been established by both parties in the House.[37]

Thus, we can draw a contrast between the practices of recent and earlier years with respect to formal party leaders other than the Speaker:

(1) Floor leaders in the 20th century are officially designated; in the 19th, they were often informally designated, indefinite, shifting or even competitive, and based on such factors as personal prestige, speaking ability, or Presidential favor.[38]

(2) Floor leaders in recent years are separated from the committee system and elected by party members; earlier they were prominent committee chairmen who were given their posts by the Speaker, sometimes as a side-payment in the formation of a coalition to elect the Speaker.[39]

(3) Floor leaders today rely upon whip systems; before 1897 there were no formally designated whips.

A third indicator of the growth of internal organization is the growth of resources assigned to internal House management, measured in terms of personnel, facilities, and money. Visitors to Washington are not likely to forget the sight of the five large office buildings, three of them belonging to the House, that flank the Capitol. The oldest of these on the House side was built just after the turn of the century, in 1909, when a great many other of our indices show significant changes.

Reliable figures, past or present, on personnel assigned to the House are impossible to come by; but it is unlikely that a commentator today would agree with the observer early in this century who said:

It is somewhat singular that Congress is one of the few legislative bodies that attempts to do its work almost entirely without expert assistance – without the aid of parliamentary counsel, without bill drafting and revising machinery and without legislative and reference agencies, and until now it has shown little inclination to regard with favor proposals looking toward the introduction of such agencies.[40]

Indeed, the only major contemporary study we have of congressional staff speaks of present "tendencies toward overexpansion of the congressional staff," and says that "Three-fourths of the committee aides interviewed" thought that professional staffs of committees were sufficiently large to handle their present work load.[41]

Needless to say, that work load has grown, and, though it is impossible to say precisely by how much, congressional staffs have grown as well. This is roughly reflected in figures that are more or less comparable over time on that portion of the legislative budget assigned to the House. These figures show the expected increases. However, except for the jump between 1945 and 1946, reflecting the new provisions for staff aid of the Legislative Reorganization Act, the changes in these figures over time are not as abrupt as is the case with other of our time series. Nor would changes over time be even as steep as they are in Table 4.6 (pp. 110–11) if these figures were corrected for changes in the purchasing power of the dollar. So we must regard this indicator as weak, but nevertheless pointing in the expected direction.

FROM PARTICULARISTIC AND DISCRETIONARY TO UNIVERSALISTIC AND AUTOMATED DECISION MAKING

The best evidence we have of a shift away from discretionary and toward automatic decision making is the growth of seniority as a criterion determining committee rank and the growth of the practice of deciding contested elections to the House strictly on the merits.

The literature on seniority presents a welter of conflicting testimony. Some commentators date the seniority system from 1910;[42] others say that seniority as a criterion for determining the committee rank of members was in use well before.[43] Woodrow Wilson's classic account of *Congressional Government* in 1884 pays tribute both to the independence of the committees and their chairmen and to the absolute discretion of the Speaker in the committee appointment process.[44] It is clear that the Speaker has no such power today. In another paper my colleagues and I present a detailed preliminary tabulation and discussion on the extent to which seniority in its contemporary meaning was followed in the selection of committee chairmen in the most recent 40 Congresses.[45] The central finding for our present purposes (summarized in Table 4.7 and Figure 4.5, pp. 112–13) is that the seniority system – an automatic, universally applied, nondiscretionary method of selection – is now always used, but that formerly the process by which chairmen were selected was highly and later partially discretionary.

109

Table 4.6. *The growth of internal complexity: expenditures made by the House of Representatives*

Fiscal year	Expenditures (1000s dollars)	Fiscal year	Expenditures (1000s dollars)
1872	1,952	1910	4,897
1873	3,340	1911	5,066
1874	2,678	1912	4,741
		1913	5,148
1875	2,030	1914	5,012
1876	2,201		
1877	2,232	1915	5,081
1878	2,183	1916	4,917
1879	2,230	1917	5,400
		1918	5,331
1880	2,137	1919	5,304
1881	2,191		
1882	2,188	1920	7,059
1883	2,339	1921	6,510
1884	2,405	1922	6,001
		1923	6,588
1885	2,466	1924	6,154
1886	2,379		
1887	2,232	1925	7,761
1888	2,354	1926	7,493
1889	2,416	1927	7,526
		1928	7,623
1890	2,567	1929	7,813
1891	2,520		
1892	2,323	1930	8,260
1893	2,478	1931	8,269
1894	2,844	1932	8,310
		1933	7,598
1895	2,945	1934	7,154
1896	2,843		
1897	3,108	1935	8,007
1898	2,948	1936	8,377
1899	3,063	1937	8,451
		1938	8,139
1900	2,981	1939	8,615
1901	3,066		
1902	3,088	1940	9,375
1903	3,223	1941	9,511
1904	3,247	1942	9,678
		1943	9,361
1905	3,367	1944	10,944
1906	3,517	1945	11,660
1907	3,907		
1908	4,725	1946	14,243
1909	5,005	1947	16,012

Table 4.6. *(Continued)*

Fiscal year	Expenditures (1000s dollars)	Fiscal year	Expenditures (1000s dollars)
1948	18,096	1958	39,524
1949	18,110	1959	43,882
1950	20,330	1960	44,207
1951	21,053	1961	47,324
1952	23,474	1962	50,295
1953	23,622	1963	52,983
1954	23,660	1964	55,654
1955	26,610	1965	58,212
1956	34,587	1966 (est.)	65,905
1957	36,738	1967 (est.)	70,883

Sources: U.S. Executive Office of President. Bureau of the Budget. *The Budget of United States Government*. Annual Volumes for 1921–1967. Washington, U.S. Government Printing Office U.S. Treasury Department. *Combined Statement of Receipts, Expenditures and Balances of the United States Government*. Annual volumes for 1872–1920. Washington, U.S. Government Printing Office.

The figures for before 1911 can be interpreted as indicating the use of the Speaker's discretion in the appointment of committee chairmen. After 1911, when committee appointment powers are vested in committees on committees, the figures principally reflect the growth of the norm that no one man should serve as chairman of more than one committee. Congressmen often sat on a large number of committees, and senior men rose to the top of more than one committee, but allowed less senior men to take the chair, much as the custom presently is in the U.S. Senate. After 1946, when the number of committees was drastically reduced, this practice died out, and a strictly automated system of seniority has asserted itself.

The settlement of contested elections on some basis other than the merits seems in earlier years to have been a common phenomenon. To this point, we can bring the testimony of a number of quotes and anecdotes, widely separated in time. Here are a few examples:

1795:   A foreshadowing of future developments arose in the contested election of Joseph B. Varnum, of Massachusetts, in the Fourth Congress. This case became the focus of a struggle for power between the Federalists and the Anti-Federalists. It is an early instance of the triumph of the rule that all too often might makes right, at least in the settlement of election contests in the House of Representatives.

Table 4.7. *The growth of universalism: violations of seniority in the appointment of committee chairman, U.S. House of Representatives 1881–1963*

Percentage of Committees on which the chairman was not selected by seniority, averaged by decades

Congress	47–51	52–56	57–61	62–66
Years	1881–89	1891–99	1901–09	1911–19
Average violations of seniority	60.4	49.4	19	30.8
Congress	67–71	72–76	77–81	82–88
Years	1921–29	1931–39	1941–49	1951–63
Average violations	26	23	14	0.7

Varnum's election was contested on the principal ground that the Board of Selectmen of his home town (of which Board he was a member) had returned sixty votes more than there were qualified voters in the town. Since he had been elected with a certified overall plurality of eleven votes, investigation was warranted. Theodore Sedgwick, leader of the Federalists in the House, suggested that testimony be taken... inasmuch as the House alone had the power to compel the town clerk to produce the records containing the names of the illegal voters, if indeed any existed. Varnum, an Anti-Federalist, strongly protested against such a procedure.... He proposed...that petitioners...should present the names of the illegal voters, if they could do so.... This was impossible, since only the town clerk had access to the voting records of the town. The Anti-Federalists, who controlled the House at the time, on a party-line vote sustained Varnum's objections...in fact, the controlling faction even went so far as to adopt a resolution, again by a partisan vote, declaring that "the charges against [Varnum] are wholly unfounded...." "Thus, amidst an outburst of derisive laughter, the incident closed like a harliquinade."[46]

1860's: I served in my second term on the Committee on Elections.... Election cases in the House up to that time were...determined entirely by party feeling. Whenever there was a plausible reason for making a contest the dominant party in the House almost always awarded the seat to the man of its own side. There is a well-authenticated story of Thaddeus Stevens, that going into the room of the Committee on Elections, of which he was a member, he found a hearing going on. He asked one of his Republican colleagues what was the point in the case. "There is not much point to it," was the answer. "They are both damned scoundrels." "Well," said Stevens, "which is the Republican damned scoundrel? I want to go for the Republican damned scoundrel."[47]

1869: All traces of a judicial character in these proceedings are fast fading away.... Each case is coming to be a mere partisan struggle. At the dictate of party majorities, the Committee [on Elections] must fight, not

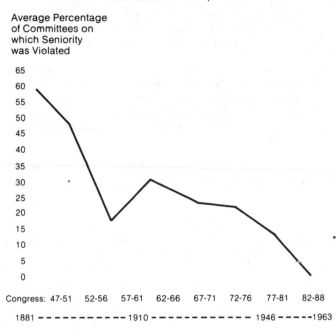

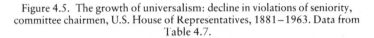

Figure 4.5. The growth of universalism: decline in violations of seniority, committee chairmen, U.S. House of Representatives, 1881–1963. Data from Table 4.7.

follow, the law and the evidence.... This tendency is so manifest... that it has ceased to be questioned, and is now but little resisted... [E]fforts...to hold the judgments of the Committee on Elections up above the dirty pool of party politics have encountered such bitter and unsparing denunciation, and such rebuke for treason to party fealty, that they are not likely often to be repeated.[48]

1890: The [elections] committee usually divides on the line of party...and the House usually follows in the same way.... The decision of election cases invariably increases the party which organized the House and... appoints the majority of the Committee on Elections. Probably there is not an instance on record where the minority was increased by the decision of contested cases.... It may be said that our present method of determining election cases is...unjust to members and contestants and fails to secure the representation which the people have chosen.[49]

1895: A most casual inspection of the workings of the present system of deciding election contests will show that it barely maintains the form of a judicial inquiry and that it is thoroughly tainted with the grossest partisanship.... When it is alleged that members of a minority do not generally contest seats, a striking tribute is paid to the partisanship of the present system.[50]

1899: The Republican majority in this House [56th Congress] was reduced about fifty from the previous Congress, but before the [first] session closed, a dozen or more Democrats lost their seats in election contests, which gave the Republicans a comfortable majority with which to do business.[51]

1905: Today it is simply a contest between two parties for political influence and the rewards of office, or sometimes a contest between the majority in the House and a constituency of the minority party.... In the period [1865–1905, 39th through 58th Congresses]...the majority deprived itself of seats only nine times, while it deprived the minority of seats eighty-two times.[52]

A journalist writing at the beginning of the twentieth century summarizes the situation as he had encountered it over a twenty-year period:

It may be said...that there is no fairness whatever exercised in...contests for seats, especially where the majority needs the vote for party purposes. Hundreds of men have lost their seats in Congress, to which they were justly entitled upon all fair, reasonable, and legal grounds, and others put in their places for purely partisan reasons. This has always been so and doubtless will continue so....[53]

In fact, it has not continued so; nowadays, contested elections are settled with much more regard to due process and the merits of the case than was true throughout the nineteenth century. By 1926, a minority member of the Committee on Elections No. 1 could say:

In the eight years I have served on Elections Committees and six years upon this Committee, I have never seen partisanship creep into that Committee but one time. There has not been any partisanship in the Committee since the distinguished gentleman from Utah became Chairman of that Committee. A Democrat was seated the last time over a Republican by this Committee, and every member of the Committee voted to seat that Democrat.[54]

This quotation suggests a method by which the development of universalistic criteria for settling contested House elections can be monitored, namely, measuring the extent to which party lines are breached in committee reports and in voting on the floor in contest cases. I have made no such study, but on the basis of the accumulated weight of contemporary reports such as I have been quoting, I predict that a time series would show strict party voting in the 19th century, switching to unanimity or near-unanimity, in most cases, from the early years of the 20th century onward.

Attempts to establish legal precedents for the settlement of contested elections date from the recommendations of the Ames Committee in 1791. In 1798 a law was enacted prescribing a uniform mode of taking testimony and for compelling the attendance of witnesses. This law was required to be renewed in each Congress and was allowed to lapse in

Table 4.8. *The growth of universalism: contested elections in the House by decades, 1789–1964*

Congress	Number of contested seats	Mean seats in House for decade	% seats contested per Congress*
1– 5 (1789–1798)	16	89.8	3.56
6–10 (1799–1808)	12	126.6	1.90
11–15 (1809–1818)	16	166.4	1.92
16–20 (1819–1828)	12	202.6	1.18
21–25 (1829–1838)	11	230.0	.96
26–30 (1839–1848)	17	231.8	1.46
31–35 (1849–1858)	23	233.0	1.98
36–40 (1859–1868)	73	196.4	7.44
41–45 (1869–1878)	72	273.0	5.28
46–50 (1879–1888)	58	312.2	3.72
51–55 (1889–1898)	87	346.8	5.02
56–60 (1899–1908)	41	371.4	2.20
61–65 (1909–1918)	36	417.4	1.72
66–70 (1919–1928)	23	435.0	1.06
71–75 (1929–1938)	25	435.0	1.14
76–80 (1939–1948)	15	435.0	.68
81–85 (1949–1958)	12	435.0	.56
86–88 (1959–1964)	8	437.0	.90

* Column 2 divided by column 3, over the number of Congresses (5 except in last instance).
Sources: Dempsey, *op. cit.*, Appendix I, and George B. Galloway, *History of the U.S. House of Representatives* (House Document 246, 87th Congress, 1st Session) (Washington: U.S. Government Printing Office, 1962), pp. 215–216.

1804. Bills embodying similar laws were proposed in 1805, 1806, 1810, 1813, and 1830. Not until 1851 was such a law passed, which provided for the gathering of testimony forming the bases of the proofs of each contestant's claim, but not for rules concerning other aspects of contested elections. More significant, however, was a clause permitting the House to set the law aside in whole or in part in specific cases, which apparently the House availed itself of with some regularity in the 19th century. With a few modifications this law is still in effect.[55]

The absolute number of contests shows a decrease in recent decades, as does the number of contests in relation to the number of seats. This suggests that the practice of instigating contests for frivolous reasons has passed into history; contemporary House procedures no longer hold out the hope of success for such contests.[56] Table 4.8 and Figure 4.6 give the figures, by decades.

There is today, certainly, no wholesale stealing of seats. If any bias

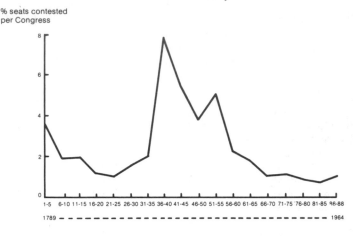

% seats contested
per Congress

Figure 4.6. The growth of universalism: contested elections in the House by decades, 1789–1964. Data from Table 4.8.

exists in the system, it probably favors the protection of incumbents irrespective of party,[57] and hence (we may surmise not incidentally) the protection of the boundaries of the organization.

CAUSES, CONSEQUENCES, CONCLUSIONS

It seems reasonable to conclude that one of the main long-run changes in the U.S. House of Representatives has been toward greater institutionalization. Knowing this, we may wish to ask, at a minimum, three questions: What caused it? What follows from it? What can this case tell us about the process in general? It is not from lack of space alone that our answers to each of these questions will be brief and highly speculative.

Not much, for example, is known about the causes of institutionalization. The best theoretical guess in the literature is probably Durkheim's: "The division of labor varies in direct ratio with the volume and density of societies, and, if it progresses in a continuous manner in the course of social development, it is because societies become regularly denser and generally more voluminous."[58] "Density" in at least some sense is capable of being operationalized and measured separately from its institutional consequences. For present purposes, the proposition can probably be rendered as follows: As the responsibilities of the national government grew, as a larger proportion of the national economy was affected by decisions taken at the center, the agencies of the national government institutionalized.[59] Another, complementary, translation of the density theorem would be that as organizations grow in size, they

116

tend to develop internally in ways predicted by the theory of institutionalization. Size and increasing work-load seem to me in principle
measurable phenomena.[60] Size alone, in fact, seems almost too easy.
Until a deliberative body has some minimum amount of work to do, the
necessity for interaction among its members remains slight, and, having
no purpose, coordination by means of a division of labor, rules and
regulations, precedents and so on, seem unlikely to develop. So a
somewhat more complicated formula has to be worked out, perhaps
relating the size of an organization to the amount of work it performs
(e.g., number of work-days per year, number of full-time as opposed to
nominal members, number of items considered, number of reports
rendered) before the strength of "density" and "volume" can be tested as
causes of the process of institutionalization.

A discussion of the consequences of the House's institutionalization
must be equally tentative. It is hard – indeed for the contemporary
observer, impossible – to shake the conviction that the House's
institutional structure does matter greatly in the production of political
outcomes. A recent popular account begins:

A United States Congressman has two principal functions: to make laws and to
keep laws from being made. The first of these he and his colleagues perform only
with sweat, patience and a remarkable skill in the handling of creaking
machinery; but the second they perform daily, with ease and infinite variety.[61]

No observer who focuses upon policy results, or who cares about the
outputs of the American legislative process, fails to note the "complicated forms and diversified structure" which "confuse the vision, and
conceal the system which underlies its composition."[62] All this is such
settled knowledge that it seems unnecessary to mention it here. Still, it is
important to stress that the very features of the House which casual
observers and freshman legislators find most obtrusive are principal
consequences of (among other things) the process we have been
describing.[63]

It is, however, not merely the complexity or the venerability of the
machinery that they notice. These, in our discussion so far, have been
treated as defining characteristics rather than consequences of institutionalization. What puzzles and irks the outside observer is a partial
displacement of goals, and a focus of resources upon internal processes at
the expense of external demands, that come as a consequence of
institutionalization. This process of displacement is, of course, well
known to social theory in other settings.[64] A closer look at the general
character of this displacement is bound to suggest a number of additional
consequences.

For example, representatives may find that the process of institutionalization has increased their incentives to stay within the system. For them, the displacement of resources transforms the organization from a convenient instrument for the pursuit of social policies into an end value itself, a prime source of gratification, of status and power.[65]

The increasing complexity of the division of labor presents an opportunity for individual Representatives to specialize and thereby enormously increase their influence upon a narrow range of policy outcomes in the political system at large. Considered separately, the phenomenon of specialization may strike the superficial observer as productive of narrow-minded drones. But the total impact of a cadre of specialists operating over the entire spectrum of public policies is a formidable asset for a political institution; and it has undoubtedly enabled the House to retain a measure of autonomy and influence that is quite exceptional for a 20th century legislature.[66]

Institutionalization has, in the House, on the whole meant the decentralization of power. This has created a great many important and interesting jobs within the House, and thus increased the attractiveness of service therein as a career. Proposed reforms of Congress which seek to move toward a recentralization of Congressional power rarely consider this fact. But it is at least possible that some moves to restore discretion to the Speaker, or to centralized party agencies outside Congress, would reduce the effectiveness of Congress far below the level anticipated, because the House would come to be less valued in and of itself, its division of labor would provide less of a power base for subject matter specialists, and the incentives to stay within the organization would sharply decline.

Thus we can argue that, along with the more obvious effects of institutionalization, the process has also served to increase the power of the House within the political system and to spread somewhat more widely incentives for legislators to participate actively in policy making.

A final possible consequence of institutionalization can be suggested: that the process tends to promote professional norms of conduct among participants. Indeed, something like these norms are built into the definition of institutionalization by some commentators.[67] But the built-in norms typically mentioned in discussions of "organization men" have to do with the segmental, ritualized interaction that characterizes organizations coordinated by hierarchical means; slightly different predictions about norms would have to be made for more decentralized, more egalitarian institutionalized legislative bodies.

In fact, there is coming to be a sizeable body of literature about the norms of professional legislative conduct. Time and again, the norms of predictability, courtesy, and reciprocity are offered by professional legislators as central to the rules of the legislative game.[68] Thus, we can suggest a hypothesis that the extent to which these norms are widely applied in a legislative body is a direct function of that body's structural institutionalization. Appropriate tests can be made cross-sectionally, by comparing contemporary legislatures that vary with respect to boundary-maintenance, internal complexity, and universalistic-automated internal decision making. Historically, less satisfactory tests are possible, since a number of vagaries enter into the determination of what is recorded and what is not, and since antecedent factors may account for both structural and normative institutionalization. This makes it hard to estimate the dispersion and importance of norms of conduct.

Nevertheless, the history of the House does suggest that there has been a growth in the rather tame virtues of reciprocity, courtesy, and predictability in legislative life since the turn of the century. Clem Miller describes human relations in the House of today:

One's overwhelming first impression as a member of Congress is the aura of friendliness that surrounds the life of a congressman. No wonder that "few die and none resign." Almost everyone is unfailingly polite and courteous. Window washers, clerks, senators – it cuts all ways. We live in a cocoon of good feeling....[69]

No doubt there are breaches in the fabric of good fellowship, mostly unpublicized, but the student of Congress cannot refrain even so from comparing this testimony with the following sampling of 19th century congressional conduct:

Upon resuming his seat, after having replied to a severe personal arraignment of Henry Clay, former Speaker White, without the slightest warning, received a blow in the face. In the fight that followed a pistol was discharged wounding an officer of the police. John Bell, the distinguished Speaker and statesman, had a similar experience in Committee of the Whole (1838). The fisticuffs became so violent that even the Chair would not quell it. Later in the day both parties apologized and "made their submissions." On February 6, 1845, Edward J. Black, of Georgia, "crossed over from his seat, and, coming within the bar behind Joshua R. Giddings as he was speaking, made a pass at the back of his head with a cane. William H. Hammett, of Mississippi, threw his arms round Black and bore him off as he would a woman from a fire...."
When Reuben M. Whitney was before a committee of investigation in 1837, Bailie Peyton, of Tennessee, taking offense at one of his answers, threatened him fiercely, and when he rose to claim to committee's protection, Mr. Peyton, with due and appropriate profanity, shouted: "You shan't say one word while you are in this room; if you do I will put you to death." The chairman, Henry A. Wise, added: "Yes; this insolence is insufferable." As both these gentlemen were armed with deadly weapons, the witness could hardly be blamed for not wanting to testify before the committee again.
"These were not pleasant days," writes Thomas B. Reed. "Men were not nice in their treatment of each other."[70]

Indeed they were not: Nineteenth century accounts of Congressional behavior abound in passages like these. There is the consternation of members who put up with the presence on the floor of John Randolph's hunting dogs.[71] There is the famous scene on May 22, 1851, when Representative Preston Brooks of South Carolina entered the U.S. Senate and beat Senator Charles Sumner senseless with a cane,[72] and the record contains accounts of more than one such occasion:

When Matthew Lyon, of Kentucky, spat in his face, [Roger] Griswold [of Connecticut, a member 1795–1805] stiffened his arm to strike, but remembering where he was, he coolly wiped his cheek. But after the House by its vote failed to expel Lyon, he "beat him with great violence," says a contemporary chronicle, "using a strong walking-stick."[73]

With all the ill will that the heat of battle sometimes generates currently, the House has long since left behind the era of guns and dogs, canings and fisticuffs, that occupied so much of the 19th century scene. No doubt this reflects general changes in manners and morals, but it also reflects a growth in the value of the House as an institution capable of claiming the loyalty and good behavior of its members.[74] The best test of the hypothesis, to be sure, remains the cross-sectional one. If American state legislatures, for example, can be found to differ significantly with respect to structural institutionalization, they may also be found to vary concomitantly with respect to the application of the norms of professional legislative life.[75]

Finally, the study of the institutionalization of the House affords us a perspective from which to comment upon the process in general. First, as to its reversibility. Many of our indicators show a substantial decay in the institutional structure of the House in the period surrounding the Civil War. In sheer numbers, the House declined from 237 members in the Congress of 1859 to 178 in the Congress of 1861; not until a decade later did the House regain its former strength. Frivolous contests for seats reached a height in this period, and our rank-and-file boundary measures reflect decay as well. It may be true, and it is certainly amusing, that the strength of the British Admiralty grows as the number of ships declines;[76] but that this illustrates an inflexibly narcissistic law of institutional growth may be doubted. As institutions grow, our expectations about the displacement of resources inward do give us warrant to predict that they will resist decay, but the indications of curve-linearity in our present findings give us ample warning that institutions are also continuously subject to environmental influence and their power to modify and channel that influence is bound to be less than all-encompassing.

Some of our indicators give conditional support for a "take-off" theory of modernization. If one of the stigmata of the take-off to modernity is the rapid development of universalistic, bounded, complex institutional forms, the data presented here lend this theory some

120

plausibility.[77] The "big bang" seems to come in the 1890–1910 period, on at least some of the measures.

In conclusion, these findings suggest that increasing hierarchical structure is not a necessary feature of the institutionalization process. Organizations other than bureaucracies, it seems clear, also are capable of having natural histories which increase their viability in the modern world without forcing them into uniformly centralized patterns of authority.

NOTES

["this REVIEW" = *American Political Science Review*]

1 A good recent summary of literature bearing on this point as it applies to the study of political development may be found in Samuel P. Huntington, "Political Development and Political Decay," *World Politics*, 17 (April, 1965), 386–430.

2 Robert A. Dahl speaks of "the three great milestones in the development of democratic institutions – the right to participate in governmental decisions by casting a vote, the right to be represented, and the right of an organized opposition to appeal for votes against the government in elections and in parliament." In enumerating these three great achievements of democratic government, Dahl also implies that they are embodied principally in three main institutions: parties, elections, and legislatures: Robert A. Dahl (ed.), *Political Oppositions in Western Democracies* (New Haven and London: Yale University Press, 1966), p. xi. See also William Nisbet Chambers "Party Development and the American Mainstream," especially pp. 18–19, in Chambers and Walter Dean Burnham (eds.), *The American Party Systems: Stages of Political Development* (New York: Oxford, 1967).

3 See for example, Nelson W. Polsby, "Congressional Research and Congressional Data: A Preliminary Statement" (mimeo) delivered at the Conference on Congressional Research, sponsored by the Inter-university Consortium for Political Research and the Social Science Research Council at the Brookings Institution, Washington, D.C., April 3–4, 1964; H. Douglas Price, "The Congressman and the Electoral Arena" (mimeo, 1964); and T. Richard Witmer, "The Aging of the House," *Political Science Quarterly*, 79 (December, 1964), 526–541.

4 Sir Henry Sumner Maine, *Ancient Law* (London: John Murray, 1908), pp. 220–325.

5 Ferdinand Tönnies, *Community and Society (Gemeinschaft und Gesellschaft)* (East Lansing: Michigan State University Press, 1957). See, in particular, the introductory commentary by Charles P. Loomis and John C. McKinney, "The Application of Gemeinschaft and Gesellschaft as Related to Other Typologies," *ibid.*, pp. 12–29.

6 Max Weber, *The Theory of Social and Economic Organization* (Glencoe: The Free Press, 1947), pp. 328ff.

7 Emile Durkheim, *The Division of Labor in Society* (Glencoe: The Free Press, 1947).

8 C. Northcote Parkinson, *Parkinson's Law* (Boston: Houghton Mifflin, 1957).

9 The only successful modern attempt I am aware of that employs a classical theory of institutionalization in an empirical study of something other than a bureaucracy is Harold W. Pfautz's "Christian Science: The Sociology of a Social Movement and Religious Group" (unpublished Ph.D. dissertation, Department of Sociology, University of Chicago, 1954). See also Harold W. Pfautz, "The Sociology of Secularization: Religious Groups," *The American Journal of Sociology*, 41 (September, 1955), 121–128, and Pfautz, "A Case Study of an Urban Religious Movement: Christian Science" in E. W. Burgess and D. J. Bogue (eds.), *Contributions to Urban Sociology* (Chicago and London: University of Chicago Press, 1963), pp. 284–303.

10 On Clay, see Bernard Mayo, *Henry Clay: Spokesman of the New West* (Boston: Houghton Mifflin, 1937); Glyndon G. Van Deusen, *The Life of Henry Clay* (Boston: Little, Brown, 1937); Mary Parker Follett, *The Speaker of the House of Representatives* (New York: Longman's, Green, 1896), pp. 69–82; and Booth Mooney, *Mr. Speaker* (Chicago: Follett, 1964), pp. 21–48.

11 This pattern has been suggested before, by Douglas Price and myself, in unpublished papers (see Footnote 3). It is apparently not unique to the House. David Rothman, on what seem to me to be tenuous grounds, suggests something similar for the U.S. Senate in *Politics and Power: The U.S. Senate 1869–1901* (Cambridge: Harvard University Press, 1966). Consider, for a better example, where the United States gets its military leaders today and compare with this observation on the Mexican war period:

> The President [Polk] now undertook to offset this Whig advantage by making a number of Democratic generals. . . . He thereupon proceeded to name numerous Democrats to command the new divisions and brigades. . . . Even this flock of Democratic generals did not erase Polk's fears. After he had committed the command to Scott he considered giving the top authority to a civilian. He wanted to commission Senator Thomas Hart Benton a lieutenant general, and give him overall command. . . .

(Roy F. Nichols, *The Stakes of Power: 1845–1877* [New York: Hill and Wang, 1961], pp.16, 17.) One would expect civilians to serve high in the officer corps in wars of total mobilization, such as the Civil War and World War II, but not in a conflict involving only a partial mobilization, such as the Mexican War, Korea or Viet Nam. Nevertheless, the full professionalization of our army took place only in this century. During the Spanish-American War, another war of partial mobilization, the business of fighting was still carried on partially by militia and by federal volunteer regiments – irregulars – who fought side by side with, but independently of, regular troops. See Walter Millis, *Arms and Men* (New York: G. P. Putman's Sons, 1956), pp. 167–210. See also a contemporary Washington newsman's report: Arthur Wallace Dunn, *From Harrison to Harding* (New York: G. P. Putnam's Sons, 1922), Vol. I, pp. 240ff, 272–274. Dunn says (Vol. I, pp. 240–41): "From the very beginning politics cut a leading part in the war. The appointments of generals and many other officers were due to influence rather than to merit or fitness. . . . One of these [appointments] was General Joe Wheeler, a member of Congress from Alabama. When he appeared with the twin stars of a major general on his shoulders, he joyously exclaimed: 'It is worth fifteen years of life to die on a battlefield'. . . . 'He will have twenty thousand men under him [remarked a critic] who do not share his opinion, and they will not care to lose fifteen years of their lives to give Joe Wheeler a glorious death.' " See also Samuel P. Huntington, *The Soldier and the State*

(Cambridge: Harvard U. Press, 1957), esp. pp. 222–269. Huntington dates the rise of the American military as a profession from after the Civil War.

Consider also the following observation about the U.S. Supreme Court: "In the early years, resignations tended to occur for all sorts of reasons; Chief Justice Jay resigned to assume the governorship of New York, for example. But as the Court's prestige increased, justices found fewer reasons to step down from the bench": Samuel Krislov, *The Supreme Court in the Political Process* (New York: Macmillan, 1965), p. 9. David Danelski has suggested in a personal communication that while in its earliest years, the U.S. Supreme Court was neither a prestigious nor well-bounded institution, it became so more rapidly than the House, as the following table indicates:

Decade appointed	Number of justices appointed	Average tenure
1789–99	12 justices	10.3 years
1800–09	4	25.0
1810–19	2	29.0
1820–29	3	18.0
1830–39	6	20.3
1840–49	4	18.7
1850–59	3	12.3
1860–69	5	21.0
1870–79	5	18.0
1880–89	7	13.6
1890–99	6	16.1
1900–09	4	14.2
1910–19	7	15.0
1920–29	5	14.0
1930–39	6	20.0 + (Black and Douglas still on)
1940–49	8	9.4

It is, of course, not uncommon for students of the Court to view the leadership of Chief Justice Marshall as highly significant in stabilizing the role of the Court in the political system and in enlarging its influence. Other indicators useful in tracing the institutionalization of the federal judiciary might be to study changes in the professional training of persons who have become federal judges, the increase in the number of judges on inferior federal courts, the codification of procedures for dealing with constitutional questions, the routinization of procedures for the granting of certiorari, and the growth of a bureaucracy to administer the federal court system. See, *inter alia*, Mr. Justice Brandeis' dissent in *Ashwander* vs. *T.V.A.* 297 U.S. 346–348; Edwin McElwain, "The Business of The Supreme Court as Conducted by Chief Justice Hughes," *Harvard Law Review*, 63 (November, 1949), 5–26; Merlo J. Pusey, *Charles Evans Hughes* (New York: Macmillan, 1951), Vol. II, pp. 603–690; Frederick Bernays Wiener, "The Supreme Court's New Rules," *Harvard Law Review*, 68 (November, 1954), 20–94; and Chief Justice Vinson's address before the American Bar Association,

"The Work of the Federal Courts," September 7, 1949, reprinted in part in Walter F. Murphy and C. Herman Pritchett (eds.), *Courts, Judges and Politics* (N.Y.: Random House, 1961), pp. 54–58.

12 The combined totals of standing committees and subcommittees might be a better guide; but reliable information about subcommittees only exists for the most recent two decades.

13 I believe the word is George Galloway's. See *Congress at the Crossroads* (New York: Crowell, 1946), p. 340.

14 It certainly is, on the other hand, in the present-day United Kingdom, where purely legislative committees are regarded as a threat to the cohesion of the national political parties because they would give the parliamentary parties special instruments with which they could develop independent policy judgments and expertise and exercise oversight over an executive which is, after all, not formally constituted as an entity separate from Parliament. Thus committees can be construed as fundamentally inimical to unified Cabinet government. For an overview see Bernard Crick, *The Reform of Parliament* (Garden City: Doubleday Anchor, 1965); *The Political Quarterly*, 36 (July–September, 1965); and Andrew Hill and Anthony Whichelow, *What's Wrong with Parliament?* (Harmondsworth: Penguin, 1964), esp. pp. 64–82. See also a most illuminating essay by Robert C. Fried on the general conditions under which various political institutions (including legislatures) are strong or weak within their political systems: *Comparative Political Institutions* (New York: Macmillan, 1966), esp. p. 31.

15 Ralph V. Harlow, *The History of Legislative Methods in the Period Before 1825* (New Haven: Yale, 1917), pp. 127–128. See also Joseph Cooper, "Jeffersonian Attitudes Toward Executive Leadership and Committee Development in the House of Representatives 1789–1829," *Western Political Quarterly*, 18 (March, 1965), 45–63; and Cooper, "Congress and Its Committees in the Legislative Process" (unpublished Ph.D. dissertation, Department of Government, Harvard University, 1960), pp. 1–65.

16 On changes in the use of select committees, Lauros G. McConachie says: "Business of the earlier Houses went to hosts of select committees. At least three hundred and fifty were raised in the Third Congress. A special committee had to be formed for every petty claim. A bill founded on the report of one small committee had to be recommended to, or carefully drafted by, yet another committee. But the decline in the number of these select committees was strikingly rapid. In twenty years, at the Congress of 1813–1815 with its three war sessions, it had fallen to about seventy": *Congressional Committees* (New York: Crowell, 1898), p. 124. See also Galloway, *op. cit.*, p. 88.

17 DeAlva Stanwood Alexander, *History and Procedure of the House of Representatives* (Boston: Houghton Mifflin, 1916), p. 228.

18 Harlow, *op. cit.*, pp. 141.

19 *Ibid.*, pp. 120–150.

20 *Ibid.*, p. 151.

21 *Ibid.*, pp. 157–158.

22 Wilfred E. Binkley, *President and Congress* (New York: Vintage, 1962), p. 64.

23 Of Randolph's initial appointment as chairman of the Ways and Means Committee, in the Seventh Congress, Noble Cunningham writes: "in view of the close friendship of [Speaker] Macon and Randolph, it is unlikely that

Jefferson had any influence in the choice of Randolph as Chairman of the Ways and Means Committee": *Jeffersonian Republicans in Power* (Chapel Hill: University of North Carolina Press, 1963), p. 73. See also Henry Adams, *John Randolph* (Boston: Houghton Mifflin, 1886), pp. 54–55, 123–165ff; and Adams, *History of the United States of America During the Administrations of Thomas Jefferson and James Madison* (New York: Boni, 1930), Vol. III, p. 128.

24 This interpretation is the brilliant achievement of James S. Young in *The Washington Community: 1800–1828* (New York: Columbia University Press, 1966). It harmonizes with Richard P. McCormick's notion of a series of historically discrete American party systems. See McCormick, *The Second American Party System* (Chapel Hill: University of North Carolina Press, 1966).

25 See Wilfred Binkley, "The President and Congress," *Journal of Politics*, 11 (February, 1949), 65–79.

26 See Young, *op. cit.*, pp. 131–135.

27 William Nisbet Chambers, *Political Parties in a New Nation* (New York: Oxford, 1963), p. 194.

28 See Nelson W. Polsby, Miriam Gallaher and Barry Spencer Rundquist, "The Growth of the Seniority System in the Selection of Committee Chairman in the U.S. House of Representatives" (mimeo., October, 1967).

29 *Ibid.* Chang-wei Chiu says, "The power of appointing committees by the Speaker was a real issue in the attempts to reform the House. In the eyes of the insurgents no change would be of any real and permanent value to the country if that change did not take away from the Speaker the power of appointing standing committees": *The Speaker of The House of Representatives Since 1896* (New York: Columbia University Press, 1928), pp. 71–72.

30 Harlow, *op. cit.*, p. 176.

31 Cunningham, *op. cit.*, p. 74. The quotation is from a letter from Roger Griswold to John Rutledge, December 14, 1801.

32 See Jefferson's letters to Barnabas Bidwell and Wilson Cary Nicholas cited in *ibid.*, pp. 89–92. Also Henry Adams, *History, op. cit.*, Vol. III, pp. 166–171.

33 Randall Ripley, in his forthcoming Brookings study, *Party Leadership in the House of Representatives* (mimeo, 1966) says: "The Majority leader did not become a separate and consistently identifiable party figure until some time around the turn of the century." Ripley also discusses the indeterminacy of the minority leadership in the mid-19th century. Of an earlier period (1800–1828) Young (*op. cit.*, pp. 126–127) writes: "Party members elected no leaders, designated no functionaries to speak in their behalf or to carry out any legislative task assignments. The party had no whips, no seniority leaders. There were no committees on committees, no steering committees, no policy committees: none of the organizational apparatus that marks the twentieth-century congressional parties...." On pp. 127–130 Young argues that although there were a number of party leaders in the House, there was no fixed majority leader. "[W]hile the names of Randolph, Giles, Nicholas and Rodney appear more frequently, at least twenty Republican legislators in the eight years of Jefferson's administration are either explicitly identified as leaders in the documentary record or are associated with activities strongly suggesting a role of presidential spokesmanship" (p. 130).

34 From 1865–1869, for example, Thaddeus Stevens left the chairmanship of Ways and Means (a post he had held from 1861–1865) to become chairman

of the new Committee on Appropriations. See Samuel W. McCall, *Thaddeus Stevens* (Boston: Houghton Mifflin, 1899), pp. 259–260. McCall says, oddly, that at the time the Appropriations Committee was not very important, but this is hard to credit. From 1895–1899, Joseph G. Cannon was floor leader and chairman of Appropriations. See Edward T. Taylor, *A History of the Committee on Appropriations* (House Document 299, 77th Congress, 1st Session) (Washington, Government Printing Office, 1941).

35 See George Rothwell Brown, *The Leadership of Congress* (Indianapolis: Bobbs-Merrill, 1922), pp. 175–177, 183–184; Oscar King Davis, "Where Underwood Stands," *The Outlook* (December 23, 1911), 197–201. At p. 199: "Every move Mr. Underwood has made, every bill he has brought forward, he first submitted to a caucus. . . . Not until the last man had had his say was the vote taken that was to bind them all to united action in the House. Every time that vote has been either unanimous or nearly so, and invariably it has approved Mr. Underwood." See also Binkley, "The President and Congress," *op. cit.*, p. 72.

36 See Ripley, *op cit.*; Hasbrouck, *op. cit.*, p. 94; and Alex M. Arnett, *Claude Kitchin and the Wilson War Policies* (Boston: Little, Brown, 1937), pp. 42, 71–72, 75–76, 88–89 and passim.

37 See Randall B. Ripley, "The Party Whip Organization in the United States House of Representatives" this REVIEW, 58 (September, 1964), 561–576.

38 See, e.g., Alexander, *op. cit.*, pp. 111–114. "[W]ith very few exceptions, the really eminent debaters. . .were in the Senate; otherwise, MacDuffie [who served 1821–1834], Chief of the Hotspurs, could scarely have justified his title to floor leader," p. 114.

39 *Ibid.*, p. 110: "In selecting a floor leader the Speaker often names his party opponent."

40 James W. Garner, "Executive Participation in Legislation as a Means of Increasing Legislative Efficiency," *Proceedings of the American Political Science Association at its Tenth Annual Meeting* (Baltimore: Waverly Press, 1914), p. 187.

41 Kenneth Kofmehl, *Professional Staffs of Congress* (Lafayette, Indiana: Purdue University Press, 1962), pp. 97–99. The quotation is at p. 99. Kofmehl presents a short, nonquantitative historical sketch of the growth of committee staffs on pp. 3–5. See also Samuel C. Patterson "Congressional Committee Professional Staffing: Capabilities and Constraints," a paper presented at the Planning Conference of the Comparative Administration Group, Legislative Services Project, Planting Fields, New York, December 8–10, 1967; and Lindsay Rogers "The Staffing of Congress" *Political Science Quarterly*, 56 (March, 1941), 1–22.

42 George B. Galloway, *op. cit.*, p. 187; George Goodwin, Jr., "The Seniority System in Congress" this REVIEW, 53 (June, 1959), p. 417.

43 Chiu, *op. cit.*, pp. 68–72; James K. Pollock, Jr., "The Seniority Rule in Congress," *The North American Review*, 222 (1925), 235, 236; Asher Hinds, "The Speaker of the House of Representatives," this REVIEW, 3 (May, 1909), 160–161.

44 Woodrow Wilson, *Congressional Government* (New York: Meridian Books, 1956) (First edition, 1884). See, for example, on pp. 85–86: "The Speaker is expected to constitute the Committees in accordance with his own political views. . .[and he] generally uses his powers as freely and imperatively as he is expected to use them. He unhesitatingly acts as the legislative chief of his

party, organizing the Committees in the interest of this or that policy, not covertly or on the sly, as one who does something of which he is ashamed, but openly and confidently, as one who does his duty...." Compare this with p. 82: "I know not how better to describe our form of government in a single phrase than by calling it a government by the chairmen of the Standing Committees of Congress. This disintegrate ministry, as it figures on the floor of the House of Representatives, has many peculiarities. In the first place, it is made up of the elders of the assembly; for, by custom, seniority in congressional service determines the bestowal of the principal chairmanships...."

45 Polsby, Gallaher, and Rundquist, *op. cit.*

46 John Thomas Dempsey, "Control by Congress over the Seating and Disciplining of Members" (unpublished Ph.D. dissertation, The University of Michigan, 1956), pp. 50–51. The final quotation is from Alexander, *op. cit.*, p. 315.

47 George F. Hoar, *Autobiography of Seventy Years* (New York: Scribner, 1903), Vol. I, p. 268. Hoar claims that during the time he served on the Elections Committee in the Forty-second Congress (1871–73), contested elections were settled on the merits.

48 Henry L. Dawes, "The Mode of Procedure in Cases of Contested Elections," *Journal of Social Science* (No. 2, 1870), 56–68. Quoted passages are at p. 64. Dempsey, *op. cit.*, pp. 83–84, identifies Dawes as a one-time chairman of the House Committee on Elections. See also C. H. Rammelkamp, "Contested Congressional Elections," *Political Science Quarterly*, 20 (Sept., 1905), 434–435.

49 Thomas B. Reed, "Contested Elections," *North American Review*, 151 (July, 1890), 112–120. Quoted passages are at pp. 114–117. See also Alexander, *op. cit.*, p. 323.

50 Report from Elections Committee No. 3, Mr. McCall, chairman, quoted in Rammelkamp, *op. cit.*, p. 435.

51 O. O. Stealey, *Twenty Years in the Press Gallery* (New York: published by the author, 1906), p. 147.

52 Rammelkamp, *op. cit.*, pp. 421–442. Quoted passages are from pp. 423 and 434.

53 Stealey, *op. cit.*, p. 147.

54 Quoted in Paul De Witt Hasbrouck, *Party Government in the House of Representatives* (New York: Macmillan, 1927), p. 40.

55 See U.S., *Revised Statutes of the United States*, Title II, Ch. 8, Sections 105–130, and Dempsey, *op. cit.*, pp 55–60. For indications of attempts to routinize the process of adjudication by setting up general criteria to govern House disposition of contested elections, see two 1933 cases: Gormley vs. Goss (House Report 893, 73rd Congress; see also 78 *Congressional Record*, pp. 4035, 7087, April 20, 1934) and Chandler vs. Burnham (House Report 1278, 73rd Congress; see also 78 *Congressional Record*, pp. 6971, 8921, May 15, 1934).

56 On the relatively scrupulous handling of a recent contest see Richard H. Rovere, "Letter from Washington," *The New Yorker* (October 16, 1965), 233–244. Rovere (at p. 243) identifies criteria governing the report on the 1965 challenge by the Mississippi Freedom Democratic Party to the entire Mississippi House delegation in the following passage: "...the majority could find no way to report favorably [on the challenge] without, as it seemed

to them, abandoning due process and their constitutional responsibilities. Neither, for that matter, could the minority report, which went no further than to urge continued study."

57 See, e.g., the assignment of burden of proof in Gormley vs. Goss and Chandler vs. Burnham, *loc, cit.*

58 Durkheim, *op. cit.*, p. 262. Durkheim in turn cites Comte as describing this mechanism. Weber's notion, that the central precondition for the development of bureaucratic institutions is the money economy, strikes me as less interesting and less plausible. See H. H. Gerth and C. Wright Mills (eds.), *From Max Weber: Essays in Sociology* (N.Y.: Oxford University Press, 1946), pp. 204–209. See, however, Weber's comment (p. 211): "It is obvious that technically the great modern state is absolutely dependent upon a bureaucratic basis. The larger the state, and the more it is or the more it becomes a great power state, the more unconditionally is this the case."

59 Cf. Young, *op. cit.*, pp. 252–253, who seems to put great stress on public attitudes and local political organization as causes of the growth in the influence of the central government.

60 George Galloway's *History of the U.S. House of Representatives*, 87th Congress, 1st Session, House Document No. 246 (Washington: U.S. Government Printing Office, 1962), pp. 215–216, has a convenient scorecard on the size and party composition of the House for the first 87 Congresses. Mere size has been found to be an indifferent predictor of the internal complexity of bureaucratic organizations. See Richard H. Hall, J. Eugene Haas and Norman J. Johnson, "Organizational Size, Complexity, and Formalization," *American Sociological Review*, 32 (December, 1967), 903–912.

61 Robert Bendiner, *Obstacle Course on Capitol Hill* (N.Y.: McGraw-Hill, 1964), p. 15.

62 Woodrow Wilson, *op. cit.*, p. 57.

63 This is not to say, however, that the policy output of the House is exclusively determined by its level of institutionalization. The 88th, 89th and 90th Congresses all represent more or less equivalent levels of institutionalization, yet their policy outputs varied greatly. Nevertheless if the casual observer asked why it took thirty years, more or less, to get the New Deal enacted in the House, and what sorts of strategies and circumstances made the legislative output of the 89th Congress possible, answers would have to refer quite extensively to structural properties of the institution.

64 See, e.g. Peter M. Blau, *The Dynamics of Bureaucracy* (Chicago: University of Chicago Press, 1955), *passim*; Philip Selznick, *TVA and the Grass Roots* (Berkeley: University of California Press, 1953), esp. pp. 250ff.

65 See Philip Selznick, *Leadership in Administration* (Evanston: Row, Peterson, 1957).

66 This position disagrees with Sidney Hyman, "Inquiry into the Decline of Congress," *New York Times Magazine*, January 31, 1960. For the argument that 20th century legislatures are on the whole weak see David B. Truman, "The Representative Function in Western Systems," in Edward H. Buehrig (ed.), *Essays in Political Science* (Bloomington: Indiana University Press, 1966), pp. 84–96; Truman, *The Congressional Party* (New York: Wiley, 1954), pp. 1–10; Truman, "Introduction: The Problem and Its Setting," in Truman (ed.), *The Congress and America's Future* (Englewood Cliffs: Prentice-Hall, 1965), pp. 1–4. For the beginning of an argument that the U.S.

Congress may be an exception, see Nelson W. Polsby, *Congress and the Presidency* (New York: Prentice-Hall, 1964), pp. 2, 31–32, 47–115.

67 See Weber, *op. cit.*, p. 69, pp. 330–34; and Gerth and Mills, *op. cit.*, pp. 198–204.

68 See, for example, Donald Matthews, "The Folkways of the U.S. Senate," this REVIEW, 53 (December, 1959), 1064–1089; John C. Wahlke, Heinz Eulau, William Buchanan, and Leroy C. Ferguson, *The Legislative System* (New York: Wiley, 1962), pp. 141–169; Alan Kornberg, "The Rules of the Game in the Canadian House of Commons," *The Journal of Politics*, 26 (May, 1964), 358–380; Ralph K. Huitt, "The Outsider in The Senate," this REVIEW, 55 (September, 1961), 566–575; Nicholas A. Masters, "Committee Assignments in The House of Representatives," this REVIEW, 55 (June, 1961), 345–357; Richard F. Fenno, Jr., "The House Appropriations Committee as a Political System: The Problem of Integration," this REVIEW, 56 (June, 1962), 310–324.

69 Clem Miller, *Member of the House* (John W. Baker, ed.) (New York: Scribner, 1962), p. 93. See also pp. 80–81 and 119–122.

70 Alexander, *op. cit.*, pp. 115–116. The internal quotations are from John Quincy Adams' *Diary* and from an article by Reed in the *Saturday Evening Post*, December 9, 1899.

71 Mayo, *op. cit.*, p. 424; William Parkes Cutler and Julia Perkins Cutler (eds.), *Life, Journals and Correspondence of Reverend Manasseh Cutler* (Cincinnati: Robert Clark and Co., 1888), Vol. II, pp. 186–189.

72 A motion to expel Brooks from the House for this act was defeated; but soon thereafter Brooks resigned anyway. He was subsequently reelected to fill the vacancy caused by his resignation. See *Biographical Directory of The American Congress, 1774–1961* (Washington: Government Printing Office, 1961), p. 604.

73 Alexander, *op. cit.*, pp. 111–112. Other instances of flagrant misbehavior are chronicled in Ben Perley Poore, *Perley's Reminiscences of Sixty Years in the National Metropolis* (Philadelphia: Hubbard, 1886), Vol. I, pp. 394–395; and William Plumer, *Memorandum of Proceedings in the United States Senate* (Everett Somerville Brown, ed.) (New York: Macmillan, 1923), pp. 269–276.

74 A report on decorum in the 19th Century House of Commons suggests that a corresponding toning down has taken place, although Commons was palpably a good bit less unruly to start with. Says an ecstatic commentator, "Like so much else that is good in the institutions of Parliament, the behaviour of the House has grown straight, or, like a river, purified itself as it flowed": Eric Taylor, *The House of Commons At Work* (Baltimore: Penguin, 1961), pp. 85–87. Anthony Barker says: "The close of the 19th Century has been described by Lord Campion as the ending of informality and the beginning of rigid government responsibility for policy in the procedures of the House of Commons": " 'The Most Important And Venerable Function': A Study of Commons Supply Procedure," *Political Studies*, 13 (February, 1965), p. 45.

75 Perhaps secondary analysis comparing the four states (California, New Jersey, Tennessee, Ohio) in the Wahlke, Eulau, Buchanan, and Ferguson study (*op. cit.*) will yield an acceptable test of the hypothesis. This study has good information on the diffusion of legislative norms; it is less strong on structural data, but these might be relatively easy to gather.

76 Parkinson, *op. cit.*, p. 39.
77 The growth of political institutions does not play a particularly important part in the interpretation offered by W. W. Rostow in *The Stages of Economic Growth* (Cambridge: Cambridge University Press, 1960), see, e.g., pp. 18–19, but these may afford at least as good support for his theory as some of the economic indicators he proposes.

5

A rational choice perspective on congressional norms

BARRY R. WEINGAST

Theoretical work by several authors suggests that a minimum winning coalition (*MWC*) will determine the decisions of a legislature making distributive policy (Riker, 1962; Buchanan and Tullock, 1962; Riker and Ordeshook, 1973; Aumann and Kurz, 1977; see also Bott, 1953). These scholars conclude that the majority will adopt distributive policies that benefit themselves at the expense of the minority. These authors also predict that majorities will be of the barest possible size, since *MWC* maximizes the per capita gains for the winners.

Empirical studies of Congress uniformly find that the *MWC* prediction is simply wrong. Nearly all studies report that members of legislatures seek unanimity and are reluctant to exclude minorities from the benefits of distributive legislation (e.g., Ferejohn, 1974 on Public Works; Fenno, 1966 on Appropriations; Fenno, 1972 on Interior; Manley, 1970 on tax policy; Schattschneider, 1935 on the traditional tariff; and Froman, 1967 on member's private bills). This phenomenon is referred to as the universalism norm.[1] Even in the more general case of legislative party relations, studies have repeatedly shown that the majority parties in Congress attempt to work with the minority parties rather than to override them (e.g., Fenno, 1966, p. 164; Ferejohn, 1974, chaps. 8 and 10; Manley, 1969; Mayhew, 1966; and Froman and Ripley, 1965).

This paper presents a modification of the theory of the legislature which retains the assumption of self-interested maximizing behavior, but yields predictions consistent with empirical observation. In addition, this perspective suggests rationales for other features of Congress that are commonly reported in the empirical literature: the existence of various

American Journal of Political Science, Vol. 23, No. 2, May 1979. Reprinted by permission of the University of Texas Press. The author is grateful to Robert Bates, John Ferejohn, Morris Fiorina, Bengt Hölmstrom, Roger Noll, Robert Parks, James Quirk, Trout Rader, and Kenneth Shepsle for helpful comments at various stages of this paper.

"norms," "roles," and "expectations." These features are interpreted as the informal rules or institutions of the legislature. It is argued that rules will be chosen which further the interests of the legislators. This point will be returned to in the final section following the discussion of the choice of a universalism norm. The next few sections attempt to resolve the above paradox by showing why this particular norm is chosen.

PREVAILING THEORIES

A policy is distributive if the benefits accruing to one area can be varied without affecting the benefits received by other areas. Such policies exhibit high divisibilities so they can be disaggregated and dispensed unit by unit, thereby concentrating the benefits while spreading the costs through general taxation. These policies are in contrast to "public goods" which must be provided to all citizens or to none. The term was originally coined for nineteenth century land policies, but as Lowi (1964, p. 690) notes, it can be

easily extended to include most contemporary public land and resource policies; rivers and harbor ('pork barrel') programs; defence procurement and R & D; labor, business, and agricultural 'clientele' services; and the traditional tariff.[2]

In analyzing distributive policies, formal theories of legislative behavior concentrate upon the consequences of simple majority rule. To develop the context of these models, consider a legislature with N members, each with a consistent set of preferences over policies and outcomes.[3]

The legislature can be modeled as an n-person cooperative game. It is a majority rule game with some special features, and will be called the Distributive Legislative Game (DLG). It is represented as follows. Each representative, i, proposes a project or program with total benefits b, total costs c, and $b > c$.[4] Further, suppose that the benefits from the ith project accrue solely to district i and that the taxation system spreads the costs evenly over all districts. Notice that the DLG's taxation mechanism restricts the possibilities for side payments. This feature, along with the lack of the zero sum condition, distinguishes the DLG from the simple majority rule games analyzed by Riker and Buchanan and Tullock.

The vector valued characteristic function is

$$v_i(S) = b - \frac{|S|}{N}c \qquad \text{for } i \in S, |S| > \tfrac{1}{2}N$$

$$v_i(S) = -\frac{|S|}{N}c \qquad \text{for } i \notin S.$$

Thus, if i is a member of the winning coalition, he receives the benefits of his project, b, and pays his share of the total costs which is one-Nth of $|S|$ projects, each of which costs c. If i is not a member of the winning coalition, he pays his share of the total costs and receives no benefits.

If a single legislator proposes his project, it will be defeated by $N - 1$ votes to one vote (the payoffs to all other districts are negative). Since no single project will be authorized, legislators may turn to a logrolling mechanism. In this context, logrolling is the process by which groups of representatives cooperate to pass each other's projects. Any coalition composed of more than half the legislators can assure passage of their projects and is called a winning coalition.

Both Riker and Buchanan and Tullock, analyzing a zero sum majority rule game, conclude that coalitions will be of minimum size, or $\dfrac{N + 1}{2}$ legislators. That is, the set of MWC is identified as the "solution" to the legislative game and is considered to be stable in the following sense. All that is needed to ensure an outcome is the barest of majorities. If a set amount is to be divided up, increasing the number of members in the coalition will serve only to decrease the payoff to some or all of the members of the winning coalition. If a coalition forms that is bigger than the minimum size, then a subset (i.e., another coalition) of these legislators can increase their own payoff by excluding some members of the larger coalition. Which of the many minimum winning coalitions will actually form is not suggested; the theory merely predicts that the winning coalition that does form will be in this set.

Several scholars question whether MWC characterizes majority rule decisions on theoretical grounds (e.g., Butterworth, 1971; Frolich, 1975; Shepsle, 1974). However, these criticisms pertain to analysis of a zero sum majority rule game with side payments. The following proposition shows that these criticisms are irrelevant in the current context. Because the zero sum condition is not imposed and because the taxation mechanism of the DLG restricts side payments in a particular manner, a much stronger rationale exists for considering the MWC as the solution set.

Proposition 1: Assuming that each legislator seeks to maximize the net benefits which accrue to his district, the set of MWC constitutes the core of the DLG. Further, any coalition not in this set is dominated by all members of this set.

Proof: Throughout, let $S \in MWC$ and let $A \notin MWC$. One coalition dominates another if its members comprise a majority (i.e., it is winning) and if these members prefer this coalition over the other.

Case I: $|A| < |S|$. By definition, S is minimum winning, so A cannot be winning; therefore, S defeats A. Case II: $|A| > |S|$. $\forall\ i \in S$, either $i \in A'$ or $i \in A \cap S$, where A' is the complement of A. To show dominance, simply note that all $i \in S$ prefer S to A. If $i \in A'$, he prefers S since

$$b - \frac{|S|}{N}c > -\frac{|A|}{N}c;$$

If $i \in A \cap S$, he prefers S since

$$b - \frac{|S|}{N}c > b - \frac{|A|}{N}c.$$

Conversely, no $S \in MWC$ is dominated by A (s.t. $|A| > |S|$). Case III: $|T| = |S|$. Finally, no $S \in MWC$ strictly dominates any other $T \in MWC$. Since S and T each comprise more than half the members, $S \cap T \neq 0$. $\forall\ i \in S \cap T$, i is indifferent between the two coalitions because they both yield the same payoff.   Q.E.D.

Thus, the set of MWC possesses an important stability property in the DLG which doesn't hold for simple majority rule games. This result serves as compelling reason to suppose that MWC characterizes outcomes of DLG. Any winning coalition which is not minimum can be beaten by an MWC; that is, a majority of members always prefers a minimum winning coalition to any other. Further, once an MWC forms, no other coalition can upset it. This last property does not hold in the contexts analyzed by Riker (1962) and Buchanan and Tullock (1962).

MODIFYING THE THEORY

The preceding theory fails to explain universalism, i.e., the tendency to seek unanimous passage of distributive programs through inclusion of a project for all legislators who want one. Indeed, this tendency constitutes evidence against the model. In exploring the observed data, it becomes apparent that the model fails to give consideration to an obvious feature of a representative process – the payoffs to a representative and to his district may differ. While the district may wish to enrich itself at the expense of the rest of the country, the representative wishes to retain the prestige and power which accompanies continued membership in the legislature. This feature, when explicitly incorporated into a model of the legislature, destroys the MWC theory and gives rise to the norm of universalism.

The model that follows is based upon several assumptions. The first is that representatives seek reelection. Although this need not be an end in itself, it is necessary to continue the utility derived from the prestige and power of a membership in the legislature.[5] The second assumption is that districts respond positively to beneficial legislation: the greater the net benefits received by the district the more likely they are to reelect their representative. Further, decisions made by the electorate are based on the net benefits accruing to them without consideration of the effects on other districts. While the model distinguishes the intentions of the electorate and the representatives, it does assume that their interests are related: the representative seeks to be returned to office and his electoral fortunes are related to the benefits he brings home to his district. The more successful he is at getting projects built, the greater his chances of remaining in the legislature.

The major implication of these assumptions for the analysis of distributive policy is that representatives pursuing their own interests will prefer institutional arrangements (or norms) which increase their chances of success in gaining benefits for their districts. Universalism is such an institution. Rational self-interested legislators have compelling reasons to prefer decision making by maximal rather than minimal winning coalitions.[6]

Since different rules define different legislative games, the choice between various institutions is a choice between games. The Universalism Legislative Game (*ULG*) is an alternative legislative institution to compare with *DLG*. Assume, again, that each legislator has a project worth b to his district with costs c ($b > c$) which are spread across all districts through general taxation. Further, *ULG* allows each legislator to include his project in an omnibus-type proposal.

The legislators, in choosing their operating rules, must decide which game to play, *DLG* or *ULG*. Each legislator will evaluate the alternatives in terms of the *ex ante* expected payoffs.[7]

Consider the decision of legislator i. Under *ULG* his district's payoffs are known with certainty and are $b - c$ (which is the benefits minus the district's share of the total costs, or one Nth of N projects which cost c).

In contrast, outcomes under *DLG* are characterized by *MWC*. The net payoff to the districts of the *MWC*'s members will be $b - \dfrac{(N + 1)c}{2N}$ which is the benefits from the project minus the district's share of the total costs $\left(\text{or one Nth of } \dfrac{(N + 1)c}{2N}\right)$. The payoff to the legislator is a greater chance of reelection for ensuring a project for his district.

For members not in the coalition, the payoff to their districts will be negative. They pay their share of the total costs, $\dfrac{1}{N}$th of $\dfrac{N + 1}{2}c$ projects for a net payoff of $-\dfrac{(N + 1)c}{2N}$. For these legislators, the payoff is an increased chance of defeat for having obtained a negative payoff for the district.

A priori, of course, no legislator can be sure that he will be a member of the winning coalition, and hence of how distributive programs affect his chance of reelection. From this standpoint, if all such coalitions are equally likely,[8] any given legislator has a $\frac{(N + 1)}{2N}$ chance of being in the winning coalition.[9]

The following theorem shows that under these circumstances all legislators will prefer *ULG* to *DLG*.

UNIVERSALISM THEOREM: If legislators maximize the net benefits which accrue to their districts, and if all minimum winning coalitions are equally likely, then *ULG* dominates *DLG* for all legislators (i.e., the expected net benefits are greater under *ULG* than *DLG* for all legislators).

Proof: Let EP_D be the expected payoff under *DLG* for legislator i. If $i \in MWC$, then his payoff is $b - ac$ where $a = \frac{(N + 1)}{2N}$; however, if $i \notin MWC$, then his payoff is $-ac$. Since his chances of being included in the MWC are $\frac{N + 1}{2N} = a$ (see footnote 9 for the derivation of this result),

$$EP_D = a(b - ac) + (1 - a)(-ac)$$
$$= ab - a^2c - ac + a^2c$$
$$= a(b - c).$$

Next, let EP_U be the expected payoff under *ULG*. This yields legislator i $b - c$ in all cases (i.e., $EP_U = b - c$). Finally,

$$EP_U - EP_D = (b - c) - a(b - c)$$
$$= (1 - a)(b - c) > 0.$$

Q.E.D.

Under *ULG*, the expected payoff to each district is greater than under *DLG*, and moreover, each legislator is more likely to be reelected.

The pursuit of reelection is not the only reason legislators would rationally choose to institutionalize and maintain a tradition of unanimous coalitions.[10] In addition to increasing the *ex ante* probability of reelection, unanimity reduces the uncertainties they face if *MWC*s are to be formed. Risk averse legislators presumably favor reductions in their risk of defeat. Also, institutionalizing the coalition of the whole reduces the time and energy used to negotiate the formation of the winning coalition. This time can be used pursuing actions related to other objectives of the members.

Once universalism has been accepted as an institutional rule, the legislator must decide whether to include a project (previously, the decision also included the choice of a strategy to become part of the MWC). This decision can be modeled as a noncooperative game and has a Nash equilibrium solution. The choice is whether to propose a project, given that all other districts are getting a project. As long as the project brings a net benefit to the district, it is in the interests of the representative to propose one.

Consider again N legislators indexed by i. Each could propose a project bringing benefits, b_i, and costs, c_i. The decision for any legislator, j, is between the following strategies: (1) Propose a project and receive net benefits $b_j - \frac{1}{N} \times (\Sigma_i c_i)$; or (2) Fail to propose a project and simply bear the district's share of all other costs $-\frac{1}{N} \times \left(\sum_{i \neq j} c_i \right)$.

Strategy (1) is preferable to (2) as long as b_j is greater than $\frac{1}{N} c_j$ or, in words, the benefit/cost ratio of the project is greater than $1/N$. Thus the equilibrium strategy is a project for every district as long as one can be found that provides benefits that exceed $1/N$th of the costs.

A natural objection to the preceding analysis poses short-term against long-term rationality. In the long-term all the legislators do better under universalism. But in the short-term what prevents an impetuous group of legislators from proposing a bill with projects for just a bare majority? Obviously, a universalistic rule must include further features that give individual legislators an incentive to follow the rule at all times. What "maintenance mechanisms" are there to support this norm?

One possible answer lies in the procedural rules and institutional structure of the legislature. For example, a rule may be adopted to prevent poaching. If a member attempts to remove a project by floor amendment or otherwise obstruct the process, then remove his project instead. Though this rule is rarely needed, it is invoked on occasion. Ferejohn reports that Senator Proxmire's attempts to reduce the pork resulted in the curtailment of his pet project (Ferejohn, 1974, pp. 114–15). More recently, Senator Buckley of New York proposed a series of amendments removing a project or two for every state from the public works legislation. Only the two amendments removing projects from New York passed. Similarly, this rule provides potential penalties to a member seeking to build a MWC. Those who make the attempt may only make themselves worse off through the exclusion of their district's project.[11]

A second, noninstitutional factor inhibits attempts to form *MWCs*: the repetition inherent in the legislative process. In the next session a new *MWC* might form. If exclusion from the legislative benefits implies a much greater risk of defeat, then legislators will be even more reluctant to make the attempt for short-run gain out of fear of losing next time.

In order for the legislature to adopt universalism, legislators must perceive that the benefits of projects generally exceed the costs. Assuming each legislator's project has the same benefits, b, and costs, c, the proposal to adopt universalism yields net benefits to each legislator of $b - \dfrac{1}{N} \times NC$, in contrast to *MWC* expected benefits of $\dfrac{N+1}{2N}b - \dfrac{N+1}{2N}c$. The former exceeds the latter only if b is greater than c. Hence a rational legislator will vote to adopt universalism only if the expected benefits are positive. Yet this conclusion is at odds with scholarly observations of many distributive policies. The very term "pork barrel" connotes expenditures that are not economically warranted. Empirical studies abound with examples of public works for which the "benefits" exceed the costs only because of the wildest assumptions that lie behind the calculations.

Two factors help explain why universalism persists after the objective basis for its adoption has vanished. First, over time, projects are chosen with successively lower rates of return. This reflects rational legislators choosing those projects with the greatest net benefits first. As the process continues, the net benefits of the projects decline and eventually become negative.

Once universalism is adopted, cooperative action by all legislators is no longer required, and each proposes his projects individually. As the projects being proposed no longer meet the criterion $b > c$, the process takes on the familiar form of the prisoner's dilemma. Acting individually, legislators will still continue to propose projects (until $b < \dfrac{1}{N}c$, since each district bears only one Nth of the costs of its own projects). Consequently, the institution may remain after it has ceased producing net benefits.

Constituents will not necessarily find it rational to hold their representative responsible for the persistence of pork after the entire program ceases to provide them with net benefits. A representative is only one vote in the legislature. Acting by himself, though perhaps making a valiant attempt (as either Proxmire or Buckley may have been doing), one vote is not likely to alter policy. At the same time, as long as he goes along, he retains the ability to get his district its share which partially negates the liability of the entire program. As Noll and Fiorina argue, constituents may indeed be satisfied with this type of role as long as there is some advantage to incumbency. If voters perceive their ability to change the system, acting through their legislator, to be negligible, it is rational for them to (reluctantly) approve of this role.[12]

Second, the political benefits and costs may differ from the economic benefits and costs. This explanation remains vacuous without a particular model of how these systematically differ. The following discussion suggests but one way in which this might occur.[13]

Legislators rarely receive 100 percent of the vote.[14] Sixty percent is usually considered a large plurality. Since most districts are not composed of a homogeneous group of constituents, representatives cannot hope to capture 100 percent of the vote. A legislator is successful in obtaining reelection if he builds a majority coalition or constituency within his district. The basis of this coalition is an amalgam of positions on issues, including issues other than distributive programs, such as regulatory or redistributive policies.[15] Thus a representative may consciously choose a supporting constituency that contains only a comfortable majority of the district population. This implies that the institution of universalism may continue even though the net return on projects is negative. If a representative has built a supporting constituency that represents, say 60 percent of his district, then projects with negative rates of return may still be included if the benefits can be concentrated among the supporting coalition, and if $b > .6c$ for all legislators.[16]

Eventually, electoral incentives will favor removing pork barrel expenditures when net benefits become sufficiently negative. A new cooperative action may remove or alter the nature of the now counterproductive institution, thereby increasing the flow of net benefits to the constituencies. This can be accomplished by canceling the program or by altering its scope and jurisdiction. The latter alternative has the potential to widen the set of possible projects to include some with positive net benefits.

Indeed, widening the scope of the process rather than dismantling a committee's jurisdiction has occurred frequently in recent years. As Ferejohn reports, "The Corps' function has expanded...dramatically in the last thirty years. Projects for the protection of wildlife, the construction of recreation facilities, the improvement of water supply and quality, and the stimulation of regional economic development have all been authorized by Congress for the Corps of Engineers during this time period.... This expansion has enabled the Corps to avoid cutting back its budget and staff as earlier functions have declined in importance" (Ferejohn, 1974, p. 8). In particular the recent amendments to the Water Pollution Control Act (1956 and especially 1972) authorizing construction of sewage treatment plants gave the Corps a boost as their more traditional function has become less valuable.

These modifications to the theory of the legislature provide a rationale for the pork barrel as a structure to serve member goals. It further predicts that this system cannot remain unaltered indefinitely. The process must either be halted entirely or dramatically changed once the total system becomes inefficient.

POLICY CONSEQUENCES

In addition to affecting member goals differently from unmodified majority rule, universalism has an effect on policy outcomes. In the case of no constituency differentiation within the district, the pork barrel system becomes an electoral liability once the benefits are no longer greater than their costs. This provides an incentive to alter the process as was discussed above. In contrast, under MWC the process will not become a liability until the benefits are less than $\frac{(N+1)}{2N}$% of the costs.

Since $\frac{N+1}{2}$ projects are built under MWC, a district receiving a project pays only $\frac{1}{N}$ of $\frac{N+1}{2}c$. Consequently, the net benefits to the district are positive if $b > \frac{N+1}{2N}c$. This implies that pork barrel will continue longer under unmodified majority rule than under universalism. Alternatively, more inefficiency (or pork) is possible under MWC than universalism.

The results remain if the possibility of the political rewards differing from the economic rewards is assumed. Recall that a congressman who has built a supporting constituency of 60 percent of his district receives positive benefits under universalism as long as $b > .60c$.[17] With this supporting constituency, under MWC rules, a project will yield positive political rewards of $b > \frac{N+1}{2N} \times .60c$ or $b > .6\frac{(N+1)}{2N}c.$ $\left(\text{e.g.,}\right.$ if $N = 100$, then $.6\frac{(N+1)}{2N}c < \frac{1}{3}.\left.\right)$

The conclusion that simple majority rule allows more inefficient policies than unanimity is not new. Buchanan and Tullock (1962, pp. 10–14, and chap. 5) argue that unanimity is required to ensure that only efficient projects will be chosen. Their conclusion and the results of this paper are derived from similar models so this inconsistency is not surprising.

The literature is not fully supportive, however. Barry (1965, pp. 250–

56, 317–18) argues that unanimity has the greatest potential for pork since it distributes a "veto" to every voter. Each individual, pursuing his own self-interest, is likely to demand special benefits in return for his cooperation. Unanimity maximizes the pork if all voters pursue this strategy. However, in terms of the rational actor paradigm, this argument makes little sense. If all voters pursue the strategy of choosing a project such that $\frac{1}{N}c < b < c$ then any one individual can make himself better off by vetoing the whole proposal. Since all are demanding pork, the payoff to any individual voter will be $b - \frac{1}{N} \times Nc = b - c < 0$; vetoing the whole collection yields him zero.[18]

One possible way of interpreting Barry's (1965) claim is to examine a legislature where the majority rule is qualified to allow a subset of voters a veto.[19] Those legislators possessing veto power may be able to extract more pork than unmodified majority rule. For example, assume majority rule subject to only one legislator's veto. This legislator must be in the MWC which forms, and may demand more projects than any other legislator, potentially increasing the pork barrel. A more detailed investigation of this social choice rule is beyond the scope of this paper.

CONCLUSION

This paper provides an instrumental basis for the social-psychological norms observed in most real world legislatures. In doing so, it follows Fenno and others in interpreting these norms as the informal structure or rules of the legislature.[20] In the *Power of the Purse*, Fenno begins the discussion of the House Appropriations Committee's structure in these terms.

In the first place, the Committee must develop an institutional decision-making structure. In the second place, the Committee must maintain or stabilize the decision-making it created. (p. 127)...The basic elements of the Committee's internal structure are its differentiated roles...Roles consist of clusters of norms (p. 128).

Next,

The idea of control mechanisms completes the definition of an operative norm. Two such mechanisms are of special importance to the Committee on Appropriations. The first is the socialization process...the second is the sanctioning mechanisms applicable to all members of the Committee which operates to reward the observance of appropriate norms and punish deviations from them (p. 208).

As argued here, legislators find it in their own self-interest to establish norms and form institutions to further their goals. Observing that different institutions imply different outcomes, which affect member goals differentially, a rationale exists for establishing one set of norms over another.[21]

This perspective suggests possible explanations for other norms discussed in the literature. The informal rules of the legislature further collective goals and individual members' goals. Consider the dual norms of specialization and reciprocity which support the committee system.[22] These norms foster the development of legislative expertise in a specific area so that complex proposals on diverse subjects can be considered simultaneously. Consequently the Congress as a whole need not consider each bill and individual representatives need not study and research the details of all legislation. The reciprocity rule provides the incentives to specialize by delegating the decision power of the legislature in a particular area to a specific committee. Individual members thereby gain greater influence in a particular area. Since representatives tend to be members of committees related to their constituency's interests (Fenno, 1973), members can use this influence to shape policies closer to their constituency's needs or preferences than if these policies were to be drafted by a random collection of members.[23] Individual legislators consequently have an incentive to support the committee system by following the reciprocity rule. Thus, like the universalism norm, the specialization and reciprocity norms have an effect on a representative's electoral fortunes and on the nature of the policies written by the legislature.

NOTES

1 This paper follows Mayhew and Polsby in distinguishing between "universalism" and "reciprocity." The former is used to describe unanimous inclusion of representatives' projects in omnibus-type legislation produced by one committee; the latter is used as representatives' deferential behavior toward the legislation of other committees. See Mayhew (1974, p. 114) and Polsby (1968). This distinction is made because the phenomena and their rationales are different. Compare this paper with the discussion of reciprocity in Weingast (1978). Most authors do not distinguish between these phenomena. For example, see Matthews (1960, compare pp. 99–100 with p. 147) and Froman (1967, compare pp. 15–17 with p. 22).
2 The categorization of public policies as either distributive, regulatory, or redistributive is developed in this article.
3 N is assumed to be an odd number throughout. This is solely for ease of exposition; all of the results hold if N is even.
4 The results which follow necessitate the assumption that each legislator's proposal has the same benefits and costs. See Fiorina (1978).
5 See Fenno (1972) for a more general discussion of legislators' goals. In Fenno's scheme, the reelection goal is but one of three goals. Mayhew (1974,

Part I) places the assumption of single purposeful behavior in context by discussing its advantages and disadvantages.

6 The following argument provides a rationale for Mayhew's claim:

> On legislators supplying particularized benefits, two points may reasonably be made. The first is that it is vital for members to win victories; a dam is not good unless it is authorized and built. The second is that winning victories can be made quite easy. The best way for members to handle the particularized is to establish universalistic standards (Mayhew, 1974, p. 114).

7 The following decision calculus is actually a special case of the Deegan-Packel Index (Deegan and Packel, 1977). More generally, see Plott (1972) for a discussion of individual choice among constitutional provisions. See also Roth (1977).

8 Though an unrealistic assumption because it ignores institutional features such as parties, committees, seniority, etc., this assumption is commonly employed in probability models of legislative behavior. For example, see Rae (1969), Taylor (1969), Curtis (1972), Badger (1972), and Schofield (1972).

9 Proof that if all coalitions are equally likely, the probability of inclusion for any given members is $(N + 1)/2N$. Let $M = (N + 1)/2$ be the minimum number which comprises a majority. The total number of minimum winning coalitions is $\binom{N}{M}$. The total number of minimum winning coalitions in which a given representative is not a member is $\binom{N-1}{M}$. Thus,

$$1 - \frac{\binom{N-1}{M}}{\dfrac{N}{M}}$$

is the probability that a given representative will be included in the minimum winning coalition which eventually forms. Reducing, this becomes

$$1 - \frac{\dfrac{(N-1)!}{M!(N-1-M)!}}{\dfrac{N!}{M!(N-M)!}} = 1 - \left(\frac{N-M}{N}\right) = \frac{N + 1}{2N}$$

10 The question of maintenance will be pursued shortly.

11 A full exposition of the institutions supporting universalism is beyond the scope of this paper. See Ferejohn (1974) for a discussion of the actual rules supporting the Public Works legislation.

12 Noll and Fiorina (1978) develop this point in greater detail in the context of a formal model. For an interesting interpretation on the changing role of representatives from policymakers to errand boys, see Fiorina (1977a, 1977b).

13 Developing models of the divergence between the economic and the political costs and benefits deserves greater attention. Two outstanding approaches not discussed in the text are Hinich's study of food regulation by the FDA and Haveman's work on the Army Corps of Engineers. See Hinich (1975) and Haverman (1965).

14 This section relies on Fenno (1977) and Fiorina (1974).

15 See Lowi (1964) for discussion of this classification.

16 If the benefits are perfectly concentrated among the legislator's supporters

then the cost to the supporters is 60% of $(1/N)Nc$. Consequently, they receive positive net benefits at the expense of the rest of the district and all other districts if $b > .6c$.

17 Thus, the political net benefits are $b - .6c$.

18 Pennock (1970) disagrees with Barry's (1965) arguments and supports Buchanan and Tullock (1962). See also Ferejohn (1974, "Conclusion") for a further contrast between the two approaches.

19 It is possible Barry had this in mind. He writes,

> The nearer a system comes to requiring unanimity for decisions, the more prevalent we may expect to find the "pork barrel" phenomenon. The United States comes nearer to a "unanimity system" than any other Western democracy; it also suffers most from the "pork barrel" problem.... (1965, p. 317).

In the above example, the individuals with the veto power are the relevant committee chairman, ranking minority member, president, etc.

20 Arrow (1963) argues similarly for the case of medical ethics; Harsanyi (1969) presents an insightful rational choice interpretation of social norms and values; and Barry (1970) devotes most of *Sociologists, Economists and Democracy* to contrasting the rational choice approach against the sociological. The first two scholars, and Barry at times, provide a partial synthesis of the two approaches. They interpret social values or norms within the rational choice framework as rules governing behavior. As such, the rules must be explained in terms of the benefits and costs which they provide for the group and the individuals following the rules. Schelling (1963) argues a similar thesis.

21 Mayhew (1974) devotes the second half of his excellent essay to a discussion of how the structure of Congress is designed to further member goals.

22 For a further elaboration on the rational choice perspective on the reciprocity system, see Weingast (1978).

23 Fenno (1966) makes a similar argument for the House Committee on Appropriations. One of the Committee's prime methods of controlling spending under Chairman Cannon was to assign members to subcommittees unrelated to their districts' interests. See Ferejohn (1974, Chap. 9) for evidence supporting this claim in the case of pork barrel legislation.

REFERENCES

Arrow, Kenneth A. 1963. Uncertainty and the welfare economics of medical care. *American Economic Review*, 53 (December 1963): 941–73.

Aumann, Robert, and Mordecai Kurz. 1977. Power and taxes. *Econometrica*, 45 (July 1977): 1137–62.

Badger, Wade W. 1972. Political individualism, positional preferences, and optimal decision-rules. In Richard G. Niemi and Herbert F. Weisberg, eds., *Probability models of collective decision making*. Columbus: Charles E. Merrill.

Barry, Brian M. 1965. *The political argument*. London: Routledge and Kegan Paul.

1970. *Sociologists, economists and democracy*. London: Sollier-Macmillan.

Bott, Raoul. 1953. Symmetric solutions to majority games. In H. W. Kuhn and A. W. Tucker, eds., *Contributions to the theory of games*, II. Princeton: Princeton University Press.

A rational choice perspective

Buchanan, James M., and Gordon Tullock. 1962. *The calculus of consent*. Ann Arbor: University of Michigan Press.

Butterworth, Robert. 1971. A research note on the size of winning coalitions. *American Political Science Review*, 65 (September 1971): 741–47.

Curtis, Richard B. 1972. Decision-rules and collective values in constitutional choice. In Richard G. Niemi and Herbert F. Weisberg, eds., *Probability models of collective decision making*. Columbus: Charles E. Merrill.

Deegan, John Jr., and Edward W. Packel. 1977. A new index for simple n-person games. Mimeograph. University of Rochester.

Fenno, Richard F. 1966. *Power of the purse*. Boston: Little, Brown and Company.

1973. *Congressmen in committees*. Boston: Little, Brown and Company.

1977. Congressmen and their constituencies: An exploration. *American Political Science Review*, 71 (December 1977): 883–917.

Ferejohn, John F. 1974. *Pork barrel politics*. Stanford: Stanford University Press.

Fiorina, Morris P. 1974. *Representatives, roll calls, and their constituents*. Lexington: Lexington Books, D.C. Heath and Company.

1977a. The case of the vanishing marginals: The bureaucracy did it. *American Political Science Review*, 71 (March 1977): 177–81.

1977b. *Congress: Keystone of the Washington establishment*. New Haven: Yale University Press.

1978. "Legislative facilitation of government growth: Universalism and reciprocity practices in majority rule institutions." Social Science Working Paper #228, California Institute of Technology, Pasadena, California.

Frohlich, Norman. 1975. The instability of minimum winning coalitions. *American Political Science Review*, 69 (September 1975): 943–46.

Froman, Lewis A. Jr. 1967. *The congressional process: Strategies, rules and procedures*. Boston: Little, Brown and Company.

Froman, Lewis A., and Randall B. Ripley. 1965. Conditions for party leadership: The cases of the house democrats. *American Political Science Review*, 59 (March 1965): 52–63.

Harsanyi, John C. 1969. Rational choice models of political behavior vs. functionalist and conformist theories. *World Politics*, 21 (July 1969): 513–38.

Haveman, Robert H. 1965. *Water resource investment*. Nashville: Vanderbilt University Press.

Hinich, Melvin J. 1975. A social choice model for consumer support for food regulation. Mimeographed. Virginia Polytechnic Institute.

Lowi, Theodore J. 1964. American business, public policy, case studies and political theory. *World Politics*, 16 (July 1964): 690.

Manley, John F. 1969. Wilbur D. Mills: A study in congressional influence. *American Political Science Review*, 62 (June 1969): 442–64.

1970. *The politics of finance*. Boston: Little, Brown and Company.

Matthews, Donald R. 1960. *U.S. senators and their world*. New York: Vintage.

Mayhew, David R. 1966. *Party loyalty among congressmen*. Cambridge: Harvard University Press.

1974. *Congress: The electoral connection*. New Haven: Yale University Press.

Niemi, Richard G., and Herbert F. Weisberg. 1972. Editors, *Probability models of collective decision making*. Columbus: Charles E. Merrill.

Noll, Roger G., and Morris P. Fiorina. 1978. Voters, legislators, and bureaucrats: A rational choice perspective on the growth of bureaucracy. *Journal of Public Economics*.

Pennock, J. Roland. 1970. The "pork barrel" and majority rule: A note. *Journal of Politics*, 32 (May 1970): 709–16.

Plott, Charles R. 1972. Individual choice of a political-economic process. In Richard G. Niemi and Herbert F. Weisberg, eds., *Probability models of collective decision making*. Columbus: Charles E. Merrill.

Polsby, Nelson W. 1968. The institutionalization of the house of representatives. *American Political Science Review*, 62 (March 1968): 144–68.

Rae, Douglas. 1969. Decision-rules and individual values in constitutional choice. *American Political Science Review*, 63 (March 1969): 40–56.

Riker, William H. 1962. *The theory of political coalitions*. New Haven: Yale University Press.

Riker, William H., and Peter C. Ordeshook. 1973. *An introduction to positive political theory*. Englewood Cliffs: Prentice-Hall.

Roth, Alvin E. 1977. The Shapley value as a Von Neumann-Morgenstern utility. *Econometrica*, 45 (April 1977): 657–64.

Schattschneider, E. E. 1935. *Politics, pressures and the tariff*. Englewood Cliffs: Prentice-Hall.

Schelling, Thomas C. 1963. *The strategy of conflict*. New York: Oxford.

Schofield, Norman J. 1972. Is majority rule special? In Richard G. Niemi and Herbert F. Weisberg, eds., *Probability models of collective decision making*. Columbus: Charles E. Merrill.

Shepsle, Kenneth A. 1974. On the size of winning coalitions. *American Political Science Review*, 68 (June 1974): 505–24.

Taylor, Michael. 1969. Proof of a theorem on majority rule. *Behavioral Science*, 14 (May 1969): 228–31.

Weingast, Barry R. 1978. Reciprocity, committees, and public policy. Mimeograph. Center for the Study of American Business, Washington University.

6

Congressmen and committees: a comparative analysis

RICHARD F. FENNO, JR.

This book* rests on a simple assumption and conveys a simple theme. The assumption is that congressional committees matter. The theme is that congressional committees differ. Both are commonplace. But the book has been written because those who think committees matter and those who think committees differ have not yet fully accommodated one to the other – not intellectually and not in practice.

Generalizations about congressional committees are numerous and familiar. The oldest and most familiar is Woodrow Wilson's book-length assertion that committees dominate congressional decision making. A corollary states that committees are autonomous units, which operate quite independently of such external influences as legislative party leaders, chamber majorities, and the President of the United States. Other staples of committee commentary hold: that members specialize in their committee's subject matter, and hence that each committee is the repository of legislative expertise within its jurisdiction; that committee decisions are usually accepted and ratified by the other members of the chamber; that committee chairmen can (and usually do) wield a great deal of influence over their committees. A broader generalization holds that Congress, and by extension its committees, is gradually losing policy-making influence to the executive branch.

Most of our empirical generalizations are of the same order. Each one is uttered as if it were equally applicable to all committees. And taken together, they convey the message that committees are similar. Our recent studies of individual committees have taught us, to the contrary, however, that committees are markedly different from one another. Indeed, as we shall show, committees differ in all the respects previously

* From Richard F. Fenno, Jr., *Congressmen in Committees* (pp. xiii–xvi, 81–114, 137–38). Copyright © 1973 by Little, Brown and Company (Inc.). Reprinted by permission.

mentioned – their influence in congressional decision making, their autonomy, their success on the chamber floor, their expertise, the control exercised by their chairmen, and their domination by the executive branch. If such is – even partially – the case, the need for a new set of generalizations is obvious. One immediate temptation, of course, is to scrap all our familiar generalizations in favor of a single statement asserting the uniqueness of each committee. But that is a counsel of despair; political scientists ought not to eschew the possibility of making limited comparisons before they have tried. This book should be read as one such effort – to describe and generalize about committee similarities and differences at a level somewhere between that which assumes committee uniformity and that which assumes committee uniqueness.

The need for a middle range of generalizations is not purely academic. Reform-minded members of Congress and citizen groups have also viewed committee operations from the perspectives of uniformity and/or uniqueness, and they have been as ill served by this outlook as the scholar. Every congressman knows that committees are dissimilar. Assertions to that effect are hard currency on Capitol Hill. "Committee behavior all depends on the chairman and every chairman, of course, is different." Or, "Committee behavior all depends on the subject matter and every committee, of course, handles a different policy area." Why, then, when they prescribe committee reform, do congressmen abandon their own wisdom and insist on applying every reform in equal dosages to every committee? The answer may be partly intellectual in nature – that they cannot conceive of committee similarities and differences in such a way as to formulate a mixed strategy of reform. It is as if the practitioner were waiting for the student to equip him with a middle range of categories in which to think and make his prescriptions. Thus, the political scientist's search for explanation may be related to the reformer's search for change.

Our theme is, then, that committees differ from one another. And, we shall argue, they differ systematically. We shall examine their similarities and differences with respect to five variables – member goals, environmental constraints, strategic premises, decision-making processes, and decisions. We shall pursue the following line of argument. The members of each congressional committee have certain goals that they want to achieve through membership on a committee. If there is a high level of consensus on goals, they will organize their committee internally in ways that seem likely to aid them in achieving these individual goals. However, each committee operates within a distinctive set of environmental constraints – most particularly the expectations of influential external groups. Committee members will, therefore, also organize their committee internally in ways that seem likely to satisfy the expectations of

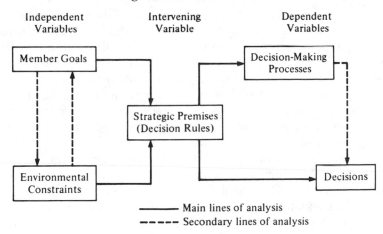

Figure 6.1. Analytic scheme for comparing committees

these groups that make up their environment. The members of each committee will develop strategies for accommodating the achievement of their individual goals to the satisfaction of key environmental expectations. These strategies become the proximate premises on which each committee's internal decision-making processes are based. From these strategies, operationalized as decision rules, flow committee decisions. In our explanatory scheme, then, member goals and environmental constraints are the independent variables; strategic premises (or, decision rules) are an intervening variable; and decision-making processes and decisions are dependent variables.

We shall use this scheme to analyze six committees of the House of Representatives as they functioned in the period from 1955 to 1966, from the 84th through the 89th Congresses. They are the Committees on Appropriations, Education and Labor, Foreign Affairs, Interior and Insular Affairs (hereafter referred to as the Interior Committee), Post Office and Civil Service (hereafter referred to as the Post Office Committee), and Ways and Means.... No claim is made for the representativeness of the time span or the sample. But we would argue that in both respects our data are sufficient to support an initial foray into comparative analysis....

DECISION-MAKING PROCESSES

Within certain constraining norms established by the House – norms which act as homogenizing influences – the members of each committee are free to devise whatever internal structure they wish. Accordingly they search for a structure that will help them implement their decision rules – especially as those rules reflect a strategy for achieving their personal goals. A committee will alter its internal structure when a solid majority of members feel that it no longer serves their objectives, provided only that they can agree on an alternative. No decision-making structure will completely satisfy all interested parties. At any point in time, therefore, a committee's structure is only an approximation of an arrangement that would give everyone everything he wants. So long as the members regard it as "good enough" or "satisfactory" or "better than any other practicable possibility," the internal structure displays a certain degree of stability. While the structure is stabilized, we can generalize about it and describe the committee's normal decision-making process. We can also describe incremental changes in that process. That is what we shall be doing in this chapter. Our description will focus on...important aspects of committee decision making. They are: *partisanship and participation-specialization....*

As a prefatory note, however, we should remember that every committee's internal structure is bounded by certain formal and informal norms of the parent chamber. One homogenizing constraint comes indirectly from the congressional electorate, which decides at the polls which party shall control all House committees. Other constraints come directly from House rules. Some internal committee procedures – concerning meeting days, parliamentary practice, record keeping, reporting, for example – are fixed by the House. Committee size and party ratios are set by the House and altered through time by amicable bargaining among the leaders of the two parties....

Of all the House-imposed constraints, the most consequential is the informal seniority rule for the designation of the committee chairman (and ranking minority member). Because of his prerogatives, prestige, and leadership opportunities, the chairman is normally the most influential member of a committee. It may be that he is, in every respect, cut from the mold of his committee and would be its members' choice for chairman. But the seniority rule brings him to his pre-eminence through a concatenation of electoral and actuarial fates wholly beyond the control of the other committee members. In this sense, the rule stands as a formidable limitation on the ability of a committee's members to shape their internal structure. On the other hand, seniority choices should not be viewed as wholly fortuitous. If a man has chosen membership on a given committee and served on it for a long period of time, the chances are excellent that he will share the goals, the perceptions of the environment, and the strategic premises held by most of his fellow members. Still, there is no guarantee of such agreement. The probabilities, we would guess, are highest on committees having high consensus and House-oriented strategic premises and are lowest on committees with low consensus and non-House-oriented strategic premises. When disagreement exists, as in the case of the three chairmen we have mentioned, Murray, Barden, and Powell, it can have major consequences for committee decision making.

Partisanship

If a committee's decision rules help to explain internal structure, we would expect to find, obviously, that *partisanship* is greatest inside committees that adopt decision rules calling for it. Two of our six committees, *Ways and Means* and *Education and Labor* prescribe for themselves "the prosecution of policy partisanship." These are the same two committees whose members... have the strongest partisan leanings and are the most ideologically divergent of the six. By all accounts, Ways and Means and Education and Labor are more partisan than the other four. One measure of these differences in internal partisanship is presented in Table 6.1. We have analyzed the committee reports for all bills deemed sufficiently important by *Congressional Quarterly Almanac* to warrant description in its yearly catalogue of "major legislation."[1] We have calculated, first, the number of reports on which there was any recorded disagreement on the committee's final decision and, second, the number of these disagreements on which a majority of one party was found recorded in opposition to a majority of the other party. The latter we call "party disagreements." Whether measured by absolute numbers, percentages, or ratios, Ways and Means and Education and Labor display a much greater degree of partisanship, at the decision stage, than any of the other six committees. In both cases, it is a response to the partisan elements in their environments – elements more prominent in these two committees than in the other four.

Though the two committees share a high degree of partisanship at the point of *decision*, the importance of partisanship during the *deliberative* stage of committee work differs radically from one committee to the other. Ways and Means members limit the play of partisanship to the final stages of decision making and do most of their work in a non-partisan atmosphere. Education and Labor proceeds, at all stages, in an atmosphere charged with partisanship. The two committees are, therefore, as different in their decision-making styles as they are similar in their voting splits. And the difference, we would argue, can be explained wholly on the basis of contrasting member goals and environmental constraints.

Ways and Means members want influence in the House, a goal that forces an internal concern for their reputation in the House and for

Table 6.1. *Disagreement and partisanship in Committee reports –*
1955–1966

	Total major legislation	Percentage recorded disagreements	Percentage party disagreements	Party disagreements as percentage of all recorded disagreements
Ways and Means	114	52% (59)	26% (30)	50%
Education and Labor	96	56% (54)	25% (27)	50%
Interior	78	35% (27)	8% (6)	22%
Post Office	42	38% (16)	7% (3)	19%
Foreign Affairs	66	24% (16)	5% (3)	19%
Appropriations	154*	7% (11)	0% (0)	0%

Note: Original appropriation bills only.

winning on the House floor. Only if the committee, as a collectivity, retains the confidence, respect, and support of the House will the individual Committee member gain the influence he seeks. To this end, members carefully circumscribe internal partisanship and try to behave in what House members will regard as a responsible, responsive manner. "The House says, here is a bunch of smart guys; we won't tamper too much with what they do." "The House knows we won't pull any fast ones." Education and Labor members, desirous of making good policy, feel no necessity for self-imposed, House-oriented restraints on their partisanship. They acknowledge the practical force of outside partisan constraints…and the philosophical right of each member to define "good" public policy for himself. But neither of these limits on partisanship betrays a collective concern for the Committee as an institution – for its reputation or its influence in the House. And both are compatible with heavy dosages of partisanship at every stage of decision making.

Normal decision making in the Ways and Means Committee is described by a staff member:

I think you will find that Ways and Means is a partisan committee. There are usually minority reports. But partisanship is not that high when they discuss the bill and legislate. About 95 per cent of the time, the members deliberate the bill in a nonpartisan way, discussing the facts calmly. Then toward the end (John) Byrnes (ranking Republican) and the Republicans may go partisan. The things the Committee deals with are big Administration issues, so you are bound to get minority views and partisanship. But Byrnes likes to take a nonpartisan attitude toward things and it gets partisan only toward the end.

The governing rule is what Manley calls the norm of "restrained partisanship" – "that members should not allow partisanship to interfere with a thorough study and complete understanding of the technical complexities of the bills they consider."[2] The "restrained" phase of decision making is a positive response to House demands for responsible behavior. More than any other committee, Ways and Means members see themselves as working *for* the House. "On our Committee, we have a responsibility to the House; we have to do the best we can." The closed rule, of course, provides strong reinforcement for this perception. If Committee bills are to be offered on a take-it-or-leave-it basis, members must make certain that they are "taken" and without unnecessary misgivings. By following the norm of restrained partisanship, Committee members can implement both decision rules – writing a bill that will pass the House and prosecuting policy partisanship. And they can achieve the House influence they seek.

Education and Labor operates under quite a different set of ground rules. Ways and Means members pointed out the contrast. Said one: "We always try for a consensus. Now you take Education and Labor. They never try for a consensus; they battle it out." And a Ways and Means Republican recalls the behavior of a Democratic newcomer fresh from years of service on Education and Labor, saying:

In our hearings and in our meetings he was taking up a lot of time making partisan speeches and raising partisan issues. I went to (Chairman) Wilbur (Mills) and asked him, "What's the matter with————? All this partisanship." Wilbur said, "He'll be all right once he learns the traditions of the Committee. He just doesn't understand yet that we don't fight about those things over here."

"Over there," on Education and Labor, members normally fight about anything at any stage. In the words of one veteran, "You can't get a resolution praising God through this Committee without having a three-day battle over it." When conflicts are not partisan, they are centered on individual ideological preferences, as each member fights for his own version of good public policy. As another senior member put it, "It's a free-for-all; every man for himself." Whether decision making features partisan policy making or policy individualism, there are no informal traditions of restraint, only the formal rules whereby policy victories are won by majority vote.

Within the frame of electoral constraints and individual members' willingness, party majorities will push their advantage to the utmost and at all stages. In the 89th Congress, Republicans were allowed only ritual involvement in subcommittees and less than that in full committee. A Democratic subcommittee chairman described decision making at that level:

We talk it over. I'll say to him (ranking Republican), "Do you want to fight it out here or in the full committee? You know and I know that I have the votes." He'll say, "I know you have, but let me make my record." I'll say, "Do you want to call up your amendments in subcommittee?" He'll say, "Yes." I'll say, "Do you want to vote on your amendments?" He'll say, "Yes." So we go through that in subcommittee. And as soon as we get a quorum, we vote our bill right through.

A Republican described full committee activity:

We met from 11:00 till 12:00. We reported out three bills in that time and one of them was the repeal of 14B – the most controversial piece of legislation our Committee has this session. We took 30 minutes on that. Sometimes, they seem to be in a hurry and when they're in a hurry they just go ahead and report it out. You have five minutes of debate, someone moves the previous question, and it's all over. They've got the votes, and when they want to do it they can.

The 89th Congress represents the extreme case. But in 1961, for example, Chairman Powell evicted the minority staff from their rooms in the Committee office, precipitating a rancorous running feud between himself and ranking Republican Carroll Kearns for the remainder of the 87th Congress. And in the 88th Congress, for example, Committee Democrats marked up the poverty bill in party caucus while Committee Republicans picketed (with a sign saying, "Open the door, Adam") outside the locked door protesting their exclusion. ("The Republicans screamed," said a Democrat, "but it's good for them, it's therapeutic.") No one would mistake these vignettes for pictures of life on the Ways and Means Committee. But the point is, of course, that Education and Labor members have policy goals they want to achieve and gladly wage a no-holds-barred struggle to achieve them. They will battle for their goals via massed partisan phalanx or extrapartisan guerrilla skirmishing, as conditions of external partisanship and individual philosophy may dictate.

Our other four committees display a good deal less internal partisan-ship than these two. On the evidence of Table 6.1, by far the least partisan of the six is the Appropriations Committee. The measures used in Table 6.1 probably exaggerate its lack of partisanship somewhat, because the Appropriations Committee happens to have a particularly strong internal norm proscribing the writing of minority reports – even when internal disagreement exists. On the other hand, however, the existence and apparent success of the norm is evidence of a strenuous effort to dampen such internal partisanship as may exist. Whether or not the distance between Appropriations and the next three Committees is as great as Table 6.1 portrays, there is little doubt that Appropriations is far less partisan in its decision making than the two Committees we have discussed. Its members have all the same incentives for nonpartisanship as Ways and Means. In pursuing their goal of House influence, they lean hard on executive budgets. But unless they can win House support for their decision, neither the committee collectively nor the members individually will be influential. So Appropriations members become as concerned as Ways and Means members for their reputation and their success in the House. One requisite, they believe, is the curbing of internal partisanship, to the end that the Committee will come to the floor united (or, at least, apparently united) in support of its recommendations. Under such circumstances they will maximize the likelihood of winning on the floor. Unlike Ways and Means, however, Appropriations members face few external demands for partisanship; so they try to minimize partisanship at the point of decision as well as at the deliberative stage. Their guiding rule is the norm of "minimal partisanship," a stronger and more pervasive injunction than that of "restrained partisanship."

Two freshman members, recently transferred from Education and Labor, described Appropriations Committee decision making according to this norm – the first at the subcommittee level and the second in full committee:

If there's a difference of opinion, we may pass on and then come back to it later. Usually we come to an agreement and compromise things out. Most subcommittee reports are unanimous reports. I never saw a unanimous report on anything on Education and Labor. I guess you could say there's a lot less partisanship on Appropriations.

On Education and Labor there was a healthy partisan division. But on this Committee there are no Democrats or Republicans. There's harmony. There's no two-party system on Appropriations. In full Committee, the chairman of the subcommittee gets up and then the ranking minority member of the subcommittee. And they say what a good job the other has done. They scratch each other's backs. There's never any dissent. Only once in two years has there been any difference.

Partisanship does, of course, occur, just as nonpartisanship occurs on Education and Labor. But the ratios of partisanship to nonpartisanship in the internal operations of the two Committees are the exact reverse of one another, as any congressman moving from one to the other can – plainly and vividly – see. And these contrasting ratios can be explained, again, by different member goals and different environmental contexts.

The ideological convergence of Appropriations Committee members eases their internal effort to minimize partisanship. The same phenomenon plays an even more important part in accounting for the low levels of partisanship on the *Foreign Affairs Committee*. Committee Democrats and (especially) Committee Republicans have markedly more liberal leanings than their respective party colleagues in the House. And liberals (in the period 1955–1966), we assume, were more likely to define the foreign aid program – the Committee's central issue – as good public policy. Partisanship has been relatively unimportant in decision making for the basic reason that, throughout the period, all but two or three Democrats and a majority of Republicans have supported the foreign aid program. In twelve years, as Table 6.1 shows, the Committee recorded only three party disagreements. One (1961) involved foreign aid policy; but it recorded Republican objections to President Kennedy's proposed method for financing the Development Loan Fund, not opposition to the program itself. Insofar as foreign aid dominates the work of the Committee (and it does), a bipartisan majority has felt little inducement to prosecute partisanship as a means of implementing its key decision rule.

Prior to full committee markup (i.e., decision-making session) on the foreign aid bill, the Democrats caucus to see if they can reach a consensus on the amount of the authorization they will support and to discuss amendments any of them intends to propose. Pro-aid Republicans are not invited; to this extent partisanship does affect Committee decision making. But sympathetic Republicans have plenty of opportunity to offer amendments at the markup and usually can get them accepted. The "hopelessly split" Republicans do not caucus as a group, but the anti-foreign aid "minority of the minority" does, to decide which amendment to offer, how to vote, how to focus their attack. If they need staff help, they must get it from the Committee's totally nonpartisan staff. But they normally do not find partisanship a useful vehicle for the promotion of their policy goals. In the words of a State Department official, "They oppose on conservative grounds, not on partisan grounds." And a veteran leader of the anti-aid group summed up: "Foreign·Affairs is partisan sometimes, but it's not the same as Education and Labor or Banking and Currency or Ways and Means. Less partisan than these... most of the time it comes down to a question of individual opinion rather than a party question."

Partisanship on Education and Labor and Ways and Means, we have seen, is primarily a response to environmental partisanship. Foreign Affairs works in response to executive-led coalitions that make strenuous efforts in exactly the opposite direction – seeking bipartisan, consensus support for their foreign policy initiatives. Executive branch prescriptions of nonpartisanship are closely bound to the more general argument that the Committee should support the President, regardless of his party. And these sentiments evoke a sympathetic response inside the Committee. The day he took over chairmanship of the Committee, under a Republican president, Dr. Thomas Morgan said:

I intend to try to further bipartisanship on the Committee; and the aid bill will be presented on that basis in the House. I have always believed in the old Vandenberg theory of bipartisanship.[3]

156

And seven years later, a Committee member described the practice thus:

There's a feeling on the Committee that you don't want to exacerbate partisan feelings if you don't have to. That's the feeling. And after all...(the majority of Republicans) we get them, so you don't want to drive them away.... Doc will say many times, "It makes no difference; under Eisenhower, Kennedy, or Johnson we did this." He'll often make this appeal. I've heard it several times when some partisan questions will be raised. I won't say he does it every time there is a conflict, but he sets the atmosphere of the Committee. There's a feeling that the executive has to have a free hand here, as much as possible.

"Sometimes, of course, the members get partisan," said a State Department leader, "but they'll never admit it. Partisanship is a dirty word on the Committee and nobody wants to be called a partisan." He was, of course, happy about the condition, concluding, "Nonpartisanship is usually observed on the Committee and that's the important thing." Surely the Committee members' foreign aid policy goals and their environmental pressures are both conducive to a low level of partisanship. And this will continue until such time as a Committee majority can decide what strategy it will substitute for the executive "free hand."

In Table 6.1, the *Post Office Committee* displays the same low degree of partisanship at the stage of decision as Foreign Affairs. Its three partisan reports were written during the Eisenhower years, when the Committee's clientele-oriented Republicans followed their President, providing a majority for pay increases (1955) and rate increases (1956, 1957) deemed too low and too high, respectively, by the affected postal groups. Eight Democrats joined their clientele allies in opposing each Committee action. In the election year of 1960, all but one Republican and Chairman Murray stood with the clientele groups and against the President on the postal pay raise bill; and a bipartisan Committee majority spearheaded the successful override of Eisenhower's veto of that bill. Since then, Committee Democrats and Republicans have operated in an atmosphere of low partisan intensity – broken only by a small but unorganized minority of the minority. For a group whose strategic premises involve the close adherence to clientele desires, partisanship is not relevant. "No, no, it's not partisan," said one Republican, "because with the exception of two or three mavericks, the members realize the power of the postal workers." The 1965, anti-Murray rule changes were voted in by sixteen of seventeen Democrats and five of eight Republicans – including the ranking minority member.

In terms of their individual goals, no two sets of committee members could be farther apart than those serving on Post Office and Foreign Affairs. One group wants committee service to help them get re-elected; the other group wants to help make policy on an international scale. We found their environments, however, to be strikingly similar. Relative to the other four committees, these two inhabit simple, monolithic environments – the one strongly dominated by a small set of clientele groups, the other strongly dominated by the executive branch. For both committees, the dominant environmental element has worked hard to depress partisanship, thereby helping to account for the low levels of partisanship in both cases. It seems reasonable for any environmental element (other than the political party) to want to keep down conflict inside the Committee if the element has a strong, monopolistic position in the environment. For the exacerbation of partisanship means that two opposing positions will be argued, in which case the monopoly-like external element stands to lose some of its support and some of its pre-eminence. Besides, parties become useful as leaders of policy coalitions only when some organization is needed to aggregate plural environmental interests. All other things being equal, we might speculate, the more monolithic the committee environment, the less the partisanship inside the Committee.

Interior Committee members uniformly describe their Committee as low in partisanship. And the reason is clear. Neither of its decision rules could be implemented under conditions of partisanship. Its members could not meet their re-election goals, and the clientele groups with which they are in greatest sympathy would not be served. To the contrary, cross-party cooperation is absolutely essential if members are to get projects for their districts and extend sympathetic treatment to Western-oriented interests. The direct relationship between individual member goals and bipartisan internal decision making was stated by two members.

There's a kind of cohesiveness in the Committee that overrides partisan considerations. The key here is that there aren't any ideological issues. You don't hear the Republicans saying we can't afford this or that. And the reason is that everyone has a project in his district that he wants or will want.

Interior is not partisan like some other committees here. You don't have the bitter partisan fights you do on some committees.... Look at the membership. Most of the members are from the seventeen western states. The issues are thrashed out in the Committee. If you can't get a whole loaf take half a loaf, if you can't get a half take a slice, and if you can't get a slice take a crumb.... There's no friction, you see, and that's how you get cooperation. The man you squash today, so to speak, you may need his help tomorrow.

Its members have been attracted to Interior precisely because they sought loaves, half-loaves, slices, and crumbs; and they have devised an appropriately low-partisan decision-making process through which to obtain them.[4] As far as the protection of Western interests are concerned, there, too, partisanship would be counterproductive, because the conflicts, as we have seen, simply do not cut that way. A Committee member explained: "What you get is not Republicans fighting Democrats, but conservationists against the commercial users. These things cross party lines. You get Easterners versus Westerners."

It is a further indication of success in depressing partisanship that Wayne Aspinall, Chairman of the Committee through 1972 and an ardent Westerner, worked so amicably and cooperatively with ranking Republican John Saylor, an ardent Easterner. Said a Republican:

Saylor and Aspinall work so completely together it wouldn't make any difference who was chairman. They don't let politics in. When someone brings up something political, they put the lid on right away. It couldn't be less partisan.

The two men had some strong policy disagreements – over conservation and public power; and in that sense, the preceding comment overstates its case. What Aspinall and Saylor shared was a desire to maintain the Committee's reputation for careful, expert, and independent handling of its legislation and, consequently, the confidence of the House. To this end, they worked in conspicuous harmony on all internal procedural matters and compromised on substantive matters wherever possible. Aspinall yielded to Saylor because Saylor's support on the House floor helped legitimize the Committee product in the eyes of non-Westerners. Saylor yielded to Aspinall because he could not beat Aspinall head-on in the Committee; and by acting as "constructive critic" internally he could help to shape bills substantively, while at the same time preserving sufficient external unity to retain the Committee's floor reputation. Saylor, it should be noted, comes from a coal mining area in Pennsylvania and has his own constituency-re-election goals to achieve on the Committee.

This strong House orientation of the Interior Committee derives not, as with Ways and Means and Appropriations, from any special House interest in the Committee's work. It emerges rather, as we noted earlier, out of the Committee's strategy for insuring passage of its many small bills and allaying non-Western fears regarding its few controversial ones. We might generalize from the three committees that, however derived, a strong committee concern for its success (i.e., winning, plus respect and confidence) on the House floor acts as one of the most important regulators of internal committee partisanship. All things being equal, the greater their concern for floor success, the more a committee's members will act to depress internal partisanship.

Participation-specialization

Because of the overwhelming magnitude of its task and its large size, the *Committee on Appropriations* divides its labor among a dozen or so

Table 6.2. *Subcommittee and full-committee meetings, 88th Congress*

	Number of subcommittee meetings	Number of full-committee meetings	Total number meetings	Subcommittee meetings as a % of total
App.	590	24	614	96
E.&L.	363	40	403	90
Int.	374	82	456	82
P.O.	119	44	163	73
F.A.	186	135	321	58
W.&M.	0	180	180	0

Note: Figures for Table 6.2 are from Joint Committee on the Origanization of Congress, *Final Report on Organization of Congress*, 89th Congress, 2nd Session (Washington: U.S. Government Printing Office, 1966), p. 65.

subcommittees, ranging in size between five and eleven members. Each subcommittee has jurisdiction over a cluster of executive agencies, and each produces a separate appropriation bill. The work of the Committee – holding hearings, examining budgets, marking up bills – is done in and by the subcommittees. Furthermore, subcommittee members lead the discussion in full committee, dominate debate on the floor, and go to conference with the Senate on their particular bill. Each Committee member serves on two or three subcommittees. And he participates in Committee decision making almost exclusively in his subcommittees and through his subcommittees. Table 6.2 compares the number of subcommittee and full committee meetings for each committee in 1963 and 1964, thereby providing a crude indication of the locus of internal participation. It shows that the Appropriations Committee had the greatest number of subcommittee meetings, the fewest number of full committee meetings, and the highest ratio of subcommittee to all committee meetings of any of the six committees.

Though one cannot infer this from Table 6.2, Appropriations members have made a virtue out of a necessity by achieving the House influence they seek in the context of subcommittee participation. They have made the subcommittee structure work to promote their individual goals by giving to each member nearly certain influence within the restricted scope of his subcommittee activity. In order to preserve the subcommittee structure and member influence within it, the Committee has elaborated a more complex set of informal decision-making norms than have the other five committees.

First, there is the norm of subcommittee autonomy which restricts participation to one's own subcommittee. Said a veteran member of the Treasury-Post Office subcommittee.

Why you'd be branded an imposter if you went into one of those other subcommittee meetings. The only time I go is by appointment, by arrangement with the chairman at a special time. I'm as much a stranger in another subcommittee as I would be in the legislative committee on Post Office and Civil Service. Each one does its work apart from all others.

Second, there is the norm of reciprocity, whereby all nonsubcommittee members accept the recommendations of the subcommittee in the full committee. "It's a matter of 'if you respect my work, I'll respect yours.'" "It's frowned upon if you offer an amendment in the full committee when you aren't a member of the subcommittee."

Third, there is the norm of specialization, which grows out of sub-committee autonomy and operates as a rationale for reciprocity. Each subcommittee specializes; and nonsubcommittee members defer to expertise. "It's considered presumptuous to pose as an expert if you aren't on the subcommittee." "You don't go barging into another man's field unless something is patently wrong."

Fourth, there is the norm of apprenticeship, which holds that new comers should spend a little time learning committee norms and sub-committee subject matter before they start participating fully in its work. As two subcommittee veterans advised freshmen:

Work hard, keep quiet, and attend committee sessions. We don't want to listen to some new person coming in here. But after a while, when you know what you are doing, we'll listen to you.

Follow the (subcommittee) chairman until you get your bearings. For the first two years, follow the chairman. He knows. He's been around a long time. Then take more of a part yourself.

When these four decision-making norms are combined with the norm of minimal partisanship, then the internal structural conditions for sub-committee unity, full committee unity, full committee influence, and, ultimately, individual member influence are present.

For the two dozen or so subcommittee chairmen and ranking minority subcommittee members, observance of these participation-specialization norms brings almost certain influence in the House – as much as most full committee chairmen or ranking minority committee members. Appropriations newcomers are not always happy about the restricted scope of their participation. "It's frustrating as hell. You feel shut out – and you are!" But if they are content (as most are) to endure a brief apprenticeship, the rewards of influence soon become evident. A second-year man described the sequence:

The first year you let things go by. You can't participate. But you learn by watching the others operate. The next year you know what you're interested in and when to step in. For instance, I've become an expert in the school lunch program. The (subcommittee) chairman said to me, "This is something you ought to get interested in." I did, and now I'm the expert on the subcommittee. Whatever I say on that, the other members listen to me and do what I want.

So long as his subcommittee regards him as the specialist, and so long as full Committee members defer to the subcommittee, this one Committee member may be the most influential man in Congress on the school lunch program. He may even find this small area of influence useful in dealing with other members of the House. And these are, after all, the goals that led him to the Committee in the first place.

The Committee members' strategic premises do not require any one particular internal structure to secure their implementation. But the arrangements we have just described, along with minimized partisanship, appear well enough suited for such implementation to underwrite their continued observance. For example, members perceive of their subject matter as manageable by a series of independent decisions, all of which can be made by compromising along a dollars-and-cents continuum. These perceptions and the decision making by autonomous and unified subcommittees provide strong mutual reinforcement. For another example, a restricted scope of decision making helps members obtain the kind of intimate, detailed knowledge of an agency that facilitates budget cutting. Members believe that in order to uncover unnecessary expenditures, one must "dig, dig, dig behind closed doors day after day" in "the salt mines of Congress." And they use their knowledge of "the facts" and their style of "hard work" to help sell the House on the necessity for budget reductions.

There is, of course, the chance that the opposite result may develop out of intensive subcommittee specialization – what we have called elsewhere "the interest-sympathy-leniency syndrome"[5] – and bring program support without budget reduction. Subcommittee assignments are patterned so as to hedge against this syndrome by assigning some members to subcommittees in which they have no personal experience and in which their constituency has no interest. And the apprenticeship period is used by elders to socialize the newcomers in the perceptual and logical underpinnings of budget cutting. On the evidence, they have a good deal of success; but if they fail, the very compartmentalization of the Committee keeps any spending virus isolated – this took place, during the period studied, in two subcommittees, Health, Education, and Welfare and Agriculture.[6] In the end, of course, the Committee's decision rules call for a balance between budget reducing and program support decisions, and the subcommittee structure gives some support to each.

In many ways, participation and specialization practices on the *Interior Committee* are a pale imitation of those on Appropriations. For instance, Interior has a similarly durable subcommittee structure, which is the main locus of every member's participation. When the Committee was formed by the Legislative Reorganization Act of 1946, it was a confederation of six previously existing standing committees. Two of the six were combined, a new one was added, and the pre-1947 standing-committee structure became the subcommittee structure of the new committee. A tradition of moderate subcommittee autonomy and influence sprang from these roots and has continued since. Subcommittees are not as compartmentalized as they are on Appropriations, mainly because there are only six, and every member sits on three of them. Ranging in size from sixteen to twenty-one members, they are more nearly a replica of the full committee than any Appropriations subcommittee could be. Hence, the elaborate system of norms to insure subcommittee autonomy and influence are absent from Interior. Nonetheless, like Appropriations, decisions tend to be made in subcommittee and accepted by the full committee. Two subcommittee chairmen explained:

I'd say that in my twelve years on the Committee, eighty per cent of the bills, once they go through the subcommittee and are reported out, go through the full Committee with no problems. The membership overlaps so much on our subcommittees, you don't run into trouble with the full Committee. Most of the bills are reported to the full Committee unanimously.

About 95 per cent of the time the subcommittee recommendation on what policy ought to be reported out (to the floor) is accepted; but if you are talking about the actual substance and wording of the bill, then I'd reduce the figure to about eighty per cent.

Sometimes major controversial bills, e.g., the Wilderness Bill, are considered immediately in full Committee. Even considering occasional deviations, the percentage of subcommittee meetings is high, as revealed in Table 6.2.

For the individual member, concerned particularly about constituency benefits, the subcommittee system provides an avenue for extensive participation. Each member states his preferences for subcommittee assignment, on the basis of his constituency's interests. The chairman grants as many as he possibly can; and members are quite satisfied with their assignments. Once on a subcommittee, a member often has opportunities to hold *ad hoc* subcommittee hearings on district projects in the district itself, with all the attendant benefits of local publicity. Specialization in one's subcommittee work and reciprocity across specializations are present, just as they are on Appropriations. But on Interior, specialization is primarily the result of each member's constituency-based interest in his subcommittee area. And deference to specialization plus reciprocity within and across subcommittees will often take the form of a member-to-member negotiation for exchanges of support for their constituency projects. For instance:

Mr. Burton (R. Utah): I think the Dixie Project has worked its natural course and it is before us today and we hope that we can have your support.

Mr. Udall (D. Arizona): I think when the roll is called up yonder, that I will be found in support of the legislation or something very much like it....

Mr. Burton: I want my colleague to know that I am sure when the roll is called up yonder, he will find me in support of his aspirations as far as water is concerned....

Mr. Udall: I am hopeful that we can work this thing out so that both Dixie and projects we need lower down on the Colorado can help each other.[7]

Advice from Committee veterans to Committee newcomers is liberally sprinkled with hints like these on how to secure one's projects: "He'd better make sure he's up on what affects his district or he won't have to worry about anything else. He'd better specialize in constituency matters." "I'd put that (constituency specialization) at the top of the list. That's number one. And be tolerant with other people who have different interests back home to worry about." The advice takes and works. "I can't think of a committee where there's more cooperation or camaraderie than ours," exulted one Westerner. "More legislation is passed by the Interior Committee than by any other one." Decision-making characteristics of this sort are as useful to the individual member with senatorial ambitions as they are to the member seeking re-election to the House.

The Interior Committee member, unlike his Appropriations Committee counterpart, is quite free to determine for himself the scope of his participation. Nor is his participation seriously restricted by his juniority. Committee elders advise the newcomer to "do your homework," "read the previous hearings and reports," "study, study, study" – and in this way they mean to emphasize that subject matter competence, not social philosophy, is the relevant basis for achieving one's goals on the Committee. They do not mean to impose an apprenticeship; the necessity for achieving one's individual goals before the next election will not permit it. Accordingly, a central tenet of internal decision making is, "Everyone has an equal right to be heard. No one's throttling anyone on Interior." And freshmen consider themselves equal participants. "I feel no constraints," said a first-term Republican about subcommittee hearings. "You have to wait your turn to ask questions, and they start with the senior members. I understand it's not like that on all committees – some chairmen run all over you if you're a freshman." Newcomers consider Interior "the best training ground for active participation and debate in the House."

If members are to achieve their individual, project-oriented goals and at the same time process their distinctively large number of bills, participation must not only be equal but orderly and efficient as well. The Committee was one of the first (if not the first) in the post-1947 period to write its own set of supplementary (to those of the House) rules providing for majority control of Committee activity, while protecting individual member rights. These rules are – in the formal sense at least – a model for participatory democracy; and they were copied by Education and Labor and Post Office during their later democratizing efforts. Once the rules were written, the Committee proceeded to adhere religiously to them. And this adherence gives to the Committee its distinctive self-image as orderly, efficient, and fair. "Everything is formal. You have to raise your hand, get recognition, yield the floor, and all that." "The chairman bangs the gavel and we go through every step. We can skip a step only by unanimous consent, and this is not taken unless the ranking minority member is there. It's very strict and fair." "We just go through every bill line by line. Every member has a chance to offer amendments, just as they do on the floor, under the five-minute rule – Republicans and Democrats right down the line."[8] Observance of these careful parliamentary procedures helps, obviously, to dampen partisanship. It would be hard to devise an alternate internal structure better suited to the implementation of members' goals and environmental demands. "You ask around Capital Hill," said one, "and you'll find that Interior probably does the best job of them all. As for efficient handling of the work load and that sort of thing, we are very fast."

Education and Labor is the third committee which appears to operate with an active subcommittee structure. And while it is true, as Table 6.2 indicates, that most of its members' time is spent in subcommittee activity, the participation-specialization characteristics of Education and Labor are very different from those of Appropriations or Interior. Prior to 1959, the Committee operated with *ad hoc* subcommittees set up to deal with specific bills. In 1959 it established five permanent standing subcommittees. In 1961, these were changed to six – three for labor policy and three for education policy – of about ten members each. To this core has been added, from time to time, less permanent ones, for a total of nine in 1961 and eight in 1965. Only the poverty bill (in 1965–66) was taken directly to the full committee. The 1959 and 1961 rules changes were designed, in part, to insure the widest possible participation of all members. And such is the case. Every member serves on two or three subcommittees; members say that "you can get practically any subcommittee you want so everybody is happy with his assignments." Unlike Appropriations, and more, even, than Interior, "everybody gets his shots in" on Education and Labor. A new member of the Committee declared:

165

I never dreamed the older members would have allowed us freshmen to contribute so much and participate and get into the legislative process as much as we have. I thought we would have to break the seniority system. But on my subcommittees I participate, get amendments passed, and open doors I never thought I could. I was amazed at how little restraint and restriction is placed on us. I think Education and Labor is unique in the use that is made of freshmen.

Life on the Committee, members say, is "just the opposite of what the myth and fiction of seniority would have you believe," "Freshmen even get to go to conference on this Committee." There would seem to be ample opportunity for each member to pursue his policy goals. Indeed, there is far more opportunity than the formal subcommittee structure reveals.

In the first place, subcommittees are not autonomous, as in the case of Appropriations, but highly permeable. A member commented:

I have friends on all the other subcommittees. I talk with them constantly about what is going on and we plot strategy. I'm very seldom surprised by anything that comes out of any of them.... I'm chairman of a labor subcommittee, but I'll fight like hell for things I want in education. I'm having an argument now with the subcommittee on higher education. I think I've won, but if I haven't I'll go to the full committee and raise hell there.

In the second place, unlike both Appropriations and Interior, subcommittee decisions carry very little weight in the full committee. "On some two-bit, piddling little bill, the full committee will say, 'that's what the subcommittee recommends, we'll vote it through.' But on major bills, the subcommittee has no standing with the full committee." A veteran describes the full committee meeting:

The members of the subcommittee always have the first crack at the legislation they report. They explain it and they are allowed to talk first. Then everyone pitches in. We question the subcommittee, we crossexamine the subcommittee, and they'd damn well better be able to answer the questions. That's true of the freshmen, too – they participate as much as anyone else.... Everybody gets in the swim in full committee. Very few pieces of legislation get through the full committee the way they come out of subcommittee. Maybe a few noncontroversial bills, but not the major ones. They are all amended in full committee. Sometimes I wonder why we have subcommittees at all.

The fact that a member participates extensively in his subcommittee does not mean, on Education and Labor, that he cannot also participate intensively in the work of other subcommittees – at subcommittee or full committee level.

On Appropriations, participation is restricted; on Interior, it is less restricted; on Education and Labor, it is unrestricted. Appropriations and Interior members restrict their participation, in the interest of their individual goals – in one case to enhance House influence, in the other case to attend to one's constituency. Education and Labor places no restrictions on participation so that its members can be free to pursue their interest in good public policy. Their lowest-common-denominator decision rule, calling for policy individualism, requires this kind of internal structure. Thus we are brought back again to the Committee members' view of their subject matter as essentially ideological and hence quite manageable in terms of their prior experience and social philosophy. If every member's policy opinion is as valid as the next fellow's, why should anyone be denied the opportunity to pursue his policy goals at any point in decision making? Given the extent of members' participation, it is impossible to develop a high level of specialization or expertise. There would be little reward for these in terms of members' goals, for they would not bring deference on policy. Again their perception of subject matter is important.

Expertise? Hell, everyone thinks he's an expert on the questions before our Committee. On education, the problem is that everyone went to school. They all think that makes them experts on that. And labor matters are so polarized that everyone is committed. You take sides first and then you acquire expertise. So no one accepts anyone as impartial.

When Committee members say that they "specialize" in education or labor matters, they mean that they have a special interest in one field or the other. They do not mean that others defer to them in decision making. Nor, of course, do members defer to the committee's staff. One reported: "The staff isn't very influential. I doubt if anyone relies on them on policy. They may furnish technical information, that's all. Policy positions are pretty well taken beforehand." It is a self-fulfilling evaluation, therefore, when members criticize, as they do, the quality of the staff. Staff turnover is, under such working circumstances, predictably high.[9] Of course, members will sometimes defer to the political judgment or the political blandishments of party leaders. But that is a different matter.

On those occasions when partisanship is not totally controlling, the Committee's high-participation, low-specialization characteristics will dominate internal decision making. A participating Health, Education, and Welfare executive supplied the following perspective on the process:

Our greatest trouble with the committee is that they are a bunch of smart asses – they think they know everything there is to know and the trouble is they don't. They don't do their homework, they don't know what is in the bill when they pass it or after they pass it even. When they get in executive session, they all think they are experts and no one will listen to anyone else. It's wild. They will nitpick on some little item for two hours and then pass the whole rest of a two billion dollar bill out in forty-five minutes. They have a very cavalier attitude toward staff. The staff is weak generally and wouldn't dare talk up to these strong

167

personalities. The staff doesn't count for anything – compared to the staff on the Senate side. House committee members don't even know what they are talking about. In some ways it may be good. If a member is with us, he goes all the way. But if he gets the bit in his teeth and wants some very bad amendment, he won't listen to reason. He may shout and bang his fist on the table and very often no one in the committee will want to take him on. No one knows what he's talking about anyway, so he gets by. There is nothing we can do about it. The work habits of the members are terrible and it makes for bad legislation. These habits become the norm.... The younger members of the committee have a unique opportunity. They can get amendments in the bill, amendments galore. They can speak up and participate all over the place. Nothing about being seen and not heard on this committee. They can make speeches knowing that no one will contradict them, because nobody knows enough. No one knows the bills. For the freshmen, this is very exhilarating, but from our viewpoint it is demoralizing. It is hardly a good legislative process. These young people learn that they don't have to do any work. They can just come in and sound off. Legislation is not passed on the basis of reasoned arguments. It is a matter of who can shout the loudest or bang his fist the hardest.

To a considerable extent Committee members are doing what they came on the Committee to do. The process is not, as with Interior, orderly and efficient. As a Democrat serving on both committees put it:

We do give careful consideration to (Interior) legislation. Every "t" is crossed; every "i" is dotted; every comma is in the right place... On Education and Labor, we don't consider all bills thoroughly. The "t's" aren't crossed; the "i's" aren't dotted; and the commas aren't there.

But Education and Labor decision making is, say the members, "stimulating," "exciting," "explosive," "pyrotechnical." And most of them like it. "It's never a dull committee," said one, "it isn't like Appropriations, which would be awfully boring – to me anyway." An alumnus of the Committee, now unhappily ensconced on Appropriations, agreed: "Education and Labor was creative and exciting work. It's considered an honor and a promotion to go on Appropriations. But I feel lik a glorified accountant."

Ways and Means is one of the very few House committees (three in the 88th Congress) that function without subcommittees. Its relatively small size makes feasible full committee decision making. And the rationale offered by Committee members emphasizes their perception of their policy subjects as of immense national importance. Therefore, so the members reason, every member must legislate on the basis of first-hand knowledge of every subject.

The things we deal with are so important and have such major consequences that we don't use subcommittees. I wouldn't want to have to rely on subcommittees for bills with such consequences.... We want to know what's going on.

The historic tradition of the Committee is that each member is an integral part of the Committee. It's a small committee and each member has to keep informed on everything.

So long as there are no subcommittees, specialization will remain at a low level on Ways and Means. As the work of Education and Labor makes clear, there is no inexorable logic linking subcommittees and specialization. But Ways and Means members often make the link in explaining the absence of specialization: "The Ways and Means Committee does not specialize because we don't have any subcommittees." "I am so damn glad we don't have subcommittees, because if you broke things down into three or four parts you wouldn't know what's going on.... All the members want to know what's going on in everything." It is probably true that if the incentive to specialize exists, subcommittees are a necessary condition of that specialization. At present the incentive does not exist on Ways and Means. Neither influence in the House, nor writing a bill that will pass, nor prosecuting partisanship requires specialization. The first two can be achieved by the kind of responsible, carefully architected judgment expected by the House, and the second can be achieved by observing party allegiance in voting. So long as the full Committee performs accordingly, incentives for subcommittees and/or specialization will continue to be absent.

Members participate in lengthy full-committee executive sessions. So also, for most of the deliberative phase, do executive officials (and sometimes clientele groups). This is the stage at which bipartisan consensus building is emphasized, and everyone participates freely. For the newcomer, however, an apprenticeship norm – less restrictive than that of Appropriations – exists. The idea is that it takes time to acquire a good working grasp of the Committee's complicated subject matter and to develop good judgment in handling it. While learning, say the Committee's elders, freshmen should participate modestly and knowledgeably.

I'd advise a new member to work as hard as he could and get familiar with everything.... I wouldn't advise anyone to specialize in minutiae...you just can't do it.... If he wants to be effective, he will have to master the subject. He can participate, but if he's wise he'll comment only if he knows what he's talking about. He'd better not show his ignorance. I tell him to listen to the more senior members and follow their advice, pretty much. After all, we've been around for years and over everything time after time.

He'd be a fool to jump right in except for asking questions for information. I'd tell him to participate right away, however. No reason why he shouldn't be active right away. The members with the seniority know the subject pretty well and they lead things. I wouldn't tell him to specialize in anything; just be familiar with everything we do.

These prescriptions call for knowledge and participation but not specialization.

New members share the perception of subject matter that regulates their participation. They are impressed, if not overwhelmed by its difficulty. "The Committee won't hear much from me for a while." "I study hard." If they are frustrated, it is not because (as with Appropriations newcomers) their participation is restricted to a few subjects but because they have such a wide range of subjects to master. "I used to leave the meetings with a headache, truly a headache." On the other hand, they feel that as soon as they know what they are doing they can participate. "If I have any questions, I can ask them. I get a chance to participate... no problems." And participation is bipartisan. "In Committee deliberations," wrote a Republican freshman to his constituents, "I have as much chance to influence legislation as anyone else. This has given me many personal satisfactions I would not have had on a more partisan committee." The Committee's apprenticeship norm is nothing more than a reminder of the more basic self-restraining "responsibility" norm. All members accept this as necessary to the achievement of their individual goal of influence in the House.

On the *Foreign Affairs Committee*, as the figures in Table 6.2 suggest, the important arena for participation is the full committee. Second only to Ways and Means, Foreign Affairs has the most active full committee and the highest percentage of full committee meetings of the six committees. Desirous of making public policy and able to agree on the extent of their activity only on the foreign aid bill, all members naturally want to participate fully in this one important decision of the year.

If you had subcommitttees, the full committee would take it apart all over again. It's the one bill of the year. It's not like Education and Labor, where you have all those big bills. You can't reverse this process and have subcommittees. We have only the one big bill every year.

In 1957, the foreign aid bill was broken up into segments and parceled out to regional subcommittees. But when the bill reached the House floor, the subcommittee chairmen defended their respective segments with such varying degrees of skill, enthusiasm, and knowledge that the whole thing "fell of its own weight" for lack of coherence and coordination. Only a very few members still think subcommittees would help on this important bill. Indeed, so ingrained is the tradition of handling important matters in the full Committee that the Peace Corps, the Arms Control and Disarmament Agency, and resolutions such as Tonkin are also treated in full committee.

The Committee has a fairly elaborate array of standing subcommittees (nine in the 88th Congress) supplemented on occasion by special *ad hoc* subcommittees (one in the 88th Congress). Some of them are regional in their jurisdiction (e.g., Europe, Inter-American Affairs) and some pertain to the problem areas (e.g., International Organization, State Department). Members serve on from two to four of these and experience little difficulty getting placed on the subcommittees that most interest them. The crucial fact about these subcommittees is simply that very little happens there. With the exception of the subcommittee handling State Department regulations, they report out almost no legislation. Their function is one of information gathering, to which end they hold hearings and consume information. Members speak of them as "more for research and study than legislation" or "more conversational than legislative." They also describe them as "really minor things dealing with picayune matters." "Africa never meets except to welcome an ambassador."

I've been on the Europe subcommittee for five months and I haven't even heard NATO mentioned, haven't even heard the word. I read my hometown newspaper to find out what's happening to NATO. . . . The subcommittees have displayed absolute irrelevancy in foreign affairs, amazing irrelevancy.

Lacking a legislative charter and inclined to spend time on less than central matters, subcommittees tend to become "inactive," "dormant," or "slow." In the 89th Congress, three subcommittees did not meet at all, and a fourth was nearly defunct. One had not met for five years. Subcommittee chairmen lack incentive – "if you are a beaver, you can call a lot of meetings. I don't." Ordinary members succumb to more pressing priorities. "Once we are finished with the foreign aid bill, you can't get the members to come. They think it's all over and they have too many other things to do." In such a context members have plenty of opportunity to participate and to specialize. But in such a context neither activity will help them meet their individual policy goals. Nor, for those members pursuing outside career ambitions, does attentiveness to detailed subcommittee work seem productive in running for the Senate.

The only participation that counts occurs on the foreign aid hearings and markup. And here, specialization counts for little. Everyone participates equally, and no apprenticeship of any sort obtains. As on Education and Labor, the other policy-oriented Committee, expertise and deference are nonoperative. "You can go on there and become an expert overnight." "Every man is his own foreign policy expert." In the hearings, the Committee operates under the five-minute rule for questioning witnesses, with Democrats and Republicans taking turns, "from left to right, very fair." Some members chafe under the five-minute restriction, applied more out of consideration for key executive branch witnesses than for meaningful Committee member participation. "The five-minute rule means you can't ever develop a line of questioning. The witness will filibuster on one question; he won't really answer it, and then he's out of time." But the restriction hits all members equally. Full Committee markup sessions are more leisurely and less restrictive. Any member can offer as many amendments as he wants and no one is cut off from speaking on the amendment. A member who sits on Foreign Affairs and Interior described the two markups as "completely different":

Interior (is run) strictly according to the rules. We meet at 9:45 and that doesn't mean 10 o'clock. Nobody speaks out of turn – no one. You have to have the proper recognition to speak, to offer amendments. On the other hand, Foreign Affairs – we sit around and have general discussion. How they ever keep a record of that I'll never know. It's the most disjointed, disconnected committee.

Foreign Affairs is a policy-oriented committee, lacking a complete set of decision rules; Interior is a constituency-oriented committee, with an operational set of decision rules.

Given all that we have said about member support for foreign aid, the main proceedings in full committee are an anticlimax. On the main lines of disagreement, positions have been established in their respective caucuses by the majority and by the "minority of the minority." Executive officials sit in the anteroom if information be needed. All that cannot be predicted are the "country amendments," often the result of constituency interest, which committee members want to append and executive officials wish to avoid. A Democratic administration stalwart described this aspect of the markup:

Someone's got some silly amendment he's offering because he already has a press release out on it and he wants to say he tried to get the Committee to do this or that but they rejected it – or maybe they didn't. He's running against Tito this week or Sukarno or Castro. Maybe he's just been to Togoland and seen a "Yankee go home" sign; or he's mad because they tore down our library and he wants to get back at "never-never land." ...I lean back to take a look at who's not there, who's asleep and not paying attention, who's ready to spring an amendment from his vest, who's breathing heavy, and whose nostrils are dilated.... You have to watch out.

Shades of decision making inside Education and Labor! But these are minor flurries over details, not the main contest. That has already been settled. In the end, Foreign Affairs seems much less participatory than Education and Labor and provides much less involvement, as we have already said. Two members who transferred from Education and Labor to Foreign Affairs summed up: "Education and Labor was a much more active Committee. The legislation flows through there like water." "On Education and Labor, I was *too* busy. On Foreign Affairs, all we do is handle the foreign aid bill and go on trips."

For the *Post Office Committee*, as for Foreign Affairs, internal norms are less important for understanding participation and specialization than is the sheer amount of Committee activity. As Table 6.2 indicates, Post Office has been, in terms of the number of meetings, the least active of the six committees. Table 6.1 reveals, relatedly, that Post Office reported out the fewest pieces of "major legislation" of the six committees, with Foreign Affairs reporting the next fewest. Post Office members attributed much of this inactivity to the internal stalemate over strategy between Chairman Murray and the clientele-oriented members. At least, this was a cause of inactivity susceptible to internal remedy. And it was to raise the level of Committee activity and thereby increase overall member participation and member specialization that a large majority of members voted to adopt the Committee Rules of 1965.

The major change was the creation, for the first time, of eight standing legislative subcommittees. Prior to 1965, the Committee had had only four subcommittees, all of them "investigative" rather than legislative. On legislative matters, *ad hoc* subcommittees would be created and subsequently disbanded. The net result was to restrict member participation, member specialization, and legislative volume. Two of the rebellious leaders vented member complaints.

Murray would appoint some fluffy subcommittee, a temporary sort of thing, with mostly newcomers. They'd issue some half-assed report which no one would read.... We'd read the hearings and then come in and vote. Of course there wasn't that much legislation to handle.... With the old subcommittees, they were temporary and you couldn't learn about any one thing. But with permanent subcommittees, you can absorb information from the witnesses and you can become an expert.

We have two functions: one, legislate, two oversight. And we weren't performing either. During the last two years our Committee passed eighteen bills. Now, I don't rank effectiveness by numbers but many of these were minor little things. We're a third-rate committee and I think we should be a first-rate one. Look at what we handle. The most important thing we wanted, and there were lots of things, was subcommittees so we could specialize and do our job.

Under the new rules, every member sat on three subcommittees, and as an inducement to support the rule changes, the 1965 freshmen were given their first and second choice of subcommittees. The number of subcommittees was dictated not by natural subject matter division but by the desire to secure the allegiance of the eight most senior Democrats. The remainder of the rules, copied closely from those of the Interior Committee, were designed to bring order, dispatch, and fairness into full-committee procedures, which had become meandering and dilatory under the purposeful neglect of Chairman Murray.

If it be asked why Post Office members did not seek to increase their overall level of activity before 1965, a major reason is simply that most members of the Committee, as we have said, are not terribly interested in the Committee. They do not come to it with purpose, they give it less of their time than their other committee, they use it for constituency advantage while they serve on it, and they leave it as soon as they can. This scenario is not valid for all members, but for enough so that any serious commitment to internal change was hard to come by. Table 6.3 presents some corroborating evidence. Post Office has the highest average turnover of the six committees, and the highest percentage of freshman appointees. Turnover among majority party Democrats (who were most likely to favor change) was especially high, averaging 49 per cent for the five sessions, as against 27 per cent for the Republicans. These conditions militate against a large number of interested members – against the solidification of a revolutionary leadership and of followers with strong incentives to participate in a revolt. Common inertia and respect for tradition doubtless often played a part. So, too, did the occasional success of the Committee's majority in working around their recalcitrant chairman.

When the change came, the overall aim seemed to be increase the Committee's gross level of activity and, particularly, to render greater assistance to clientele groups. The vehicle was the new subcommittee system. And the method was the assertion of leverage over the executive branch. In the 89th Congress, the Committee's activity level rose palpably. A top Post Office Department official reported the reverberations.

Once a congressman gets a subcommittee, he has to come up with some plan for the betterment of mankind. Or else he will go back to campaign and his opponent will say, "He's chairman of a subcommittee and what legislation has he brought out – nothing. . . ." That's what has happened on Post Office and Civil Service now and it's keeping us in the Post Office hopping.

Committee members felt rejuvenated and began to zero in on their traditional adversary, the Post Office Department. Prior to 1965, they felt, "Post Office paid no attention to the Committee; it was a withering arm of the House." But in the 89th Congress, "We are driving them crazy now; they are really worried. We are criticizing now, you see. We have the power and are they ever worried?" Here is how a veteran committee leader discussed the transition:

You aren't a member of Congress and you would have had just as much influence as I had. The Department would just promulgate rules. They were happy – what the hell. (Postmaster General) Gronouski is coming here tomorrow and you know what I'm going to tell him? "It's a new day. Things have changed. They aren't going to work the way they used to."[10]

More than accomplishing anything specific, Committee members seemed

174

Table 6.3. *Committee turnover*

		Percentage new members per Congress – 85th–89th					Percentage freshmen among total no. of appointees	
	85	86	87	88	89	Avg.		1955–1966
P.O.	40	44	44	40	36	41	74	58/78
Int.	16	39	39	46	42	36	73	64/88
E.&L.	23	30	29	32	23	27	69	52/75
F.A	19	28	27	24	17	23	30	21/69
W.&M.	4	36	16	20	28	21	4	2/52
App.	12	24	8	24	32	20	14	14/100

Note: This computation does not take into account anyone who remained on a committee less than six months. If it took them into account, turnover figures for Post Office would be even higher.

pleased to be in motion and making progress. "We were a third-rate committee; we are a second-rate one now."

That the Committee can ever become a first-rate one or that internal specialization will ever give it much independent leverage over the executive branch seems doubtful. So dominated by clientele groups is their environment and so easy is it to meet their individual goals by yielding to such domination, it does not appear that they have any durable incentives for developing an independent competence. "The Post Office Committee is the creature of outside groups" summed up a veteran member. "They found out years ago that if they could control our membership, they could control our product. They have to; we're their lifeblood.... And they've been very successful at it." The monolithic environment, in short, dampens internal participation and specialization, regardless of stirrings among the members.

Again, the similarity with Foreign Affairs is compelling. As a companion piece to the foregoing comment, a Foreign Affairs member summarized: "One generalization you can make is that the Committee is more reflective of the executive than any Committee I know of. We do just about what the State Department tells us, and we don't do anything they don't want us to." And a member who serves on both committees sees environmental dominance as rendering them "two of the most insignificant committees in the House." He said: "Foreign Affairs is a disgrace because all Doc Morgan does, just like a rubber stamp, is give the Administration everything it wants.... Post Office is a disgrace in a different way. Individual members are owned by the postal unions. Post

Office is subservient to the unions." The judgment is harsh, but the comparison is apt. Their many decision-making similarities result from the strong conditioning force of similarly monolithic environments....

Summary

We have tried to demonstrate, in this chapter, that each committee's internal decision-making processes are shaped by its members' goals, by the constraints placed upon the members by interested outside groups, and by the strategic premises that members adopt in order to accommodate their personal goals to environmental constraints. One overall comparative dimension suggested by the independent variables of the analysis involves the relative impact of the members themselves and of external groups on decision-making processes. We might think of the dimension as decision-making *autonomy*. The greater the relative influence of the members, the more autonomous the committee; the greater the relative influence of outside groups, the less autonomous the committee. Making only the grossest kinds of distinctions, it appears that Ways and Means, Appropriations, and Interior are more autonomous decision makers than Foreign Affairs, Education and Labor, and Post Office. That is, members of the first three committees have a more independent influence on their own decision-making processes than do the members of the second three. For Ways and Means, we might mention the restraints on partisanship and the leadership of Wilbur Mills; for Appropriations, there are the specialization and internal influence of its subcommittees; for Interior, there are its participatory democracy and the leadership of Wayne Aspinall. The sources of committee autonomy are not always the same, but the result – a marked degree of internal, member control of decision making – is the same. With the other three committees, it is the environmental impact on decision making that seems most noteworthy. For Foreign Affairs, it is executive domination; for Education and Labor, it is the permeation of partisan policy coalitions; for Post Office, it is clientele domination. The three more autonomous committees emphasize expertise in decision making more than the three less autonomous ones, suggesting that perception of subject matter is related to decision-making processes.

The clustering of committees with regard to decision-making autonomy parallels the clustering noted in the last chapter, based on some similarities and differences in the committees' decision rules. Appropriations, Ways and Means, and Interior have, in common, a consensus on decision rules, a House-oriented set of decision rules, and decision-making autonomy. The three characteristics are probably closely interrelated. But the main thrust of our argument would be that the first two contribute to the third. When a committee's members agree on what they should do, they are more likely to be able to control their own decision making than when they cannot agree on what to do. When a committee's decision rules are oriented toward success (i.e., winning plus respect and confidence) on the House floor, the committee will have a greater desire to establish its operating independence than when its strategies are not especially concerned with floor success. House members, we recall, *want* their committees to be relatively autonomous, relatively expert decision makers. They are more likely, therefore, to follow and to respect committees that can demonstrate some political and intellectual independence of outside, non-House groups. Whether or not distinguishing the two clusters of committees will, in turn, help us to differentiate and explain committee decisions is a question we will keep in mind. . . .

NOTES

1 The totals in the first column of Table 6.1 are not exactly the same as the twelve-year totals listed under "Major Legislation" in the *Almanacs*. When committee reports could not be located, those bills were omitted from the tabulation.

2 John Manley, "The House Committee on Ways and Means: Conflict Management in a Congressional Committee," *American Political Science Review* 59, no 4 (December 1965): 929.

3 *New York Times*, February 9, 1958, p. 62.

4 It is interesting in the light of James Murphy's recent work emphasizing partisanship on the House Public Works Committee that two Interior members who also sit on Public Works should spontaneously comment about Interior, "It's not a partisan committee. It's just the opposite from Public Works." Public Works would appear to be populated by constituency-oriented members and to operate amid highly partisan environmental constraints. Its strategic premises are, therefore, a kind of cross between Interior's project-oriented guidelines and Education and Labor's party-oriented guidelines – in Murphy's terms "routinization" and "partisanship." See "The Empty Pork Barrel: Partisanship and Routinization in House Public Works Committee Decision Making," a paper presented at the American Political Science Association meeting, Washington, D.C., 1968.

5 Richard Fenno, *The Power of the Purse* (Boston: Little, Brown, 1966), p. 141.

6 *Ibid.*, pp. 212–214, 364.

7 Committee on Interior and Insular Affairs, *Hearings on the Dixie Project, Utah*, before the Subcommittee on Irrigation and Reclamation, 88th Congress, 2nd Session (Washington: U.S. Government Printing Office, 1964), p. 76.

8 Excellent examples can be found in: Committee on Interior and Insular Affairs, *Hearings on Marketing Area of the Bonneville Power Administration* before the Subcommittee on Irrigation and Reclamation, 88th Congress, 1st

Session (Washington: U.S. Government Printing Office, 1963), pp. 12, 107–109, 253.

9 Of the six men who acted as professional staff for each of the standing subcommittees when they were established in the 87th Congress, only one remained at the beginning of the 88th Congress – and he had changed from an education to a labor subcommittee. Of the six who manned the standing subcommittees in the 88th Congress, three stayed to begin the 90th Congress. And of those, only one remained at the outset of the 91st Congress. During the four Congresses from 1961 to 1968, every standing subcommittee had *at least* three different staff men in charge of its operations.

10 An early example of this "new day" will be found in Committee on Post Office and Civil Service, *Hearings on Zip Code System in the United States Postal Service*, 89th Congress, 1st Session (Washington: U.S. Government Printing Office, 1965) pp. 9–18; 445–448.

7

Democratic committee assignments in the House of Representatives: strategic aspects of a social choice process

DAVID A. ROHDE AND KENNETH A. SHEPSLE

Since Woodrow Wilson wrote *Congressional Government*, the dominance of the standing committees in the House of Representatives in determining legislative outcomes has been accepted by students of Congress. In light of recent studies of groups of House committees[1] and in-depth studies of individual committees,[2] the generalization about the central role of committees in the legislative process remains intact. These studies, however, indicate that there are major differences among these "little legislatures" in regard to their organization and behavior, and that these differences are in part a function of differences in their memberships. Furthermore, as Charles Clapp has said,

Not only is the fate of most legislative proposals determined in committee: to an important degree the fate of individual congressmen may be decided there too. A person's congressional career may rest largely on the kind of committee post he is given.[3]

Therefore, given the importance of committee membership, both in policy making and in determining the success of individual congressmen's careers, the process by which members are assigned to committees is of the greatest importance.

A good deal of research has been devoted to the committee assignment

Reprinted from *American Political Science Review* 67, no. 3 (September 1973): 889–905. We would like to express our gratitude to Richard Fenno of the University of Rochester and John Manley of Stanford University for making available to us the request data for the 87th, 88th, and 90th Congresses, and to Robert Salisbury of Washington University, St. Louis, for the request data from the 86th Congress. We also wish to acknowledge the research assistance of Robert Delgrosso of Michigan State University. We finally want to thank Richard Fenno, Morris Fiorina of the California Institute of Technology, and the two anonymous referees for their helpful comments on previous versions of this study. An earlier draft of this paper was presented at the 67th Annual Meeting of the American Political Science Association, Chicago, September 7–11, 1971.

process in the House.[4] Most of this research, however, has been based on the *results* of the process, i.e., the committee assignments that were actually made. For example, the desirability of committees has been measured in terms of the proportion of the freshmen on each committee, or the number of transfers from a committee versus the number of transfers to it. The variable missing from such treatments has been the desires of the members. Also, success in achieving committee assignments has been treated in only the most general terms, again because of the absence of data on what committees members requested.

The purpose of this paper is to analyze committee assignments by focusing on this "missing link." Our subject will be the committee assignments of Democratic members of the House of Representatives. Committee assignments, as Clapp's observation above suggests, are valued, are in limited supply, and are allocated by rather well-defined mechanisms and procedures. By viewing committee assignments as the culmination of a special sort of allocation process, we shall be in a position to *explain* the results of this process, the *descriptions* of which have constituted the bulk of research on this topic to date. It is explanations we seek, and we find more general theories of social choice particularly well-suited for this purpose. More specifically, we examine the data of committee assignments in terms of actors in pursuit of personal goals, constrained only by scarcity and institutional procedures. We will consider the process from the point of view of the members requesting assignment and the members who make the assignments: who wants what committees, and whose requests are satisfied. The basic data which will be employed are the requests for committee assignments, by all House Democrats, made to the Democratic Committee on Committees in the 86th–88th and 90th Congresses.

DEMOCRATIC COMMITTEE ASSIGNMENTS[5]

In the House, the Democratic Committee on Committees is made up of the Democratic members of the Ways and Means Committee.[6] At the beginning of each Congress they are faced with the task of filling vacancies on the other standing committees of the House. Each member of the Committee is assigned a geographic zone, containing his own state and perhaps others, and he is responsible for handling requests for assignments from members in his zone.[7]

Some time after the November election, new Democratic congressmen submit to the Committee on Committees their requests, in order of preference, for committee assignments. At the same time, returning congressmen may submit requests for second assignments or for transfers from committees they held in the previous Congress.

180

Democratic committee assignments in the House

After members submit requests, lobbying for assignments begins. Many representatives seeking assignments write letters to some or all members of the Committee on Committees, setting forth arguments on their own behalf. Many also pay personal visits to the members of the Committee (especially their zone representative), to the Democratic leaders, and to the chairmen of the committees they are requesting. Often letters are written to members of the Committee on Committees to support the cause of some requesters. Typically these letters come from the deans of state delegations (either from themselves alone or on behalf of the whole delegation), from party leaders or office-holders outside the House, from committee chairmen and from leaders of interest groups relevant to the work of the committees requested.

At the beginning of the Congress, the size of committees as well as party ratios are set by negotiation between the leaders of both parties.[8] Thus the members of the Committee on Committees are faced with the task of filling the vacancies on the standing committees which have resulted either from the failure of some Democratic members to return or from the creation of new positions. The Committee meets in executive session, and each of the committees is called up (usually alphabetically). For each committee the members proceed in order of seniority to nominate candidates from their zone.[9] The names of nominees are written on a blackboard, and they are discussed by the members. After nominations are completed, the members vote by secret ballot.

Finally, after the Committee on Committees has filled all the vacancies, their decisions are placed before the Democratic Caucus for ratification. This is, however, almost always a *pro forma* action.

For our purposes, then, the time sequence of the committee assignment process, which culminates in the creation of a committee structure for a new Congress, may be characterized by the following stages:

1. the committee configuration in the previous Congress;
2. an election;
3. requests for assignments by newly elected members and by returning members who held assignments in the committee configuration of the previous Congress;
4. the establishment of size and party ratios for committees in the new Congress;
5. committee assignments by the Democratic Committee on Committees for the new Congress.

Stage 1 provides initial conditions which are "disturbed" by an election (stage 2). The election disturbs the initial committee structure in several obvious ways. First aggregate party proportions in the chamber are altered, requiring the renegotiation of the committee structure by party leaders: committee sizes and party ratios are fixed at this stage (stage 4). Second, individual and aggregate election results effect a change in the opportunity structure in the chamber. Individual defeats of party members in the election create party committee vacancies (which may or may not be lost to the party depending on the aggregate election results and its effect on stage 4). At the outset of the new Congress, then, there are unfilled committee vacancies and demand for those slots by newly elected and returning members (as expressed at stage 3).

Our concern in this paper is with the process of committee assignments for the Democrats. We take the first, second and fourth stages of the process as exogenous to our concerns (though, as we suggested earlier, stage 4 may well be conceived of as endogenous, since it is probable that deviations from the aggregate party ratio on any given committee are partly a result of the configurtion of requests at stage 3). Before getting into the details of our analysis, we should first outline the general theoretical context within which we view the requests of the members and the decisions of the Committee on Committees.

MEMBER GOALS AND COMMITTEE ASSIGNMENTS

As the title of this paper implies, we view the committee assignment process as an instance of "social choice" (or "collective decision making"). That is, a group (the Committee on Committees) is charged with allocating the valuable resources (places on committees) of the collectivity (the Democratic members of the House). We view the participants in the process as rational actors, that is, actors who have goals that they want to achieve, and who, when confronted with a decision-making situation, examine the available alternatives and choose the alternative which seems most likely to lead to the achievement of those goals.

On the question of goals, Richard Fenno has argued that "of all the goals espoused by members of the House, three are most basic. They are re-election, influence within the House and good public policy. There are others; but research on the House acknowledges these to be the most consequential."[10] If this view is accepted, we may now consider each of the participants in the assignment process and show how the outcomes of that process affect their goals.

(1) *Requesters.* The impact of committee assignments on the members requesting those assignments is so obvious that it hardly needs to be discussed. If a congressman holds any or all of the goals mentioned above, his committee assignment will have a substantial impact on the probability of achieving them.

182

A "good" assignment may greatly enhance his value to his constituents and provide unusual opportunities to publicize his activities in Congress; here he can develop the expertise and the reputation as a "specialist" that will enable him to influence his colleagues and important national policies.[11]

(2) *The Committee on Committees.* The interest of members of the Committee on Committees in what assignments are made is less direct than that of the requesters, but important nonetheless. If a member has a general interest in the policy area of a particular committee, he may support the assignments of congressmen whose views are most congruent with his own. Furthermore, when a piece of legislation important to a member of the Committee on Committees comes before the House, he may call in debts owed to him by congressmen he has sponsored for committee assignments in order to influence such legislation.[12]

(3) *The Leadership.* The filling of committee vacancies is also important to the Democratic leadership, for much the same reasons as it is to the members of the Committee on Committees.

Committee assignments are vital to the leadership in two ways. First, to the degree that the leadership affects assignments it has an important resource for doing favors for members, for rewarding members for past favors, and for establishing bonds with members that may provide some leverage in future legislative situations. Second, committee assignments are vital to the policy for which the leadership is responsible.[13]

(4) *State Delegations.* Members of a state delegation have an interest in other delegation members serving on committees which affect the interests of their state. Such members serve as a source of information about the committee's business and a resource for influencing the course of legislation on that committee.[14]

This discussion could be extended to include the committee chairmen and persons outside the House (e.g., interest groups), but the essence of our point is established. How committee slots are assigned is of vital interest to many individuals and groups, because those assignments will have an impact on the achievement of their goals within the House.

DATA AND ANALYSIS

The empirical analysis, which constitutes the bulk of this current study, employs *request* data from four Congresses. In all, we have data on the committee requests, in order of preference, of 106 freshmen and 89 nonfreshmen Democratic representatives. It is important to reiterate the distinctiveness of these data. Ordinarily, analyses of committee assignments are based on the *results* of the process, from which inferences about the process are drawn.[15] By using request data, however, we are in a position to assess the extent to which the process links requests on the one hand with final assignments on the other. Moreover, we may now determine who benefits and who is harmed by the assignment process, not in terms of so-called objective standards of "good" and "bad" assignments, but rather in terms of the subjective preferences of the actors affected. All these possibilities permit somewhat keener insights into the characteristics of this important internal process.

The first aspect of the assignment process we will consider is the requests themselves: what committees are requested most often, and how many requests are made. For this part of the analysis we will consider only the requests of freshman congressmen. Nonfreshmen already hold committee assignments and, because of service restrictions,[16] are prevented from applying for certain committees (unless they are trying to transfer from the committee they hold).[17]

Table 7.1 presents these data on freshman requests. The first column gives the total number of requests for each of the standing committees. The second column gives the percentage of all requesters who applied for a slot on each of the committees. The last column indicates the percentage (and number) of all requests that were the requesters' first choices. Thus, 15 congressmen (nearly 14 per cent of all freshmen) requested Agriculture Committee slots. It may be further noted, however, that of these 15 requests, 7 were first preference requests.[18]

Although this table does indicate the distribution of preferences for the various standing committees, consideration of aggregate demand to determine committee desirability is potentially misleading. First, the distribution of preferences reflects the *opportunity structure* as well as the preference structure, so that observations about committee popularity on this basis are necessarily ambiguous.[19] Second, even if we discount the effects of opportunity, the aggregate demand for a committee vacancy may not accurately reflect the intensity of preference for that vacancy. To take one example, although aggregate demand for Agriculture and Post Office-Civil Service is approximately the same (14 per cent and 12 per cent, respectively), there is a great difference in the proportion of those requests that are first choices (47 per cent and 23 per cent, respectively).

More important than the two previous points, however, is that attempts to provide an aggregate measure of committee desirability are inconsistent with the conception of the legislator's behavior as goal-directed. All congressmen are not the same. Their goals differ, and the kinds of constituencies they represent vary. Thus, we would expect committees to have *differential* appeal to different types of congressmen.

The next two tables lend credence to this expectation. While it is difficult to measure the personal goals of legislators, it is probably safe to

Table 7.1. *House committee requests and first-choice preferences of freshmen*

Committee	Total requests	Percentage requesting[a]	Percentage of requests first choice (N)[b]
Agriculture	15	14	47 (7)
Appropriations	12	11	42 (5)
Armed Services	26	24	26 (12)
Banking and Currency	34	32	41 (14)
District of Columbia	3	3	0 (0)
Education and Labor	17	16	29 (5)
Foreign Affairs	23	21	61 (14)
Government Operations	8	7	13 (1)
House Administration	1	1	0 (0)
Interior and Insular Affairs	20	19	50 (10)
Interstate and Foreign Commerce	34	32	38 (13)
Judiciary	25	23	36 (9)
Merchant Marine and Fisheries	5	5	20 (1)
Post Office and Civil Service	13	12	23 (3)
Public Works	29	27	31 (9)
Science and Astronautics	15	14	33 (5)
Un-American Activities	2	2	0 (0)
Veterans Affairs	8	7	13 (1)

Note: Number making requests = 108.
[a] Since requesters submitted multiple requests, this column sums to more than 100%.
[b] The number totals to 109 because one requester asked for "Foreign Affairs or Agriculture," and so both requests were considered first choices.

assume that most freshmen are initially concerned with firming up relationships with their constituencies. This is probably a minimal requirement for the pursuit of policy goals and internal House influence, and is, of course, directly relevant to the goal of reelection. Thus, we can classify members according to the kinds of districts they represent in order to demonstrate the extent to which "committee popularity" varies with constituency types.

In Table 7.2 we have classified districts according to region and population per square mile. Although the classification is crude and the choice of variables somewhat arbitrary,[20] this scheme suffices to exhibit the very real differences in committee appeal. We have listed those committees requested (at any preference level) by 30 per cent or more of the members in each category containing at least seven requesters.[21] Immediately one notes that committees differ greatly in their relative attractiveness to the various groups of representatives. Interior is one striking example. That committee was the most requested for both

Table 7.2. *House committees most requested by freshmen
(controlling for region and population density)*

Region	Density[a]	Committee	Percentage requesting
South (N = 18)	Sparse	Interstate Comm.	45
		Banking and Curr.	39
		Public Works	33
Midwest (N = 7)	Sparse	Interior	57
		Interstate Comm.	57
		Public Works	43
West (N = 16)	Sparse	Interior	75
		Public Works	38
East (N = 8)	Medium	Armed Services	50
South (N = 9)	Medium	Interstate Comm.	44
		Foreign Affairs	33
Midwest (N = 9)	Medium	Judiciary	44
		Public Works	44
		Ed. and Labor	33
		Interstate Comm.	33
East (N = 5)	Concentrated	Banking and Curr.	40
		Interstate Comm.	40
		Judiciary	33
West (N = 7)	Concentrated	Banking and Curr.	71
		Interstate Comm.	71
		Ed. and Labor	57
		Foreign Affairs	43

[a] See footnote 20 for definitions.

Midwestern and Western congressmen from sparsely populated districts. These members, moreover, accounted for 80 per cent of the total requests for that committee (16 of 20). The reason is clear: Congressmen from these constituencies can probably serve the interests of their districts better on that committee than on any other. In the words of one Western representative on the committee:

I was attracted to it, very frankly, because it's a bread and butter committee for my state. I guess about the only thing about it that is not of great interest to my state is insular affairs. I was able to get two or three bills of great importance to my state through last year. I had vested interests I wanted to protect, to be frank.[22]

Other specific examples may be cited. Public Works is requested by 17 of the 41 representatives from sparsely populated districts in the South,

Midwest, and West, and they account for 59 per cent of the requests for that committee. Banking and Currency, part of whose jurisdiction includes housing legislation, was the most requested committee by members from districts with concentrated populations in both the East and West.

Thus, as these data demonstrate, there is indeed a difference in the attractiveness of committees to various groups of representatives, and in most instances there is a clear relationship between the type of district represented and the committees most requested.

Table 7.3 provides even more direct evidence on this score. For five selected committees, we partitioned members into two groups – interesteds and indifferents – depending on constituency characteristics.[23] Although the relationship between ascribed interest and request behavior varies from committee to committee, it is always in the predicted direction and quite strong. The ratio of the proportion of interesteds applying for a committee to the proportion of indifferents applying varies from a low of nearly 2 to 1 (Armed Services) to a high of more than 16 to 1 (Agriculture). Moreover, a high proportion of requests for each committee is accounted for by interested requesters.[24]

These findings lead us to the following conclusions: Since the attractiveness of a committee does vary from member to member, a broad-gauged, systemic property like "committee desirability" may not be appropriate for an understanding of congressional behavior. A few committees (e.g., Appropriations, Ways and Means) may be almost universally desired, but beyond these few, the attractiveness of a committee, and the value of an assignment to it, may depend solely on the interests and preferences of the member under consideration. While to an urban congressman an assignment to Agriculture might be viewed as disastrous, a farm-belt member might prefer it second only to an appointment to Appropriations.

To this point we have been characterizing the empirical request configuration. Before we turn to the data on assignments proper, we should report several additional features of this configuration as it relates to the opportunity structure of the House.

Clearly the decision about *which* committees to request is a complex strategic one for a member to resolve. Additionally, however, he must decide the strategic question of *how many* committees to include in his preference ordering. In many instances (at least with regard to freshmen) the final preference ordering submitted comprises the entire "information environment" of the Committee on Committees. In any event, it does provide one of the few pieces of hard data on members' desires. The extent to which a goal-directed member chooses to vary that information environment, then, becomes an important strategic consideration.

187

Table 7.3. *Requests by freshmen for selected House committees*
(controlling for interesteds and indifferents)

	Requested		Not requested		Total		Percentage of requests by interesteds
	N	%	N	%	N	%	
Banking and Currency							
Interesteds	17	47	19	53	36	100	65
Indifferents	9	20	36	80	45	100	
Total	26	32	55	68	81	100	
Education and Labor							
Interesteds	11	30	25	70	36	100	79
Indifferents	3	7	42	93	45	100	
Total	14	17	67	83	81	100	
Interior and Ins. Aff.							
Interesteds	11	65	6	35	17	100	69
Indifferents	5	8	59	92	64	100	
Total	16	20	65	80	81	100	
Armed Services							
Interesteds	9	30	21	70	30	100	50
Indifferents	9	18	42	82	51	100	
Total	18	22	63	78	81	100	
Agriculture							
Interesteds	11	33	22	67	33	100	92
Indifferents	1	2	47	98	48	100	
Total	12	15	69	85	81	100	

Note: See footnote 23 for definitions.

(Shortly we examine the relationships among length of preference ordering, assignment success, and other features of the opportunity structure.)

Initially we consider this decision as faced by freshmen and nonfreshmen. The strategic problems facing these two groups are very different. The freshman has no committee assignment at all. He desires a good committee, but he knows for certain that he will be assigned to *some* committee. That is, any committee assignment is possible, the range of alternatives open to the Committee on Committees is maximal, and the member is entirely at the Committee's mercy. The nonfreshman, on the

Table 7.4. *Number of requests by freshmen and nonfreshmen*

Number of requests	Freshmen		Nonfreshmen	
	N	%	N	%
1	24	22	7	82
2	15	14	9	10
3	49	45	3	3
4 or more	20	19	4	5
Total	108	100	87	100

Note: Here also the two unassigned nonfreshmen are included with the freshmen (see note 17).

other hand, already has a committee, one which he may keep as long as he wishes. Thus, he need not worry about being given a committee less desirable than the one he holds.

Therefore, if the member assumes that, circumstances permitting, the Committee on Committees will attempt to satisfy his request (obviously he must assume this, or else it would be irrational to bother making any requests at all), the two groups are likely to follow different strategies regarding the number of requests they make. Freshmen are likely to offer the Committee on Committees a wider range of alternatives (i.e., make more requests), while nonfreshmen will probably be much more specific in their requests. As Table 7.4 shows, the data are in accord with these expectations. Only 22 per cent of the freshmen make only one request, while 82 per cent of the nonfreshmen do so.

Within the freshman category in Table 7.4, there is considerable variation in the number of requests.[25] Some of this variation in request behavior reflects variations in opportunities confronting members.[26] The data of Table 7.5 are wholly consistent with this hypothesis. In this table we look at two features of the opportunity structure (unfortunately, our total N is too small to permit the meaningful introduction of other relevant features). The first is whether a member is confronted by competition for his first-choice committee by another member of his state delegation. Since the only way a member can get assigned to a committee is to be nominated by his zone representative, a member's probability of getting a particular assignment is substantially reduced if the zone representative or the Committee on Committees must choose among two or more members from the same state. Therefore, we would expect a member to "hedge his bets" – that is, make a greater number of requests – if another member from his state is requesting his most-preferred committee.

Table 7.5. *Number of House committee requests by freshmen (controlling for state vacancy and state competition on first-choice committee)*

Number of requests	State vacancy				No state vacancy			
	State compet.		No state compet.		State compet.		No state compet.	
	N	%	N	%	N	%	N	%
1	0	0	5	42	1	9	18	26
2	0	0	4	33	3	27	7	10
3	8	67	1	8	4	36	32	47
4 or more	4	33	2	17	3	27	11	16
Total	12	100	12	100	11	99[a]	68	99[a]

Note: Five members whose most-preferred committee had no vacancies are omitted here.
[a] Error is due to rounding.

The second feature of the opportunity structure that may influence the decision concerning the number of requests a congressman makes is the source of vacancies. It is apparent that at least the large states regard themselves as entitled to one or more seats on important committees, and that members, when requesting assignments, feel that a claim made on "their state's" vacancy is a persuasive argument in their favor.[27] Thus a member whose most preferred committee (as revealed by him in his preference ordering) contains a state vacancy may be more likely to list few options, *ceteris paribus*, than other members.

As Table 7.5 reveals, when a state vacancy exists, the presence of state competition makes a great deal of difference in the number of committees requested. With state competition, no member makes fewer than three requests, but without state competition, 75 per cent do so. When no state vacancy exists, state competition has no effect; 36 per cent make fewer than three requests with state competition, and 36 per cent make fewer than three requests without it. (There is a large difference, in the predicted direction, in the number that make a *single* request.) Furthermore, in the absence of state competition, a member is much more likely to submit fewer than three requests if there is a state vacancy than if there is not (75 per cent versus 36 per cent). Thus, as we expected, both the existence of state competition and the presence of a state vacancy exert an independent impact on the number of committees requested by freshmen.

So far, we have examined the committee assignment process from the

Table 7.6. *Number of House committee requests and assignment success (freshmen and nonfreshmen)*

Number of requests	A. Freshmen Member received							
	First choice		Other choice		No choice		Total	
	N	%	N	%	N	%	N	%
1	18	75	—	—	6	25	24	100
2	6	40	5	33	4	27	15	100
3	16	34	15	32	16	34	47	100
4 or more	9	45	8	40	3	15	20	100
Total	49	46	28	26	29	27	106	99[a]

Number of requests	B. Nonfreshmen Member received							
	First choice		Other choice		No choice		Total	
	N	%	N	%	N	%	N	%
1	32	45	—	—	39	55	71	100
2	1	11	5	56	3	33	9	100
3 or more	2	22	5	56	2	22	9	100
Total	35	39	10	11	44	49	89	99[a]

[a] Error is due to rounding.

point of view of the requester. We now consider who is successful in getting the assignments he requests, viewing the process in terms of the goals of the members of the Committee on Committees and the leadership.

Above we stated that the member must assume that, if circumstances permit, the Committee on Committees will try to satisfy his request. We also argued that the number of requests a member makes depends on certain strategic considerations, and thus we implicitly argued that a member would think that his probability of getting *some* requested committee depends (at least in part) on the number of requests made. In Table 7.6 we present data relating to these points. Freshmen and nonfreshmen are treated separately to prevent seniority from contaminating the results.

When the data are examined we find that in regard to freshmen our first statement is more correct than our second. That is, almost three-fourths of the freshmen do get *some* committee that they requested, and

Table 7.7. *Seniority and success in assignment to House committees*

Number of previous terms	Member received							
	First choice		Other choice		No choice		Total	
	N	%	N	%	N	%	N	%
0	49	46	28	26	29	27	106	99[a]
1	19	41	8	17	19	41	46	99[a]
2	9	43	1	5	11	52	21	100
3 or more	7	32	1	5	14	64	22	100[a]
Total	84	43	38	20	73	37	195	100

[a] Error is due to rounding.

the probability of getting *no* choice is affected little by the number of requests. For nonfreshmen, on the other hand, more requests do increase chances of some success.

The most striking finding in Table 7.6, however, results from our treating freshmen and nonfreshmen separately. Contrary to what one might expect in a body in which seniority is often important, freshmen are much more successful in getting requested assignments than are nonfreshmen. This finding is reinforced by the data in Table 7.7, which shows assignment success by amount of seniority. We find that the probability of receiving *no* request monotonically *increases* as seniority increases.

This result should not be entirely unexpected, for many references in the literature on committee assignments claim that seniority is often ignored when circumstances dictate. For example, Clapp claims that

given a contest for an important committee assignment, in which returning members of Congress may wish to transfer from another committee and find themselves competing with each other and with freshmen congressmen, seniority is not infrequently brushed aside, if it will not bring about the outcome desired by those making the decision.[28]

Another observer of the process stated:

Seniority may control if all other things are equal. But other things usually are not equal. Sometimes you begin to think seniority is little more than a device to fall back on when it is convenient to do so.[29]

To assess the accuracy of this last statement, we examined a situation where it is more likely for "other things" to be "equal": the case when two members from the same state are competing for the same committee. We looked at all committees that had vacancies, and determined for each

Table 7.8. *State competition, seniority, and success in House committee assignment (all committees with vacancies)*

	Member assigned		Member not assigned		Total	
	N	%	N	%	N	%
No same state competition	103	36	187	64	290	100
Same state competition; competitor not more senior	20	26	56	74	76	100
Same state competition; competitor more senior	1	7	13	93	14	100
Total	124	33	256	67	380	100

requester whether another member from the same state was applying for that committee, and if so, whether the other member was more senior. The relevant data are presented in Table 7.8. It is clear that a request for which there is no same state competition has a likelihood of about one chance in three of being granted. When there is competition, however, a member has about one chance in four of success if his competitor is not more senior, while he has only one chance in fourteen if the competitor *is* more senior. Thus in this instance, where "other things" are more likely to be "equal," seniority may become very advantageous, although it is generally not.

What then are the things that in other situations are *not* "equal"? That is, in terms of the goals of members who determine committee assignments, what factors cause them to ignore seniority? Clearly, many kinds of interacting and even conflicting motivations may influence the members of the Committee on Committees. Thus it is dangerous to posit either a single motive for all members of the Committee on Committees or even for any one member. Still, it is not unreasonable to assess the extent to which the data support any of these motives.

The first motive or goal for Committee on Committees members we have posited might be termed the *management goal*. The Committee on Committees, in this view, is concerned solely with satisfying requester demands. Thus, it acts as an "impersonal" preference aggregation device in an effort to keep requesters happy. In reporting on this motive, we find it useful to contrast it with another, the *constituency interest goal*. According to this goal, committee makers ignore request data, concerning themselves instead with matching individual members to committee vacancies on the basis of constituency characteristics and interests. The data relevant to this comparison are presented in Table 7.9. For

Table 7.9. *Interesteds, requests, and success in House committee assignments (freshmen)*

Interested[a] requested	Yes Yes	Yes No	No Yes	No No	Total
Committee					
Banking and Currency	47	0	33	3	15
	(17)	(19)	(9)	(36)	(81)
Education and Labor	64	4	67	2	14
	(11)	(25)	(3)	(42)	(81)
Interior and Ins. Aff.	64	17	20	3	14
	(11)	(6)	(5)	(59)	(81)
Armed Services	33	0	11	2	6
	(9)	(21)	(9)	(42)	(81)
Agriculture	27	14	100	4	11
	(11)	(22)	(1)	(47)	(81)

Note: Each cell gives percentage of N assigned to that committee (N in parentheses).
[a] See footnote 23 for definition of interesteds.

the committees investigated in Table 7.3 we partitioned freshmen[30] members according to two criteria: whether they qualify as interested and whether they requested the committee. The results suggest that the management goal dominates the constituency interest goal. In most instances (the small Ns make firm conclusions difficult), interested-requesters get the nod. Moreover, for *every* committee, requesting-indifferents are more successful than nonrequesting-interesteds. Minimally, we conclude that committee makers do not take member requests lightly – that, in requesting a committee, a member is not waltzing before a blind audience.

A third obvious candidate as a motivational hypothesis for members of the Committee on Committees is *party maintenance*. Whether a member is interested in influencing policy outcomes or in influence for its own sake, one thing that in part determines the amount of such influence is the majority or minority status of his party. A member has more influence if he is Speaker than if he is Minority Leader, more influence if he is chairman of a committee than if he is ranking minority member, and probably more influence if he is on the majority side of the committee than if he is in the minority. Therefore it is in the interest of most Committee members to help insure the reelection of party colleagues. Thus the question arises, who needs the most help? Clearly, the members most in need of help are those who were elected by the smallest margin. *Ceteris paribus*, a member elected with 51 per cent of the vote is more

Table 7.10. *Margin of election and success in House committee assignments (freshmen and nonfreshmen)*

| | A. Freshmen Member received | | | | | | | |
| | First choice | | Other choice | | No choice | | Total | |
District is	N	%	N	%	N	%	N	%
Marginal	31	56	10	18	14	25	55	99[a]
Safe	18	35	18	35	15	29	51	99[a]
Total	49	46	28	26	29	27	106	99[a]

| | B. Nonfreshmen Member received | | | | | | | |
| | First choice | | Other choice | | No choice | | Total | |
District is	N	%	N	%	N	%	N	%
Marginal	7	39	5	28	6	33	18	100
Safe	28	39	5	7	38	54	71	100
Total	35	39	10	11	44	49	89	99[a]

[a] Error is due to rounding.

likely to be defeated than one elected with 61 per cent. Thus, we would expect members from marginal districts to be more successful than members from safe districts. (We have termed a district marginal if the member was elected with less than 55 per cent of the vote.)

As the data in Table 7.10 show, our expectations are correct. Marginal freshmen are slightly less likely to fail to receive a requested committee and are much more likely to receive their first choice than are safe freshmen.

Marginal nonfreshmen are *much* less likely to receive no choice than are safe nonfreshmen, but they are about equally likely to receive their first choice as are safe nonfreshmen. We also find that some of the difference in success between freshmen and nonfreshmen disappears here – that is, safe freshmen are treated about the same as marginal nonfreshmen. When one recalls that these nonfreshmen, even though they are marginal, have demonstrated (at least once) their ability to get re-elected, it does not seem surprising that these two groups are about equally successful.

The perceived stand of the individual member on specific issues is yet another basis on which committee makers may determine assignments.[31] Their prime concern here is the degree to which members will support the party position on issues which come before the standing committees

Table 7.11. *Region and success in House committee assignments*
(freshmen and nonfreshmen)

| | A. Freshmen Member received | | | | | | | |
| | First choice | | Other choice | | No choice | | Total | |
Region[a]	N	%	N	%	N	%	N	%
South	8	31	7	27	11	42	26	100
Non-South	41	51	21	26	18	23	80	100
Total	49	46	28	26	29	27	106	99[b]

| | B. Nonfreshmen Member received | | | | | | | |
| | First choice | | Other choice | | No choice | | Total | |
Region[a]	N	%	N	%	N	%	N	%
South	7	27	2	8	17	65	26	100
Non-South	28	44	8	13	27	43	63	100
Total	35	39	10	11	44	49	89	99[b]

[a] The South includes the eleven states of the Confederacy.
[b] Error is due to rounding.

(*party support goal*). While detailed considerations of individual committees are beyond the scope of an initial study such as ours, two pieces of evidence may shed some light on this question. Generally speaking, southern Democrats are less likely to support their party's position than are northern Democrats. Therefore, whether we consider the granting of a specific request a reward for past behavior or an attempt to gain influence over future behavior, the leadership should be less likely to intervene with the Committee on Committees on behalf of a southerner than a northerner. Moreover, since the Democratic members of the Ways and Means Committee are more liberal and more supportive of their party than is the average House Democrat,[32] those members, even when acting on their own, are likely to be more favorably disposed toward the requests of northern Democrats than toward those of southerners. Therefore, we would expect southerners to be less successful than northerners in obtaining requested committees.

As Table 7.11 shows, the data support this hypothesis. For both freshmen and nonfreshmen, southerners are more likely than nonsoutherners to receive *no* request. They are less successful than their colleagues from other regions in getting their first choices as well. One might wonder, however, whether this finding of lesser success among southern-

Table 7.12. *Region, margin of election, and success in House committee assignments (freshmen)*

| Region[a] | A. Marginal districts Member received | | | | | | | |
| | First choice | | Other choice | | No choice | | Total | |
	N	%	N	%	N	%	N	%
South	1	25	0	0	3	75	4	100
Non-South	30	59	10	20	11	22	51	101[b]
Total	31	56	10	18	14	26	55	100

| Region[a] | B. Safe districts Member received | | | | | | | |
| | First choice | | Other choice | | No choice | | Total | |
	N	%	N	%	N	%	N	%
South	7	32	7	32	8	36	22	100
Non-South	11	38	11	38	7	24	29	100
Total	18	35	18	35	15	29	51	99[b]

[a] The South includes the eleven states of the Confederacy.
[b] Error is due to rounding.

ers does not simply repeat our finding concerning marginal varsus safe districts. That is, since southerners are more likely to come from safe districts,[33] they may be less successful than nonsoutherners simply because they are elected by larger margins. To examine the possibility we present in Tables 7.12 and 7.13 data on region, margin of election, and assignment success for freshmen and nonfreshmen, respectively.

Since there are few marginal freshmen southerners, and no marginal nonfreshmen southerners, we will focus our discussion on members from safe districts. As the data demonstrate, even when marginal members are removed, southerners are less successful than are nonsoutherners. Among both freshmen and nonfreshmen, safe southerners are more likely to receive no request than are safe nonsoutherners, and are less likely to receive a first request. The evidence is unequivocal: Region has a strong, independent impact on committee assignment success, even when election margin is controlled.[34]

The second piece of evidence bearing on the party support goal is presented in Table 7.14. To construct this table we examined the party support scores of nonfreshmen requesters[35] for each of the Congresses in the sample, and compared the assignment success of those whose support surpasses the mean for the party in the previous Congress with those who

Table 7.13. *Region, margin of election, and assignment success in House committee assignments (nonfreshmen)*

	A. Marginal districts Member received							
	First choice		Other choice		No choice		Total	
Region[a]	N	%	N	%	N	%	N	%
South	0	—	0	—	0	—	0	—
Non-South	7	39	5	28	6	33	18	100
Total	7	39	5	28	6	33	18	100

	B. Safe districts Member received							
	First choice		Other choice		No choice		Total	
Region[a]	N	%	N	%	N	%	N	%
South	7	27	2	8	17	65	26	100
Non-South	21	47	3	7	21	47	45	101[b]
Total	28	39	5	7	38	54	71	100

[a] The South includes the eleven states of the Confederacy.
[b] Error is due to rounding.

gave the party less than the mean support. In each of the four Congresses, high party supporters were more successful in securing assignments (i.e., being granted any one of their requests) than low party supporters. Part E of this table gives the aggregate totals: 58 per cent of the high party supporters, as opposed to 37 per cent of the low party supporters, secured a requested committee.

SUMMARY AND CONCLUSIONS

In this paper we have viewed the Democratic assignment process as an instance of social choice. We have examined the process from the point of view of the members requesting assignments and of the members making assignments. We have assumed that both groups are goal-directed and that an understanding of their behavior derives from an analysis of alternative goals and alternative means (behaviors) of achieving them.

In regard to those members requesting assignments, we have shown that their choice of committees is related to the type of district they represent. Also, the data indicate that the decision concerning the number of requests to make appears to be affected by certain strategic

Table 7.14. Party support and success in House committee assignments (nonfreshmen)

A. 86th Congress

	Assigned	Not assigned	Total
Supporter[a]	62 (8)	38 (5)	100 (13)
Nonsupporter	40 (2)	60 (3)	100 (5)
Total	56 (10)	44 (8)	100 (18)

B. 87th Congress

	Assigned	Not assigned	Total
Supporter	50 (8)	50 (8)	100 (16)
Nonsupporter	45 (5)	55 (6)	100 (11)
Total	48 (13)	52 (14)	100 (27)

C. 88th Congress

	Assigned	Not assigned	Total
Supporter	62 (8)	33 (5)	100 (13)
Nonsupporter	40 (4)	60 (6)	100 (10)
Total	52 (12)	48 (11)	100 (23)

D. 90th Congress

	Assigned	Not assigned	Total
Supporter	60 (9)	40 (6)	100 (15)
Nonsupporter	0 (0)	100 (4)	100 (4)
Total	47 (9)	53 (10)	100 (19)

E. All Congress

	Assigned	Not assigned	Total
Supporter	58 (33)	42 (24)	100 (57)
Nonsupporter	37 (11)	63 (19)	100 (30)
Total	51 (44)	49 (43)	100 (87)

[a] Supporters are members whose party support scores were above or equal to the mean for the party for the previous Congress. Cell entries are percentages; Ns are in parentheses.

considerations such as whether the requester is a freshman, whether there is a vacancy from his state on his most preferred committee, and whether another member from his state is competing with him for his most preferred committee.

We next considered the making of assignments. Here we found that about three-fourths of the freshmen are granted some committee they requested. The data showed, however, that nonfreshmen are much less successful. Indeed, the probability of success decreased as seniority increased; therefore other·factors were sought in order to explain assignment success. We considered several alternative goals for committee makers – the management goal, the constituency interest goal, the party maintenance goal, and the party support goal – and found strong support in the data for most of them. However, the interaction (and collinearity) among goals precludes any unqualified conclusions.

The assignment process in the House of Representatives is obviously complex, and it is affected by a host of factors, some of them detailed in the body of this paper. Our purposes here have been severalfold. First, we believe it is useful to view the assignment process as an institutionalized allocation process involving goal-seeking actors, scarce but valued commodities, and behavioral constraints. Second, given this view, we have sought to supply a "missing link" in the literature on committee assignments, namely the preferences of committee requests. Not only does this link provide some interesting insights about one group of actors in the process (requesters); additionally, it provides empirical knowledge about the constraints and information confronting the other significant group in the process – the committee makers. Third, the heuristic use of a social choice construct and the new data on the preferences of committee requesters have brought into focus and provided some order to the complex of strategic factors involved in this process.

The questions for future empirical analysis appear to be almost limitless. For example, future research should consider, instead of surrogate variables like region, the position of members on specific issues before and after the assignment decision. Another aspect to be examined is the behavior of individual members of the Committee on Committees. What requesters from which zones are most successful? Do zone representatives appear to nominate members whose views are like their own? A third aspect of the process which deserves further consideration is the opportunity structure: Are members who are granted their first choice more likely to make further requests in the future, and if so are they very successful? Are members who receive no request initially granted a good assignment at some later time, or are they perpetually unsuccessful?

The research reported here is not distinctive in one respect: It raises as many questions as it answers. Nevertheless, we feel this study has provided some initial direction for a more comprehensive, formal understanding of the committee assignment process, and thus of internal relationships in the House as a whole. In this fashion, we believe, students of the public sector will begin to ascertain some of the operating characteristics of its institutions and thus be in a better position to make sound evaluations and prescriptions.

NOTES

1 Richard F. Fenno, Jr., "Congressional Committees: A Comparative View," a paper presented at the 66th Annual Meeting of the American Political Science Association, Los Angeles, September 8–11, 1970; George Goodwin, Jr., *The Little Legislatures* (Amherst: University of Massachusetts Press, 1970).

2 Richard F. Fenno, Jr., *The Power of the Purse: Appropriations Politics in Congress* (Boston: Little, Brown and Co., 1966); John Manley, *The Politics of Finance: The House Committee on Ways and Means* (Boston: Little, Brown and Co., 1970).

3 *The Congressman: His Work as He Sees It* (New York: Doubleday and Co., 1963), p. 207.

4 The classic treatment of the process is Nicholas A. Masters, "Committee Assignments in the House of Representatives," *American Political Science Review*, 55 (June, 1961), 345–357. Assignments are discussed at length in Clapp, *The Congressman*, pp. 207–240, and Goodwin, *The Little Legislatures*, pp. 64–79. Some recent studies include Louis C. Gawthrop, "Changing Membership Patterns in House Committees," *American Political Science Review*, 60 (June, 1966), 366–373; Charles Bullock and John Sprague, "A Research Note on the Committee Reassignments of Southern Democratic Congressmen," *Journal of Politics*, 31 (May, 1969), 493–512; Charles Bullock, "Correlates of Committee Transfers in the United States House of Representatives," a paper delivered at the Annual Meeting of the Midwest Political Science Association, Chicago, April 29–May 1, 1971; Charles Bullock, "The Influence of State Party Delegations on House Committee Assignments," *Midwest Journal of Political Science*, 15 (August, 1971), 525–546; and Charles Bullock, "Freshman Committee Assignments and Reelection in the United States House of Representatives," *American Political Science Review*, 66 (September, 1972), 996–1007.

5 In addition to our own data, this description relies heavily on Masters, "Committee Assignments," and on Clapp, *The Congressman*, Chapter 5.

6 The Democratic delegation on Ways and Means is made up almost entirely of members drawn from the South and Border States and from the large industrial states. They are elected to membership by a vote of the full Democratic caucus. During the period covered by this study the committee was dominated by the Southern and Border State group, who were greatly overrepresented compared to their proportion of the Democratic delegation in the House. In the 86th–88th Congresses, they had 8 members out of the total of 15, and in the 90th Congress they had 7 of 15. For a discussion of assignments to Ways and Means, see Manley, *Politics of Finance*, pp. 22–38.

7 Zone assignments in the 86th Congress are listed in Masters, "Committee

Assignments," p. 347. The number of states represented varies greatly, with Keogh of New York, for example, representing only his own state, while Metcalf of Montana represents seven small Western and Midwestern states.

8 While party ratios usually reflect the partisan division in the House, it is not unlikely that the decisions on both these questions are influenced by the leadership's knowledge of the requests of the members of their party.

9 It is important to note that the only way a requester can be nominated for a committee post is to be nominated by his zone representative.

10 Fenno, "Congressional Committees," p. 3.

11 Clapp, *The Congressman*, p. 207.

12 It is clear that such debts are recognized, and that they are called in. One member, commenting on the influence another member had within the House, said, "Much of his power rests with the fact he is on Ways and Means. Since that Committee determines committee assignments, he is in a very important and strategic spot. He makes his deals with various groups as to which people he will support for certain spots. Naturally when the time comes that he wants something, he can make a request and people reciprocate." Quoted in Clapp, *The Congressman*, pp. 29–30.

13 Manley, *Politics of Finance*, p. 24.

14 See Bullock, "The Influence of State Party Delegations."

15 Most of the individual committee studies (e.g., Fenno, Manley) also draw on interviews with committee members to generalize about what led them to seek assignment to the committee and why they were successful.

16 The standing committees of the House are divided into three classes: exclusive, semi-exclusive, and nonexclusive, and there are rules which govern assignments to each class. Members of exclusive committees may serve on no other committee. Members of semi-exclusive committees may be given a second assignment only on a nonexclusive committee; and members of nonexclusive committees may be given second assignments on any semi- or nonexclusive committee. During the period covered by this study the committees in these classes were: *exclusive:* Appropriations, Rules, and Ways and Means; *semi-exclusive:* Agriculture, Armed Services, Banking and Currency, Education and Labor, Foreign Affairs, Interstate and Foreign Commerce, Judiciary, Public Works, and Science and Astronautics; *nonexclusive:* District of Columbia, Government Operations, House Administration, Interior and Insular Affairs, Merchant Marine and Fisheries, Un-American Activities, and Veterans Affairs. In addition, Post Office and Civil Service was changed from semi-exclusive to nonexclusive status at the beginning of the 88th Congress. Finally, the twenty-first standing committee, Standards of Official Conduct (established in 1967) seems to occupy a special status since it is a third assignment for a number of members.

17 We do, however, include the requests of two nonfreshmen who were first elected in special elections near the end of a Congress. They were not assigned to any committees then, and thus they are in the same position as freshmen.

18 The reader will note that only 18 committees are listed in Table 7.1. Ways and Means is excluded here, and throughout the rest of the analysis, because its vacancies are filled by the caucus. Rules and Standards of Official Conduct are excluded because they were never requested, by either freshmen or nonfreshmen. In regard to Rules, this absence of requests probably reflects the special importance this committee has to the leadership, since almost never is a vacancy on Rules filled by a member not first sponsored by the

leadership. See Clapp, *The Congressman*, p. 218; and Manley, *Politics of Finance*, p. 77.

19 Thus a problem with using requests or appointments as a measure of committee desirability results from anticipated reactions. A freshman will probably refrain from requesting the committee he most wants if he believes there is no chance of getting it. Table 7.1 seems to support this view in regard to requests for Appropriations, which (along with the other two exclusive committees) is generally recognized to be the most sought-after committee. It is, however, also recognized that freshmen have little chance to be appointed. (Indeed, in the four Congresses analyzed here, no freshman was appointed.) There does not, however, seem to be any evidence of anticipated reaction in regard to requests for other committees.

20 Differences among districts on a regional basis are well known, hence the selection of that variable. Regions are defined as follows: *Northeast:* Conn., Del., Me., Mass, N.H., N.J., N.Y., Penn., R.I., Vt.; *Border:* Kent., Md., Mo., Okla., W.Va.; *South:* Ala., Ark., Fla., Ga., La., Miss., N.C., S.C., Tenn., Tex., Va.; *Midwest:* Ill., Ind., Ia., Kan., Mich., Minn., Neb., N.D., Ohio, S.D., Wisc.; *West:* Alaska, Ariz., Cal., Colo., Haw., Ida., Mont., Nev., N.M., Ore., Utah, Wash., Wyo.

Population per square mile was selected to tap the relatively urban or rural nature of districts. While percentage urban would have been a preferable measure in this regard, such data were available on a district basis only for the 88th and 90th Congresses. To operationalize this variable the districts were divided into three categories: sparse (less than 100 persons per sq. mi.), medium (100–999 persons per sq. mi.), and concentrated (1,000 or more persons per sq. mi.). Population data were obtained from *Congressional District Data Book: Districts of the 87th Congress* (for the 86th and 87th Congresses) and from *Congressional District Data Book: Districts of the 88th Congress* and its supplements (for the 88th and 90th Congresses). Both books and the supplements are published by the Bureau of the Census.

21 The excluded categories and the number of members in each were: East, sparse (3); Border, sparse (4); Border, medium (5); West, medium (3); Border, concentrated (0); South, concentrated (0); Midwest, concentrated (4).

22 Quoted in Fenno, "Congressional Committees," p. 6.

23 These committees were selected because of the availability of constituency data which seemed reasonably related to representatives' probable interest in the committee. We borrowed the terms "interested" and "indifferent," and the basic ideas on measuring interest, from Charles Bullock (see "Correlates of Committee Transfers," pp. 22–23), although our specific measures are somewhat different. Bullock, in turn, adopted the terms from David R. Mayhew, *Party Loyalty Among Congressmen* (Cambridge: Harvard University Press, 1966).

Data on constituency characteristics were obtained from the *Congressional District Data Book: Districts of the 88th Congress* and its supplements. In this source data were available on freshmen representatives in the 86th and 87th Congresses only if they came from states which were not redistricted after the 1960 census. Therefore the number of members considered in Table 7.3 is 81 instead of 108.

For each committee a constituency measure was selected, and each representative's district was ranked as either above or below the national average on that measure. If the district was above the national average, the congressman was classed as an interested; if the district was below the national average, the congressman was classed as an indifferent. The measures of the committees are as follows (national averages are in parentheses); Banking and Currency and Education and Labor, percentage of population residing in urban areas (69.9 per cent); Interior and Insular Affairs, land area of district (8,159 sq. mi.); Armed Services, percentage of the total labor force who are members of the armed forces (2.5 per cent); and Agriculture, percentage of the employed civillian labor force employed in agriculture (6.6 per cent).

24 The proportion of Armed Services requests made by interesteds is by far the lowest. This is probably because interest in this committee is determined by other things besides a relatively large number of servicemen in a district (e.g., large defense plants or a hope of attracting defense bases or plants to a district in the future).

25 We restrict the following discussion to freshmen because the argument about a nonfreshman's ability to be more specific in his requests applies as well here as it did above.

26 Here we consider opportunities to depend upon certain objective conditions, such as number of vacancies for a given committee (supply), number of requests (demand), and service restrictions regarding dual requests (formal rules), and upon informal norms which may guide the allocation of committee vacancies, such as "same-state" norms for appointment.

27 See Bullock, "The Influence of State Party Delegations," and Clapp, *The Congressman*, pp. 220, 238.

28 Clapp, *The Congressman*, pp. 226–227.

29 Quoted in Clapp, *The Congressman*, p. 226. We should note here that the data in Tables 7.6 and 7.7 indicate only overall success and not success in those instances where the requests of freshmen and nonfreshmen are in direct competition. Masters states that "when two or more members stake a claim to the same assignment, on the ground that it is essential to their electoral success, both party committees usually, if not invariably, will give preference to the member with longer service" (Masters, "Committee Assignments," p. 354). We do not know what arguments were made about electoral success, but in our data 50 nonfreshmen were in competition with one or more freshmen for assignments to semi- or nonexclusive committees which had insufficient vacancies to satisfy all requests. Of these 50 members, 23 were passed over in favor of freshmen. This does not include instances where the passed-over member received another, more preferred, assignment.

30 We restrict our attention here to freshmen not only because of the effects of seniority on both request behavior and success, but also because the situation is much more complex in regard to nonfreshmen. Minimally we would have to control for whether a representative is already a member of a committee for which he would be classified as an interested. Further, we would probably want to control for whether the requests made are for transfers or dual service assignments. Also we would want to exclude prestige committee requests. These controls would make the Ns so small and would break them into so many categories that a meaningful test would be impossible.

31 In addition to our discussion of member goals above, see Masters, "Committee Assignments," pp. 354–355, and Clapp, *The Congressman*, pp. 228–230.

32 See Fenno, "Congressional Committees," pp. 33–34, and Manley, *Politics of Finance*, pp. 29–32.

33 Using a different definition of safe seats, Wolfinger and Hollinger found that while southerners held only 38 per cent of the Democratic seats in the 88th Congress, they held 63 per cent of the safe seats. See Raymond E. Wolfinger and Joan H. Hollinger, "Safe Seats, Seniority, and Power in Congress," in *New Perspectives on the House of Representatives*, ed. Robert L. Peabody and Nelson W. Polsby, 2nd ed. (Chicago: Rand McNally, 1969), pp. 60–61.

34 This finding is all the more striking in light of the southern Democrats' dominance of the Committee on Committees during this period (see footnote 6). It is, admittedly, dangerous to treat a variable like region as a surrogate for, in this case, expected policy behavior. Support for party policies clearly varies within regions. Moreover, other informal, nonpolicy, behavioral norms are likely to cloud the relationship between region and appointment success. A clear indication of this intraregional variation is the rather startling differential in success between members from the South and those from

Table A. *Assignment success, region, and zone representative's state delegation (member received)*

	First choice		Other choice		No choice		Total	
	N	%	N	%	N	%	N	%
A. Freshmen, non-South								
Same state[a]	16	52	8	26	7	23	31	101[b]
Not	25	51	13	27	11	22	49	100
Total	41	51	21	26	18	23	80	100
B. Freshmen, South								
Same state	5	46	4	36	2	18	11	100
Not	3	20	3	20	9	60	15	100
Total	8	31	7	27	11	42	26	100
C. Non-Freshmen, non-South								
Same state	13	46	3	11	12	43	28	100
Not	15	43	5	14	15	43	35	100
Total	28	44	8	13	27	43	63	100
D. Non-Freshmen, South								
Same state	3	30	2	20	5	50	10	100
Not	4	25	0	0	12	75	16	100
Total	7	27	2	8	17	65	26	100

[a] Same state means that the member making the request and his zone representative are from same state.

[b] Error due to rounding.

outside the South when we control for the state of their zone representative. As the data in Table A show, the southern member who is from the same state as his zone representative is much more likely to secure a requested assignment than are his southern colleagues who are not from the same state as their zone representatives. Whereas 60 per cent of the freshmen who are *not* from the same state as their zone representative fail to receive any committee request, only 18 per cent of those from the zone representative's state delegation are in the same unenviable position. The differential is somewhat smaller for nonfreshmen (75 per cent versus 50 per cent receive no request), but the pattern is the same. For members from outside the South, however, this differential does not appear. There is virtually no difference between the success of members who are from the same state as their zone representative and that of members who are not.

35 We exclude the two nonfreshmen elected in special elections near the close of the preceding Congress, for whom there were no party support score data. For each Congress, a member's party support score is tabulated from his voting behavior in the previous Congress. Party support data are found in the appropriate volumes of the *Congressional Quarterly Almanac:* vol. XIV (1958), pp. 124–125; vol. XVI (1960), pp. 140–141; vol. XVIII (1962), pp. 764–765; vol. XXII (1966), pp. 1030–1031.

8

Reforming the structure of the House appropriations process: the effects of the 1885 and 1919–20 reforms on money decisions

DAVID BRADY AND MARK A. MORGAN

The budget process in the United States House of Representatives has undergone a number of major structural changes since the Civil War. Each of these changes was enacted by a majority of the members of the House and, we assume, was enacted for a purpose. Although political scientists have a good idea about the effects of the 1974 reforms on budgetary matters, very little is known about the effects of the other great changes in the structure of the appropriations process. Yet there are strong similarities both in the exogenous circumstances of the reforms and in the proposed structural changes. To understand both why structural changes occur and what effects they have on appropriations decisions it is necessary to examine the range of budgetary and appropriations reforms.

In this paper we investigate two major reforms: the 1877–85 move to decentralize and the 1919–20 decision to recentralize the appropriations process. Our investigation entails an analysis of the 1865 to 1877 period as a baseline for analyzing the effects of the 1877–85 and 1919–20 reforms. We examine the causes and effects of reforms in light of the relationship between (1) reforms and the state of government finances, (2) structural changes and appropriations decisions, and (3) the House and the Appropriations Committee. We approach the problem from a perspective based loosely on rational choice. Specifically, we assume that the reforms were designed and voted in by members to achieve results that they perceived as beneficial to themselves. We begin with a historical review of the appropriations process from 1865 to the post–World War II period, paying special attention to what House members perceived the

The authors are especially indebted to Professors Rick Wilson and Joseph Cooper for their careful reading of the manuscript and their many helpful comments.

issues and solutions to be (Ostrom 1980). We then formulate and test hypotheses concerning the relationships outlined above.

BACKGROUND

In 1865 the House of Representatives created a separate Appropriations Committee. Until that time moneys had been appropriated by the Ways and Means Committee. The creation of a separate committee did not generate much controversy or occupy much of the House's time. The rationale for its creation was that Ways and Means members could not possibly find enough time to both raise and spend revenues; thus, specialization was required. The chairman of the Ways and Means Committee (Thaddeus Stevens, R-Penn.), which was losing power, spoke in favor of the new committee. The only argument raised against it was that the same end could be achieved by enlarging the Ways and Means Committee, and only one member spoke in opposition. The resolution passed easily.

One of the major factors associated with the need for the Appropriations Committee was the Civil War. Prior to 1861 the sums of money needed to run the government were minimal; but the huge increases necessary to fund the war overburdened the Ways and Means Committee. The relatively high national debt in 1865 made economy in government necessary, and the members were convinced that a specialized committee on appropriations could provide a solution.

In the ensuing decade the Appropriations Committee took its role as watchdog of the Treasury seriously. In 1876 the committee enhanced its power by leading the fight to pass the Holman Rule, which gave the committee the right to reduce expenditures in general appropriations bills. Prior to the passage of this rule, the committee's authority concerning such bills was limited to recommending salary increases. The Holman Rule effectively gave the committee greater power to reduce executive branch budget estimates. It also permitted the committee to add amendments to bills – effectively allowing it to legislate as well as appropriate.

Those in favor of the Holman Rule won the roll-call vote, with 156 voting yes, 102 no; 32 did not vote. The vote was highly structured by party identification – slightly over 90 percent of the Democrats voted yes; over 90 percent of the Republicans, no. The partisan nature of the vote was not surprising given that the Democrats had been in a continual minority on questions of federal intervention in expanding industrial interests, land grants to railroads, the creation of land-grant colleges, and homestead policy. All of these policies had cost money and had been opposed by the congressional Democratic party (Brady 1982). The passage of the Holman Rule was, however, a Pyrrhic victory. In 1877 the House voted to allow a rivers and harbors bill to bypass Appropriations (Wander 1981).

In the 46th Congress (1879–81)[1] the House enacted a major revision of the rules. Among the proposed changes none generated more debate than the special rules giving the right to appropriate money to the Agriculture Committee and (on river and harbor legislation) to the Commerce Committee. Other committees – Post Office and Post Roads, the military committees and Indian Affairs – also sought the right to appropriate; but only agricultural and rivers and harbors legislation was favored. The debate centered on Rule XI, clause 7; in each case it was proposed to give the relevant committee "the same privileges in reporting bills and making appropriations...as it accorded to the Committee on Appropriations" (*C.R.*, 46th Cong., p. 684).

The argument for passage of the reforms centered on two issues. The first and foremost was the claim that the Appropriations Committee was too powerful; the second was that it used various rules and techniques to bottleneck bills until late in the session. Underlying these two claims was the notion that Appropriations was not funding worthwhile projects and services. Opponents of the reforms, among whom were some of the most powerful House members, argued that decentralization would open the doors to the Treasury. Ultimately, the only committees to receive the right to appropriate on their own were Agriculture and, for the rivers and harbors bills, Commerce. Each of the other committees was denied the right to appropriate on its own. However, the losers in the 46th House (1880) would surface again in the 49th House (1885–87).

In the 47th and 48th Houses the move to decentralize the appropriations power grew in strength, as attested to by the creation in 1883 of a Rivers and Harbors Committee. On December 14, 1885, the 49th House began to debate a rule change that would give five other committees the right to appropriate funds. The arguments on both sides were much the same as the arguments offered in 1880. Opponents argued that when the rivers and harbors bill had gone to special committees the effect had been to raise appropriations and to fund trivial projects. They claimed that in 1884 the pork barrel for rivers and harbors had appropriated millions more than President Arthur requested and then passed the increase over his veto. Moreover, they claimed bills were passed before estimates had been received. Unlike 1880, however, the forces seeking to limit Appropriations' power now were in the majority. The rules changes allowing other committees to appropriate were all passed, although the debate over changes was a lengthy one and divided party members.

The majority on the Rules Committee had proposed extensive rules revisions, which among other things eliminated much of the legislative effect of the Holman Rule and gave the power to appropriate the following bills to the relevant committees: consular and diplomatic to Foreign Affairs, post office bills to Post Office and Post Roads, the Indian bill to Indian Affairs. The new system had eight committees that could fund programs. Appropriations was responsible for about one-half, and the other seven committees one-half. This system was to remain in place until 1920.

The 35 years following this reform were years of impressive economic growth, both private and governmental. Woodrow Wilson's progressivism and America's entry into World War I resulted in great increases in federal expenditures. After the war the Republicans won control of the House (in 1918) for the first time in eight years; and under the leadership of Representative Good (R-Iowa), chairman of the Appropriations Committee in the 66th House, the Republicans sought major reforms in the budget process. The Budget Act of 1919 created the Bureau of the Budget and gave the executive branch greater control over estimates and expenditures. A crucial part of the budget reform was the recentralization of appropriations decisions in the Appropriations Committee. However, the Republicans separated the committee changes (H.R. 324) from the 1919 act. Their rationale was that there was greater bipartisan support for it and more heated opposition to recentralizing power in Appropriations. And, indeed, the debate on the Budget Act was characterized by support for the act but opposition to H.R. 324, which was not yet under consideration.

The formal debate on H.R. 324 did not occur until June of 1920, well after the 1919 Budget Act had passed. Those in favor of recentralizing the money power in the Appropriations Committee argued that (1) with eight committees appropriating in different ways it was impossible "to visualize the financial situation of the Nation" (Madden, R-Ill; C.R., 66th Cong., p. 8109); (2) the present system led to extravagance and waste (Good, R-Iowa; C.R., 66th Cong., p. 8116); and (3) the government's work must be conducted "along business lines, unmindful of the ambitions of men" (Good, R-Iowa; C.R., 66th Cong., p. 8117). Those opposed to the reform argued the old refrains: (1) Appropriations would have too much power; "To my surprise, notwithstanding the fact that autocracy is generally looked upon with scorn and contempt, it appears here in a more malignant from than ever" (C.R., 66th Cong., p. 8109). (2) Certain projects and areas would be underfunded. Unlike 1885, these arguments were not compelling. The final vote was 200 in favor of H.R. 324 and 117 against. The vote was not entirely a party vote, though Republicans voted strongly for it. The resultant recentralized system stayed in place until at least 1946, and the more likely end point is 1974.

DESIGN AND DATA ANALYSIS

Our basic assumption is that the structure of the House and its committees makes a difference in terms of both the decisions made and who benefits from the decisions. The tenor and tone of the debates surrounding the reforms of 1876, 1880–85, and 1920 show that the representatives themselves saw structural changes as affecting decisions. Based on the work of Shepsle (1978), Shepsle and Weingast (1981), and Ostrom (1980) and on the members' comments during the debates, we can generate a number of testable hypotheses.

The first area of concern is the relationship between exogenous economic variables and the endogenous structuring of the appropriations process. The major economic variables used in this study are governmental finances and the public debt. Specifically, we have collected data on whether the government was running surpluses or deficits and what was per capita national debt over the 1867 to 1930 time period. The argument is that the status of governmental finances will affect the House's structural decisions. When the government is running deficits and the public debt is high one would expect the pressures on the House to favor retrenchment of expenditures. On the other hand, when the government has a surplus and the public debt is low the pressures on the House should be to expand expenditures. We cannot show a clear causal relationship between these external variables and specific structural changes; rather, the intention is to show that the forces for structural changes vary with the state of the federal government's finances. When said finances are in good shape, pressure to change structures to accommodate increased expenditures will be ascendant; when they are in poor shape, pressure to change structures in order to decrease expenditures will be ascendant. Thus, though we cannot show cause we can indicate the conditions under which structural change is likely to occur.

Second is the relationship between structural changes and appropriations decisions. In the 1867 to 1877–85 period, when Appropriations had control over expenditures, we expect that the committee will have attempted to maximize its power by cutting department requests and funding programs at a rate lower than the House wished. In addition, as the debates revealed, the Appropriations Committee's use of the Holman Rule for legislative purposes would further increase the committee's power. In short, during the pre-1880–85 reform period the Appropriations Committee should have acted as a bottleneck to legislation, thus enhancing its own power.

In the 1877–85 to 1920 period, when there were from three to eight separate committees appropriating, we expect to find the special interest committees funding programs more generously than did Appropriations

211

in the preceding period. Such increased funding, we expect, results in higher yearly increases in the total budget as well as higher increases in special interest appropriations. Testing these hypotheses entails examining both the total appropriations pattern and agricultural and rivers and harbors appropriations over the entire period to determine the effects of structural changes on decisions. The case of rivers and harbors appropriations is especially interesting because these expenditures have been regarded as a classic case of pork barrel politics (Buchanan and Tullock 1962; Ferejohn 1974; Shepsle and Weingast 1981). The costs for such programs are diffuse, especially before individual taxes formed any portion of governmental revenues, and the benefits are district-specific. Under rules where such expenditures are made by committees clearly and specifically attached to the involved interests, there should be an increase in expenditures and/or the number of funded projects. In short, we expect to find changes in decisions occurring concomitantly with changes in the structure of committees and, if the comments of the representatives voting to recentralize appropriations in 1919–20 were correct, a decrease in the rate of expenditures following 1920.

Third is the relationship between the House and the appropriating committees. Fenno (1966) and Schick (1980) have shown that the main constituency of the Appropriations Committee is the House membership, and one of Congress's goals is to "spend on its preferred programs, even if it must weaken the appropriations process in order to get its way" (Schick 1980, p. 417). The desire of members to fund their programs was present in earlier eras, as the debates over the reforms of the late nineteenth and early twentieth century clearly show. The House's continuing concern over the power of the Appropriations Committee allows us to test for relationships between appropriating committees' reports and House action under different structural conditions.

The final area of concern is the overall relationship among the exogenous economic variables, structural change, and appropriations decisions. We do not propose to put forward a model of these relationships, given the preliminary nature of the work and the difficulty in making the data district-specific. For example, to show that when the Rivers and Harbors Committee had appropriations power expenditures were greater than when the Appropriations Committee had funding power does not prove that individual members were maximizing. In order to show maximization the data would have to be compiled on a district-level basis. Shepsle, Wilson, and Weingast have constructed such a data set, and we await the results of their analysis. Our purpose here differs in that we seek to portray in broad strokes the effects of structural changes on money decisions and to indicate that the political actors making the structural changes were cognizant of their likely effects.

Reforming the House appropriations process

GOVERNMENT FINANCES AND THE REFORMS OF 1880–1885 AND 1919–1920

The decision to create a separate Appropriations Committee in 1865 came at a time when, due largely to the Civil War, budget deficits and national debt were at a high and Congress and the country were anxious to reduce expenditures. In the next 20 years the American economy was transformed. A comparison of the decade from 1850 to 1860 with the decade 1865–75 makes clear that the Civil War contributed to the industrialization of the United States. The three major indicators of industrial production used by economic historians are pig iron, bituminous coal, and railroad construction. Between 1850 and 1860 pig iron production increased 50 percent, bituminous coal production increased about 95 percent, and 20,000 miles of railroad track were laid. In contrast, between 1865 and 1875, pig iron production increased over 100 percent, bituminous coal increased over 150 percent, and over 40,000 miles of railroad tracks were built. This expansion of the American economy generated budget surpluses and lowered per capita national debt. In fact, from 1867 until 1894 the federal government ran budget surpluses each year, and in the process the per capita national debt fell linearly from $70.91 in 1867 to $17.80 by 1890. Thus, at precisely the time (1877–85) when House majorities were objecting to Appropriations' tight control over expenditures (from 1867 to 1878 federal expenditures decreased from $155.9 million to $145.3 million) the government was running surpluses and dramatically reducing the national debt.

In contrast to these favorable economic figures, the reforms of 1919 and 1920 were characterized by unfavorable economic figures. The cost of fighting World War I had by 1919 generated a $13,370,638,000 deficit and a per capita national debt of $242.54. Under these conditions it is reasonable to assume that there were pressures to retrench governmental expenditures. In addition, for the first time in the history of the United States both an individual and a corporate income tax had been collected to fund the war effort.

STRUCTURAL CHANGES AND COMMITTEE DECISIONS

Budget estimates from departments during the 1866 to 1880 period are neither readily available nor, when discovered, systematic enough to generate a valid time series. However, as the final appropriations bills make evident, there was no real increase in federal expenditures during the era of Appropriations Committee control. The committee utilized parliamentary timing and techniques as well as bargaining in the

213

conference committees to bottleneck money decisions. The result of these tactics was to increase the power of the committee over legislation. After 1872 the committee began to report its bills late in the legislative session – within two weeks of adjournment; and after the passage of the Holman Rule, the committee on four occasions added amendments to bills that prohibited final House-Senate passage. In the four years from Holman to the 1880 rules changes the committee three times kept yearly omnibus rivers and harbors bills from passing. Committee members also were able to keep amendments from being offered, either by timing the bills for late introduction or by exercising the special rules and privileges given to Appropriations legislation. Membership on the committee was restricted to representatives with relatively long tenure in the House, and apparently to those with fiscally conservative views. The available hearings on the appropriations bills and the debates show committee members always speaking for the need to economize or "retrench governmental expenditures." Debates on rivers and harbors and levee construction on the Mississippi River over the 1867–76 period invariably show committee members to be opposed to excessive spending on "creeks and miniature, trivial rivers." Their success in keeping the "Treasury from being opened to a committee scramble" is attested to by the minimal increases in governmental expenditures over the period.

The opening of the appropriations process to Rivers and Harbors in 1877 and Agriculture in 1880, and then in 1885 to five other committees, tied the appropriations powers to special interests. If the literature on structure-affecting decisions and the remarks of the House members opposing decentralization are correct we should find:

a higher average annual percentage increase in appropriations during the 1880 to 1916 period compared to the preceding 1866 to 1880 period

an immediate increase in expenditures for those departments and agencies directly under the control of an appropriating committee

the increases in appropriations that were the result of the structural changes to be independent of the state of the government finances

in the case of rivers and harbors bills, the reforms of 1880 and the House's general acceptance of the practice in 1885 yielding an increase in both the number of projects and the amounts expended.

We now turn to an analysis of these hypotheses.

Expenditures in the pre- and post-1880–1885 reform periods

In 1877 the House had passed special rules so that the rivers and harbors appropriation could bypass the Appropriations Committee. In 1880 the House passed a revision of the rules that allowed committees other than

Reforming the House appropriations process

Appropriations to pass money bills. The granting of monopoly rights to the committees responsible for rivers and harbors and agriculture bills was a major change signaling discontent with Appropriations' decisions. The 1885 rules changes, which extended monopoly rights to five other committees, were the logical cumulation of the changes made in 1880. The 1919-20 rules changes recentralized power over appropriations and should have resulted in a decrease in the average annual increment in the federal budget. Given that these rule changes alter the incentive structure of individual representatives, we expect to observe changes in the appropriations decisions associated with the different structures. Because change can be in either the intercept or the slope of the annual percentage increase or decrease in the federal budget, it is necessary to specify the changes we expect to observe. We expect that the structural reforms of 1867 will yield a significant downward slope. The shift in 1877 that allowed another committee to appropriate on its own should result in a significant positive change in the intercept because the House formally limited the power of the Appropriations Committee. However, the slope for the post-1876 period should not be significantly different because almost 90 percent of the total appropriations were still under the power of Appropriations. In short, the changes associated with limiting the Appropriations Committee's power will be short-term. The culmination of the movement to limit the power of Appropriations occurred in 1885, and we expect the slope of the post-1885 structural change to be positive and significant. Likewise, the 1919–20 change to recentralize power in Appropriations should result in a negative slope change.

In order to test these hypotheses we use disjoint piecewise regression analysis (Judge et al. 1983, p. 378; Kiewiet and McCubbins 1985a). We are interested in assessing the effects of structural reforms on budget changes over time, and we have an annual measure of the amount appropriated by the relevant committees. The dependent variable is the percent change in the budget from one year to the next; $t_2 - t_1/t_2$. Using percent change as a dependent variable both gives us a real measure of change and avoids statistical problems associated with first differencing. The independent variables are the reforms themselves and the associated changes in the incentives to committee members. Since we are using percent change as the dependent variable we can use an ordinary least squares estimation rather than first-order difference generalized least squares techniques. Preliminary data analysis revealed some obvious autocorrelation problems; thus, we use the Cochrane–Orcutt (1949) method for resolving the problem, and the results reported in the Table 8.1 are corrected via Cochrane–Orcutt. The effects of World War I on budget were removed by excluding the figures from 1916 through 1919.

With one exception the results are as predicted. The creation of a

Table 8.1. *The effect of structural reforms on money decisions,*
1967–1934

Reforms	B	(*t*)	Intercept	(*t*)
1867–1875	−.10	(−9.6)**		
1876	−.02	(−1.06)	.62	(3.85)*
1885	.16	(15.6)**	−.03	(−.17)
1920	−.12	(−3.5)*	.41	(2.43)*

Note: $R^2 = .94$; $N = 61$; $D - W = 2.1$.

separate Appropriations Committee with an emphasis on protecting the Treasury resulted in a significant and negative slope −.10 in appropriations. The recognition by the House in 1876 that the Appropriations Committee was not appropriating enough funds resulted in the predicted jump in the intercept (.62), and the full-fledged shift to a decentralized appropriations system yielded a positive and significant change in slope (.16). The shift to a decentralized system in 1920 resulted in the predicted significant decrease (−.12) in the slope of the line. The only aberration is that the intercept change for 1920 (.41) was significant at the .05 level. This shift is due to two factors. First, the effect of World War I on the budget obviously shifts the level of appropriations upward. Second, the cost of building a majority to pass the decentralizing reform was to increase the level of appropriations in the first budget passed under the new structure. Another indicator of the bargaining necessary to recentralize appropriations power was the increase in the size of the Appropriations Committee from 21 to 35 members. Shifting the data for the first budget to 1923 drops the intercept change to .07, which is not significant. In short, this test strongly supports our theory that changes in the structure shifted members' incentives to appropriate, and members behaved in a rational fashion.

The results for the total appropriations, though corroborative, do not prove the point because the total appropriations reflect the decisions both of special interest committees and of the Appropriations Committee. If structure affects decisions, then we should see immediate effects from the rules changes in 1877 and 1880 on the appropriations for both rivers and harbors and agriculture legislation. The argument is that in the 1867 to 1876 period the Appropriations Committee preserved and enhanced its power by monopolizing the appropriations agenda (Shepsle 1978, pp. 129–30, elaborates on this argument). Such monopoly rents were earned and used by committee members who converted them into institutional influence (Shepsle 1978, p. 129). During the heyday of Appropriations, the committee membership was small and came from a relatively limited number of senior members. Membership on Appropriations was not easy to obtain, and thus, in Shepsle's terms, influence was not dissipated. The reforms of 1880, though not increasing the membership of Appropriations, dissipated their influence by allowing over 30 other members (membership of Commerce and Agriculture) influence over money decisions. The 1885 change to allow five other committees to appropriate further dissipated the Appropriations Committee powers by both decreasing (by about half) the scope of their influence and increasing the number of members with influence over appropriations. In addition, the members of the new committees were self-selected, and therefore the likelihood that they would favor changing expenditure patterns increased.

Shepsle (1978, pp. 129–30) argues that when a committee is permeable (easy to gain membership on) the power of the committee is diminished. In the 1867–79 period, the committee was not permeable. There were 75 appointments to the Appropriations Committee; 58 men filled these positions. Thus, of the 1,300-odd members of the House during this period, less than 5 percent had a seat on Appropriations. In any given House less than 4 percent of the members could have a seat on Appropriations. In the contemporary House about 13 percent of the House membership has a seat on Appropriations (55 of 435). It is clear that appointment to the Appropriations Committee did not come easily in the period in which Appropriations had sole control over money bills. When the House voted in 1880 and in 1885 to divide the appropriations power it increased the permeability of the monopoly greatly. The 150-odd members of the 49th House appropriating committees constituted over 45 percent of the total House membership. Such changes in the number of individuals with a share of the appropriations process could only result in changed expenditure patterns. Fenno suggests this result when he comments on the difficulties in the Appropriations Committee in the 80th House (1947–49) due to the influx of new members (1966, p. 52). Under conditions of decentralized monopoly control, extreme permeability, and self-selected membership, the members of the new monopoly committees could be expected to enhance their influence by increasing appropriations in their domains.

Agriculture and rivers and harbors

The House Agriculture Committee made the first agriculture appropriation in 1880, and so no pre- and poststructural change test is possible. Given this date, however, the expectation is that agriculture appropriations will rise faster than the overall appropriations during the 1880 to 1920 period. Rivers and harbors bills had a legislative history dating back to the 1820s, and as a result a pre- and post-1877 reform analysis is possible. The expectation is that the committee responsible for the appropriation, beginning in 1877 (first budget, postreform), increases both the number of individual projects funded and the number of dollars spent. The rationale is straight forward. A House majority voted special monopoly rights to the committees in order to avoid the Appropriations Committee's fiscal conservatism; the "new" committees could enhance their influence and House support for their influence by expanding the number of recipients and increasing expenditures.

Testing the hypothesis for agricultural appropriations was relatively simple, given that each year from its inception (1880) there was both an agricultural and a total appropriations bill passed. If our thesis is correct, the annual increase in moneys for agriculture should be higher than the increase in total appropriations for the years 1880 to 1910. This is, in fact, a conservative test because about one-half of the total appropriations came from committees that had the same interest in increasing appropriations as did Agriculture. We are predicting that increases in agricultural appropriations will be higher than average in a period of high increases and that the percentage of the total budget devoted to agriculture will rise rapidly.

Testing these hypotheses entailed running separate regression analyses on the changes in the budget per year $(t_2 - t_1/t_2)$ for both agricultural appropriations and the overall budget. The specific hypothesis is that the slope for agricultural appropriations will be greater than the slope for overall appropriations. The results clearly support the hypothesis. The average change in agricultural appropriations is almost twice the change in the overall appropriation voted by the House. A brief look at these figures is illustrative. The average increase for agriculture exceeds the same figure for total appropriations eight of nine times from 1881 to 1889; on six occasions the increase is greater than 10 percent, and on three of these, greater than 50 percent. In the 1890 to 1916 period the agricultural appropriation exceeded its overall counterpart two-thirds of the time, with about one-half of these being greater than 10 percent and five being greater than 25 percent.

Figure 8.1 shows the rise of agricultural appropriations as a part of the overall budget. The figure shows that over the 1880 to 1916 period agricultural expenditures rose dramatically. In terms of cumulative increases in budgets over the period, agriculture rose 9,188 percent compared to a 452 percent increase in total expenditures. Thus, regardless of how calculated, the agricultural appropriations rose more dramatically than did total appropriations in the 1880–1916 period.

The test for the hypothesis concerning rivers and harbors legislation is twofold: (1) We present two graphic plots of the number of projects

218

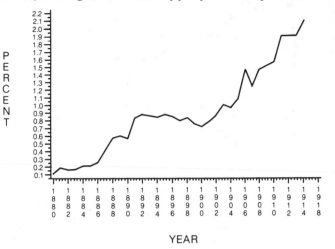

Figure 8.1. Agricultural appropriations as a percentage of total appropriations, 1880–1916

funded in omnibus rivers and harbors bills from 1867 to 1887 and the amounts of money expended in the same period; (2) we make a tabular analysis of rivers and harbors expenditures from 1867 to 1915. The expectation is that both the number of projects and the amounts expended dramatically increase in 1880 and again in 1886 and 1887 after the House's majority made decentralized appropriations a general principle. Figures 8.2 and 8.3 show the number of projects funded by bill from 1867 to 1887 and the amount of money expended over the same period. Table 8.2 shows the average appropriation for rivers and harbors omnibus bills from 1867 to 1876, 1877 to 1886, and 1887 to 1915. In addition, the table shows the ratio of growth for each of the three periods.

Figures 8.2 and 8.3 demonstrate the increases both in projects funded and in amounts spent beginning in 1880. The number of projects funded increased from slightly over 200 in 1879 to over 350 in 1880 and from approximately 330 in 1886 to over 400 in 1887. The amount appropriated moves from less than $7 million in 1880 to about $11 million in 1882 and over $15 million in 1887. It is clear that the change in structure generated immediate increases in numbers of projects funded and slightly more gradual increases in amounts appropriated.

Table 8.2 shows a large percentage increase (84.3 percent) in the 1877 to 1886 period, when the appropriations power was limited to three committees. The average appropriation in this period was $14.65 million, compared to $7.18 million in the period of Appropriations'

219

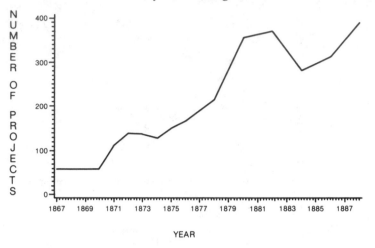

Figure 8.2. Number of rivers and harbors projects appropriated, 1867–87

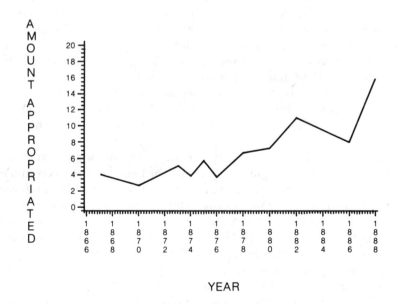

Figure 8.3. Total amount appropriated for rivers and harbors projects, 1866–88 (in millions of dollars)

220

Table 8.2. *Rivers and harbors: annual increase in expenditures compared to total expenditures, 1867–1916*

Years	Congress	Percent increase	Average approp. (%)	Total approp. (% increase)	Difference in % approp. to R&H
1867–1876	41st–45th	−23.1	7.18	−13.1	−10.0
1877–1886	46th–49th	84.3	14.65	18.4	69.6
1887–1915	50th–63rd	345.6	30.12	309.3	36.3

control. During the 1887 to 1915 period the average appropriation was $30.12 million. Comparable figures for the total budget increases in the same three periods reveal that during the heyday of Appropriations rivers and harbors expenditures went up less than the total budget (actually were cut more), whereas during the second period rivers and harbors expenditures went up 70 percent more than total outlays. In the period of full decentralization the rivers and harbors expenditures went up only 36 percent more than total outlays. The results show that in the period of several appropriating monopolies, expenditures in special areas rose more quickly than did total expenditures, with the largest differences coming in the period of limited monopolies. Piecewise regression analyses of the entire 1867 to 1919 time series corroborate these findings for both numbers of projects and amounts appropriated. That is, the slope changes in the post-1877 and post-1887 periods are significant at the .05 level, and the intercept for 1887 is statistically significant.

It is of course possible that the rise in expenditures shown herein simply reflects the rise in governmental surpluses over the period. There are, however, theoretical reasons to believe that such is not the case. Shepsle and Weingast (1981) argue that structure has effects that can be independent of exogenous effects. If they are correct, then the rise in agricultural and rivers and harbors outlays need not move with the status of government finances. In order to test this hypothesis we collected the yearly figures on governmental surpluses and/or deficits and normalized both the state of government finances and rivers and harbors expenditures by creating Z scores for both. The surplus measure is an extremely useful measure because from 1867 to 1893 the federal government ran surpluses, and the increased appropriations over the 1880 to 1915 period may be the result of member spending to reflect the available surplus. If, as we suspect, it is not, plotting the Z scores for both surpluses and rivers and harbors expenditures should show expenditures increasing at a faster rate than a simple reflection of available revenue would predict. Simple regression analysis was run on both sets of Z scores, and the results show that the slope of the rivers and harbors appropriations is positive after 1877 and relatively unrelated to government surpluses or deficits. Until 1872 the standardized scores for rivers and harbors funding are lower than the scores for budgetary surplus, meaning that the Appropriations Committee was not funding rivers and harbors bills with an eye to budgetary surpluses. In the 1874 to 1876 period, rivers and harbors funding runs slightly higher than the standardized budget scores; however, the two move together reasonably well in this period. The 1877 to 1885 period also shows rivers and harbors scores generally moving with the budget scores, although slightly higher. After the House's approval in 1885 of the decentralized appropriations process the two figures diverge sharply. That is, at precisely the point where budget revenues drop, the appropriations for rivers and harbors increase, indicating that the structural changes act independently of the government's financial situation.

Given the importance of asserting that structure acts independently of exogenous variables, we conducted a second test. The data on governmental surpluses/deficits used above are for all revenues combined minus expenditures. The Congress had control over only about half of these revenues – the tariffs – and the question of protective versus not-protective tariffs had long been a divisive one (Brady 1982). Thus, one might well hypothesize that special appropriations moved with tariff revenues rather than general revenues, the argument being that since Congress controlled tariff revenues through tariff bills it could fund special interests like agriculture and rivers and harbors by adjusting tariff bills as conditions dictated. If structure is independent of revenue generated by tariffs, then appropriations for agriculture and rivers and harbors should increase under the decentralized appropriations structure. In order to test this argument we converted the total value of tariff revenues received by year into their natural logarithms, then converted the total dollars appropriated for agriculture and rivers and harbors in a similar manner. We then regressed the results for each data set from 1867 to 1916.

The results clearly show that appropriations move independently of tariff revenues. The slope for tariffs is only .012 over the entire period whereas the comparable slope for rivers and harbors is .025. More importantly, there is the expected jump shift at the inception of the special power to appropriate independently. The slope for the post-1877 rivers and harbors appropriations is .031, clearly indicating independent effects. The slope for agricultural appropriations (1880 to 1916) is .056 with a major upward shift occurring in the 1886–88 period immediately after a House majority approved the fully decentralized appropriations system. The slope differences between the two appropriations lines relative to the steady state slope observed for the tariff revenue line shows that the structural changes of the 1880–85 period resulted in increased expenditures that were independent of tariff revenues.

Regional and pork barrel politics

We have argued that the reasons underlying this result are that the 1877 and 1885 reforms created new monopolies and that the members of the specialized committees self-selected their committee assignments specifically to appropriate more money. It was only by appropriating more money that members could satisfy the House, which created their monopolies, and build personal influence. Because both rivers and harbors and agricultural legislation affected directly almost all congressional districts, we expected and found (for rivers and harbors) an increase in the number of projects funded. Rivers and harbors legislation is of special interest because it is a classic case of specific benefits (projects in districts) coming from diffuse unspecified sources (Buchanan and Tullock 1962). This argument suggests that prior to the 1880 rule changes the Appropriations Committee would have decided rivers and harbors expenditures in a non–pork barrel fashion. Given the relatively high levels of party voting prevalent in this era and the strong "bloody shirt" politics of the 1867–76 period, we expect rivers and harbors legislation to have a strong regional flavor prior to the late-1870s to 1880 period. Table 8.3 shows the number of projects and the total dollar value by region for the 1867 to 1886 period.

The data show that for more than half of this period the eastern and midwestern sections received more projects and money than did southern and border state regions. It was not until 1878 that the South received a million dollars or more in projects. The Midwest received this amount in each appropriation and the East in three-quarters of the appropriations during the 1867 to 1886 period. In the first postreform appropriations (1878) both the southern and border state regions received substantial boosts; the East and Midwest were cut back in dollars while the number of projects increased.

The sectional bias after the Civil War and before the 1876 compromise is a function of committee assignments. From 1867 (39th House) until 1873 (42nd House) no southerner had a seat on Appropriations, and seven of the nine members came from midwestern (four) and eastern (three) states. It is not until the 1878–80 period that the South receives substantial representation on the Appropriations Committee. When in the 46th House the decision was made to allow Commerce to appropriate for rivers and harbors, the South had 20 percent of the committee seats and Border state representatives had 25 percent of the seats. The

Table 8.3. *Rivers and harbors: number of projects and total dollars appropriated by region, 1867–1886*

Year	East		Midwest		South		Border		West	
	(n)	($)	(n)	($)	(n)	($)	(n)	($)	(n)	($)
1867	23	1.59	33	2.21	1	.20	1	.08	1	.03
1870	31	.83	35	1.43	7	.27	2	.13	1	.03
1871	44	1.26	40	1.48	17	.51	4	.10	3	.24
1872	55	1.36	55	1.71	23	.86	3	.10	4	.23
1873	55	1.55	37	1.94	20	.81	11	.62	3	.17
1874	47	.90	47	1.96	20	.72	5	.14	5	.17
1875	55	1.30	52	2.39	26	.94	9	.87	7	.31
1876	34	.92	58	1.55	32	.91	6	.18	13	.24
1878	49	1.84	74	2.14	60	1.63	17	.89	7	.19
1880	79	1.66	102	1.90	105	2.20	33	1.06	13	.40
1882	91	2.22	87	2.72	119	3.34	36	1.70	16	.97
1884	61	1.93	72	2.28	97	2.58	25	1.83	19	.81
1886	87	2.58	66	1.50	114	2.80	23	.72	9	.35

Note: Dollar amounts are in millions.

immediate effect on appropriations is evident in the table. Though we cannot show decisively that after 1877 rivers and harbors decisions were based on members maximizing, we can conclude that at the aggregate level many of the signs of a universal pork barrel (Shepsle and Weingast 1981) are present.

The evidence for the effects of structural change on money decisions is impressive. Decentralizing the appropriations power by creating seven committees with monopoly control over special interests resulted in higher increases in the total budget outlays, higher increases in appropriations for rivers and harbors and agriculture independent of government's financial position, and clear indications of pork barrel politics in the rivers and harbors bills. But what of the Appropriations Committee's behavior during the period in which power was decentralized? If the committee behaved differently from the specialized committees, the case for structural change would stand in great relief. The only money bill that was controlled by appropriations throughout the 1867–1915 period is the Legislative Appropriations Act. The committee retained control over "deficiency and sundry civil" appropriations, but these bills cannot be compared over time. The only comparable data are, then, the House Appropriations Committee's funding of the legislative budget.

Over the 1860 to 1915 period the House grew from 243 members to 435 members, an increase of about 89 percent. One would therefore

Table 8.4. *Average percent change in legislative budgets, 1867–1878*
and 1880–1915

Years	Structure	Mean change	Standard deviation
1867–1879	Appropriations sole power	−.21	12.6
1880–1915	Appropriations shares power	2.62	3.9

expect pressures from House members to increase the legislative budget. Moreover, during this period the workload of the Congress increased greatly (Cooper 1975), which should have generated increased demand for resources. Table 8.4 shows the average annual increase in legislative appropriations over the years 1867–1915.

The table shows that the Appropriations Committee's behavior did not vary greatly over the entire time period. In the first period the average increase was −.21 whereas in the second period the average increase was only 2.62 with a lowered standard deviation. These figures are all the more impressive when compared to the average increases in total appropriations (over 6 percent) and in agriculture and rivers and harbors (over 10 percent) over the 1880–1915 period. In short, the behavior of the committee did not change markedly during an era when specialized committees increased appropriations greatly. The committee members by their behavior during the period justified the conclusions of Good and other reformers that Appropriations would be a "watch dog of the Treasury."

APPROPRIATING COMMITTEES AND THE HOUSE

The reforms of 1880 and 1885 were in large part a question of the power of the Appropriations Committee. A majority of the House in 1880 and again in 1885 wished to strip power from the committee and to distribute it across a wider spectrum of the membership. Thirty-odd years later, another majority voted decisively to return the appropriating power to the committee in an attempt to retrench expenditures and manage the war debt. In one sense the questions about the power of the Appropriations Committee are fundamentally questions about levels of funding for programs of concern to House members. There appears to be constant pressure on the committee to increase appropriations in order to satisfy House members. When asked why the Appropriations Committee had approved such large increases in the federal budget during the 1960s, chairman George Mahon (D-Tex.) replied:

We do need to impose greater discipline on our ourselves.... But when we deal with all of the 435 Members of this body, then we have to do the best we can under the circumstances. The Congress and the country must come to the position of supporting a greater degree of restraint than we now have.

Schick 1980, p. 439

Fenno (1966) also documents the pressure on the committee to fund programs and (1973) makes the House membership the committee's primary constituency. It seems to be the case that the Appropriations Committee's relationship with the House has always been of primary importance. "The Committee is subject to two sets of expectations – one holding that the Committee should supply money for programs authorized by the Congress and the other holding that the Committee should fund these programs in as economical manner as possible" (Fenno 1966, p. 410).

The committee's dilemma is that its members' power is enhanced when it can act as a bottleneck to legislation and can successfully reduce expenditures. The House majority that reduced the committee's powers in 1880 and 1885 obviously felt that the committee had not appropriated enough to satisfy members' demands for funding. We have seen that the effect of the structural changes of 1880–85 was to increase expenditures, particularly in areas where special interest committees were formed. We have not, however, examined the relationships among appropriating committees, executive department requests, and House action.

The underlying cause of the reforms of 1880 and 1885 was Appropriations' failure to adequately fund projects. The debates of 1880 and 1885 demonstrated the strength of members' objections to Appropriations' policies. When the House created a new set of monopoly committees based on special interests they expected a rise in expenditures; and, as we have seen, they got it. When, in turn, they recentralized authority in the president and in the Appropriations Committee they expected a lower rate of growth in expenditures, and that obtained. If the creation of special interest committees with monopoly appropriating powers yielded these results in the aggregate, the effects should also show in the relationships among executive department requests, committee action, and House reaction to committee reports. The expectations are that (1) during the period of special interest monopoly appropriating committees' executive budgets often increase; (2) in the postreform era (from 1921) executive requests are cut far more often than raised; (3) in the period of monopoly committees the House is more inclined to cut committee requests or alternatively to raise them less; and (4) in the postreform period the House is more inclined to raise committee reports.

In order to test these hypotheses we collected executive department requests, appropriating committee reports of funding, and the House's floor action on committee reports for the years 1888 to 1948. It would have been preferable to have the same data from 1867 onward, but both budget requests and committee reports are spotty, and thus comparisons to the post-1888 period are inappropriate. The data for committee action on executive requests were collected for all rivers and harbors and agriculture bills and the legislative budget bill. The data sets are complete (1888–1948) for the agriculture and legislative appropriations. Unfortunately, the rivers and harbors bills are not comparable after 1921; thus, we use rivers and harbors expenditure data only up to 1916. Utilizing both the legislative and agriculture histories over the entire period gives us the actions of the Appropriations Committee.

There are 30 separate agricultural appropriations in the 1888–1916 period; of these the Agriculture Committee cut the department request 17 times and raised it 13. On nine occasions the committee changed the request by greater than 10 percent, six times raising and three times lowering it. In contrast, during the 1920 to 1948 period there were 29 committee actions on requests, and of these 25 were cuts and four were raises. There were eight cuts of 10 percent or greater and two raises of over 10 percent. In terms of a simple count of cuts and raises, the Agriculture Committee raised estimates far more often than did the Appropriations Committee; and when they made nonincremental decisions raises outnumbered cuts two to one. In contrast, when the Appropriations Committee acted in a nonincremental fashion they cut requests at a four-to-one ratio to raises.

The same analysis of the legislative appropriations reveals a different result. In 31 decisions during the 1886–1916 period Appropriations cut requests 28 times; in 29 decisions during the 1920 to 1948 period, 25 times. In both periods the committee cut requests by over 10 percent on a number of occasions, and in neither period did they raise requests by over 10 percent. Data by committee and period on average change of requests are presented in Table 8.5.

The results show that the Appropriations Committee actions in regard to requests are consistent over the entire period. Requests in both periods were cut, regardless of the interest involved. The cuts averaged 3.3 percent in agriculture and 5.2 percent in the legislative requests during the 1920 to 1948 period. In contrast, when agricultural requests were handled by the Agriculture Committee, requests were raised by an average of 3.5 percent. The Rivers and Harbors Committee was more extreme, raising presidential requests by an average 24.5 percent, although the variance of 60.8 shows that great swings in action on requests were prevalent. In sum, the results show that different structures resulted in different treatment of budget requests, and that the difference is in the expected direction.

227

Table 8.5. *Selected appropriating committees: average annual change in requests*

Years	Appropriations Committee only (legislative)		Agriculture (1888–1910) Appropriations (1920–1948) (agriculture)		Rivers & Harbors (rivers & harbors)	
	(mean) change	(s.d.)	(mean) change	(s.d.)	(mean) change	(s.d.)
1886–1916	−3.5	2.6	3.5	14.5	24.5	60.8
1920–1948	−5.2	7.8	3.3	13.7	na	na
Difference	−1.7		−6.8		na	na

The question of House floor action on committee reports is complicated by the fact that in most cases throughout its history the House has accepted with little modification the committee report. The reasons for this behavior are reasonably straightforward. First, the floor is not a very good place to take on a detailed appropriations bill because the committee members have expertise and generally the noncommittee members do not have the time or expertise to fight. Second, the structuring of the House's rules both on the floor and in the Committee of the Whole favored the appropriating committee. Third, and most important for our purposes, the structure of the committees making the expenditure has been approved by a majority of members. Under these conditions it is not surprising that the House's actions on committee reports not greatly alter committee decisions. Nevertheless, we expect that whatever variance is left to be explained will be in the hypothesized direction. That is, the House will increase committee appropriations less in the 1888–1916 period than in the post-1921 period. In this analysis we include the House's reactions to the total budget as a baseline for the analysis of specific appropriations. Table 8.6 shows the average annual change in committee reports by area and by committee over the two separate structures.

House floor action on committee bills does not alter committees' decisions much in either period. This is attested to by the low average change figures. However, what limited changes there are move in the predicted direction. The House added an average of .325 to agriculture appropriations coming from the Agriculture Committee; when the Appropriations Committee handled the agriculture bill the House added

Table 8.6. *Average annual changes in selected committee reports by the whole House*

Years	Appropriations Committee only		Agriculture (1888–1916) Appropriations (1920–1948)		Rivers & Harbors		Mixed (1888–1916) Appropriations (1920–1948)	
	(legislative)		(agriculture)		(rivers & harbors)		(total)	
	(mean) change	(s.d.)	(mean) change	(s.d.)	(mean) change	(s.d.)	(mean) change	(s.d.)
1888–1916	−.08	1.26	.38	1.70	.41	1.96	−.01	1.02
1920–1948	.08	.49	.43	6.04	na	na	.58	2.10

an average of .425 to the committee report. The figures for the total budget follow the same pattern. Specifically, when appropriations bills were mixed the House cut reports .01 on the average whereas in the post-1921 period they added an average .58 to reports. On the legislative budget the Appropriations Committee's decisions were cut an average .08 in both periods. Interestingly, and somewhat in contrast to these results, in spite of the large increases in rivers and harbors appropriations over the 1887–1916 period the House increased appropriations slightly.

THE SPECIAL CASE OF THE 1919–1920 REFORMS

The structural reforms of 1877 to 1885 are readily understandable in terms of members' desire to increase expenditures benefiting their constituents. Once the system was fully in place, about one-half of House members had a direct vote in appropriating funds. The recentralizing reforms of 1919–20 clearly eviscerated a system that spread decisional power over a large number of members. Why would a majority of the House agree to change the rules so as to create a new monopoly-rights committee with a reduced membership? The 1919–20 budget reforms were led by Representative Good and supported by the Republican leadership; thus, one might expect the reform to have been passed on a straight party vote. Such was not the case. The final vote, 200 for and 117 against, was not entirely a party vote: although over 80 percent of the Republicans voted for the reform, there was also solid Democratic support for the reform. Most interesting is the extent to which members of the committees about to lose power voted for the resolution. One might have expected Republican members of these committees at least to be cross-pressured to support the reform because the party leadership supported the charge. However, Democratic members might be thought to have clear reasons to vote against the reform. Interestingly, a majority of both Republicans and Democrats on the appropriating committees voted for the reform. The pattern was not, of course, unmixed. The three senior Republicans on Agriculture voted against the resolution, as did the two ranking Democrats on Agriculture. On the other appropriating committees a majority of the senior members, including chairmen and ranking members, voted to strip their own committees of appropriations power. How can these results be explained in light of our views of reforms?

Under the decentralized appropriations process each of the special interest committees had a monopoly over appropriations related to their interest. Members in those committees selected themselves, largely on the basis of interests in their districts. There were, for example, no representatives from urban districts on Agriculture; and in three Houses we have examined carefully, each member of Rivers and Harbors had at least one Corps of Engineers project. Given these conditions, there is little or no constraint on committee members to reduce expenditures. In fact, since the members of Agriculture know that Rivers and Harbors' and Naval Affairs' expenditures will rise, they are induced to vote greater expenditures in agriculture. The steady rise in expenditures benefiting constituent groups generated concern on the part of the House. By the time of the 1910–11 revolt against the Speaker, the House had created a number of committees to oversee expenditures in the various departments of government, and in 1912 they created a Select Committee on the Budget. The rationale as early as 1912 was that expenditures were getting out of hand.

This condition was exacerbated by the expenditures necessary to fund the First World War. The deficit budgets of 1917, 1918, and 1919 (over $40 billion) created an untenable fiscal situation. The behavior of the special interest committees during the 1917–19 period contributed to the sense of crisis. The agricultural budget increased 36 percent and rivers and harbors appropriations increased 20 percent at a time when per capita national debt rose from $28.77 to $242.54. The formal resolution (H.R. 324) in the 66th House to recentralize power in Appropriations came from the Select Committee on the Budget. The best explanation for the 1919–20 reform is that members recognized the dire financial straits the country was in, and they knew that only under conditions where all committees were constrained would there be the possibility of a solution. Under the decentralized monopoly structure it was not likely that expenditures would be checked; given these circumstances and the status of the government's finances, something had to change. A majority voted to restructure appropriations. The result, as has been shown, was a decrease in the rate of growth of government expenditures over a decade in which the economy grew rapidly. Recentralizing power in Appropriations meant a reduction in the number of members with a portion of the appropriations power; more importantly, the 35 members of Appropriations could increase their influence by reducing department requests, thus decreasing the rate of growth of expenditures. In short, when a majority of members perceived the magnitude of the problem, they shifted the problem to a centralized Appropriations committee and the responsibility away from themselves!

A micro factor that helps explain the House's decision to change the appropriations process was the changed nature of revenue sources. Shepsle and Weingast (1981) in their discussion of universal pork barrel use a term in their system of equations that implicitly represents a member's ability to calculate the benefits to his or her district based on what contributions the district makes to the federal budget through income taxes. Given this, a member can rationally decide pork barrel issues. Prior to the introduction of income taxes the revenues of the government were untargeted. That is, funds were generated from sources not directly attributable to members' districts. Under this condition members would be more likely to vote for increases in funds benefiting their districts. The costs of World War I made income taxes, both corporate and individual, an important source of government revenue; and though we cannot prove that members foresaw the greater costs to their districts, it is apparent from the debate of 1920 that some members recognized the argument. Representative Madden (R-Ill.), one of the reform's prime movers, argued:

Only a few years ago we had but 300,000 taxpayers.... Today we have 3,400,000 and it will not be long before we have 5,000,000 and these taxpayers are all alert to the need for economy. Extravagance such as has never been known before has existed throughout the Nation for a long period, and today we are confronted with a deficit more than $3,500,000,000. It is only by the most rigid system of economy that we can hope to pay this deficit with the revenues at our command. ...unless we register our votes in favor of this resolution we will have said by our actions that we are not in favor of economical reform in Government.

C.R., 66th Cong.; p. 8109

Though it cannot be proved that his explanation contributed to the final vote, it is a plausible explanation and one that some important members of the House accepted.

A SUMMARY

The results reported in this paper support the position of what some call the new institutionalism; that is, that endogenous structural factors have independent effects on policy outcomes. The decentralization of the appropriating power resulted in just what its proponents desired – an increase in expenditures. The increased expenditures were distributed by members through their committees to relevant constituents. The decentralization system with its built-in spending incentives began to create budget problems as early as 1910, and the House created committees to oversee expenditures. World War I created a deficit of unprecedented scope, and in the 1919–20 period the budget system was recentralized. The rationale for recentralizing was that only by shifting responsibility to one committee could expenditures be reduced. The results showed that those favoring budgetary restraint via centralizing responsibility were correct and that the new Appropriations Committee cut executive requests because doing so enhanced its power (Fenno 1966). Thus, in each reform proponents and opponents of the reforms knew what they wanted and created appropriate structural incentive systems.

The results constitute only a preliminary run at understanding a crucial era in the development of the United States House of Representatives. The post-Civil War era in American politics has often been noted for its benchmark characteristics. Wiebe refers to the era as *The Search for Order* (1966). Polsby documents "The Institutionalization of the House" during the 1890–1910 period (1968). Burnham (1970) and Schattschneider (1960) argue that there is a pre- and post-1896 system. Clearly, the era from 1877 to 1920 is replete with events that determined the shape of the modern House of Representatives. Though we cannot claim definitive understanding, we can outline an approach to the era that is compatible with other "new institutional" studies of the contemporary Congress. (See especially Ferejohn 1974; Kiewiet and McCubbins 1985a, 1985b., Shepsle 1979; Shepsle and Weingast 1981.)

We believe that the most fruitful approach to understanding the change in this era is as follows: In any given time period, "motivational, institutional, and environmental features hang together in a sort of equilibrium, with changes in one effecting and constraining adoptive responses in the others" (Rohde and Shepsle 1985). The post-Civil War period featured major changes in the House's environment, with the industrialization and rationalization of the economy and the changes in the electorate (both structural and behavioral) playing major roles. Structural reforms in the Congress are not limited to those discussed in this paper but also include Reed's rule changes, the heyday of the Speaker, the rise of House careerists, and the decline of the Speaker, among others. We assume that individual members' desires for election, reelection, and influence remained constant, with behavior varying only in how electoral and internal incentive structures shaped the way in which desires could be attained. This approach suggests that research in this period should specifically focus on how changes in the environment shaped reforms in the House's internal structure, and in turn how both together shaped public policy outputs.

NOTE

1 Congress in the nineteenth century did not meet as does the contemporary Congress. A Congress elected in 1878 would not sit in Washington until December of 1879. Thus, we list the Congress and the years it sat (in parentheses) as follows: 55th House (1897–99), although it was elected in 1896. If the reference is to a congressional election it is given as follows: 46th House (1880), or 55th House (1896).

REFERENCES

Brady, D., with J. Stewart. 1982. "Congressional Party Realignment and Transformations of Public Policy in Three Realignment Eras." *American Journal of Political Science* 26, 333–360.

Buchanan, James M., and Gordon Tullock. 1962. *Calculus of Consent.* Ann Arbor: University of Michigan Press.

Burnham, W. 1970. *Critical Elections and the Mainsprings of American Politics.* New York: Norton.

Clausen, Aage. 1973. *How Congressmen Decide: A Policy Focus.* New York: St. Martin's Press.

Cochrane, D., and G. Orcutt. 1949. "Application of Least Squared Regressions to Relationships Containing Auto-correlated Error Terms." *Journal of the American Statistical Association* 44, 32–61.

Cooper, Joseph. 1970. "The Origins of the Standing Committees and the Development of the Modern House." Houston: Rice University Press.

1975. "Strengthening the Congress: An Organizational Analysis." *Harvard Journal of Legislation* 12, 307–368.

1977. "Congress in Organizational Perspective." In Lawrence Dodd and Bruce Oppenheimer, eds., *Congress Reconsidered.* New York: Praeger.

Dodd, Lawrence, and Bruce Oppenheimer, eds. 1981. *Congress Reconsidered.* 2nd ed. Washington, D.C.: Congressional Quarterly Press.

Fenno, Richard. 1966. *The Power of the Purse: Appropriations Politics in Congress.* Boston: Little, Brown.

1973. *Congressmen in Committees.* Boston: Little, Brown.

Ferejohn, John. 1974. *Pork Barrel Politics.* Palo Alto: Stanford University Press.

Fiorina, Morris, and Charles Plott. 1978. "Committee Decisions under Majority Rule: An Experimental Study." *American Political Science Review* 72, 575–598.

Brady and Morgan

Judge, G., W. Griffiths, C. Hill, and C. Tsoung. 1983. *The Theory and Practice of Econometrics.* New York: Wiley.

Kiewiet, Roderick, and Mathew McCubbins. 1985a. "Congressional Appropriations and the Electoral Connection." *Journal of Politics* 47, 59–82.
1985b. "Presidential Influence on Congressional Appropriations Decisions." Paper presented at the annual meeting of the American Political Science Association.

McConachie, Lauros. 1898. *Congressional Committees: A Study of the Origin and Development of Our National and Local Legislative Methods.* New York: Crowell.

Mann, Thomas, and N. Ornstein, eds. 1981. *The New Congress.* Washington, D.C.: American Enterprise Institute.

Orfield, Gary. 1975. *Congressional Power: Congress and Social Change.* New York: Harcourt Brace Jovanovich.

Ostrom, Vincent. 1980. "Artisanship and Artifact." *Public Administration Review* 40, 309–317.

Polsby, Nelson, 1968. "The Institutionalization of the House of Representatives." *American Political Science Review* 62, 144–168.

Rohde, David, and Kenneth Shepsle. 1985. "The Ambiguous Role of Leadership in Woodrow Wilson's House." Paper delivered at the American Political Science Meetings, New Orleans.

Schattschneider, E. E. 1960. *The Semi-sovereign People,* New York: Holt.

Schick, Allen. 1980. *Congress and Money: Budgeting, Spending, and Taxing.* Washington, D.C.: Urban Institute.

Shepsle, Kenneth. 1978. *The Giant Jigsaw Puzzle.* Chicago: University of Chicago Press.
1979. "Institutional Arrangements and Equilibrium in Multidimensional Voting Models." *American Journal of Political Science* 23, 27–59.

Shepsle, Kenneth, and Barry Weingast. 1981. "Political Preference for the Pork Barrel: A Generalization." *American Journal of Political Science* 25, 96–112.

Wander, William. 1981. "Patterns of Change in the Congressional Budget Process, 1865–1974." Paper delivered at the annual meeting of the American Political Science Association, New York.

Wiebe, Robert, 1966. *The Search for Order.* New York: Hill & Wang.

Wilson, Woodrow. 1885. *Congressional Government.* Cleveland: World-Publishing.

9

The decline of party in the U.S. House of Representatives, 1887–1968

DAVID BRADY, JOSEPH COOPER, AND PATRICIA A. HURLEY

Voting on the basis of party in the contemporary U.S. House of Representatives is low when compared with similar institutions in other Western democracies (Jewell and Patterson, 1973; Turner and Schneier, 1970). Many scholars have commented on the consequences of the lack of partisan voting in Congress (Schattschneider, 1950; Burns, 1963, ch. 1). In general all have agreed that, given the disunity of the congressional parties, there must be ceaseless maneuvering to form majorities capable of governing. Some contemporary studies have refined this thesis by showing that partisanship varies across issue dimensions, and by degree of substance (Clausen, 1973; Froman and Ripley, 1965). However, political scientists have neglected an important aspect of voting on the basis of party in the House; namely, long-term trends in the overall levels of partisan strength. The work of Lowell (1902), Turner and Schneier (1970), and Shannon (1968) has highlighted some of the variations in overall levels of partisanship in the House but there are still more gaps than data. In short, we have not followed the admonition of V.O. Key (1964, p. 668) that the long-run view may yield an estimate of the role of party far different from that which emerges from the microscopic examination of yesterday's votes in the House or Senate.

Previously published work on partisanship in the House shows that there is considerable variation over time (Turner and Schneier, 1970; Shannon, 1968). Nonetheless the data are fragmentary, with the result that important information bearing on the character and patterns of change is not readily available. Moreover, insufficient attention has been paid to the fact that the impact of party on congressional voting is complex and multifaceted. Thus, often overlooked is that partisan voting involves and is determined by both the degree of intraparty unity and the

Reprinted from *Legislative Studies Quarterly* 4, no. 3 (August 1979): 381–408.

degree of interparty conflict (Cooper, Brady, and Hurley, 1977). For example, high levels of party unity on votes of low divisiveness do not testify to the strength of party as a determinant of voting, but rather to bipartisan or unanimous voting. Similarly, votes that combine high degrees of divisiveness with restricted degrees of internal unity also indicate that elements of weakness exist in the strength of party as a determinant of voting. In short, then, the impact of party on voting results from the combined effects of two facets or dimensions of voting. Both of these dimensions are important and must be taken into account. Stuart Rice (1928) recognized this problem when he developed an index of party likeness to complement his index of cohesion. John Grumm (1964) and Duncan MacRae (1970) have also contributed to our understanding of the multifaceted character of party as a basis for voting in legislatures. In this paper we use both unity and conflict measures as well as an overall measure of party strength that combines the two dimensions to examine the changing role of party in the House. The time period analyzed in this paper is 1887 (50th House) to 1968 (90th House).

Our strategy for analyzing the role of party in the House over time is to first discuss the character and pertinence of various measures of partisan voting and then to present party cohesion (unity), party voting (conflict), and party strength (overall) scores in the House from 1887 (50th House) to 1968 (90th House) and to comment on the changing patterns of partisan voting over time based on this record. Then, using the variables culled from contemporary legislative behavior research and utilizing regression techniques, an explanation of changes in levels of party strength is put forward. The importance of such an analysis is threefold: (1) if an explanation using variables culled from contemporary research can account for variance over time, the generalizability of current approaches and findings will be extended; (2) if the explanation can account for changing levels of partisan voting, then our understanding of its changing role in the House is improved; and (3) if the explanation is predictive then we can determine, within limits, under what conditions partisan voting will increase in the contemporary era.

THE HISTORICAL RECORD OF PARTY IN THE HOUSE

The four most commonly used measures of partisanship in Congress are the index of cohesion, the party vote score, the party unity score, and the index of likeness. As indicated above, the index of cohesion is simply an overall measure of partisan unity or cohesion on roll call votes.[1] The party vote score is a measure of the degree to which the parties differ from one another on roll call votes. As initially formulated by Lowell (1902), it measures the percentage of the time that 90 percent of one party opposes 90 percent of the other on roll call votes. In recent decades, however, party votes have generally been measured as the percentage of the time that 50 percent of one party opposes 50 percent of the other on roll call votes (Turner and Schneier, 1970). The party unity score measures unity or cohesion on party votes. As currently used, it measures the degree to which fellow partisans vote together on roll calls in which 50 percent of one party opposes 50 percent of the other.[2] The index of likeness is similar to the party vote score in its object. It focuses on division or conflict and measures the degree to which the parties differ from one another on roll call votes.[3]

It is obvious from our brief descriptions of these measures that they focus on different dimensions of partisan voting. The measures focus on either the unity dimension or the conflict dimension. Only the party unity measure taps a part of both dimensions – i.e., party unity on conflict roll calls – but it does so in a limited or segmented fashion. As a consequence, we need to supplement existing measures of the separate dimensions of partisan voting with a measure that combines their effects. In the following analysis, we therefore utilize measures of intraparty unity, interparty conflict, and a combined or overall measure of party strength.

Our measure of intraparty unity is the simple Rice index of cohesion, which is based on the percentage of Democrats and Republicans respectively who vote alike on a given roll call. Interparty conflict is measured by the percentage of times a majority of one party opposes a majority of the other party, and in Table 9.1 the percentage of times 90 percent of one party opposes 90 percent of the other party. The party strength variable is measured by multiplying the average party cohesion scores by the percentage of (50 percent vs. 50 percent) party votes in a given House. This measure is multiplicative because, of course, cohesion and conflict are interactive and not additive; that is, in order for party conflict to exist, the congressional parties must be unified and opposed. Thus the higher the party conflict score, the higher the intraparty cohesion and the interparty conflict; the lower the score, the less intraparty cohesion and/or interparty conflict. In sum, by using all three measures we get a more accurate picture of changing patterns of the impact of party on congressional voting.

Levels of party cohesion, party voting, and party strength from the 50th to the 90th Houses are shown in Table 9.1. The cohesion score was obtained by computing a simple index of cohesion (percent voting yea and nay) for both parties on all roll calls in each of the forty-one Houses. These data were also used to calculate the Rice cohesion score, the percentage of roll calls where a majority of one party opposed a majority of the other party, and the percentage of roll calls where 90 percent of one party voted against 90 percent of the other party. Finally, on the basis of these results, party strength scores for each House were calculated.

While the data in Table 9.1 show a decline in partisan voting over time in the House, the decline in party voting (conflict) and party strength (overall) is more pronounced than is the case for party cohesion (unity). We should note that we might expect the unity measures to lag behind the divisiveness measures since the index of cohesion gives credit for intraparty agreement that derives from bipartisan agreement. Aside from the overall trend, Table 9.1 indicates that the years from 1910 to 1940, the years from the overthrow of House Speaker Joe Cannon to the accession of Speaker Sam Rayburn, stand as a period of transition from the high scores of the era of party government to the far lower scores of the contemporary, decentralized House. In addition, the data indicate that the decline in partisanship, though continuing, has not occurred at a steady rate, but rather has proceeded at different rates in different decades. For example, it was checked somewhat by the Warren Harding landslide in 1920 and the emergence of the New Deal coalition in the 1930s.

In order to more precisely document the decline in partisan voting, the trend element was removed from the data on party voting and party strength by regressing both scores against time. The critical values for both regressions are the intercept, which is the value of party voting and party strength when time is set equal to zero, and the slope of the line (B), which is the change in party voting and party strength as time changes one unit. If there has been decline in partisanship, then the value of the slope should be negative; as time increases, the predicted values of partisanship should decrease. The results of both regressions show the severity of the decline. The intercept for party voting is 64.9 and the slope of the regression line is $-.52$. This clearly shows a decline in the levels of party voting over time. The data also indicate an approximately 25-year period when party voting was high (roughly 1890 to 1915) and a roughly 30-year low period (1940 to 1968). In short, party voting in the House has been declining in a linear fashion.

The results for both Democratic and Republican party strength show the same pattern. The intercept for Democratic party strength is 49.5 and the slope of the regression line is $-.49$. The intercept for Republican party strength is 54.6 and the slope is $-.62$. Both sets of results show that the overall impact of party on voting has clearly declined over time, and that the decline is linear. Thus, it seems fair to conclude that partisanship in the House, however measured, has declined.

What accounts for the decline of partisanship in the U.S. House over this time period? In order to answer this question, we turn to contemporary legislative behavior research to cull out the variables

Decline of party in the House, 1887–1968

Table 9.1. *Party voting, cohesion, and strength in the House of Representatives: 50th (1887) to 90th (1967) Houses*

Year elected	Congress	Party votes (proportion) 50% vs. 50%	90% vs. 90%	Average cohesion Dem.	Rep.	Party strength Dem.	Rep.
1886	50	51.1	8.7	58.9	77.8	30.9	39.8
1888	51	78.9	42.5	70.5	86.2	56.1	67.9
1890	52	45.4	4.2	55.9	73.8	25.2	33.3
1892	53	44.8	6.1	73.0	73.3	32.9	32.9
1894	54	68.5	24.8	67.3	58.0	46.2	40.0
1896	55	79.8	50.2	74.6	84.3	60.0	67.2
1898	56	77.2	49.8	73.8	83.8	57.0	64.7
1900	57	67.0	38.9	75.0	87.6	50.3	59.0
1902	58	89.7	64.4	83.2	83.9	74.7	75.6
1904	59	73.5	34.6	80.9	79.1	59.9	58.5
1906	60	57.1	26.3	78.6	89.3	45.0	50.7
1908	61	79.2	29.4	78.5	67.4	62.4	52.9
1910	62	59.5	23.0	69.8	73.5	42.0	44.4
1912	63	61.4	19.9	63.2	72.0	38.4	43.9
1914	64	58.6	21.7	67.0	72.1	39.5	42.5
1916	65	42.7	9.4	72.9	67.3	31.4	28.8
1918	66	44.9	14.9	67.2	75.4	30.2	33.8
1920	67	59.9	35.2	70.8	76.1	42.6	45.6
1922	68	58.7	13.4	59.4	73.9	41.9	43.7
1924	69	43.7	5.3	55.3	72.5	24.2	32.1
1926	70	48.6	5.6	64.6	65.1	31.9	31.9
1928	71	58.2	13.6	67.5	68.1	39.4	39.4
1930	72	57.7	13.8	60.0	57.0	34.8	33.1
1932	73	70.6	18.9	68.3	70.2	48.3	49.7
1934	74	59.9	14.2	64.4	68.0	38.4	40.8
1936	75	63.9	11.8	56.6	68.7	36.5	44.2
1938	76	71.4	17.6	65.4	74.2	46.2	52.5
1940	77	41.5	10.5	62.9	72.3	26.5	30.2
1942	78	49.4	9.6	59.9	73.0	29.4	35.8
1944	79	48.1	12.1	64.4	69.4	30.7	33.1
1946	80	44.8	12.7	65.1	76.5	29.3	33.8
1948	81	50.9	6.5	63.0	67.6	32.1	35.0
1950	82	64.1	4.9	61.8	65.2	39.7	41.6
1952	83	44.9	5.4	60.9	73.8	27.5	33.3
1954	84	42.3	6.7	68.5	61.4	29.0	25.6
1956	85	49.2	5.2	59.9	56.9	29.4	27.9
1958	86	52.8	5.0	62.5	62.3	33.4	32.9
1960	87	48.8	5.8	73.2	64.3	35.8	31.4
1962	88	51.7	8.6	73.5	67.4	38.5	34.8
1964	89	47.1	1.8	70.6	70.4	33.4	32.9
1966	90	35.8	2.9	67.7	68.3	24.5	24.5

associated with partisanship, and then formulate an explanation of party based on this literature.

LEGISLATIVE BEHAVIOR RESEARCH AND PARTY VOTING

The dominant view of contemporary political scientists holds that legislative behavior and legislative outputs are a result of various combinations of external and internal variables. That is, legislators must deal with groups, institutions, and forces that are formally external to the legislative body as well as groups, norms, and forces that are part of the internal organization of the legislative body.

Perhaps the most important external variable, at least in terms of time devoted to it by congressmen, is elections (Mayhew, 1974). While research directly linking voting behavior to elections has not revealed any clear pattern of relationships, there is evidence that freshmen congressmen vote in accordance with the party position more often than do their senior counterparts. The percent of freshmen in the House is an important variable because it measures the extent of electoral change. The higher the percent freshmen, the greater the electoral change; the lower the percent freshmen, the more stability. Weinbaum and Judd (1970) suggest that freshmen congressmen are more susceptible to party cues because they are not yet socialized to such cues as committees and state delegations. Moreover, it is during landslide and realigning elections that large numbers of freshmen congressmen are recruited, and some authors have suggested a connection between new members, partisan voting, and policy changes (Brady and Lynn, 1973). In his analysis of freshmen members in the 89th House, Fishel (1973, p. 163) asserts that "few groups could better meet the assumptions of responsible party government theorists than did these freshmen.... Democratic freshmen certainly provided the winning margins." Thus the number of freshmen congressmen may well be related to the levels of partisan voting in the House over time.

Contemporary political scientists have also found that party homogeneity, an external variable, and centralized leadership structure, an internal variable, seem to stand out as predictors of party voting in legislatures. MacRae (1952) found that in the Massachusetts legislature high levels of partisan voting were associated with homogeneous political parties located at different points on an SES continuum, and with a strong centralized leadership system. LeBlanc (1969), in a comparative study of twenty-six state Senates, found that partisan voting was higher in states where the constituency bases of the legislative parties were homogeneous and recognizably different from one another. Jewell and Patterson's (1973, p. 422) summary of party as a basis for voting

240

research also states that homogeneous parties and centralized leadership are most predictive of partisanship. Research on the U.S. Congress reveals the same general results.

The analysis of why partisan voting is low in the U.S. Congress is perhaps best summed up by Ralph Huitt (1961, p. 334):

The reformers model (party responsibility) has failed to attract support in Congress because it does too much violence to the political context in which members operate – that is, to the relationships of the members with the constituencies which they serve and must please, and to the internal power systems of the respective houses.

He goes on to argue that constituency-party cross pressuring and the decentralized leadership structure with power residing in committees are the specific factors accounting for low levels of party responsibility in Congress. In sum, party homogeneity, electoral change, and leadership structure are viewed as important determinants of party in the House. The House in the modern era certainly has been characterized by heterogeneous parties (especially the Democrats), low membership turnover, and a weak, decentralized leadership structure.

Two other external variables that impact the level of partisan voting in the House are the extent to which the parties are in conflict and the partisan affiliation of the president. The first variable – partisan conflict – taps the degree of ideological conflict between the parties as electoral coalitions; the greater the difference between parties, the greater the impact of party on voting in the House. Thus, during an era of intense partisan differences (e.g., 1894 to 1900, 1930 to 1938), partisan voting in the House should be high. The second variable – president's party – also impacts partisan voting in the House; if the president and the majority in the House share party affiliation, partisanship is likely to rise and vice-versa. The president's legislative requests set an agenda for the majority party and, with the backing of the president, the majority leadership has a critical source of leverage that acts to increase party cohesion (Truman, 1959; Sorauf, 1972, pp. 333–334). Additionally, the minority party may unite in opposition to the presidential program and thus contribute to higher levels of partisanship.

Our analysis utilizes the external and internal factors discussed above to account for variance over time in levels of aggregate partisan behavior in the House. Specifically, party homogeneity, party conflict, the partisanship of the president, and electoral change or membership turnover are the external variables used to explain aggregate partisan behavior. The internal variable used is centralized leadership structure as measured by the Speaker's prerogatives and the strength of the party caucus. Our strategy is first to determine if the external variables alone can be fit to a main effects regression model and then add the internal variables to determine their impact on party cohesion, party voting, and party strength. The question of the relative impact of the external and internal variables is of course both relevant and important. To determine the relative impact of these variables we shall first analyze separately both the external and internal variables and then put forward and test a model that sorts out the relative effects of the external and internal variables.

External variables and party voting

The first external variable to be used is party homogeneity. There is, of course, a problem in finding a measure of party homogeneity over time, since homogeneity might be measured in any number of ways. In a time series analysis of the type presented here, party homogeneity can only be crudely approximated since one needs a summary measure for each House under consideration and that measure must be roughly comparable over time. Since our purpose is to demonstrate that partisanship varies with homogeneity, a crude measure can show whether the direction of the hypothesis is correct. For the Democratic party, during the period under consideration we can use the traditional Northern/Southern and Border state division to estimate party homogeneity. As the percentage of Southern and Border or Northern Democrats rises above 50 percent, Democratic constituencies become more similar. Thus, if three-fourths of the congressional Democrats come from Northern (or Southern and Border) states, the dominant faction in the party is more homogeneous than if only 55 percent come from Northern states. Our measure of homogeneity taps the dominant faction of the party by measuring the percentage above 50 percent the dominant faction constitutes. For example, if 65 percent of the Democrats come from Southern and Border states, the value is 15, whereas if 75 percent come from the same states, the value is 25.

For the Republicans, party homogeneity is also measured by a regional split, although the cleavage is not so well defined as for the Democrats. Our measure is the percentage of congressional Republicans coming from Eastern or non-Eastern states. While the meaning of this regional split is not as constant over the time period under consideration as is the North-South Democratic split, it has been considered as a viable way of characterizing the Republican alignment in the House (Deckard and Stanley, 1974). The hypothesis is that as party homogeneity increases, levels of partisanship also increase.

The second external variable is electoral change. We have operationalized electoral change in terms of membership turnover, or the percentage of freshmen congressmen. The hypothesis is that the higher the percent freshmen, the higher the level of partisanship. The partisanship of the incumbent president is operationalized as a dichotomous variable. When the president and the House majority is truncated (that is, the president and the House minority are the same party) the variable equals zero. The assumption is that when the president is of the same party as the majority in the House, the level of partisanship will be higher. The final external variable is the degree of party conflict. This variable is operationalized by using Ginsberg's (1972) measure of party conflict on economic issues.[4] The hypothesis is that the greater the level of party conflict, the greater the level of party strength.

In order to test these hypotheses, multiple regression analysis was employed. Party cohesion, party voting, and the combined party strength variable were regressed on the four external variables. Table 9.2 presents the results.

The results for party cohesion (unity dimension) show that, for the Democrats, party conflict, dominant faction, and the partisanship of the president have the predicted relationships. The greater the party differences, the more homogeneous the party, and the presence of a Democratic president are all associated with greater party unity. The electoral turnover variable does not behave in the posited manner. However, for the Republicans, electoral turnover and partisanship of the president are positively related to party cohesion. While both the dominant faction and the party conflict variables are positively related to party cohesion, they have relatively high standard errors. Thus, the relationship must be discounted.

The results for party voting (conflict dimension) show that partisan electoral conflict, electoral turnover, and partisanship of the president are in that order positively related to party splits for both parties. The dominant faction variable does not add much predictability or explanatory power to the party voting equations. The multiple R's for both parties are above .65 indicating a respectable fit of the data.

The party strength section of Table 9.2 (overall impact) shows important differences between the parties. Republican party strength is about equally affected by electoral party conflict, electoral turnover, and the partisanship of the president, with dominant faction insignificant. Democratic party strength is most significantly affected by electoral party conflict, with partisanship of the president and dominant faction having significant but secondary effects on party strength. In both regressions the multiple R's are .71 indicating a reasonable fit.

In sum, the table shows that the external variables have differential effects depending upon the facet of partisan voting being measured, and differential effects depending upon which political party is under

243

Table 9.2. *Impact of external variables on party cohesion, voting, and strength*

External variables	B		Beta		Standard Error	
	Dem.	Rep.	Dem.	Rep.	Dem.	Rep.
Party cohesion						
Electoral turnover						
(percent freshman)	−.11	.38	−.14	.44	.11	.13
Partisanship of president	3.02	7.85	.18	.42	2.29	2.51
Dominant faction	.20	.26	.23	.20	.12	.19
Party conflict	19.56	5.90	.48	.13	6.17	6.78
(constant)	51.28	38.81				
Multiple R					.58	.63
Party voting						
Electoral turnover	.38	.39	.26	.28	.19	.20
Partisanship of president	6.19	6.25	.20	.20	3.49	3.95
Dominant faction	.22	−.02	.13	.01	.20	.29
Party conflict	32.89	33.15	.43	.43	10.48	10.65
(constant)	23.52	37.85				
Multiple R					.68	.65
Party strength						
Electoral turnover	.18	.50	.14	.37	.17	.18
Partisanship of president	6.00	9.37	.21	.32	3.42	3.59
Dominant faction	.28	.15	.19	.07	.18	.27
Party conflict	35.91	28.74	.52	.39	9.21	9.68
(constant)	5.36	6.87				
Multiple R					.71	.71

consideration. The important point is that each of the external variables has some effect on partisanship in the House. Thus it is clear that the external variables we have culled from the literature have some longitudinal validity. Of course, the weights differ depending upon both party and which dimension of party strength is under consideration. In addition, the results show that when electoral turnover is high, parties are homogeneous and in conflict, and the president is of the same party, then party cohesion, party voting, and party strength are also likely to be high. The long-run decline in party strength in the House is clearly related to the increased stability of the membership, a decline in electoral party homogeneity and conflict, and an increasing tendency to have a president of one party and a Congress of the other party. All of these, in turn, are characteristics of the post-World War II House.

One possible objection to these results is that the regression results obtained are the result of a spurious correlation of both the dependent and the independent variables with time, or what Campbell and Stanley (1963, p. 20) call "history as a threat to validity." To overcome this difficulty in the following section, we operationalize time in terms of the changes in the internal structure of the House, and add it to the regression analysis as an independent variable.[5]

Internal structure and voting patterns

The analysis clearly shows that the external variables affect partisanship in the House. The analysis as presented thus far is deficient, however, in that it says nothing about internal variables, which others have shown to be related to levels of partisan voting. The internal variable we have chosen to test is centralized leadership structure, as measured by the Speaker's formal prerogatives and the strength of the party caucus. Operationalizing the formal powers of the Speaker and the strength of the caucus presents two problems. First, over the time period under consideration, these two variables combine to form three distinct periods of internal structure. The first period, 1886–1910, corresponds to an era in which the Speaker's prerogatives were substantial and the party caucus was strong. When these conditions are present the levels of party cohesion, party voting, and overall levels of party strength should be high. During the second period, 1911–1939, decentralization of power to committee chairmen took place due to the reduction in the Speaker's powers and the declining role of the caucus. However, the caucus was utilized occasionally during this era, thus distinguishing it from the 1940–1968 period. This last period is characterized by decentralized leadership structure and the atrophy of the caucus (Cooper, 1970; Diamond, 1976, pp. 112–116). Under these conditions party cohesion, party voting, and overall levels of party strength can be expected to be low.

Second, these variables can only be measured on a nominal scale and hence do not meet the assumptions of regression analysis, which requires interval level data. The problem was solved by incorporating the three periods of internal structure into the analysis as dummy variables. This is a technique used often in econometrics for introducing nominal variables into regression analysis (Blalock, 1972, pp. 498–502). Dummy variables are binary, taking a value of one if a condition is met, zero if it is not. Two dummy variables are necessary in order to represent the three periods of diverse organizational situations or conditions. Specifically, this analysis includes two dummy variables: one takes on a value of one for the condition of strong centralized leadership structure as measured by the Speaker's formal powers (50–61st Houses, or 1887–1910), and zero for non-centralized leadership. The second dummy takes the value of one for the condition of substantive use of the caucus by the party (the 50–61st Houses and 62nd–75th Houses, or 1887–1938) and zero for the 1939–1968 time period. Thus we have three distinct periods: the first (50 to 61st Houses) has both a strong Speaker and use of the caucus, the second (62nd to 75th Houses) has some substantive use of the caucus, and the third (76th to 90th Houses) has neither characteristic of centralized leadership.

Our use of dummy variables assumes equal slopes; that is, there is no interaction between the two dummy variables. In this case only the constant term will be affected. The intercept for the modern era is the base to which we compare the effects of the other two sets of structural conditions. The intercepts for these two eras are obtained by adding the coefficient of the appropriate dummy to the value of the intercept obtained when $D_1 = D_2 = 0$. Our hypothesis is that in the years of centralized leadership power in the House, with both a strong Speaker and a strong caucus present, party cohesion, party voting, and party strength should be higher than in the other two eras regardless of the effects of the external variables; thus, we expect the highest intercept. In the years after the revolt against the Speaker, party discipline was still relatively strong, although less rigid than it had been perviously. While party unity and conflict in the House were not as high as in the previous era, the effects of party organization were more strongly felt than in the current House. We expect an intercept lower than that of the previous years, yet higher than that which the modern House will exhibit. In the modern House, where committees are the central actors, and where party leadership is decentralized, we expect the lowest levels of partisan voting and consequently, the lowest value for the intercepts. The results of the dummy variable regression are presented in Table 9.3.

The results for party voting (conflict dimension) and party strength (overall impact) fit the hypothesis exactly. That is, party voting and party strength are highest in the 1890–1910 period and lowest in the 1940–1968 period. In regard to party cohesion (unity dimension) differences exist between the 1911–1939 and 1940–1968 periods but they are not significant. This reflects the fact, noted earlier, that party cohesion has not declined to the extent that party voting and party strength have declined. The major factor underlying the lesser decline in party cohesion is the over-time increase in the number of unanimous (less than 10 percent dissenting) roll calls. The results here thus can be discounted since they reflect a limitation in the measure and we can conclude that our findings do indicate that internal variables affect partisanship in the House.

Both sets of variables – internal and external – have been shown to be related to our measures of party as a determinant of voting in the House.

Table 9.3. *Effects of internal variables on partisanship in the U.S. House as measured by intercepts*

Internal variables	Party voting	Party cohesion		Party strength[a]	
		Dem.	Rep.	Dem.	Rep.
1890–1910 Centralized leadership plus caucus	66.6	71.6	77.9	48.43	52.14
1911–1939 Caucus	55.6	64.3	69.5	35.88	38.67
1940–1968 Neither centralized leadership nor caucus	49.5	65.3	68.2	32.27	33.76

[a] Divided by 100.

The more important question is what is the relationship between the external and internal variables and which has the greater relative weight in explaining partisanship in the House. In the final section we propose a model to account for partisan voting in the House and then test the model. Since our concept of party strength taps both the unity and conflict dimensions of partisanship in the House and can be operationalized to provide an overall measure of the impact of party, we shall rely on it alone in defining and testing the model.

A MODEL OF PARTY STRENGTH

In seeking to identify the relative influence of external and internal factors as determinants of party strength, our presumption is that external factors possess the greater importance and impact. This presumption derives from the character of democratic legislatures as organizations and the resulting conditions or requirements for centralizing power within them.

In the House, as in other democratic legislatures, party plays a primary role in ordering and integrating internal structures and processes (Cooper, 1975). On the one hand, party exists as the most stable and comprehensive basis of coalition, thus providing the most stable and comprehensive basis for organizing and assembling majorities. On the other hand, party's status as the most potent legislative coalition makes its leaders the prime leaders of the House; as such, they are the prime wielders of whatever forms of leadership power its structures and processes create and allocate. As a consequence, the degree to which power can be centralized in the House, the degree to which rewards and penalties can be generated by formal and/or party structures and concentrated in the hands of party leaders, rests substantially on the potential of party as a voting coalition.

In part, this is true because the party coalition alone has the ability to provide shared policy goals of sufficient breadth and permanence to induce individual members to accept highly differential distributions of power, despite the limitations on voting choices and coalition building that they entail. In part, however, it is also true because operation on the basis of party alone can legitimize continuing impairment of the formally equal and independent status of members by appealing to an alternative version of democratic values that equates representative government with party rule.

Centralized power thus rests on the willingness of party members to operate the House on the basis of party. This is not to deny that to concentrate organizational rewards and penalties in the hands of party leaders is to give them substantial leverage over rank-and-file members. Nonetheless, the structural arrangements in the formal and/or party systems that generate and confer such leverage cannot be created or maintained if party members do not possess a high degree of willingness to pursue policy goals in concert on a permanent or continuing basis; that is, in democratic legislatures, such as the House, even centralized power structures must be continually renewed and sustained by majority support on the floor and in caucus. High concentrations of power in the hands of party leaders are accordingly always open to challenge. Moreover, leadership power easily becomes vulnerable whenever an appreciable minority of party members begin to feel that party rule vitiates policy goals that they and their constituents hold dear. If, in line with such sentiments, party members begin to accept and assert traditional, individualistic conceptions of representation, they deny legitimacy to concentrated forms of leadership power.

If it is true, then, that centralized power ultimately rests on the willingness of party members to vote on the basis of their party affiliation, it is also true that such inclinations do not arise out of thin air. Rather, the ability of party to motivate members to sacrifice their independence and flexibility for the purpose of attaining collective goals and to legitimize such sacrifices rests on similarities in policy orientation and interest among party members; these, in turn, rest on similarities in basic values and goals among the electoral coalitions that elect them to office.

In summary, we may think of centralized power as a potential that is bounded by the potential for voting on the basis of party and see this latter potential itself as bounded by the character of the electoral coalitions that elect members to office. Stated in this way, we may recognize that the degree of leverage the party leadership derives from structural arrangements always contributes to party strength, to the actual degree of voting on the basis of party. Indeed, in periods when a high degree of power can be concentrated in the hands of party leaders, the result is not only to insure that the full potential for voting on the basis of party will be realized, but also to make it possible to artificially extend or exaggerate such voting. In contrast, when leadership power is decentralized, it becomes difficult to realize the potential that does exist and the sheer political skill of party leaders becomes of critical importance in providing the bare margins needed for victory.

Nonetheless, we may also recognize that the degree to which power can be concentrated in the hands of party leaders is itself dependent on the potential of party as a voting coalition and that the limits or constraints here are very demanding. Substantial levels of party unity and conflict can accordingly exist and persist without spawning or involving highly centralized power structures. In contrast, the potential for voting on the basis of party must be very strong to provide a foundation for such structures because of the limitations they impose on individual members and the appeal of traditional concepts of representation.

Last but not least, our approach gives us additional perspective on the leverage the president obtains from the fact that he now monopolizes the role of national party leader and serves as the prime instrument for focusing and expressing the communalities that exist in his party coalition. In the absence of centralized leadership power within the House, the president must and does serve as a surrogate for it whenever his party is in control.

The model we propose therefore accords primacy to external factors. It postulates that the impact of internal organizational factors rests on and is constrained by the character of electoral variables and that the impact of external factors is of greater proportions. The former postulate derives from our contention that both the materials with which the leadership must work and the means or instruments of power available to it are electorally determined or constrained. The latter postulate derives from our recognition of the fact that the constraints on highly centralized forms of leadership power are very demanding and usually not satisfied. As a consequence, though the incremental contributions of party leaders are often critical to provide the margins of victory, their ability to make substantial, independent contributions to heightening levels of party voting is generally limited. Figure 9.1 shows the hypothesized relationships.

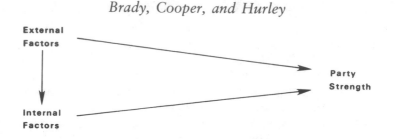

Figure 9.1. A model of factors affecting party strength

Testing the model

To confirm or verify our model, we need to establish both that external variables are positively related to internal variables and overall party strength and that their impact is of greater causal significance. In order to operationalize the external variables, we created a summary index for the external variables by combining each of the separate variables in the following manner. If in a given House electoral turnover was above the over-time mean, a 1 was assigned; if the value of electoral turnover was below the mean, a 0 was assigned. Similarly, if the value of the party conflict and dominant faction variables were above the mean, a value of 1 was assigned for each variable. If the president and the House majority were of the same party, a value of 1 was assigned. Thus, a given House could have an index value that ranged from 0 to 4. The hypothesis is that as the external index value rises, party strength will also rise.

The internal variables are operationalized essentially as they were in the previous section. A value of 0 means that the House had neither centralized leadership nor a strong caucus. A value of 1 means that the House had either strong centralized leadership or a strong caucus, while a value of 2 means that both centralized leadership and a strong caucus were present. Party strength was then regressed against these variables and Figure 9.2 shows the results.

The results support the hypotheses for the Democratic party strength model. The external variables index is strongly correlated with both internal factors and party strength. The internal variables index is also related to party strength but not as strongly as is the case for the external variables. Moreover, the external factors have an indirect effect on party strength through the internal factors. Thus for the Democrats the results support the model; namely, while both internal and external factors affect party strength, the external factors are more important.

The model does not work quite as well for the Republicans. The external factors are positively related to both the internal and the party strength variables but the internal variable has a stronger relationship

Decline of party in the House, 1887–1968

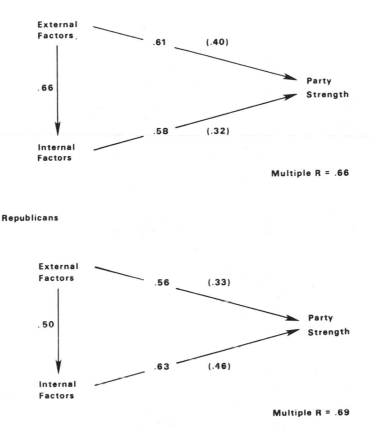

Figure 9.2 The effect of external and internal variables on party strength
(numerals are Pearson's *r*; betas are given in parentheses)

with party strength than does the external variable index. This, of course, presents a problem because our model posits that the external factors will be more strongly related to party strength than the internal structural variable.

A part of this dilemma is the time frame used in this paper. That is, during the 1890 to 1910–11 period, when under Reed and Cannon the Speaker was in his "heyday," the parties were ideologically divided and highly polarized (Brady and Althoff, 1974). Thus the r between the internal and external variable is quite high (r = .91) and it is difficult to sort out the separate effects of the two variables on party strength. The fact that the model fits the data for the Democrats but not the

251

Republicans indicates that the 1890 to 1910–11 time period is problematic. Dropping the 1890 to 1910–11 time period and running the regression over the 1912–1968 time period shows that for the corrected time period the model fits the data. The r between external factors and party strength is .51, while the same r for the internal variable is .40 and the beta's corroborate this difference.

Thus far, our evidence supports our model, but remains inconclusive. In spite of the corrected results for the 1912–1968 period, the question of the relative strength of the internal and external variables remains problematic. Therefore, we decided to run another test to determine relative strength.

The problem is to determine which set of variables – external or internal – has a greater impact on party strength. Our model posits that the internal factors are an intervening variable between the external factors and party strength. In order to test this relationship we have chosen to use a technique devised by Cnudde and McCrone (1969), which avoids spuriousness problems associated with partial correlation and beta analysis. The strategy employed in this test is to partial, using unstandardized regression techniques to determine if the internal structural variable significantly reduces the magnitude of the effect of the external variables on party strength. Our application is two-fold. First, we regress party strength against each component of the internal variable – caucus strength and centralized leadership; then we used a .05 confidence limit for the B's and partial, using the external index as the partial. The model predicts that the external variable will significantly reduce the relationship between the internal variables and party strength. Second, we regress party strength on each of the components of the external variable – electoral turnover, presidential partisanship, party conflict, and dominant faction. Then using the same .05 confidence limit for the B's we partial using the internal variable. The model predicts that the internal variable will not significantly reduce the effect of all the external factors on party strength. Table 9.4 presents the results of the analysis in the form of a summary table.

Partialing for the external variable shows that the effect of the internal factors is significantly reduced for both parties. Thus, the results are in the predicted direction. Partialing for the internal variable indicates that the effect of electoral turnover and party conflict on party strength is significantly reduced for both parties. However, the relationships between president's party, dominant faction, and party strength are not significantly reduced when the internal variable is controlled.

So much, then, for confirming discrete relationships posited by our model. As a final and critical step in testing it, its predictive value should be considered, for if we can show that our model has such value, we can

252

Decline of party in the House, 1887–1968

Table 9.4A. *Summary of the effects of controlling for the external variable on the relationship between internal factors and party strength*

Internal factors	Democrats	Republicans
Caucus strength	Significant reduction*	Significant reduction*
Centralized leadership	Significant reduction*	Significant reduction*

Table 9.4B. *Summary of the effects of controlling for the internal variable on the relationship between external factors and party strength*

External factors	Democrats	Republicans
Electoral turnover	Significant reduction	Significant reduction
Partisanship of president	No significant reduction*	No significant reduction*
Dominant faction	No significant reduction*	No significant reduction*
Party conflict	Significant reduction	Significant reduction

* Predicted direction.

transcend the confines of statistical operations and demonstrate its relevance for understanding the empirical world. We can argue that not only is our model valid, but more importantly it is useful.

The regression results from Table 9.3 give a predicted level of party strength for each House, which may be higher or lower than the observed level of party strength for that House. To determine which Houses best fit the regression we ran an analysis of the regression residuals for party strength. In doing so, since we have determined the external variables to be the more important, we entered them first in the regression and entered the internal variables second. In short, rather than using a step-wise regression, our model determined the order of entry of the variables. Figures 9.3 and 9.4 show the results for the Democrats and the Republicans.

In general, the results indicate that party strength is predicted accurately by the external and internal variables we have chosen and ordered. The only Houses not predicted within plus or minus one standard deviation for both parties are the 50th (1887), 53rd (1892), and 58th (1902) Houses. In both the 50th and 53rd Houses the equation predicts greater party strength than is present, while the equation predicts less party strength than is present in the 58th House. The lower levels of party strength in the 50th and 53rd Houses are explainable for Democrats in terms of divisions over the questions of Populism (bimetallism, protective tariffs, etc.), while results for Republicans reflect

253

```
                                    (n = 25)
                                       89
                                       88
                                       87
Lower Levels of                        86              Higher Levels of
Party Strength than Predicted          85              Party Strength than Predicted
                                       84
                                       82
                                       81
                                       80
                                       79
                                       78
                                       75
                                       74
                                       72
                                       71
                                       68
                                       67
                                       66
                      (n = 6)          65
                         90            64
                                                    (n = 4)
       (n = 3)           83            63
                         77            62              61              (n = 3)
        53               70            59              56              76
        52               69            57              55              73
        50               60            54              51              58

    Within -2.00     Within -1.00   Within + or -.50   Within 1.00    Within 2.00
                                   Standard Deviations
```

Figure 9.3. Distribution of residuals for Democrats

similar divisions particularly over gold versus silver. In both of these Houses many of the roll calls were aimed at procedural delay and Democratic cohesion was low on these roll calls as well as on the substantive questions mentioned earlier. The higher than predicted levels of party strength in the 58th House were in all probability the result of Czar Cannon's first term as Speaker. In this Congress, levels of party voting reached an all-time high and the number of roll calls was restricted to eighty-six as Cannon established his supremacy early. Further, the roll calls themselves were often procedural in nature, focusing on the Speaker's control of the body and Cannon used the caucus to impose the party line.

The results also show that for the Democrats the equation under-predicts party strength in the 73rd (1932) and 76th (1938) Houses and overpredicts it for the 52nd (1890) House. In the latter case, the explanation is the same as discussed above. The remaining cases reflect the impact of novel conditions in the 1930s. The 73rd was F.D.R.'s first House and his record in the first 100 days need not be recounted here. In the 76th House, the Republicans made their first significant gains in the House since 1928, and sought to undo much of the New Deal. The result

		(n = 25)		
Lower Levels of Party Strength than Predicted		89 88 87 86 85 84 83 82 81 80 79 78 75 74 72 71 68	Higher Levels of Party Strength than Predicted	
	(n = 8)	67 66 64	(n = 5)	
	90 77 70 69 65 63	62 61 60	76 73 56	(n = 1)
(n = 2) 53 50	54 52	59 57	55 51	58
Within -2.00	Within -1.00	Within + or -.50	Within 1.00	Within 2.00

Standard Deviations

Figure 9.4. Distribution of residuals for Republicans

was higher Democratic cohesion and an underpredicted party strength score.

These exceptions, however, should not be permitted to obscure our overall results. In thirty-five of forty-one cases for Democrats and in thirty-eight of forty-one cases for Republicans, our model can be used to predict party strength within plus or minus one standard deviation.

CONCLUSION

In this article we have argued that both external and internal variables impact the level of party strength in the House, but that external variables, and particularly electoral variables, are the more important. We have ordered these propositions in the form of a model, tested the model, and also established its predictive value.

Given our model and the supporting evidence, it is not surprising that centralized leadership power in the U.S. House of Representatives is infrequent and prone to breakdown. Indeed, to assert this point is only to reassert a traditional interpretation of the impact of the scope and complexity of American electoral politics. Our model, however, permits us to do more than simply reemphasize aspects of traditional wisdom that have been obscured by the rich but diverse nature of contemporary research. It also permits us to shed some light on the politics of the current House.

If we accept the prime importance of factors such as the degree of intraparty homogeneity and interparty conflict at the electoral level, evidence of increasing fractionalization in the politics of the current House becomes readily understandable. Such fractionalization, it should be noted, is revealed not only in voting patterns (Sinclair, 1977), but also in the mushroom growth of a dozen or so ad hoc groups or caucuses (Commission on Administrative Review, 1977). Fractionalization in both these regards is attributable to a decline in the strength and comprehensiveness of the communalities in interest and viewpoint that unite majority party members in the House and distinguish them from their minority opponents. The result is not only less stability and consistency in majority formation under the aegis of the leadership, but also the institutionalization of other bases of alliance through the creation of ad hoc groups.

Similarly, the increasing tendency of House members to run simply as individuals and their ability to render themselves immune from even severe reversals in party fortunes at the presidential level is also attributable to the weakening hold of party at the electoral level. Declines in party coherence and conflict at the electoral level lead to declines in reliance on party as a vehicle for collective position-taking and action at the legislative level; these lead, in turn, to decreasing relevance and significance for party as a factor in electoral judgments. In short, the reason for the disappearance of the marginals and the increased strength of incumbents does not lie simply in the joint effects of bureaucratic expansion, constituent service, and increased staff and office allowances (Fiorina, 1977). Rather the explanation lies to an equal, if not even greater degree, in the broad and defining alterations of context produced by the decline of party as a basis for collective action and judgment at both the electoral and legislative levels.

Last, but certainly not least, our analysis aids in appraising the significance of the reemergence of the Democratic caucus in the House. The reemergence of the caucus in 1969 after decades of dormancy seems at first glance highly anomalous in a period of party weakness and decline. Yet the mystery is easily solved once it is recognized that the modern caucus is a quite different entity than its traditional forebears; it serves not as an instrument for enhancing leadership power and centralized decision making, but rather as another arena for factional conflict.

It is thus no accident that soon after the reestablishment of regular caucus meetings, the caucus voted to abolish the traditional two-thirds rule and thereby removed the historic mechanism for binding party members to support party decisions. Nor is it an accident that the caucus has functioned as an instrument of two overlapping groups – Northern liberals and junior members. The former have used it to limit the power of Southern chairmen and the latter to wrest a greater share of influence from senior members. In sum, then, the modern caucus is a product of tensions rather than unities within the majority party coalition (Cooper, 1975). It provides an arena for conflict and not an instrument for integration, thus threatening leadership power more than reinforcing it. In truth, the caucus has a life and a politics of its own and the hold of the leadership over it is often quite tenuous. The character and significance of the modern caucus are thus not at variance with the premises and propositions of our analysis, but rather far more understandable once interpreted in terms of our model.

NOTES

1 In this paper we use the Rice index of cohesion, which measures the degree of intraparty cohesion, as the degree to which members of the same party vote together on a given issue. This index is formed by dividing the number of majority votes (intraparty) by the total number of party votes cast, subtracting 50 from this, and finally multiplying this figure by two. Zero cohesion is the index value when a party is split 50-50; perfect cohesion (100) is the index value when all members of a party vote in the same way.

2 This is the measure that the *Congressional Quarterly* uses in determining its party vote scores.

3 In this paper we use the index of party likeness, which measures the degree of similarity between two legislative groups. It is obtained by calculating the percentage of members of each group that voted in favor of the measure, subtracting the smaller number from the larger, and subtracting the remainder from 100.

4 Ginsberg measured party differences by content analyzing party platforms from 1844 to 1968. For the specifics the reader is referred to the original articles (Ginsberg, 1972, 1976).

5 In the following analysis, we deal with time in two separate ways. The assumption behind both views is that time itself is a vacuous concept causing nothing; rather, it is a relatively arbitrary division (1 year, 2 years, etc.). Thus we believe that the decline in party strength is not a function of time but rather a function of changes in the environment within which the House functions. In order to deal with time, we created two sequential variables – one measures change in the independent variable; the other is simply the dummy variable for internal structure in the House. The correlations of these variables with time were .92 and .94 respectively. Since these correlations are so high we assume that they better account for the pattern of party strength and that time need not be included in the tables presented. For those that might still argue that time is relevant in the section where we test the model, we entered time as the

last variable in the regression equation and it increased explained variance by only .002. Thus we felt safe in concluding that the decline in party strength reported in this paper *is not* a function of time except in an ersatz sense.

REFERENCES

Blalock, Hubert M. 1972. *Social Statistics*. 2nd ed. New York: McGraw-Hill.

Brady, David W. and Naomi Lynn. 1973. "Switched Seat Congressional Districts: Their Effects on Party Voting and Public Policy," *The American Journal of Political Science* 17 (August, 1973): 528–543.

Brady, David W. and Phillip Althoff. 1974. "Party Voting in the U.S. House of Representatives 1890–1910: Elements of a Responsible Party System," *Journal of Politics* 36 (August, 1974): 753–774.

Burns, James M. 1963. *The Deadlock of a Democracy*. Englewood Cliffs: Prentice-Hall.

Campbell, Donald T. and Julian C. Stanley. 1963. *Experimental and Quasi-Experimental Designs for Research*. Chicago: Rand-McNally.

Clausen, Aage R. 1973. *How Congressmen Decide: A Policy Focus*. New York: St. Martin's.

Cnudde, Charles F. and Donald J. McCrone. 1969. "Party Competition and Welfare Policies in the United States," *American Political Science Review* 63 (September, 1969): 858–866.

Commission on Administrative Review. 1977. "Background Information on Administrative Units, Members' Offices, and Committee and Leadership Offices," *House Document* 95–178. Washington, D.C.: US GPO.

Cooper, Joseph. 1970. *The Origins of the Standing Committees and the Development of the Modern House*. Houston: Rice University Studies.

 1975. "Strengthening the Congress: An Organizational Approach," *Harvard Journal on Legislation* 12 (April, 1975): 307–368.

Cooper, Joseph, David W. Brady, and Patricia A. Hurley. 1977. "The Electoral Basis of Part Voting," in Louis Maisel and Joseph Cooper, eds., *The Impact of the Electoral Process*. Beverly Hills: Sage, pp. 133–165.

Deckard, Barbara and John Stanley. 1974. "Party Decomposition and Region: The House of Representatives, 1945–70," *Western Political Quarterly* 27 (June, 1974): 249–264.

Diamond, Robert A., ed. 1976. *Origins and Development of Congress*. Washington, D.C.: Congressional Quarterly, Inc.

Fiorina, Morris P. 1977. *Congress: Keystone of the Washington Establishment*. New Haven: Yale University Press.

Fishel, Jeff. 1973. *Party and Opposition: Congressional Challengers in American Politics*. New York: David McKay.

Froman, Lewis A., Jr. and Randall B. Ripley. 1965. "Conditions for Party Leadership: The Case of the House Democrats," *American Political Science Review* 59 (March, 1965): 52–63.

Ginsberg, Benjamin. 1972. "Critical Elections and the Substance of Party Conflict: 1844–1968," *Midwest Journal of Political Science* 16 (November, 1972): 603–625.

 1976. "Elections and Public Policy," *American Political Science Review* 70 (March, 1976): 41–49.

Grumm, John G. 1964. "The Means of Measuring Conflict and Cohesion in the Legislature," *Southwestern Social Science Quarterly* 44 (March, 1964):

377–388.

Huitt, Ralph K. 1961. "Democratic Party Leadership in the Senate," *American Political Science Review* 55 (June, 1961): 333–344.

Jewell, Malcolm E. and Samuel C. Patterson. 1973. *The Legislative Process in the United States.* New York: Random House.

Key, V. O. 1964. *Politics, Parties, and Pressure Groups.* 5th ed. New York: Thomas Crowell.

LeBlanc, Hugh L. 1969. "Voting in State Senates: Party and Constituency Influences," *Midwest Journal of Political Science* 13 (February, 1969): 33–57.

Lowell, A. Lawrence. 1902. "The Influence of Party upon Legislation in England and America," *Annual Report of the American Historical Association for 1901* 1 (1902): 321–543.

MacRae, Duncan. 1952. "The Relation Between Roll Call Votes and Constituencies in the Massachusetts House of Representatives," *American Political Science Review* 46 (December, 1952): 1046–1055.

1970. *Issues and Parties in Legislative Voting: Methods of Statistical Analysis.* New York: Harper and Row.

Mayhew, David R. 1974. *Congress: The Electoral Connection.* New Haven: Yale University Press.

Rice, Stuart A. 1928. *Quantitative Methods in Politics.* New York: Alfred A. Knopf.

Schattschneider, E. E. 1950. "Toward a More Responsible Two Party System," *American Political Science Review* 44 (Supplement).

Shannon, W. Wayne. 1968. *Party, Constituency, and Roll Call Voting.* Baton Rouge: Louisiana State University Press.

Sinclair, Barbara D. 1977. "Who Wins in the House of Representatives: The Effects of Declining Party Cohesion on Policy Outputs, 1959–1970." *Social Science Quarterly* 58 (June, 1977): 121–129.

Sorauf, Frank J. 1972. *Party Politics in America.* 2nd ed. Boston: Little, Brown and Company.

Truman, David B. 1959. *The Congressional Party: A Case Study.* New York: John Wiley.

Turner, Julius and Edward V. Schneier, Jr. 1970. *Party and Constituency: Pressures on Congress.* Rev. ed. Baltimore: Johns Hopkins University Press.

Weinbaum, Marvin G. and Dennis R. Judd. 1970. "In Search of a Mandated Congress," *Midwest Journal of Political Science* 14 (May, 1970): 276–302.

10

Joseph G. Cannon and Howard W. Smith: an essay on the limits of leadership in the House of Representatives

CHARLES O. JONES

That the House of Representatives is characterized by bargaining has been well established by many scholars of that institution[1] and suggests that leaders of that body must be skilled negotiators. Ultimately each representative, even the freshman, has some bargaining power (at minimum – his vote). It is on this basis of bargaining that the "middleman" thesis of congressional leadership has been developed.[2] Rightly or wrongly House leaders must attend to their majorities.

Two types of majorities in the House are of interest here – procedural and substantive. Procedural majorities are those necessary to organize the House for business and maintain that organization.[3] They are formed at the beginning of the session. Leaders are selected and provided with a number of bargaining advantages so that the House may perform its functions in the political system. Normally, membership of procedural majorities and minorities coincides with that of the two political parties.[4]

Substantive majorities are those necessary to pass legislation in the House. Whereas procedural majorities are relatively stable in membership, the make-up of substantive majorities may well differ issue to issue, since many substantive measures cut across party lines. Leaders are expected to build substantive majorities – employing the many bargaining advantages provided by their procedural majorities. They are not expected, nor do they normally have the power, to force members into substantive majorities.

House leaders must take care not to lose touch with any sizeable segment of their procedural majorities. On most issues they will find the basis for substantive majorities in their own party. Obviously, party

Reprinted from *Journal of Politics* 30, no. 3 (August 1968): 617–46. Financial support for this study was provided by the American Political Science Association's Study of Congress, Professor Ralph K. Huitt, Director, and the Institute of Government Research, University of Arizona. I wish to acknowledge the comments of Richard Cortner, Conrad Joyner, John Crow, Phillip Chapman, and Clifford Lytle.

members have views on the substantive matters before the House. If he wishes to remain in office, a leader must hold himself accountable to his procedural majority when building substantive majorities and accommodate important substantive changes among segments of his procedural majority. House leaders have latitude in their behavior, to be sure, and the process of defeat and/or reform is often painfully slow, but the leader who maintains himself in a responsible position of authority over a long period of time must be adaptive, communicative, accommodating, and accountable.

What if a House leader fails to behave in this way? In the short run, it probably will not make much difference. In the long run, however aberrant behavior is bound to cause trouble for the leader with segments of his procedural majority. If it is a case of a leader exceeding the authority given to him, or failing to meet the expectations of his followers, he may simply be removed. But what if he has developed sources of power which make him independent of his procedural majority? That is, he is exercising authority which is real – it is incorporated into the position he holds – but is contextually inappropriate because it violates the bargaining condition in the House. Under these circumstances removing the leader is not the whole solution. One may expect some House members to be concerned enough about the potential of divorce between the procedural majority and its leader to press for reform. One may further expect that in these situations the House will define the limits of leadership in that body as it debates reform.

There are two spectacular cases of "excessive leadership" in the House in this century. Joseph G. Cannon, as Speaker, had become an exceptionally powerful figure in American politics. He had a wide variety of sanctions available and he used them all. Nearly 50 years later, Howard W. Smith, as Chairman of the Committee on Rules, also had an impressive array of prerogatives – all of which he used to his advantage. The purposes of this essay are to examine the authority of these two men, how they exercised this authority in relationship to their procedural majorities, and the reaction and ultimate loss of their majorities. The findings not only tend to support the "middle-man" hypothesis but provide a clearer indication of its meaning as defined by the members themselves.

THE CASE OF UNCLE JOE CANNON

The House leadership situation in 1910 should have satisfied many of the responsible party scholars. There was no question that the Speaker was responsible for leading the House. Since his election in 1903, Speaker

Joseph G. Cannon had enjoyed rather substantial procedural majorities and due to the growth of the speakership and Cannon's interpretation and use of his powers, a procedural majority carried with it awesome authority. He could appoint committees – including the chairmen – determine the schedule of business, recognize members on the floor, appoint members to conference committees, dispense favors of various kinds.

Cannon's exercise of power

Particularly significant was Speaker Cannon's power as chairman of the Committee on Rules. The Committee was small – never over five members prior to 1910. The three-to-two edge of the Republicans was potent, however, since the Speaker appointed the members carefully – insuring that they agreed with his views.[5] Champ Clark's view of the Committee was widely shared: "I violate no secret when I tell you the committee is made up of three very distinguished Republicans and two ornamental Democrats. [Laughter]...there never would be a rule reported out of that committee that the Speaker and his two Republican colleagues do not want reported."[6]

During Speaker Cannon's reign, four Republicans served on the Committee on Rules in addition to the Speaker himself – John Dalzell, Pennsylvania; Charles Grosvenor, Ohio; James S. Sherman, New York; and Walter I. Smith, Iowa. These members had considerable seniority (overall the average number of terms served by Committee members was approximately three times that of other House Republicans) and therefore also were high ranking on other important standing committees.

A second center of power which the Speaker dominated was the Committee on Ways and Means. It was the custom to have the Chairman of Ways and Means serve as the majority floor leader. Sereno Payne, New York, served Cannon in these two important posts during his speakership. There was considerable overlapping membership between Rules and Ways and Means. Between 1903 and 1907, Dalzell and Grosvenor were second- and third-ranking Republicans on Ways and Means. Dalzell remained in both positions throughout Cannon's speakership.[7]

The list of grievances against Cannon and his lieutenants on Rules and Ways and Means lengthened with each year of his speakership. A frequent complaint was that Speaker Cannon abused House Rule X, which gave him the power to appoint the standing committees. He had made some spectacular appointments and adjustments prior to 1909 – selecting Tawney, Minnesota, as Chairman of Appropriations in 1905, even though Tawney had never served on that committee; Overstreet, Indiana, as Chairman of Post Office and Post Roads in 1903, even though Overstreet had never served on that committee; and Scott, Kansas, as Chairman of Agriculture in 1907 over Henry, Connecticut (whom Cannon removed completely from the Committee) and Haugen, Iowa. In 1909, however, Speaker Cannon appeared to shift assignments about at will. Though seniority was not an inviolable rule at this time, it was relied on as a significant factor in committee assignments.[8] Twelve Republicans had not voted for Cannon for Speaker in 1909 and seniority was certainly no protection for them. Table 10.1 provides some examples of actions taken by the Speaker in the 61st Congress.

Speaker Cannon was not above delaying the appointment of committees until his wishes on legislation had been met. In the famous 61st Congress, he appointed the important Rules and Ways and Means Committees on March 16, the second day of the session. Most of the remaining appointments had to wait until the Payne-Aldrich tariff bill was in the conference committee – nearly five months after the session began.[9]

Joe Cannon did not limit himself to managing committee appointments. He also managed the output of the House. George Norris describes one of his early experiences on the House Committee on Public Buildings and Grounds. The Committee discussed drafting a public building bill and Norris soon learned that the Speaker would ultimately decide whether the Committee should proceed or not. "The senior Democratic member of the committee, Representative Bankhead of Alabama...actually made a motion that the chairman of the committee should seek a conference with the Speaker and ascertain whether or not we should be allowed to have a public building bill at that session."[10]

There were many examples of the frustrations of the insurgents in dealing with Speaker Cannon's Committee on Rules during the debate in 1910 to remove the Speaker from that Committee. One involved a first-term congressman from New York, Hamilton Fish. He had unsuccessfully sought to get a hearing before the Committee on a resolution which called on the Committee on Post Office and Post Roads to inquire into the feasibility and the desirability of establishing a parcel-post system. The colloquy between Fish and Walter I. Smith, Iowa, a member of the Committee on Rules, is worth recording here as an example of how various senior members would treat a freshman.

Mr. SMITH. I deny that a hearing has ever been refused.

Mr. FISH. Mr. Speaker, I have the evidence in writing that I asked a hearing and none has been granted me.

Mr. SMITH. Well –

Mr. FISH. I will ask the gentleman, in the six weeks that the resolution has been before the Committee on Rules why he has not answered my request and given me the privilege of a hearing?

263

Table 10.1. *Examples of violations of seniority principle in committee assignments, 61st Congress*

Member	Committee and rank (60th Congress)	Committee and rank (61st Congress)	Comments
Cooper, Wisc.	Insular Affairs, Chmn.	Elections #3, 2nd Foreign Affairs, 10th	Cooper had been Chairman since 56th Congress.
Fowler, N. J.	Banking & Currency, Chmn. Reform of Civil Service, 2nd	Insular Affairs, 11th Reform of Civil Service, 2nd	Fowler had been Chairman since 57th Congress. Vreeland, N. Y., made Chairman. Not on Banking & Currency before. Was lowest on Appropriations in 60th.
Haugen, Iowa	Agriculture, 2nd War Claims, 2nd Expenditures in Interior Dept., Chmn.	Agriculture, 4th War Claims, 3rd	Haugen had been passed over in 60th in Agriculture. In 61st two lower-ranking members moved ahead of him. Same on War Claims – thus denying him Chairmanship.
Lovering, Mass.	Coinage, Weights & Measures, 4th Interstate & Foreign Commerce, 5th	Coinage, Weights & Measures, 4th Manufacturers, 4th	Lovering had previously been removed from Banking & Currency (59th).
Morse, Wisc.	Indian Affairs, 10th War Claims, 9th	War Claims, 4th Manufacturers, 6th Private Land Claims, 4th	
Murdock, Kans.	Post Office and Post Roads, 9th	Post Office and Post Roads, 12th	Six new members plus one who was below Murdock in 60th, were placed ahead of him.
Norris, Nebr.	Election of Pres., V. Pres. & Repres., 3rd. Public Bldgs. & Grounds, 6th Labor, 7th	Coinage, Weights & Measures, 7th Private Land Claims, 2nd Revision of the Laws, 6th	

Sources: Various volumes of the *Congressional Directory* and Paul D. Hasbrouck, *Party Government in the House of Representatives* (New York: Macmillan, 1927).

Mr. SMITH. Does the gentleman ask that question?
Mr. FISH. Yes; why have you not given me a hearing?
Mr. SMITH. I wrote the gentleman in person that while I did not approve of a parcel post myself I was opposed to suppressing any measure, and that I was willing to give him a hearing and report the bill adversely.
Mr. FISH. I would ask the gentleman, then, why he did not give me a hearing?
Mr. SMITH. The gentleman never appeared and asked for a hearing.
Mr. FISH. But I have written time and time again asking for it.
Mr. SMITH. Oh, written –[11]

Fish's subsequent question to John Dalzell, also a member of the Rules Committee, regarding how a member extracted a bill from a committee which did not wish to report it, went unanswered.

Managing the work assignments of congressmen, managing their work, and managing the rules by which their work would be done – such were the powers of the Speaker. Yet still other sanctions were available to him. Speakers have always had a number of temporary and honorary appointments which they can make. In some cases these are much sought after – for publicity, prestige, or for some other special purpose. Norris reports one such appointment which he sought. William C. Lovering, Massachusetts, a close friend of Norris and an early insurgent congressman, died February 4, 1910. Norris wished to be appointed to the committee representing the House at the funeral.

I hoped the Speaker, recognizing my close ties with Mr. Lovering, would accord me the privilege of paying my respects to a very dear friend, as a member of the House committee. Without seeing the Speaker about it personally, I had one or two friends approach him; and they reported he refused absolutely to approve my selection. It was a long time before the deep resentment which this aroused in me disappeared.[12]

This awesome list of powers exceeded that exercised by any previous Speaker. It was exceedingly difficult for the insurgent members to "force" the Speaker to accommodate their views because (1) he had so many sanctions available and could discipline not only them but any members who might otherwise be enticed to join them, and (2) the insurgent Republicans did not want to defeat Cannon so as to elect a Democratic Speaker, who would likely be no more accommodating to their views. Thus, Cannon had a considerable advantage and could ignore the changes occurring within his own procedural majority – he had developed a certain amount of independence from that majority.

The warning signals

Speaker Cannon and the regular Republicans had ample warning of the unrest among their more progressive brethren during the 60th and 61st

Congresses. In fact, members made no effort to hide their dissatisfaction in speeches on the House floor. Twelve insurgents refused to vote for Cannon for Speaker at the opening of the special session in 1909, called by President Taft to consider the tariff. And a combination of insurgents and Democrats defeated the motion to adopt the rules of the preceding Congress. Minority Leader Champ Clark followed this victory with a resolution which would have increased the size of the Committee on Rules, removed the Speaker from the Committee, and taken from the Speaker his power of appointing all committees except Ways and Means. With insurgent support, the stage was set for revolution at that moment, but John J. Fitzgerald (D-New York) and 22 bolting Democrats voted with the majority of Republicans to defeat Clark's move and Cannon was saved. Fitzgerald then offered a compromise motion of his own which established a unanimous consent calendar, a motion of recommital (for use by the minority), and increased the majority necessary to set aside Calendar Wednesday.[13]

Calendar Wednesday itself had been adopted at the close of the 60th Congress and though it did not meet the reform standards of the insurgents, there were strong hopes that it would limit Cannon's power. These hopes were dashed rather soon and rather decisively. A call of standing committees every Wednesday allowed committee chairmen to take bills which had been reported off the calendar for House consideration. With the changes as a result of the Fitzgerald compromise, the procedure could be dispensed with only by a two-thirds majority. A variety of devices was used to neutralize the procedure – adjournment required only a simple majority and was used to avoid Calendar Wednesday; bills of great length and complexity were called up and debated on successive Calendar Wednesdays (all nine Calendar Wednesdays were devoted to one bill in the third session of the 61st Congress).[14]

The Consent Calendar was more of a victory for the rank-and-file. There was a unanimous consent procedure in existence wherein any member could move consideration of a bill. The Speaker, theoretically, had no greater power of objection than any other member. In practice, however, the Speaker required advance notice of a unanimous consent request before he would recognize it. Thus, members had to clear such requests with Cannon before they could even be recognized on the floor.[15] The rules change created a Calendar for Unanimous Consent. The Speaker's consent was no longer required for a unanimous consent motion.

It was unlikely that these reforms would satisfy those members who were increasingly alienated from their own party. The 1908 elections resulted in a further reduction of the size of the House Republican majority. Cannon had a slim 29-vote majority in his first term as Speaker.

Roosevelt's election in 1904 brought with it a 114-vote majority for Republicans in the House. This was reduced to 58 in 1906 and to 47 in 1908. Many of the new Republicans elected in 1906 and 1908 were from states in the Middle West and were soon to join veteran insurgents like Henry Cooper, Wisconsin; Gilbert Haugen, Iowa; and George Norris, Nebraska. Thus, not only was Cannon's majority being reduced but regular Republicans were being replaced by members who were potential threats to Cannon's leadership. The result was that if enough members absented themselves on crucial votes, the insurgents would hold the balance of power. For the insurgents the time had come. Speaker Cannon would be taught some fundamental lessons about leadership in the House of Representatives. Though he had developed impressive power as Speaker and found that he didn't have to make accommodations to a changing procedural majority in the short run, there were other alternatives available to the insurgents. They could always take their one bargaining advantage — the vote — and join the Democrats to curb the powers of the Speaker.

The revolt

The full-scale revolt against Cannon began on March 16, 1910. Though the details of the revolt are adequately recorded in a number of sources,[16] a brief resumé of pertinent facts is necessary. March 16 was Calendar Wednesday. Mr. Crumpacker (R-Indiana) called for the consideration of House Joint Resolution 172 on the 1910 census.[17] Mr. Fitzgerald (D-New York) made the point of order that a call of the committees was in order, under the Calendar Wednesday procedure. Speaker Cannon overruled the point of order, noting that "a certain class of business, like election cases, like matters arising in impeachment, and like legislation relating to apportionment or the taking of the census as to the population, have invariably been admitted as involving *constitutional privilege*, presenting a privilege higher than any rule of the House would give."[18] (Emphasis added.) Fitzgerald appealed the ruling of the chair to the House. Crumpacker moved that the matter be postponed until Thursday — thus postponing the appeal to the chair as well. Fitzgerald objected. Cannon overruled his objection but the House supported Fitzgerald and refused to allow the matter to be postponed. After some debate, the appeal to the House was voted on and Cannon was defeated, 112 to 163, as 42 Republicans voted with the Democrats. Cannon then made the dramatic announcement: "The decision of the Chair does not stand as the decision of the House."[19]

On March 17, Crumpacker again attempted to bring his resolution before the House. Cannon refused to rule. He put the question to the

House: "Is the bill called up by the gentleman from Indiana in order as a question of constitutional privilege, the rule prescribing the order of business to the contrary notwithstanding?"[20] The House, in no mood to let the Speaker snatch victory from defeat, responded negatively. The House then passed the following revised version of the question, as put by Oscar W. Underwood (D-Alabama): "Is the House joint resolution called up by the gentleman from Indiana in order now?"[21] Note that no mention was made of the Constitution in the Underwood resolution. It simply asked if the Crumpacker resolution were in order "now." William R. Gwinn, in his account of the overthrow, observes that the House had "endorsed the proposition that his [Crumpacker's] resolution was privileged under the Constitution..."[22] and, as is discussed below, George Norris later so argued. Technically, however, the House never did rule that the Crumpacker resolution was privileged.

Following the debate on House Joint Resolution 172, Norris pulled from his pocket a resolution to change the rules of the House. In his autobiography, Norris observes:

> ...I had carried it for a long time, certain that in the flush of its power the Cannon machine would overreach itself. The paper upon which I had written my resolution had become so tattered it scarcely hung together.[23]

Norris announced: "Mr. Speaker, I present a resolution made privileged by the Constitution." In Crumpacker's effort to have his census resolution considered on Calendar Wednesday, Norris found a way to circumvent the House Committee on Rules for effecting a rules change. His "privileged" resolution would reorganize the Rules Committee by increasing its size, having members selected by groups of state delegations, and removing the Speaker from the Committee. Norris argued that his resolution was privileged under the Constitution because in Article I, Section 5, paragraph 2, it stated "Each House may determine the rules of its proceedings." The Speaker ordered the clerk to read the resolution. "The moment the reading clerk saw it he smiled, for he recognized the fact that the great fight on the rules of the House was on."[24]

The turnabout was a strange one indeed. Speaker Cannon had ruled that Crumpacker's resolution was privileged but was overruled by the House. Norris had voted against the Speaker. On March 17, the House *voted against* Cannon's question which explicitly stated that the resolution was in order *under constitutional privilege* but voted in favor of the more ambiguous motion which simply stated that the Crumpacker resolution was in order. Norris waltzed through all of this with the head-spinning logic that his resolution was privileged because the Crumpacker resolution was in order. And there was no difference between the two resolutions resulting from the fact that Crumpacker's had been in committee and Norris' had not (a critical fact if his resolution was to survive).

If it [Crumpacker's] was privileged it was privileged because the Constitution made it so, and having decided that it was privileged, because the Constitution made it privileged, its privileged character was not added to by the fact that it had been referred to a committee and a report made by the committee.[25]

As indicated here, there is considerable doubt that Crumpacker's resolution *was* ruled by the House to be privileged. If it was not, then Norris and Cannon might well be faced with a complete reversal of positions – Cannon denying Norris' request because the House had not allowed the Crumpacker resolution to be privileged matter, and Norris arguing that the Crumpacker resolution had been ruled as privileged, even though Norris had not agreed that it should be.

Cannon, in his book written by L. White Busbey, argues that Norris was right. Not because Norris' resolution was as privileged as Crumpacker's but rather because:

The House having made itself ridiculous in the space of two days and publicly declared that it was bound by no rules and had no regard for logic or consistency, why should it not continue to maintain the record?[26]

The Cannon forces stayed with their original position, however – that the Crumpacker resolution was privileged. They then proceeded to argue that the Norris resolution was not. The difference was in the wording of the two relevant sections of the Constitution. "The actual enumeration *shall be made*. . ." (Article I, Section 2, Clause 3) but "Each House *may* determine the rules. . ." One was interpreted to be compelling, and thus privileged; the other was a right, could be accomplished at any time, and was not privileged.

Thus began the debate which was to terminate on March 19 with important rules changes that would have a serious impact on party government in the House of Representatives. There were six unsuccessful attempts to recess throughout the evening, on into the night, and the next morning. At 2:02 p.m. on March 18, a motion to recess until 4:00 p.m. was finally approved. The House had been in session over 26 hours. The House again recessed at 4:00 p.m. until March 19 at noon. Speaker Cannon then ruled that "the [Norris] resolution is not in order." Norris appealed the decision of the chair and the Speaker was overruled (162 Republicans supporting Cannon and 34 Republicans voting with 148 Democrats against him). An amended version of the Norris resolution then passed the House 193 to 153. A total of 43 insurgent Republicans crossed over on this key vote to defeat the Speaker. Speaker Cannon then invited a resolution which would declare the speakership vacant and call

Charles O. Jones

for an election. Such a resolution was introduced by Burleson (D-Texas) and was overwhelmingly defeated. Only eight insurgents voted against Cannon.

Defining the limits of leadership

In debate the Cannon forces set forth the following argument – basically a party responsibility position with important modifications. The people had elected a majority of Republicans to the House of Representatives. That majority had selected a leadership group which acted for the party and therefore for the country. There is a necessary coincidence between electoral majorities, procedural majorities, and substantive majorities which must not break down. That is, no member may leave the majority without severe penalty. Those members who reject the party leadership are rejecting the Republican party and its mandate from the people to manage the House and its work. The leadership would provide mechanisms whereby individual members could make their opinions known. Mr. Fassett of New York spoke for the Cannon forces:

> We are robust partisans, every one of us.... I take it that no Democrat was elected to cooperate with our party nor was any Republican elected to hand over the Republican control of this House to our political opponents.... A man ought to have opinions and convictions. He ought not to be a political chocolate eclair.... In my judgment, the place to adjust differences of opinion on unimportant questions, and on important questions of public policy and party policy is not in public, where one minority uniting with another minority may make a temporary majority; but in the family caucus...[27]

Mr. Gardner of Michigan noted the importance of two parties which put the issues before the people in debate and the threat caused by actions of the sort contemplated by Norris.[28] Mr. Nye of Minnesota observed that "Parties are a necessity, and the great power and effectiveness of the Republican party has been largely its cohesiveness. Its followers have stood shoulder to shoulder and fought the battle against a political foe.[29]

But it was left to Speaker Cannon, following his defeat, to summarize the position most eloquently.

> The SPEAKER. Gentlemen of the House of Representatives: Actions, not words, determine the conduct and the sincerity of men in the affairs of life. This is a government by the people acting through the representatives of a majority of the people. Results cannot be had except by a majority, and in the House of Representatives a majority, being responsible, should have full power and should exercise that power; otherwise the majority is inefficient and does not perform its function. The office of the minority is to put the majority on its good behavior, advocating, in good faith, the policies which it professes, ever ready to take advantage of the mistakes of the majority party, and appeal to the country for its vindication.[30]

Joseph G. Cannon and Howard W. Smith

After his defeat, Cannon surprised both his friends and his enemies by entertaining a motion to declare the office of Speaker vacant so that the new majority could proceed to elect a new Speaker. It was a perfectly consistent maneuver on his part – consistent with his notion of party leadership in the House of Representatives. If a new majority had formed, and the recent vote indicated to him that such was the case, then that new majority "ought to have the courage of its convictions, and logically meet the situation that confronts it." Though Cannon's action was consistent with his notions of party leadership, it is likely that this move was less honest consistency than it was impressive strategy. If he felt strongly about the logic of his theory of party leadership, he could have easily resigned. He did not resign, however, because, in his words, he declined "to precipitate a contest upon the House...a contest that might greatly endanger the final passage of all legislation necessary to redeem Republican pledges..." and because resignation would be "a confession of weakness or mistake or an apology for past actions."[31] Neither reason is convincing. A lengthy and divisive contest could as easily ensue as a result of declaring the office vacant. Cannon himself noted that he was entertaining the motion so that the new majority could proceed to elect another Speaker. There was no reason to think that Cannon would be the only nominee. Further, if Cannon was consistent with the party responsibility theory, he would have resigned, not because of his analysis of his personal weakness or strength or because of his view of whether he had made mistakes or not, but due to the simple fact that on a paramount issue, *he had been defeated*. Other considerations were irrelevant.

In short, Cannon, and probably his cohorts, believed more in strong, personal party leadership with limited accountability to party membership, let alone the nation as whole, than they did in the classic party responsibility position. There is abundant evidence for this interpretation in their behavior before 1910, in the actions of the cabal before the debate in 1910, and in the Cannon maneuver following his defeat. He chose the strategy of entertaining the motion to declare the office vacant so that he might regain control of the situation. At the time, it looked very much as though he might succeed. As he proudly notes in his autobiography: "I was given more votes than at the beginning of Congress and when I went back to resume the Chair I received a demonstration from both sides such as the House has seldom witnessed."[32]

It was precisely this "limited accountability" interpretation of party leadership in the House which defeated Cannon. It was not, and is not, consistent either with the structure of the House as noted above or the "middle-man" concept of leadership which is fostered by this structure. The insurgents articulated an interpretation much more consistent with

271

the structure of the House. Whether theirs was a good or bad theory; whether it was well articulated or not; these are not relevant to the present argument. Though their position was much less tidy, and required considerable painful unraveling in the 1910 debate, it was more in the mainstream of the traditions of party leadership in Congress.

The insurgents argued that Cannon and his supporters had simply gone too far. Each congressman is an individual who is potentially part of a majority – procedural or substantive. On substantive issues, the insurgents argued, the Republican leadership was not attuned to new attitudes among Republicans. Leaders were using sanctions provided by procedural majorities to force – rather than build – substantive majorities. Leaders who do not attend to new opinions, and recognize their force, must face the consequences of losing their procedural majorities. Mr. Lindbergh of Minnesota argued the case for the insurgents as follows:

> . . . when I look back over the proceedings of this House, and when I know, and the entire country knows, that by indirection the will of this House has been thwarted time and time again, then I say, when we have a resoluton before us, which proposes to do by direction the will of the House, it is time now and here on this occasion to manifest our power, to enforce the rule of the majority, in the language that has frequently been expressed by the able Speaker of this House. I say now and here, in the light of what has occurred over and over again, in defeating, in holding back, in preventing bills that have been introduced in this House, which were in accord with the wish of the entire country at large – I say, when those bills have time and time again been pigeonholed by select committees, that now. . .the House can by a direct vote do directly the will of the House. . .[33]

John Nelson of Wisconsin also stated the insurgents' case vigorously. He observed that their duty was unpleasant – but that theirs had been an unpleasant experience in the House for some time. They had foregone the many privileges of the "regulars" – e.g., patronage and power – for the sake of principle. Their punishment was severe for failing to "cringe or crawl before the arbitrary power of the Speaker and his House machine." Nelson then discussed the problems of majorities, rules, leadership, and representation.

> The eloquent gentleman from New York [Mr. Fassett] says the majority must control, but what is the majority? Speaker Reed emphatically said:
> There is no greater fallacy than this idea that majority and minority are predicated on political parties only.
> Why should the subject of the rules be a party matter? At what convention did the Republican party adopt the present rules of the House? The Speaker says he represents the majority. But how? He and his chief lieutenants – favorites or personal friends, a small minority within the majority – call themselves the party and then pass the word on to the rank and file of the Republican membership to line up or be punished. What is the controlling force? Party principles? No. The

272

Speaker's power under the rules.... We are no less Republicans because we would be free Members of Congress. We do not need to be kept on leading strings. We are free representatives of the people, and we want freedom here for every Member of every party.[34]

It seems quite clear that Nelson's remarks may be interpreted in line with the analysis suggested here. Cannon's exercise of power was inconsistent with the bargaining condition in the House and therefore "free representatives" would form a new majority which would change the sanctions available to the Speaker.

The argument of the Democrats was very much like that of the insurgents. Oscar W. Underwood was led to conclude that leadership in the House should not be centered in the speakership – at least as it was exercised by Cannon. The Cannon "system" had to be overthrown.

We are fighting a system, and that system is the system that enables the Speaker, by the power vested in him, to thwart and overthrow the will of the majority membership of this House. We recognize to-day that there has to be leadership; that some man must be the leader of the majority and some man must be the leader of the minority, but we say the place for that leadership *is not in the Chair*.[35] (Emphasis added.)

In summary, the insurgent Republican members were led to take the drastic action of leaving their party to join the Democrats on a major procedural change because they were convinced that the Speaker's authority had allowed him to ignore segments of his procedural majority. They were unable to reach him directly in pressing for representation of their views. As their numbers grew, they merely waited for the right moment – primed to take action sometime to make the Speaker more accountable. Mr. Norris' resolution served as the catalyst for action.

THE CASE OF JUDGE SMITH

In 1961, the House voted 217 to 212 to enlarge the Committee on Rules from 12 to 15 members. By this action, the House took the first of a series of steps to curb the power of the Committee and its chairman, Howard W. Smith of Virginia. The Committee had, since 1937, developed an anti-administration nature. Southern Democrats and Republicans joined to defeat presidential proposals. There was considerable evidence to suggest that these actions more often than not had the tacit support of a bipartisan majority in the House. As Lewis J. Lapham concluded:

...it is perfectly true that a very good case can be developed for supporting the proposition that the Rules Committee, though out of sympathy with the majority party program as defined by the President and his supporters, did in fact faithfully represent majority sentiment in the House.[36]

Adolph Sabath (D-Illinois) chaired the Committee every Congress, except the 80th, between 1939 and 1952. Though he personally supported Democratic presidents and their programs, he was extremely weak and ineffective as Chairman. Lapham observed that "the *Congressional Record*, since 1939, is replete with candid admissions by Mr. Sabath that he was 'helpless' in the face of an obstinate majority on the Committee which he could not control."[37]

In 1953, conservative Republican Leo Allen (Illinois) again chaired the Committee, as he had in the 80th Congress. And in 1955, after the Democrats recaptured control of Congress in the 1954 elections, Howard W. Smith became chairman. Smith had been influential on the Committee before his accession to the chairmanship. He and Eugene E. Cox of Georgia were the principal leaders of the Southern Democratic-Republican coalition during Sabath's long tenure as chairman. Smith was first appointed to the Committee in 1933 – over the objections of the then-Speaker, Henry T. Rainey of Illinois. As chairman, Smith was free to exercise his considerable powers to stifle legislation which he and his southern Democratic and Republican colleagues opposed. In some cases the legislation was part of President Eisenhower's program – in other cases attempts by the Democratic majority in the House to enact their own legislation.

Smith's procedural majority was of a different sort than that provided Speaker Cannon. Whereas Cannon was elected to office, Smith achieved his position of leadership through seniority. Thus, in accepting seniority as a procedure for committee chairmanships, the Democrats had to accept Howard W. Smith as chairman of the Committee on Rules. To "defeat" Smith, the Democrats would have to strike a blow against the whole seniority system. Thus, Smith, like Cannon, had a considerable advantage. He had a certain amount of independence from his procedural majority. Up to a point, he could afford to ignore it in exercising the considerable reservoir of power in the Committee on Rules. He proceeded to do just that.

Chairman Smith's exercise of power

How did Smith develop and use his powers? Two careful students of the House Committee on Rules, James A. Robinson and Walter Kravitz, have examined the influence of the Committee on legislation during this period.[38] Both indicated the wide variety of powers available to the Committee at the height of its influence. The more overt actions were to refuse to grant a hearing for a rule and to refuse to grant the rule. During the 84th Congress, Robinson found that only four requests for hearings were refused and 11 rules were denied. During the 85th Congress, 20 requests for hearings were refused and 9 requests for rules were denied. In addition to these more obvious exercises of power, the Committee could force changes in the legislation as a condition for granting a rule, they could delay granting a rule until the mood of the House changed for some reason, they could grant a rule with conditions for debate which the authors did not want, they could threaten to refuse a rule. All of these tactics were relied on during the 84th and 85th Congresses. And, as is indicated by both Robinson and Kravitz, the legislation which was affected was often important legislation – the doctors' draft, housing, statehood for Alaska and Hawaii, aid to education, civil rights, depressed areas aid, presidential disability, absentee voting, appropriations measures, federal judgeships.

Warning signals again

In 1958, the Democrats won a sweeping victory throughout the nation. They increased their margin in the House by 49 seats and their margin in the Senate by 17 seats. A number of Democratic liberals in the House went to the Speaker and proposed that the party ratio on the Committee on Rules be changed from eight Democrats and four Republicans to nine and three. They further pressed for the return of the 21-day rule. Speaker Rayburn convinced them that they should not press for the changes. He assured them that legislation would be brought out of the Committee.[39]

The 1958 elections were of considerable importance to Chairman Smith and his power base. It was at this time that his procedural majority began to change drastically. There were 48 congressional districts in which Democrats replaced Republicans. What was the significance of this trade for Chairman Smith? The *Congressional Quarterly* provides economy support and opposition scores for the 85th Congress and for the first session of the 86th Congress.[40] The 48 House Republicans who were replaced by Democrats in 1958 had an average economy score of 42.9 and an average economy opposition score of 42.0 in the 85th Congress. Their Democratic replacements in the 86th Congress, 1st session, had an average economy score of 9.3 and an average economy opposition score of 86.3. Obviously this new group of congressmen was considerably more liberal than the Republicans who left Congress in 1958, and markedly less dependable for Chairman Smith.

If Chairman Smith wished to retain his position of power in the long run, several developments made it evident that he would have to make some accommodations during the 86th Congress. Speaker Rayburn had given the reformers his assurance that important legislation would not be delayed and thus had put his prestige on the line. The new Democrats were anxious to develop a legislative record for the 1960 presidential elections. Criticism of the Chairman and his committee had continued to mount during the 85th Congress. And, the new Democrats had served notice of their intentions with their reform suggestions during the early days of the 86th Congress (much as the progressive Republicans had placed Speaker Cannon on notice 50 years earlier).

The record shows, however, that Chairman Smith continued to block legislation. He relied on the same techniques as before, despite the fact that a new, restive majority was emerging in the House – a majority which ultimately could deprive Chairman Smith of much of his influence through procedural changes. During the 86th Congress, the Committee on Rules denied 31 requests for hearings and 11 requests for rules. As before, the Committee was a major factor in practically all significant legislation to come before the House – either by preventing its consideration on the floor or by influencing the substance of the legislation. But the most controversial action of the Committee was that taken in 1960 to defeat the first broad scale federal aid to education bill since the Morrill Act of 1862. Following the passage of the bill in both houses, the Committee on Rules invoked its power to deny the request for a rule allowing the House of Representatives to agree to a conference so as to resolve the differences between the House and Senate versions of the bill. The result, of course, was to kill the bill. By this action, the Committee on Rules seemed to place itself above majority action by *both* the House and the Senate. It became obvious to the liberal and moderate Democrats that Chairman Smith was not going to make accommodations. They concluded that their only alternative was to curb the power of Chairman Smith and his Committee on Rules.

The limits of leadership reemphasized

The 1960 elections brought to the White House an energetic young President of the twentieth century. He had campaigned on a platform of "action." Though his majority in the House was 20 less than the Democratic majority of the 86th Congress, it was still sizeable and it was made up of many members who were extremely critical of the Committee on Rules. If the President's program was to receive favorable consideration in Congress, it would have to receive favorable consideration in the Committee on Rules. Unless changes were made, it was unlikely that the Committee would be so cooperative.

The results of the power struggle between the young President, his Speaker, and Chairman Smith have been well chronicled and thus only the sequence of events needs repeating here.[41] Our interest is not in the details of what happened but rather in the arguments which were made, since these arguments should provide clues in defining the limits of power

Joseph G. Cannon and Howard W. Smith

Table 10.2 *Sequence of events in decline of power of House Committee on Rules, 1961–1965*

Event	Date	Vote
Enlargement of Committee from 12 to 15 for 87th Congress	January 31, 1961	217-212 GOP-22-148 Dem-195-64
Permanent enlargement of Committee from 12 to 15	January 9, 1963	235-196 GOP-28-148 Dem-207-48
Reinstitution of the 21-day rule and transfer of power regarding sending bills to conference[a]	January 4, 1965	224-201[b] GOP-16-123 Dem-208-78

[a] The second change permitted the Speaker to recognize a member to offer a motion to send a bill to conference.
[b] On a motion to close debate. Rules changes actually passed by voice vote.

for leaders in the House. A brief sequence of events is provided in Table 10.2.

As might be expected there are parallels between the debate in 1910 and the debates during the 1961–1965 period (of which the 1961 debate was the most crucial). As in 1910, those who pressed for change in 1961 argued in favor of leadership accountability to the majority. The Committee on Rules was a roadblock to the majority. It was not allowing the House to vote on measures which a majority in the House wished to vote on. Despite the fact that the majority party had a 2 to 1 majority on the Committee, Chairman Smith and second-ranking Democrat, William Colmer (Mississippi), would frequently vote with the four Republicans on important legislation to prevent it from coming to the floor. John A. Blatnik (D-Minnesota), head of the Democratic Study Group, and therefore a principal leader in adopting the rules changes, stated the case as follows:

My constituents did not cast a free ballot for the office of U.S. Representative to Congress to have the functions of that Office limited by one or two or even six other Members. They understand that in a body as large as this the majority shall be established in caucus and put forward in the form of legislation by the leadership chosen by the majority. It is difficult to explain to them how 2 members of the majority [Smith and Colmer] can desert the majority's program, join with 4 members of the minority and among them determine the course of action of 431 other Members of this House. . . . Does their judgment supersede the cumulative judgment of the legislative committees? Do they have some inherent right . . . to determine the course of legislation . . . ? It would appear that they at least think so.[42]

Thus, though Blatnik, and others who pressed for change, agreed that any leader or any leadership committee had latitude in exercising power, they also agreed that there should be limits beyond which leaders are not permitted to go. To the reformers, the Committee on Rules ultimately should be a part of the majority leadership. That meant something very specific. For example, to Paul J. Kilday (D-Texas), it meant that:

...the Committee on Rules is an arm of the leadership of the majority party. ...one who assumes membership on the Committee on Rules must be prepared to exercise a function of leadership. His personal objection to the proposal is not always sufficient reason for him to vote to deny the membership of the whole House the opportunity to express its approval or, equally important, the opportunity to express its disapproval.[43]

Speaker Rayburn expressed much the same sentiment:

I think that the Committee on Rules should grant that rule whether its membership is for the bill or not. I think this House should be allowed on great measures to work its will, and it cannot work its will if the Committee on Rules is so constituted as not to allow the House to pass on those things.[44]

Frequent references to 1910 were made. At the time "too much control was centered in the Speaker...." "Today...we fight a system which has deposited too much power in the Committee on Rules..."[45] according to Sidney R. Yates (D-Illinois). What is the definition of "too much power?" It is that situation when leaders have been permitted to exercise greater authority than was intended by the procedural majority in the House.

The limited accountability theory restated

The arguments of Smith and his supporters also bore the characteristics of the 1910 debate. Speaker Cannon believed in limited accountability and so did Smith. Though their positions of leadership were different, and therefore one would not expect exact parallels between the two situations, the two had similar views of leadership and accountability. To Chairman Smith, the whole effort to enlarge the Committee was both unnecessary and premature. In a series of circumlocutions (some of which were contradictory), Smith and his cohorts argued as follows:

1. The Committee has been wrongly charged – it does not block important legislation which requires "emergency action." As Clarence Brown (R-Ohio), ranking Republican on the Committee on Rules, and close colleague of Chairman Smith, noted: "In my nearly a quarter of a century of service here, I have never known of a single instance, when the House leadership desired a bill to be brought to a House vote, that such measure was not voted upon."[46]

2. The Committee will delay on measures which are not "emergency" measures but "nothing is lost and much is gained by delay. . . . 'haste make waste'. . .John Nance Garner. . .once was reported to have said, 'The country never suffers from the things that Congress fails to do.'"[47]

3. The majority can always work its will – it can go around the Committee on Rules by relying on Calendar Wednesday, discharge petition, and suspension of the rules.

4. Much more legislation is killed in other standing committees than in the Committee on Rules.

5. How can the president know that his program will not be enacted? He has just arrived on the scene. It would be better to leave the "packing" resolution on the calendar for two years and then assess the situation when the evidence is in.

6. The Chairman is willing now to insure that "no obstacles" would be interposed "to the five major bills that the President has publicly announced as his program for this session."

This example of a Smith accommodation is very revealing and brings us to an analysis of his broader view of his position of leadership. He did not consider it necessary generally to work with his party leaders and membership in passing legislation but he was willing to allow five major bills to reach the floor. This offer was considered "audacious" by the reformers. Blatnik expressed their views:

Who else would have the audacity and arrogance to even suggest that in exchange for our agreeing to the status quo they would permit us to consider five pieces of legislation said to be the cornerstone of the new administration's domestic program? This offer was an insult to the House and its Members. The fact that it was a bona fide and sincere attempt only heightens the frightening picture of two men telling a nation that they will permit five bills to pass if they can reserve their right to kill off any others that do not meet with their approval.[48]

How could this type of proposal be offered by Smith? Clearly, he saw it as a definite concession. "All of the five bills which the President has announced as his program for this session. . .are five bills that I am very much opposed to. . . ."[49] Smith did not consider that he had an obligation to support his party's legislation just because he chaired the committee which scheduled that legislation.

When I made this pledge to the Speaker and to the Members of this House, it is a pledge I made when I first became chairman of the Rules Committee. That is, *I will cooperate with the Democratic leadership of the House of Representatives just as long and just as far as my conscience will permit me to go.*[50] (Emphasis added.)

The convenience of holding oneself accountable to "conscience" is that only the individual himself is involved in defining accountability. This self-interpretation was the very thing that was objected to by the reformers. It meant that the majority could not be assured of cooperation from one of their leaders. Speaker Rayburn, among others, expressed his concern.

The gentleman from Virginia says that he is not going to report anything that violates his conscience and then winds up his talk on the floor by saying you have nothing to fear from the action of the Committee on Rules.[51]

In 1963 the Committee on Rules was permanently expanded to 15 members. Many of the same arguments were invoked but the political situation had changed. The reformers could now defend their experiment – pointing out that the dire predictions of those opposed in 1961 had not come true. Even the Republicans seemed to accept the 15-member committee, though they tried to have the party division changed from 10 Democrats and 5 Republicans to 9 Democrats and 6 Republicans. The best the opponents of a 15-member committee could do was to reiterate their earlier arguments and note that the committee's performance in the 87th Congress was little different than before – it, too, blocked legislation.[52] For Judge Smith's part, he focused his attention on southern Democrats, warning that:

...this matter of packing the Rules Committee affects more closely our area of the country than anywhere else.... I hope that none of my southern friends are going to be complaining around here when certain measures come up, and come up quite promptly, if the Committee on Rules is packed again.... I hope that at least those Members who voted against the packing before will see fit to do the same thing again, because I believe *it is vital to the interests of their States*....[53] (Emphasis added.)

The Chairman also addressed the new members of the 88th Congress. He warned them that unwise fiscal legislation would soon be introduced.

Are you going to yield up every little leverage or every little weapon you may have to defeat measures so unsound? Are you going to yield some of your prerogatives and privileges here today that are going to adversely affect your people for the next 20 years? If you do, *that is your business and none of mine*.[54] (Emphasis added.)

Howard W. Smith proved himself to be an unintentioned prophet. By a margin of 39 votes (see Table 10.2), the House did make an attempt to clarify the distinction between its business and that of Judge Smith. Thus occurred the second important increment in the decline of the chairmanship of the Committee on Rules.

The third increment came in 1965. With very little debate, the House re-invoked the 21-day rule[55] and took away the Committee on Rules' power, when any member of the House objected, to grant rules to send a bill to conference (or to agree to the Senate version). In both instances, the powers of the Speaker were increased. To Clarence Brown (R-Ohio) this raised the spectre of the all-powerful Speaker before 1910. In a colloquy with Speaker McCormack, he observed:

You are too nice a fellow. But I am thinking about some dirty dog that might come along some other time and say here is a nice little wrinkle in the rule which we can use to block this legislation.

In other words, should we give that power to every Speaker in the future? We gave that power to "Uncle Joe" Cannon and Tom Reed as the gentleman recalls. We gave them too much power.[56]

Ironically, Brown failed to perceive that his colleague, Howard W. Smith, also had been given more power than was compatible with the structure, organization, and composition of the House of Representatives. Smith had developed independence from those who ultimately had provided him with this position of authority. Smith's refusal to heed the warning signals of substantive shifts in his procedural majority resulted in changes which forced him to be more dependent on this majority or face a serious loss of influence in the process of building substantive majorities.

CONCLUSIONS

In 1910 and 1961 the House of Representatives acted to curb the power of two generally well-loved and admired leaders – Joseph G. Cannon and Howard W. Smith. These men had realized the full potential of the authority inherent in their respective positions in the House. Though in different ways, they both had become virtually independent of their procedural majorities. Defeating them would not have solved the problems raised by their exercise of power. Thus, the House took the more drastic action of making procedural changes to guarantee the predominance of the condition of relatively free bargaining, with leaders acting as "middle-men."

Though it is not possible as a result of this inquiry to set forth a handbook for successful leadership in the House, it is possible to draw some inferences concerning the limits which must be observed by the "middle-man" type of leader. First, the procedural majority is of major significance for House leaders since the sanctions it allows determine the limits on leaders in forming or thwarting substantive majorities. In order to protect his position, the House leader must be exceptionally protective of this procedural majority – developing techniques which will inform him as to substantive changes which have occurred within various segments of the majority, and making a requisite number of adaptations.

Second, there are cases, as noted here, where leaders have developed, over a period of time, the authority of the position to the extent that they seemingly are independent of the procedural majority. Their exercise of power eventually leads some members to the conclusion that procedural changes are necessary to prevent a recurrence of such independent action. If there are enough members of the majority who perceive violations of bargaining behavior on the part of leaders over a period of time, they may take extreme action to force compliance with their expectations. These instances are of major significance for the study of the House since they provide important clues as to how that body defines leadership for itself.

Third, all House leaders have considerable latitude in using the sanctions provided by procedural majorities in building substantive majorities. In the short run, therefore, leaders thwart the emergence of new majorities. Furthermore, leaders are normally given ample warning of dissatisfaction before action is taken. If the leader persists in ignoring these signs (or in simply failing to read them properly), he will be defeated. If, in addition, he has assumed so much power that he is protected from his procedural majority, the reform condition is set and changes will be made eventually.

Fourth, both cases cited here suggest that leadership positions of great, absolute authority in the House of Representatives are contextually inappropriate. Congressional political parties are coalitions of members, each of whom has some bargaining power. Thus, conditions in the House are not conducive to the exercise of power with such limited accountability to major segments of the procedural majority, as in the two cases cited here.

Fifth, one is inevitably led to inquire whether Speaker Cannon and Chairman Smith could have avoided the consequences which ultimately developed. If the analysis of this essay is accurate, the answer must be "yes." They could have avoided the reforms by accepting the conditions of leadership in the House and behaving accordingly. Had they been more flexible, they would likely have not only avoided being "reformed" but also have preserved more power for themselves in the long run. Speaker Sam Rayburn, the model "middle-man," could have counseled them both on such matters.

NOTES

1 For a sample of this literature see: David B. Truman, *The Governmental Process* (New York: Knopf, 1951); Bertram M. Gross, *The Legislative Struggle* (New York: McGraw-Hill, 1953); Robert L. Peabody and Nelson

W. Polsby, eds., *New Perspectives on the House of Representatives* (Chicago: Rand-McNally, 1963); and particularly Robert L. Peabody, "Organization Theory and Legislative Behavior: Bargaining, Hierarchy and Change in the U.S. House of Representatives," unpublished paper delivered at the Annual Meeting of the American Political Science Association, New York, 1963.

2 The "middle-man" thesis of congressional leadership is discussed in David B. Truman, *The Congressional Party: A Case Study* (New York: Wiley, 1959). See also Samuel C. Patterson, "Legislative Leadership and Political Ideology," *Public Opinion Quarterly*, Vol. 27 (Fall, 1963), 399–410.

3 Richard F. Fenno, Jr., has eloquently discussed the organizational problems of the House in his essay in David B. Truman, ed., *The Congress and America's Future* (Englewood Cliffs, N. J.: Prentice-Hall, 1965).

4 Lewis A. Froman, Jr., and Randall B. Ripley note that the two parties maintain the highest level of cohesion on procedural questions. See "Conditions for Party Leadership: The Case of the House Democrats," *American Political Science Review*, Vol. 59 (March, 1965), 52–63. Much of this essay tends to support their general argument.

5 Cannon allowed the Democrats to select their members, though he did not have to make this concession. He did so because he thought that by giving the minority leader this power, the Democrats would fight over committee assignments. See William R. Gwinn, *Uncle Joe Cannon: Archfoe of Insurgency* (New York: Bookman Associates, 1957), p. 97.

6 *Congressional Record*, 61st Cong., 2d sess., March 17, 1910, p. 3294.

7 Cannon also preferred to have his whip on Ways and Means. James Tawney (Minnesota), James Watson (Indiana), and John Dwight (New York), all were on that Committee while serving as Whip under Cannon.

8 For discussions of seniority and its development, see George Goodwin, "The Seniority System in Congress," *American Political Science Review*, Vol. 53 (June, 1959), 596–604; George B. Galloway, *History of the House of Representatives* (New York: Crowell, 1961); and particularly Nelson W. Polsby, "The Institutionalization of the U.S. House of Representatives," *American Political Science Review*, Vol. 62 (March, 1968), 144–168.

9 See Paul D. Hasbrouck, *Party Government in the House of Representatives* (New York: Macmillan, 1927), p. 37.

10 George Norris, *Fighting Liberal* (New York: Macmillan, 1945), p. 109.

11 *Congressional Record*, 61st Cong., 2d sess., March 17, 1910, p. 3300.

12 Norris, p. 144.

13 Hasbrouck, pp. 4–6.

14 The principal student of these changes is Joseph Cooper. See "Congress and Its Committees," unpublished Ph.D. dissertation, Harvard University, 1961. See also Chang-wei Chiu, *The Speaker of the House of Representatives Since 1896* (New York: Columbia University Press, 1928), Chapter VI. Actually, for rather complicated reasons, the insurgents hadn't voted for Calendar Wednesday; see Cooper, Ch. II.

15 Hasbrouck, p. 126.

16 One can consult any number of sources on the 1910 revolt. Those highly recommended include: Hasbrouck; Chiu; Gwinn; Norris; Kenneth Hechler, *Insurgency* (New York: Columbia University Press, 1941); George R. Brown, *The Leadership of Congress* (Indianapolis: Bobbs-Merrill, 1922); Charles R. Atkinson, *The Committee on Rules and the Overthrow of Speaker Cannon* (New York: Columbia University Press, 1911), plus the several

biographies and autobiographies of those who participated. For a listing of the latter see Charles O. Jones and Randall B. Ripley, *The Role of Political Parties in Congress: A Bibliography and Research Guide* (Tucson: University of Arizona Press, 1966).

17 Gwinn suggests that this move was prearranged between Crumpacker and Cannon. See p. 206.

18 *Congressional Record*, 61st Cong., 2d sess., March 16, 1910, p. 3241.

19 *Ibid.*, p. 3251.

20 *Congressional Record*, 61st Cong., 2d sess., March 17, 1910, p. 3287.

21 *Ibid.*, p. 3289.

22 Gwinn, p. 207.

23 Norris, p. 126

24 *New York Times*, March 18, 1910, p. 1.

25 *Congressional Record*, 61st Cong., 2d sess., March 17, 1910, p. 3292.

26 L. White Busbey, *Uncle Joe Cannon: The Story of a Pioneer American* (New York: Holt, 1927), p. 254.

27 *Congressional Record*, 61st Cong., 2d sess., March 17, 1910, p. 3302.

28 *Ibid.*, p. 3305.

29 *Congressional Record*, 61st Cong., 2d sess., March 19, 1910, p. 3430.

30 *Ibid.*, p. 3436.

31 *Ibid.*, p. 3437.

32 Busbey, p. 266.

33 *Congressional Record*, 61st Cong., 2d sess., March 17, 1910, p. 3300.

34 *Ibid.*, p. 3304.

35 *Congressional Record*, 61st Cong., 2d sess., March 19, 1910, p. 3433. Interestingly, Underwood later became the principal leader of the House during the 62nd Congress as majority leader. The Democrats were in a ticklish spot. They wanted to emphasize the internal divisions in the Republican Party so as to win the 1910 elections, but did not want the Republicans either to get credit for reform or to reunite after reform. One news story suggested that the Democrats wanted Cannon to win, so as not to lose an issue in 1910 (*New York Times*, March 19, 1910). The Democrats also had to consider the problems for themselves of a drastic change in the Speaker's power, should they gain control of the House in 1910.

36 Lewis J. Lapham, "Party Leadership and the House Committee on Rules," unpublished Ph.D. dissertation, Harvard University, 1954, p. 137.

37 *Ibid.*, p. 123.

38 See James A. Robinson, *The House Rules Committee* (Indianapolis: Bobbs-Merrill, 1963); and the several useful unpublished research papers on the House Committee on Rules produced by Walter Kravitz of the Legislative Reference Service, Library of Congress. See also, Christopher Van Hollen, "The House Committee on Rules (1933–1951): Agent of Party and Agent of Opposition," unpublished Ph.D. dissertation, Johns Hopkins University, 1951.

39 See Congressional Quarterly, Inc., *Congress and the Nation*, p. 1425. See also William MacKaye, *A New Coalition Takes Control: The House Rules Committee Fight 1961* (New York: McGraw-Hill, 1963).

40 *Congressional Quarterly Almanacs*, Vols. 14 and 15.

41 Note in particular, in addition to Robinson and MacKaye, the two articles in Peabody and Polsby – one by Peabody and one by Peabody and Milton C. Cummings, Jr.; and Neil MacNeil, *Forge of Democracy: The House of*

Representatives (New York: MacKay, 1963), Ch. 15.

42 *Congressional Record*, 87th Cong., 1st sess., January 31, 1961, pp. 1582–1583.

43 *Ibid.*, p. 1574.

44 *Ibid.*, p. 1579.

45 *Ibid.*, p. 1581.

46 *Ibid.*, p. 1575.

47 *Ibid.*, p. 1577.

48 *Ibid.*, p. 1583.

49 *Ibid.*, p. 1576.

50 *Loc. cit.*

51 *Ibid.*, p. 1580.

52 Particularly noted was the defeat of the federal aid to education bill in the Committee in 1961. Though a bargain had been struck between pro- and anti-parochial school aid members, the parochial aid proponents were not convinced that they would get what they wanted. Thus, a liberal, Democratic, Catholic member of the Committee on Rules, James Delaney of New York, voted with the conservatives to kill the bill. See H. Douglas Price, "Race, Religion, and the Rules Committee," in Alan F. Westin, ed., *The Uses of Power* (New York: Harcourt, Brace, 1962); and Robert Bendiner, *Obstacle Course on Capitol Hill* (New York: McGraw-Hill, 1964).

53 *Congressional Record*, 88th Cong., 1st sess., January 9, 1963, p. 18.

54 *Loc. cit.*

55 The 21-day rule had been implemented during the 81st Congress and abandoned in the 82nd Congress. It has since been abandoned in the 90th Congress.

56 *Congressional Record*, 89th Cong., 1st sess., January 4, 1965, p. 22.

11

*Presidential leadership in Congress: securing
commitments*

TERRY SULLIVAN

"Listen Lyndon," [Senator Wirtz] said, . . ."if I have learned anything at all in
these years, it is this: you can *tell* a man to go to hell, but you can't *make* him go."
    I thought of that story many times during my presidency. It seemed particularly
apt when I found myself in a struggle with the House or the Senate.
                                                    Lyndon Johnson, *The Vantage Point*

In order to govern, get reelected, and serve their own policy goals,
presidents must be able to form coalitions within Congress. This is not
always easy since in the American system the goals of presidents and
members of Congress need not, and often do not, coincide. The
Constitution created an institutional structure in which executive and
legislative branches serve different constituencies, their modes of election
vary, and the scope of their ambitions is constrained in different ways.
Presidents must be able to overcome these institutional barriers in order
to secure enough commitment to form a governing coalition. And they
must often be able to *convert* opponents in Congress to their cause in
order to form those coalitions.

This is a study of how presidents form governing coalitions in this
environment. It explores whether or not three specific forces in decision

    I would like to thank Ken Collier, who has worked on this project in various
capacities. I am also grateful for the suggestions of my colleague Mathew McCubbins.
Other helpful suggestions were received from Benjamin I. Page, Charles Cnudde, Jim
Alt, Gary Cox, Melvin Hinich, Lawrence C. Dodd, and several anonymous referees
my coeditor obtained for this paper. The Everett Dirksen Center, the University
Research Institute at the University of Texas, and the Lyndon Baines Johnson
Foundation supported some phases of this research. I am also very thankful for the
assistance I have received from the archivists at the LBJ Presidential Archives: Nancy
Smith, Linda Hansen, and Claudia Anderson. Finally, I would like to express my
thanks to Alan Meltzer, director, and the Center for the Study of Public Policy,
Graduate School of Industrial Administration, Carnegie-Mellon University, who
supported me as a fellow while I completed this paper.

making – *institutional structure, constituency "trust,"* and *substantive compromise* – play a role in presidential influence. These forces are examined in the context of a simple model of congressional decision making that emphasizes the role of reelection as a central institutional force. To test whether these three new forces play a role in securing conversions, data on the initial positions of members and change in their positions were gathered from *headcounts* collected by Lyndon Johnson's Office of Congressional Relations (OCR) during the 90th Congress (1967–68). These headcounts are polls of the House membership taken periodically (and confidentially) in order to inform the president and the congressional leadership about the expected positions of members on various issues as the coalition process proceeded.

PROPOSITION OF THE MODEL

As yet, no theory exists about how presidents lead in the Congress, except to say that presidents must be able to persuade (Neustadt 1960). A good place to begin an exploration of such presidential influence is with the constitutional structure of governing and the nature of congressional decision making. Both constrain presidential influence. And the nature of both is somewhat understood.

A simple model of legislative leadership

To understand presidential (or any other) leadership in Congress it is necessary to have a theory of how members make decisions. The theory employed here assumes that members engaged in forming coalitions are guided by a desire to maximize their expected election return, which serves as a source of consistency in behavior. This was the intent of the founders: to rest the structure of policy making on the desire to be reelected.[1] The anecdotal literature on congressional behavior is also filled with enough such incidents to make this assumption a reasonable one.[2]

The president and the members of Congress have in common the fact that they are both elected. They share a common fate with regard to the electorate. This shared fate might be tapped by the president. For example, similar constituent bases may unify the two behind a common political outlook. A member may share with the president preferred positions on basic issues such as proper economic policy, civil rights, or foreign policy because they both draw their strength from the same interests. These kinds of common outlooks form a useful *context* for coalition building between the two actors, each tending to assume the other's preferred position while at the same time acting to stabilize their

287

relationship, their current positions tending to coverage over the long run (though not necessarily in the short term).

The effect of such contextual forces is widely understood. Indeed, variables commonly associated with these forces (e.g., *party*, some measure of *ideology*, and *region*) make up the mainstay of any empirical study of congressional decision making. Along with these kinds of forces, congressional decision making is also affected by more short-term forces, which give the president temporary strengths or weaknesses in the leadership process. Since members and presidents are often inextricably linked together by the electorate, the ebb and flow of immediate presidential fortunes loom large as a consideration for members. When the president is very popular, members want to be closely associated with the administration, especially members of the president's party. In bad times, they will want to distance themselves from the president. A few of these more immediate forces are widely recognized as important – for example, the current level of *presidential popularity* and the current *state of the economy*. The simple model of legislative decision making, and thus of securing commitments, rests upon these standard forces associated with the nature of constituencies and the desire to be reelected.

Three additions to the simple model

In addition to the simple model of constituency forces, three other forces may play a role. These are particularly important to the president's ability to secure commitments. The first is *institutional structure*. The other two forces, which affect the flexibility of the president and members and are based upon a constitutional balance of power between them, are *constituency trust* and *substanitive compromise*.

The genius of the constitutional framework is epitomized by the system of checks and balances between the executive and the legislative. Although the two branches must compete for control of the policy agenda, the system makes it impossible for one actor to produce policies (and the resultant political credit) without the favorable intervention of the other. Which policy outcome is selected, then, hangs upon the relative influence of one branch over the other. The ability of the president to secure commitments from members may depend either upon the freedom of the members to respond favorably to the administration's appeals or, conversely, upon the ability of the membership to extract a compromise of the administration's proposal.

Institutional structure as a force. Constituency representation plays an important role in a member's electoral career, but that is not the only career a member has. A member may represent a committee or a party as well as a district. And this representation also affects decision making. In the House, structure decentralizes control over the agenda by creating a number of positions of responsibility throughout the committee system and the party organization. Holding such a position affords a member the resources with which to affect the coalition process by controlling the agenda.[3]

In utilizing their control over the agenda, members depend upon the organization and mechanisms of leadership accommodation and compromise. It is assumed that this use necessarily redefines the member's calculus, acting as an inducement to being more supportive. In a study of the former Speaker's constituency relationships, Champagne describes Sam Rayburn's perspective on this influence in the following way:

In essence, he told his constituents that a leader must be a part of a team. Sometimes that team went against his wishes and the district's wishes, but it was necessary to go along on some distasteful policies in order to have impact on others. He also pointed out that some of those distasteful policies were a product of team compromise which he had been able to make less distasteful than they would have been without his influence. [1984, p. 138]

It is expected that the higher one travels in the hierarchy, the more likely it is that one's claims on policy credit are associated with the success of the president's program. Thus, the first hypothesis to test is

Hypothesis 1: Institutional position will positively affect the likelihood a member will commit to the administration position.

Of course, institutional position is a secondary consideration – one must first serve one's constituents before serving influence. Since it is a secondary objective, it seems reasonable to expect that

Hypothesis 2: The strength of institutional position will be less than that of the constituency forces (and those variables associated with these forces).

Constituency "trust" as a force. Constituency forces (whether contextual or immediate) play an important role in decision making because members are vulnerable to their electorates. Obviously, these forces are less important whenever members are secure in their constituency. Obtaining this degree of support is the process of receiving constituent "trust." Fenno, in his ground breaking study of "home styles" (1978, pp. 56–57), says that

Members of Congress go home to present themselves...and to win the accolade: "he is a good man".... Their object is to present themselves in such a way that the inferences drawn by those watching will be supportive. The representative's word for these supportive inferences is trust. When a constituent trusts a House member, the constituent is saying something like this, "I am willing to put myself in your hands temporarily; I know you will have opportunities to hurt me;...I

289

assume – and I will continue to assume until it is proven otherwise – that you will not hurt me;...I'm not going to worry about your behavior.

Trust acts as a buffer modifying the "main" effect of the constituency variables.

In addition, trust makes it possible to respond more positively (or at least more freely) to the institutions of power: party leaders, the president, and so on. Secure from defeat, a member may act more independently of constituency forces. On the other hand, those more closely threatened by defeat are far more likely to exhibit inflexibility in dealing with administration requests for support whenever they would violate constituency interest. With these two kinds of trust effects in mind, it should be expected when presidents seek commitments that[4]

Hypothesis 3: "Safe" members are more able to weather short-term fluctuations in presidential popularity or the economy than are "marginal" members, and they are more likely to be guided by the basic, contextual forces within their constituencies.

Substantive compromise as a force. One way in which a president can secure commitments from nonsupporters is through the proposition or, alternatively, the acceptance of compromises.[5] Through the use of compromise, the president may move the administration's bill closer to the preferred proposal of some target group. Thus, a compromise can be expected to amplify the contextual forces that underlie the preferences of that group and to increase differentially the probability that members of the target group will make commitments at a higher rate than the membership in general; that is,

Hypothesis 4: Liberal compromises should amplify the tendency for those with liberal ideological identifications to commit to the administration, and conservative compromises should dampen the tendency of liberals to commit.

Measures and data

Given the hypotheses stated about these three forces, the model tested is

$$
\begin{aligned}
P_{commit} = \alpha &+ \gamma_{ij}(\beta_1 PARTY + \beta_2 ADA + \beta_3 REGION) \\
&+ \delta_j(\beta_4 UR + \beta_5 IR + \beta_6 GALLUP + \beta_7 DIST) \\
&+ \beta_{25} LEADER + \beta_{26} COMMV + \beta_{27} CONTROL + e
\end{aligned}
$$

The model takes the basic theory of constituency forces and adds to it several new variables (some associated with the three new forces, plus a variable associated with the need for statistical *control*) in order to predict the probability (P) that a member will commit to the administration's position when that member responded to the initial headcount with a nonsupportive position. In general, the empirical model employs standard representations (or measures) of the forces in the theory. For example, the model employs a member's party membership as a basic differentiation between members. It is common to use a rating score provided by the Americans for Democratic Action (ADA) in order to measure a member's ideological orientation. Regional identification is measured in a common way and represented in the model by REGION. The previous month's rate of unemployment and inflation (UR and IR) are used as measures of the state of the economy. Presidential popularity is measured in two ways, by the monthly approval rating of the president (in this case, Lyndon Johnson) on the Gallup poll (GALLUP) and by the margin of victory by which the president (Johnson) carried the member's district in the previous presidential election year, 1964 (DIST).

Two measures of institutional position are employed, representing the majority party and the committee system. Holding an office in the Democratic party organization (LEADER) is taken as a good measure of a member's institutional position within the party hierarchy. For positions within the committee system hierarchy, the special nature of that system must be taken into account. In the committee system, some committees are more central to policy making than others, and seniority within a committee is indicative of some position. So an appropriate measure of institutional position with the committee system had to account for this duality. A "committee value total" (COMMV) was calculated from a members's committee seniority and the Bullock committee value, which is based upon requests for transfer of assignment to that committee (Bullock 1962). A member's total committee value was determined by dividing a member's rank within the committee's caucus by the number of members of that caucus. The additive inverse of this value was then added to one and multiplied by the Bullock value for the committee. All values for the member, given multiple committee assignments, were then added together to represent the member's total value. Thus, a senior member on a committee was always ranked above others on that committee, but the importance of the various committees was also considered so that a less senior member on a very important committee might score higher than a moderately senior member on an unimportant committee.

Members adopting some initial position close to that of the administration are more easily converted than are those who are ardent opponents. In order to avoid the masking that this effect might have on assessing the other variables, a "control" variable (CONTROL), accounting for the member's initial position prior to conversion, was introduced into the model.

The constituency variables are modified by interaction with two of the three new variables. These variables, *compromise* and *trust*, are called "switching variables," because they affect the main variables differently depending upon which group of members is involved or "switched to." When members are attempting to decide which coalitions to join and which kinds of commitments to make, these forces in their decision calculus are bound to interact with the others. One force then amplifies the effect of the other making the effect of the latter far greater for that member than it is in general for most members. These variables are represented by the symbols γ and δ respectively.

The switching variable for trust is the simplest to describe. It takes on different values (j subscript) depending upon the different level of constituency trust secured by the member: A member is either "safe" or "marginal." This characteristic then interacts with the rest of the main variables as noted. The second switching variable is more complicated since it adds the effect of compromise to the effect of trust. The second switching variable takes on different values (i and j subscripts) depending upon the different kinds of compromises arrived at and the different levels of constituency trust secured. So, the i subscript takes on values associated with compromise types (liberal leaning, no compromise, and conservative leaning), while the j subscript takes on the values associated with trust.

In order to test the model just introduced, data were collected from archival files at the Lyndon B. Johnson Presidential Archives. To Johnson, making Congress do his bidding required a special working arrangement – one of constant attention. Headcounting and his OCR were the technique and instrument for maintaining this attention. A headcount polled the members of Congress in order to ascertain their current positions on some specific legislative issue. Typically, members were asked a question or series of questions intended to reveal their positions. Member's responses were recorded on a worksheet, which listed all of the current membership of the House arranged by state and party. These positions were coded as one of seven possible responses: "Right," "Leaning right," "Possible," "No response," "Absent," "Leaning wrong," "Wrong."

Once a worksheet was filled out, the arduous process of assessment, strategy development, and securing commitments could begin. The objective was to develop a package strong enough to attract and hold a voting majority on the floor. For purposes of assessment and strategy, it is apparent that the OCR considered all those who were not solidly committed to the administration's bill to be "nonsupporters" in need of clarification and coversion: To LBJ a member was either "Right" or in need of persuasion.[6]

The administration's efforts at clarification and conversion were often followed by another poll of members. Sometimes, this involved recontacting the entire membership. Other times (and more often), the administration monitored only those from whom it had not received initial commitments of support. This new information would be recorded in an updated version of the original worksheet, indicating the position of each member. Taken together, these efforts resulted in a multiple or "sequenced" counting effort leading up to a "final" count completed just before floor consideration of the bill. These sequenced counts provide an interesting historical record of the coalition-building process, pinpointing members' policy positions over time and documenting whether a member committed to the administration.

The counts employed in this study cover 42 different subjects related to 27 bills (see the Appendix for a list of counts). Of the 42 counts, 28 are sequenced efforts averaging about 27 days between the initial and the final count. On the average count, about 134 members could be expected to support the administration's proposal initially. This figure is 84 shy of the 218 voted needed for an assured victory. If the administration considered as nonsupporters all of the other members who were not "Right," then those 84 votes had to be secured from the remaining 301 members. It is this pool of members, the nonsupporters on each issue, that provided the data to test the model.

Pooled together, the nonsupportive responses were then divided into three policy subpools in order to avoid a technical problem with statistical analysis of differing policy dimensions.[7] The three subject areas are Civil Rights, Foreign Policy, and Governing the Economy.[8] In general, the empirical results are reported for the Governing the Economy data. Results in the other two issue dimensions were virtually identical.

Occasionally, White House sequenced counts excluded Republicans, at least in the initial stages. On the 28 sequenced efforts, for example, 54.6 percent of the Republicans were coded as "No response" on the initial count. And Republicans accounted for more than 70 percent of the "No response" responses on 16 of the final counts. This clearly suggests that about half the time the Administration did not attempt to convert the opposition party. On other counts, obviously, Republicans were contacted. Adding all Republicans would bias the tests in one direction, whereas excluding all Republicans would bias them in another direction. Excluding members from the data is an admittedly arbitrary decision but one that is intended to lead to confidence in the results. Whenever at least 70 percent of the Republican caucus is recorded as "No response" on the final sequenced count, all Republicans were excluded from the data base on that bill. Using the 28 sequenced efforts created a data base for the study of conversion with 6,887 incidents of initial nonsupport. Eventually, data selection and deletions within the various statistical programs reduced this set to 6,089 cases, divided into the three policy groups: Civil Rights, 1,882; Foreign Policy, 1,321; and Governing the Economy, 2,886.

THE EMPIRICAL RESULTS

Hypotheses

Given the measures used in this study, the four hypotheses discussed earlier suggest the following specific expectations.

1. *The importance of institutional position*: A nonsupporter who holds an office in the Democratic leadership should more readily convert than one who does not. Likewise, a senior member of the committee system should more readily convert than one with less at stake; that is, the coefficient for both the variables LEADER and COMMittee Value should be positive (+).[9]

2. *The relative importance of institutional position*: Constituency variables should have larger standardized coefficients[10] than the institutional variables in general.

3. *The importance of constituency trust*: Trust should dampen the impact of the more immediate constituency variables while amplifying the impact of the contextual constituency variables. The coefficients on safe-switching variables should be smaller than for marginal switching variables on UNEMPLOYMENT rate, INFLATION rate, LBJ's GALLUP popularity, and DISTrict % for LBJ in 1964. The coefficients on the contextual variables (PARTY, ADA Ideology, and REGION) should be greater for the safe-switching variable than for the marginal-switching variable; for example, ADA Ideology-Safe should be greater than ADA Ideology-Marginal, PARTY-Safe should be greater than PARTY-Marginal, et cetera.

4. *The importance of substantive compromise*: Administration compromises should enhance the commitments of the targeted groups. For example, the coefficient for Liberal Compromises on ADA Ideology should be positive and greater than those for No Compromises and Conservative Compromises and ADA Ideology.

Table 11.1 reports a PROBIT[11] test of the hypotheses about securing commitments. The theory seems to be extremely well supported. The model performed well and accounted for a great deal of the information found in the data. For example, although it is not the most accurate

Table 11.1. *PROBIT model of conversion on Governing the Economy, 90th House*

Main variable	Switches Trust	Compromise	Stand. coeff.	Stand. error	t
PARTY	Safe	/Lib compromise	.3191	.4673	4.292***
	Safe	/No compromise	.2676	.1415	4.549***
	Safe	/Con compromise	.4957	.2033	7.414***
	Marginal	/Lib compromise	.0450	.5127	1.058
	Marginal	/No compromise	.2106	.1853	3.661***
	Marginal	/Con compromise	.2312	.2443	4.467***
ADA Ideology	Safe	/Lib compromise	.3868	.0076	7.316***
	Safe	/No compromise	.2179	.0013	7.622***
	Safe	/Con compromise	.4734	.0021	13.179***
	Marginal	/Lib compromise	.1155	.0058	4.197***
	Marginal	/No compromise	.1243	.0014	4.130***
	Marginal	/Con compromise	.2937	.0023	9.403***
REGION	Safe	/Lib compromise	−.1524	.0411	2.675**
	Safe	/No compromise	−.0337	.0159	−.742
	Safe	/Con compromise	.0513	.0197	1.169
	Marginal	/Lib compromise	.1159	.0485	3.010***
	Marginal	/No compromise	.0638	.0215	1.436
	Marginal	/Con compromise	.1648	.0295	4.056***
UNEMPLOYMENT	Safe		−1.5207	.1305	−6.444***
	Marginal		−2.1034	.2012	−5.809***
INFLATION	Safe		−1.3065	.0992	−8.690***
	Marginal		−.9389	.1284	−5.065***
GALLUP	Safe		.8106	.0061	6.765***
	Marginal		.4200	.0074	2.926**
DIST % LBJ	Safe		.0744	.0028	.919
	Marginal		.7336	.0045	5.833***
LEADER in Dem. party			.0637	.3479	2.392*
COMMittee value			−.403	.0759	−1.043
CONTROL for initial position			−.3224	.0211	−8.932***

Note: *t*-values significant at better than: * .05; ** .01; *** .001.
n of cases: 2886
Standardized constant: −1.3084
LIKELIHOOD RATIO STATISTIC: 1161.50058
Degrees of freedom: 29 significance: 0.0000
Yule's Q: 0.93948
Phi: 0.56538   Pseudo *R*-square: 0.45107
% Predicted: 0.88462

reflection of the power of a PROBIT model, the "pseudo *R*-square" statistic for the model was fairly high at 0.45.

The importance of institutional position. The first hypothesis was not supported by the test. In the three issue areas, there were a total of six opportunities for the hypothesis to be tested – two institutional variables in three issue areas. Of these only one appeared as an important variable: party hierarchy played a significant role in converting members on those bills associated with the issue of Governing the Economy. But, in general, there is very little support for the idea that institutional position plays a role in conversion.

The second hypothesis, dealing with the relative importance of the constituency variables, is clearly supported since these variables were generally significant influences on conversion. Indeed, in each of the three issue areas, constituency variables were the most significant in effecting commitments to the administration's position. In particular, if the compromise switch is held constant and the various constituency-trust combinations are examind, the immediate constituency variables are seven of the top eight most effective variables. Among the safe-switching variables on Governing the Economy issues, for example, the four most effective variables are the UNEMPLOYMENT rate (-1.52), the INFLATION rate (-1.31), GALLUP popularity (.82), and PARTY identification (.50); the first three are immediate constituency variables.

There are other interesting patterns among the constituency variables. For example, the fact that the effects of the two economy variables are negative suggests that a deterioration in the economy, along either of the measured dimensions, hurts the administration's ability to persuade and convert. Apparently, this relationship holds for both Foreign Policy and Governing the Economy but not for the area of Civil Rights. On Civil Rights issues, an improvement in employment strengthens the administration's ability to secure commitments whereas changes in the inflation rate do not appear to play any significant role. Although these two effects may be somewhat specific to historical circumstances surrounding the Johnson administration, it would be inappropriate to dismiss the policy implications of these findings so quickly.

The other constituency variables, namely, the contextual variables, performed as expected for the most part and were consistent with commonly held theory about their influence in the member's decision calculus. For example, of the 18 main variable/switching contextual combinations (e.g., ADA Ideology/Safe/Liberal compromise) in the Governing the Economy issue area, 14 played a significant role, and the direction of each of these significant variables was as expected. The variable representing ideological orientation performed more consistently than did the other contextual variables. Indeed, of the 14 combinations for REGION in the three issues, only five performed well; for the Civil Rights set of issues, for example, all four of the regional combinations were statistically insignificant, as were most of the PARTY combinations. On Civil Rights apparently only ideological orientation among the contextual variables played an important role in securing commitments.

The importance of constituency trust. Although there are some interesting results to report where constituency trust is concerned, the empirical evidence provides only some support for the hypothesis. For example, the hypothesis was that trust would insulate members from the effects of changes in the immediate constituency variables. To support this, the coefficients for, say, UNEMPLOYMENT on the safe switch should be smaller than the coefficients for UNEMPLOYMENT with the marginal switch. There are six pairs of trust switching immediate constituency combinations that have significant coefficients. On these six pairs, the hypothesis was supported on four; it was not supported on the pairs for INFLATION and LBJ's GALLUP popularity on the Governing the Economy set of issues. On the other hand, one pattern that is consistent across all of the issue areas is that changes in unemployment have a greater effect on the conversion of marginal members than on the conversion of safe members. Marginal members, already deeply in trouble, are much more willing to commit to the administration's position on all issues as the unemployment rate begins to creep upward.

One empirical result worth noting is the interaction between trust and immediate constituency variable measuring the president's coattails. This effect can be seen by examining the marginal combinations with DISTrict percentage for LBJ in the three issue equations. For Governing the Economy, as on Civil Rights, the effect is quite obvious. In both of these issue groups, the safe switching variable is not significant whereas the marginal-switching variable *is* significant for this coattails main variable. This would indicate that, especially on domestic issues, presidential coattails do affect the tendency of members to support the administration when the member's own electoral situation is considered. As might be expected, a marginal member, regardless of party, is particularly vulnerable to a president who is popular in the district.

Another result worth focusing on is the interaction between trust and the variables measuring the immediate constituency force associated with the state of the economy, in particular the UNEMPLOYMENT rate. In general the rate of unemployment plays a significant role in securing commitments. But its relation to the member's career in the constituency is also impressive. In each of the three issue areas, marginal members were more sensitive to the effects of unemployment than were safe members. Conversion among marginal members attributable to increases in unemployment has the largest coefficient in each of the three issues areas.

The interaction between trust and the contextual variables is slightly less difficult to assess. The hypothesis suggests that for these more long-term forces, trust should amplify their main effects. To support the hypothesis, then, coefficients for the safe switch on a variable should be greater than that for the marginal switch on the same variable. There are 11 such comparisons to make involving significant variables in the three issue areas; on eight of these the hypothesis is supported. The issue area that posed the most problems was Foreign Policy. Apparently, on this issue marginal members are more responsive to the administration than safe members; contextual variables are more similar to immediate variables than usual.

The importance of substantive compromise. The main question in assessing this hypothesis is whether the coefficients indicate that the compromise actually garnered targeted support. In general, the hypothesis is supported by the tests conducted, although the tests do pose some problems for interpretation. Though most of the coefficients have the proper sign (liberal compromises increase the probability of conversion as a member's liberal ideological orientation increases), some of the relationships between the various compromise switches are not as expected. For example, the coefficient for liberal compromise-switching ADA Ideology is consistently greater than the coefficient for the no compromise-switching ADA Ideology. And, except for Governing the Economy issues, the coefficient for no compromise-switching ADA Ideology is greater than for conservative-switching ADA Ideology, suggesting that a liberal compromise increases the chances of liberal commitments more than does holding firm on the proposal, which in turn increases the chances of liberal commitments more than does offering a conservative compromise.

On the other hand, for the Governing the Economy issues, offering a conservative compromise performed *better than any of the other options including liberal compromises.* Moreover, the sign on the conservative-switching ADA Ideology variable is consistently in the unexpected direction on all three issues areas (for safe members, Governing the Economy, +50; Civil Rights, +.03; and Foreign Policy, +.31). The offering of conservative compromises appears to have resulted in *continued liberal conversion* in all three issue groups. This may suggest that ideological liberalness plays such a strong role in conversion that making conservative compromises does not lead to disaffection of the liberal wing in the House. This interpretation is not supported in the data since, on two of the issue groups (Governing the Economy and Foreign Policy) the effect on liberals for conservative compromises was *greater* than the coefficient for no compromise at all. This could mean, however, that the conservative compromise strategy is employed on the bills on which any successful compromise that saves the bill is welcome by all members of the administration's coalition, including liberals. Thus, the liberals are rallying around the Johnson administration's compromise in order to stem off some worse alternative – in the politician's verncular, they are getting "half a loaf."

A second possibility involves strategic manipulation. On those issues where conservative compromises are employed to bring additional support to the bill, liberals initially may be taking positions in nonsupport of the administration's proposal although they would prefer the proposal to the current status quo ante. Their objective in acting in this fashion is either to commit the administration to a more hard-line position on the bill or to forestall any potential conservative compromise. But when the administration does in fact compromise with the conservatives in order to gain their votes, these strategic liberals are called on either to support the administration's bill or to leave the government's policy at the status quo. And since the compromise is better than no bill, these strategic liberals "convert" to the administration's proposal. Hence, in those situations that create conservative compromises, a large contingent of liberals have had their bluff called by the administration.

A note about the control variable

This hypothesis was supported on each of the issue groups on securing commitments. The more inclined to the "Right" position a member was initially, the more likely the administration could secure a commitment from the member as the governing coalition was being developed. That result was expected, and because it was borne out there is good reason to believe that the control worked.

LEADERSHIP IN THE CONSTITUTIONAL SYSTEM: ART AND SCIENCE

Presidential success within the constitutional system depends greatly upon legislative support. This study suggests some of the ways in which a president may successfully bridge the constitutional gap between the two institutions. Apparently bridging that gap depends upon the ability of the leadership to tap the forces of influence in Congress, in particular those associated with constituency. This ability to bridge the gap can be an art, as in the nature of compromise, or a science. The evidence that has been provided here suggests that the science of securing commitments is possible and possibly not that far beyond reach.

The main forces that an administration can most rely on in securing commitments are related to the congressional responsibility for representation. Presidents may develop some of their most successful conversion strategies by basing them upon a mutual identification with the constituencies within a member's district. This kind of shared identity accounts for the strength of many of the most commonly understood forces in the congressional process. For example, partisan and ideological identifications play a consistent role in securing the commitments of members to the administration's proposal. It also accounts for the amount of attention that administrations pay to maintaining contact with the various local groups. That continual contact at the local level not only maintains an effective reelection machine for the administration but also serves to fuse the congressional and presidential fates in a way that the president can then tap.

The research here also suggests that the distinction made between types of constituency forces is an important one to maintain. There is a clear difference in the impact of these two types. The constituency variables associated with the "context" of presidential-congressional relations (party, ideology, and region) seem to play a much smaller role in securing commitments than do the more immediate and short-term constituency variables having to do with the president's popularity or the shape of the economy. It could be that the kinds of forces characterized here as contextual are associated more with shaping *core support*, the consistent levels of initial support that the administration can count on, issue after issue, and less with securing commitments. If that were true, then these contextual forces probably define the outer bounds of strategic action and compromise on the part of the administration. Party and ideology are fixed forces that the administration cannot easily manipulate to its advantage, although some kinds of agenda manipulation are possible (e.g., having one kind of issue come to Congress before another kind of issue). In any case, these kinds of forces are like large ships in the ocean; they cannot be turned around on a moment's notice but require a long lead time and plenty of maneuvering room before results can be observed. On the other hand, a survey of how the membership is distributed across these kinds of contextual variables will act as a good descriptor of the president's initial core support.

In general, however, the more immediate constituency variables are much more manipulable and, apparently, carry a larger clout in securing commitments. One of these kinds of forces that is very subject to manipulation is the president's popularity. Another is the short-term forces associated with the state of the economy. Presidential standing with the public – somewhat outside specific election constituencies – has an interesting effect on legislative support. It plays a consistent though comparatively smaller role in securing commitments. Presidents who can tap the public's mood in an electrifying way are apt to greatly lessen their troubles with Congress. Presidents who wish to build a record on major, controversial issues are then best advised to bring up these issues early in their administrations for two reasons. First, with the usual postelection popularity that a president enjoys and with the opposition party in relative disarray (lacking a clear leader), the administration should be best able to secure commitments. This would be particularly true for presidents of a different party from the congressional majority, since presumably the two would differ on a variety of fundamental dimensions. Second, presidents need to act early on their most controversial legislative proposals because the very controversial nature of these issues is likely to erode presidential standing over time, with a resultant decline in the ability to secure commitments. Again, the president of a minority party particularly needs to bring forward the most controversial proposals early. The risk, of course, with this tack is that controversial proposals may serve to mobilize the opposition congressional party in a way that overcomes its natural disarray following the loss of the national standard bearer and the subsequent competition for the helm of the party.

The advantage of popularity (or the appearance of popularity), at least from the perspective of the administration, is that it is manipulable. Administrations can control some aspects of what goes into presidential popularity. Easy and relatively untrammeled access to the media affords the president the best opportunity to control an important aspect of the legislative struggle. Given its effect on congressional support, presidents are well served to expend a sizable effort on manipulating public standing, especially in specific congressional districts. Johnson, for example, invested a large amount of effort in affecting public standing and the appearance of popularity. The administration maintained extensive contacts with the various polling organizations, including assisting them in question writing and analysis. In addition, presidents would be well advised to pinpoint key congressional districts, whose members cannot be counted on as consistent core supporters but who might be high on an "index of persuadibility." The districts of these members might be singled out for special attention. A trip to such a district early in the administration, when the president's standing is naturally high, could possibly establish a lasting picture of constituency popularity in the minds of the members, which would be efficacious in securing commitments.

Of course, all that an administration does to manipulate popularity need not be accomplished early in the life of the administration. For example, foreign initiatives or adventures, which are often quite popular and tend to drive up presidential popularity, can occur at any time during an administration. The research here suggests that such instigators of popularity should be followed by difficult policy initiatives. In this light, two conclusions can be drawn about presidents and popularity. First, since presidential popularity is highest at inauguration, Presidents Johnson, Carter, and Reagan were right to attack their most difficult policy questions early, when their influence over legislative support was highest – at least in terms of popularity. And, second, given the typical decline of presidential popularity over the life of an administration, constitutional reforms that would lengthen the term of office and then fix it at one term would be disastrous to presidential influence in Congress. The advantage of a second term, if one can get it, is that a second election victory creates a second period of high popularity and disarray among the competition. It is the only way in which a president can get a second chance to bring popularity to bear on the legislative process in a regular fashion without a great deal of manipulation, except of course a long campaign. Without the second term, the president would work Congress with one hand tied.

The empirical results also suggest that presidents wishing to increase their leadership success may be able to do so by effecting an economic upswing. Because inflationary pressures from expanded employment tend to lag behind an expansion, a desire for *legislative* success at the end of a congressional term as well as electoral success may explain the tendency of presidents to favor expansion of the economy in the last year of their administrations. And since reducing unemployment plays a much bigger role in convincing marginal members than does reducing inflation, presidents leading congressional minorities or, like LBJ, presidents trying to maintain the unprecedented gains in congressional seats of a landslide election have the greatest incentive to expand employment in order to increase legislative commitments to the administration.

The importance of such an upswing, however, may depend upon what kinds of issues are the most significant at the time. Though the evidence appears to suggest that administrations in general may support in-creasing employment, a stricter reading may suggest that Democratic administrations may want to focus exclusively on jobs only whenever civil rights is a key issue in their coalition strategy. Obviously, because employment contractions affect blacks most directly, the Democratic coalition is much more vulnerable to that problem when civil rights issues are on the agenda. On the other hand, if governing the economy is critical, the administration's hand is strengthened whenever *any* kind of progress is made.

Apparently, forces associated with the nature of the institutional career – with party and committee hierarchy – are not related to coalitional behavior in Congress. There was little evidence that these forces played any kind of significant role in securing commitments. It is possible, of course, that the real effect of institutional position is in how it affects initial support. Leaders, for example, seem bound to represent the wishes of the administration, regardless of their own personal ideal points. In a way, the lack of an institutional effect is unfortunate from the perspective of the leadership, since institutional career is one of the few variables over which the leaders have complete control. This finding would suggest that the general strategy (popular with the current House leadership) of coopting new members by assigning them policy responsibilities through membership on party task forces is not likely to reap any benefits (cf. Sinclair 1981). In addition, this finding would cast doubt on those models of congressional decision making that assume that members are motivated by a variety of interests, including power within the institution (e.g., Fenno 1973 or Kingdon 1973).

One force that is constantly overlooked in the literature on coalition formation is constituency trust and, in particular, the vulnerability of marginal members. That is understandable, for there has been very little evidence that marginality plays a significant role in any aspect of congressional decision making, particularly voting. The results produced in this analysis, however, suggest that marginality does play a role in the congressional process. Securing constituency trust affords members the ability to make decisions on the basic of their basic policy preferences. Thus, trusted members are less influenced by immediate events and more affected by compromises and substantive arrangements. Obviously, a coalition leadership must take the mix of trusted versus marginal members into account as it develops its legislative strategies for securing commitments. The larger the proportion of safe nonsupportive members, the more likely it will be that the administration will seek to secure a substantive compromise since events cannot affect these members greatly whereas substantive changes (i.e., moving the proposal closer to their ideal point) might. The larger the proportion of marginal nonsupportive members, the more likely the administration is to rely upon existing conditions (to which these members are more vulnerable) and persuasion as a means of securing commitments.

One interesting aspect of "trust" is its manipulative nature. If constituents, voters, and groups of voters are motivated to support one candidate over another on the basic of those net benefits from government activities that are secured through the auspices of the two candidates, then a member can develop a high degree of expected electoral support through the supply of goods and services to the constituency. It is certainly the case that leaders, and especially the president, have a great deal of influence over the distribution of such largesse. An effective strategy, therefore, when the economy is failing or when popularity is slipping is to prop up marginal members – those most likely to respond adversely to these changes. A less sure strategy, but possibly a more long-term-effective one, is for the administration to pinpoint marginal members from the very outset and pander to their needs, regardless of party. Over the life of the administration this may make more sense, legislatively, than trying to target those districts for defeat of the incumbent.

Another thing this research has highlighted is the perplexing problem of compromise. The results on substantive compromise suggest the immense complexity of the legislative situation and the introduction of compromises. All manner of compromise seemed to have the same effect on securing commitments. At present, the only suggestion that can be gleaned from the performance of these variables is that some kind of strategic behavior might be affecting the results. Regardless of the best interpretation, the results on compromise suggest that administrations need good information about the nature of members' districts in order to properly assess their anticipated initial positions on issues. Only with this kind of information is it possible for the administration to interpret properly the distribution of initial support in a way that will allow it to employ compromise in a systematic manner. Until more information about the nature of constituency influence on initial positions can be obtained, the art of compromise must remain just that.

Earlier it was suggested that a systematic characterization of the distribution of members across the various contextual variables was probably a good and quick first step to estimating initial core support. Equally important to describe is the anticipated distribution of immediate variables, which would project, for the administration, members' expectations of the upcoming election. Although the contextual variables are fairly fixed, and thus easily estimated but not too easily affected, the immediate variable change over time as the larger socioeconomic situation changes. At the beginning of any administration, therefore, one can easily identify the distribution of potentially supportive factions on the basis of the contextual variables, but it is not so easy to do the same for the immediate variables at the beginning of any administration because expectations about the economy are so infirm. Rather, an administration must anticipate what the economy will do and how the president's popularity will fluctuate over time. Presidents would be better served, then, to have the Council of Economic Advisors and the Treasury staffed with more economic forecasters and fewer economic policy entrepreneurs. Their forecasts could then be better fed into the administration's strategic calculations about when to bring issues to the attention of Congress.

Given the results of this study, it would be important to spend some time on forecasting and tracking the proportion of marginal members as one of the major descriptors of the administration's strategic situation. A good deal of special attention has been paid to this variable, not simply because securing commitments is one of the few areas of the legislative process in which it appears to make a difference but also because trust seems to stand on the interface between immediate and contextual constituency forces. Like the contextual variables, the degree of "trust" a member has been able to secure from his constituents is fairly fixed, but like the immediate constituency variables, trust may develop and change over time.

The potential for presidential leadership, then, can be described by these dimensions. They define the nature of ideal points and the location of core supporters, the potential flammability of the immediate situation, and the degree of manipulation the leadership might expect to exert on the system. With this definition of the legislative situation, it would be possible to extend the electoral connection, as it is argued here, into the realm of presidential decisions about which policy proposals to pursue, which compromises to accept, and which members to convert.

APPENDIX: SUBJECTS OF INITIAL COUNTS

Leadership signal	OCR headcount subject
1967	
FAVOR	OEO Reauthorization Bill*
FAVOR	Open Housing
FAVOR	Elementary and Secondary Education Reauthorization*
FAVOR	$250 billion funding for InterAmerican Development Bank*
FAVOR	$350 billion funding for InterAmerican Development Bank*
FAVOR	D.C. Reorganization Plan*
FAVOR	Increase in Debt Limit*
FAVOR	Seven-year Debt Limit
FAVOR	D.C. Reorganization Plan Conference*
FAVOR	Rail Dispute Bill*
FAVOR	Rat Extermination Bill*
FAVOR	Omnibus Crime Act*
OPPOSE	Burnes amendment to DOD Appropriations
FAVOR	Conference Report on DOD Appropriations*
FAVOR	'67 Model Cities Appropriations*
FAVOR	'67 Rent Supplements Appropriations*
FAVOR	Conference Report on Independent Offices Appropriations*
FAVOR	Highway Beautification Reauthorization*
OPPOSE	Amendments to OEO
OPPOSE	Recommittal of OEO Bill
FAVOR	Conference Report on OEO*

Leadership signal	OCR headcount subject
1968	
FAVOR	Export-Import Bank
FAVOR	Truth-in-Lending*
OPPOSE	Revolving Credit amendment to Truth-in-Lending*
FAVOR	A general tax increase
FAVOR	Tax Surcharge in final passage, House
FAVOR	Tax Reform and the Surcharge as reported in Senate*
FAVOR	Gold Cover Act*
FAVOR	Conference Report on Open Housing*
FAVOR	'68 Model Cities Appropriations*
FAVOR	'68 Rent Supplements Appropriations*
FAVOR	'68 cut in HUD Appropriations*
FAVOR	Lower Colorado River Basin Act*
FAVOR	Land and Water Conservation Act*
OPPOSE	Motion to table Surcharge Conference Report
FAVOR	4-year Farm Bill
OPPOSE	Farm Bill amendments
OPPOSE	Recommittal on Foreign Aid Authorization*
FAVOR	Foreign Aid Authorization*
FAVOR	Gun Registration
FAVOR	Gun Control Act*
FAVOR	International Development Association

Note: Asterisk (*) indicates count was sequenced by OCR.

NOTES

1 Madison, speaking of the House of Representatives but in a manner applicable to all elected officials, says in *The Federalist* no 57, that the institutions of American government are "so constituted as to support in the members an habitual recollection of their dependence on the people. Before their elevation can be effaced by the exercise of power, they will be compelled to anticipate the moment when their power is to cease, when their exercise of it is to be reviewed, and when they must descend to the level from which they were raised; there forever to remain unless a faithful discharge of their trust shall have established their title to a renewal of it."

2 In addition to the anecdotal literature, there is a large body of research on this topic; see, for example, the Mayhew selection in Chapter 1 of this volume.

3 A member central to the coalition process is a "key coalitional actor." Elsewhere, a link between institutional position and being a key actor has been demonstrated (Sullivan 1984).

4 The terminology "safe" and "marginal" members has to do with the margin by which a member was last reelected by his constituents. A trusted member is one who has a substantial reelection margin, i.e., is trusted greatly by the constituency. Typically, a safe margin is considered to be any in which the

winner's proportion of the two-party vote is at least 20 percentage points over his closest competitor. In this study, 35.4 percent of the membership were "marginal" members. On the average, these were elected by a margin of 10.2 percentage points.

5 For an interesting analysis of the nature of such compromises, see Dodd and Sullivan 1979 and Enelow 1984.

6 An aide to Johnson, Douglas Cater (1964), noted that "a President, Democrat or Republican, finds himself measuring Congress in terms of the coalitions *for* him and *against* him on specific issues" (emphasis added).

7 Since the pool of data is culled from counts on different subject areas (e.g., civil rights and foreign policy), there is not likely to be one common pool of statistical "variance" or deviation from the average response. The technical term for this problem is "heteroscedasticity," and its presence in the pool of data violates one of the basic assumptions, which guarantee that the statistical techniques used here will produce valid results.

8 This trichotomous division is similar to one first reported in Clausen (1973). Although the method for this distinction was different, there were enough similarities between the two divisions to permit using these labels.

9 The direction of the coefficient is an important test, statistically, of the hypothesis. Another important test of a hypothesis is whether the coefficient for a particular variable is "statistically significant" or whether it is different from 0.0. A variable is typically defined as statistically significant if its significance level is less than or equal to 0.01.

10 There is, of course, a controversy over whether it is possible to assess the relative importance of a variable based upon the size of any kind of coefficient. Since they are affected by the unit of measurement, the basic regression and probit coefficients cannot be employed to test this and other similar hypotheses. The size of the basic coefficient for ideology, for example, would vary by an order of 100 if the percentage score the ADA provides were recorded as a percentage (e.g., 0.85) or as a whole number (e.g., 85.0). Standardization to the size of the variable's variance is a common technique to adjust variables to control for this measurement effect, and this adjustment will be used in this situation.

11 PROBIT is a special technique for dealing with models in which the dependent variable is theoretically a probability – e.g., the probability of converting to the administration's proposal – but is actually observed "dichotomously," i.e., the member either converts or not. The results of the model – the coefficients it produces for the variables – can be interpreted, after the appropriate statistical manipulations, to suggest the amount of change in probability associated with a single unit change in the value of the independent variable, e.g., a change in ideological orientation.

REFERENCES

Bullock, Charles. 1962. "House Careerists: Changing Patterns of Longevity and Attrition." *American Political Science Review* 67:1295–1300.

Cater, Douglas. 1964. *Power in Washington*. New York: Random House.

Champagne, Anthony. 1984. *Congressman Sam Rayburn*. New Brunswick: Rutgers University Press.

Clausen, Aage. 1973. *How Congressmen Decide: A Policy Focus*. New York: St. Martin's Press.

Dodd, Lawrence C., and Terry Sullivan. 1979. *Partisan Vote-Gathering in the House: Concepts, Models, Measures, and Propositions*. APSA Convention paper, Washington, D.C.

Enelow, James. 1984. "A New Theory of Congressional Compromise." *American Political Science Review* 78, no. 3, 708–18.

Fenno, Richard F., Jr. 1973. *Congressmen in Committees*, Boston: Little, Brown. 1978. *Home Style: House Members in Their Districts*. Boston: Little, Brown.

Hamilton, Alexander, John Jay, and James Madison. 1961. *The Federalist Papers*. Edited by Clinton Rossiter. New York: NAL.

Kingdon, John, 1973. *Congressmen's Voting Decisions*. New York: Harper & Row.

Neustadt, Richard. 1960. *Presidential Power*. New York: Wiley.

Sinclair, Barbara. 1981. "The Speaker's Task Force in the Post-reform House of Representatives." *American Political Science Review* 75, no. 1, 397–410.

Sullivan, Terry. 1984. *Procedural Structure: Success and Influence in Congress*. New York: Praeger.

The impact of institutional arrangements: implications for the study of Congress

Each House may determine the Rules of its Proceedings, punish its Members for disorderly Behavior, and, with the concurrence of two-thirds, expel a Member.

U.S. Constitution, Article I, section 5

But the great security against a gradual concentration of the several powers in the same department consists in giving to those who administer each department the necessary constitutional means and personal motives to resist encroachments of the others. The provision for defense must in this, as in other cases, be made commensurate with the danger of attack. Ambition must be made to counteract ambition. The interest of the many must be connected with the constitutional rights of the place. It may be a reflection on human nature that such devices should be necessary to control the abuses of government. But what is government itself but the greatest of all reflections on human nature? If men were angels no government would be necessary.   James Madison, *Federalist*, no. 51

Part III examines how institutional arrangements influence the choices and strategies of members and, importantly, how they ultimately affect policy choices. In particular, it explores the possible ways in which institutional arrangements impart a stability to collective choices. For stability in collective choice is not happenstance; stability is unlikely without some institutional arrangements to foster it. This is the basic problem discussed in Part III: how do legislative institutions facilitate stable decision making?

THE LOGIC OF MAJORITY RULE: A BASIC INTRODUCTION

In studying legislatures the basic theoretical problem, as surveyed by Thomas Schwartz, is that majority-rule decisions are unstable. The general instability of pure-majority rule was discovered by the marquis de Condorect in the eighteenth century and is known as the "classical voting paradox." Because this instability poses problems for any sort of predictive theory of politics, we shall elaborate here on the classical voting paradox.

Suppose, for simplicity, that we have a legislature composed of only three members: member 1, member 2, and member 3. Suppose that this three-person legislature is considering what type of weapons systems to deploy in building its national defense. The choice is between buying a new missile system and buying a new supersonic bomber. Member 1 would like to purchase just one new defense system and prefers the missile system to the bomber system. On the other hand, member 1 would prefer to purchase both new weapons than to get none at all. Member 2 has a strong preference for buying the bomber: Member 2 would prefer the bomber to the missile system but would rather acquire both than not get the bomber. Member 2, however, would prefer the missile system to nothing at all. Member 3 favors a strong national defense and prefers buying both systems to buying either system alone. On the other hand, member 3 prefers the missile system to the supersonic bomber in a choice between the two. Again, member 3 would prefer deploying the bomber to deploying neither.

We can label the four alternatives among which the legislature must choose:

A: missile system and no supersonic bomber
B: no missile system and the supersonic bomber
C: missile system and a supersonic bomber
D: no missile system and no supersonic bomber

Using these labels as shorthand for the alternatives being considered, we can write each legislator's preference ordering over A, B, C, and D. Member 1 prefers A and, exclusive of policy A, member 1 prefers B to C to D. Thus, we can order member 1's preferences over the four alternatives: A is preferred to B, which is preferred to C, which is preferred to D. In voting, then, member 1 would vote for A against B, C, or D and would vote for B if the choice were between B and C or B and D. Member 1 would also vote for C if the choice were limited to C and D.

We can also order member 2's preferences: B is preferred to C, which is preferred to A, which is preferred to D; and member 3's: C to A to B to D. Since each legislator would prefer any of the alternatives (A, B, or C) to D, we can ignore D in the rest of the example, as D would never be chosen.

If these members were to vote between A and B, then A would defeat B (by a vote of two to one), since both members 1 and 3 prefer A to B, whereas only member 2 prefers B to A. Likewise, in a vote between B and C, B would win, with members 1 and 2 voting for B. On the other hand, in a vote between C and A, C would defeat A with members 2 and 3 voting for C.

In this example, if the first vote were between A and B, then A would be chosen. Member 2, however, would prefer C to A. Member 2 also knows that member 3 would vote for C against A. Thus, once A defeats B member 2 can propose that the legislature consider A and C. This time, however, C defeats A. Once C is chosen, then member 2 can propose B, which also has the support of member 1. In the vote between B and C, B would defeat C. But now member 1 can propose A, which as before would defeat B. Thus, the policy choice in this legislature will *cycle* from A to C to B and back to A. In this situation, no choice is ever *stable*: someone can always propose an alternative that defeats the policy just chosen.

If the Condorcet example looks contrived, it is. It turns out, however, that the problem of instability is not. In general, problems of stability, as surveyed by Schwartz in Chapter 12, can exist in almost all collective choice environments. "Disequilibrium or the potential that the status quo be upset," according to William Riker, "is the characteristic feature of politics" (Riker 1980).

If disequilibrium is *the* characteristic feature of politics, one should ask why there is so much stability in the policies chosen by Congress. Indeed, it seems paradoxical that simple models of legislative decision making yield results so at odds with real-world observations. In Chapters 13 and 14 Kenneth Shepsle and Keith Krehbiel seek to resolve this paradox. They suggest that institutional arrangements – rules of procedure and organization, norms of behavior, and constraints upon legitimate and legal legislative activity – adopted by all legislative bodies serve to prevent instability in majority-rule decision making.

Shepsle presents an insightful and subtle model of how institutional arrangements in Congress serve to induce stability in policy outcomes. Though it makes no important assumptions about the motivations of either constituencies or political actors, Shepsle's model of the Congress is structurally rich. It includes a committee system, a system of "exclusive" jurisdictions, self-selectivity onto committees by members, and rules about proper amendments (called "germaneness"). In conjunction with an innocuous assumption about the preferences of members, Shepsle shows how institutional structures limit the decision-making potential of various groups. In particular, he demonstrates how a committee can use some substantial procedural protections to protect its bills once they reach the floor. This is a paper that proves one of the oldest homilies of political science: that "procedure shapes policy."

Krehbiel's model of decision making is very similar to Shepsle's, with the exception that Krehbiel assumes that the committees are capable of making sophisticated decisions about whether to report legislation based upon their judgment of the likely outcome if a proposal *were* to reach the floor. What his model indicates is that it is reasonable to expect that the committee system in Congress fosters certain kinds of rules and procedures. Krehbiel's model of policy stability indicates that if committees develop strategies for reporting bills only when they are able to dominate the larger body's considerations, then they do not require extensive forms of procedural protections to attain success. On the other hand, committees like those "policy" committees, which Fenno identified as regularly split over policy issues, require substantial protections in order to have their policy recommendations pass the House. In the absence of such protections, then, these committees are likely to suffer repeated defeats on the floor.

Returning to the Condorcet example, suppose the choice of defense policy by the three-person legislature is constrained by a set of decision rules. This set of rules prescribes the ways in which policy choices may be made by the legislature. Suppose there are four simple rules for legislative deliberations:

1. A committee consisting only of member 1 recommends the alternative (from A, B, C, D) for floor consideration.
2. Only the committee (member 1) can propose alternatives on defense issues for floor consideration.
3. The alternative is voted upon the floor under a "closed rule"; that is, no amendments are allowed.
4. If the alternative proposed by the committee is defeated, then no weapon system will be bought; that is, D is the status quo.

Under these rules the committee (member 1) will propose A. Since all three members prefer A to D (the status quo), A will be adopted. Since, by the rules, no alternative can be offered against A, A will be stable. Though the majority-rule cycle is not broken, the *policy cycling* that results will have been broken. As in this example, what Shepsle and Krehbiel show is that rules, such as jurisdictional arrangements and germaneness restrictions, common to all legislative bodies provide some stability to majority-rule decision making.

It is important to note that many of the arguments presented in this volume, and elsewhere, depend upon an assumption of stability in legislative decisions. If legislative decisions are so unstable as to be frequently overturned, then the science of politics proposed in this volume will be untenable: insofar as there is no equilibrium to legislative decision making, the behavior of the legislators will be intractable. Thus, the arguments presented by Shepsle and Krehbiel are *fundamental* to understanding Congress and its members.

But there is yet another problem: Institutions are themselves choices. Insofar as institutional rules and arrangements induce unique stable policy choices in Congress, then the manner in which the rules themselves are chosen must be considered. William Riker (1980, p. 445) argues that preferences over policy outcomes, combined with expectations about institutionally induced outcomes, lead naturally to an induced set of preferences over institutional arrangements.

Rules or institutions are just more alternatives in the policy space and the status quo of one set of rules can be supplanted with another set of rules. Thus the only difference between values and institutions is that the revelation of institutional disequilibrium is probably a longer process than the revelation of disequilibrium of tastes.... If institutions are congealed tastes and if tastes lack equilibria, then also do institutions, except for short-run events.

The question now becomes: What are the forces that bring stability to the choice of institutions?

If two institutions produce two different stable policy outcomes, then individual members prefer one of the institutions to the other if and only if they prefer the outcome under that institution to the outcome under the other. If the collective choice is cyclic over outcomes (collectively, A is preferred to B, which is preferred to C, which is preferred to A) then this cyclicity will be *inherited* in the social preference over institutions (see Shepsle 1983).

To return to the Condorcet example, if there are three institutional arrangements, R, S, T, that lead uniquely to the policy outcomes A, B, and C, respectively, then the instability exhibited there reemerges. In the example the three members of the legislature had preferences over outcomes. As shown earlier the collective choice in the Condorcet example is cyclic: through a sequence of proposals the majority-rule outcome in this three-member legislature can take on any value.

If the members of the legislature know that choosing R as their institutional arrangement will produce the policy outcome A (or if they choose S then B will come about, whereas T will yield C), then their preferences over institutions will be determined by their preferences over alternative policies. We can, then, represent their preferences over institutions as shown in Table III.1.

In voting over institutional arrangements R will defeat S (members 1 and 3 voting for R, member 2 against); S will defeat T (members 1 and 2 voting for S); and T will defeat R (members 2 and 3 voting for T, member 1 voting against). Thus, in this example, any institutional arrangement

Part III

Table III.1.

	Member 1	Member 2	Member 3
First preference	R	S	T
Second preference	S	T	R
Third preference	T	R	S

can be defeated by another and replaced. No particular institutional structure, then, will be any more stable than the choice over policy was in the Condorcet example. And, if policy choices are made under these institutional rules, they too will be unstable.

What this example points up are the limitations of Shepsle's argument. Institutional rules and arrangements can serve to induce stability in policy outcomes in majority-rule legislatures. But, when the set of institutional rules are themselves chosen by the legislature, *the choice of institutions is likely cyclic*, leading to instability in the legislature's policy choice.

There are reasons, however, to believe that the institutional arrangements by which policy choices are made will be stable. Shepsle (1983) has argued "that agent calculations about institutional arrangements differ from those about policy alternatives" (p. 33) and that the difference in these calculations "begins to drive a wedge between choice of policy and choice of institutional arrangements" (p. 32): the calculations involved in the choice of institutional structure differ from those involved in the choice of policy. In Chapter 13, Shepsle shows that when structure-induced equilibria exist, they rarely are unique. In other words, a given institutional arrangement may lead to several policy outcomes. Shepsle (1983, p. 41) has suggested that this may lead individual members to be uncertain about what the adoption of some institutional structure implies in policy terms. It seems plausible that, if legislators are uncertain about the ultimate policy consequences of different institutional arrangements, the choice of institutions may be stable. Indeed, Weingast in Part II argues that uncertainty, beforehand, over which minimum winning coalition will ultimately prevail induces a preference by individual members for a specific, for-certain, sharing rule.

To returning again to the Condorcet example, suppose that the institutional arrangements R, S, and T no longer lead to unique policy outcomes. Assume instead that R leads either A or B; S leads to either A or B; T leads to either B or C; and the members do not know beforehand which policy will result from which institutional arrangement. The preferences of the three members over the choice of institutions will be as shown in Table III.2.

Impact of institutional arrangements

Table III.2

	Member 1	Member 2	Member 3
First preference	R or S	T	T
Second preference	T	R or S	R or S

Because member 1 prefers A most of all he is indifferent between institutions R and S as they both may lead to A. Thus, his first preference may be either R or S. On the other hand, T will clearly be his second preference, as the best he can do under the institution T is the alternative to B. Likewise, members 2 and 3 will both prefer T to R or S and will be indifferent between R and S. Thus, institutional arrangement T defeats both R and S and is *stable*. Uncertainty on the part of members concerning which policy alternative an institutional arrangement may yield short-circuits the instability over the choice of institutions.

Shepsle (1983) has built on an idea present in Weingast's article in Part II (see also Weingast 1983). In Chapter 5 Weingast suggests that institutional rules and norms arise through an effort on the part of legislators to create a system of rules that enables agreements made between members to be enforceable. The problem, as Shepsle points out, is that there is no "exogenous enforcement mechanism, like an umpire or a court of law" to enforce agreements between members (1983, p. 33). In order to get bills passed that are important to them, members must seek the cooperation of other members. Coalitions must be built, agreements must be made, in order for necessary legislation to be enacted. Without a means of enforcing agreements, however, cooperation among members "will normally be truncated in frequency, scope, and duration" (p. 35). "Some exchanges... which are regarded as beneficial to the cooperating parties, will not take place because of (self) enforcement problems" (p. 37).

Shepsle conjectures that the development of political institutions and norms, and so on, is partly a response to cooperation problems. Since office holders do not always know how conflicts will shape up, they develop regularized methods that enable cooperation, on the one hand, while insuring against reneging, opportunism, and other adverse circumstances on the other (p. 38).

Thus, institutional arrangements developed to solve these cooperation problems may endure. Institutional solutions to the cooperation problem are chosen in advance of the policy choice. At the time of this choice it is uncertain what policy outcomes will be stable under the proposed rules. Indeed, it is not even certain which policy issues will emerge. Later, the gains from trade available under an existing cooperative structure

315

may outweigh the gains to be made from changing the institutional arrangement.

The point here is not that institutional arrangements are forever stable and unchanging: they do evolve. The point is that institutional arrangements are inertial. Once the arrangement is chosen, members will respond by choosing their strategies contingent upon the set of rules. In a very real sense members will make investments; trade votes and collect IOUs; start the ball rolling on some legislation; put in their time apprenticing on some committee. Also, external actors – the president, interest groups, and agencies – will make investments and will choose strategies contingent upon the existing institutional arrangement. Members and external actors will come to have a *vested interest* in the existing institutional arrangement, one that yields a stream of benefits from past investment. A new equilibrium of "tastes" will emerge supporting the institutional status quo. Thus, institutions will be "locally" stable. Again, however, they will not be static. New entrants (such as a large influx of freshman congressmen) may upset the balance of preferences and lead to a change.

REFERENCES AND SUGGESTED READINGS

Cooper, Joseph. 1970. "The Origins of the Standing Committees and the Development of the Modern House." *Rice University Studies* 56, no. 3.

*Galloway, George. 1961. *History of the U.S. House of Representatives*. New York: Crowell.

Hamilton, Alexander, John Jay, and James Madison. [Any edition.] *The Federalist*.

Harlow, Ralph. 1917. *The History of Legislative Methods in the Period before 1825*. New Haven: Yale University Press.

Hasbrouck, Paul D. 1927. *Party Government in the House of Representatives*. New York: Macmillan.

McConachie, Lauros G. 1898. *Congressional Committees: A Study of the Origins and Developments of Our National and Local Legislative Methods*. New York: Crowell.

Riker, William. 1980. "Implications from the Dis-equilibrium of Majority Rule for the Study of Institution." *American Political Science Review* 74: 432–47.
    1983. "Political Theory and the Art of Heresthetics." In *Political Science: The State of the Discipline*, ed. A. Finifter. Washington, D.C.: American Political Science Association.

Shepsle, Kenneth. 1978. *The Giant Jigsaw Puzzle: Democratic Committee Assignments in the Modern House*. Chicago: University of Chicago Press.
    1983. "Institutional Equilibrium and Equilibrium Institutions." Paper presented at the 1983 meeting of the American Political Science Association, Chicago.

Sinclair, Barbara. 1982. *Congressional Realignment, 1925–1978*. Austin: University of Texas Press.
    1983. *Majority Party Leadership in the U.S. House*. Baltimore: Johns Hopkins

University Press.

Sullivan, Terry. 1984. *Procedural Sturcture: Success and Influence in Congress.* New York: Praeger.

Weingast, Barry. 1983. "The Industrial Organization of Congress." Mimeographed. St. Louis: Washington University.

*Wilson, Woodrow. [1885] 1973. *Congressional Government.* Gloucester, Mass.: Peter Smith.

12

Votes, strategies, and institutions: an introduction to the theory of collective choice

THOMAS SCHWARTZ

Like markets, voting transforms individual preferences into a collective choice – a choice attributable to all of certain actors but to no one of them. Although such a choice reflects votes and votes reflect preferences, preferences alone do not determine votes and votes alone do not determine the final choice. A new body of political theory – the theory of "social choice" or "collective choice" – has shown that voting does not transform individual preferences into a collective choice so automatically or straightforwardly as some political analysts may have thought: institutional details and strategic decisions play starring roles, and the transformation sometimes works in unexpected, puzzling, and arguably anomalous ways. This theory is especially promising for the study of Congress, a voting body chosen by voting, rich in procedural complexity and strategic opportunity, and long the object of empirical scrutiny.

What follows is less a comprehensive survey of the rapidly growing literature on collective-choice theory or its applications than an attempt to make some of the most theoretically important and analytically useful aspects of it intuitive, transparent, accessible, and – dare I hope? – exciting. Besides fundamentals, I have emphasized aspects directly related to congressional scholarship, including the other essays in Part III.

MAJORITY RULE AND TWO-ALTERNATIVE COLLECTIVE CHOICE

In a broad sense, *majority rule* is rule by majorities, a form of government in which any majority can do what it pleases. In a narrower sense, majority rule – *simple*-majority rule, to be exact – is a particular voting rule for choosing between two feasible alternatives, which may be candidates for an office, passage and defeat of a motion, or whatnot. Given any voting rule or other collective-choice process, let us say that an alternative x is *collectively preferred* to another alternative y, or that x

beats y, if the rule chooses x when x and y alone are feasible; and that x and y are *collectively indifferent*, or *tied*, if neither beats the other. According to simple-majority rule, x beats y if the number of votes for x exceeds the number for y, and x ties y if these numbers are the same.

Simple-majority rule holds a distinguished position among voting rules. When a choice is made between two alternatives by voting, simple-majority rule is almost invariably used. We tend instinctively to identify pairwise collective choice with simple-majority choice and political democracy with majoritarianism. Why?

Characteristic properties of simple majority rule

The following answer is adapted from K. O. May (1952). Suppose n voters, Messrs. $1, 2, \ldots, n$, are to make a collective choice between two alternatives, represented by the numbers 1 and -1. Let 0 represent a tie. A *vote combination*, representing a possible way Messrs. $1, 2, \ldots, n$ can vote or abstain, is an n-fold combination, or *vector*, $(x_1, \ldots, x_n)$ in which each x_i is 1 (a vote for 1 by Mr. i), -1 (a vote for -1), or 0 (abstention by Mr. i). *Any* two-alternative voting rule may be represented by a function f such that:

(F) f is a function of vote combinations, and for every vote combination $(x_1, \ldots, x_n)$, $f(x_1, \ldots, x_n)$ is equal to 0, 1, or -1.

What further properties might we want or expect f to possess? These three have strong claims on our intuitions:

(A) $f(x_1, \ldots, x_i, \ldots, x_j, \ldots, x_n) \equiv f(x_1, \ldots, x_j, \ldots, x_i, \ldots, x_n)$
(Anonymity).

(N) $f(-x_1, \ldots, -x_n) \equiv -f(x_1, \ldots, x_n)$ (Neutrality).

(T)   If $f(x_1, \ldots, x_n) = 0$ and $(y_1, \ldots, y_n)$ is the result of replacing one or more 0's by 1 in $(x_1, \ldots, x_n)$, leaving all else the same, then $f(y_1, \ldots, y_n) = 1$ (Fragility of Ties).

Property (A) says f treats voters equally: if any two voters switch votes, the collective choice remains the same. Property (N) says f treats alternatives equally: if every vote is reversed, so that 1's become -1's and -1's become 1's, the choice is thereby reversed (or remains the same if it was 0). Property (T) says ties are easily broken: if there is a tie and some erstwhile abstainers then vote for 1, other things remaining unchanged, that is enough to break the tie in 1's favor. A voting rule that lacked any of these properties would have a built-in bias against some voters or alternatives, thereby allowing elections to be decided to some degree by factors other than votes, or it would be gratuitously indecisive, allowing

319

ties to persist in the face of new information that plainly tilted the balance in one direction.

Simple-majority rule obviously has all these properties. It holds its distinguished position because it is the *only* two-alternative voting rule with all these properties. To prove this, we must assume that f satisfies (F)–(T) and show (a) that if $(x_1, \ldots, x_n)$ is a vote combination containing just as many 1's as -1's, then $f(x_1, \ldots, x_n) = 0$; (b) that if $(x_1, \ldots, x_n)$ contains more 1's than -1's, then $f(x_1, \ldots, x_n) = 1$; and (c) that if $(x_1, \ldots, x_n)$ contains fewer 1's than -1's, then $f(x_1, \ldots, x_n) = -1$.

Proof of (a). Because $(x_1, \ldots, x_n)$ has just as many 1's as -1's, $(-x_1, \ldots, -x_n)$ is the result of switching the first 1 vote with the first -1 vote, the second 1 vote with the second -1 vote, etc. By (A), such switching leaves the choice unaffected. So

$$f(x_1, \ldots, x_n) = f(-x_1, \ldots, -x_n)$$
$$= -f(x_1, \ldots, x_n) \qquad \text{by (N)}$$
$$= 0$$

since only 0 is its own negative.

Proof of (b). Suppose $(x_1, \ldots, x_n)$ contains k more 1's than -1's. Let $(x'_1, \ldots, x'_n)$ be the result of replacing the first k 1's in $(x_1, \ldots, x_n)$ by 0. Then $(x'_1, \ldots, x'_n)$ has just as many 1's as -1's, and so, by (a),

$$f(x'_1, \ldots, x'_n) = 0.$$

Thus, by (T), since $(x_1, \ldots, x_n)$ is the result of replacing some 0's in $(x'_1, \ldots, x'_n)$ by 1,

$$f(x_1, \ldots, x_n) = 1.$$

Proof of (c). Since $(x_1, \ldots, x_n)$ has fewer 1's than -1's, $(-x_1, \ldots, -x_n)$ has *more* 1's than -1's. By (b), then,

$$1 = f(-x_1, \ldots, -x_n)$$
$$= -f(x_1, \ldots, x_n) \qquad \text{by (N)}$$

so $\qquad f(x_1, \ldots, x_n) = -1 \qquad$ Q.E.D.

Other two-alternative voting rules

If (F)–(T) are uniquely satisfied by simple-majority rule, which of these conditions are violated by other familiar two-alternative collective-choice rules?

Condition (T) is violated by survey procedures designed to reckon the collective preference between alternatives (candidates, policies, soft drinks, radio stations) by polling a sample rather than an entire population. Let f represent such a procedure, and suppose $f(0, x_2, \ldots, x_n) = 0$

and Mr. 1 does not belong to the sample. Then, contrary to (T), $f(1, x_2, \ldots, x_n) = 0$ as well.

Condition (N) is violated by any *special*-majority rule (two-thirds, three-quarters, unanimity, etc.). Suppose f represents two-thirds majority rule: 1 beats -1 (the status quo or default alternative) if two-thirds of nonabstainers vote for 1; otherwise, -1 beats 1. And suppose $(x_1, \ldots, x_n)$ is a vote combination in which the voters are evenly divided. Then, since 1 does not command a two-thirds majority in $(x_1, \ldots, x_n)$, $f(x_1, \ldots, x_n) = -1$. But 1 does not command a two-thirds majority in $(-x_1, \ldots, -x_n)$ either, and so, contrary to (N), $f(-x_1, \ldots, -x_n) = -1$ as well. Special-majority rules have a built-in conservative bias – a bias in favor of the status quo, or collective inaction. This is true, in particular, of the unanimity rule prescribed by classical social-contract theory for constitutional choices.

Condition (A) is violated by any rule that weights the votes of different voters differently. Let f represent the rule by which stockholders choose one of two slates of corporate directors, and suppose Mr. 1 owns a majority of shares. Then $f(1, -1, x_3, \ldots, x_n) = 1$ but, contrary to (A), $f(-1, 1, x_3, \ldots, x_n) = -1$.

Condition (A) is violated as well by the standard Anglo-American procedure for choosing one of two parties to control a legislature: voters are partitioned into districts, each of which elects a representative belonging to one of two parties (1 and -1), and the party winning a majority of votes in each of a majority of districts wins control of the legislature. Let f represent such a procedure, and suppose there are three districts, one comprising Messrs. 1, 2, and 3, another comprising Messrs. 4, 5, and 6, and the third comprising Messrs. 7, 8, and 9. Then:

$$f(1, 1, -1, 1, -1, -1, 1, -1, -1) = -1$$

but

$$f(1, 1, -1, 1, 1, -1, -1, -1, -1) = 1.$$

That violates (A) because the second vote combination can be got from the first just by switching the votes of Messrs. 5 and 7.

This example shows that a system of equal-size districts (the "One Man, One Vote Rule") does not ensure that voters count equally. It also shows that elections by single-member districts can choose a ruling party opposed by a majority: $f(1, 1, -1, 1, 1, -1, -1, -1, -1) = 1$, although $(1, 1, -1, 1, 1, -1, -1, -1, -1)$ contains a majority of -1's. That often happens in the states. It happened nationwide in 1984: the Republicans won a scant majority of votes for the U.S. House of Representatives, but the Democrats kept a clear majority of seats. (For in-depth studies of two-alternative collective choice, see Murakami 1968 and Fishburn 1973, pp. 13–68.)

PARADOXES OF COLLECTIVE CHOICE

When we jump from two alternatives to three or more, there occurs a phenomenon, widely regarded as a paradox, that has lain at the center of theoretical speculation since the marquis de Condorcet discovered it near the end of the eighteenth century. As generalized in varied ways, beginning with Kenneth Arrow's seminal contribution (1952, 1963), this phenomenon is often described as a kind of indeterminateness, incoherence, or collective irrationality.

The classical voting paradox

Suppose three voters, any majority of whom can do what they please, are to choose among three alternatives, which they rank in order of preference as follows:

Mr. 1	Mr. 2	Mr. 3
x	y	z
y	z	x
z	x	y

A majority (Messrs. 1 and 3) prefer x to y, another majority (Messrs. 1 and 2) prefer y to z, and a third majority (Messrs. 2 and 3) prefer z to x: under majority rule, the collective preference is *cyclic*, and every feasible alternative is *unstable* in the sense that another one beats it. Such is the *classical voting paradox*, discovered by Condorcet (for historical details, see Black 1958, pt. 2). Its theoretical significance is fourfold:

1. Instability makes it hard to predict what will be chosen: every possible prediction is opposed by some majority, and it is majorities generally (we have assumed) that rule.

2. The *latent* instability in this example – the power and incentive of some groups to overturn any feasible choice – may occasion a great deal of *manifest* instability – the continual overturning of choices by dint of successive realignments. True, policy change is sometimes a good thing, and a political system that allows change in the face of strong opposition thereby institutionalizes those realignments and exercises in reform that would otherwise occur in a more violent way. But continual change can be costly and can prevent any government program from being carried out.

3. If, perhaps because of May's theorem, we take majority preference as the measure of better-to-worse in point of social welfare, then there is

no social welfare optimum – no socially best alternative – in the example.

4. Because social preference can be cyclic, social choice does not always meet the minimum condition of "rationality" customarily required of individual choice: unlike a "rational" individual, a majoritarian government cannot always make a choice to which it prefers no alternative. In other words, majoritarian governments cannot in general be modeled as maximizers of anything.

How general is this phenomenon of cyclic collective preference, or unstable collective choice? For one thing, it is not peculiar to the three-voter case. Here is a four-voter example:

Mr. 1	Mr. 2	Mr. 3	Mr. 4
x_1	x_2	x_3	x_4
x_2	x_3	x_4	x_1
x_3	x_4	x_1	x_2
x_4	x_1	x_2	x_3

For *any* number of voters *greater* than four, Figure 12.1 (in which *m* is a bare majority) shows how to construct a majority-preference cycle among just three alternatives.

The phenomenon is yet more general. Cycles do not just occur under majority rule. Consider any collective-choice rule satisfying this condition:

> If all but one voter prefer *x* to *y* while he prefers *y* to *x*, then *x* beats *y* (Virtual Unanimity).

Let any number *n* of voters have the preference orderings of a set of *n* alternatives shown in Figure 12.2. When $j < n$, every voter prefers x_j to x_{j+1} unless x_{j+1} is the first alternative in his ordering, that is, all voters but Mr. $j + 1$ prefer x_j to x_{j+1}. And all but Mr. 1 prefer x_n to x_1. So by Virtual Unanimity, x_1 beats x_2, x_2 beats $x_3, \ldots, x_{n-1}$ beats x_n, and x_n beats x_1 – another cycle.

Although many collective-choice processes besides majority rule satisfy Virtual Unanimity, not all do. Any voting rule that gives individual veto power to one or more voters, such as the rule used in the U.N. Security Council and the rule for amending the Articles of Confederation, obviously violates Virtual Unanimity. So does any constitution that protects individual rights: if the choice of *x* in preference to *y* would violate Mr. 1's right against self-incrimination, for example, then *y* beats *x* under the U.S. Constitution even if Messrs. 2,..., *n* all prefer *x* to *y*.

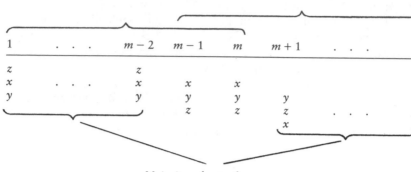

Figure 12.1

1	2	...	i	...	n
x_1	x_2	...	x_i	...	x_n
x_2	x_3		x_{i+1}		x_1
.	.		.		.
.	.		.		.
.	.		.		.
x_{i-1}	x_i		x_n		x_{i-2}
x_i	.		x_1		x_{i-1}
.	.		.		.
.	.		.		.
.	x_n		.		.
x_n	x_1	...	x_{i-1}	...	x_{n-1}

Figure 12.2

Impossibility theorems

The problem is more general still. Several so-called *impossibility theorems*, beginning with that of Schwartz (1970), show that collective-preference cycles and therewith unstable collective choices can occur under any voting rule (or collective-choice process) meeting mild conditions of "reasonableness" – conditions so mild they are satisfied alike by brutal tyrannies, corrupt oligarchies, and ideal constitutional democracies. These theorems are variations on Arrow's celebrated impossibility theorem. Arrow's theorem does not show, however, that cycles can occur; its conclusion, as you will see, is weaker than that.

Arrow (1963) considered a rule whereby Messrs. $1, 2, \ldots, n$ make

324

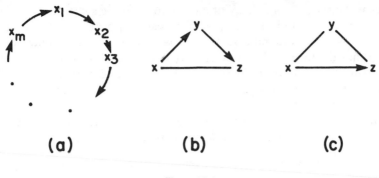

(a)   **(b)**   **(c)**

Figure 12.3

collective choices from finite subsets of a given "universal set" of alternatives and assumed:

(1) The universal set contains three or more alternatives.

(2) The rule applies to all possible combinations of individual preference orderings (orderings by Messrs. $1, 2, \ldots, n$) of the universal set (Unrestricted Domain).

(3) No individual is so powerful that, for *every* pair of alternatives x and y, x beats y under *every* combination of preference orderings in which he prefers x to y while everyone else prefers y to x (Nondictatorship, slightly modified).

(4) x beats y whenever *everyone* prefers x to y (pairwise Pareto Principle).

(5) The collective preference between two alternatives never depends on individual preferences regarding *other* alternatives (pairwise version of Independence of Irrelevant Alternatives).

Arrow deduced that, for some combination of individual preference orderings, the relation of collective preference or indifference is *nontransitive*, which means that at least one of the three cases depicted in Figure 12.3 (in which "→" represents collective preference and "—" collective indifference) arises. Only (a) is a cycle. Only in case (a) does some set of alternatives lack a stable choice. But Arrow did not show that (a) can arise, only that at least one of the three cases can arise – maybe just (c).

To put the theorem another way, Arrow assumed (1)–(5) plus:

(6) If x beats y and y beats or ties z (i.e., z does not beat y), then x beats z (Transitivity, or Collective Rationality),

and deduced a contradiction, demonstrating that no collective-choice rule can satisfy (1)–(6). Any violation of (6) must be a case in which (i) x beats y, y beats z, and z beats x; or (ii) x beats y, y beats z, and x ties z; or (iii) x beats y, y ties z, and z beats x; or (iv) x beats x, y ties z, and x ties z. But (i) has the form of (a) (a cycle), (ii) and (iii) the form of (b), and (iv) the form of (c). So every violation of (6) is a case of type (a), (b), or (c). Note that (i) is not just a cycle but a *tricycle*, one comprising three alternatives.

An especially simple if not terribly appealing addition to (1)–(5) that lets us deduce that a cycle can arise is the following:

(7)   No two alternatives are ever tied (Pairwise Resoluteness).

For (7) rules out (ii)–(iv), which involve ties, ensuring that any violation of (6) must be of type (i), a tricycle.

The theorem of Schwartz (1970), which shows that a cycle can arise, replaces (1) and (7) with:

(1′)   The universal set contains at least n alternatives (n being the number of voters).

(7′)   If all but one individual prefer x to y, then x does *not tie* y (either x beats y or y beats x) (Minimum Resoluteness).

In other words, Arrow's inconsistency survives when we replace (1) by (1′), add (7′), and replace (6) (Transitivity) by the weaker:

(6′)   It never happens that x_1 beats x_2, x_2 beats $x_3, \ldots, x_{m-1}$ beats x_m, and x_m beats x_1 (Acyclicity).

I will prove Arrow's theorem by assuming (1)–(6) and deducing three consequences, the third of which contradicts (3) (Nondictatorship). First, two definitions: A *profile* is a combination of n preference orderings, one for each individual, of the universal set of alternatives. A group g of individuals is *decisive* for x versus y if, and only if, x beats y under *every* profile in which the members of g all prefer x to y while the other individuals all prefer y to x. According to (4), the group of all n voters is decisive for every pair of alternatives. According to (3), no single individual (or, to be unnecessarily exact, no single individual's unit set) is decisive for every pair of alternatives (which is not to say that no individual is decisive for *any* pair).

Consequence 1. Suppose g is a group of individuals and p a profile in which the members of g all prefer x to y, everyone else prefers y to x, and x *beats* y. Then g is decisive for x versus y.

Proof. What must be shown is that x beats y for *every* profile q in which the g's all prefer x to y while everyone else prefers y to x. But this follows from (5) (Independence) since x beats y under p and Messrs.

$1, 2, \ldots, n$ have the same preferences between x and y in q as they have in p. Q.E.D.

Consequence 2. Suppose Mr. i is decisive for x versus y. Then (a) Mr. i is decisive for x versus any alternative z different from x; (b) Mr. i is decisive for any z different from y versus y; and (c) Mr. i is decisive for any alternative z versus any other alternative w.

Proof. (a) Trivial if $z = y$. Otherwise, there is a profile of the form:

Mr. i	Everyone else
x	y
y	z
z	x

By (2), the collective-choice rule applies to this profile. Since Mr. i is decisive for x versus y, x beats y, and by (4) (Pareto Principle), y beats z, so by (6) (Transitivity), x beats z, and thus, by Consequence 1, Mr. i is decisive for x versus z.

(b) Trivial if $z = x$. Otherwise, there is a profile of the form:

Mr. i	Everyone else
z	y
x	z
y	x

Since Mr. i is decisive for x versus y, x beats y, and by (4), z beats x, so by (6), z beats y, and thus, by Consequence 1, Mr. i is decisive for z versus y.

(c) By (1), the universal set contains an alternative t different from x and z. By (a), since Mr. i is decisive for x versus y, he also is decisive for x versus t, whence he is decisive for z versus t by (b), and thus, by (a), he is decisive for z versus w. Q.E.D.

Consequence 3. Someone is decisive for every pair of alternatives (contrary to (3)).

Proof. By (4), the group of all individuals is decisive for every pair. Hence, there must exist a *minimum decisive group*: a group g that is decisive for some pair, say x versus y, while no smaller group is decisive for any pair. By (4), g cannot be empty; say Mr. i belongs to g. By (1) and (2), the collective-choice rule applies to some profile of the following form:

Mr. i	$g-i$	Everyone else
x	z	y
y	x	z
z	y	x

327

where $g-i$ comprises everyone in g but Mr. i. By Consequence 1, if z beat y, $g-i$ would be decisive for z versus y. But that is impossible because no group smaller than g is decisive for any pair. So z does not beat y: y beats or ties z. But because g is decisive for x versus y, x beats y. Hence, by (6) (Transitivity), x beats z, and thus, by Consequence 1, Mr. i is decisive for x versus z. By Consequence 2, therefore, he is decisive for every pair.

Q.E.D.

The theorem of Schwartz (1970), which shows that collective preference can be cyclic, not just nontransitive, says that (1′), (2)–(5), (6′), and (7′) are jointly inconsistent. To prove this, let us first see which consequences of Arrow's conditions follow from the revised set of assumptions. Consequence 1 does because its proof did not invoke (6) (Transitivity). Consequence 2(a) did invoke (6) at one point: we showed that x beats y and y beats z and inferred, by (6), that x beats z. The weaker (6′) (Acyclicity) just lets us infer that z does not beat x. But since Mr. i alone prefers x to z, (7′) (Minimum Resoluteness) tells us that either x beats z or z beats x. It follows that x beats z, as required. Similarly for Consequence 2(b). And Consequence 2(c) was deduced from 2(a) and 2(b) without further use of (6). So Consequence 2 still holds.

But in the previous subsection we saw that there must be a cycle under some profile, assuming (1), (2), and Virtual Unanimity. Since the existence of a cycle contradicts (6′), it suffices to deduce Virtual Unanimity. Suppose, then, that all but one individual, Mr. i, prefer x to y, while he prefers y to x; to deduce that x beats y. But by (7′), *either* x beats y or y beats x. And by Consequence 1, if y beat x then Mr. i would be decisive for y versus x, and so, by Consequence 2, he would be decisive for every pair of alternatives, contrary to (3). Hence, y does not beat x, and thus x beats y.

Q.E.D.

I conclude this section with a glimpse at more advanced results. The theorem of Schwartz (1970) actually was more general than the one just proved: it used a drastically weakened version of (5) and allowed (although it did not require) interpersonal comparisons of preference intensity. Mas Collel and Sonnenschein (1972) proved that cycles can arise after assuming that $n \geq 4$, strengthening (3) a bit, and replacing (7′) with:

(7″)   If x beats or ties y and if one individual changes his relative ranking of x and y in x's favor (all else remaining the same), then x beats y – so that a single voter can break any tie (Positive Responsiveness).

Although dropping (1′) was an improvement, (7″) is quite strong: it is satisfied by simple-majority rule but not by sample surveys – as I explained earlier in connection with the kindred condition (T). This limitation is inessential, however: assuming that $n \geq 5$, Schwartz (1982*b*) showed that (7'') can be replaced with:

(7''')   If x beats or ties y and if a coalition comprising a *fifth of all individuals* switches from a preference for y over x to a preference for x over y (all else remaining the same), then x beats y.

What you have seen so far is not that collective choices are *always* unstable, or even that they are *ever* unstable, but only that they *can* be unstable, depending on individual preferences and the feasible set (the set of feasible alternatives): the actual profile might yield no cycle; if it does, the actual feasible set might not contain that cycle; and if it does, it might also contain a stable alternative foreign to the cycle. But according to the theorem of Schwartz (1982*b*), based on (7'''), the cycle can be so constructed that it precisely exhausts *any given set*, finite or infinite, of three or more alternatives. The instability revealed by this theorem still depends, however, on individual preferences: for all the theorem tells us, the actual profile might never produce an unstable choice. (On impossibility theorems, see Arrow 1963; Plott 1976; Schwartz 1985*a*, 1985*b*; and Sen 1983.)

STABILITY AND INSTABILITY

We do know something, however, about the conditions under which instabilities actually occur, or are likely to occur, not just about their institutional possibility.

Stability in one dimension

Following Hotelling (1929), let the feasible set comprise all points along a line, which we might think of as the liberal-conservative continuum. Suppose every voter has an "ideal point" on this line and likes alternatives less and less the farther they lie from his ideal point. Given this "one-dimensional spatial model," we can show that a stable alternative exists under majority rule. We can even identify it.

A *median* of voters' ideal points is an ideal point m such that no majority of voters have their ideal points to the left of m or to its right. There must exist one or two median ideal points. Hotelling proved that such a median, as well as any point between two such medians, must be stable under majority rule: no majority of voters prefer any point to it.

Proof. Let m be such a point and r any point to the right of m. Then the voters with ideal points at or to the left of m prefer m to r. These voters are at least half the electorate inasmuch as no majority have their ideal points to the right of *m*. Since at least half the electorate prefer *m* to *r*, no majority prefer *r* to *m*. Similarly, if *l* is any point to the left of *m*, then no majority prefer *l* to *m*. So *m* is stable. Q.E.D.

Although Hotelling assumed that the feasible set comprises *all* points on a line, we can assume instead that there are finitely many feasible alternatives, each occupying a point on the line. By reasoning much like Hotelling's, Black (1948, 1958) showed that any median of voters' *favorite feasible alternatives* is stable.

The basic idea behind Hotelling's result has been applied by Downs (1957, esp. p. 115) to elections with two candidates (or parties) each of whom must decide what position to occupy on the liberal-conservative continuum, with the sole goal of winning. To simplify a bit, suppose there is a unique median, *m*, of voters' ideal points. If *l* is a point to the left of *r* and closer than *r* to *m*, those voters with ideal points at or to the left of *m* prefer *l* to *r*. Since they are a majority, *l* beats *r*. Similarly, *r* beats *l* if *r* is closer to *m*. So each candidate has an incentive to take a position closer than his opponent's to *m*. Therefore, candidate positions will tend to converge to *m*, providing voters with an echo, not a choice.

Instability in more than one dimension

The tidy stability property of majority voting for points along a line cannot be extended to points in a space of two or more dimensions, a fact revealed by a number of spatial instability theorems but most simply by that of Davis, De Groot, and Hinich (1972): Suppose the feasible alternatives are all the points in a two-dimensional space (or coordinate system) in which each voter has an ideal point and likes alternatives less and less the farther they lie from that point. The two dimensions might represent the social and economic liberal-conservative continua. A *median in all directions* is a point *m* such that, for every line through *m*, no majority of voters have their ideal points on one side of this line. The theorem says that a point is stable under majority rule only if it is a median in all directions.

Proof. Suppose *x* is *not* a median in all directions: there is a line *L* through *x* and a majority *M* of voters with ideal points on one side of *L*. Then parallel to *L* there must be a line *L'* that lies strictly between *L* and the ideal points of *M*. Drop a perpendicular from *L'* to *x*, as in Figure 12.4. The point at which the perpendicular intersects *L'* is closer than *x* to *M*'s ideal points. So the members of *M* all prefer that point to *x*: *x* is not stable. Q.E.D.

Although it states a necessary condition for *stability*, the result just proved really is an *in*stability theorem because the condition is so severe: however we rotate a line at a stable point, we will never find a majority of

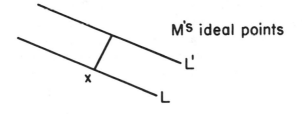

Figure 12.4.

voters' ideal points on one side. This requires quite a balanced spread of ideal points, ruling out almost any preferential clustering of voters in terms of ideology, geography, economic interest, party loyalty, or plain chance.

Other spatial instability theorems are stronger in some ways, although less simple to prove. Plott's (1967) celebrated condition of pairwise symmetry, which requires a stable point to be a seesaw fulcrum on which every ideal point different from it is balanced with one other ideal point, is more severe than that of being a median in all directions. Although it is only a sufficient condition for stability, Enelow and Hinich (1983) have turned it into a necessary condition as well by tacking on some qualifications. McKelvey (1976) proved that if (as is likely) no point in a multidimensional space containing voters' ideal points beats all other points under majority rule, then there exists not only a cycle but one that eats up the entire space. Schofield (1978) and Cohen (1979) have proved interesting variations on this theme.

The spatial instability theorems do not show that the potential instability revealed by the impossibility theorems is always or even often realized. For their assumptions are much stronger than those used in the impossibility theorems: individuals are assumed to have ideal points, or points of satiation, precluding the interpretation of spatial dimensions as economic goods; the collective-choice rule is assumed to be majoritarian (an assumption that can be weakened somewhat for certain theorems); and what is most questionable, the feasible set is assumed to be the whole space, or at least (for some theorems) a convex subset thereof. (A set of points is *convex* if, for any two points in the set, the line segment joining them also is in the set.)

Although political analysts have considerable latitude in identifying "the" feasible set in any given case (Schwartz 1986; sec. 10.1), the feasible sets commonly identified are finite, and they are constrained in innumerable ways. Often a feasible set comprises the candidates for some office, often the motions voted on in some legislature or committee. In either case it is finite. True, the set of all possible platforms a candidate might conceivably adopt and the set of all possible motions a legislature or committee might conceivably pass are infinite. But even if these sets could be construed as *feasible* sets, they cannot be convex because platforms and motions must be formulated in English and there are only countably many English sentences (an infinite number smaller than the infinite number of points on a line).

Instability and vote trading

Conditions for instability are also specified by a set of theorems based not on the spatial representation of alternatives and preferences but on vote trading. Independently discovered by Kadane (1972), Oppenheimer (1972), and Bernholz (1973), then generalized by Schwartz (1977), this type of theorem asserts that, given certain assumptions, any collective choice is unstable for which *vote trading* is essential.

An *outcome* is a vector $(x_1, \ldots, x_k)$ consisting of one position on each of k *issues*. Let $m = (m_1, \ldots, m_k)$ be the *no-trade outcome* – the outcome that would be chosen in the absence of any vote trading. We need two assumptions:

(8)   If x_i is a position on the ith issue other than m_i, then m beats $(m_1, \ldots, x_i, \ldots, m_k)$.

This says that if a position on a given issue that would be defeated in the absence of vote trading is combined in an outcome with only the no-trade positions on all other issues, then that outcome is beaten by the pure no-trade outcome.

(9)   Suppose $x(a_i)$ and $x(b_i)$ are two outcomes differing only in that a_i is the ith component of $x(a_i)$, and b_i the ith component of $x(b_i)$, and suppose $y(a_i)$ and $y(b_i)$ are two other outcomes differing in the same way. Then if $x(a_i)$ beats $x(b_i)$, $y(a_i)$ beats $y(b_i)$ (Separability).

This says that the collective preference on any issue is independent of the positions chosen on other issues.

It follows from (8) and (9) that any outcome other than m, hence any outcome for which vote trading is essential, must be unstable: some outcome beats it.

Proof. Let $x = (x_1, \ldots, x_i, \ldots, x_k)$ where $x_i \neq m_i$. By assumption (8),

$$m = (m_1, \ldots, m_i, \ldots, m_k) \text{ beats } (m_1, \ldots, x_i, \ldots, m_k),$$

whence it follows, by (9), that

$$(x_1, \ldots, m_i, \ldots, x_k) \text{ beats } (x_1, \ldots, x_i, \ldots, x_k) = x \qquad \text{Q.E.D.}$$

Although stated in terms of vote trading, this theorem really is more general than such language implies. For the effect of vote trading can be achieved by making a "package" motion to begin with – one that combines positions from different issues – and virtually all legislative motions are packages of some sort.

Like the spatial instability theorems, this one rests on highly restrictive assumptions. Although majority rule was not assumed, (8) required a unique no-trade outcome (no ties), whereas (9) required separability of collective preference – which means, for example, that a committee of banquet planners who collectively prefer red wine to white with meat must also prefer red wine to white with fish. And implicit in the statement of the theorem was the assumption that every outcome – every combination of positions on the k issues – is feasible (since otherwise the outcome that beats x might not be feasible).

To be sure, nothing prevents us from interpreting each issue as a set of *feasible positions*. But a *combination* of feasible positions (an outcome) need not itself be feasible. A position on one issue that exhausts a given budget and a position on a second issue that exhausts that budget are each feasible (affordable), but their combination is not. Constitutionally, lengthy confinement and hanging may be singly feasible as penalties for a crime but not jointly feasible (it may be "cruel and unusual" to lock someone up for 30 years and then hang him).

The Universal Instability Theorem of Schwartz (1981; 1985; 1986, sec. 11.2) generalizes this last theorem by dropping the separability and no-tie assumptions and allowing the feasible set to be *any set of outcomes whatever*. Details are beyond the scope of this survey.

STRATEGY

Although collective choices depend on preferences and institutions (voting procedures), democratic institutions are not algorithms into which we can simply plug preferences and reckon final outcomes. For collective choices also depend on strategic maneuvers of various sorts.

Strategic voting

Voting rules transform votes into choices, but preferences alone do not always determine votes. Voters sometimes have an incentive to misrepresent their true preferences – to vote *strategically* rather than *sincerely*, thereby "manipulating" the voting rule – in order to secure a collective choice they prefer to that which would otherwise have been made. Three examples follow.

Example 1. In a congressional primary, a candidate with a majority of

333

votes wins, but if none has a majority, a runoff is held between the top two candidates (the two with the most votes). There are eight voters (or equal-size groups) with the following preference orderings of three candidates:

Mr. 1	Mr. 2	Mr. 3	Mr. 4	Mr. 5	Mr. 6	Mr. 7	Mr. 8
x	x	x	y	y	z	z	z
z	z	y	x	x	y	y	y
y	y	z	z	z	x	x	x

If everyone votes sincerely, Messrs. 1–3 will vote for x, Messrs. 4 and 5 for y, and Messrs. 6–8 for z, so that no candidate has a majority and x and z enter a runoff, which x wins. Since Messrs. 6–8 prefer y to x, however, they have an incentive to misrepresent their true preference and vote strategically for y. If even one of them does so, y rather than z will join x in the runoff, and since a majority prefer y to x, y will win.

Example 2. A three-member legislature or committee have the following "voting paradox" preference orderings of a bill b, an amended version a, and the status quo q:

Mr. 1	Mr. 2	Mr. 3
b	a	q
a	q	b
q	b	a

There are two votes, or *divisions*: the first between b and a, the second between the winner in that contest and q. This agenda order is represented by the following agenda tree (or "extensive form" of the "voting game"):

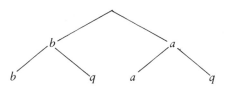

The first level of this tree represents the vote (division) between b and a; the second, the vote between q and either b or a – whichever wins in the first vote. If everyone votes sincerely, b wins at the first division (since it beats a) and q at the second, so that q is the final choice. But if Mr. 1, who likes b best but prefers a to q, votes strategically for a rather than b at the first division, a wins the first vote and goes on to win the second.

If one can play this game, so can all. Suppose everyone votes strategically. Then the three voters will not necessarily compare b with a at the first division. Instead, they will look ahead to the consequence of choosing b and the consequence of choosing a. If b were chosen at the first division, q would be chosen at the second, and if a were chosen at the first division, it would win at the second as well. So a voter will vote for b at the first division if he prefers q to a, and for a if he prefers a to q. Let us summarize this by saying that q is the *strategic equivalent* of b, and a of itself, at the first division. Because a beats q, a would win in the end if everyone voted strategically.

In general, if there are k divisions, the strategic equivalent of an alternative x at the $(k-1)$th division is the collectively preferred of the two alternatives that would be compared at the kth division if x were chosen at the $(k-1)$th, the strategic equivalent of x at the $(k-2)$th division is the collectively preferred of the strategic equivalents of the two alternatives that would be compared at the $(k-1)$th division if x were chosen at the $(k-2)$th, and so on up to the first division. When everyone votes strategically, then, the final choice is the collectively preferred of the strategic equivalents of the two alternatives compared at the first division. We can find it by reading the agenda tree from the bottom up. To do so, we need only know the collective preference, not the individual orderings. On the other hand, the assumption of uniform strategic voting requires voters to have a great deal more knowledge than they may actually have in many cases. (On agendas and strategic voting, see Farquharson 1970; McKelvey and Niemi 1978.)

Example 3. There are three legislative districts, D_1, D_2, and D_3. It is certain that D_1 will reelect its popular incumbent, a Communist, and that D_2 will reelect its left-of-center moderate incumbent. In D_3, your district, there are two candidates, a moderate liberal and a Baby-Eating Fascist, celebrated for having ridiculed Ghengis Khan as a mealy-mouthed pinko. Your own ideal point lies between those of the left-moderate D_2 incumbent and the moderate-liberal D_3 candidate, and it is slightly closer to that of the D_2 incumbent, as shown in Figure 12.5. If the moderate-liberal wins D_3, his ideal position becomes the legislative median and, therefore, wins in any legislative vote. But if the Fascist wins D_3, the left-moderate D_2 incumbent's ideal position becomes the legislative median, hence the winning position in the legislature. Therefore, since you prefer the left-moderate position to the moderate liberal position, you have an incentive to vote strategically for the Fascist, whom you loathe, rather than the moderate liberal, whom you prefer.

Vote trading, too, is a kind of strategic voting. By contrast with the examples just above, it is *cooperative* rather than *individual* strategic voting.

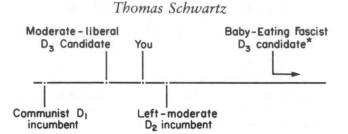

* Unfortunately, limitations of space make it impossible to display the position of the Baby-Eating Fascist without making the rest of the diagram submicroscopic.

Figure 12.5

The extent of manipulability

Is the possibility of manipulating an outcome by individual strategic voting peculiar to certain voting rules? Can a voting rule be devised that always elicits truthful statements of preferences – a rule under which no one can, by misrepresenting his preferences (by voting strategically), thereby secure a collective choice he prefers to that which would have been reached had he voted sincerely?

It seems not. To see why, let all profiles comprise only *linear* orderings – ones in which no two alternatives are ranked at the same level. Consider any voting rule applicable to all finite, nonempty subsets of a given universal set of alternatives and satisfying Arrow's conditions (1) (≥ 3 alternatives), (2) (Unrestricted Domain), and (3) (Nondictatorship), plus three more:

(4′)   If x belongs to a set A of two or more alternatives and *everyone* prefers *every other* member of A to x, then the collective choice from A remains unchanged when x is deleted from A.

(7*)   The rule prescribes a unique choice from every finite, nonempty set of alternatives (i.e., there never exist two or more permissible choices) (Resoluteness).

(10)   Suppose x_1 is the collective choice from A under a profile p_1, and x_2 the choice under a profile p_2 that differs from p_1 only in Mr. i's preference ordering. Then x_2 is not preferred to x_1 according to Mr. i's p_1 ordering, and x_1 is not preferred to x_2 according to Mr. i's p_2 ordering (Nonmanipulability).

Condition (4′) is obviously a bit stronger than (4) (Pareto Principle). Because (7*) rules out multiple permissible choices in general, it does so in particular for two-member feasible sets, which is to say that it rules out all *ties*. Thus, (7*) is even stronger than (7). Condition (10) says that the voting rule is *nonmanipulable*: no individual can, by misrepresenting his preferences (as his p_2 ordering rather than his "true" p_1 ordering, say), thereby secure a choice (x_2) he prefers to that which would otherwise have been reached (x_1).

These conditions are inconsistent: any voting rule satisfying (1)–(3), (4'), and (7*) must be manipulable.

We can prove this by deducing Arrow's conditions (1)–(6), which we know to be inconsistent, from (1)–(3), (4'), (7*), and (10). Since (1)–(3) are among Arrow's conditions and (4) obviously follows from (4'), it suffices to deduce (5) (Independence) and (6) (Transitivity).

To deduce (5), suppose x beats y, and let Messrs. $1, 2, \ldots, n$ change their preference orderings any way you please but *without* altering their preferences *between x and y*. What must be shown is that x still beats y after the change. Suppose on the contrary that y beats x after the change ((7*) rules out ties). Let Mr. i be the first voter (in order from Mr. 1 to Mr. n) whose change of preference ordering reverses the collective preference. Then by (10), y cannot be preferred to x according to Mr. i's original ordering and x cannot be preferred to y according to his new ordering. Hence, since the relative positions of x and y are the same in both orderings, neither alternative is preferred to the other according to Mr. i's original ordering. But that is impossible since preference orderings are linear and $x \neq y$.   Q.E.D.

To deduce (6) (Transitivity), recall from our discussion of Arrow's Theorem that, in the absence of ties (which (7*) rules out), (6) is violated only if there is a *tricycle* under some profile. Suppose, contrary to (6), that some profile yields a tricycle:

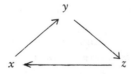

By (7*), the voting rule chooses one alternative, say x, from among the three. Change the profile by pushing y to the bottom of everyone's ordering. I will first show that x is still the collective choice. Suppose not. Let Mr. i be the first voter (in order from Mr. 1 to Mr. n) whose change of preference ordering changes the collective choice. By (10), the new choice cannot be preferred to x according to Mr. i's original ordering, and x cannot be preferred to the new choice according to Mr. i's new ordering. Hence, since nothing was raised above x in constructing Mr. i's new ordering, x cannot be preferred to the new choice according to Mr. i's original ordering either. So neither x nor the new choice is preferred to the other according to Mr. i's original ordering. But that is impossible since the new choice is different from x. Consequently, x remains the collective choice after y is pushed to the bottom of everyone's preference ordering. Thus, by (4'), x remains the collective choice under the new profile when y is deleted, that is, x beats z under the new profile. But that is impossible, by (5), since z beats x under the original profile and voter preferences between z and x are the same in both profiles.   Q.E.D.

The general manipulability of voting rules was first demonstrated by Gibbard (1973) and Satterthwaite (1975). Although their theorem differs in detail from the one just proved, it too assumes (7*) (Resoluteness), an exceedingly severe condition. I know of no real-world voting rule that satisfies (7*). Interestingly, the *only* way to manipulate plurality rule, the most common election rule in English-speaking countries, is to make or break a "generalized tie" – a multiple permissible choice, proscribed by (7*). Condition (7*) rules out much of the real world. However, Schwartz (1982*a*) proved the above theorem without (7*) or any weakened version thereof – adding some mild assumptions about individual preferences between multimembered sets of alternatives. Details are beyond the scope of this paper.

Agenda manipulation

Besides preferences, institutions (or rules), and voting strategies, collective choices depend on strategies of another sort: the manipulation of *agendas*. Committee chairmen, legislative leaders, and other officials can sometimes affect collective choices by their control, partial or complete, of agendas. This can take three forms: (i) *set manipulation* – manipulating a choice by controlling what gets on the agenda (which alternatives qualify as feasible), (ii) *order manipulation* – manipulating a choice by controlling the order of voting, and (iii) *question-manipulation* – manipulating a choice by combining legislative items in a single question or dividing an item into separate questions. Let us examine each in turn.

Set manipulation. Suppose you are able to decide what gets on an agenda. Obviously, then, by keeping something off, you can prevent its choice. Obviously, too, you can ensure the choice of one alternative or prevent the choice of another by placing on the agenda an alternative that would be chosen if included. Less obviously, you can ensure or prevent the choice of a given alternative by including or excluding another alternative that would not be chosen anyway. Suppose there is a cycle:

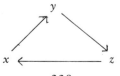

And suppose *x* would be chosen if all three alternatives were feasible. Then by excluding *y*, you can prevent *x*'s choice since *z* beats *x* – which means that *z* would be chosen if *x* and *z* alone were feasible. Likewise, by including *y* you can ensure the choice of *x* rather than *z*.

The conditions under which set manipulation is minimized are surprisingly severe (Schwartz 1976, 1985*a*, sec. 10.2). Among other things, they require Arrow's full Transitivity condition. As you just saw, the existence of a cycle gives the set manipulator considerable power.

Order manipulation. Suppose the cycle above arises under majority rule. And suppose the agenda, or voting order, pits *x* against *y*, then the winner in that contest against *z*, as in this agenda tree:

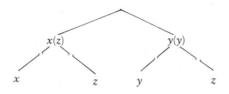

Strategic equivalents are listed in parentheses: at the first division, *z* is the strategic equivalent of *x*, and *y* the strategic equivalent of itself, because *z* would win at the second division if *x* were chosen at the first whereas *y* would win at the second division if chosen at the first. If everyone voted sincerely, *x* would win at the first division and *z* at the second. If everyone voted strategically, *y* would win at the first division (since *y* beats *z*) and go on to final victory.

Now consider a different order of voting: *y* against *z*, then the winner against *x*.

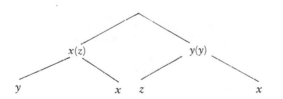

Under sincere voting, *y* would win at the first division, *x* at the second. Under strategic voting, *z* would win at the first division (*z* beats *x*) and also the second. So under sincere voting, the first agenda yields *z* whereas the second yields *x*, and under strategic voting, the first agenda yields *y* whereas the second yields *z*. He who controls the order of voting partly decides the outcome.

Thomas Schwartz

Question manipulation. Suppose an agricalatural price support measure and a food stamp measure are each supported by a minority and the two minorities together are a majority. Then both measures can pass by means of a vote trade. The same effect might be achieved by a legislative committee that reports both measures in a single bill (at least under a closed rule). That is one kind of question manipulation. Alternatively, the defeat of both measures might be secured (assuming no vote trades) by reporting them as separate bills or by a motion or parliamentary ruling to "divide the question" – the other kind of question manipulation.

DEMOCRATIC FAILURES

Despite the ostensibly majoritarian character of our electoral and congressional voting rules, these rules can produce choices that seem antidemocratic – contrary to the "popular will." A *Condorcet winner* is a feasible alternative that beats all others under majority rule. The classical voting paradox shows that there does not always exist a Condorcet winner. Sometimes, however, a Condorcet winner does exist but is not chosen: the actual choice is opposed by some majority although an alternative choice is unopposed. A *Pareto-efficient* feasible alternative is one to which no other feasible alternative is unanimously preferred. Sometimes the collective choice is Pareto *in*efficient: every voter would be happier with an alternative choice. I offer five examples.

Example 1. Liberal, moderate, and conservative candidates contest a congressional seat. The liberal receives the most votes, the moderate the fewest, none a majority. Under plurality rule, the liberal wins. Taken together, however, the moderate and conservative voters are a majority who prefer the moderate to the liberal, whereas the moderate and liberal voters are a majority who prefer the moderate to the conservative. So the moderate candidate, who lost, is the Condorcet winner. And if a runoff were held between the top two candidates (the liberal and conservative), the Condorcet winner would still lose. Just this pattern of voting occurred in the 1972 Chilean presidential election and, with the conservative receiving the most votes, in the 1970 U.S. senatorial election in New York State: in each case the moderate candidate – the apparent Condorcet winner – received the fewest votes. Such squeezing out of the middle also is a frequent feature of U.S. presidential primaries.

Example 2. As we saw in the first section, even if only two parties run in each congressional district, it can happen that one receives a majority of votes nationwide while the other receives a majority of votes in a majority of districts, thereby winning control of Congress, contrary to the party preference of a majority of voters (who may, however, care more about individual candidates than parties).

340

Example 3. A three-member legislature votes on three bills, *a*, *b*, and *c*, to which the members assign values, in millions of dollars, as follows:

	Mr. 1	Mr. 2	Mr. 3
a	4	4	−9
b	4	−9	4
c	−9	4	4

Since each bill benefits some majority, all three pass. As a result, everyone loses $1 million (4 + 4 − 9). This outcome is Pareto inefficient: everyone prefers the defeat of all three bills to the passage of all three.

The example is similar to the extreme case of a market failure: each action benefited its participants (the winning majority) but imposed an external cost on the nonparticipant (the losing minority); and although everyone participated in some actions, the external cost he bore from the action in which he did not participate outweighed the internal benefits he received from those in which he did participate.

It is essential to the example that each bill represents a project or program that is not cost effective: the aggregate cost exceeds the aggregate benefit. It seems reasonable, however, for each winning majority to raise the scale of its project above a cost-effective level because the losing minority subsidizes the cost.

It is worth noting that, although regulation by majority-ruled government is often prescribed as the cure for market failures, majority rule always imposes external costs on losing minorities except when majorities are unanimous (whereas the *requirement* of unanimity would increase the incidence of private-sector externalities). It is worth noting, too, that a Pareto-efficient outcome can be achieved in the example by a three-man vote trade (resulting in the defeat of all three bills) or a two-man trade (resulting in the passage of one bill, and with it a much greater external cost). Party discipline also would secure the passage of just one bill.

Example 4. A legislature votes on a bill and two amendments, *x* and *y*. four outcomes are possible:

b: the bill without amendments
bx: the bill perfected just by *x*
by: the bill perfected just by *y*
bxy: the bill perfected by both amendments
q: the status quo ante

At the first division, *b* is pitted against *bx*. If *b* wins, it is pitted against *by* at the second division, and if *bx* wins, it is then pitted against *bxy*. At the third division, the second-division winner is pitted against *q*. Every voter

341

prefers *by* to *bxy* to *bx* to *b* to *q*. So *by* is the Condorcet winner, and every other alternative is Pareto inefficient. The agenda tree, with strategic equivalents in parentheses, is shown in Figure 12.6.

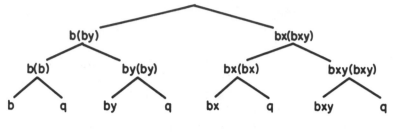

Figure 12.6

Under sincere voting, *bx* wins at the first division and *bxy* at the second and third: the Condorcet winner is rejected and a Pareto-inefficient alternative chosen.

To be sure, this particular affliction can be cured by strategic voting: *b* wins at the first division (because *by* beats *bxy*), and *by*, the Condorcet winner, wins at the second and third divisions. But consider:

Example 5. A three-member legislature is to choose among seven alternatives:

c: a bill
a: *c* perfected by an amendment
b: *c* perfected by a substitute amendment
x: a substitute bill
y: *x* perfected by an amendment
z: a substitute for *x*
q: the status quo ante

According to Rule 14 of the U.S. House of Representatives (on congressional procedures, see Sullivan 1984), the order of voting is as follows:

1st division: *a* versus *b*
2nd division: winner at 1st division versus *c*
3rd division: *x* versus *y*
4th division: winner at 3rd division versus *z*
5th division: winner at 2nd division versus winner at 4th division
6th division: winner at 5th division versus *q*

Here are the legislators' preference orderings and the relation of majority preference:

342

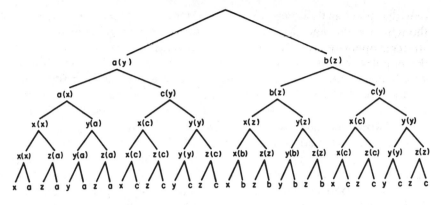

Figure 12.7

Mr. 1	Mr. 2	Mr. 3	Majority preference
a	*b*	*x*	*a*
c	*y*	*a*	*c*
z	*c*	*z*	*z*
b	*x*	*y*	*b*
y	*a*	*c*	*y*
x	*z*	*b*	*x*
q	*q*	*q*	*q*

Majority preference is depicted by an arrow and, in the absence of any arrow, by height on the page. The agenda tree, with strategic equivalents in parentheses, is shown in Figure 12.7. I omitted the representation of the sixth division because *q* is beaten by every other alternative. The final choice is *z* under strategic voting. But *z* is Pareto inefficient: everyone prefers *a* to *z*. Interestingly, *a* would have been chosen under sincere voting. (Much recent research [esp. Banks 1985, Miller 1980, Shepsle and Weingast 1984] has argued that legislative agendas are better behaved under strategic voting than this example shows, yielding outcomes that are, among other things, Pareto efficient. The mistake seems attributable to an overly restrictive formal assumption about the class of binary trees that can represent legislative agendas. On congressional agendas, see Ordeshook and Schwartz 1987.)

CONCLUSION

That the institutions of representative democracy are prone to instability and manipulation does not mean that political analysis is impossible, only that good analysis depends, to a greater degree than some may have thought, on the fine details of institutions, political alignments, and strategic opportunities. Despite producing outcomes that ostensibly flout the popular will, these institutions may be far preferable, even from a strictly democratic point of view, to the feasible alternative institutions. On the other hand, a Marxist or other critic of representative democracy might make clever use of some of the anomalies discussed above; the debate would be interesting. My own reaction is that the apparent shortcomings of voting procedures are the price of securing the Madisonian goal of "republican government," which is not to reckon the "popular will" but to prevent tyranny: the easier it is to alter and manipulate political outcomes – the greater the opportunities for realignment and strategic maneuver – the less concentration of power there will be (cf. Riker 1982, pp. 233–53).

REFERENCES

Arrow, Kenneth J. 1952. *Social Choice and Individual Values*. 1st ed. New York: Wiley.
1963. *Social Choice and Individual Values*. 2nd ed. New Haven: Yale University Press.
Banks, Jeffrey S. 1985. "Sophisticated Voting Outcomes and Agenda Control." *Social Choice and Welfare* 1:295–306.
Bernholz, Peter. 1973. "Logrolling, Arrow Paradox, and Cyclical Majorities." *Public Choice* 15:87–95.
Black, Duncan. 1948. "On the Rationale of Group Decision-Making." *Journal of Political Economy* 56:23–24.
1958. *Theory of Committees and Elections*. Cambridge: Cambridge University Press.
Cohen, Linda. 1979. "Cyclic Sets in Multidimensional Voting Models. *Journal of Economic Theory* 20:1–12.
Davis, Otto, Morris H. De Groot, and Melvin Hinich. 1972. "Social Preference Orderings and Majority Rule." *Econometrica* 40:147–57.
Downs, Anthony. 1957. *An Economic Theory of Democracy*. New York: Harper & Row.
Enelow, James M., and Melvin J. Hinich. 1983. "On Plott's Pairwise Symmetry Condition for Majority Rule Equilibrium." *Public Choice* 40:317–21.
Farquharson, Robin. 1970. *Theory of Voting*. New Haven: Yale University Press.
Fishburn, Peter C. 1973. *The Theory of Social Choice*. Princeton: Princeton University Press.
Gibbard, Allan. 1973. "Manipulation of Voting Schemes: A General Result." *Econometrica* 41:587–601.
Hotelling, Harold. 1929. "Stability in Competition." *Economic Journal* 39: 41–57.
Kadane, J. B. 1972. "On Division of the Question." *Public Choice* 13:47–54.
Kelley, Jerry S. 1978. *Arrow Impossibility Theorems*. New York: Academic Press.
McKelvey, Richard D. 1976. "Intransitivities in Multi-Dimensional Voting

Models, and Some Implications for Agenda Control." *Journal of Economic Theory* 2:472–82.

McKelvey, Richard D., and Richard G. Niemi. 1978. "A Multistage Game Representation of Sophisticated Voting for Binary Procedures." *Journal of Economic Theory* 18:1–22.

Mas Collel, Andreu, and Hugo F. Sonnenschein. 1972. "General Possibility Theorems for Group Decision." *Review of Economic Studies* 39:185–92.

May, K. O. 1952. "A Set of Independent, Necessary, and Sufficient Conditions for Simple Majority Decision." *Econometrica* 20:680–84.

Miller, Nicholas R. 1980. "A New 'Solution Set' for Tournaments and Majority Voting." *American Journal of Political Science* 24:68–96.

Murakami, Yasusuke. 1968. *Logic and Social Choice*. New York: Dover.

Oppenheimer, Joe A. 1972. "Relating Coalitions of Minorities to the Voter's Paradox; or, Putting the Fly in the Democratic Pie." Paper presented to the annual meeting of the Southwest Political Science Association, San Antonio, March.

Ordeshook Peter C., and Thomas Schwartz. 1987. "Agendas and the Control of Political Outcomes." *American Political Science Review* 81.

Plott, Charles. 1967. "A Notion of Equilibrium and Its Possibility under Majority Rule." *American Economic Review* 57:788–806.

1976. "Axiomatic Social Choice Theory: An Overview and Interpretation." *American Journal of Political Science* 20:511–96.

Riker, William H. 1982. *Liberalism against Populism*. New York: Freeman.

Satterthwaite, Mark A. 1975. "Strategy-Proofness and Arrow's Conditions: Existence and Correspondence Therorems for Voting Procedures and Social Welfare Functions." *Journal of Economic Theory* 10:187–217.

Schofield, Norman. 1978. "Instability of Simple Dynamic Games." *Review of Economic Studies* 45:575–94.

Schwartz, Thomas. 1970. "On the Possibility of Rational Policy Evaluation." *Theory and Decision* 1:89–106.

1976. "Choice Functions, 'Rationality' Conditions, and Variations on the Weak Axiom of Revealed Preference." *Journal of Economic Theory* 13:414–27.

1977. "Collective Choice, Separation of Issues, and Vote Trading." *American Political Science Review* 71:999–1010.

1981. "The Universal Instability Theorem." *Public Choice* 37:487–501.

1982*a*. "No Minimally Reasonable Collective Choice Process Can Be Strategy-Proof." *Mathematical Social Science* 3:57–72.

1982*b*. "A Really General Impossibility Theorem." *Quality and Quantity* 16:493–505.

1985. "The Meaning of Instability." Paper presented to annual meeting of American Political Science Association, New Orleans, August.

1986. *The Logic of Collective Choice*. New York: Columbia University Press.

Sen, A. K. 1983. "Social Choice Theory." In Kenneth J. Arrow and Michael D. Intrilligator, eds., *Handbook of Mathematical Economics*, vol. 3. Amsterdam: North Holland.

Shepsle, Kenneth A., and Barry R. Weingast. 1984. "Uncovered Sets and Sophisticated Voting Outcomes with Implications for Agenda Institutions." *American Journal of Political Science* 28:49–74.

Sullivan, Terry. 1984. *Procedural Structure*. New York: Praeger.

13

Institutional arrangements and equilibrium in multidimensional voting models

KENNETH A. SHEPSLE

Theories of social choice are concerned with the operating characteristics and equilibrium properties of collective decision-making arrangements. At a very general level, as exemplified in the famous work of Arrow (1963), we have failed to understand how collective decision-making arrangements operate because they lack equilibrium properties. Indeed, a fundamental lesson of his inquiry is that an institutional arrangement lacking some (perhaps distasteful) constitutional restrictions or failing that, a basic value consensus, is *inherently* inexplicable in its operation.

In light of Arrow's Possibility Theorem, one major direction of scholarship has sought to isolate the characteristics of that value consensus. Represented most elegantly by the theorem of Sen (1966) and broadly summarized in Sen (1970), Pattanaik (1971), and Fishburn (1973), this literature focuses on the properties of a collection of individual preference orderings that induce equilibrium states in an aggregation mechanism. It turns out, however, that in at least one interesting choice environment – that in which the alternatives are a compact subset of a multidimensional Euclidean space – the restrictions on preferences are extraordinarily severe (Kramer, 1973). Related research on majority rule and other binary decision rules in multi-

American Journal of Political Science, Vol. 23, No. 1, February 1979. Reprinted by permission of the University of Texas Press. The author is Professor of Political Science at Harvard University. Earlier versions of this paper were presented at the annual meetings of the American Economic Association, New York, December, 1977 and the Public Choice Society, New Orleans, March, 1978. The author is grateful to the Carthage Foundation for sponsoring this research and to Professors John Aldrich of Michigan State University, John Ferejohn and Morris Fiorina of California Institute of Technology, Howard Rosenthal of Carnegie-Mellon University, and Robert Parks, Trout Rader, Barbara Salert, and Barry Weingast of Washington University for useful conversations and comments.

dimensional alternative spaces has produced a similar conclusion (Plott, 1967; Sloss, 1973; McKelvey and Wendell, 1976; Slutsky, 1977b; Matthews, 1977). In all of these works, in order for equilibrium to obtain, preferences must exhibit an extremely precise symmetry which is unlikely to emerge in natural decision-making settings and, even if it should, is extremely sensitive to slight perturbations (McKelvey, 1977; Cohen, 1977). It now appears that further characterizations of the value consensus required for choice equilibrium will, in essence, consist of "mopping up" exercises. Equilibrium of a social choice process *depends* on the configuration of preferences but can only rarely be *guaranteed* by that configuration. We must search elsewhere to understand how collective choices are arrived at.

In recognition of this theoretical cul de sac, some recent efforts have been made to model institutional arrangements more directly. As Zeckhauser and Weinstein (1974, p. 664) note,

the relatively infrequent appearance of [disequilibrium in the form of] cyclical majorities in functioning legislatures cannot be explained by some geometric property of individuals' preferences.... [M]atters such as procedural rules and institutional constraints provide key insights into real-world social choice phenomena.

Two such efforts, those of Slutsky (1975, 1977a) and Denzau and Parks (1973), attempt to provide the structure for a political economy in which tax prices and levels for public goods, and after-tax income, prices, and quantities for private goods are all in equilibrium (in the sense that public sector levels are majority winners, the public budget is balanced, private goods markets are cleared, profits maximized, and no citizen bankrupted). To circumvent the difficulties surrounding public sector voting equilibrium, they resort to restrictions on the domain of public sector choices. Space does not permit me to review their work more fully here, so let me only note that their respective general equilibrium orientations tend to submerge matters of institutional structure in the public sector, matters I wish to make more prominent in this paper. Therefore, in what follows, I focus exclusively on the internal structure of a generic collective decision-making institution. While this institution looks very much like a legislature, I shall argue below that it shares many interesting characteristics in common with other kinds of decision-making arrangements. The basic point of this paper is that institutional structure – in the form of rules of jurisdiction and amendment control – has an important independent impact on the existence of equilibrium and, together with the distribution of preferences, co-determines the characteristics of the equilibrium state(s) of collective choice processes.

347

Kenneth A. Shepsle

1. MOTIVATION, NOTATION, EXAMPLES

We consider a generic decision-making institution composed of n members, $N = \{1, 2, \ldots, n\}$ and a binary choice procedure $C(x, y)$ that determines choices between pairs of alternatives. The space of alternatives is a compact, convex subset R^m of m-dimensional Euclidean space. Each $i \epsilon N$ has a complete, transitive, binary preference relation, $\geqslant_i$, defined on all $x, y \in R^m$, and represented by an ordinal utility function $u_i \colon R^m \to R$ which is maximized on R^m at $\bar{x}^i = (\bar{x}^i_1, \ldots, \bar{x}^i_m)$.

Winners

A point $x \in R^m$ is said to be a *global binary winner* if and only if $x \cap_{y \in R^m} C(x, y)$. More generally, x is said to be an *A- restricted winner* if and only if $x \cap_{y \in A} C(x, y)$, for some $A \subseteq R^m$. Clearly global winners are A-restricted winners under the most demanding domain requirement $-A = R^m$. Shortly we give a substantive interpretation to A, relating it explicitly to institutional arrangements. First, however, we define the institution's choice function, $C(x, y)$.

Throughout this paper we focus on decisive *majority* coalitions, though not necessarily of the pure majority rule form. With some changes it may be possible to generalize results to other collections of decisive coalitions. For $B \subseteq N$ let $|B|$ represent the number of $i \in B$ and let $|x \geqslant_i y| = |\{i | x \geqslant_i y\}|$. The following A- restricted winners are defined.[1]

DEFINITION:

Strong Majority Condorcet:	$E_1 = \{x \epsilon A | \forall y \epsilon A, y \neq x,$
(*Weak*)	(E_2) $\qquad\qquad |x > y| > \frac{n}{2}\}$
	$(\geqslant)$
Strong Plurality Condorcet:	$E_3 = \{x \epsilon A | \forall y \epsilon A, y \neq x, |x > y|$
(*Weak*)	(E_4) $\qquad\qquad > |y > x|\}$
	$(\geqslant)$
Strong Majority Core	$E_5 = \{x \epsilon A | \forall y \epsilon A, |y > x| > \frac{n}{2}\}$
(*Weak*)	(E_6) $\qquad\qquad\qquad (\leqslant)$

It is clear that a strong winner of each type is also a weak winner of that that type $- E_1 \to E_2, E_3 \to E_4, E_5 \to E_6$. Moreover, $E_1 \to E_3 \to E_5$ $(E_2 \to E_4 \to E_6)$. For $A = R^m$, McKelvey and Wendell (1976, Theorem 1.1) demonstrate that whenever $\geqslant_i$ is strictly convex—$x \neq y$ and $y \geqslant_i x$

imply $[tx + (1-t)y] >_i x$ for any $t \in (0, 1)$—all strong (weak) winner types are equivalent:

$$E_s = E_1 = E_3 = E_5$$
$$E_w = E_2 = E_4 = E_6$$

More generally, for A-restricted winners we have

THEOREM 1.1: *If $\geq_i$ is strictly convex and A a convex set, then $E_1 = E_3 = E_5$ ($E_2 = E_4 = E_6$).*

Proof: We already have $E_1 \rightarrow E_3 \rightarrow E_5$ from the definitions, so demonstrating that $E_5 \rightarrow E_1$ establishes the result. Suppose the contrary – $x \in E_5$ but $x \notin E_1$. $x \notin E_1$ implies there exists a $y \in A$ with $|x > y| \leq \frac{n}{2}$. Thus, $|y \geq x| \geq \frac{n}{2}$ since A is convex, pick a $y' \in A$ with $y' = tx + (1-t)y$, $t \in (0, 1)$. From the strict convexity of $\geq_i$, $y \geq_i x$ implies $y' >_i x$. Thus $|y' > x| > \frac{n}{2}$ and $x \notin E_5$, a contradiction. The proof for weak winners is developed in a similar fashion.   Q.E.D.

Notice that the equivalence of the strong (weak) winners need not obtain if A is not convex, for then it would only be by accident that a point $y' \in A$ with the appropriate properties exists.[2]

Jurisdictional restrictions

The focus of this paper (and the main departure from traditional social choice theory) is on the consequences of constraints on contests between competing proposals. Restrictions on contests derive from the rules by which the decision-making agenda is constructed and are often most conspicious in the structural arrangements into which decision-making groups constitute themselves. Particularly noteworthy in this respect are the mechanisms of decentralization that are employed to expedite complex decision making. Examples abound: a committee system in a legislature; a collection of schools, colleges, and departments in a university; a system of divisions in a firm; an arrangement of bureaus in an agency; the "separation of powers" within a national government; a federal organization for layers of government; and so on.

What distinguishes these mechanisms of decentralization is that they are division-of-labor instruments. The different committees of a legislature or departments of a university have different (though not necessarily disjoint) domains of responsibility or jurisdictions. Of course, the idea of *jurisdiction* is quite independent of division-of-labor structural arrangements. The formal agenda of an ordinary business meeting, with its separate categories of activity – old business, new business, officers' reports, etc., suggests a separation of activities into jurisdictions without a structural division-of-labor. While a matter of new business may not be brought up (i.e., is out of order) during the session on old business and vice versa, the entire membership of the organization participates in both deliberations.

In order to keep the ideas of jurisdiction and division-of-labor distinct, we define two finite coverings.[3]

DEFINITION: *Call the family of sets* $C = \{C_j\}$ *a committee system if it covers* $N = \{1, 2, \ldots, n\}$

Example 1.1 (*Committee-of-the-Whole*): Let the family of sets consist of a single set $C = \{N\}$. This is known as the committee-of-the-whole and, in traditional social choice theory, is the main structural arrangement, usually labeled committee, society, electorate, etc. It is a trivial partition of N.

Example 1.2 (*Legislative parties*): Let the family of sets $C = \{C_j\}$ be the party groupings of a legislature. The family of legislative parties is normally a partition inasmuch as each legislator affiliates with one and only one legislative party.

Example 1.3 (*Committee system of the U.S. House of Representatives*): Let the family $C = \{C_j\}$ represent the collection of standing committees of the U.S. House of Representatives. Here C is a covering but not a partition since most $i \in N$ serve on more than one standing committee.

A committee system, as these examples illustrate, is a division-of-labor arrangement that distributes members to structural decision-making subunits of the organization. The notion of jurisdiction is defined next.

DEFINITION: *Let* $E = \{e_1, \ldots, e_m\}$ *be an orthogonal basis for* R^m, *where* e_i *is the unit vector for the* i^{th} *dimension. Call the family of sets* $J = \{J_k\}$ *a jurisdictional arrangement if it covers* E.

Thus each jurisdiction $J_k \in J$ is a subspace of R^m. Three examples in R^3 will illustrate the range of alternatives.

Example 1.4 (*Global Jurisdiction*): Let the family of sets consist of a single set $J = \{\{e_1, e_2, e_3\}\}$. The space of alternative, R^3, falls entirely within a single jurisdiction. Together with Example 1.1, this arrangement characterizes the context of social choice that is prevalent in the literature.

Example 1.5 (*Simple Jurisdictions*): Let $J = \{J_1, J_2, J_3\}$ with $J_k = \{e_k\}$. Here each jurisdiction is simply a single dimension of R^3.

Institutional arrangements in voting models

Example 1.6 (Overlapping Jurisdictions): Let $J = \{J_1, J_2\}$ with $J_1 = \{e_1, e_2\}$, $J_2 = \{e_2, e_3\}$. This jurisdictional arrangement is descriptive of arrangements in the U.S. House and U.S. Senate, where jurisdictional overlaps of committees are considerable.

In the remainder of this paper, attention is devoted to the case of *simple jurisdictions* with comparisons made between committee-of-the-whole decision arrangements and arbitrary committee systems. The existence of equilibrium will be established in each case with differences between the equilibria noted.

For an arbitrary committee system C and jurisdictional arrangement J, the correspondence $f: C \to J$ associates (sets of) jurisdiction(s) with the $C_j \in C$. Several points are in order. First, each $C_j \in C$ is mapped into at least one $J_k \in J$. It then has jurisdiction over the dimensions in J_k. Thus if some subset of the $i \in N$ comprises C_j and f takes C_j to $J_k = \{e_1, e_2\}$ then C_j has jurisdiction over the points in R^m spanned by e_1 and e_2; they are of the form $(x_1, x_2, x^\circ_3, \ldots, x^\circ_m)$ where the x°_i are components of some predetermined status quo (see below). Second, the correspondence permits a $C_j \in C$ to be associated with several J_k's. One of special interest to us is the situation involving the committee-of-the-whole and simple jurisdictions. There $C_j = N$ and $J = \{\{e_1\}, \{e_2\}, \ldots, \{e_m\}\}$. The points in C_j's jurisdiction are of the form $(x_1, x^\circ_2, \ldots, x^\circ_m)$ or $(x^\circ_1, x_2, x^\circ_3, \ldots, x^\circ_m)$ or $\ldots$ or $(x^\circ_1, 2x^\circ_2, \ldots, x^\circ_{m-1}, x_m)$ – points that alter the status quo in at most one dimension. Contrast this arrangement to the one considered in traditional social choice theory in which $J = \{\{e_1, e_2, \ldots, e_m\}\}$: there, all points in R^m fall in C_j's jurisdiction. Third, it is possible for a particular $e_i \in E$ to be contained only in J_k for which $f^{-1}(J_k)$ is undefined. That is, some dimensions of the choice space may be contained in jurisdictions associated with no $C_j \in C$. Short of revolution or more peaceful constitutional change, the status quo level on this dimension is immutable.

The status quo and the organizational agenda

The prevailing social state is a point $x^\circ \in R^m$. The status quo represents the cumulation of historical decisions that has brought the organization to x°; it characterizes the current level on each of the m dimensions of the choice space. The organizational agenda for changes in x° is controlled by the $C_j \in C$ and is channeled by jurisdictional arrangements. The set of feasible changes in x° is the set of points that alter x° in no more than one jurisdiction:

DEFINITION: *A proposal is a change in x° restricted to a single jurisdic-*

351

tion. The set of proposals is $P = \{x | x = x^\circ + \Sigma\lambda_i e_i, I \subseteq J_k$ for some $\underset{i \epsilon I}{}$

$J_k \epsilon J\} \subseteq R^m$.

Committees may recommend changes in x° to the parent organization from among the proposals falling within their assigned jurisdictions. Committees, in this view, are instruments that generate proposed changes. Their actions are constrained by their respective jurisdictions and their own internal decision-making rules.

Amendment control

We have defined $f(C_j)$ as the dimensions constituting the jurisdiction of $C_j \epsilon C$. Let $g(C_j)$ represent the set of proposals available to C_j when the status quo is x°:

$$g(C_j) = \{x | x = x^\circ + \Sigma_i \lambda_i e_i, e_i \epsilon f(C_j)\}$$

Suppose now that C_j proposes some $x \epsilon g(C_j)$ to the parent body.[4]

DEFINITION: *For any proposal $x \epsilon g(C_j)$, the set $M(x) \subseteq R^m$ consists of the modifications N may make in x. $M(x)$ is said to be an amendment control rule.*

The idea here is the following: C_j proposes some $x \epsilon g(C_j)$ to the parent body; before x is compared to x° it may be modified by N; either x or some $x' \epsilon M(x)$ is then compared to x°.

An amendment control rule represents the extent to which an organization can monitor and change the proposals of its subunits. In some instances, a parent organization is little more than a holding company for its subunits, voting the latter's recommendations "up" or "down":

DEFINITION: *A committee's proposal is said to be governed by the closed rule if $M(x) = \emptyset$ for all $x \epsilon g(C_j)$.*

Example 1.7 (Romer and Rosenthal): Romer and Rosenthal construct a model in which a group, called the *agenda setter*, proposes an alternative – a change in the status quo – which is either accepted or rejected by the collectivity. They have in mind decision settings illustrated by school tax choices in many school districts. There the agenda setter is usually the school board which proposes a property tax rate. By referendum the citizens of the school district decide whether to adopt the recommendation of the school board; if they do not, then the rate to which the tax reverts is usually constitutionally-specified.[5]

Example 1.8 (Tax Legislation in the U.S. House): Though by no means a hard and fast rule, it has been the usual practice in the U.S.

House to provide legislative proposals of the Ways and Means Committee with a closed rule. No modifications, unless acceptable to a committee majority, are permitted.

The closed rule is obviously the most restrictive constraint on the discretion of the parent organization to modify committee proposals. At the other extreme there is the open rule:

DEFINITION: *A committee's proposal is said to be governed by the open rule if $M(x) = R^m$ for all $x \in g(C_j)$.*

Example 1.9 (U.S. Senate Riders): The rules of procedure in the U.S. Senate permit the modification of proposals through the addition of riders. As a consequence, a major piece of legislation, e.g., the extension of the Voting Rights Act, may be tagged on as a rider to a fairly innocuous bill, e.g., a District of Columbia Public Library authorization.

Between the open and the closed rule lie alternative amendment control rules which may be partially ordered by set inclusion. One that deserves special distinction is that of germaneness:

DEFINITION: *A committee's proposal is said to be governed by a jurisdictional germaneness rule if $M(x) = \{x' | x'_i = x_i^\circ \text{ if } e_i \notin f(C_j)\}$.*

The jurisdictional germaneness rule permits amendments of $x \in g(C_j)$ only along those dimensions that fall in the jurisdiction of the committee proposing x. A slightly different rule of relevancy is the following.

DEFINITION: *A committee's proposal is said to be governed by a proposal germaneness rule if $M(x) = \{x' | x_i' - x_i^\circ \text{ if } x_i = x_i^\circ\}$.*

If jurisdictions are simple (example 1.5), then proposal germaneness and jurisdictional germaneness are equal; otherwise proposal germaneness is a proper subset of jurisdictional germaneness. For example, if $f(C_j) = \{e_1, e_2\}$ and C_j proposes $x = (x_1, x^\circ_2, x^\circ_3, \ldots, x^\circ_m)$ – i.e., only a change in the first of C_j's two dimensions – then jurisdictional germaneness entails $M(x) = \{x' | x' = x^\circ + \lambda_1 e_1 + \lambda_2 e_2\}$, whereas proposal germaneness requires $M(x) = \{x' | x' = x^\circ + \lambda_1 e_1\}$. In effect, germaneness rules are open rules restricted either to the dimensions of C_j's jurisdiction or to the dimensions on which C_j's proposal alters x°.

2. STRUCTURE-INDUCED AND PREFERENCE-INDUCED EQUILIBRIUM

We have, to this point, sought to characterize some salient aspects of organization, namely structural and jurisdictional decentralization. To summarize briefly, an institutional choice situation is described by

1. a status quo, $x° \in R^m$;
2. a covering $C = \{C_j\}$ on the set of institutional actors;
3. a covering $J = \{J_k\}$ on the choice space R^m, describing the jurisdictional constraints on challenges to $x°$;
4. a correspondence, f, mapping elements of C to (subsets of) elements of J; and
5. an amendment control rule, $M(x)$, defined for $x \in g(C_j)$, describing the alternatives against which N may compare any proposal made by a $C_j \in C$.

In this section a model of organization possessing these characteristics is offered and its equilibrium states defined.

DEFINITION: *A proposal $x \in R^m$ is called a replacement for $x°$ if*
(i) *$x \in g(C_j)$ for some $C_j \in C$*
(ii) *$x = C_j(x, x°)$*
(iii) *$x \in C(x, x')$ for all $x' \in M(x)$, and*
(iv) *$x = C(x, x°)$* (2.1)

In order to replace $x°$, a proposal must, first, be *feasible* in the sense of (i). It is in this sense that jurisdictional arrangements channel (constrain) change. Letting $C_j(\cdot, \cdot)$ be a binary choice function for C_j, (ii) requires that proposal $x \in g(C_j)$ be preferred to $x°$ by a decisive coalition in C_j. Thus, not only do jurisdictional arrangements *channel* proposals; they empower *veto groups* as well. (iii) requires that x survive when compared to all admissible alterations $x' \in M(x)$; that is, x must be a maximal element of $\{x\} \cup M(x)$. Finally, by (iv), x must be preferred to $x°$ by a decisive subset of N.[6]

This suggests the following equilibrium notions:

DEFINITION: *The status quo $x°$ is vulnerable if there exists a replacement for it or if there exists an $x \in g(C_j) \cap C_j(x, x°)$ and an $x' \in M(x)$ with $x' \in C(x', x) \cap C(x', x°)$.*

That is, $x°$ is vulnerable if there is a point that dominates it in the sense of (i)–(iv) above or if there is a proposal of some C_j an amended version of which dominates it.

DEFINITION: *The status quo $x°$ is a structure-induced equilibrium if and only if it is invulnerable.*

By a somewhat circuitous route, it may be shown that a structure-induced equilibrium is a particular form of A-restricted winner defined in section 1. It is not particularly instructive to dwell on these details except to note the contrast between a structure-induced equilibrium and a global binary winner:

DEFINITION: *The status quo $x°$ is a preference-induced equilibrium if and only if it is a global binary winner* $- x° \in \bigcap_{x \in R^m} C(x, x°)$

THEOREM 2.1: *If $x°$ is a preference-induced equilibrium then it is a structure-induced equilibrium, but not the converse.*

Proof: $x°$ a preference-induced equilibrium $\rightarrow x° \in \bigcap_{x \in R^m} C(x, x°) \rightarrow$ $x° \in C(x, x°)$ for any $x \in C_j(x, x°)$ and $x° \in C(x', x°)$ for any $x' \in M(x)$ for any $x \in C_j(x, x°) \rightarrow x°$ invulnerable $\rightarrow x°$ a structure-induced equilibrium. The converse fails in general since there can be a structure-induced equilibrium $x°$ and another point x for which $x = C(x, x°)$ but $x° \in g(C_j)$ for no C_j. Q.E.D.

Example 2.1: In R^3, suppose $N = \{1, 2, 3\}$ with utility maxima, respectively, at $(1, 0, 0)$, $(0, 1, 0)$, $(0, 0, 1)$ and spherical indifference loci. The Pareto optimal surface is the triangle connecting these points (see Figure 13.1). It is easy to show that, for $C(\cdot, \cdot)$ the simple majority rule, no preference-induced equilibrium exists. Consider now $x° = (0, 0, 0)$, a jurisdictional covering $J = \{\{e_1\}, \{e_2\}, \{e_3\}\}$, the committee-of-the-whole $- C = \{N\}$, and a germaneness rule to amendments. The point $x°$ is a structure-induced equilibrium since all proposals (and amendments) are of the form $x° + \lambda_i e_i$ and, for any such proposal with $\lambda_i \neq 0$, at least two individuals prefer $x°$. That is, $x°$ is preferred by a majority to all proposals of the form $(x, 0, 0)$, $(0, x, 0)$ or $(0, 0, x)$. Interestingly there exist points on the shaded triangle unanimously preferred to $x°$, but jurisdictional constraints and amendment rules prohibit their consideration. If, instead of $(0, 0, 1)$, 3's ideal point were $(t, 1\text{-}t, 0)$, $t \in [0, 1]$, then that point, a convex combination of the ideal points of 1 and 2, would be a preference-induced equilibrium and, by Theorem 2.1, a structure-induced equilibrium as well.

3. SIMPLE JURISDICTIONS AND GERMANENESS: CONDITIONS FOR EQUILIBRIUM

The main focus is on a jurisdictional scheme $J = \{\{e_1\}, \{e_2\}, \ldots, \{e_m\}\}$ of single-dimensional jurisdictions and the germaneness rule defined in section 1. The particular committee system remains implicit for now. The following definitions and lemma are useful for the main result of this section.

DEFINITION: *For status quo $x°$ and jurisdiction e_j, let the induced ideal point in the jth direction for $i \in N$ be $x^{*i} = (x_1^{*i}, \ldots, x_m^{*i})$ where $x_k^{*i} = x_k°$; $k \neq j$, and $u_i(x^{*i}) = \max_j [u_i(x_1°, \ldots, x_j, \ldots, x°_m)]$. More*

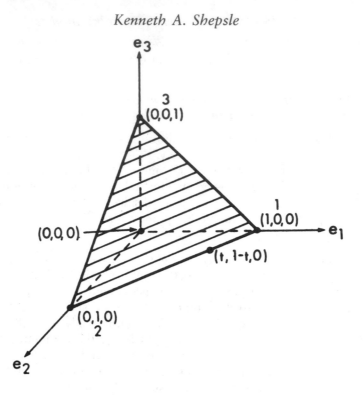

Figure 13.1

generally, x^{*i} is the induced ideal point on an arbitrary set X if $u_i(x)$ is maximized on X at $x = x^{*i}$.

DEFINITION: *A utility function $u_i(x)$ is strictly quasi-concave if and only if, fox $x \neq y$, $u_i(x) \geqslant u_i(y) \rightarrow u_i(x') > u_i(y)$ for any $x' = \lambda x + (1-\lambda)y$, $\lambda \in (0, 1)$.*

DEFINITION: *Let $X = \{x | x = \lambda y + (1-\lambda)z, y, z \in R^m, \lambda \in [0, 1]\}$ be the line connecting arbitrary points y and z. A preference representation on X is said to be single-peaked if and only if, for all $x \in X$, $x \neq x^{*i}$, $u_i[\alpha x + (1-\alpha)x^{*i}] > u_i[\beta x + (1-\beta)x^{*i}]$ whenever $0 \leqslant \alpha \leqslant \beta \leqslant 1$ and x^{*i} is the induced ideal point on X.*

LEMMA 3.1: *If $u_i: R^m \rightarrow R$ is strictly quasi-concave and continuous for $i \in N$, then the preference representation for i on any line X is single-peaked.*

Proof (see Figure 13.2): For any line, its intersection with R^m (a compact, convex set) is itself compact and convex. Since u_i is continuous it has a maximum on this set (see Nikaido, 1972, Theorem 1.1). The

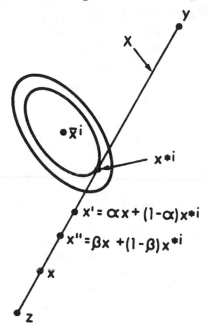

Figure 13.2

uniqueness of the maximum follows from the strict quasi-concavity of u_i. Hence an induced ideal point, x^{*i}, exists and is unique. Let $x'' = \beta x + (1-\beta)x^{*i}$ for arbitrary $x \in X$. By construction, $u_i(x^{*i}) \geq u_i(x'')$ and, by strict quasi-concavity, $u_i(x') > u_i(x'')$ for $x' = \lambda x^{*i} + (1-\lambda)x''$, $\lambda \in (0, 1)$. From the definition of x'', it follows that $x' = \lambda x^{*i} + (1-\lambda)[\beta x + (1-\beta) x^{*i}] = (1-\lambda)\beta x + [\lambda + (1-\lambda)(1-\beta)]x^{*i} = \alpha x + (1-\alpha)x^{*i}$ where $\alpha = (1-\lambda)\beta > \beta$. From the above definition, u_i is single-peaked.   Q.E.D.

THEOREM 3.1: *Let* $X_j^* = \{x_j^{*1}, x_j^{*2}, \ldots, x_j^{*n}\}$ *be the set of* j^{th} *components from the induced ideal points of the* $i \in N$ *in the direction* e_j *from status quo* x°. *For one-dimensional jurisdictions, a germaneness rule for amendments, and any committee system,* x° *is a structure-induced equilibrium if, for all* j, $x_j^\circ = median\ X_j^*$.   (3.1)

Proof: From Lemma 3.1, the u_i are single-peaked on any line of the form $X = \{x|x = x^\circ + \lambda e_j\}$. From Black's well-known theorem on single-peaked preference representations, if $x_j^\circ = median\ X_j^*$ then x° defeats all points in X. If condition (3.1) holds for all j, then, given the jurisdictional constraint and the germaneness rule for amendments, x° is invulnerable. From the earlier definition, it is a structure-induced equilibrium.

Q.E.D.

The theorem establishes that condition (3.1) is *sufficient* for $x°$ to be an equilibrium when the jurisdictions are the individual basis vectors and a germaneness rule governs amendments. It is not a necessary condition, as the following corollary suggests and Theorem 3.2 proves.

COROLLARY 3.1: *(3.1) is necessary condition for $x°$ to be a structure-induced equilibrium under the committee-of-the-whole arrangement.*

The proof is omitted. The corollary suggests that not only must a preferred alternative to $x°$ exist for the latter to be vulnerable; it must be *proposed* by a committee with appropriate jurisdiction or "reached," via the amendment process, from an appropriate committee proposal. Under the committee-of-the-whole procedure, $x°$ is a structure-induced equilibrium only if (3.1) holds, since $x°_j \neq$ median X_j^* implies there exists a $y = x° + \lambda e_j$ with $y_i =$ median X_i^* and any member of at least a simple majority of N eligible to propose it – i.e. the "committee" (N, itself) will approve $y = (x_1°, \ldots, y_i, \ldots, x_m°)$ which, in turn, is passed over $x°$ by the parent organization (again N).

The full implications of the veto-power of committees, and consequently their capacity to create equilibria, are provided in Theorem 3.2. Let

$$S_j = \{x | x = x° + \lambda e_j, \lambda \neq 0, x = C_j(x, x°)\}$$

be the set of modifications of $x°$ in its jurisdiction preferred to the status quo by C_j. From the strict quasi-concavity of the u_i, $i \in C_j$, and Lemma 3.1, it is straightforward to show that S_j is an open interval (possibly degenerate) for $C_j(\cdot, \cdot)$ the simple majority rule for committee j. Similarly, let

$$T_j = \{x | x = x° + \lambda e_j, \lambda \neq 0, x = C(x, x°)\}$$

be the set of modifications in $x°$ along e_j preferred by N. Finally, define

$$R_j(x) = \begin{cases} M(x) \cup \{x\} & \text{if } x \in S_j \\ \emptyset & \text{if } S_j = \emptyset \end{cases}$$

Now we may state

THEOREM 3.2: *For the jurisdictional arrangement consisting of the basis vectors of R^m and a germaneness rule for amendments, $x°$ is a structure-induced equilibrium if and only if, for every j and every $x \in S_j$,*

$$R_j(x) \cap T_j = \emptyset.$$

Proof: (1) Necessity. Suppose $x' \in R_j(x) \cap T_j$. Since $R_j(x)$ is the union of two sets (it cannot be empty under the supposition) there are two cases to consider: (i) $x' = x$ and (ii) $x' \in M(x)$. We establish necessity for (i); it also holds for (ii) but the proof is omitted here. Thus, if $x' = x$, then there exists an $x \in S_j \cap T_j$. $x \in S_j \rightarrow x \in g(C_j)$, $x = C_j(x, x^\circ)$. $x \in T_j \rightarrow x = C(x, x^\circ)$. Therefore, according to (2.1), either x is a replacement for x° or there is an $x' \in M(x)$ with $x' \in C(x', x) \cap C(x', x^\circ)$, i.e., x' defeats both x and x°. In either case, x° is vulnerable. It is, therefore, not a structure-induced equilibrium and necessity is established.

(2) Sufficiency. Suppose x° is not a structure-induced equilibrium. Then x° is vulnerable. Then either there exists a C_j and an $x \in g(C_j)$ satisfying (2.1) – that is, a replacement for x° – or there exists a C_j and an $x \in g(C_j)$ with an "amended version" $x' \in M(x)$ such that $x' \subset C(x, x')$ $\cap C(x', x^\circ)$. In either case, there is a C_j and an $x \in S_j$ for which $R_j(x) \cap T_j \neq \emptyset$. Sufficiency is established. \hfill Q.E.D.

It should be noted that Theorem 3.1 is, in fact, a direct consequence of Theorem 3.2, so that the latter may be regarded as a generalization of the former to any $C = \{C_j\}$. In particular, if $x^\circ_j = \text{median } X_j^*$ for all j, then $T_j = \emptyset$ and the condition of Theorem 3.2 is satisfied, independent of the committee structure or of the recommendations of any $C_j \in C$. In effect, Theorem 3.1 identifies x° as an equilibrium when it is a "partial median" in the sense of Hoyer and Mayer (1974).[7] In their Theorem 2, however, they prove that a partial median, in the absence of jurisdictional restrictions on comparisons, is an equilibrium *only if* it is a *total median* – the median in *every* direction, not just in the directions of the basis vectors. And, in order for a total median to exist, a strong symmetry of preferences – a condition formulated elegantly by Slutsky (1977b) – is required. Jurisdictional restrictions on comparisons obviate this *necessity* – if preferences exhibit symmetry *within* jurisdictions (and they always will with unidimensional jurisdictions), then x° is an equilibrium. This is precisely what Theorem 3.1 tells us.

Further consequences of Theorem 3.2 are instructive:

COROLLARY 3.2: *x° is a structured-induced equilibrium whenever $S_j = \emptyset$ for all j. In this case the $C_j \in C$ are veto groups.*

COROLLARY 3.3: *If $M(x)$ entails only germaneness and $S_j \neq \emptyset$, then x° is a structure-induced equilibrium if and only if $x^\circ = \text{median } X_j^*$.*

Corollary 3.2 indicates the real import of structural arrangements. If, for no $\lambda \neq 0$, there is an $x = x^\circ + \lambda e_j$ which a majority of C_j prefers to x° – that is, if $x^\circ_j = \underset{i \in C_j}{\text{median}} \{x_j^{*i}\}$ – then x° is invulnerable in the jth direction. The normative import of C_j "keeping the gates closed" in its agenda role for the parent organization depends, in some sense, upon

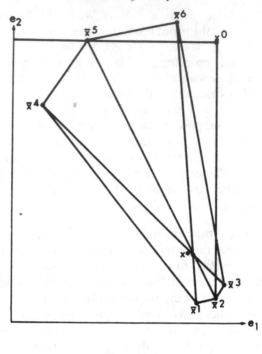

Figure 13.3

the deviation between median X_j^* and median $\{x_j^{*i}\}$. Example 3.1
$$i \in C_j$$
suggests that if there are distinct biases in the committee assignment process, this deviation can be considerable.

Example 3.1: In Figure 13.3 there are six voters with circular indifference contours and ideal points as indicated. The point x^* *is* a total (and hence a partial) median – for any vector originating at x^*, at most three voters prefer a point along that direction over x^*; x^* is a weak equilibrium in the sense of the definition in section 1 and Theorem 1.1. Suppose now that there is a committee system $C = \{C_1, C_2\}$, with $C_1 = \{1, 2, 3\}$, $C_2 = \{4, 5, 6\}$ and $f(C_1) = e_1$, $f(C_2) = e_2$. The point $x^\circ = (\bar{x}_1^2, \bar{x}_2^5)$ is a structure-induced equilibrium (so is x^*), since both committees will "keep the gates closed" – $S_1 = S_2 = \emptyset$. Also note that x° does not lie in the convex hull of the six ideal points – the Pareto set.

In the same fashion that Theorem 3.2 generalizes Theorem 3.1, Corollary 3.2 stands as a generalization of Corollary 3.1. In particular, the only way for $S_j = \emptyset$ to hold under the committee-of-the-whole committee system is when (3.1) is satisfied.

From Theorem 3.2, it is apparent that a structure-induced equilibrium

360

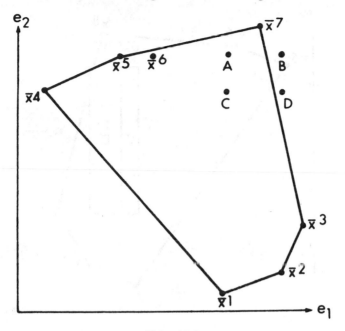

Figure 13.4

may satisfy $R_j(x) = \emptyset$ for some j and $T_j = \emptyset$ for other j. That is, $x_j^\circ =$ median X_j^* for some j and $x_k^\circ =$ median $\{x_k^{*i}\}$ for all remaining k. If
$$i \subset C_k$$
each $C_j \in C$ has a uniquely defined median in the jth direction, and N has a unique median X_j^* for each j, then there are as many as 2^m structure-induced equilibria (under the germaneness rule and simple jurisdictions).

Example 3.2: In Figure 13.4, $C_1 = \{1, 2, 3\}$ has jurisdiction e_1 and $C_2 = \{4, 5, 6, 7\}$ has jurisdiction e_2, and each $i \in N$ has circular indifference contours and ideal point as illustrated. Point C is the point at which $T_j = \emptyset$ for all j; point B has the property that $S_j = \emptyset$ for all j; points A and D mix these properties – A has $S_2 = T_1 = \emptyset$ and D has $S_1 = T_2 = \emptyset$. Note that two of the four equilibria are not Pareto optimal and that none of four are, in any sense, "centrally" located.

Finally, if either committee or parent organization median in any jurisdiction is nonunique, there will be a dense set of equilibria associated with that jurisdiction; instead of point A, B, C, D, as in Figure 13.4, there will be regions.

Example 3.3: In Figure 13.5, $N = \{1, \ldots, 8\}$, $C_1 = \{1, \ldots, 4\}$, $C_2 = \{5, \ldots, 8\}$, each $i \in N$ has circular indifference contours with ideal point as indicated, and the jurisdictions of C_1 and C_2 are e_1 and e_2, respectively. The regions A, B, C, D are the structure-induced equilibria

361

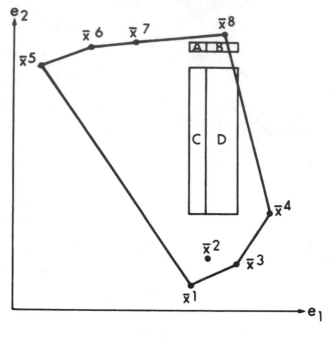

Figure 13.5

for this problem (their descriptions parallel those in Example 3.2). In contrast to the previous example, "almost all" of the structure-induced equilibria are Pareto optimal. Indeed, a substantial proportion of the Pareto surface consists of equilibria.

Corollary 3.3 strengthens Theorem 3.1 and generalizes Corollary 3.1. It strengthens Theorem 3.1 in the sense that, under a germaneness rule for amendments, unless a $C_j \in C$ is at a maximal element along e_j distinct from median X_j^* (in which case $S_j = \emptyset$), then condition (3.1) is *necessary* as well as sufficient. It generalizes Corollary 3.1 providing the condition, *viz.* $S_j \neq \emptyset$, that renders (3.1) necessary for equilibrium for arbitrary committee systems (not just the committee-of-the-whole arrangement).

Corollary 3.3, however, does strain the assumption of nonsophisticated behavior by committees. In particular, it is entirely imaginable that a highly unrepresentative committee's efforts to move the status quo along the line $x° + \lambda e_j$ to the point $x' = x° + \lambda' e_j$ will backfire in that its proposal will be amended under the germaneness rule to $x'' = x° + \lambda'' e_j$ and passed by N, where $x' \underset{C_j}{>} x° \underset{C_j}{>} x''$ ($>$ is $>_i$ for all $i \in C_j$). There are, then, occasionally strong disincentives to proceed sincerely in

362

revealing that, in fact, $S_j \neq \emptyset$. More precisely, whenever x° lies between the maximal elements[8] of C_j and N along $x^\circ + \lambda e_j$, sincere behavior by C_j is penalized. However, only under rather strong assumptions about information (knowing, for instance, the distribution of preferences of the parent body on the issue at hand) do the incentives for nonsincere behavior become unequivocal. While much is made in the Congressional literature of the wily, sophisticated, committee chairman, antenna carefully attuned to the "will" of the House, e.g., Wilbur Mills of the House Ways and Means Committee (see Manley, 1969), the representativeness of this caricature is in some doubt.

4. SIMPLE JURISDICTIONS AND GERMANENESS: EXISTENCE OF EQUILIBRIUM

The results of the previous section provide some of the characteristics of structure-induced equilibria when they exist. In this section we establish their existence. Unlike preference-induced equilibrium, their existence does *not* depend upon a knife-edge assumption about the distribution of preferences.

In order to illustrate the existence result it is useful to distinguish between $\bar{x}_j^i$ and x_j^{*i}. The former is the jth component of i's ideal point; it is independent of x°, the status quo, and always exists. The latter is the solution to the following *maximization problem*:

Find x^{*i} such that
$$u_i(x^{*i}) = \underset{j}{\text{Max}} [u_i(x^\circ_1, x^\circ_2, \ldots, x^\circ_{j-1}, x_j, x^\circ_{j+1}, \ldots, x^\circ_m) \tag{4.1}$$

That is, x_j^{*i} is the jth component of the *induced ideal point* in the jth jurisdiction when the levels for all other dimensions are maintained as in the status quo. For many of the examples of the last section, in which individuals were assumed to have circular indifference contours, $x_j^{*i} = \bar{x}_j^i$. This equality, called *separability*, holds under more general conditions, and implies that preference as between two points that differ in at most one jurisdiction is independent of the *levels* of variables in other jurisdictions. For the case of general jurisdictions, separability is defined as follows:

DEFINITION: *Let an arbitrary jurisdiction consist of $\{e_1, \ldots, e_i\}$. Furthermore, define the following points:*

$x = (x_1, \ldots, x_j, z_{j+1}, \ldots, z_m)$
$y = (y_1, \ldots, y_j, z_{j+1}, \ldots, z_m)$
$x' = (x_1, \ldots, x_j, z'_{j+1}, \ldots, z'_m)$
$y' = (y_1, \ldots, y_j, z'_{j+1}, \ldots, z'_m)$.

Kenneth A. Shepsle

A *preference representation* u_i is *separable by jurisdiction* if and only if $u_i(x) \geq u_i(y) \rightarrow u_i(x') \geq u_i(y')$.

This concept will be utilized in the corollary to the existence theorem below.

The issue of existence of a structure-induced equilibrium reduces to the following question: Does a point exist that is simultaneously invulnerable in all jurisdictions? Theorem 4.1 answers this question in the affirmative.

THEOREM 4.1 (*Existence*): *If the preferences of each $i \in N$ are representable by a strictly quasi-concave, continuous utility function, if the basis vectors of R^m constitute committee jurisdictions, and if a germaneness rule governs the amendment process, then structure-induced equilibria exist.*

We prove this theorem shortly. In order to obtain some intuition about the theorem and its proof, we first establish the following corollary:

COROLLARY 4.1: *If the preferences of each $i \in N$ are representable by a strictly quasi-concave, continuous utility function separable by jurisdiction, if the basis vectors of R^m constitute committee jurisdictions, and if a germaneness rule governs the amendment process, then a vector of medians* $\mu = (\mu_1, \mu_2, \ldots, \mu_m)$, *where* $\mu_j = \text{median } \{\bar{x}_j^1, \bar{x}_j^2, \ldots, \bar{x}_j^n\}$, *exists and is a structure-induced equilibrium.*

Proof: The median vector μ exists since, by construction, $\bar{x}^i$ exists for each $i \in N$ (a strictly quasi-concave, continuous function has a maximum on a compact set) and the median of a well-ordered finite set exists (though it need not be unique). From Theorem 3.1, $\mu^* = (\mu_1^*, \mu_2^*, \ldots, \mu_m^*)$, where $\mu_j^* = \text{median } \{x_j^{*1}, x_j^{*2}, \ldots, x_j^{*n}\}$, is a structure-induced equilibrium. But, by jurisdictional separability, $\bar{x}_j^i = x_j^{*i}$ so that $\mu = \mu^*$. Thus μ is a structure-induced equilibrium and, as demonstrated above, μ exists. Q.E.D.

In effect this corollary states that when preference "types" are restricted to those representable by a utility function separable by jurisdiction (essentially either spherical indifference contours or ellipsoids the major and minor axes of which are parallel to the basis vectors), then a structure-induced equilibrium exists. In this instance, *jurisdictional arrangements not preference distributions create equilibrium.* This stands in stark contrast to the strict requirements on preferences required for a preference-induced equilibrium. The restriction of preference "types" in corollary 4.1 inherent in the separability condition confuses the issue because the conclusion generalizes to a much broader class of preference characteristics. This is the import of Theorem 4.1 which we now prove.

364

Institutional arrangements in voting models

The strategy for proving Theorem 4.1 is first indicated. For any jurisdicton e_j the maximization problem (4.1) is solved for each $i \in N$ for all combinations of levels for other jurisdictions. This traces out the X_j^{*i} surface for each $i \in N$ and $e_j \in E$. The strict quasi-concavity and continuity of the u_i and the compactness of R^m imply that (4.1) has a unique solution. From these surfaces, the median in the jth jurisdiction $X_j^M = \text{median } \{X_j^{*1}, \ldots, X_j^{*n}\}$ may be traced. The intersection of the X_j^M surfaces $j = 1, \ldots, m$, is a structure-induced equilibrium.

Example 4.1: The procedure is illustrated for three individuals and two dimensions in Figure 13.6, parts (a) and (b). For various levels on the e_2 dimension, each i's solution to the maximization problem (4.1), based on his indifference curves in part (a), traces out his most-preferred level on the e_1 dimension. These are drawn in part (b) as X_1^{*1}, X_1^{*2}, and X_1^{*3}. Notice that Mr. 3, whose preferences are separable, prefers a fixed level on e_1, no matter what the e_2 level. By a similar procedure, for various e_1 levels, the maximization problem yields a solution in e_2, tracing out the curves X_2^{*1}, X_2^{*2}, X_2^{*3}. For various levels of e_2, median $X_1^{*i} = X_1^M$ and, for various levels of e_1, median $X_2^{*i} = X_2^M$. These are
$$\begin{array}{c} i \in N \end{array}$$
simply segments of the individual curves. The point $x^\circ \in X_1^M \cap X_2^M$ is the unique point of intersection. From the definition of the X_j^M curves, it is obvious that x° is a structure-induced equilibrium – since it lies on both median curves it is invulnerable in both jurisdictions. Notice, in part (a), the disparity between x° and μ (the vector of medians of the ideal points). When separability does not hold (only Mr. 3 has separable preferences), μ no longer has equilibrium properties.

The proof of Theorem 4.1, then, requires that we establish a nonempty intersection for the X_j^M surfaces. In Figure 13.6 there is a singleton intersection; this follows from the fact that, in that particular example, the median mappings $X_1^M : e_2 \rightarrow e_1$ and $X_2^M : e_1 \rightarrow e_2$ are single-valued. However, X_j^M need not be single-valued (even though the individual maximization surfaces, X_j^{*i}, are). X_j^M, that is, is generally a *correspondence*, as illustrated in Figure 13.7, a contingency that may occur, for example, when there are an even number of voters. In this case the equilibria are *weak* (see section 1).

The proof of Theorem 4.1 is facilitated by three lemmas.

LEMMA 4.1: X_j^{*i} *is continuous and single-valued for each $i \in N$ in each $e_j \in E$.*

Proof: X_j^{*i} is the function which graphs solutions to the maximization problem (4.1), for $i \in N$, for all combinations of levels of $e_k (k \neq j)$. Since u is *strictly* quasi-concave, X_j^{*i} is single-valued. Since u_i is continuous, so is the solution to (4.1).   Q.E.D.

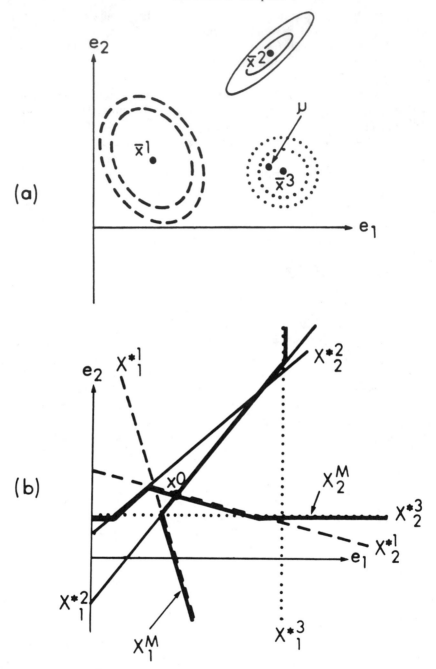

(a)

(b)

Figure 13.6

366

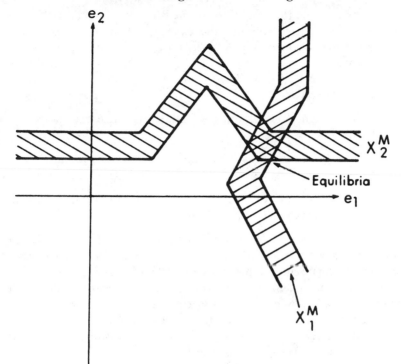

Figure 13.7

LEMMA 4.2: X_j^M is upper semicontinuous for all j. If it is single-valued, then it is continuous.

The proof is omitted, but several remarks are made. Whenever, for any combination of levels on other dimensions, there is an odd number of distinct images of the X_j^{*i}, then there will be a unique median – X_j^M will be single-valued for that combination of levels on other dimensions (see Figure 13.6). X_j^M will simply be "pieces" of continuous functions (the X_j^{*i}'s). It is clearly continuous along each piece, as well as where two pieces "join." Hence it is everywhere continuous. Even in those instances where X_j^M is a correspondence, mapping a particular combination of levels on other dimensions into a range of points along e_j, that range will be closed. Hence it is upper semicontinuous.[9]

LEMMA 4.3: $\cap_j X_j^M \neq \emptyset$.

Proof: The argument behind this proof exploits well-known fixed point theorems. In particular, if the X_j^M are continuous and single-valued and

R^m is compact, then the conditions of the Brouwer Fixed Point Theorem are met. This theorem implies the existence of a fixed point, i.e. a nonempty intersection of the X_j^M. If, on the other hand, the X_j^M are upper semicontinuous correspondences, and R^m is compact, then the conditions of the Kakutani Fixed Point Theorem are met, implying a nonempty intersection.[10]   Q.E.D.

Proof of Theorem 4.1: Lemmas 4.1–4.3 guarantee the existence of points in $\cap_j X_j^M$.

Let x be one of those points. Consider $x' = x + \lambda e_{j'}$, for any j'.
$x \in \cap_j X_j^M \to x \in X_{j'}^M$. From Lemma 3.1, the u_i are single-peaked on $x + \lambda e_{j'}$. Therefore, $x \in X_{j'}^M \to x = C(x, x')$ for all $j \to x$ is invulnerable $\to x$ is a structure-induced equilibrium.   Q.E.D.

The main point of this essay has now been established. *Jurisdictional arrangements and rules of procedure (amendment control) create equilibrium.* Theorem 4.1 provides the grounds for concluding that a social choice arrangement consisting of *any* collection of individual preferences, each representable by a continuous, strictly quasi-concave utility function, possesses an equilibrium state under majority rule. This is true for *any* committee system for which the jurisdictions are single-dimensional and a germaneness rule for amendments is in effect.

This result can be extended modestly as follows:

COROLLARY 4.2: *If X_j^M is single-valued for all j, then the X_j^M intersect in a unique point and that point is a strong equilibrium.*

The uniqueness of the intersection does *not* imply that it is a unique structure-induced equilibrium. Let $\{x\} = \cap_j X_j^M$, with $x = (x_1, \ldots, x_m)$ and, by definition of X_j^M, $x_j = \underset{i \in N}{\text{median}} \{x_j^{*i}\}$.

Let $y_i = \underset{i \in C_j}{\text{median}} \{x_j^{*i}\}$ and $y = (x_1, \ldots, x_{j-1}, y_i, x_{j+1}, \ldots, x_m)$. The point *may* be a structure-induced equilibrium. Certainly if preferences are separable by jurisdiction then y *is* a structure-induced equilibrium. The fact we exploited in establishing existence is that there is always a point from which no majority of the *parent organization* desires change (in any jurisdictionally permissible direction). From Theorem 3.2 and its corollaries, however, we know that equilibria may arise for other reasons.

A final generalization is suggested by some earlier work of Slutsky (1975, 1977a). Let $V = \{v_1, \ldots, v_k\}$ be any collection of linearly independent vectors in R^m. From linear independence, $k \leq m$. The $v_j \in V$ are permissible directions of change.

COROLLARY 4.3: *If the preferences of $i \in N$ are representable by a continuous, strictly quasi-concave utility function in the subspace of R^m spanned by the $v_j \in V$, if the v_j constitute jurisdictions, and if a germaneness rule governs amendments, then*

(i) *structure-induced equilibria exist, and*
(ii) *a point $x°$ is a structure-induced equilibrium if and only if, for all $v_j \in V$ and all $x \in S_j$, $R_j(x) \cap T_j = \emptyset$ (where R_j, S_j, and T_j, are defined as in Theorem 3.2).*

5. DISCUSSION

In this concluding section there are several loose ends to be dealt with. First, the question of sensitivity is raised. The model of social choice offered in this paper is more institutionally detailed than its predecessors. Indeed, that is the central thrust of the paper — institutional details matter. But how much? How sensitive is the existence of equilibrium and its properties to the specifics of institutional arrangements? This raises a second, related question. What are the effects of institutional "reforms"? In particular, and this is the obverse of the previous question, under what conditions are equilibria invariant under institutional "reforms"? Finally, the prospects for exploiting the general framework of section 2 to establish results for more complex or troublesome institutional arrangements are briefly explored.

Robustness of structure-induced equilibria

With single-dimensional jurisdictions and a germaneness rule governing the amendment process, any collection of voters whose preferences are represented by strictly quasi-concave, continuous utility functions, and any committee system, yields structure-induced equilibria.

1. Existence is insensitive to changes in the distribution of ideal points or to changes in other properties of the utility functions: In contrast to preference-induced equilibrium, the existence of structure-induced equilibrium does not depend on preference distributions. Changes in preference distributions or other utility properties do not endanger the existence of equilibrium, though they may change its location (see below). Even some of the properties assumed above for the proof of existence — continuity and strict quasi-concavity of the u_i — may be relaxed to some degree so long as the upper semicontinuity of each X_j^M is preserved.

2. The location of structure-induced equilibria may depend on preference distributions: As Theorem 3.2 and its corollaries suggest, the equilibrium properties of a status quo, $x°$, depend on the relationship of

its *jurisdictional projections*, x°_j, to median $\{x_j{}^{*i}\}$ and median $\{x_j{}^{*i}\}$.
$$i \in N \qquad\qquad i \in C_j$$
To the extent that changes in preference distributions alter either of these relationships, then the location of equilibrium shifts. However, distributional changes that leave these relationships intact will not affect the location of equilibrium.[11]

3. *The existence of equilibrium does not depend upon the particular committee system* $C = \{C_j\}$: The point x with $x_j = $ median $\{x_j{}^{*i}\}$
$$i \in N$$
always exists and is a structure-induced equilibrium, no matter what committee system is in effect. Particular committee systems produce *additional* equilibria, but associated with every committee system is the equilibrium point identified above.

4. *The location of equilibrium is affected by the committee system in effect*: Corollary 3.1 indicates that (3.1) is a necessary condition a point must satisfy in order to be an equilibrium under the committee-of-the-whole arrangement. It is *not* necessary under alternative committee arrangements. The set of equilibria associated with a given committee system is different from, though shares common elements with, the set of equilibria associated with some other committee system. In this sense, structural arrangements matter.

5. *Both existence and location of equilibrium depend on the rule governing the amendment process*: Consider the following straightforward result.

THEOREM 5.1: *If the conditions of Theorem 4.1 hold except that $M(x)$ = R^m – the open rule – and if $S_j \neq \varnothing$ for some j, then x° is a structure-induced equilibrium if and only if it is a preference-induced equilibrium.*

For a given committee, C_j, $S_j \neq \varnothing$ whenever $x_j^\circ \neq$ median $\{x_j{}^{*i}\}$. With
$$i \in C_j$$
our assumption of nonstrategic behavior, if this condition holds for *any* C_j, then it will propose an alternative to x°. With $M(x) = R^m$, any amendment to the proposal, even a nongermane one, is in order. Thus, whenever $S_j \neq \varnothing$ for some C_j, committees and jurisdictions no longer serve to structure social comparisons. Social intransitivities are no longer mitigated by structural or jurisdictional arrangements. Generic cycling predominates unless the severe conditions that assure a preference-induced equilibrium prevail. The only role played by the structural arrangement is associated with the conditions $S_j = \varnothing$, *viz.*, if this holds, and only if this holds for all C_j, then structure-induced and preference-induced equilibria are not equivalent.

On the other hand, for the closed rule – $M(x) = \varnothing$ – it may be shown that structure-induced equilibria always exist and, in fact, those produced by the germaneness rule are a proper subset of those produced by the closed rule. The closed rule gives much stronger veto power to committees – a point recently examined by Romer and Rosenthal (forthcoming) – and, as a consequence, produces a large (and always nonempty) equilibrium set.[12]

6. *Both existence and location of equilibrium depend on the jurisdictional arrangement*: The unidimensional nature of jurisdictions has permitted us to exploit the "good behavior" of simple majority choice functions when individual preferences are single-peaked. Now consider the following extreme, but otherwise straightforward result.

THEOREM 5.2: *If the conditions of Theorem 4.1 hold except that, for a particular $C_j \in C$, $f(C_j) = \{e_1, \ldots, e_m\}$ (that is, $g(C_j) = R^m$), then, if $S_j \neq \varnothing$ for this C_j, then $x°$ is a structure-induced equilibrium if and only if it is a preference-induced equilibrium.*

This result once again underscores the important "channeling" role played by jurisdiction (and structure). If the binary comparisons the parent organization is allowed to make are not sufficiently restricted then the prospects for equilibrium increasingly depend upon preference distribution requirements. In the extreme (Theorem 5.2), they are necessary and sufficient. One line of inquiry worth pursuing is the nature of cycling as a function of jurisdictional restrictions; this line has been pursued, in the absence of any jurisdictional considerations, by McKelvey (1976, 1977), Cohen (1977), and Schofield (1977).

This brief treatment of robustness suggests that, even when structural and jurisdictional matters are given more attention, equilibrium is still a delicate affair. The results of section 2, 3, and 4 need to be generalized, a point we turn to shortly. In another sense, however, the lack of robustness further underscores the main thesis offered here. Structural and jurisdictional arrangements offer the prospect of equilibrium; they are alterable properties of institutions (as preferences probably are not) and thus are potential instruments of equilibrium (disequilibrium) in the hands of institutional designers; and finally, even if they do not assure equilibrium, they undoubtedly affect (constrain) the form of disequilibrium.

Structure-induced equilibrium and institutional reform

Traditional social choice theory, to the extent that its main elements are limited to individual preferences, a preference aggregation mechanism, and decisive coalitions, is unlikely to have much bearing on substantive debates about institutional reform. The latter deal mostly with the structure of choices permitted an organization (as well as its decisive coalitions) (see Rohde and Shepsle, 1978). Hence a theory which elevates

371

institutional features is to be welcomed if it can contribute to these debates an understanding of how institutional practices work (and to whose advantage). While I do not claim to have provided this theory, the structure offered in section 1, or some variation, is one promising line of attack. For now let me focus on one issue involving institutional reform.

In both houses of the United States Congress, the last few years have witnessed the salience of jurisdictional realignments for standing committees. To obtain some purchase on this problem, consider the jurisdictional arrangement $J° = \{J_k\}$, with each $J_k \in J°$ a single basis vector in $E° = \{e_1, \ldots, e_m\}$. Associate, under the conditions of Theorem 4.1, a structure-induced equilibrium, $x°$. Question: What happens when each jurisdiction vector is rotated by θ degrees? Call the associated jurisdictional arrangement, basis, and equilibrium, respectively, J^θ, E^θ and x^θ. From Corollary 4.3, x^θ exists. But what is the relationship of x^θ to $x°$? We have the following result:

THEOREM 5.3: *If the conditions of Theorem 4.1 hold, and if $x°$ is a preference-induced equilibrium, then it is invariant under jurisdictional rotations.*

A preference-induced equilibrium (which is a structure-induced equilibrium – see Theorem 2.1) remains are under rotations of jurisdictional vectors; it depends in no way on jurisdictional arrangements. In general, however, $x° \neq x^\theta$. Letting $\epsilon: J \to R^m$ be the correspondence which associates the equilibrium state(s) identified in Theorem 4.1 with jurisdictional arrangement J, the following question is posed: Under what conditions does ϵ possess continuity-like properties? That is, for example, when is $\lim_{\theta \to 0} \epsilon(J^c) = \epsilon(J°)$?[13] Put in substantive terms, this sort of question seeks to distinguish the class of jurisdictional reforms that have an impact on outcomes from those that are merely cosmetic.

Concluding observations

The theoretical concepts of section 1 have been offered in order to elevate institutional properties in the debate on social choice. The overly atomistic representations of traditional social choice theory and general equilibrium theory are troublesome to political scientists who see a world of individuals whose choices are constrained by the operating characteristics of political and economic institutions.[14]

Currently I am preparing papers on alternative amendment procedures (see Shepsle, 1978), complex jurisdictions, jurisdictional change, and hierarchies of decentralization. In each case the idea is to identify equilibria if they exist or to trace the path of disequilibrium if they do not. Underlying these projects is the expectation that weakening an otherwise rarely explored[15] axiom of Arrow – the Social Completeness Axiom – in the "right" way, and in effect capturing the ways in which institutional structure, jurisdiction, and other operating characteristics channel and constrain social comparisons, social choice in institutionally-rich contexts can be understood.

NOTES

1 These definitions are adapted from McKelvey and Wendell (1976).

2 Notice also for choice processes in which simple majority coalitions are not decisive that strong (weak) winners are not equivalent.

3 A *finite covering* of a set B is a finite collection $\beta = \{\beta_j\}$, where $\cup_j \beta_j = B$. If, in addition, $\beta_i \cap \beta_j = \phi$ for all β_i, $\beta_j \in \beta$, then β is a *partition* of B. Technically, $\cup_j \beta_j \supseteq B$ is all that is required for β to cover B, but this technically is of no consequence in what follows.

4 For the moment we defer consideration of the internal procedure by which C_j arrives at x as its proposal.

5 It may be the prevailing rate or some other predetermined rate. In Oregon, Romer and Rosenthal report, if a school tax rate proposal fails, then it reverts to some low tax rate that generates only the level of revenue mandated by earlier statute.

6 Throughout, the assumption of *sincere behavior* is maintained. When called to make a choice, each $i \in N$ consults $\geqslant_i$ and chooses in a manner consistent with it. By immediate implication, if x° is not a maximal element of $g(C_j)$ for some C_j, and if the maximal set of $g(C_j)$ is nonempty, then a proposal by C_j is forthcoming.

7 Hoyer and Mayer define a *partial median* in terms of any basis for R^m. A point is a partial median if it is the median along each of the m lines defined by the basis vectors. The one-dimensional jurisdictional arrangements are such a basis. Also see Davis, Hinich and Ordeshook (1970).

8 Along any line in R^m, the majority rule choice function is transitive, owing to the single-peakedness of the $\geqslant_i$; since R^m is compact, the choice function has a maximal element.

9 *Upper semicontinuity* is defined in most topology and mathematical economics texts, e.g., Berge (1963, p. 109), and Nikaido (1968, p. 65). A correspondence $\Phi: X \rightarrow Y$ (Y compact) is said to be upper semicontinuous if $\{x^i\}$ is a sequence in X with $x^i \rightarrow x$ and $\{y^i\}$ is a sequence in Y such that $y^i \in \Phi(x^i)$ and $y^i \rightarrow y$ implies $y \in \Phi(x)$. This is equivalent to requiring the graph of $\Phi(x)$ to be closed – see Figure 13.7.

10 After constructing this argument I discovered it was nearly identical to a result proved elegantly by Kramer (1972), Theorem 1', though for different purposes. The details of the proof are found there.

11 These assertions, and those that follow, depend on the other conditions of the relevant theorems holding. In other words, this "sensitivity analysis" is conducted one condition at a time.

12 For a comparison of amendment rules, see Shepsle (1978).

13 One could pose a related question for the correspondence ϵ' that associates *all* the structure-induced equilibria of a particular jurisdictional arrangement.

14 See my comments in Shepsle (1977).
15 The one exception of which I am aware is Fishburn (1974).

REFERENCES

Arrow, Kenneth A. 1963. *Social choice and individual values.* 2nd ed. New York: Wiley.

Berge, Claude. 1963. *Topological spaces.* New York: Macmillan.

Cohen, Linda. 1977. The structure of maximum majority rule cycles. Paper presented at the Annual Meeting of the American Economic Association, New York, December 26–30, 1977.

Davis, Otto A., Melvin J. Hinich, and Peter C. Ordeshook. 1970. An expository development of a mathematical model of the electoral process. *American Political Science Review*, 64 (June 1970): 426–449.

Denzau, Arthur and Robert Parks. 1973. Equilibrium in an economy with private and spatial political dimensions. Paper presented at the Winter Meeting of the Econometrics Society, 1973.

Fishburn, Peter C. 1973. *The theory of social choice.* Princeton: Princeton University Press.
1974. Impossibility theorems without the social completeness axiom. *Econometrica*, 42 (July 1974): 695–704.

Hoyer, R. W. and Lawrence S. Mayer. 1974. Comparing strategies in a spatial model of electoral competition. *American Journal of Political Science*, 18 (August 1974): 501–523.

Kramer, Gerald H. 1972. Sophisticated voting over multidimensional choice spaces. *Journal of Mathematical Sociology*, 2 (1972): 165–180.
1973. On a class equilibrium conditions for majority rule. *Econometrica*, 2 (March 1973): 285–297.

McKelvey, Richard D. 1976. Intransitivities in multidimensional voting models and some implications for agenda control. *Journal of Economic Theory*, 12 (June 1976): 472–482.
1977. General conditions for global intransitivities in formal voting models. Paper presented at Annual Meeting of the Public Choice Society, New Orleans, March. 1977.
and Richard E. Wendell. 1976. Voting equilibria in multidimensional choice spaces. *Mathematics of Operations Research*, 1 (May 1976): 144–158.

Manley, John. 1969. Wilbur D. Mills: A study in congressional influence. *American Political Science Review*, 63 (June 1969): 442–464.

Matthews, Steven. 1977. The possibility of voting equilibria. Unpublished paper, California Institute of Technology.

Nikaido, Hukukane. 1963. *Convex structures and economic theory.* New York: Academic Press.

Pattanaik, Prasanta K. 1971. *Voting and collective choice.* Cambridge: Cambridge University Press.

Plott, Charles R. 1967. The notion of equilibrium and its possibility under majority rule. *American Economic Review*, 57 (September 1967): 787–806.

Rohde, David W. and Kenneth A. Shepsle. 1978. Thinking about legislative reform. In Leroy Rieselbach, ed., *Legislative reform.* Boston: Lexington.

Romer, Thomas and Howard Rosenthal. Political resource allocation, controlled agendas, and the status quo. *Public Choice*, (Winter 1978).

Schofield, Norman. 1977. Local acyclicity and the null dual set in dynamic games. Paper presented at Mathematical Social Science Board Conference on Game Theory and Political Science, Hyannis, Mass. July, 1977.

Sen, Amartya K. 1966. A possibility theorem on majority decisions. *Econometrica*, 34 (April 1966): 491–499.

1970. *Collective choice and social welfare.* San Francisco: Holden-Day.

Shepsle, Kenneth A. 1977. The future of public choice: A political scientist's views. Banquet address, Meetings of the Public Choice Society, New Orleans, 1977.

1978. Institutional structure and policy choice: Some comparative statics of amendment control procedures. Paper presented at Conference on Political Science and the Study of Public Policy, Hickory Corners, Michigan, May 1978 and at the Annual Meeting of the American Political Science Association, New York, September 1978.

Sloss, Judith. 1973. Stable outcomes in majority rule voting games. *Public Choice*, 15 (Summer 1973): 19–48.

Slutsky, Steven M. 1975. Majority rule and the allocation of public goods. Unpublished Ph.D. dissertation, Yale University.

1977a. A voting model for the allocation of public goods: Existence of an equilibrium. *Journal of Economic Theory*, 14 (1977). 299–325.

1977b. Equilibrium under plurality voting. Paper presented at Annual Meeting of the Public Choice Society, New Orleans, March, 1977.

Zeckhauser, Richard J. and Milton C. Weinstein. 1974. The topology of Pareto-optimal regions with public goods. *Econometrica*, 42 (July 1974): 643–666.

14

Sophisticated committees and structure-induced equilibria in Congress

KEITH KREHBIEL

Other articles in this book vividly illustrate the ways in which institutions in general constrain political behavior and shape political outcomes. With respect to Congress in particular, two distinct approaches to the study of institutions emerge. Shepsle's pioneering work on structure-induced equilibria is theoretical; Fenno's and Polsby's studies are products of close and careful observations of Congress. No doubt some readers have a predilection for one approach or the other. Regardless of which is favored, differences between the observations of the latter and the theory of the former are bothersome. Fenno's committees are all different; Shepsle's are all the same. Polsby's Congress changes over time; Shepsle's abstract institution is static. In the extreme, such differences create skepticism about the usefulness of abstractions, such as finite coverings, correspondences, and orthogonal bases, for understanding Congress.

To demand that Shepsle's theory pertain to all sessions of Congress or to all decision-making settings within any given session is, of course, unreasonable. But in light of the indisputable empirical truths that Congress does change and congressional committees do differ, a more modest challenge is appropriate: to demonstrate the empirical relevance of formal theories of institutions. Accordingly, this article explores the question of whether a theory of legislatures, á la Shepsle, can usefully and intelligibly accommodate the diversity in real-world legislatures while retaining its ability to predict political outcomes. I argue that Shepsle's theory is useful for understanding Congress in spite of its limitations and simplifications. Some of these are defended and others are modified. Ultimately, I show how an extension of the theory, though abstract, nevertheless says something concrete about how the institutionalization of Congress stabilizes congressional outcomes.

I am indebted to Richard Fenno and Kenneth Shepsle for constructive comments.

Structure-induced equilibria

The essay begins with a relatively nontechnical review of Shepsle's theory and its main result and proceeds to extensions of the theory to situations in which committees are more attentive and responsive to the preferences of noncommittee members. Theoretical results are presented for *simple institutional arrangements* (SIAs) with sophisticated committees.[1] Finally, Fenno's House committees and Polsby's comments on institutionalization are reconsidered in light of the revised theory.

INGREDIENTS

An implicit assumption in Shepsle's theory is that political outcomes, such as congressional decisions, result from three types of ingredients: the *preferences* of decision makers for various policies; the *institutional features* that specify when, how, and by whom decisions are made; and the *strategies* decision makers employ within the confines of institutional features in their attempts to obtain preferred outcomes. Shepsle's main theoretical result is that the imposition of institutional features – most notably the committee system and jurisdictional system – says a lot about which policies are selected. Specifically, these institutional ("structural") features create ("induce") a predictable and stable outcome ("equilibrium") in a large class of situations in which their absence would guarantee virtually complete unpredictability and instability of outcomes. Since the theory places few constraints on the configurations of decision makers' preferences, institutional features are properly credited for inducing equilibria. Thus, to the degree that the assumptions of the theory are defensible, the importance of institutional features cannot be doubted.

Of course, neither Fenno nor Polsby doubts the importance of institutional features. Polsby, for example, writes that "[i]t is hard – indeed for the contemporary observer, impossible – to shake the conviction that the House's institutional structure does matter greatly in the production of political outcomes" (Chapter 4). This is not to say, however, that observers of Congress are at ease with Shepsle's theoretical characterization of preferences, institutions, and strategies. Thus the question: How closely does Shepsle's institutional arrangement resemble the U.S. Congress? To answer the question we shall consider the theory in light of Congress itself. Unlike Shepsle, who demands a high level of generality from his theoretical results, I introduce the ingredients of the theory at a relatively specific, concrete, and nontechnical level. The assumptions to be examined, respectively, are about preferences, institutional features, and strategies. Only in the latter case are significant deviations from Shepsle made.

377

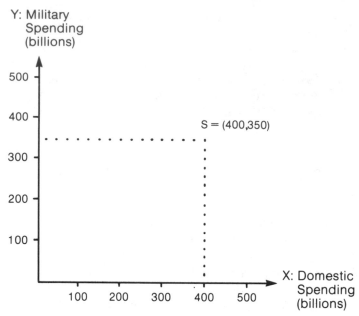

Figure 14.1. A two-dimensional policy space

Preferences

The initial assumption is that a legislature consists of a set of members who make decisions about different policies. Specific policies are represented as points in a geometric (Euclidean) space; issues are represented as different dimensions in the space. Figure 14.1 is a simple two-dimensional example in which the only policies on which the legislature makes decisions are domestic spending and military spending. Domestic spending is represented by the horizontal (X) axis; military spending is represented by the vertical (Y) axis. Any point on an axis represents a policy, that is, a decision to spend the amount specified by the numerical value of the point. Selection of an overall spending policy consists of selecting a point in this two-dimensional space. The point S, for example, represents domestic expenditures of $400 billion and military expenditures of $350 billion.

Different members typically want different policies. Similarly, any individual member prefers some policies to others. Assume that there is a minimal degree of consistency in each individual's preferences that can be represented on each separate dimension as a *single-peaked preference curve.* Consider the preferences of a single legislator on domestic spending. Suppose that the level of domestic spending he prefers most is

378

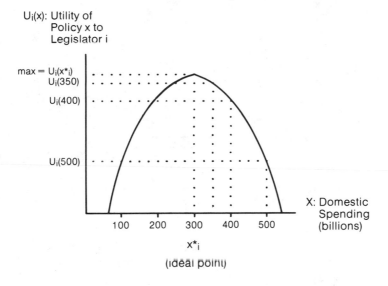

Figure 14.2. A single-peaked preference curve. With the increasing distance
between a policy and the ideal point, lx* −xl, the utility of *i* for the policy,
$U_i(x)$, necessarily declines.

$300 billion. In Figure 14.2, domestic spending is again represented by
the horizontal axis, but now the vertical axis reflects the degree to which
the member likes (or derives utility from) various policies on the
horizontal axis. The graph of the legislator's preference curve for
domestic spending is straightforward. Notice that the curve reaches its
sole maximum directly above the $300 billion point on the policy axis.
Thus, the point x_i^* at $300 billion on the horizontal axis is the *ideal point*
of legislator *i*. Because *i*'s utility for other policies always decreases
as points get farther from x_i^* – for example, $U_i(x_i^*) > U_i(350) >
U_i(400) > \ldots > U_i(500)$ – the preference curve has a *single* peak.

Single-peakedness makes sense in most political situations in which
quantity is involved. Although receiving somewhat more (or less) of
something than one ideally wants is somewhat undesirable, it is
nevertheless preferable to getting *much* more (or much less) than the
ideal amount. The relationship between preference (as represented by
utility on the vertical axis) and policy distance (as represented by the
absolute values of the differences of two given policies on the horizontal
axis) thus becomes clear. For any two policies *A* and *B* with numerical
values on a dimension *X*, and for a legislator *i* with an ideal point x_i^* and
a single-peaked symmetric preference curve, we deduce that *i* prefers *A* to
B if and only if the distance from *A* to x_i^* is less than the distance from *B*

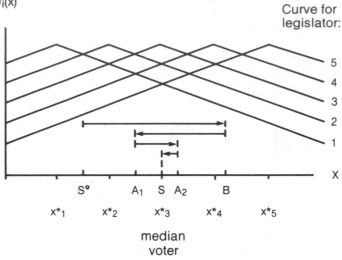

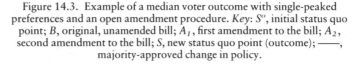

Figure 14.3. Example of a median voter outcome with single-peaked preferences and an open amendment procedure. *Key: S°*, initial status quo point; *B*, original, unamended bill; *A₁*, first amendment to the bill; *A₂*, second amendment to the bill; *S*, new status quo point (outcome); ——, majority-approved change in policy.

to x_i^*. Using "$\succ_i$" to mean "is preferred by i to," we formally state:

$$A \succ_i B \text{ if and only if } |A - x_i^*| < |B - x_i^*|.$$

Consistency of preferences can be defined and represented formally in a number of ways besides single-peakedness (e.g., convex indifference contours), but this relatively simple notion of decreasing utility with increasing distance from the ideal point is sufficient for exposing and extending Shepsle's model. The theoretical significance of the assumption of single-peakedness is illustrated in Figure 14.3. Five members have single-peaked preferences with peaks at their respective ideal points, $x_i^* \ldots x_5^*$. $S°$ represents existing policy (status quo point), and B represents a proposal (bill) to change $S°$. Suppose that whenever a member has a chance to vote for one of two alternatives, he votes for the alternative he prefers: that is, the one that when projected upward reaches a higher point on his preference curve. Then, under common amendment procedures, something predictable happens. In a vote that pairs $S°$ against B, B obtains the votes of members 3, 4, and 5 and wins. The arrow from $S°$ to B reflects this change in policy. Suppose, however, that B can be amended. Members 1 and 2 see that A_1 is preferable not only for themselves but also for member 3, so they propose it as an amendment to B, whereupon members 1, 2, and 3 vote to accept it. Next, members 4 and 5 might counterpropose A_2, which with member 3's vote defeats A_1. This process might continue, but by now the dynamic, if not the outcome, is clear. Eventually member 3's ideal point will be offered and selected as an amendment, after which *no* point will defeat it. The result is that the old status quo point, $S°$, moves to the outcome, which by definition becomes the new status quo point, S.

The general statement of this phenomenon is Black's (1958) median voter theorem, so called because it says that with members arrayed on a policy dimension in such a way that their preferences are single-peaked, and with an open amendment process such as the one just described, the outcome is always the ideal point of the *median voter* – the voter for whom half of the other voters' ideal points are on each side of his. Surprisingly, this rather simple result is instrumental for many of the more complicated, institutionally rich results in Shepsle's article.

Institutional features

The nature of legislators' preferences over alternatives in a policy space is one of the most basic ingredients of political decision making and, not coincidentally, the one on which most formal political theory focused prior to Shepsle. However, there is more structure to congressional decision making than preferences alone can reflect. Fenno's and Polsby's research provides details of several "structurers." The committee system divides labor by assigning different members to different committees. The jurisdictional system insures that different committees work on different problems and decide on different policies. Thus, actual decision making in Congress is at least a two-stage process: Committee members (a subset of the full membership) decide first; the full membership then accepts, rejects, or – depending upon the rules – amends the decision of a committee. Among other things, the rules determine the circumstances under which members may or may not offer amendments to committees' legislation. Shepsle shows that institutional features, too, can be expressed formally. The following examples bring the discussion closer to Congress.

A committee is a subset of legislators; the *committee system* is the mechanism that divides the full membership into subgroups. For example, the committee system assigns William Gray, Jim Wright, Jack Kemp,...to the Budget Committee; Jamie Whitten, Silvio Conte, David Obey,...to the Appropriations Committee; John Dingell, James Broyhill Henry Waxman,...to the Committee on Energy and Commerce, and so on.

The *jurisdictional system* is structurally similar to the committee system but assigns policy dimensions, instead of legislators, to committees. Tax policy is assigned to the Ways and Means committee, thereby granting Ways and Means the exclusive privilege of making initial proposals (bills) on tax policy. Similarly, education policy and labor policy are matters taken up by the Education and Labor Committee; defense policy is the jurisdiction of the Armed Services Committee; and so on.

This characterization of committee and jurisdictional systems is remarkably flexible. Legislators are not prohibited from serving on more than one committee; indeed, almost all congressmen serve on two or more committees. Similarly, a dimension of the policy space may be assigned to more than one committee. For example, the Science and Technology Committee in the House has jurisdiction over some matters of education – such as authorizations for the National Science Foundation, which funds several science education programs – even though the Education and Labor Committee claims the same jurisdiction (with mixed success).

Complicated jurisdictional arrangements confound not only the efforts of members of Congress to pass legislation but also the attempts of political scientists to predict congressional outcomes. Therefore, it is understandable that while present theoretical tools permit definition of complex combinations of committee and jurisdictional systems, present theoretical results rest on assumptions of simpler institutional arrangements. One such assumption is that a special, restricted combination of committee and jurisdictional systems is in effect. This is defined as a *simple institutional arrangement* (SIA).

To understand precisely what an SIA is, recall that the policy space is n-dimensional. Although Figure 14.1 shows only two broadly defined dimensions, the congressional policy space is often better represented as several narrower ones. For example, total domestic spending is an amalgam of spending decisions by several committees. The Judiciary Committee makes initial decisions on authorizations for the Justice Department; the Energy and Commerce Committee makes initial decisions on toxic waste cleanup, and so on. The assumption of SIAs pertains to the relationship between, and the numbers of, committees and jurisdictions. Specifically, an institutional arrangement is considered simple if each committee has one and only one unique unidimensional jurisdiction: committees do not share jurisdictions, and no committee's jurisdiction contains more than one policy dimension. This implies a one-to-one-to-one relationship between committees, jurisdictions, and policy dimensions. Simple institutional arrangements, therefore, are very simple – so simple, in fact, that one may argue that they bear little resemblance to Congress. Congress, unlike SIAs, has some multidimensional and overlapping jurisdictions, and some recent reforms have made

382

them more common. Nevertheless, there are several reasons for focusing on SIAs.

First, all models are simplifications. If a model abstracts essential features from a real-world situation, then simplicity is no detriment.[2] To specify the essential features entails judgment, of course, but few congressional scholars would omit the committee and jurisdictional systems from their list of essential features. Therefore, we seem to be off to a good start.

Second, closer consideration of behavioral as well as structural features of Congress suggests that the assumption of unidimensional and nonoverlapping jurisdictions may not be so unrealistic after all. Even though jurisdictions of specific committees may not be unidimensional in the sense that the Education and Labor Committee, for example, writes legislation on both education and labor policy, there is a tendency for committees to address one policy at a time. The existence of multidimensional jurisdictions, then, does not imply that committees with such jurisdictions produce multidimensional legislation.

Third, even if policies within broad areas such as education, labor, energy, and transportation are technically multidimensional, legislators often evaluate policies as if they were unidimensional. For example, during the second session of the 98th Congress, the maritime authorization bill (HR 5723) contained specific provisions for construction subsidies, loan guarantees, and development funds (all for American shipbuilders), as well as restrictions on foreign flag vessels. Theoretically, each provision might be considered a separate dimension: the amount of construction subsidies, the degree to which loans are guaranteed, and so on. In practice, however, most members probably evaluated the legislation more parsimoniously; their main interest was in how much the provisions as a whole helped American shipbuilders. Therefore, the situation approximates a unidimensional one, even though a strict interpretation casts it in a multidimensional framework.[3]

Finally, legislators may also address relatively complex and possibly multidimensional legislation by ignoring all but one major dimension. Legislation is often noncontroversial on all but a single provision, in which case the array of preferences on the single controversial dimension is all that matters in practice. An example is the House Judiciary Committee's treatment of the Senate's authorization bill for the Justice Department (S. 951). The bill contained many provisions, but only one aroused much attention: a provision that would have ended court-ordered busing for the purpose of achieving racial balance in schools. Thus, as with the shipbuilding example, the way in which legislators are likely to perceive bills often makes a putatively multidimensional decision unidimensional in practice. In sum, although neither Shepsle nor

383

I would argue that *all* congressional committee and jurisdictional arrangements fall into the class of SIAs, a sufficient number do so that we may cautiously proceed with the assumption.

Strategies

Thus far we have seen how the committee and jurisdictional systems determine the assignment of members and policies to committees, thereby imposing some order on congressional decision making. Little has been said, however, about how members may (and may not) behave in these minimally structured settings. Which institutional features analogously structure strategies on the floor as committee and jurisdictional systems structure committee members' initial choices about policy? One answer is the rules. In two-stage decision making, rules shape strategies by defining the set of alternative proposals that members in the second (floor) stage may offer to the bill reported by committee in the first stage. Shepsle discusses several kinds of "amendment control rules," three of which are most prevalent in Congress: open, germaneness, and closed. The meaning of each becomes clear in the context of the policy space.

The open rule is the least constraining rule. In a multidimensional policy space, it permits any amendment. Thus, when it is in effect, as is normal in the Senate, amendments may be offered by any member on the floor who is recognized by the chair. Moreover, the amendment need not pertain to the legislation under consideration. An amendent to a jobs bill, for example, might call for the repeal of withholding of taxes on interest and dividends.[4]

The germaneness rule also permits amendments, but it requires that they pertain closely to the issue under consideration. In SIAs, the germaneness rule allows any amendment that leaves policy unchanged on all dimensions other than those under consideration in the current bill. If, for example, the House is operating under the germaneness rule (as it normally does) and is debating a bill for appropriations for military assistance to El Salvador, members are permitted to propose amendments changing the level of assistance to El Salvador. A proposed amendment to reduce subsidies to tobacco farmers in North Carolina, however, would be nongermane and in violation of the rule. The germaneness rule, then, provides some opportunities for noncommittee members to shape legislation but constrains their efforts to the issue at hand.

No such opportunities are available under the closed rule, which dictates that members on the floor simply accept or reject the committee bill. Strategic opportunities for noncommittee members, therefore, are minimal. In contrast, strategic opportunities for the committee that reports the bill are sometimes substantial:

The continuum that emerges from the discussion of rules is the degree of restrictiveness or openness of the rule. As rules change from closed to germaneness to open, more amendments are permitted, and the requirement that the policy content of the amendments pertain closely to the legislation is relaxed. Although the rules represent only three points on the continuum, (and only two are considered below), the continuum reflects other, relatively complicated congressional rules. Scholars who observe congressional rules firsthand and write about them more concretely classify the rules in a manner consistent with the continuum. For example, in a series of studies of "complex rules" in the House, Bach (1981*a*, 1981*b*) discusses rules as being either "expansive" or "restrictive." The degree of expansiveness or restrictiveness is consistent with movement toward the open or closed end of the continuum.

STRUCTURE-INDUCED EQUILIBRIA

The previous section reintroduced the principal ingredients in Shepsle's theory. This section reconsiders its main result: the existence of structure-induced equilibria. The discussion and demonstrations are designed to answer several questions. First, exactly how do the institutional features, such as committee system, jurisdictional system, and rules, channel outcomes to specific points or regions in the policy space? Second, what does it mean for an outcome to be an equilibrium? Finally, how credible is the result in light of what Fenno, Polsby, and others write about Congress?

Outcomes under the germaneness rule

In Figure 14.4, x's represent ideal points of committee members and o's represent ideal points of legislators who participate in decision making only on the floor.[5] CM represents the ideal point of the committee median voter, FM is the ideal point of the floor median voter, S^o is the status quo point at the initial time period, and B is the bill reported to the floor by the committee.

According to Shepsle's assumptions, decision making proceeds as follows. First, the committee convenes and decides to report its median proposal to the floor; thus, the bill is located at CM. This is a straightforward application of Black's theorem within committee. Once it is sent to the floor, the bill is subject to amendment under the germaneness rule, so floor members may propose any amendment that changes policy on only this dimension. Again, Black's theorem generates the prediction: the

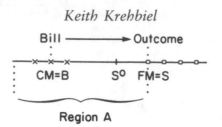

Figure 14.4. Two-stage decision making under the germaneness rule and Shepsle's assumption of sincere behavior. *Key*: *x*, ideal point of a committee member; *o*, ideal point of a noncommittee member; *CM*, ideal point of the committee median voter; *FM*, ideal point of the floor median voter; *B*, original, unamended bill; S^o, initial status quo point; *S*, new status quo point (outcome); ——, change(s) in policy from amendments.

amendment process continues until a majority votes in favor of the floor median proposal (*FM*), after which no proposal defeats it. The outcome, therefore, is *FM*, which in turn becomes *S*, the new status quo point.

The occurrence of such an outcome under the germaneness rule is straightforward. That the outcome is an equilibrium is somewhat more complicated. We therefore examine in some detail what it means for an outcome to be in equilibrium. This entails consulting, backtracking, and sometimes negating Shepsle's key definitions. The aim is to devise a generally applicable test for situations, such as figure 14.4, in which we wish to determine whether an outcome, *S*, after some prior session of decision making is a structure-induced equilibrium. Shepsle states that

DEFINITION 1. "The status quo...is a *structure-induced equilibrium* [SIE] if and noly if it is invulnerable" (Chapter 13).

Working backward and paraphrasing, we obtain

DEFINITION 2. The status quo is *vulnerable* (and hence not an SIE) if either condition *R* or *RA*, defined as follows, is satisfied:
R: there exists a *replacement*, that is, a point that
    (1) is in the jurisdiction of the committee,
    (2) the committee chooses over the status quo,
    (3) the House chooses over all valid amendments and over the status quo.
RA: there exists a *replacement by amendment*, that is, a point that
    (1) is in the jurisdiction of the committee,
    (2) the committee chooses over the status quo,
    (4) has a valid amendment that the House chooses over the point and over the status quo.

Conversely,

DEFINITION 3. The status quo is *invulnerable* (and hence an SIE) if neither R *nor* RA is satisfied, that is, if
$\sim R$: there is *no replacement*, that is, no point such that (1), (2), and (3) above are each satisfied,
and
$\sim RA$: there is *no replacement by amendment*, that is, no point such that (1) and (2) and (4) above are each satisfied.[6]

Notice how the formalization simplifies matters. Because conditions (1) and (2) are identical under replacement (R), replacement by amendment (RA), no replacement ($\sim R$), and no replacement by amendment ($\sim RA$), the same labels are used. But notice also the differences between replacement and replacement by amendment (and their negations) due to conditions (3) and (4). A replacement is a point that defeats all competitors; a replacement by amendment is a point chosen by a committee for which there is an amendable version that defeats both the original point (the bill) and the status quo.[7]

With reference to these definitions, existence and nonexistence of SIE in various settings are easily demonstrated. Shepsle rigorously proves the existence of SIE in settings such as Figure 14.4, so we cannot doubt existence in these situations. Nevertheless it is a useful exercise to focus on the definition of invulnerability to see *why* S cannot be replaced – either directly or by amendment.

Clearly, there are points in the jurisdiction of the committee, and there are points that a majority on the committee prefers and would choose over the status quo. *Any* point to the left of S (region A) is preferable to the committee because CM, and therefore a committee majority, is to the left of S. Since conditions (1) and (2) are satisfied, both (3) and (4) must be contradicted to demonstrate invulnerability of S. Conditions (3) and (4) both require that the floor choose the replacement (or an amended version thereof) over the status quo. But recall that the new status quo lies precisely at the floor median position. Black's theorem tells us that *no* point can defeat the median voter's ideal point. So $S = FM$ can be replaced neither by a committee's bill nor by some amendment to the committee's bill. This indeed contradicts conditions (3) and (4) and demonstrates that there is no replacement, and no replacement by amendment, for S. Therefore, S is invulnerable and, according to definition 1, an SIE.[8]

The implication of this finding for the larger legislature is that attempts to change S always fail if the specified institutional arrangement is in effect, if the configuration of preferences does not change, and if members continue to exercise the strategies assumed by the theory. The key is that the combination of committee and jurisdictional systems structures the legislature in such a way that the same process of decision making goes on independently in several committees and jurisdictions. Therefore, not only is the S on this dimension invulnerable; *all* S's in jurisdictions governed by the germaneness rule are in equilibrium. But importantly, the equilibrium is induced by a special combination of structural features: the committee system, the jurisdictional system, and th germaneness rule.

Outcomes under the closed rule

Careful readers will have noticed some potentially important qualifications in the previous argument. One is the restricted focus on the germaneness rule. Indeed, Shepsle's main theorems about SIE pertain only to situations in which the germaneness rule is in effect. Are structure-induced equilibria guaranteed to exist in closed rule settings also? Figure 14.5 and the restatement of Shepsle's definitions provide the answer. The configuration of preferences is identical to that in figure 14.4, but the initial status quo point, S^o, is different. As before, the assumptions dictate that the bill is at the committee median position. But now members cannot amend it. In an up-or-down vote on the bill, everyone to the right of FM as well as the floor median voter himself votes nay and the bill is defeated. The outcome and new status quo point are therefore the same as the initial status quo point. On the grounds that $S = S^o$, may we infer that this presumably stable point is an SIE? Not until the test is applied.

Returning to definition 2 (vulnerability), we first search for a replacement. If it is found, then S is vulnerable and cannot be an SIE. Here too there are points in the jurisdiction of the committee that the committee would choose over the status quo. Any point on the line except for S itself is a valid committee proposal, so condition (1) is satisfied.[9] Condition (2) is satisfied also; all points in region A would be chosen by the committee over S because each such point receives a majority of the committee's votes. Next, condition (3) requires that some point that satisfies (1) and (2) defeats all possible amendments and the status quo point. Since there can be no amendments under the closed rule, the first part of (3) is trivially satisfied. Furthermore, with respect to the second part of (3), several points defeat the status quo. One obvious candidate whose attractiveness was demonstrated in the discussion of the germaneness rule is FM, which indeed would defeat S on the floor. Therefore, we have found a replacement and shown S to be vulnerable and thus not an SIE.[10]

The seemingly limited applicability of structure-induced equilibria to germaneness situations suggests at least one of two things, both of which

Structure-induced equilibria

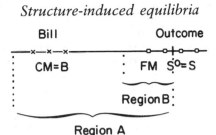

Figure 14.5. Two-state decision-making under the germaneness rule and Shepsle's assumption of sincere behavior. *Key*: *x*, ideal point of a committee member; *o*, ideal point of a noncommittee member; *CM*, ideal point of the committee median voter; *FM*, ideal point of the floor median voter; *B*, original, unamended bill; *S°*, initial status quo bill; *S*, new status quo point (outcome); ———, change(s) in policy from amendments.

turn out to be closely related to institutionalization and the stability of congressional outcomes. First, perhaps closed rule situations are fundamentally less predictable and stable than germaneness rule situations. The existence of SIE in the latter but not in the former supports this conjecture. Alternatively (but not necessarily contrastingly), perhaps the assumptions of the theory about legislators' strategies are not plausible in light of what Fenno and others write about congressmen. We address assumptions about strategy next, after which we are better equipped to reconsider institutionalization and stability of outcomes.

SOPHISTICATION IN COMMITTEES

A perplexing feature of the situations in Figures 14.4 and 14.5 is the myopic behavior of the committees. Why would experienced and knowledgeable committees act as these committees acted? In Figure 14.4, the committee reported a bill consistent with its members' preferences but substantially different from what members on the floor wanted. Thereafter, the bill was amended substantially, much to the chagrin of the committee. With a similar lack of foresight, the committee in Figure 14.5 reported a bill destined to fail, when, at minimum, it could have reported a bill equal to *FM* and obtained an outcome preferable to all committee members – indeed, preferable to a majority of members of the legislature, too. The issue, then, is whether decision makers in the first (committee) stage of a two-stage decision-making process take into account probable second-stage actions. Fiorina and Plott (1978, p. 593) concisely outline the problem:

[N]aturally occurring political committees do not exist in splendid isolation. Instead, they are frequently embedded in some larger ongoing institutional context. This embedding raises the following potentially critical question: if the

389

committee decision is regarded by the members as only one stage in a sequence of games, might behavior in the committee reflect strategic considerations from the larger game? If so, a model which explains the behavior in the larger game might produce implications for the committee stage which differ substantially from those implied by models successful in explaining the process of isolated committees.

Maintaining our congressional focus, we now address several related questions: What are some alternative strategies exercised in committees? What are the necessary conditions for the exercise of foresight in uniquely beneficial ways? Finally, when and why do different strategies result in different outcomes? Though the questions are phrased somewhat abstractly, the underlying motivation could hardly be more concrete and is nicely summarized in excerpts from Manley's classic study (1969, p. 448) of Wilbur Mills and the Ways and Means Committee:

"As I see it," Mills has said, "our job is to work over a bill until our technical staff tells us it is ready and until I have reason to believe that it is going to get enough support to pass. Many of our bills must be brought out under a closed rule, and to get and keep a closed rule you must have a widely acceptable bill. It's as simple as that.... It's a waste of time to bring out a bill if you can't pass it."

And to insure passage in the House, Mills was acutely attuned to House members' preferences. To quote one of his colleagues: "He counts the heads in the Committee and he counts the heads in the House; he's always counting" (p. 446).

The revised theory incorporates the two key elements of strategy to which Manley alludes: a willingness of committee members to win, and their corresponding attentiveness to preferences of legislators outside of the committee. It does so, however, by building onto, rather than reconstructing, Shepsle's theory.

Traditionally, theorists of voting discuss two strategies: sincere voting (sometimes called "naive" or "myopic") and sophisticated voting (sometimes called "strategic"). A voter who employs a sincere strategy when faced with two alternatives always votes for the alternative he prefers, even though its winning at the immediate stage of voting may in effect ensure its replacement by some inferior proposal at some subsequent stage. In contrast, the sophisticated voter votes for the alternative that he thinks will ultimately lead to the selection of a preferable alternative. Sophisticated strategies therefore often prescribe ostensible misrepresentation of one's preference at some stages of voting.

Using the same rationale as that used in the conventional definitions of sophisticated voting, we shall define a new form of sophistication that is uniquely suited to simple institutional arrangements in which either the germaneness or the closed rule is in effect. Just as sophisticated voting in the conventional sense requires that voters are aware of how the outcome of immediate votes affects the choices available in subsequent stages, sophistication of committees requires foresight on the part of committee members. In particular, we assume that members of a sophisticated committee ask: If we select a bill for referral to the floor, can it win, or how will it be amended? If the members judge that the bill cannot win or that it will be amended in an unsatisfactory manner (relative to other feasible alternatives, including the status quo), then the sophisticated committee may adopt another course of action or, possibly, inaction.

The development of precise definitions of sophisticated committee behavior takes place in two stages. First, examples are studied and general definitions of situations that are *ripe for sophisticated behavior* are stated for germaneness and closed rules. Second, a single, complete definition of committee sophistication is stated in terms of the two definitions of ripeness.[11]

Committee sophistication under the germaneness rule consists of knowing when to obstruct, that is, to choose not to report a bill to the floor because of the expectation that it would be amended unacceptably. Reconsider the decision-making situations in Figure 14.4. Under Shepsle's assumptions, the committee myopically reports its median motion, after which the amendment process on the floor causes the bill to converge to the floor median. With a modicum of foresight, however, the committee would choose not to report a bill at all. As a result, $S°$ would remain in effect and a committee majority would be more satisfied with the outcome. (Note that the example is not as contrived as it may appear. For example, even if the rightmost committee and floor members were interchanged, a majority on the committee would still prefer the status quo outcome under obstruction to the floor median outcome under referral.)

If committee sophistication under the germaneness rule consists of knowing when to obstruct, then a precise specification of the conditions under which obstruction is favorable for a majority on the committee is a necessary step toward defining committee sophistication. The key points are FM, CM, and $S°$. The key decision maker is the committee median voter, who considers the relative distances between his ideal point and FM and $S°$ – distances that determine his preference between alternatives. In general, if the committee median voter prefers the initial status quo ($S°$) to the floor median voter's ideal point (FM), the situation is ripe for obstruction. Only then does a majority of committee members prefer $S°$ to FM. Stated formally in terms of distance:

DEFINITION 4. A situation under the germaneness rule is *ripe for obstruction* if and only if $|CM - S°| < |CM - FM|$.

391

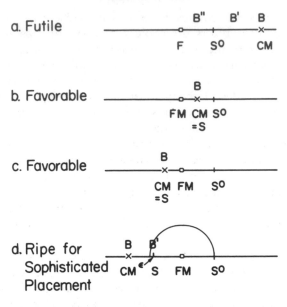

Figure 14.6. Possible situations under the closed rule.
$B' = FM - |FM - S°| + \epsilon$ is the sophisticatedly placed bill.

Incorporation of foresight into the committee decision-making calculus is beneficial in some closed rule situations, too. But sophistication under the closed rule involves not the binary choice of whether or not to obstruct but, instead, the choice of where to place the bill. Although this form of sophistication is relatively complicated, the examples in Figure 14.6 lead to a general definition of situations that are ripe for sophisticated placement. Again, the relative locations of *CM*, *FM*, and *S°* determine the strategic possibilities. The exploratory procedure is to fix *FM* and *S°* and to move *CM* from right to left, continually considering the strategic situation of the committee.

Whenever the status quo is in the middle position of the three key points, as in 14.6*a*, the committee position is hopeless and its actions, unless perverse, are inconsequential. For example, *B* = *CM* loses on the floor because a majority of voters necessarily are on or to the left of *FM*, which in turn is to the left of *S°*, the sole alternative to *B*. Such is the case even if the committee moderates its proposal, as with *B'*. In fact, the committee's bill wins only if placed to the left of *S°*, such as *B''*. But the victory is hollow, since at least half of the committee members prefer no bill (*S°*) to *B''*. Clearly, this situation is futile for the committee.

In 14.6*b*, however, *CM* is between *FM* and *S°*, and the inability of floor members to amend the committee's bill is an obvious advantage for the committee. Since the floor median voter is· on the far side of the bill (relative to $S°$), a winning coalition for the bill over the status quo is guaranteed and the committee obtains its median outcome. The situation is similar in Figure 14.6c in which FM is in the middle. But because the floor median voter still prefers CM to $S°$, the committee is again in a favorable position. Indeed, the committee's situation is so favorable that it need not exercise foresight in order to produce a winning bill; even Shepsle's sincere committees would obtain committee median outcomes.

Finally, in Figure 14.6d the committee members can benefit from the judicious exercise of foresight and a willingness to jettison its median bill in favor of one that is strategically placed. A necessary condition is for FM to occupy the middle position. Given that, the sufficient condition is determined by the relative distances $|CM - FM|$ and $|FM - S°|$. If the former is greater than the latter, as in 14.6d, then the committee can exploit the situation. We know that the committee loses if it reports its sincere bill, $B = CM$, since such a proposal is farther from the floor median voter's ideal point than is the status quo. Sophisticated committee members, however, have the foresight to obviate such an outcome by moderating their bill so that the floor median voter barely prefers the strategically placed bill, B', to the status quo. Spatially, the bill should be slightly closer to FM than FM is to $S°$. Arithmetically, the bill is $B' = FM - |FM - S°| + \varepsilon$, where ε is a distance minimally detectable to the floor median voter. If B' were referred to the floor, it would secure the votes of a majority of voters, and the majority coalition in the committee would be more satisfied with this outcome than with $S°$.

The discussion of Figure 14.6 is condensed and generalized in three definitions, the last of which is the basis for the subsequent definition of committee sophistication.

DEFINITION 5. A committee's situation is *futile* under the closed rule if
(a) $CM > S° \geqslant FM$, or
(b) $CM < S° \leqslant FM$.
($S°$ is in the middle.)

DEFINITION 6. A committee's situation is *favorable* under the closed rule if
(a) $FM \leqslant CM \leqslant S°$ or $FM \geqslant CM \geqslant S°$, or
(b) $CM \leqslant FM < S°$ and $|CM - FM| < |FM - S°|$, or
(c) $CM \geqslant FM > S°$ and $|CM -FM| < |FM - S°|$.
(CM) is in the middle, or FM is in the middle and nearer to CM than to $S°$.)

DEFINITION 7. A situation is *ripe for sophisticated placement* under the closed rule if

393

(*a*) $CM < FM < S°$ or $CM > FM > S°$, and

(*b*) $|CM - FM| \geq |FM - S°|$.

(*FM* is in the middle and is at least as far from *CM* as from *S°*.)

Now, with reference to the definitions of ripeness under each rule, we define committee sophistication.

DEFINITION 8. A *committee is sophisticated* if it exploits ripe situations as follows:

(*a*) If the situation is ripe for obstruction (definition 4), it reports no bill.

(*b*) If the situation is ripe for sophisticated placement (definition 7), it reports:

(i) $B = FM - |FM - S°| + \varepsilon$, if $FM > CM$, and

(ii) $B = FM + |FM - S°| - \varepsilon$, if $FM < CM$.[12]

A crucial concluding point is that although the term "committee sophistication" may seem anthropomorphic, *individuals'* preferences nevertheless remain the primary determinants of committee decisions. For example, if under the germaneness rule, a committee obstructs, it does not do so because the committee as a single entity prefers obstruction; a committee, strictly speaking, cannot have *a* preference. Rather, it obstructs because a majority of its *members* each prefers the outcome under obstruction (*S°*) to the expected outcome (*FM*) if they were to report a bill. Similarly, under the closed rule, a committee that places its bill sophisticatedly does so not because such a choice is dictated by some amorphous committee preference; it does so because a majority of individuals (quite possibly with diverse preferences) each benefits from such placement.

NEW SIAs WITH NEW SIE

Now that we have fully exposed the ingredients of preferences, institutional features, and strategies, it is possible to explore the diversity and the relevance of the extended theory. Figure 14.7 highlights the extension from Shepsle's two institutional arrangements with sincere behavior, which differ only according to the rule governing the amendment process, to my four simple institutional arrangements, which are determined by both rules and strategies. The focus on committees as key institutional features in the congressional process suggests that the usefulness of the theory is proportional to the ease and meaningfulness with which actual congressional committees can be assigned to one of the four cells. For example, which committees receive closed rules for their legislation? Which committees engage in sophisticated behavior?

Structure-induced equilibria

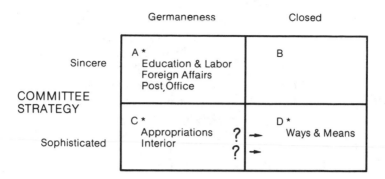

Figure 14.7. Simple institutional arrangements and Fenno's committees.
*Existence of structure-induced equilibria.

Although the figure contains some answers to these questions, the discussion of why certain committees were placed into certain cells is deferred until some loose ends of the extended theory are tied up.

Recall that Shepsle restricted his attention to the top half of Figure 14.7, and that his theorems on the existence of SIE pertained only to germaneness situations (SIA *A*). Furthermore, it was demonstrated above that in closed rule settings with committee members who vote sincerely (SIA *B*), SIE do not exist in general. The natural follow-up is to assess the equilibrium properties of SIAs *C* and *D* to see whether the existence of SIE is attributable to rules only (e.g., SIE exist under the germaneness rule but not under the closed rule) or, perhaps, to some heretofore unspecified *combinations* of rules and strategies.

The procedure for determining whether SIE exist in settings in which committees are sophisticated is only slightly different from the earlier one. The central thrust of Shepsle's definitions remains intact, but the meaning of condition (2) in definitions 2 and 3 is different under the assumption of committee sophistication. Implicit in condition (2) is the committee's choice function, which tells which of any two points a committee chooses. In the context of the definition, one such point is $S°$. In Shepsle's institutional arrangements, the committee's choice is always determined exclusively by the preferences of committee members. When committees are sophisticated, however, the committee's bill is not always the median, as committee members' preferences alone dictate. Rather, the choice is conditioned also by noncommittee members' preferences, which determine whether a situation is ripe, nonripe, futile, or favorable; and which inform the committee what will happen to various feasible bills on the floor. The revised choice function for the committee is included in definition 8, which is used when examining the equilibrium properties of the new SIAs.

In SIA C (sophisticated committees, germaneness rule), the situation must of course be ripe or not ripe. If it is not ripe, committee behavior is identical to that in SIA A, in which Shepsle proved the existence of SIE. Therefore, only situations that are ripe for obstruction, such as Figure 14.4, need to be addressed. Since sophisticated committees obstruct in such situations, the outcome under sophistication would remain at $S°$ instead of moving to FM. Thereafter, the point would remain fixed. But the question is not simply whether the outcome is durable but more importantly whether it is invulnerable in Shepsle's sense. The answer is yes, for the simple reason that choice of some point over the status quo by the committee is a necessary condition for vulnerability. Since a sophisticated committee never chooses any point over $S°$ in situations ripe for obstruction (definition 8a), the necessary condition for vulnerability is not satisfied. $S°$ therefore is invulnerable and an SIE. More generally, type-C SIAs always have SIE. Considered jointly with Shepsle's result, then, this finding indicates that the ability of the germaneness rule to induce equilibrium is not strategy-dependent; sincere and sophisticated behavior alike result in SIE when the germaneness rule is in effect.

Only one institutional arrangement remains: closed rule situations in which committees are sophisticated. One of three situations must exist: futile, favorable, or ripe. In futile situations, such as Figure 14.6a, the committee senses its futility, minimizes decision costs, and reports no bill. As in the germaneness situation, then, condition (2) cannot be satisfied and $S°$ is invulnerable in closed rule, futile situations.[13]

In favorable situations (Figures 14.6b and 14.6c), either $S° = CM$ to begin with or it moves to CM after one session. In neither case will a sophisticated committee report a bill. So this outcome, too, fails condition (2) for vulnerability and is therefore an SIE.

Finally, under ripe situations (Figure 14.6d), the strategically placed bill becomes the new status quo point, S, after one session, whereupon the situation changes from ripe to futile. Since we just showed that the status quo point in futile situations is an SIE, the demonstration is complete. No matter what the initial situation – futile, favorable, or ripe – after one and only one session of decision making there exists a structure-induced equilibrium in SIA D, as well as in SIAs A and C.

IMPLICATIONS AND EVIDENCE

Although intuitively one might expect that incorporation of diverse strategies would undermine the predictability and stability of political outcomes, the theoretical analysis suggests the opposite. If anything, outcomes under sophisticated behavior ought to be *more* stable than outcomes under sincere behavior. It remains to be seen, however, whether there is an empirical basis for the theoretical speculation.

Polsby's study offers persuasive evidence that the contemporary House has become "institutionalized." Boundaries are well defined, in part because turnover has declined and members' incentives to stay in the system have increased. Concomitantly, the House became internally complex; committees are no longer ad hoc tools of the leadership but rather are permanent, increasingly specialized units with fixed jurisdictions and membership determined primarily by "automatic rather than discretionary methods." A major effect of such change has been to "facilitat[e] the growth of stable ways of doing business." Polsby's reasoning (not to mention his choice of words) paves the way for a practical response to the quest for theoretical relevance. Specifically, might there be a relationship between Polsby's observed "stable ways of doing business" and various formal theorists' stable outcomes or, more concisely, between institutionalization and equilibria? If a connection does exist – and it seems that all of us suspect that it does, though perhaps for somewhat different reasons – then how might theory and data be combined to support its existence?

Based on the fact that committees are the central components both of the institutionalized House and of SIAs, an answer is sought by examining the fit between committees in Congress and committees in simple institutional arrangements. To the degree that congressional committees belong to *stable* institutional arrangements (that is, SIAs with SIE), the hypothesis that institutionalization contributes to stable outcomes receives support. We therefore expect to see committees in cells with SIE (*A*, *C*, and *D*) but not in cells without SIE (*B*). (Or, if there were committees in *B*, we would expect to see erratic outcomes on issues over which those committees have jurisdiction.)

Fenno's six committees make a readily available and well known sample for this exercise. Initially, the committees are classified as sophisticated or sincere according to the degree to which their members have reached a consensus on their decision rules. Fenno (1973, p. 80) writes that decision rules differ widely but are nevertheless generalizable.

Despite the uniqueness of each committee's decision rules, two interesting patterns did emerge – interesting because both of them distinguish Appropriations, Ways and Means, and Interior on the one hand from Education and Labor, Foreign Affairs, and Post Office on the other. Each of the first three committees has achieved a consensus on its decision rules; each of the latter three committees has not. Furthermore, the decision rules of the first three committees are all, in one way or another, oriented toward insuring success on the House floor; the decision rules of the latter three are not.

The absence of a consensus on decision rules in the Education and Labor, Foreign Affairs, and Post Office committees is evidence of sincere behavior by committees. Without the consensus, members of the committee are not likely to recognize and exploit ripe situations. They are too preoccupied with the "harsh rules of policy combat" in the committee stage to worry about whether, or in what amended state, their bills will pass on the floor. Fenno's quotation (in Chapter 6 of this volume) and interpretation of a member of one such committee supports the characterization of these committees as strategically sincere.

On Education and Labor, members normally fight about anything at any stage. In the words of one veteran, "You can't get a resolution praising God through this Committee without getting a three-day battle over it."... As another senior member put it, "It's a free-for-all; every man for himself."

But in the Ways and Means, Appropriations, and Interior committees, the desire for success on the floor, and a recognition that success requires the exercise of a specific set of decision rules in committee, are evidence of sophisticated committee behavior. If committee members want their committee's position to prevail on the floor, and know how to make it prevail, then they must possess the foresight characteristic of sophisticated behavior. Thus, Fenno (1973, p. 240) writes that

[a] set of decisions coming from an influence-seeking, House-oriented, corporate committee will be packaged for the floor more carefully than will a set of decisions emerging from a policy-seeking non-House-oriented, individualistic committee.

These excerpts – and the rich set of observations on which they are based – support the placement of Appropriations, Ways and Means, and Interior committees in the lower, sophisticated portion of Figure 14.7, whereas Education and Labor, Foreign Affairs, and Post Office more plausibly belong in one of the top cells.

Categorization on the basis of rules is less clear-cut, whereas *pure* closed rules are rarely granted to legislation (Oleszek 1984). Recall, however, that a continuum underlies what is presented in Figure 14.7 as a dichotomy. Thus to the extent that some committees are relatively likely to receive closed rules for their legislation – as the Ways and Means Committee was when Fenno studied it (but see Rudder 1977) – *or* to the extent that committees tend to receive relatively closed rules (rules that restrict the number of amendments or inhibit the offering of amendments), the committees belong on the closed end of the continuum. With this interpretation and further support from Fenno (chapter 6), Ways and Means is placed in SIA *D*.

More than any other committee, Ways and Means members see themselves as working *for* the House. "On our Committee, we have a responsibility to the House; we have to do the best we can." The closed rule, of course, provides strong reinforcement for this perception. If Committee bills are to be offered on a take-it-or-leave-it basis, members must make certain that they are "taken" without unnecessary misgivings.

Classification of the committees on Interior and Appropriations is confounded by the fact that neither committee regularly receives closed rules. However, when Fenno studied them, both committees were sufficiently cognizant of and responsive to preferences of noncommittee members that, in practice, their legislation was rarely amended successfully and significantly.[14] Fenno writes that the Interior Committee "cultivates an image of routinized, expert deliberations" (1973, p. 63) and that the effect of its image is to reduce controversies on the floor. For example "in 1965, Wayne Aspinall said that since he had become Chairman [of Interior] (in 1959) he had 'only lost two bills – two inconsequential bills' " (p. 260). And in his earlier study of the Appropriations Committee, Fenno reported that about 90 percent of its dollars-and-cents recommendations were accepted without change on the floor (1966, p. 450). So there can be little doubt that these two committees belong in SIAs *C or D*. Whether classification in *D* is more appropriate than in *C* remains an open question, depending on how one wishes to define rules. Strictly speaking, they are germaneness rules; practically speaking (for reasons the present theory does not incorporate), they were relatively closed during the period in question.[15]

Fortunately, occasional gray areas and simplifications do not undermine the two larger findings. First is the close correspondence between Fenno's permeable committees and type-*A* SIAs, and between his corporate committees and sophisticated SIAs (types *C* and *D*). Second is the broader observation that, according to this sample of committees, the dominant institutional arrangements in Congress exhibit stable *mixes* of institutional and strategic features. Three of four SIAs yield structure-induced equilibria, and no committee (either in this sample or in Congress itself, for that matter) belongs in the sole, potentially unpredictable SIA.

To conclude, reconsider Shepsle's profound synopsis that "institutional arrangements...conspire with the preferences of individuals to produce structure-induced equilibrium." Now, in light of theoretical extensions bolstered by Fenno's and Polsby's empirical insights, the set of conspiring ingredients seems to be larger and the resulting equilibria more pervasive. Not just preferences and institutional arrangements but also *strategies* conspire to produce predictable and stable outcomes.

Combined with the observed incidence of stable institutional arrangements in Congress, this revised synopsis should help to reduce skepticism about the empirical relevance of emerging formal theories of legislatures.

NOTES

1 The forthcoming definition of sophisticated committees is similar to that of Denzau and Mackay (1983) but was developed independently in Krehbiel (1983), from which other parts of this essay are adapted. Interested readers are encouraged to study Denzau and Mackay's article, which contains an expected utility formulation of committee strategy.

2 See Fiorina (1975) for an extended argument.

3 See "House Bill Drops Ship-building Subsidies," *Congressional Quarterly Weekly Report*, October 2, 1982, p. 2443. For other examples, see "Turf Fight Results in Limited Highway Funds," ibid., October 9, 1982, pp. 2635–36, and "Senate Eases Foreign Bribery Law," *New York Times*, November 24, 1981, D1.

4 See "Interest Withholding Dispute Stalls Senate Action," *Congressional Quarterly Weekly Report*, March 12, 1983, pp. 491–94.

5 The remainder of the essay focuses on unidimensional situations and assumes that members' preferences on one dimension are not affected by policy on any other dimension (i.e., preferences are separable). Bear in mind, however, that many decisions can be made simultaneously in different committees and jurisdictions. Together with the special properties of SIAs, this insures that all results can be generalized to n dimensions.

6 Definition 3 is the negation of definition 2. Its form is somewhat different since the statements "$\sim(p$ or $q)$" and "$\sim p$ and $\sim q$" are logically equivalent. Thus, vulnerability is R or RA; invulnerability is $\sim(R$ or $RA)$, which is equivalent to $\sim R$ and $\sim RA$.

7 Shepsle does not use the term "replacement by amendment," but his verbal explanation of the second part of the definition of vulnerability is consistent with the term.

8 If in Figure 14.4 $S°$ were equal to CM, this status quo point, too, would be an SIE, albeit for a different structural reason. Specifically, $S° = CM$ could not be replaced because of condition (2). There is no point that the committee would select over its median. Note, however, that although this SIE has a *retentive* property (i.e., it cannot be replaced), it does not *attract*. That is, given any value of $S° \neq CM$, CM cannot become the outcome under the assumption of the model, unless (by chance) CM exactly equals FM.

9 S is excluded because Shepsle defines a proposal as a *change* in the status quo.

10 More generally, any point in the closed interval comprising region B is a replacement for $S°$, where the lower boundary of the region is defined as the point at which the floor median voter is indifferent between that point and $S°$. A final technicality is that theoretically it is possible for closed rule settings to have an SIE. But the necessary condition that $S°$ exactly equals FM is not likely to occur under the closed rule, just as $S° = CM$ in germaneness settings is rare (see note 8). In both cases, the equilibria retain but do not attract. Henceforth, we restrict our focus to SIEs that retain *and* attract.

11 Throughout the discussion we assume that members' preference curves are not only single-peaked but also symmetric. This assumption can be relaxed

and the definitions can be generalized, but generalization requires more complicated notation and sacrifices the straightforward notion of preference as a function of policy distance.

12 For theoretical completeness (and out of practical interest) we define committee sophistication in nonripe situations also. In nonripe situations under the germaneness rule, the committee reports CM; it knows the bill will converge to FM during the amendment process but in actual settings may reasonably expect it not to converge entirely, since noncommittee members sometimes appear to defer to committees. In closed rule, futile situations, the committee does not report a bill; it knows the bill is doomed so chooses to reduce its workload. In closed rule, favorable situations, the committee reports no bill if $CM = S°$ and reports CM otherwise.

13 Alternatively, a definition of committee sophistication might state that the committee reports CM even though it knows it will lose. Condition (2) is then satisfied, but neither condition (3) nor (4) is. There would be no replacement because the parent body always chooses $S°$ over CM; nor could there be replacement by amendment, since there can be no amendment. Thus, with either definition, SIE exist in futile situations.

14 More recently, appropriations bills are regularly modified on the floor. See Bach (1985).

15 A related exclusion is the choice of rules which, in practice, is endogenous (e.g., negotiated between committee chairmen and the Rules Committee) rather than given.

REFERENCES

Bach, Stanley, 1981*a*. Special Rules in the House of Representatives: Themes and Contemporary Variations. *Congressional Studies* 8:37–58.

1981*b*. The Structure of Choice in the House of Representatives: The Impact of Complex Special Rules. *Harvard Journal on Legislation* 18:553–602.

1985. Representatives and Committees on the Floor: Amendments to Appropriations Bills in the House of Representatives, 1963–1982. Paper presented at the annual meeting of the American Political Science Association, New Orleans.

Black, Duncan. 1958. *The Theory of Committees and Elections.* Cambridge: Cambridge University Press.

Denzau, Arthur T., and Robert J. Mackay. 1983. Gatekeeping and Monopoly Power of Committees: An Analysis of Sincere and Sophisticated Behavior. *American Journal of Political Science* 27:740–61.

Fenno, Richard F. 1966. *The Power of the Purse: Appropriations Politics in Congress.* Boston: Little, Brown.

1973. *Congressmen in Committees.* Boston: Little, Brown.

Fiorina, Morris P. 1975. Formal Models in Political Science. *American Journal of Political Science* 19:133–59.

Fiorina, Morris P., and Charles R. Plott. 1978. Committee Decisions under Majority Rule: An Experimental Study. *American Political Science Review* 72:575–98.

Krehbiel, Keith. 1983. Decentralization, Representativeness, and Congressional Reform. Ph.D. dissertation, University of Rochester, Department of Political Science.

Manley, John F. 1969. Wilbur D. Mills: A Study in Congressional Influence.

American Political Science Review, 62:442–64.

Oleszek, Walter J. 1984. *Congressional Procedures and the Policy Process.* 2nd ed. Washington, D.C.: Congressional Quarterly Press.

Rudder, Catherine. 1977. Committee Reform and the Revenue Process. In *Congress Reconsidered.* ed. Lawrence C. Dodd and Bruce I. Oppenheimer, pp. 117–39. Washington D.C.: Congressional Quarterly Press.

The impact of institutional arrangements on the development of public policy

The legislative department derives a superiority in our governments from other circumstances. Its constitutional powers being at once more extensive, and less susceptible of precise limits, it can with the greater facility, mask, under complicated and indirect measures, the encroachments which it makes on the co-ordinate departments. It is not unfrequently a question of real nicety in legislative bodies whether the operation of a particular measure will, or will not, extend beyond the legislative sphere. On the other side, the executive power being restrained within a narrower compass and being more simple in its nature, and the judiciary being described by landmarks still less uncertain, projects of usurpation by either of these departments would immediately betray and defeat themselves. Nor is this all: as the legislative department has access to the pockets of the people, and has in some constitutions full discretion, and in all a prevailing influence, over the pecuniary rewards of those who fill the other departments, a dependence is thus created in the latter, which gives still greater facility to encroachments of the former.   James Madison, *Federalist*, no. 48

In earlier chapters Mayhew, Fiorina, Krehbiel, Polsby, and Shepsle provided conjectures about the motivations underlying the choice of institutional arrangements and the influence of chosen institutional structures on policy making. Part IV deals specifically with how Congress designs institutional arrangements to achieve favored policy outcomes.

In this century, the nexus of policy making has largely shifted from the constitutionally designated branches of government to the bureaucracy: the system of shared powers created by the Constitution has become a system of shared influence over bureaucratic decision making. Each branch of government possesses many tools with which to influence the bureaucracy; both Congress and the president attempt to design institutional arrangements to effectively oversee and control bureaucratic decision making. These institutional arrangements channel and constrain policy making within the bureaucracy in much the same manner as the institutional features disscussed by Shepsle and Krehbiel induced stability in legislative deliberations.

The papers in this part examine a small segment of the larger constitutional system. They provide a single, coherent line of reasoning concerning how Congress and the bureaucracy will interact to make public policy. They explore the notion that Congress has a dominant influence on bureaucratic decision making through the structure it designs for agencies. In delegating, Congress will not create an administrative agency and just let it choose any regulatory policy it finds acceptable, nor will Congress rely on its powers to reward and punish regulatory agencies through the appropriations or authorization process; rather, in writing the legislation that creates an agency Congress will take steps to insure its compliance. These steps are largely procedural; by structuring the decision-making procedures of the agency (e.g., by defining those things that the agency can and cannot make rules about), Congress attempts to provide an automatic means of control that fosters compliant behavior on the part of agents.

In Chapter 15, Mathew McCubbins and Talbot Page examine the ways in which Congress structures the decision-making processes within administrative agencies in an attempt to channel bureaucratic decision making toward policy choices more in line with congressional interests. Congress, they conjecture, attempts to prescribe the structure of agency policy making in four ways: (1) by constraining the range of policies the agency can choose; (2) by structuring the decision-making procedures used by the agency, for example, limiting comparisons of alternatives, prescribing due-process requirements, and establishing rules of evidence; (3) by fashioning incentives to shape bureaucratic motivations; and (4) by monitoring agency activity. They argue that the principal determinants of the choices over these four structural features are the amount of conflict of interst and the degree of uncertainty over outcomes associated with each policy issue.

In Chapter 16, McCubbins and Thomas Schwartz are concerned with the specific control problem of overseeing bureaucratic decision making. They make a technical distinction between different types of oversight. These are "police-patrol" and "fire-alarm" oversight. In the former, members of Congress actively seek out improper policy execution in the agencies: members look for trouble as a method of control much as does a prowling patrol car. In the latter, members wait for signs that agencies are improperly executing policy: members wait for an alarm to be raised by their constituents or concerned groups before they engage in control of the agencies much as the firemen in the local station await their call.

Fire-alarm oversight, they argue, has several valuable characteristics for the reelection-minded member. To begin with, members do not have to spend a great deal of time gratuitously looking for trouble, and awaiting trouble allows members the opportunity to control some aspects of the situation. The trouble that is brought to members' attention by someone else's discovery is trouble that is of concern to their constituents. Not only does solving the problem enable members to reap electoral credits, but limiting their attention to constituents' concerns enables them to engage in all of the standard practices suggested by Mayhew in Chapter 1 (advertising, claiming credit, issue-specific position taking). On the other hand, the trouble discovered by actively patrolling might not concern any constituents at all and thus yields no electoral benefit for members. McCubbins and Schwartz conclude, then, that members prefer the low-risk, high-reward strategy of fire-alarm oversight to the more risky and potentially costly police-patrol system.

Oversight, of course, is but one of the mechanisms of legislative influence on bureaucratic decisions. Agencies may also be induced to produce their own procedures in order to satisfy their own client's interests. John Ferejohn's paper seems to be a natural extension of the research on the institutions of control adopted by Congress. Ferejohn assumes that agencies have some practical discretion in the procedural structures they adopt. The model Ferejohn creates seems to imply that agencies devise a set of procedures which protects them from the uncertainty of their particular environments. In particular he argues that the agency will adopt procedures that act to mirror the forces in their external environment. By following this "structuring principle," agencies can head off any controversial decisions that might jeopardize their autonomy. Agencies that find themselves in a conflictive environment adopt intricate and labyrinthine procedures in order to survive, whereas agencies with missions entailing less controversy have relatively more freedom of action.

Roger Noll integrates and expands these theories in an attempt to model how Congress, the president, the courts, and the bureaucracy interact to make regulatory policy. Noll argues that the political foundations of regulatory policy are forged in the institutional structure of decision making created by the Constitution. The constitutional issues of concern to Noll are, of course, institutional in nature: What kind of effects can be expected if the nature of elections is varied; what consequences result from varying the degree of separations of powers in the system? Noll's paper takes a broader view of the policy process than the other articles in Part IV and extends their analyses to the broader constitutional issues.

Noll's model implies that particularistic policy outcomes are likely to result from any electoral system and thus that regulation will tend to be highly particularistic as well. This confirms the result of the electoral connection model that policy is likely to be particularistic. Noll's expansion of the basic point to encompass regulatory politics is consistent with the thrust of the other papers in this section. These indicate the tendency for the executive agencies to reflect the interests of Congress. Yet, according to Noll, the kind of particularism obtained under regulatory policy is potentially less responsive to electoral interests than are other types of policy.

Randall Calvert, Mark Moran, and Barry Weingast go on to examine empirically a model of the influence of congressional politics on bureaucratic decision making. They offer a view of policy making in which Congress, using its constitutionally mandated powers, indirectly affects policy choices within the bureaucracy. This indirect congressional control, they argue, works through the mechanism of "anticipated reaction" whereby bureaucrats anticipate congressional demands in making their policy choices. By correlating changes in the preferences of the members of the relevant congressional committees having jurisdiction over the Federal Trade Commission with the actual decisions made by the commission, they show that the decisions made by the commission indeed foreshadowed congressional demand.

R. Douglas Arnold explicitly analyzes how rules of procedure affect policy. Arnold shows that allocational formulas and individual case-by-case decision making lead to different geographic allocations of projects. He also finds support for the hypothesis that the nexus of decision makes a difference: allocations chosen by bureaucrats differ from those chosen by legislators. The difference in allocation may arise from a fundamental difference between the type of projects over which Congress delegates authority and the type of projects that Congress chooses to deal with on its own.

The chapters in Part IV examine political control of the bureaucracy and, to some extent, how the bureaucracy will adapt to these external controls. In order to get a handle on this complex topic, the authors simplified the problem by looking at only one relationship at a time, generally focusing on the ways Congress exercises control of bureaucratic policy making. This should be viewed not as a shortcoming of this literature but rather as an opportunity for further research. Through what mechanisms does the president control bureaucratic policy making? The Constitution establishes the powers and limitations of the three branches of government. Congress can do little without the cooperation of the other two branches. How does this constitutionally prescribed cooperation affect the ability of Congress or the president to influence the bureaucracy? These issues are as yet unresolved.

REFERENCES AND SUGGESTED READINGS

*Aberbach, Joel D. 1980. "Changes in Congressional Oversight." *Final Report of the Select Committee on Committees* (the Patterson Committee).

Arnold, R. Douglas. 1979. *Congress and the Bureaucracy*. New Haven: Yale University Press.

Bauer, Raymond A., Ithiel de Sola Pool, and Lewis A. Dexter. 1963. *American Business and Public Policy*. New York: Atherton.

Cooper, Joseph, and Patricia Hurley. 1983. "The Legislative Veto: A Policy Analysis." *Congress and the Presidency*, summer.

Cronin, Thomas, ed. 1982. *Rethinking the Presidency*. Boston: Little, Brown.

Dodd, Lawrence C., and Richard Schott. 1979. *Congress and the Administrative State*. New York: Wiley.

*Fenno, Richard F., Jr. 1966. *The Power of the Purse: Appropriations Politics in Congress.* Boston: Little, Brown
  1973. *Congressmen in Committees*. Boston: Little, Brown.

*Ferejohn, John. 1974. *Pork Barrel Politics*. Stanford: Stanford University Press.

*Fiorina, Morris P. 1977. *Congress: Keystone of the Washington Establishment*. New Haven: Yale University Press.

Fritschler, A. Lee. 1975. *Smoking and Politics*. Englewood Cliffs, N.J.: Prentice-Hall.

Hamilton, Alexander, John Jay, and James Madison. [Any edition.] *The Federalist*.

Hamilton, James. 1976. *The Power to Probe*. New York: Vantage Books.

Kaufman, Herbert. 1981. *The Administrative Behavior of Federal Bureau Chiefs*. Washington, D.C.: Brookings Institution.

Key, V.O. 1937. *The Administration of Federal Grants to States*. Chicago: Public Administration Service.

Kirst, Michael W. 1969. *Government without Passing Laws: Congress' Nonstatutory Techniques for Appropriations Control*. Chapel Hill: University of North Carolina Press.

Maass, Arthur. 1951. *Muddy Waters: The Army Engineers and the Nation's Rivers*. Cambridge, Mass.: Harvard University Press.

Mayhew, David. 1966. *Partly Loyality among Congressmen*. Cambridge, Mass.: Harvard University Press.

* 1974, *Congress: The Electoral Connection*. New Haven: Yale University Press.

Mosher, Frederick C. 1979. *The GAO: The Quest for Accountability in American Government*. Boulder, Colo.: Westview Press.

Ogul, Morris S. 1976. *Congress Oversees the Bureaucracy: Studies in Legislative Supervision*. Pittsburgh: University of Pittsburgh Press.

Pois, Joseph. 1979. *Watchdog on the Potomac: A Study of the Comptroller General of the United States*. Washington, D.C.: University Press of America.

Schick, Allen. 1980. *Congress and Money: Budgeting, Spending, and Taxing*. Washington, D.C.: Urban Institute.

Seidman, Harold. 1980. *Politics, Position, and Power: The Dynamics of Federal*

Organization. New York: Oxford University Press.

Sundquist, James. 1969. *Politics and Policy.* Washington, D.C.: Brookings Institution.

*Wildavsky, Aaron. 1974. *The Politics of the Budgetary Process.* Boston: Little, Brown.

Wilson, Woodrow. [1885] 1973. *Congressional Government.* Gloucester, Mass.: Peter Smith.

15

A theory of congressional delegation

MATHEW D. McCUBBINS AND TALBOT PAGE

Policy choices in the federal system often involve a delegation of legislative authority to an executive agency. This delegation enables Congress to take advantage of efficiency gains in policy making that come about through a division of labor. In delegating, however, Congress creates for itself a problem of agency: the agent to which authority is delegated may not do what Congress would like. Thus, in delegating, members of Congress make a trade-off between the costs due to agency and the gains in policy making efficiency.

In order to reduce these agency costs, Congress attempts to structure its relationship with its agents through a set of structural and management arrangements. Structural arrangements define the rules and procedures that channel and constrain the activities of the agent.[1] Management arrangements consist of the incentive and oversight mechanisms that motivate agents to take actions consistent with congressional desires.[2] This paper investigates the influence of uncertainty and conflict on the choice of these structural arrangements.

LEGISLATIVE DELEGATION

Perhaps the most common explanation for congressional delegation is complexity. The complexity of modern problems results in intricate, complex, and complicated administrative procedures and, because time and other resources are scarce, in delegation of legislative authority to administrative agencies. Certainly there is some merit in this argument; but such an explanation is far from sufficient to explain the myriad forms of regulatory intervention witnessed in this century.

Fiorina (1982a, 1982b) has hypothesized that delegation is the result of efforts on the part of legislators to shift the costs, political and otherwise, of regulating to bureaucrats (see also Aranson, Gellhorn, and Robinson 1982). Delegation in Fiorina's "shift-the-responsibility" model follows from four basic assumptions: first, that the ultimate effect of regulation is to create a distribution of benefits and costs among groups in society; second, that legislators attempt to maximize their districts' *net* benefit from regulation for which they are held accountable; third, that delegation *dilutes* the costs and benefits of regulation that constituents *attribute* to legislative action; fourth, that delegation does not change the actual policy adopted, that the agency chooses precisely the regulatory policy Congress wants. In Fiorina's model a legislator's attitude toward delegation will hinge on the trade-off between the loss in his ability to claim credit for benefits and the gain in his ability to shift the blame for costs to the agency (Fiorina 1982*b*, p. 21). Simply, the legislative choice to delegate authority to an administrative agency in preference to judicial enforcement of a legislative enactment follows when the act of delegating disguises the costs of the regulation to a larger extent than it disguises the benefits.

In studying legislative delegation Fiorina sets aside problems of agency. Administrators in Fiorina's model are *not* strategic actors but rather are mechanisms that add "political daylight between the legislators and those who feel the incidence of legislative actions" (Fiorina 1982*b*, p. 19). Conversely, we are not so much interested in why Congress chooses to delegate as in how Congress seeks to control the exercise of delegated authority by administrative entities. For our purposes the political motivations to delegate will be taken as given. It is the choice by Congress of institutions with which to control bureaucratic decision making that is the focus of this paper.

DESIGN OPTIONS

In creating administrative entities and authorizing them to make decisions within their delegated authority, Congress creates the potential for a problem of agency: the administrative entity may not do what Congress wants. A conflict may exist between the goals and aspirations of the administrators and the preferences of Congress. Two circumstances make the problem only partially solvable, from the point of view of Congress: the instruments of control are imperfect, and so is information. The problem is like walking a dog with a rubber leash on a dark night. The leash is not a perfect instrument of control to begin with, and control is made more difficult by being able to see only shadows and fragments of what is going on.

Problems of agency are of two general types: shirking and slippage. In the theory of agency the term "shirking" denotes any form of noncompliance by the agent and results from a conflict of goals. The agent may pursue his own objectives to the detriment of congressional interests: the agent's chosen policy may not be the same as the policy preferred by members of Congress. Informational asymmetries between the agent and Congress exacerbate the problem. If Congress has incomplete information concerning the activities of the agent and how such activities affect outcomes, then shirking may go partially or entirely unnoticed.

Agency slippage refers to institutionally induced problems. Administrative entities will suffer from many of the same problems other social choice institutions do: if there exists a stable legislative outcome, then slippage may occur as the result of institutionally induced biases that induce the agent to choose policies that diverge from the stable legislative policy choice. Slippage may also occur as a result of instabilities in the agent's decision processes (like those discussed by Thomas Schwartz in Chapter 12). Thus, even if commissioners within a regulatory commission each earnestly attempt to choose policies that comply with the preferences of Congress, the institutions within the commission may lead them collectively to choose policies that are not in compliance with the collective choice Congress would have preferred. Agency slippage, then, may be a problem irrespective of shirking problems.

The challenge for Congress is to choose the decision-making rules for the bureaucrats so as to mitigate problems of agency. The strategies for the congressional choice consist of the institutions that serve to establish the rules of the game of the bureaucracy.[3] In choosing these institutions, congressmen will pursue their own individual goals. These goals may consist of retaining their seats in office, serving their constituents or closely affiliated groups, or attaining their own policy interests. In choosing the rules of the game, though, congressmen also recognize that bureaucrats, in implementing the policy, will have their own goals: attaining political or policy aspirations; achieving stability in their relationship with Congress; or, possibly, increasing their budget and program jurisdiction.

We refer to the institutional arrangements by which Congress attempts to exercise control over the administration of delegated authority as the *form* of a regulatory intervention. Some of the arrangements are built into an act of Congress at the time it is passed – these we call *structural arrangements*. Others are taken during the course of agency implementation of the act – these we call *management arrangements*.

Structural arrangements

In designing a regulatory act Congress chooses the scope of the act, the regulatory instruments delegated to the agency, and the procedures required to use the instruments.

411

Scope. Congress defines the regulatory scope by specifying the domain of potential regulatory targets or problems the entity administering the regulation may address. For example, in the Toxic Substances Control Act (TSCA) Congress delegated authority to regulate approximately 50,000 chemicals in commerce but expressly limited the scope by exempting tobacco, pesticides, food additives, drugs, cosmetics, and radioactive materials (most of which are regulated by other acts). In the Resource Conservation and Recovery Act (RCRA) Congress delegated authority to regulate waste materials and their management but told the agency what chemicals to look at, what problems to address, and what objectives to seek.

Specification of scope includes the statement of the purpose of the act. In TSCA the purpose is to prevent "unreasonable risk" from chemicals to health and environment but "not to impede unduly" technological innovation. The purpose of RCRA is to "promote the protection of health and the environment" and "to conserve valuable material and energy resources." Generally speaking, statements of purpose tend to be of a sweepingly broad, "motherhood-is-good" quality, without much effect on the act itself. But when statements of purpose become incorporated in legal requirements of the act they more directly affect the scope of delegated authority. In TSCA, section 6, the administrator is told to regulate against unreasonable risks to health and environment but to do so "using the least burdensome requirements."

Instruments. In delegating authority Congress spells out the legal tools or *instruments* that an administrative agency can use to implement the act. Generally, instruments are of the following types: command and control, provisions of information, direct provision of some public good, and decentralized economic incentives.[4] The set of regulatory instruments specifies how the administrator may regulate particular problems within its regulatory scope. Congress in TSCA allows the Environmental Protection Agency (EPA) to ban or limit production and distribution of a chemical or category of chemicals; to require warnings or instructions; to require testing or monitorings; and to require record keeping and reporting. McCubbins and Sullivan (1984) have modeled the choice of regulatory instruments by reelection-seeking legislators. Command and control instruments, which provide an *indirect* means of policy implementation, are preferred, they argue, because such instruments hide the costs imposed by regulatory policies while accenting benefits delivered. Those groups bearing the cost of the regulation do not fully perceive their share, whereas the legislator can readily claim credit for benefits delivered. The *perceived* changes in welfare to affected groups, then, add up favorably for reelection-minded legislators.

Procedures. Third, Congress spells out the procedures required to use the instruments. As lawyers are fond of pointing out, procedural requirements are substantive in effect. The number and sizes of hoops to jump through shape and often constrain the delegated authority, affect the allocation of resources within the agency, and in some cases determine the regulatory outcomes. An act specifies the process of hearings, the standards of evidence and burdens of proof in decision making, the points of access for outside parties, the opportunities for judicial review, and the standards for review. Regulatory procedures specify the path of legal requirements an administrator must follow to implement a regulation (e.g., the use of some instrument on a certain target). For example, the Occupational Safety and Health Administration is prohibited from promulgating regulations on various safety issues until directed to do so by the National Institute of Occupational Safety and Health.

Besides controlling and channeling agency decision making, procedural requirements can also be used to improve information. In TSCA, the agency cannot just require testing of a chemical that "may present an unreasonable risk." Before EPA can require a chemical to be tested, it must first show by some sort of reasonable search that the required tests have not been done before or were inadequate *and* that the tests are necessary to determine if the chemical has any potentially harmful effects. The agency must also "consider all relevant factors" in determining fair-sharing of the cost of testing, when there are several firms manufacturing or distributing the chemical. Such procedural requirements to develop information as a part of rule making are designed to protect Congress (and the industry) from arbitrary actions by the agency.

In many cases procedural requirements are specified by reference to the Administration Procedures Act (APA) or the National Environmental Policy Act (NEPA). Many of the procedural requirements imposed by Congress on agency decision making are in response to court objections (see Aranson, Gellhorn, and Robinson 1982). Congress can, however, impose procedures over and beyond those required by the courts, APA, and NEPA and does so for strategic reasons.

Management arrangements

Once a regulatory act is passed, and while it is being implemented, Congress has additional means of control through rewards, sanctions, and monitoring (and of course further structural controls are not ruled out, as Congress can amend the original act).

Rewards and sanctions. Rewards and sanctions arise largely through the exercise of Congress's constitutionally defined powers of authorization, appropriation, and appointment. Calvert, Moran, and Weingast argue in Chapter 19 that many of these powers when exercised in an informal way establish a system wherein Congress wields considerable, albeit indirect, influence over the bureaucracy's choice of regulatory policy. They test several comparative static properties related to the use of these tools by Congress to affect Federal Trade Commission (FTC) decisions.

In general, Congress possesses all the powers it might ever need to insure agency compliance; and though sanctions are used infrequently, their presence creates incentives for bureaucrats to comply with congressional desires. In implementing a regulatory policy the agency will respond to the structure of incentives fashioned by Congress (see Ferejohn, Chapter 17; or Noll 1971*a*, 1971*b*). Congress holds the power of life or death in the most elemental terms throughout the existence of any agency. The power to terminate, either by refusal to renew authorization or by refusal to appropriate funds, is firmly lodged in Congress and nowhere else. That Congress is willing and able to act if the agency commits an impropriety is made clear by the examples of congressional intervention in FTC regulatory decisions concerning cigarette advertising (Fritschler 1969) or, more recently, children's television and funeral homes; or in the congressional dismantling of the Area Redevelopment Administration in 1963 (Ripley 1972).

Monitoring. Congress chooses the methods and extent of monitoring to determine whether an agency is complying with congressionally delegated goals and procedures. McCubbins and Schwartz in Chapter 16 make the distinction between two forms of oversight: "police-patrol" oversight, which is comparatively centralized, active, and direct; and "fire-alarm" oversight, which is less centralized and involves less active and direct intervention. (See also Weingast 1983.)

THE FORM OF A REGULATORY INTERVENTION

Given that Congress has a range of choice over the scope, instruments, and procedures to be delegated, is there any way to predict how Congress will choose concerning a future act or to explain systematically the pattern of previous acts? In the next two sections we offer a simple theory which, we hope, holds at least some predictive and explanatory power. In our theory, just as imperfect control and imperfect information are the fundamental problems Congress faces in delegating authority, the degree of conflict and amount of uncertainty are the principal determinants of what form of delegation Congress chooses.

Most models of policy choice presuppose a world of certainty. Legislators are seen to make policy choices with complete infomation as to their distributional, welfare, and efficiency efforts (e.g., Fiorina 1982*a*; Peltzman 1976; Stigler 1971). Legislators, however, may have incomplete information with respect to some aspects of their policy choices. This uncertainty may have to do with the nature of the problem regulation is supposed to redress (e.g., it is not know beforehand which new drugs are safe and efficacious). Alternatively, the uncertainty may have to do with the potential costs of controlling the activity to be regulated (e.g., at the time of regulation it was not known if the cost of reducing vinyl chloride emissions would be in the billions, as the industry claimed, or much less, as it eventually turned out). Legislators may be uncertain as to their subsequent ability to control the bureaucratic implementation of their chosen policy; or they may be uncertain as to the true preferences or powers of important groups. Since we are concerned with the decisions of individual legislators, we can measure uncertainty as the aggregate value of information (in utility terms) for each congressman, summed over all congressmen. The greater this sum, the greater the degree of uncertainty, from the point of view of the congressman.

Similarly, since congressmen represent different districts each with different interests, their preferences over regulatory outcomes, and hence over regulatory institutions, may sometimes be in conflict. We can measure conflict by taking the difference between the utility each legislator would receive if all other legislators cooperated by choosing actions to maximize the individual legislator's utility and the utility the legislator would receive from the noncooperative legislative outcome, summed for all legislators. If this sum is small, then what is good for one legislator is good for the others. This essentially sets up a Bayesian game between legislators and provides us with tractable definitions of our exogenous influences.

We can now informally examine the comparative static properties of changes in the regulatory scope, procedures, and substantive discretion delegated to an administrative agency with respect to changes in uncertainty and conflict of interest. How does the choice of scope, instruments, and procedures constrain and channel agency activity? Intuitively, the more instruments (bans, quotas, taxes, labels, testing and reporting requirements, etc.), the more regulatory opportunities an agency will have. However, not all regulatory actions are feasible. Before an action can be implemented it must be filtered through the required administrative procedures. What comes out might be something different something weakened, or nothing at all. The set of outcomes reachable by agency actions is the province of its *substantive discretionary authority*. This domain of policy choices is fashioned, in part, by Congress, through its particular delegation of regulatory scope and procedural require-

415

ments. The choice of regulatory scope defines the domain of feasible regulatory opportunities available to the regulatory entity, subject to procedural requirements. Procedural requirements then serve to reduce the set of outcomes reachable within this scope.

In relating uncertainty and conflicts of interest to the choice of regulatory scope and procedures, we focus on the motivations of an individual legislator. We recognize, however, that these choices are collective choices and will reflect the structure of the collective choice institutions. What we are assuming is that the collective decisions of the legislature (positively) reflect changes in an individual member's preferences. We are cautious in light of the instability results of the last two decades (e.g., McKelvey 1979). This assumption may not always be satisfied. There are good reasons, however, that it might frequently be satisfied: the rules of procedure in Congress may induce a structural equilibrium that will be responsive to changes in individual preferences (Shepsle 1979; Shepsle and Weingast 1982). Specifically, the committee system in Congress provides the institutional agenda by which legislative policies are developed. The decentralized system of semiautonomous committees and subcommittees, on which membership is largely self-selected, establishes a framework in which much of the available power over a given regulatory issue is held by just a few congressmen who care the most about it and who share similar preferences concerning its outcome (see Chapter 19, herein; Cox, McCubbins, and Sullivan 1984; Weingast 1984). This near monopoly power granted to subcommittees provides subcommittee members *individually* with extraordinary influence over the choice and implementation of regulatory policy. This tendency for decentralized policy control is further strengthened through widely accepted norms of universalism and reciprocity, wherein members of different committees, interested in different policies, implicitly logroll across issues in order to guarantee majority support for their respective proposals.

Our theory of how uncertainty and conflict affect the congressional choice of delegated authority is stated in three propositions.

Proposition 1. Under the same level of conflict, an increase in uncertainty leads Congress to delegate:
  (a) a broader scope of regulatory authority and more instruments,
  (b) more confining procedures.

With increased uncertainty, congressmen would prefer to delegate a broader scope of authority and more instruments for two reasons. First, greater uncertainty implies that the range of alternative policy choices concerning which the legislator has little or no information, and thus among which the legislator cannot discern a clear optimum, is large.

416

With little or no information with which to evaluate the possible alternatives, and with conceivably large political risks associated with uncertain choices, legislators would prefer to delegate an increasingly large domain of alternative regulatory targets to the agency. Control can be maintained, and the potential losses associated with uncertain choices can be mitigated. The legislator can claim credit for addressing an important policy problem and at the same time shirk any blame for making hard policy choices. Thus, greater uncertainty will increase the incentive for legislators to delegate a large domain of target problems to a regulatory agency. This means delegating both a larger scope and a larger set of instruments.

Second, under uncertainty there is a greater need for information because congressmen will not know beforehand what their interests will ultimately be. They would like constituents and interest groups to reveal their preferences and powers before being pinned down to particular substantive solutions to particular problems. Their need for information grows relative to their uncertainty. Congressmen and congressional staffs are capable of eliciting information concerning the various policy alternatives. Such information retrieval, however, may have high opportunity costs, taking away time and resources from other electorally oriented activities. On the other hand, the problem of choice, along with the costs of eliciting information, can be delegated to an administrative agency. Insofar as Congress can exercise a great deal of control over the activities of regulatory agencies, congressmen may prefer to delegate the regulatory choices, and therewith a large portion of the information costs, to the agency and sit back in an oversight role awaiting clarification of the issue. This costs congressmen little in terms of policy control and enables them to pass the costs of decision making on to the agency.

Increasing uncertainty leads to more restrictive procedural requirements, also for two reasons. First, as the domain of scope and instruments broadens, so does the congressional need to maintain control. Monitoring agency activities becomes of increased importance to congressmen. McCubbins and Schwartz argue that decentralized oversight techniques will be preferred by reelection-seeking legislators. Weingast (1984) similarly argues that such decentralized techniques will be effective in giving Congress control over agency activities. Decentralized oversight techniques rely, in large measure, upon labyrinthine and intrusive regulatory procedures. Thus, with increased uncertainty congressmen prefer to prescribe an increasingly extensive array of regulatory procedures for agency decision making.

Second, it also follows that reelection-seeking legislators will prefer to focus the agency's regulatory discretion away from targets with potentially high political costs. With increased uncertainty, the political risks associated with virtually all regulatory alternatives are increased. Fewer alternatives are unambiguously preferred by the membership to the status quo. More and more of the alternatives in an expanded regulatory scope are politically risky for the members. Legislators will prefer, then, to make the choices more difficult by extending the procedural requirements necessary for the promulgation of a regulation.

For example, TSCA presented Congress with a regulatory problem immersed in uncertainty and conflict. The uncertainty had to do with the nature of the problem regulation was supposed to redress, as well as with the potential costs of controlling hazards. Under section 4 of the act, EPA must promulgate test rules for those chemicals that it requires to be tested. Such tests are used to generate information about the health and environmental effects of the new chemical. The chemical manufacturing firms have to pay for the tests. Procedural safeguards were put into TSCA to prevent EPA from requiring tests that were redundant or did not produce useful information. Indeed, in the case of one of EPA's first "priority" chemicals, chloromethane, these procedural requirements were interpreted so strictly by the agency that it spent several hundred thousand dollars and several years writing the test rule (which was nearly 1,000 pages long). The cost of writing a rule requiring testing was several times the cost of performing the test.

Proposition 2. Under the same structure of information, an increase in conflict of interests leads Congress to delegate:
  (*a*) a broader scope of regulatory authority and more instruments,
  (*b*) more confining procedures.

Increased conflict also leads to the pattern of broader scope, more instruments, and narrowed procedures. With single-member districts and with constituents' interests varying across districts, increased conflict means more disagreement among groups of constituents, and hence among members of Congress, concerning what should be the regulatory mandate. This makes it harder for a decisive coalition in Congress to narrow down the range of regulatory targets to be delegated to the agency. Excluding policy alternatives that are points of controversy during the writing of the legislation will increase the likelihood of defections from the legislative coalition. Since controversial decisions need not be made during the writing of the legislation, the cooperative solution will be to leave the number of policy alternatives included in the agent's regulatory scope large.

Again, with increased agency discretion there is an increased need to exercise control over agency decision making. Problems associated with agency shirking and slippage increase with increasing discretion. There is an incentive to increase the level of regulatory procedures in order to establish a system of control over regulatory decision making. With increased conflict there are increased political risks and therewith increased incentive to direct the choice of regulation by the agency, through the imposition of extensive procedural requirements, away from potentially costly alternatives.

That increased decision uncertainty and increased conflict among members leads to an increased delegation of regulatory scope to an administrative agency is in some respects counterintuitive. With increased uncertainty and conflict come increased political risks for legislators. It is expected, then, that congressmen would want more control of the regulatory process, not less, when the stakes are high. What is argued here, however, is *not* that congressmen prefer less control in such situations but that they prefer to exercise their control, not by making potentially costly policy choices themselves but instead by exercising control over the choice of policy by a regulatory agency.

We are suggesting that with greater uncertainty and greater conflict there is a stronger incentive for Congress to pass the hot potato to the agency by broadening the scope and instruments of delegated authority. But, while passing on the hot potato, there is no need to send over a loose cannon. With one hand, Congress broadens the scope and instruments; with the other, Congress tightens the procedural requirements. What Congress gives with one hand, Congress takes away with the other.

Proposition 3. Under the same level of conflict, an increase in uncertainty leads Congress to delegate a smaller amount of substantive discretion to the agency. Similarly, under the same structure of information an increase in conflict leads Congress to delegate a narrower substantive discretion.

This proposition is basically a conjecture based on several qualitative case studies. We have noted that with increased uncertainty and/or conflict the tendencies toward broader scope and instruments and narrower procedures work in opposite directions, the first leading to more substantive discretionary authority, the second to less. It is our conjecture that the need for control (via procedures) more than offsets the legislature's inability to narrow the scope of the delegation. Thus, to insure control, the substantive discretionary authority of the agent decreases with increasing conflict and/or uncertainty (cf. McCubbins 1985).

What does this imply about the structure of various regulatory agencies? If there is more uncertainty and more conflict in environmental and health regulation than in economic regulation (e.g., regulation of a single industry, such as the regulation of the airlines by the Civil Aeronautics Board), then the model predicts a difference in the form of regulation for these two areas. Specifically, we have a series of, in principle, testable hypotheses.

1. A broader scope of substantive authority is delegated to the administrator under environmental and health compared with economic regulation.

2. There are more procedural requirements for decision making in environmental and health regulation as compared with economic regulation, more public hearings and comment, more points of access to agency decision making by outside parties, more access to judicial review, and more strenuous burdens of proof and standards of evidence.

3. Consequently, greater substantive discretion is granted to economic regulatory entities as compared with environmental and health regulatory entities.

The model also helps explain differences among existing regulatory acts in the same environmental area. TSCA was passed after six years of bitter congressional struggle. There was a great deal of explicit conflict between the Commerce Department, which reflected industry interests, and EPA and the Council on Environmental Quality, which reflected the broader interests of those at risk. These conflicts were mirrored in Congress. At the same time, several sources of uncertainty were widely perceived. There were 50 to 70 thousand chemicals in commerce (no one knew how many) that needed to be addressed because some of them (no one knew how many) were toxic (with various unknown potencies and types of toxicity). It was widely perceived that there was little toxicity information existing for the vast majority of the chemicals in commerce (this turned out to be correct), but there were widely conflicting estimates of the cost and need for testing and the cost and need for regulation.

In contrast, RCRA was enacted with little controversy. It was widely perceived (wrongly, it turns out) that management of waste materials including hazardous wastes was straightforward and the cradle-to-grave approach of the manifest system would be feasible and effective. In contrast with TSCA, there was little perceived conflict or uncertainty associated with the passage of RCRA.

The acts themselves are quite different. TSCA is known as one of the most complicated "organic" acts, with a sweeping mandate, wide scope, and a large stock of instruments – and voluminous and confining procedures. RCRA is a much simpler act, with simpler procedures and a more focused scope and set of instruments.

420

A theory of congressional delegation

The form of the legislative delegation has important implications for the performance of regulation. If an agency has stringent procedural requirements that allow little discretion, regulatory actions are likely to be few and far between. If an agency has broad discretion in its substantive authority in addition to narrow procedural discretion, there may be more attempted actions (again with few results) and, therewith, more frustrations inside the agency as well.

There are several ways to evaluate the performance of a regulatory agency.[5] It can be evaluated in terms of the economic efficiency of its regulations or its addition to social welfare. Alternatively, the agency can be evaluated from its own perspective: Did it accomplish its goals; did it generate a large number of significant regulations? Performance can be measured from the point of view of the legislature as well. Though we shall discuss a few of these views, the model is predictive in nature and does not depend on any particular definition of performance.

Economists have argued for over a decade that regulation has generally failed by relying too heavily on command and control instruments and not heavily enough on decentralized economic incentives. Kneese and Schultze (1975) suggest a reason for the "overemphasis" on command and control instruments – discipline bias: most congressmen are lawyers and their education, therefore, makes them familiar and comfortable with regulation by legal order. But, although education is likely to be a factor in the choice of regulatory instrument, would not legislators become familiar and comfortable with decentralized economic incentives if it were in their interest to choose them?

The model provides another explanation (beyond discipline bias) for congressional preferences for command and control over decentralized economic incentives in regulation. When there is more conflict and greater uncertainty, congressmen have greater concern with procedural safeguards. The very flexibility of economic incentives (the source of their strength to economists) is interpreted by the congressman as uncontrolled uncertainty. The political climate they prefer for decentralized economic incentives is one with little conflict and uncertainty. For example, in establishing the Civil Aeronautics Board, where there was relatively little conflict and uncertainty, Congress did delegate a decentralized instrument, price setting, to the agency. (But note that some of the uncertainty associated with price setting was controlled by also delegating power to restrict industry entry.)

In the agency, performance is evaluated not in terms of a global concept of economic efficiency but in terms of its own structure of incentives. To grow and prosper, the agency must show some visible signs of accomplishment toward its policy mandate and its specific goals as spelled out in its substantive authority.

To communicate with Congress and to have its accomplishments believed, it is useful for the agency to be concrete about its accomplishments. To say "We improved the public health" is too vague without considerable evidence, especially of a quantitative nature. To say "We banned dioxin" carries more weight as the achievement is easily verifiable. When there is greater conflict and more uncertainty there is greater peril for the agency and incidentally a greater need to justify its actions before Congress. To maintain the support of its congressional sponsors, without whom the agency could not survive, the agency must report, very concretely, its achievements. The agency's activities are described in terms of its "planned program achievement," or PPAs, or "beans." Beans have the advantage of being countable and verifiable. Banning dioxin is a bean. On the other hand, instituting an effluent tax is less of a bean.

Thus, the agency will respond to the form of the regulatory intervention mandated by Congress and the environmental factors of conflict and uncertainty by pursuing only the most concrete and highly visible regulations. Such regulations have disadvantages, however, as they become targets for congressional critics who represent interest groups hurt by the planned program accomplishments. The agency, realizing this vulnerability, has an added incentive to make its accomplishments defendable. Increasing the defendability of the concrete, and visible, regulations in turn adds to the already high fixed cost per regulation. The result is the 1,000-page regulation, infrequent but well fortified – and, to justify its large (fixed) cost of promulgation, often large in scale.

The strategy of a few *big* beans has led at times to a sense of frustration within the agency. Some regulatory attempts become too cumbersome to make it through the agency – for example, after 48 tries, the attempt to regulate asbestos was abandoned, having never gone beyond EPA's Office of Pesticides and Toxic Substances. It would have been a billion-dollar regulation. Other billion-dollar regulations, such as that on benzene, are remanded by the courts. And, though a few big regulations survive, only a minute fraction of the problems are being addressed.

A final characteristic of the regulatory process follows from the reliance on command and control. Having chosen, partly in response to congressional wishes, regulation by legal order, the agency often finds itself dictating specific technological solutions. To survive court tests and political pressures for defendability, the agency must understand, or claim to understand, specific technological processes as well as do the experts in the affected industry. Having maneuvered itself into a position where it needs this type of specific information, the agency puts itself at a particular disadvantage relative to the regulated firms, which specialize in this information in the course of their business.

Within Congress, performance of an agency is often evaluated in terms of whether the agency has on balance benefited the constituencies of individual congressmen. When the answer is negative, the agency is likely to find out the answer during oversight hearings, by hostile queries, by legislative veto, or by reduced authorization or reduced budget.

In sum, then, conditions of high conflict of interest and great uncertainty will lead to broad scope and many instruments, but confining procedures and, on balance, little substantive discretion for the administering agency. The relatively few regulations developed under these circumstances are likely to be quite complicated and costly. Conditions of lower conflict of interest and less uncertainty, on the other hand, will lead to greater procedural discretion over a smaller range of regulatory targets. Here, regulatory form, regulatory interventions, will tend to be more flexible and less controversial from the standpoint of both Congress and the agency.

PROSPECTS OF REFORM

We have suggested that increased conflict and uncertainty are prime ingredients of regulatory inaction. It has also been suggested that to some extent the difficulties are rooted in the American constitutional system itself. We are not suggesting, however, that environmental and health regulation has failed altogether or that its limitations are completely due to our particular system of democracy. A very large factor is the large amount of uncertainty associated with potential environmental risks. This uncertainty arises from our limited understanding of cancer mechanisms, the transport of toxic chemicals in groundwater, and so on. The uncertainty is part of the nature of the problem. It is augmented in many cases by long latency periods (20 to 40 years for carcinogens).

Nor are we suggesting that attempts to improve regulatory performance depend upon changing the basic features of American democracy. It appears that less fundamental changes that might improve the prospects of environmental regulation are possible. To illustrate the implications of our theory, let us assume that, as many economists would argue, the efficiency of environmental regulation would be improved by a greater reliance on decentralized instruments and less on command and control. If we are on the right track, decentralized instruments are not going to increase in usage merely because of economists' exhortations. The present factors of environmental uncertainty and conflict will overwhelm such a strategy. A more effective strategy for implementing decentralized incentives is to focus on ways to decrease conflict and uncertainty in environmental policy making and, more specifically, on ways in which the decentralized instruments themselves can be designed to decrease group conflict and uncertainty. For example, marketable pollution quotas decrease uncertainty as to the resulting levels of air or water quality, compared with effluent effects. Distributing quota revenues within the polluting industry may reduce group conflict. Other compensation systems may be tied to decentralized instruments promoting efficiency. Liability rules may be tied to conditions of behavior that limit liability. A current development is the rapid increase in the number and success of toxic tort suits. Though this process is decentralized, it is highly uncertain and conflict-laden. If this development continues, decentralized instruments, such as hazard taxes, implemented by government agencies may be seen as decreasing uncertainty and conflict. Moreover, uncertainty can be reduced directly by research on environmental and health effects. Just as thalidomide led to the 1962 Food and Drug Amendments and Three Mile Island led to a change in political and administrative climate for nuclear power, increases in the assessment of hazard potential change the balance of uncertainty and conflict in legislative and bureaucratic politics.

NOTES

1 David Brady and Mark Morgan examine a similar problem in how Congress structures the appropriations process in Chapter 8. Roger Noll considers the consequences of the process of structuring on regulatory policy in Chapter 18.
2 Fire-alarm oversight as discussed by Mathew McCubbins and Thomas Schwartz in Chapter 16 is an example of a management arrangement.
3 The problem of structuring the principal–agent relationship between Congress and the regulatory agency bears many similarities to the problem of structuring its relationship with its own committees (see Shepsle and Weingast 1982).
4 Congress must prescribe explicit statutory limitations on administrative discretion for the delegation of legislative authority to fit within the framework established by the courts in *Panama Refining Co.* v. *Ryan*, 1935 (243 v.s. 388), *A.L.A. Schechter Poultry Corp.* v. *United States*, 1935 (245 v.s. 495), and *Carter* v. *Carter Coal Co.*, 1936 (298 v.s. 238). Broad delegations of authority by the legislature must be accompanied with procedural protections or an opportunity for judicial review (see also *Yakus* v. *United States*, 1944 (321 v.s. 414)). However, there will still be great differences among the procedures prescribed for various acts that fit within the framework of the delegation doctrine.
5 For a discussion of definitions of regulatory performance, see Cutler and Johnson 1975. On regulatory "failure" see Noll 1971c.

A theory of congressional delegation

REFERENCES

Aranson, Peter, Ernest Gellhorn, and Glen Robinson. 1982. "A Theory of Legislative Delegation." *Cornell Law Review*, November, pp. 1–67.

Cox, Gary, Mathew McCubbins, and Terry Sullivan. 1984. "Policy and Constituency: Reelection Incentives and the Choice of Policy Intervention." *Social Choice and Welfare* 1:231–42.

Fiorina, Morris. 1977. *Congress: Keystone of the Washington Establishment.* New Haven: Yale University Press.

1982a. "Legislative Choice of Regulatory Forms: Legal Process or Administrative Process?" *Public Choice* 39:33–66.

1982b. "Group Concentration and the Delegation of Legislative Authority." Mimeograph. California Institute of Technology, Pasadena.

Fritschler, Lee. 1969. *Smoking and Politics.* New York: Appleton-Century-Crofts.

Joskow, Paul, and Roger Noll. 1978. "Regulation in Theory and Practice: An Overview." Social Science Working Paper no. 213. California Institute of Technology, Pasadena, May.

Kneese, Allen V., and Charles L. Schultze. 1975. *Pollution, Prices, and Public Policy.* Washington, D.C.: Brookings Institution.

McCubbins, Mathew. 1985. "Legislative Design of Regulatory Structure." *American Journal of Political Science* 29:721–48.

McCubbins, Mathew, and Terry Sullivan. 1984. "Constituency Influence on Legislative Policy Choice." *Quality and Quantity* 13:299–319.

McKelvey, Richard. 1979. "General Conditions for Global Intransitivities in Formed Voting Models." *Econometrica* 47:1085–1111.

Noll, Roger. 1971a. The Economics and Politics of Regulation." *Virginia Law Review* 57:1016–32.

1971b. "The Behavior of Regulatory Agencies." *Review of Social Economy* 29:15–19.

1971c. *Reforming Regulations: An Evaluation of the ash Council Proposals.* Washington, D.C.: Brookings Institution.

Peltzman, Samuel. 1976. "Toward a More General Theory of Regulation." *Journal of Law and Economics* 68:211–40.

Ripley, Randall. 1972. *The Politics of Economic and Human Resource Development.* Indianapolis: Bobbs-Merrill.

Shepsle, Kenneth. 1979. "Institutional Arrangement and Equilibrium in Multidimensional Voting Models." *American Journal of Political Science* 23:27–60.

Shepsle, Kenneth, and Barry Weingast. 1982. "Structure-Induced Equilibrium and Legislative Choice." *Public Choice* 37:503–19.

Stigler, George. 1971. "The Theory of Economic Regulation." *Bell Journal of Economics and Management Science*, Spring, pp. 3–21.

Weingast, Barry. 1984. "A Principal Agent Perspective on Congressional-Bureaucratic Relations." Paper delivered at the Fifth Carnegie Conference on Political Economy, Carnegie-Mellon University, Pittsburgh, June.

Weingast, Barry, and Mark Moran. 1981. "Bureaucratic Discretion of Congressional Control: Regulatory Policymaking by the Federal Trade Commission." Mimeograph. Center for the Study of American Business, Washington University, St. Louis.

16

Congressional oversight overlooked: police patrols versus fire alarms

MATHEW D. McCUBBINS AND THOMAS SCHWARTZ

Scholars often complain that Congress has neglected its oversight responsibility: despite a large and growing executive branch, Congress has done little or nothing to oversee administrative compliance with legislative goals. As a consequence, we are told, Congress has largely lost control of the executive branch: it has allowed the executive branch not only to grow but to grow irresponsible. In popular debate as well as congressional scholarship, this neglect of oversight has become a stylized fact: widely and dutifully reported, it is often bemoaned, sometimes explained, but almost never seriously questioned.[1]

We question it. What has appeared to scholars to be a neglect of oversight, we argue, really is a preference for one form of oversight over another, less-effective form. In so arguing, we develop a simple model of congressional choice of oversight policy, offer evidence to support the model, and draw from it further implications regarding bureaucratic discretion and regulatory legislation. More generally, we model the choice by policy makers of an optimal enforcement strategy, given opportunity costs, available technology, and human cognitive limits.

THE MODEL

Congressional oversight policy concerns whether, to what extent, and in what way Congress attempts to detect and remedy executive-branch violations of legislative goals. Our model of congressional choice of oversight policy rests on a distinction between two forms or techniques of oversight.

Reprinted from *American Journal of Political Science*, Vol. 2, no. 1 (February 1984), pp. 165–179. Partial funding for this research was provided by grants from the University Research Institute, University of Texas. We are grateful to Bruce Cain, Charles Cnudde, Morris Fiorina, Paul Kens, David Prindle, and especially Roger Noll for a number of valuable criticisms and suggestions.

Congressional oversight overlooked

Police-patrol oversight. Analogous to the use of real police patrols, police-patrol oversight is comparatively centralized, active, and direct: at its own initiative, Congress examines a sample of executive agency activities, with the aim of detecting and remedying any violations of legislative goals and, by its surveillance, discouraging such violations. An agency's activities might be surveyed by any of a number of means, such as reading documents, commissioning scientific studies, conducting field observations, and holding hearings to question officials and affected citizens.

Fire-alarm oversight. Analogous to the use of real fire alarms, fire-alarm oversight is less centralized and involves less active and direct intervention than police-patrol oversight: instead of examining a sample of administrative decisions, looking for violations of legislative goals, Congress establishes a system of rules, procedures, and informal practices that enable individual citizens and organized interest groups to examine administrative decisions (sometimes in prospect), to charge executive agencies with violating congressional goals, and to seek remedies from agencies, courts, and Congress itself. Some of these rules, procedures, and practices afford citizens and interest groups access to information and to administrative decision-making processes. Others give them standing to challenge administrative decisions before agencies and courts, or help them bring alleged violations to congressmen's attention. Still others facilitate collective action by comparatively disorganized interest groups. Congress's role consists in creating and perfecting this decentralized system and, occasionally, intervening in response to complaints. Instead of sniffing for fires, Congress places fire-alarm boxes on street corners, builds neighborhood fire houses, and sometimes dispatches its own hook-and-ladder in response to an alarm.

The distinction between police-patrol and fire-alarm oversight should not be confused with the distinction that sometimes is drawn between *formal* and *informal* oversight, which differ in that formal oversight activities have oversight as their principal and official purpose, whereas informal oversight activities are incidental to other official functions, such as appropriations hearings. Both can involve direct and active surveillance rather than responses to alarms. (See Dodd and Schott, 1977; Ogul, 1977.)

Our model consists of three assumptions.

TECHNOLOGICAL ASSUMPTION Two forms of oversight are available to Congress: police-patrol oversight and fire-alarm oversight. Congress can choose either form or a combination of the two, making tradeoffs between them in two circumstances: (1) When writing legislation, Congress can include police-patrol features, such as sunset review, or fire-alarm features, such as requirements for public hearings. (2) When it evaluates an agency's performance, Congress can either call oversight hearings to patrol for violations of legislative goals or else wait for alarms to signal potential violations.

MOTIVATIONAL ASSUMPTION A congressman seeks to take as much credit as possible for the net benefits enjoyed by his potential supporters – by citizens and interest groups, within his constituency and elsewhere, whose support can help him win reelection. This means, in part, that a congressman seeks to avoid as much blame as possible for the net costs borne by his potential supporters.

INSTITUTIONAL ASSUMPTION Executive agencies act as agents of Congress and especially of those subcommittees on which they depend for authorizations and appropriations.

The Motivational Assumption is closely tied to Mayhew's celebrated reelection model (1974) and to the blame-shirking model of Fiorina (1982a). The Institutional Assumption is found in Baldwin (1975), Ferejohn (1981), Joskow (1974), McCubbins (1982a, b), and Mitnick (1980). Although not previously stated, the Technological Assumption seems to us to be uncontroversial.

That cannot be said of the Motivational Assumption, which depicts congressmen as pure politicians, single-mindedly pursuing reelection. To this picture one might object that real congressmen are not just politicians but statesmen, pursuing justice and the public interest, acting according to various moral and ideological principles, even at some cost to their reelection prospects.

We will argue, however, that if the Motivational Assumption were replaced by the assumption that congressmen act strictly as statesmen, our conclusions regarding oversight would still be derivable, although in a somewhat different way. Our analysis has less to do with specific legislative goals than with optimal strategies for enforcing compliance with legislative goals of any sort.

CONSEQUENCES

Three important consequences follow from our model:

CONSEQUENCE 1 To the extent that they favor oversight activity of any sort, congressmen tend to prefer fire-alarm oversight to police-patrol oversight.

Our argument for Consequence 1 is that a congressman's objective, according to the Motivational Assumption, is to take as much credit as possible for net benefits enjoyed by his potential supporters and that he can do so more efficiently under a policy of fire-alarm oversight than under a police-patrol policy, for three reasons:

First, congressmen engaged in police-patrol oversight inevitably spend time examining a great many executive-branch actions that do not violate legislative goals or harm any potential supporters, at least not enough to occasion complaints. They might also spend time detecting and remedying arguable violations that nonetheless harm no potential supporters. For this they receive scant credit from their potential supporters. According to the Motivational Assumption, then, their time is largely wasted, so they incur opportunity costs. But under a fire-alarm policy, a congressman does not address concrete violations unless potential supporters have complained about them, in which case he can receive credit for intervening. So a unit of time spent on oversight is likely to yield more benefit for a congressman under a fire-alarm policy than under a policy-patrol policy. As a result, a fire-alarm policy enables congressmen to spend less time on oversight, leaving more time for other profitable activities, or to spend the same time on more personally profitable oversight activities – on addressing complaints by potential supporters. Justly or unjustly, time spent putting out visible fires gains one more credit than the same time spent sniffing for smoke.

Second, under a realistic police-patrol policy, congressmen examine only a small sample of executive-branch actions. As a result, they are likely to miss violations that harm their potential supporters, and so miss opportunities to take credit for redressing grievances, however fair the sample. Under a fire-alarm policy, by contrast, potential supporters can in most cases bring to congressmen's attention any violations that harm them and for which they have received no adequate remedy through the executive or judicial branch.

Third, although fire-alarm oversight can be as costly as police-patrol oversight, much of the cost is borne by the citizens and interest groups who sound alarms and by administrative agencies and courts rather than by congressmen themselves. A congressman's responsibility for such costs is sufficiently remote that he is not likely to be blamed for them by his potential supporters.

CONSEQUENCE 2 Congress will not neglect its oversight responsibility. It will adopt an extensive and somewhat effective (even if imperfect) oversight policy.

This is because one of the two forms of oversight – the fire-alarm variety – serves congressmen's interests at little cost. When his potential supporters complain of a violation of legislative goals, a congressman gains credit if he eliminates the cause of the complaint. By virtue of the Institutional Assumption, he often can be reasonably effective in eliminating such causes. Beyond establishing and perfecting the system and addressing some complaints, fire-alarm oversight is almost costless to congressmen: others bear most of the cost.

CONSEQUENCE 3 Congress will adopt an extensive and somewhat effective policy of fire-alarm oversight while largely neglecting police-patrol oversight.

This just summarizes Consequences 1 and 2.

MISPERCEPTION

Faced with an apparent fact he finds puzzling, unfortunate, or otherwise worthy of attention, a scientist has two alternatives: (a) to accept the fact and try to explain it, or (b) to question the *apparent* fact and try to explain its appearance. In the case at hand, students of Congress have, for the most part, chosen (a): they have uncritically agreed that Congress neglects its oversight responsibility and have tried to explain this neglect.

Here are the three main explanations found in the literature, along with a brief critical comment on each:

COMPLEXITY Because public-policy issues are so complex, Congress has had to delegate authority over them to a large, complex, technically expert bureaucracy, whose actions it is unable effectively to oversee (Lowi, 1969; Ogul, 1977; Ripley, 1969; Seidman, 1975; Woll, 1977).

Comment. Given sufficient incentives, as Fiorina (1982a) observes, Congress has found the capacity to tackle a number of complex issues itself. A striking example is the tax code (Jaffe, 1973, pp. 1189–90). What is more, there is no evident reason why Congress should respond to the complexity of issues by creating a large, expert bureaucracy without also creating a large, expert congressional staff – one sufficiently large and expert, not only to help decide complex issues, but to help oversee a large, expert bureaucracy.

GOOD GOVERNMENT To serve the public interest, Congress has established regulatory and other executive-branch agencies based on expertise and divorced from politics. Because these agencies are designed to serve the public interest, whereas Congress is influenced by special-interest lobbies, oversight not only is unnecessary but might be regarded as political meddling in processes that ought to remain nonpolitical (Lowi, 1969).

Comment. Whatever the original intent, it is no longer plausible in most cases to suppose that the public interest is best served by a

430

bureaucracy unaccountable to Congress and, therefore, unaccountable to the electorate.

DECENTRALIZATION Because congressional decisions are made, for the most part, by a large number of small, relatively autonomous subcommittees with narrow jurisdictions, general oversight committees tend to be weak (Dodd and Schott, 1979).

Comment. At most this explains why congressional oversight responsibilities are not centralized. It does not explain why they are neglected. If anything, subcommittee specialization should enhance congressional oversight over individual agencies. Subcommittees controlling authorizations and appropriations might be in a better position to do oversight than so-called oversight committees.

Regarding the apparent fact the Congress neglects oversight, we choose alternative (b) over (a): what appears to be a neglect of oversight can be explained as a preference by congressmen for fire-alarm over police-patrol oversight. We have already argued that congressmen have this preference. Scholars who decry the neglect of oversight have, we suggest, focused on a single form of oversight: they have looked only for police-patrol oversight, ignoring the fire-alarm alternative – and therewith the major part of actual oversight activity. Observing a neglect of *police-patrol* oversight, they have mistakenly concluded that *oversight* is neglected.

It has been suggested to us that scholars who have remarked congressional neglect of oversight were using the word more narrowly than we are – that they were *defining* "oversight" to mean police-patrol oversight, contrary to our Technological Assumption.

To this we have three replies: First, established usage equates oversight with the task of detecting and remedying violations of legislative goals by the executive branch.[2] No technique for accomplishing this task can be ruled out by definition. Second, the definitional equation of oversight with police-patrol oversight reflects the odd view that it is less important for Congress to make a serious attempt to detect and remedy violations of legislative goals than to employ a specific technique for doing so. Third, it would be odd to have a name for one way of detecting and remedying executive-branch violations of legislative goals but none for the general task of detecting and remedying such violations.

It has also been suggested to us that fire-alarm activities were never conceived or intended to be a form of oversight, whatever their effects.

We agree that congressmen rarely if ever refer to fire-alarm activities as "oversight," a term officially applied to subcommittees engaged in direct surveillance – in police-patrol oversight. Still, there is no evident reason for congressmen to engage in most fire-alarm activities unless they aim thereby to detect and remedy certain administrative violations of legislative goals.

Those who equate oversight with police-patrol oversight might argue that redressing grievances against the executive branch is not the same as enforcing compliance with congressional goals: the goals congressmen pursue in answering alarms related to particular laws need not be the goals they had in mind when they enacted those laws.

We see no reason to believe, however, that acts of legislation reflect well-defined or unalterable legislative goals – especially in view of the classical voting paradox and similar anomalies (Arrow, 1963; Plott, 1967; Schwartz, 1970, 1981, 1982a). Rather, legislative goals are refined, elaborated, and even changed over time in response to new problems – including complaints against executive agencies – and to changes in preferences and political alignments. In answering fire-alarms, congressmen not only enforce compliance with legislative goals; they help decide what those goals are.

Possibly those who bemoan congressional neglect of oversight would agree that fire-alarm oversight is extensively practiced but argue that it is not *effective*.

We have argued already that fire-alarm oversight is likely to be somewhat effective. The evidence presented two sections hence supports this conclusion.

Even granting that fire-alarm oversight is extensively practiced and *somewhat* effective, hence that Congress does not *neglect* its oversight responsibility, one might still wonder which form of oversight is the *more* effective. To this question we now turn.

THE GREATER EFFECTIVENESS OF FIRE-ALARM OVERSIGHT

We will argue that fire-alarm oversight is likely to be more effective, on balance, than police-patrol oversight. But this requires two qualifications: First, we do not contend that the most effective oversight policy is likely to contain no police-patrol features, only that fire-alarm techniques are likely to predominate. Second, we do not contend that a predominantly fire-alarm policy is more likely than a predominantly police-patrol policy to serve the public interest, only that it is likely to secure greater compliance with legislative goal; whether such compliance serves the public interest depends on what those goals are.

A predominantly fire-alarm oversight policy is likely to be more effective – to secure greater compliance with legislative goals – than a predominantly police-patrol policy for two main reasons:

First, legislative goals often are stated in such a vague way that it is hard to decide whether any violation has occurred unless some citizen or group registers a complaint. Such a complaint gives Congress the opportunity to spell out its goals more clearly – just as concrete cases and controversies give courts the opportunity to elucidate legal principles that would be hard to make precise in the abstract.

Second, whereas a fire-alarm policy would almost certainly pick up any violation of legislative goals that seriously harmed an organized group, a police-patrol policy would doubtless miss many such violations, since only a sample of executive-branch actions would be examined.

One who agrees with this point might still argue, on behalf of the greater efficacy of police-patrol oversight, that the citizens harmed by violations of legislative goals are not always represented by organized groups and, hence, cannot always sound a loud enough alarm to secure a redress of grievances.

Our reply is fourfold: First, nowadays even "disadvantaged" groups often have public spokesmen. Second, as we show in the following section, sometimes Congress passes legislation, as part of its fire-alarm policy, that helps comparatively disorganized groups to act collectively. Third, congressmen's extensive constituent-service activities provide even individual citizens with an effective voice against administrative agencies: case work is part (but only part) of the fire-alarm system. Finally, if the point is merely that fire-alarm oversight can be biased in various ways, then the same is true of police-patrol oversight; and although a good enough police-patrol policy would avoid bias, so would a good enough fire-alarm policy.

To be sure, fire-alarm oversight tends to be *particularistic* in the sense of Mayhew (1974): it arguably emphasizes the interests of individuals and interest groups more than those of the public at large. This is an important difference – the essential difference, we think, between the respective products of police-patrol and fire-alarm oversight. But whether it is a shortcoming of fire-alarm oversight depends on one's ideological point of view: even if fire-alarm oversight deemphasizes some public interest concerns, it gives special emphasis to a concern for the interests and rights of individual citizens and small groups – a concern well founded in American political values.

Although our model refers only to Congress, we hazard to hypothesize that as most organizations grow and mature, their top policy makers adopt methods of control that are comparatively decentralized and incentive based. Such methods, we believe, will work more efficiently (relative to accepted policy goals) than direct, centralized surveillance. This is sufficiently plausible that we wonder why students of Congress have generally assumed that congressional oversight must be of the direct, centralized police-patrol variety. Part of the reason, perhaps, is that Congress itself applies the label "oversight" to subcommittees charged with police-patrol responsibilities.

As we stated earlier, Consequences 1–3 do not depend on our Motivational Assumption, which depicts congressmen as pure politicians rather than statesmen. This is because statesmen, wishing to secure compliance with their legislative goals, would presumably adopt the most effective oversight policy, and that is likely to be one in which fire-alarm techniques predominate.

EVIDENCE

Evidence for Consequence 3 – and therewith our model – is plentiful and well known. Scholars who bemoan congressional neglect of oversight have not ignored this evidence. Rather, they have missed its significance: lacking the concept of fire-alarm oversight, they have failed to see the details of our fire-alarm system as instances of oversight activity. Here is a brief summary of the available evidence:

1. Under a fire-alarm system, complaints against administrative agencies are often brought to the attention of congressional subcommittees by lobbyists for organized groups, and to the attention of administrative agencies by congressional subcommittees. The functioning of this "subgovernmental triangle" has been well documented (Dodd and Oppenheimer, 1977; Fenno, 1966, 1973a, b; Goodwin, 1970; Ornstein, 1975; Ripley, 1969; Huitt, 1973; Matthews, 1960; Ripley and Franklin, 1976).

2. Congress has passed legislation to help comparatively disorganized groups to press their grievances against the federal government. McConnell (1966) shows how the Agriculture, Labor, and Commerce Departments act as lobbyists for farm, labor, and small-business interests. Congress has also created new programs, such as the Legal-Services Corporation, to organize and press the claims of comparatively voiceless citizens.

3. Constituent-service activities are not limited to unsnarling procedural knots. As part of the fire-alarm system, district staff and casework help individuals and groups – some of them otherwise powerless – to raise and redress grievances against decisions by administrative agencies. This casework component of legislative policy making has been examined only recently, with a primary focus on the electoral connection (Cain, Ferejohn, and Fiorina, 1979a, b; Fenno, 1978; Fiorina, 1977a; Mayhew, 1974; Parker and Davidson, 1979) and with a secondary focus on policy consequences (Fiorina, 1977a, 1982b; Fiorina and Noll, 1978, 1979a, b).

4. Often the fire-alarm system allows for the redress of grievances by administrative agencies and courts; Congress itself need not always get involved. To facilitate such redress, Congress has passed several laws, notably the Administrative Procedures Act of 1946 and the Environmental Procedures Act of 1969, that have substantially increased the number of groups with legal standing before administrative agencies and district courts regarding bureaucratic controversies (Lowi, 1969).[3] Congress has also, as in sections 4–7 of the Toxic Substances Control Act of 1976, increased the courts' powers to issue injunctions in response to alarms and has required administrative agencies to hold hearings, publish information, and invite public comment on agency decision making (McCubbins, 1982a).

5. There are numerous cases in which violations of legislative goals were brought to the attention of Congress, which responded with vigorous remedial measures. For example, Congress dismantled the Area Redevelopment Administration (ARA) in 1963, even though it had just been authorized in 1961. The ARA was encouraging industries to relocate in redevelopment areas despite clear provisions in the law to the contrary (Ripley, 1972). Congress also can redefine or reaffirm its goals by redefining or explicating the jurisdictional authority of an administrative agency. This happened with the Federal Trade Commission when it first sought to regulate cigarette advertising, children's television, and funeral homes. Sometimes such congressional intervention is legislatively mandated. Before taking action on a pending case, for example, the National Labor Relations Board must consult with the appropriate congressional committees.

6. The general impression that Congress neglects oversight, we have argued, really is a perception that Congress neglects police-patrol oversight. That impression and the evidence adduced to support it constitute further evidence for Consequences 1 and 3: they show that congressmen tend to prefer an oversight policy in which fire-alarm techniques predominate.

FURTHER IMPLICATIONS: HAS BUREAUCRATIC DISCRETION INCREASED?

Hand in glove with our stylized fact (neglect of oversight) goes another: Congress has increasingly relinquished its legislative authority to the executive branch, allowing the bureaucracy to make law (Dodd and Schott, 1979; Hess, 1976; Lowi, 1969; Woll, 1977).[4]

Although Congress may, to some extent, have allowed the bureaucracy to make law, it may also have devised a reasonably effective and noncostly way to articulate and promulgate its own legislative goals – a way that depends on the fire-alarm oversight system. It is convenient for Congress to adopt broad legislative mandates and give substantial rulemaking authority to the bureaucracy. The problem with doing so, of course, is that the bureacracy might not pursue Congress's goals. But citizens and interest groups can be counted on to sound an alarm in most cases in which the bureaucracy has arguably violated Congress's goals. Then Congress can intervene to rectify the violation. Congress has not necessarily relinquished legislative responsibility to anyone else. It has just found a more efficient way to legislate.

When legislators try to write laws with sufficient detail and precision to preclude administrative discretion, they quickly run up against their own cognitive limits: beyond a certain point, human beings just cannot anticipate all the contigencies that might arise. The attempt to legislate for all contingencies can entail unintended (and undesired) consequences. In his classic study of Anglo-American judicial reasoning, Levi (1948) makes this point about judges (lawmakers of a sort), who lay down imprecise rules, which they subsequently and gradually elaborate in response to concrete legal disputes. Oakeshott (1973) makes a similar point about political activity of all sorts: it cannot be based on precise, detailed blueprints, and so policy formulations can at best be rough summaries of experience, requiring elaboration and judicious application case by case.

The ostensible shifting of legislative responsibility to the executive branch may simply be the responsible adoption of efficient legislative techniques and the responsible acceptance of human cognitive limits – both facilitated by the fire-alarm system.

FURTHER IMPLICATIONS: THE CHOICE OF REGULATORY POLICY

When it decides regulatory issues, Congress tends to choose one of two types of regulatory instrument: command-and-control instruments and incentive-based instruments. Congress faces a similar choice when it decides, not how to regulate society, but how to regulate the regulators – when it decides, in other words, on oversight policy. For police-patrol oversight is similar to command-and-control regulatory instruments, while fire-alarm oversight is similar to incentive-based instruments.

Offhand one might suppose that just as congressmen tend to prefer fire-alarm to police-patrol oversight policies, so they would tend to prefer incentive-based to command-and-control regulatory policies. Our observations, of course, do not support this supposition (Breyer, 1982; Fiorina, 1982a; Joskow and Noll, 1978; McCubbins, 1982a; McCubbins and Page, 1982; Schultze, 1977).

436

Congressional oversight overlooked

Paradoxically, Congress's very preference for fire-alarm oversight entails a preference for command-and-control regulatory policy. For command-and-control agencies are more susceptible of case-by-case congressional intervention in response to complaints, hence more susceptible of fire-alarm control, than are courts, taxing authorities, and private individuals and firms – the principal participants in incentive-based regulatory policy.

CONCLUSION

The widespread perception that Congress has neglected its oversight responsibility is a widespread mistake. Congressional scholars have focused their attention on police-patrol oversight. What has appeared to many of them to be a neglect of oversight is really a preference – an eminently rational one – for fire-alarm oversight. That a decentralized, incentive-based control mechanism has been found more effective, from its users' point view, than direct, centralized surveillance should come as no surprise.

Besides criticizing the received wisdom regarding congressional oversight, we hope to have highlighted a neglected way of looking at congressional behavior. Sometimes Congress appears to do little, leaving important policy decisions to the executive or judicial branch. But appearances can deceive. A perfectly reasonable way for Congress to pursue its objectives is by ensuring that fire alarms will be sounded, enabling courts, administrative agencies, and ultimately Congress itself to step in, whenever executive compliance with congressional objectives is called in question. In examining congressional policies and their impact, do not just ask how clear, detailed, or far-sighted congressional legislation is. Ask how likely it is that fire alarms will signal putative violations of legislative goals and how Congress is likely to respond to such alarms.

NOTES

1 See Bibby, 1966, 1968; Dodd and Schott, 1979; Fiorina, 1977a, b, 1982b; Hess, 1976; Huntington, 1973; Lowi, 1969; Mitnick, 1980; Ogul, 1976, 1977; Ripley, 1978; Scher, 1963; Seidman, 1975; Woll, 1977. The following remarks by Pearson (1975) succinctly exemplify this view: "Paradoxically, despite its importance, congressional oversight remains basically weak and ineffective" (p. 281). "Oversight is a vital yet neglected congressional function" (p. 288).

2 A 1977 report by the U.S. Senate Committee on Government Operations stated that "Oversight involves a wide range of congressional efforts to review and control, policy implementation..." (pp. 4–5). According to Dodd and

Schott (1979), "Oversight...involves attempts by Congress to review and control policy implementation" (p. 156). Ogul (1976) defines oversight as the process by which Congress determines, among other things, whether agencies are complying with congressional intent. See also Bibby, 1966; Harris, 1964; Lees, 1977; Lowi, 1969; Ripley, 1978; Woll, 1977.

3 Ferejohn (1974) provides a good example of how the decision-making procedures of the Army Corps of Engineers were expanded to include wilderness, wildlife, and environmental group interests by the passage of the 1969 National Environmental Policy Act.

4 On related points see Fiorina (1977b), Weingast and Moran (1981), McCubbins (1982a, b), and McCubbins and Page (1982). Weingast has argued that Congress employs a number of its constitutionally defined powers in a decentralized and often unobserved way in order to exercise control over the actions of administrative agencies (Calvert, Moran, and Weingast, 1982; Weingast and Moran, 1981).

REFERENCES

Arrow, Kenneth. 1963. *Social choice and individual values.* 2nd ed. New York: Wiley.

Baldwin, John. 1975. *The regulatory agency and the public corporation: The Canadian air transport industry.* Cambridge, Mass.: Ballinger.

Bibby, John. 1966. Committee characteristics and legislative oversight of administration. *Midwest Journal of Political Science,* 10 (February 1966): 78–98.

  1968. Congress' neglected function. In *Republican papers,* edited by Melvin Laird. New York: Praeger.

Breyer, Stephen. 1982. *Regulation and its reform.* Cambridge, Mass.: Harvard University Press.

Cain, Bruce, John Ferejohn, and Morris Fiorina. 1979a. The roots of legislator popularity in Great Britain and the United States. Social Science Working Paper No. 288, California Institute of Technology, Pasadena, Calif.

  1979b. Casework service in Great Britain and the United States. California Institute of Technology, Pasadena, Calif. Mimeo.

Calvert, Randall, Mark Moran, and Barry Weingast. 1982. Congressional influence over policymaking: The case of the FTC. Paper presented at the annual meeting of the American Political Science Association, Chicago, September 1982.

Dodd, Lawrence, and Bruce Oppenheimer, eds. 1977. *Congress reconsidered.* New York: Praeger.

Dodd, Lawrence, and Richard Schott. 1979. *Congress and the administrative state.* New York: Wiley.

Fenno, Richard, Jr. 1966. *The power of the purse.* Boston: Little, Brown.

  1973a. *Congressmen in committees.* Boston: Little, Brown.

  1973b. The internal distribution of influence: The house. In *The Congress and America's future,* 2nd ed., edited by David Truman, pp. 52–76. Englewood Cliffs, N.J.: Prentice-Hall.

  1978. *Home style.* Boston: Little, Brown.

Ferejohn, John. 1974. *Pork barrel politics.* Stanford: Stanford University Press.

  1981. A note on the structure of administrative agencies. California Institute of Technology, Pasadena, Calif. Mimeo.

Fiorina, Morris, 1977a. *Congress: Keystone of the Washington establishment.* New Haven: Yale University Press.

1977b. Control of the bureaucracy: A mismatch of incentives and capabilities. Social Science Working Paper No. 182, California Institute of Technology, Pasadena, Calif.

1982a. Legislative choice of regulatory forms: Legal process or administrative process? *Public Choice* 39 (September 1982): 33–66.

1982b. Group concentration and the delegation of legislative authority. California Institute of Technology, Pasadena, Calif. Mimeo.

Fiorina, Morris, and Roger Noll. 1978. Voters, bureaucrats and legislators: A rational choice perspective on the growth of bureaucracy. *Journal of Public Economics* 9 (June 1978): 239–54.

1979a. Voters, legislators and bureaucracy: Institutional design in the public sector. In *Problemi di administrazione publica, Centro di formazione e studi per il Messogiorno*, Naples, Italy, Formes 4 (2): 69–89.

1979b. Majority rule models and legislative election. *Journal of Politics* 41:1081–1104.

Goodwin, George, Jr. 1970. *The little legislatures.* Amherst: University of Massachusetts Press.

Harris, Joseph. 1964. *Congressional control of administration.* Washington, D.C.: Brookings.

Hess, Stephen. 1976. *Organizing the presidency* Washington: Brookings.

Huitt, Ralph. 1973. The internal distribution of influence: The Senate. In The *Congress in America's future*, 2nd ed., edited by David Truman, pp. 77–101. Englewood Cliffs, N.J.: Prentice-Hall.

Huntington, Samuel. Congressional responses to the twentieth century. In The *Congress in America's future*, 2nd ed., edited by David Truman, pp. 5–31. Englewood Cliffs, N.J.: Prentice-Hall, 1973.

Jaffe, Louis. 1973. The illusion of the ideal administration. *Harvard Law Review,* 86:1183–99.

Joskow, Paul. 1974. Inflation and environmental concern: Structural change in the process of public utility price regulation. *Journal of Law and Economics,* 17 (October 1974): 291–327.

Joskow, Paul, and Roger Noll. 1978. Regulation in theory and practice: An overview. California Institute of Technology, Social Science Working Paper No. 213, Pasadena, Calif.

Less, John D. 1977. Legislatures and oversight: A review article on a neglected area of research. *Legislative Studies Quarterly* (May 1977): 193–208.

Levi, Edward. 1948. *Legal reasoning.* Chicago: University of Chicago Press.

Lowi, Theodore. 1969. *The end of liberalism.* New York: Norton.

Matthews, Donald. 1960. *U.S. Senators and their world.* Chapel Hill: University of North Carolina Press.

Mayhew, David. 1974. *Congress: The electoral connection.* New Haven: Yale University Press.

McConnell, Grant. 1966. *Private power and American democracy.* New York: Vintage Books.

McCubbins, Mathew. 1982a. Rational individual behavior and collective irrationality: The legislative choice of regulatory forms. Ph.D. dissertation, California Institute of Technology, Pasadena, Calif.

1982b. On the form regulatory intervention. Paper presented at the 1983 Annual Meeting of the Public Choice Society, Savannah, Georgia, March

24–26, 1983.

McCubbins, Mathew, and Talbot Page. 1982. On the failure of environmental, health and safety regulation. Paper presented at the 1983 Annual Meeting of the Midwest Political Science Association, Chicago, Illinois, April 20–23, 1983.

Mitnick, Barry. 1980. *The political economy of regulation.* New York: Columbia University Press.

Oakeshott, Michael. 1973. Political education. In *Rationalism in politics,* edited by Michael Oakeshott, pp. 110–36. New York: Basic Books, 1962. Reprinted in *Freedom and authority,* edited by Thomas Schwartz, 362–80. Encino, Calif.: Dickenson.

Ogul, Morris. 1976. *Congress oversees the bureaucracy.* Pittsburgh: University of Pittsburgh Press.

———. 1977. Congressional oversight: Structure and incentives. In *Congress reconsidered,* edited by Lawrence Dodd and Bruce Oppenheimer, pp. 207–221. New York: Praeger.

Ornstein, Norman, ed. 1975. *Congress in change.* New York: Praeger.

Parker, Glenn, and Roger Davidson. 1979. Why do Americans love their congressmen so much more than their Congress? *Legislative Studies Quarterly* 4 (February 1979): 53–62.

Pearson, James. 1975. Oversight: A vital yet neglected congressional function. *Kansas Law Review* 23:277–88.

Plott, Charles. 1967. A notion of equilibrium and its possibility under majority rules. *American Economic Review* 57 (September 1967): 787–806.

Ripley, Randall. 1969. *Power in the Senate.* New York: St. Martin's.

———. 1971. *The politics of economic and human resource development.* Indianapolis: Bobbs-Merrill.

———. 1978. *Congress: Process and policy.* 2nd ed. New York: Norton.

Ripley, Randall, and Grace Franklin. 1976. *Congress, the bureaucracy and public policy.* Homewood, Ill.: Dorsey.

Scher, Seymour. 1963. Conditions for legislative control. *Journal of Politics* 25 (August 1963): 526–51.

Schultze, Charles. 1977. *The public use of private interest.* Washington, D.C.: Brookings.

Schwartz, Thomas. 1970. On the possibility of rational policy evaluation. *Theory and Decision* 1 (October 1970): 89–106.

———. 1981. The universal-instability theorem. *Public Choice* 37 (no. 3): 487–501.

———. 1982a. A really general impossibility theorem. *Quality and Quantity* 16 (December 1982): 493–505.

———. 1982b. The porkbarrel paradox. University of Texas, Austin, Tex. Mimeo.

Seidman, Harold. 1975. *Politics, position, and power: The dynamics of federal organization.* New York: Oxford.

U.S. Senate. Committee on Government Operations. 1977. *Study on federal regulation, vol. II, congressional oversight of regulatory agencies.* Washington, D.C.: Government Printing Office.

Weingast, Barry, and Mark Moran. 1981. Bureaucratic discretion or congressional control: Regulatory policymaking by the Federal Trade Commission Washington University, St. Louis: Center of the Study of American Business. Mimeo.

Woll, Peter. 1977. *American bureaucracy.* New York: Norton.

17

The structure of agency decision processes

JOHN A. FEREJOHN

INTRODUCTION

This paper aims to further our understanding of the structure of agency decision making procedures: the paths that potential decisions must traverse in order to become the official acts of an agency. In democratic systems, administrative agencies rely on other political bodies for support and legitimation. Though they may be charged with the pursuit of some legislated end, the means they choose in this pursuit – their actions – are largely determined internally. That these actions can be consequential we take for granted; that they may arouse the fire of members of the three constitutional branches seems obvious as well.

For these reasons, administrative agencies generally develop methods of review and clearance for proposed actions. By determining what actions it might take, who is entitled to propose these actions, and who has the right to review and alter those proposals, an agency's practices and procedures constrain not only its behavior but also its internal distribution of power. More than that, practices and procedures also influence the criteria for making choices: the kinds of arguments considered to be persuasive in getting agency members to choose one course of action rather than another, or, its internal "culture."[1]

A complete explanation of the structure of an agency's decision processes must begin with a description of the objectives of its personnel. Given the present state of the theory of organizations, however, it seems unlikely that such a description is feasible. Therefore, we do not wish to claim that agency leaders are interested only in maximizing their budgets,

The author is Professor of Political Science and Senior Research Fellow of the Hoover Institution of War, Revolution and Peace. Work on this paper was partly supported by NSF grant #PRA8114463 to the California Institute of Technology, Pasadena, California. This paper has benefited from comments by John Bendor, Morris Fiorina, Mathew McCubbins, Roger Noll, R. Talbot Page, and Serge Taylor as well as those of an anonymous referee.

441

staff size, personal perquisites, or ideological objectives. Rather, we will assume only that (at minimum) agency personnel prefer to maintain a fair degree of internal autonomy for those in leadership positions within the agency. They prefer not to see agency decisions appealed in other forums or the policies of the agency determined by default at the "street" level. Thus, with regard to these institutional choices we expect that agency members are likely to have relatively homogeneous preferences. They may disagree as to who should share power within the agency and which goals should receive priority, but everyone wants a structure that will successfully anticipate potential sources of opposition to agency actions and alert decision makers as to the consequences of proposed decisions in time to modify them. Without such a structure, the agency will find its decisions challenged or reversed, its members demoralized, and its funding cut, or worse. In any case the ability of members to achieve program goals or to satisfy private ambitions would be greatly reduced.

TWO STRATEGIES OF DECISION MAKING

Though the internal practices and procedures of an administrative agency should be seen as endogenous, the range of alternative practices is constrained by the nature of the agency's mission[2] as well as by legal doctrine. But, at least in the current legal climate, such limitations seem to be quite unconfining. There remains substantial latitude for discretion. The range of alternatives might be seen as falling along a continuum spanned by two traditional methods of organizing agency decisions.

Each of the traditional methods – case-by-case decision making and legislative rule making – carries with it a standard set of expectations and presumptions. In case-by-case decision making there are two alternative sets of expectations depending on whether the agency is dispensing discretionary awards that claimants have no recognized moral or legal claim to or is distributing goods to those claiming to be entitled to receive them. If the agency is charged with making discretionary awards – research grants, flood control projects, or defense contracts – the expectation is that the agency will utilize its discretion in a bureaucratically rational way and that this discretionary latitude will not ordinarily be reviewable by the courts.

Alternatively, if it is in the business of distributing goods to which applicants are thought to have some sort of entitlement – welfare or disability programs would be good examples – the expectation in the courts and in the society at large is that agency decisions should be reached only after proceedings in which affected interests have rights to present arguments and to rebut evidence presented against them. Such proceedings are expected to generate a record, and that record is supposed to contain virtually everything that is relevant to the decision on the case. Ex parte interventions are generally prohibited, and the record is to form the basis for judicial review of agency decisions.

Decision making through legislative rule making carries a wholly different set of expectations. Congressional expectations[3] and judicial understandings[4] indicate that agency rule making is to possess the characteristics of legislative deliberations. There is no presumption that agency rules are to be based entirely on a formal published record or that ex parte communications are inadmissible. The scope of judicial review of such decisions is thought to be much narrower, and constitutional controls are expected to work through legislative supervision of the agency rather than through court intervention. The only formal requirement imposed on such rule making is that it provide opportunity for "notice and comment."

From the perspective of the agency and its mission, each of the traditional decision making methods exhibits characteristic disadvantages as well as advantages. Case-by-case decision-making procedures are cumbersome and expensive to operate. And, if the same sorts of information have to be developed for the record for great numbers of substantially similar cases these costs may be redundant.[5]

At the same time, case-by-case decision-making systems, by their nature, tend not to treat similar cases similarly. For that reason they are hard for agency leaders to control. Although programs that proceed by deciding individual cases may develop adjudicatory principles and precedents – what have been called internal systems of justice – that allow them to achieve some semblance of evenness in application, they must still rely upon the exercise of discretion by lower-level agency personnel. Moreover, there is a likelihood that such systems tend to weigh the interests of claimants, who may be physically present or represented by lawyers at various decision points, over those of taxpayers or of potential claimants of other programs.

On the other hand, an internal justice system can protect agency decisions from the consequences of judicial or political interference. The adjudicatory norms and formal procedural requirements – the decision culture – can make direct political interference in individual cases seem illegitimate to outsiders as well as insiders.[6] Moreover, even if outside authorities successfully intervene in a particular case, this intervention will often have little consequence for agency conduct in other cases.

Besides, the limited dockets of the courts often make judicial review quite costly and inefficacious in altering the internal decision practices of administrative agencies. In considering the Social Security Administration (SAA), Mashaw writes: "SSA's implementation of its disability

443

benefits program has generated an internal law of administration...
this law is internal in the...sense that it has remained largely unaffected by the traditional external legal control through judicial
review."[7] Kagan, writing of Nixon's Phase I price freeze program,
observes that "there was no significant interference by the courts with the
over four hundred rules and thousands of individual rulings issued by the
administrative agencies."[8]

Thus, the principal advantage of case-by-case adjudication, as a
strategy of decision, is to be found in its impermeability to external
interference. The basis of this impermeability is found in the fact that
individual agency decisions affect only small numbers of individuals.
Those aggravated by agency action have an incentive to seek redress for
the injustice done in their case rather than attack the agency's general
method of doing business. Proceeding by cases divides and isolates
potential opponents and allows the agency to proceed without worrying
about the effect of its actions on its political support. And, if a claimant is
occasionally successful in appealing an agency decision elsewhere, the
consequences for the agency are minimized.

But, precisely because administration through adjudicatory methods is
relatively well insulated from legal or political review, programmatic and
fiscal effects are difficult to control. Caseworkers and examiners will
effectively determine program characteristics, and the discretion of
higher-level administrators will be limited.

For these reasons, it is often thought that agencies, even those that
must deal with individual cases, should do their work in the open. They
should make general rules that will guide their decisions in particular
cases. These rules should be discussed in public forums, and outside
interests should have plenty of opportunity to participate in their
formulation. These sentiments are of course what led to the creation of
such practices as legislative rule making.

From the standpoint of the agency, the principal advantage of
legislative rule making is that it allows agency leaders more control over
the actions of the agency by grouping broad classes of decisions into
categories amenable to the routine application of quasi-legislatively
promulgated rules. This allows them a correspondingly greater degree of
flexibility to pursue their objectives. Besides, the quasi-legislative setting
would allow relatively easy access to organized groups with an interest in
agency proceedings. Agency leaders would, therefore, be alerted to
controversial aspects of proposed rules and be able to act to take these
into account in advance of their promulgation.

But legislative rule making has severe limitations as a political strategy.
By raising the stakes and lowering the costs of participation in decision
making, rule making tends to involve diverse interests and, therefore, a

relatively high level of controversy. Moreover, because broadly formulated rules can affect large numbers of individuals, rule making can have the effect of uniting those adversely affected by a particular rule and giving them an incentive to challenge not only the proposed rule but also the agency's authority to make such rules at all. In this sense, the adoption of a rule-making strategy forces an agency to concern itself centrally about the implications of its rule-making activity for the maintenance of its political support. In turn, one would expect agencies to be cautious about promulgating rules that could undermine its support in external political settings.

Whatever the comparative merits of the traditional systems, agencies have seldom been free to choose between them in their pure forms (as argued by McCubbins and Page in Chapter 15). Often, they have been required to consider intermediate structures of decision. Congress has inserted provisions in a number of enabling statutes requiring the use of "hybrid" forms of rule making that require formal hearings, produce a record, and must in some way or other relate promulgated rules to the record. Until recently, the courts seemed to be moving in this direction as well, by requiring administrators to conduct "paper hearings" in some cases and to take a "hard look" at available alternatives when conducting informal rule making.[9]

These developments alert us to the fact that there is a wide range of decision-making structures falling between the two pure methods already discussed and that we cannot hope to understand the choice of decision-making structure without a better understanding of these intermediate systems. Agencies choose the structure of a decision from a rich set of alternatives, and this choice is made only under relatively loose formal constraints. For this reason, we see the choice of decision-making structures as a strategic one that is guided by the objectives of agency leaders.

INTERMEDIATE STRATEGIES OF DECISION

A *structural strategy* is a review procedure through which potential agency decisions must pass. Such strategies may be unconditional or conditional. An unconditional strategy would require that all agency actions go through a particular level or type of review. An example of this is the legislatively imposed requirement that federal construction projects must have environmental impact statements. In this sense, an agency that determines its policies through informal rule making would be seen as using an unconditional strategy.

A conditional strategy requires that the characteristics of the review procedure depend on the probable impact of the proposed decision. In

445

particular, many agencies have special procedures for reviewing those proposed actions that appear likely to generate controversy in Congress or the courts. Where a rule is thought likely to provoke adverse political response, special deliberateness is called for; more clearances are required, and these often involve higher officials within the agency. In this sense, case-by-case decision making is the pure form of a conditional strategy.

Conditional strategies envision the collection of information about whether a proposal is likely to evoke controversy in the agency's environment. Agencies will therefore have procedures for obtaining this information in a routine way early in the decision process. Depending on various aspects of its environment, these methods can involve formal hearings, informal exchanges of information between agency personnel and those affected by proposed actions, or, even bringing "representatives" of affected interests inside the agency's decision process.

In effect, conditional strategies amount to hybrid systems of decision in which the scope of rule making is restricted by considerations of the characteristics of cases. By adopting a conditional strategy, an agency effectively accords "rights" to potentially affected interests. The courts have held that such adminstratively created rights may impose legal restrictions on agency decision processes.

Agencies will voluntarily adopt hybrid decision systems under roughly the same circumstances in which such a choice would be attractive to Congress or the courts. Where potentially affected interests are able to appeal agency decisions to higher political authority successfully, those interests will tend to be granted rights of access and appeal within agency processes. McCubbins and Page (Chapter 15) suggest that these conditions tend to occur in circumstances of uncertainty and conflict over the original delegation of authority to the agency and result in the congressional imposition of restrictive review procedures. In our view, whether or not Congress chooses to impose such requirements on rule making, agencies will evolve procedures that reflect the level of conflict and uncertainty in their environments. Thus, whether constraints on rule making arise legislatively or administratively would appear to depend on transient historical factors and not on any fundamental characteristics of agencies.

Conditional strategies are naturally attractive to agency leaders because they guard against ill-considered action by lower-level personnel. An automatic decision review process can reduce the influence of low- and middle-level bureaucrats (who for reasons of inexperience, greed, or sloth might be pursuing their own goals at the expense of their superiors) at the expense of increasing the agency's cost of operation and decreasing the speed at which actions can be promulgated. This will tend to increase the control that those higher in the agency have over their own fates. Because of the attractiveness of such strategies, they are frequently used, so frequently, in fact, that one can speak generally of a *structuring principle* by which is meant the general tendency of the decision review processes of administrative agencies to exhibit certain characteristic structural features.

The use of conditional strategies implies that the pattern of agency decisions will exhibit a charactistic bias. If controversial issues are placed in a separate review process from those that are noncontroversial and the number of review points for the issues in the former category is increased, agency output is likely to be substantively biased in the direction of producing decisions or regulations or projects that do not attract significant opposition from the surrounding actors. In other words, to the extent that most potentially affected interests are able to voice objections to proposed courses of action, agency actions are likely to be protective of the status quo and, in that respect, conservative.

To the extent that unconditional strategies are chosen, the output of the agency is likely to be either negligible (if the review process is very long) or so controversial as to threaten the legislative mandate of the agency itself (if the review process is relatively short or if it is insensitive to various politically important interests in the environment). Thus, the choice of conditional strategies is characteristic of "successful" agencies: those that are able to make decisions that are not reversed elsewhere in the political or legal system and that enjoy both budgetary tranquillity and an unchallenged legislative mandate.

The principle of agency structure has both static and dynamic implications. If an agency is in long-run equilibrium relative to its environment, it will tend to be structured in a way that reflects the forces in that environment. To the extent that the community of potentially affected interests is large and diverse, agencies will tend to adopt more formal or representational methods. On the other hand, those agencies whose actions largely have an impact on small and homogeneous groups will rely on informal methods for anticipating objections. In other words, the static version of the structuring principle is that the complexity of an agency's review processes will reflect the heterogeneity of its environment.

From a dynamic perspective, when an agency's environment becomes more heterogeneous the agency review processes will increase in length, formality, and complexity. For example, if Congress or the courts make it possible for previously unrepresented interests to bring suit against an agency, the agency will tend to restructure its review process in such a way as to learn of the views of this group in advance of litigation. A good recent example of this is the impact of the National Environmental Policy

Act (NEPA) on the structure of construction agencies such as the Corps of Engineers.[10]

Agencies can make mistakes or misjudgments. They may fail to develop an adequate structure for anticipating sources of opposition to potential actions, and these actions may subsequently be reversed by the courts, the president, or the Congress. Worse yet, Congress may itself choose to utilize the structuring principle (it is an organization too) in order to protect its members from ill-considered actions in an agency, as is argued by McCubbins and Page in Chapter 15. A well-known example of this is the attempt to employ the legislative veto in order to review proposed actions of the Federal Trade Commission. More frequently, as Calvert, Moran, and Weingast suggest in Chapter 19, the regular authorizations and appropriations processes provide methods that are used to review agency actions.[11] Agencies that fail to make use of the structuring principle will tend to have their legislative mandates reduced or even disappear. Agencies that use the principle in an indiscriminate way will simply be moribund, as was the old Federal Trade Commission (FTC) or as is, for practical purposes, the Office of Toxic Substances at the Environmental Protection Agency.

A corollary to this obervation is that agencies that survive for a long time should be expected to have adaptive characteristics. Bureaucratic survival implies that an agency has developed an "adequate" (i.e., conditional) decision review procedure for its environment. Younger agencies may not have had time to develop fully satisfactory review processes and so may tend either to have unconditional review processes (and be inactive) or to have their decisions constantly overturned in the courts or Congress. In any event, their review procedures should display more variance. In other words, older agencies should be relatively likely to be in long-run equilibrium whereas newer ones may not yet have fully adjusted (and may never be able to adjust) to their environments. This observation may have consequences for the empirical study of agency behavior.

The next section contains a discussion of the general characteristics of agency environments in which attention is paid to how these environments vary both in the cross-sectional and longitudinal senses. At that point we try to see how the structuring principle applies to agencies with a variety of types of legislative mandates.

AGENCY ENVIRONMENTS

Each agency is surrounded by its own set of groups and governmental institutions. These groups include what are often called clientele groups, professional organizations, the press, and other sorts of interest groups.

The structure of agency decision processes

The institutions include the Office of Management and Budget, the courts, the committees of the House and Senate, and the president as well as various other agencies. Besides these organizations, some agency environments may contain elements of state, local, or foreign governments. In a sense, each agency has its own niche, its own collection of groups that pay special attention to its activities and can affect the ability of agency members to achieve their goals. One should therefore expect the decision structure chosen by an agency to reflect the particular characteristics of its niche.

Administrative agencies are located in contexts that permit the appeal of specific agency decisions in a variety of forums. If it is sufficiently unfortunate or unwise, an agency can suffer severe consequences in these exterior forums; it can see its decisions reversed, its budget reduced, its mission shrunken or even eliminated. For this reason, if an agency head wishes to achieve programmatic or personal goals he or she must be aware of the necessity of maintaining the capacity to make effective decisions. And this necessity drives the agency in the direction of devising structural or automatic methods of anticipating potential sources of opposition to agency actions.

This discussion suggests that there are several sorts of characteristics of agency environments that can affect their behavior. The principal ones seem to be these: First, the collection of groups potentially affected by the activities of agencies varies both cross-sectionally and intertemporally. Which interests are affected by agency actitivies depends on exogenous social and economic factors as well as on the legislative mandate of the agency. Some agency environments contain a great many potentially affected groups that are in substantial conflict with each other about desirable courses for agency actions. Elsewhere in this volume, Roger Noll examines the effects of these diverse forces on the choice of regulatory mechanisms (Chapter 18).

Second, the congressional environments of agencies vary widely. Congressional committees and subcommittees do most of the overseeing of agency activities, and their makeup is typically determined through processes of self-selection. This usually produces homogeneous committees but on occasion produces some that are severely divided with respect to ideology.[12] In addition, the makeup of an agency's supervising committees influences the access of private groups to its decision processes. If its authorization and appropriations committees have homogeneous preferences with respect to its actions, groups that diverge from this consensus are likely to be ignored.

Third, national-level political actors such as the president, aspirants for presidential office, the press, or others may be specially interested in agency activities in certain circumstances. This special attention may be due to the nature of the agency's mission, to its activities, or to occurrences extraneous to the agency itself.[13]

Finally, the legal fabric applies very unevenly to agencies. Some find their conduct severely limited by the Administrative Procedures Act (APA), the NEPA, or by their own enabling legislation whereas others operate in an environment characterized by much less legal constraint. Moreover, various types of proposed actions are treated distinctly in the courts. Administrative rule-making proceedings, for example, tend to be more closely scrutinized than case-by-case adjudications.[14]

Holding constant other factors, it seems likely that variations in agency environments will affect the operation of the structuring principle in several ways. First, where the set of groups that might be affected by agency actions is relatively homogeneous, the agency review procedure should be sensitive to the desires of these interests. Thus, actions that might adversely affect these groups would tend to be "slow-tracked" or simply not pursued. To the extent that an agency failed to adapt in this manner, at some point in its history interested groups might attempt to gain control over the selection of top-level agency personnel through congressional or executive channels or even seek to reduce the effective mission of the agency in some way or other.

Second, variations in the makeup of the congressional committees supervising an agency that cause certain groups to have more and better access than others should be reflected in variations in the structure of the decision procedures. Changes in the overall pattern of recruitment to committees, electorally induced changes in the composition of Congress, court-ordered shifts in apportionment, all might be expected to have effects on the decision-making structure.

Third, a president can affect the decision review process in a variety of ways.[15] In the most direct sense, his appointees might force the restructuring of the review process by fiat. But, more subtly, the president can signal attention to agency activities, thereby escalating the costs of ill-considered actions. A good example of this was Carter's emphasis on deregulation. By giving presidential attention to the conduct of certain regulatory agencies, in particular the Civil Aeronautics Board (CAB), and by putting people sympathetic to these ideas in the agency, Carter made it possible for these agencies to undertake actions that earlier review procedures might have derailed. In particular, the CAB was able to promulgate rules in the face of substantial opposition because the president had indicated a willingness to use his resources to support these actions is a variety of ways and to reward those who performed as he wished in the area. The result of this change in the environment was a dramatic and rapid change in the activities of the CAB during Carter's administration. It is not clear, however, what effect the previously established review procedures will have on the operation of the agency when the president's attention is withdrawn.

Finally, it sometimes happens that a court decision or a legislative act substantially changes the legal context in which an agency is operating. Good examples of this have already been mentioned and include changes in the law relating to standing to sue, the passage of the APA and the NEPA. The impact of these changes has generally been to change the relative costs of litigation to various groups and thus to increase the likelihood of court review of agency action. The agencies should be expected to respond to such changes by increasing their ability to anticipate objections to their proposed decisions by the newly "enfranchised" groups. Perhaps the classic example is the response of the Corps of Engineers to the passage of NEPA. The Corps went well beyond what was required in NEPA in experimenting with "open-planning" methods as well as other techniques that involved opening up the project decision process to environmental groups. This response might be interpreted as a recognition of the changed political and (especially) legal opportunities open to these interests.

APPLICATIONS TO VARIOUS TYPES OF AGENCIES

If agency environments differ, so too does the nature of the tasks that agencies face. This variation is likely to affect the strategic choices of agency leaders. Some agencies are charged with assisting the development of local communities, others with regulating economic activities, others with producing services or levying taxes, and still others with distributing benefits to individuals. Rather than attempting to discuss the whole range of agencies, we shall restrict our attention to two broad types of agencies: operating and regulatory. Unfortunately, the diversity of agencies within these categories is sufficiently great that the discussion must retain a flavor of abstractness.

Regulatory agencies have extremely diverse missions. Some deal mostly with a single industry or with a small group of industries, whereas others are charged with regulating a very broad range of economic activity. Some engage in rate setting or allocation of monopoly rights for a single industry; others are concerned with monitoring the side effects of some industrial activity in a variety of industrial settings. Not only do they differ in the scope of their missions, but regulatory agencies exercise their authority in many distinct ways. Some, like the National Labor Relations Board, proceed by case-by-case adjudication almost exclusively; others issue broad quasi-legislative rules and attempt to enforce them in a variety of ways.

The diversity exhibited by the regulatory agencies is more than matched by the operating agencies. Any of them may engage in a variety of activities, including managing projects, operating entitlements programs, or passing out grant money to states or localities, among others. When discussing operating agencies it is useful to think of them in terms of their major programs. Thus, the Corps of Engineers is regarded as a operating agency because much of its traditional activity involves the construction of water projects, though it does engage in significant regulatory activity as well. The Veterans Administration is best seen as an entitlements agency even though it engages in construction activities, too. This simplification will allow a rather concrete discussion of stylized agencies rather than a more qualified discourse about real ones.

The structuring principle in operating agencies

The actions of construction agencies are potentially controversial in the localities affected by a proposed project. Beyond that, if a project could affect environmental or aesthetic values it is possible that some nonlocal group will take an interest in minimizing this impact. Additionally, construction agencies are favorite targets of groups interested in good or "efficient" government (including the much-feared economist's lobby).

Project planning processes in the construction agencies have historically been sensitive to local interests potentially affected by a project. Indeed, in some agencies the process by which projects are proposed requires the direct involvement of local interests together with their political representatives along with the local agency representatives. In addition, either Congress or the agency may seek further evidence that opposing views have been sought out by imposing formal requirements of local "participation," which may entail land acquisition (with the attendant use of powers of eminent domain).

In such a system it is not inaccurate to say that project planning amounts to local coalition formation. If there is significant opposition to a project in the locality, the major planning requirement is to neutralize or even bring local opponents into the coalition by adjusting the physical configuration of the project. If the interests affected by a proposed project are geographically contained, it is possible to extend access to the planning process sufficiently that this form of coalition formation is viable.

However, over the last few decades, Congress and the courts have gradually enlarged the set of interests that are entitled to express their objections to proposed agency actions either through legal challenges or through access to the congressional units that oversee the agency. Such interests now include those who do not live or work near the proposed project site and who have aesthetic or ecological concerns. Not surprisingly, these changes have had the effect of changing the project planning processes in fundamental ways. In particular, it is no longer sufficient for the coalition formation process to operate on the local level since there may be significant opposition to the project that is not represented in the locality. Moreover, it is not clear that the traditional methods of project design offer enough flexibility to accommodate this broader range of interests.[16]

Agency responses to this situation may be understood in terms of the operation of the structuring principle. The NEPA required project agencies to prepare environmental impact statements, which were intended to force agencies to consider information about the potential alterations in the environment that might be caused by a project. The requirement that such reports be prepared and that the necessary information be generated prior to their preparation forced agencies to add several steps to their project planning processes. Additionally, the preparation of the reports led to the introduction of clearance processes to review and "sign off" on the reports. Each of the stages in report preparation and clearance offered potentially affected groups opportunities to express objections to the project. This allowed the agency to anticipate objections and to identify potential opponents to a project and to find ways to accommodate these objections in the planning process.[17]

In addition, the affected agencies increased the number of environmental specialists on their staffs in order to develop an internal capability to anticipate environmental objections. Mazmanian and Nienaber report that the Corps of Engineers increased its staff of environmental specialists by a factor of six in a period of a few years immediately following the enactment of NEPA. Additionally, the agencies typically restructured themselves formally, adding environmental units in Washington, in the field, or in both. These units were generally given responsibilities in the review process, and the effect was to increase the number of review stages through which a proposed project was required to pass.[18]

The structuring principle and regulatory agencies

Although the actions of a construction agency have their strongest impact in a particular locality, the consequences of a regulatory agency's action tend to be felt by particular economic actors who are geographically dispersed. Some decisions have an impact on one or a few firms whereas others have consequences for a whole industry or even for a large segment of the economy. To some extent, the agency itself can determine the scope of its actions by deciding to regulate through case-by-case adjudication rather than through rule making.

453

But, though regulatory agencies may wish to limit the scope of their own decisions, the courts and the Congress have something to say about this, too. Through changes in the interpretation of the enabling statutes or by imposing broader procedural requirements on agencies, the courts have repeatedly acted to enlarge the set of interests that are entitled to take part in regulatory proceedings or to seek judicial review of agency decisions. Similarly, congressional committees have, on occasion, served as an appellate or review body for the actions of some agencies, sometimes pushing for broader regulations, sometimes chastising agencies for making rules of broad application.

The best-known recent examples come from the FTC, but Congress has indicated a willingness to intervene in other arenas of potential regulatory action. Interestingly, in the FTC, congressional intervention occurred when the agency chose to utilize rule making rather than case-by-case proceedings (as in the cases of children's television and the proposed regulation of funeral homes), the traditional regulatory tool used by the agency since its inception.

Because they face the possibility of legal or political challenges to their actions, regulatory agencies utilize two methods of decision making to minimize the probability of such interventions and to limit their impact when they occur. By now these are familiar. Some agencies, such as the Social Security disability program, try to minimize the chances of external intervention by resorting to case-by-case adjudication, which has the effect of narrowing the scope of individual decisions. Others, like the Occupational Safety and Health Administration (OSHA), utilize the structuring principle: They employ a decision review process that locates potentially controversial decisions and modifies or delays them to take account of opposition. Such review mechanisms tend to lengthen the decision-making process and to discriminate the controversial decisions from those that do not attract serious opposition. And, as suggested earlier, controversial actions are likely to be continually postponed if not deferred indefinitely.

Whichever strategy an agency adopts, those groups with "standing" to challenge agency decisions, either in the courts or in Congress, find it relatively easy to get the agency to take account of their stakes in agency decisions. In this sense the legal and political context in which the agency makes regulatory determinations can induce it to take account of the interests of those with politically or legally recognized interests in agency decisions. Here, regulatory bias occurs not because the regulators share any tangible interests with those being regulated but because the regulated are privileged to appeal those agency decisions they oppose. To the extent that changes in the legal or political context alter this arrangement, there will be a change in the pattern of regulation. Thus, court decisions that give consumer groups standing in challenging regulatory actions will be reflected in changes in the procedures of the regulatory agency itself.

IMPLICATIONS FOR PUBLIC ADMINISTRATION IN A DEMOCRACY

The problem of accounting for the role of administrative agencies in a democratic system has concerned students of the diverse fields of administrative law, public administration, and American politics. From the standpoint of each of these scholarly pursuits, the proper balance between the exercise of administrative discretion and legislative policy formation is hard to strike. Is an agency merely to act as a neutral "transmission belt" translating the legal expressions of the legislature into decisions on particular cases?[19] Or is it instead supposed to operate a surrogate political process that has the purpose and effect of "adjusting the competing claims of the various private interests affected by agency policy?"[20] And, if it turns out that the second possibility is the only practical one, what then becomes the distinction between the legislative and administrative processes?

Lately, political scientists have generally answered this question by responding that there is no essential difference between the two processes. Administration is just legislation by other means. Agencies make policy in the same sense that Congress does and are only as subordinate to the other constitutional organs as the requirement of maintaining political support dictates. Indeed, much of modern political science does not perceive a clear boundary between Congress and the agencies. Rather, agencies are seen as linked to their supervising committees and subcommittees and to their external clientele in an "iron triangle" or "subgovernment." The relevant delegation of authority is not therefore from Congress to the agency but from Congress to its committees and subcommittees.

Cynicism about the political nature of public administration has not, however, led to a surrender of critical perspective on administrative processes. If administrative processes are just as "political" as legislative ones, they suffer from some special defects as modes of policy formation in a democratic society. The most important of these are that administrative processes tend to contain more discretion, to be less transparent, and to permit less public participation than legislative or judicial processes.[21] Together, these defects produce a situation in which people outside the process find it relatively difficult to learn when and where and on which grounds decisions are being taken that may affect their welfare. Thus, because access to administrative processes is costly,

455

the only ones who will choose to obtain it are those with the most to gain or lose from the decisions. This situation is, of course, fertile ground for "capture" or "bias" in administrative decision making. And this description of the administrative process is the basis for the democratic critique of administration.[22]

If the democratic critique of administrative processes and the theory of agency behavior on which it is based had flourished only in the halls and seminar rooms of the nation's political science departments, judges and legislators might have contented themselves with treating administrative agencies pretty much as they had for the last century. Laws giving authority to agencies would have designated a confined area for the exercise of agency discretion, and the courts would have kept to their traditional role of permitting challenges to agency actions only on the ground that some traditional liberty or property right had been infringed. Everyone would know, of course, that agencies were legislating within their bailiwicks, but traditional rights would be protected against transgression by the application of established judicial doctrines.

For reasons that are well beyond the scope of this essay, however, the democratic critique has transcended its academic cradle and come to form the basis for a reworking of congressional, presidential, and judicial behavior vis-à-vis the administrative agencies.[23] What was this reworking in the political and legal environments of agencies, and how was it manifested?

As it became widely recognized that agency policy-making processes were biased toward those with substantial stakes in agency decisions, two alternative courses of action seemed to be attractive. Agency discretion might be restricted by the imposition of clear and unequivocal rules, made by Congress in enabling legislation, by the courts through narrow construction of legislative delegation, or by the agency itself by a strict interpretation of its legislated mission.[24] Alternatively, the constitutional organs might deliberately insert themselves into agency decision processes in such a way as to counterbalance or correct their inherent biases. To varying extents, both of these courses of action have been followed.

Each of the constitutional branches of government has tried to restrict delegations of authority to agencies by requiring that they be more detailed and precise. Thus, the past two decades have witnessed passage of the voluminous Clean Air and Clean Water acts and their amendments, in which Congress prescribed in great detail just how the EPA was to go about achieving the goals of the acts and set specific conditions and deadlines for industry compliance. Delegations of congressional authority and court decisions have also forced agencies to be much more careful about formulating and adhering to rules of internal procedure and to explain these rules to those interested in their proceedings. Within the executive branch, successive presidents have limited delegations of authority by imposing requirements that agency decision processes take account of inflation or other broad social goals in carrying out their authorized mission.

These attempts to limit the discretion of administrative agencies must fail. The political nature of public administration is rooted not only in the constitutional structure but in the interests of incumbents of all descriptions. Neither judicial pronouncements nor legislative perorations will persuade men to forgo the pursuit of their own interests as they see them.

The constitutional branches have also endeavored to enlarge and balance the set of interests able and willing to participate in agency decision processes. Several of the regulatory statutes passed in the last quarter-century contain explicit grants of hearing rights and judicial review to a wide range of individuals with interests in agency decisions. Moreover, Congress has gone as far as subsidizing interests thought to be systematically disadvantaged in agency decision-making processes, either by empowering some agencies or their parts to act as advocates in administrative processes or by methods of direct subsidy. The principal judicial endeavor has been to relax traditional rules of standing so that interests that were not previously recognized are granted rights to internal and external participation in agency decision making.

These changes have produced a discernible shift in the legal and political environments of the administrative agencies. In effect, administrative agencies are much more closely monitored by political and legal authorities now than they have been traditionally. The practice of judicial deference to agency discretion has given way to court involvement in substantive agency decision processes. The congressional practice of deference to committee-based supervision of program administration has also receded somewhat as Congress has developed practices that allow some degree of control of agencies by party majorities as well as by its standing committees.[25] Finally, successive presidents have developed practices and institutions permitting the review of proposed agency rules and procedures from the perspective of the national administration.[26] In effect, agencies have been forced to adopt hybrid forms of rule making in order to comply with the desires of their political masters. Moreover, as argued above, even where the agency is not required by external actors to adopt a hybrid form, it may well choose such a form for reasons of political prudence.

The evolution of congressional sentiment and legal doctrine in the direction of requiring agency procedures to take a hybrid form has produced a characteristic bias in agency decisions. The bias does not come from the various forms of venality such as the "revolving door" – the fact that agency leaders desire to work for regulated groups after they leave the public service – or from any monopoly of information by those most affected by agency action. Rather, the bias is produced by the fact that broadly formulated rules can generate broad opposing coalitions with an interest in preventing the imposition of the rule or at least delaying its promulgation. Such coalitions are powerful within the constitutional system, and so agencies naturally find it undesirable to arouse them needlessly. The structuring principle provides a safe and tested way to avoid doing so: by effectively putting all affected interests on the internal "road map" of decision clearance, the agency can avoid promulgating rules that threaten its basis of political support. In effect, this makes agency decisions hostage to consensus.

The result of this system of decision making is that difficult rules – controversial rules that require the coercive power of the state for their effectiveness – are continually revised and seldom implemented. The history of rule making in the environmental and safety areas area fully reflects the incapacity of the regulatory institutions to make regulations at all, let alone enforce the ones that exist. Rule making under the Consumer Product Safety Act of 1973 illustrates this difficulty. Though early members of the commission expected it to promulgate perhaps 20 mandatory safety standards a year, by 1984 the commission had managed to produce only six. And two of these were substantially struck down in the courts.[27]

Congress may enact "forcing" deadlines on agencies, and environmental groups may bring suit to enforce them, but Congress has not evidenced much willingness to do anything if the action-forcing deadlines are not met. Moreover, it is not yet clear what the courts will do with these provisions. On current evidence it appears that action-forcing provisions are largely symbolic and that everyone knows it.

It seems clear that the growing understanding of public administration has not yet equipped either the agencies themselves or other political institutions with a particularly viable manner for structuring their internal processes. Agencies can sometimes be successful if they restrict themselves to making relatively narrow determinations even if their legislative mandate is amorphous. Such agencies seem able to meet the requirements of legal viability and political support relatively easily. Their decisions, however, seem to many observers to lack the central quality of justice: that like cases be treated in like fashions.

But agencies that choose to pursue their missions by making public proclamations applicable to a broad range of cases seem to face much more difficult, perhaps even intractable situations. Broad concern with the relationship of agency decisions to democratic values requires that such agencies operate as surrogate legislatures. But, without either the legitimacy or the political independence of such bodies, the quality of rules they produce is biased toward consensus. Such a bias confers veto powers on those with a vested interest in the status quo.

NOTES

1 The notion of a decision-making culture in an agency is found in Robert Kagan, *Regulatory Justice* (New York: Russell Sage, 1978), and Jerry Mashaw, *Bureaucratic Justice* (New Haven: Yale University Press, 1983).

2 Thus, an agency charged with determining eligibility for and delivering benefits to a large subset of the population will be forced to define its internal procedures quite differently from one that has a mission of assisting the development of local communities.

3 As expressed in the deliberations over the Administrative Procedures Act as well as in the various acts that contain explicit provisions governing rule making.

4 Expressed in the *Vermont Yankee* v. *NRDC* (1978) decision. Justice Rehnquist, speaking for the majority, argued that the procedural requirements in the APA that govern informal or notice-and-comment rule making are to be construed as the "maximal procedural requirements which Congress was willing to have the courts impose upon agencies in conducting rulemaking procedures." If the courts were, instead, to "continually review agency proceedings to determine whether the agency employed procedures which were...perfectly tailored to reach what the court perceives as the 'best' or 'correct' result...the agencies...would undoubtedly adopt full adjudicatory procedures in every instance...all the inherent advantages of informal rule making would be totally lost." There remain substantial disagreements among judges and commentators on the desirability of the courts' requiring agencies to develop more complete records in the course of rule making which is governed by the APA. It is clear, however, that Congress is free to impose more stringent requirements on agencies by statute, and it has done so repeatedly in the past two decades.

5 The best-known illustration of this observation is found in the case of the regulation of natural gas producers by the Federal Power Commission. In 1954, the commission began to engage in traditional cost-of-service regulation of natural gas producers, which required the determination of allowable production costs for each producer as a basis for introducing a rate schedule. The first case to be decided, the Phillips Petroleum case, took 82 hearing days and thousands of pages of testimony. "By 1960, the Federal Power Commission had completed only 10 of these cases." This method of proceeding was seen to be altogether unworkable, and the commission undertook a rule making aimed at producing a rate schedule for whole groups of producers. Stephen Breyer and Paul MacAvoy, "Energy Regulation by the Federal Power Commission," in Stephen Breyer and Richard Stewart, eds., *Administrative Law and Regulatory Policy* (Boston: Little, Brown, 1979).

6 Congressional inquiries into agency handling of cases are usually not considered ex parte communications but are treated, instead, as "status requests." Constituents are encouraged to believe that these "status requests"

are, however, efficacious in gaining consideration by agency officials; indeed, when the Social Security Administration has received a congressional inquiry on a disability claim, it routinely notifies the congressman of the award before advising the claimant (Mashaw, *Bureaucratic Justice*, p. 71). Mashaw also reports that the Social Security disability program generates more than 100,000 casework requests per year (out of about 1.4 million new filings [p.59]). This figure contrasts with the 10,000 claims that are annually appealed to the courts.

7 Ibid., p. 213.

8 Ibid., p. 124. The rules referred to in this quotation were not the product of "informal rule makings," which have specific procedural requirements that must be met prior to their promulgation and which must be published in the *Federal Register* before they can take effect. Rather, the rules that were developed by the Cost of Living Council were what is called "interpretive guidelines," which do not yet have clear procedural requirements.

9 Court initiatives in this direction may have come to a halt with Vermont Yankee's affirmation of informal rule making. While recognizing Congress's right to impose additional statutory requirements on administrative procedures, the Court restrained judges from exploring these alternatives without explicit legislative authorization.

10 For a detailed account of some of the effects of the NEPA on project planning procedures, see Daniel Mazmanian and Jeanne Nienaber, *Can Organizations Change?* (Washington, D.C.: Brookings Institution, 1979).

11 See also Barry Weingast and Mark Moran, "Bureaucratic Discretion or Congressional Control: Regulatory Policy Making by the FTC," *Journal of Political Economy* 91 (1984):765–800.

12 See ibid., and Richard Fenno, *Congressmen in Committees* (Boston: Little, Brown, 1973).

13 See especially Terry Moe, "Congressional Control of the Bureaucracy: An Assessment of the Positive Theory of 'Congressional Dominance,' " paper presented at the annual meeting of the American Political Science Association, New Orleans, 1985.

14 See Richard Stewart, "The Reformation of American Administrative Law," *Harvard Law Review* 88 (1975):1667–1813, and Donald Crowley, "Judicial Review of Administrative Agencies: Does the Type of Agency Matter?," paper presented at the annual meeting of the American Political Science Association, New Orleans, 1985.

15 Moe, "Congressional Control."

16 In the case of the Army Corps of Engineers, there have been persistent efforts to find "nonstructural" methods of dealing with its traditional mission of controlling flood damages.

17 see Mazmanian and Nienaber, *Organizations*.

18 For a more complete account of the ways in which environmental specialists were introduced into the Corps's decision procedures, see Serge Taylor, *Making Bureaucracies Think: The Environmental Impact Statement Strategy of Administrative Reform* (Stanford: Stanford University Press, 1984).

19 This expression is taken from Richard Stewart, "Reformation."

20 Ibid., p. 1683.

21 This list of characteristics is drawn from Mashaw, *Bureaucratic Justice*.

22 The list of critics is long and distinguished and would surely include Elmo Schattschneider, *The Semi-sovereign People* (New York: Holt, 1960); Grant

McConnell, *Private Power and American Democracy* (New York: Vintage, 1966); and Theodore Lowi, *The End of Liberalism* (New York: Norton, 1969).

23 Whether the democratic critique was a cause of this shift or a convenient justification is not addressed in this essay. The fact that the argument became widely available to politicians and judges in the 1960s certainly would have allowed it to serve as a useful "explanation" for otherwise attractive courses of action, even if the argument had no real persuasive force of its own.

24 See Lowi, *End of Liberalism.*

25 The best known of these devices was the legislative veto, which allowed majorities in one or both chambers the opportunity to veto proposed regulations. Although *Chadah* v. *INS* invalidated many forms of the legislative veto, there is no question that Congress retains ample means to impose checks on agency authority to make and administer rules. On this point, see Barry Weingast, "A Principal Agent Perspective on Congressional – Bureaucratic Relations," *Public Choice* 44 (1984):147–192. More generally, as congressional decision making has migrated from committees to subcommittees, the practice of chamber deference to committee proposals has waned.

26 Among these devices are the "inflation impact statement" and the regulatory review group.

27 Terrance Scanlon and Robert Rogowsky, "Back-Door Rulemaking: A View from the CPSC," *Regulation*, July/August, 1984, pp. 27–30.

18

The political foundations of regulatory policy

ROGER NOLL

Since 1970, scholars in economics, law and political science have produced important new insights about the political causes of regulatory policies. Like much of the work in applied economics, research on the political economy of regulation normally addresses a specific policy question in a specific country, and hence, implicitly or explicitly, takes as given a particular set of political and economic institutions. Most of this research is by Americans, and so is based on assumptions about the political system that hold in few countries. Examples are the separation of powers between the executive and legislative branches of government, the special features of the American Constitution (especially the due process amendment), and the structure of the American legislative system. Consequently, the generalizability of this work is dubious.

This paper provides a step towards a more general political economic theory of regulation. First, it discusses the ways in which alternative political institutions (e.g. proportional representation versus single-member geographic districts as a means of electing a legislature) might affect regulatory policy. Second, regulatory policy will be examined in a broader context than is usual, but not so broad that it encompasses essentially all governmental activities. The purposes of both of these extensions are to internationalize this field, and to facilitate international comparisons of related policies.

The premise of this paper is that a general political economic theory of regulation can provide useful insights about how policy is formulated, and perhaps even about how more effective policies might be adopted. This view is controversial. Some disagree with any attempt to internationalize the study of political institutions such as regulation. Many

Reprinted from *Journal of Institutional and Theoretical Economics Zeitschrift für die gesamte Staatswissenschaft*, vol. 139, no. 3 (October 1983): 377–404. Exceptionally useful comments on an earlier draft were provided by Bruce Cain and John Ferejohn.

scholars of comparative political and economic systems believe that the values, cultures and political structures of countries are so different that attempts to generalize across national boundaries are worse than useless – they are perilous, for what appears to work in one context is likely to be disastrous in another. Another source of controversy is the belief that a comprehensive political theory of regulation for a specific country is a useful pursuit. For example, Wilson (1980) argues that no useful political generalizations across regulatory policies are likely to prove true. Of course, negative propositions cannot be proved, so these dissents amount to a warning that general theories of political behavior bear the burden of proof: they must provide nonobvious, empirically verifiable insights.

This paper does not attempt such a proof. It is conceptual, not empirical; it is designed to raise questions and suggest lines for further theoretical and empirical research.

The analysis builds upon the existing literature that explains changes in regulatory policy in terms of attempts by organized interest groups to obtain a favorable redistribution of wealth. It departs from this approach in several ways. First, it incorporates mass political movements, organized by political entrepreneurs, as a potential countervailing force against organized interest groups. Second, it examines the role of uncertainty and incomplete information in decisions made by voters, political actors, and bureaucrats who implement regulatory policy. Third, it takes account of how different electoral institutions may produce different incentives for political actors in selecting among alternative policies.

The paper reaches several conclusions that are at variance with received wisdom. One is that the distributional orientation of regulation is not primarily due to the influence of organized special interests, but is a characteristic of representative democracy. Second, in the long run regulation may be less sensitive to particularistic distributional pressures than other types of public policies. Third, the political conditions that lead to cartelization by regulation should also lead to subsidies of the cartel. Fourth, the variance in regulatory policies in relation to the exhibited degree of protection of particularistic interests should be lower in countries that elect legislators by proportional representation, rather than from single-representative constituencies; however, the mean effect on regulatory policies is indeterminate, as is the effect of parliamentary systems in comparison to independent executive and legislative branches.

The theoretical argument is laid out in Section II. A necessary preamble is to state the definitions and assumptions on which the theoretical argument is based. These are laid out in Section I. Section III provides a summary and conclusion.

Roger Noll

I. PRELIMINARY DEFINITIONS AND ASSUMPTIONS

In developing a political theory of regulatory policy, a necessary first step is to define regulation. For the most part, the literature on regulation typically adopts a relatively narrow definition: regulation consists of policies that are intended to correct for market failures by the promulgation and enforcement of rules constraining the behavior of some or all of the participants in a market. The litany of market failures includes natural monopoly, incomplete information, and external effects. An even more narrow definition requires that the rules be written by a regulatory agency – a bureaucracy established for dealing with particular regulatory issues. Neither definition includes policies that are regarded as alternatives to regulation, such as corrective Pigovian taxes and subsides, new laws regarding liability and negligence, nationalization and public enterprise, the creation of new property rights and a market for exchanging them, such as, for example, marketable permits to emit pollutants, or legal self-regulation by industry of various forms, including European corporatism, the National Recovery Act in the U.S. during the 1930s, and Italian syndicalism from the same era. For our purposes, the broader definition of regulation is required. Moreover, the scope of analysis must include these alternatives to regulation.

The essential feature of microeconomic models is that they focus on principles governing choice among alternatives. The decision to change regulatory policy can usefully be separated into three steps. The first is the decision to take some action that alters the performance of a class of economic activities, where performance here refers to both economic efficiency and the distribution of wealth. The second step is the selection of a policy instrument from among the ones listed above: taxes, subsidies, public enterprise – or regulatory rules. Third, once political decision makers have decided to select rules, they must decide how much authority to delegate to an implementing organization. At one extreme, a regulatory law can contain detailed rules of behavior, leaving a bureaucracy the problem of enforcing the rules and perhaps elaborating and clarifying them, but giving the agency very little opportunity to make policy. Alternatively, the law may contain very vague, general instructions to the agency, delegating to the professional bureaucracy, and even to the courts, the responsibility for constructing the behavioral rules. The latter choice gives the agency or the court a substantial role in developing regulatory policy.

Regulation, of course, is not alone in having this three-step characteristic. For example, public enterprises can be more or less closely controlled by the political process. An example is the obvious differences among Western democracies in the autonomy of national broadcasting entities. In the United States, the postal system underwent a transition in the 1970s from a cabinet department that was very closely controlled by the political process to a virtually independent public enterprise that is overseen by a new regulatory agency, the Postal Rate Commission.

An important challenge to the political economic theory of regulation is to provide insight about the rationale for decisions at each stage. When analyzing the first stage – a decision to intervene at all – the theory must incorporate the full range of policy instruments that can be used to change the outcome of a target set of markets. Hence, in his influential paper on the economic theory of regulation, Stigler (1971) adopts a definition of regulation that includes almost all forms of government activity, including commodity-specific taxes (the whiskey tax), tariffs and import quotas, certain kinds of subsidies (airport subsidies to benefit airlines as well as industry-specific subsidies, as in agriculture), some kinds of public enterprise (airports are typically owned by government entities), and the more prosaic forms of regulation (controls on prices, entry, product quality and packaging, workplace safety, land use, and emissions of pollutants).

When analyzing choices at the second and third levels – what form of instrument to use and how much authority to delegate – a further challenge arises. We need to understand how the political implications of these choices differ.

The behavioral assumptions

The microeconomic approach to political decisions not only is a theory of choice, but it presumes that the choice is rational and purposive – that its purpose is to obtain some valued end. For political leaders, the objective is presumably to enhance their future political power. Usually this is taken to be to maximize a politician's chances of remaining in power; however some may be motivated by improving their chances to advance to a political position having greater power and status. In any event, the key point is that political incentives govern the choice of policy objectives, policy instruments and assignments of responsibility for making detailed policy decisions among political leaders, the bureaucracy and the courts. Consequently, political economic theory must include a theory of the political consequences of each of these choices: the political implications of the outcomes to be expected from a choice of instrument and delegation.

The roles and powers of elected political leaders, bureaucracies and courts appear to differ substantially among nations, causing potentially important differences in the implications of a decision to create a regulatory authority. In the United States, the Constitution sets forth important limitations to the procedures adopted by regulatory agencies, the authority of the legislative branch and its ability to delegate, and the rules an agency can promulgate. The Constitution guarantees citizens equal protection under the law, and due process in matters that affect them significantly. The implications for regulation are that decisions must be based upon substantial evidence, affected parties must be given the right to participate in the process by submitting evidence and argument in support of their interests, decisions of an agency must be logically derived from its legislative mandate, and decisions are subject to judicial review should any affected party believe that these requirements have not been satisfied.

In other countries, regulation need not be so cumbersome and decision makers so constrained; however, statutes can include complex procedural requirements and extensive judicial review. Even in the United States, agencies differ in the extent to which authorizing legislation imposes procedural constraints beyond the minimum constitutional requirements. In each case, the question remains as to what political incentives cause a particular form of delegation and procedural requirements.

The assumption that the primary incentive operating upon politicians is political security and/or advancement requires some further elaboration. In Western democracies, political success depends on the electorate. Hence, a political economic theory of public policy must be built on a theory of elections and, in particular, the relationship between policy and voting behavior. This in turn requires behavioral theories of both voters and candidates.

Political economic theory assumes rational choice behavior in elections, as elsewhere. Voters are assumed to engage in political activities (voting, volunteer work, contributing to campaigns, lobbying) as part of their quest to maximize their welfare, subject to a budget constraint. Government can supply public and private goods, affect the prices and qualities of private goods supplied by others, and alter personal income through taxation, through transfer payments, and by affecting factor prices. Political economic theory assumes that voters select a strategy for political participation that takes account of the many ways in which the political process can affect their welfare.

The principal importance of the structure of the political system is through its effects on the choices available to voters and the relative importance of the various activities of government in affecting political participation. As explained in Section II, the relative importance of parties versus individual candidates for legislative office plays a central role in political economic theory. So, too, does the constitutional difference between parliamentary government versus separation of powers between legislative and executive branches.

The rationality assumption about voters is another point of controversy concerning economic theories of political behavior. The alternative view is that voting behavior is affective and has no policy significance. Each voter is identified with a rung on the socioeconomic ladder, and with full information votes for the party or candidates on the same rung. But information is incomplete, and so, as Edelman (1964) argues, voters can be misled by emotional appeals and symbolic issues. Elections then become competitions for power among elite groups; policy making divides the spoils among elites, rather than responding to the wishes of the electorate. Some hold that this makes the study of elections and voting behavior largely uninteresting and certainly pointless from a public policy point of view. The implications for regulatory policy are essentially Marxist: symbolically, regulation may be represented as a device for protecting the population from monopoly or some other market failure, but in reality it is a means for maintaining a cartel arrangement for a ruling elite (see, for example, Kolko (1963) on American railroad regulation).

At one level, the competition between the two theoretical approaches ought to be resolved by testing which better explains the development of public policy. Having competing theories is healthy for the advancement of scientific knowledge, for it sharpens hypotheses and empirical tests. At another level, however, the two approaches have less difference than might appear at the surface. As long as political parties are not symbolic entities that create the illusion of competition in the reality of a unified, homogeneous elite, competition among parties for informed, competing elites is a candidate for study using the rational choice approach. Perhaps many voters do not engage in political participation on the basis of rational choice; however, elections are decided, so to speak, "at the margin" – by the voters who have a stake in the choice – as long as parties compete and elite groups have conflicts of interest. In such a world elections may have little normative significance because many voters face little or no real stake in the outcome. But elections will have significance in deciding which directions policy will take among competing elites. This makes studying the electoral foundations of public policy worthwhile. Even after the revolution, it will be useful to know how the character of policies differs among different democratic processes.

The final important group of actors in the policy making drama is civil servants – the bureaucrats who are not elected. The tenets of economic analysis require that they be endowed with personal objectives which they rationally pursue. Unfortunately, there is considerable disagreement as to what bureaucrats maximize. The candidates are job security, permanent income (including the possibility of being hired by better-paying private sector organizations), and political advancement. Another view is that the issue can be finessed: the bureaucracy can be assumed to execute more or less perfectly the commands of the political leadership. At the opposite end of the spectrum, Niskanen's (1971) influential theory assumes that agencies maximize their budgets (or discretionary budgets), and that they possess so much power that they act as monopolists at appropriations time. This implies that bureaucrats reap most of the profits from regulation. In the American system, the regulatory agency sets a "price" for regulatory services to the legislature that strips the median legislator of all potential political gains from a regulatory program, and successful legislators must set a monopoly "price" to the interest group that seeks regulation. In a parliamentary system, the analog would be that the bureaucracy strips the government of any political gains from regulation by forcing a corresponding rise in taxation to finance the agency.

In this paper, we will assume that neither bureaucrats nor political leaders possess monopoly control over public policy. This is an assumption of inconvenience: it requires that political economic theory includes both bureaucrats and politicians, and leaves as an empirical matter ascertaining their relative influence. As further inconvenience, no restrictions will be placed on the motives of bureaucrats: they may seek security and the quiet life, greater political power within one agency or through promotion to another, or greater economic rewards in the private sector. The implications of each type of behavior will be explored in Section II.

The preceding discussion has set the stage for the next section. In summary, the important definitions and assumptions are as follows. The political economic theory of regulation deals with, first, the decision to intervene in a market, second, whether to use behavioral rules or some other policy instrument, and third, the decision about how much authority to delegate and how elaborate a procedural requirement to impose. Regulation refers to one form of altering the performance of a market: by promulgating and enforcing rules governing some aspect of the production, qualitative attributes, entry and price of an economic good that is bought and sold by others. All of the relevant actors in the theory are assumed to be rational and to be motivated by self-interest, whether voters, elected politicians, bureaucrats or people participating in regulated markets.

II. THE POLITICAL ECONOMIC THEORY OF REGULATION

If political officials are rational, the decision to regulate must be based upon a realization of the performance characteristics of regulation. These effects can usefully be classified as generic, applying ubiquitously, or particularistic, affecting a well-defined subset of society.

Breyer (1981) has introduced the notion of match and mismatch between regulatory objectives and the choice of a policy for achieving them, with a mismatch occurring when the regulatory method is not effective for attaining the objective. Breyer's concept is based upon the idea that regulation is for the purpose of correcting market failures, but here no such assumption is made. Our concern is why the choice of regulation matches political incentives operating upon elected decision makers, regardless of the match with normative economic theory. Thus, the political economic theory of regulation must begin with a characterization of what political officials are likely to expect if they decide to undertake regulation – even regulation that is an economic mismatch.

The effects of regulation

The most obvious characteristic of regulation, one that deserves mention for completeness but does not require elaboration, is that it must change the economic efficiency of a market to which it is applied. It must do so because it imposes costs: the requirements that regulated firms provide information to regulatory officials, keep informed about regulatory requirements, and maintain internal systems for assuring compliance (or, perhaps, optimal noncompliance). Even if regulation imposes a nonbinding constraint, the paper work requirement alone alters the equilibrium in the regulated market; however, again applying a rationality assumption, it is implausible that an agency would be established to impose nonbinding constraints. If regulatory constraints are binding, the net efficiency effect of regulation can be positive or negative, depending on the extent to which it actually ameliorates a market failure and the costs it imposes in doing so. These effects can usefully be thought of as the comparative statics effects of regulation: the net surplus generated by a change in policy.

The second characteristic of regulation is its effects on dynamics: the speed with which a regulated market adjusts to a new equilibrium in response to changed conditions (demand, availability of resources, technological change, etc.). Regulation slows change. It does so by creating an extra step in the process whereby an economic agent adjusts to changed circumstances. The ways in which regulation retards change vary according to the type of regulation, but all methods retard entry. Potential entrants must receive approval from regulators, a time-consuming process that also entails announcing intentions to incumbent competitors.

Although retarding rates of change is normally regarded as detracting from economic efficiency, Owen and Braeutigam (1978) point out that it does not necessarily do so. By retarding change, regulation reduces uncertainty. Exogenous shocks that upset market equilibrium are public goods, and can impose a net cost. One element of cost is associated with risk aversion, but there are others. Fluctuating markets may require frequent recontracting or other means of introducing flexibility into long-term relationships between buyers and sellers. If renegotiation is costly – or if people do not like to bargain – a process that retards adjustment to changed circumstances can produce net benefits, even if it also results in reduced short-run efficiency.

The third characteristic of regulation is that it creates and destroys wealth. Analytically, this is nothing more than restating the other characteristics: changing the efficiency of a market and its response to changed circumstances affects the wealth associated with a market. But the wealth effects of regulation go beyond its efficiency aspects. First, they are more particularistic: regulation can redistribute wealth among various participants. Second, regulation can create or redefine property rights that may or may not have efficiency consequences, but that determine the identity of those who capture the surplus generated in a market.

The mechanisms by which regulation creates and destroys wealth are numerous, and are laid out more completely in Noll and Owen (1983). Here we will use a few examples to illustrate the general process. For instance, by retarding entry, regulation creates a property right in the status quo that has market value equal to the costs of gaining regulatory approval to enter. In addition, regulation benefits suppliers who are more adept at participating in the regulated market (number of firms, price, quality of product, available production method) than at the unregulated equilibrium. For example, if regulations serves to increase product quality, firms adept at producing high quality goods will experience a windfall when regulation is imposed. The expansion of regulation also enhances the wealth of entrepreneurs who are adept at dealing with the government – elected politicians, regulators and courts – in comparison to those whose primary skill is in understanding production technology and market demand. Thus, regulated industries will, over time, evolve with different sets of winners and losers than would be the case in the absence of regulation. Consequently, in an industry that has long been regulated, some of the wealth of incumbents will depend on the continued presence of regulation.

A fourth characteristic of regulation relates to the process by which regulations are established and enforced by regulatory agencies. Although there are important differences among Western democracies in the limits placed on decisions by elected political authorities and by bureaucratic decision makers, the latter are generally more constrained than the former. More specifically, regulatory agencies are more constrained by evidence than are legislatures and other administrative organizations. (Here the term legislature is used in a general sense as the representative body that votes on legislation. It includes parliaments and other bodies that are controlled by party orgainizations, as well as autonomous legislative bodies.) Evidence is generated by two principal sources: the agency itself, and participants in the regulated market who supply the agency with information, some of which may be supplied voluntarily.

The dependence of regulatory agencies on evidence gives rise to rules regarding the weight accorded to evidence, the evidentiary requirements to sustain a court challenge to a decision, and the rights of outsiders to participate in the process (e.g. rules of standing). In this regard, regulatory processes are more court-like than legislatures or other kinds of bureaucracies; however rules of evidence and standing in courts usually are more strict than in regulatory proceedings.

The significance of procedural requirements is as follows. First, they affect the costs of effective participation: one must prove that the standing qualifications are satisfied, and must submit information that satisfies evidentiary standards. Second, they affect the potential benefits from participation: because decisions depend upon evidence, a failure to participate runs the risk that no evidence will be submitted in support of a favorable decision, even if the agency is disposed to make it. Third, they affect the character of participation: in contrast to procedures with less strict evidentiary rules (like legislatures and most other forms of bureaucracy), technical information has a relatively higher value in comparison to more informal, personal activities, such as lobbying. Thus, economists, engineers, lawyers and scientists are more influential in regulatory decisions than in legislative activities or most other forms of executive decision making.

The fifth and last characteristic of regulation is that the act of creating a regulatory agency and embarking on a new regulatory program does not necessarily require that there be immediate winners and losers in the political struggle. When legislation is passed, its opponents can be regarded as having lost; however, as Fiorina (1984) argues, what they have lost, and whether there are compensating gains, is conjectural. Consider the range of approaches available to control pollution. When regulatory laws are passed, a polluter can expect higher costs of production in the future, so in that sense can be a loser. But the stringency of regulation, generally and in each specific case, remains in doubt – and depends upon evidence and argument to be supplied to the regulator. Moreover, once a firm has had standards adopted for its

471

emissions, it has a *de facto* property right in a valuable resource – the use of waterways and airsheds to dispose of waste. This is not available to potential entrants until they, too, can run the regulatory gauntlet – with, in all likelihood, more stringent requirements being applied to them than to incumbent firms. By contrast, consider two widely discussed alternative strategies for dealing with pollutants: an emissions tax or stricter laws regarding public nuisances. In both cases, all polluting firms can expect losses, and there will be no partially offsetting benefits in terms of the creation of barriers to entry. Indeed, to the extent that entering firms face generally lower abatement cost functions, either policy could enhance the prospects of entrants. Thus, the passage of either type of legislation is an immediate loss for the losers.

In the economic regulatory domain, an alternative to regulation is public enterprise, either by nationalizing existing companies or creating a publicly-owned competitor. Once again, this is more clearly a threat to companies in the industry than would be the creation of public utility regulation to control their prices and profits.

Although each of the five characteristics of regulation holds true to some extent for all policies undertaken through a regulatory bureaucracy, each is, to a degree, under the control of the political leadership through the details of the legislation establishing the policy. The following examples illustrate means to vary these characteristics.

– The extent to which regulatory policy serves economic efficiency objectives can depend on whether regulators are required to undertake mandatory benefit-cost analyses of proposed rules.
– The degree to which regulation slows change depends on whether legislation creates a legal monopoly or contains a presumption in favor of competition, and on whether it writes rules related to performance or with respect to inputs and entry into a market.
– The manner in which regulation distributes and creates wealth depends on whether it sells or gives away its implicit property rights, and whether it has a budget for compensating losers.
– Factors affecting the weight of the evidentiary burden of an agency include its internal budget for research and analysis, the vagueness of the legislative wording of its policy objective (greater detail requires a greater burden of proof that a rule carries out the legislative mandate), and the grounds other than minimal constitutional ones that are written into legislation as a legitimate basis for appealing decisions to the courts.
– Legislation can create identifiable losers by specifying a set of minimum rules that clearly hurt someone, rather than by delegating the responsibility for writing the first generation of rules to the regulatory agency.

Political foundations of regulatory policy

In the analysis to follow, we shall assume that political actors are generally aware of these characteristics of regulatory policy, so that, given the rationality assumption, the decision to regulate represents a conscious attempt to implement a policy having these characteristics. Again following the motivational assumption, the rationale for regulation is that it is in the self-interest of legislative leaders to pick this type of policy.

The theory of participation

To identify the conditions under which regulation (or deregulation) is a rational political act in a democracy requires a theory of citizen political participation. In rational actor theory, the focus is on how citizens allocate scarce resources among political activities, assuming that they rationally pursue self-interest. We focus on participation in political activities, realizing that there are unspecified trade-offs between political participation and other ways to use resources (to generate income, to buy products, to engage in leisure). In the sense used here, political participation covers a variety of activities: voting, lobbying political leaders, contributing resources to parties and candidates, participating in policy making processes (such as regulatory proceedings), and initiating legal challenges to unfavorable policies, including regulatory rules.

Imagine each citizen as solving an optimization problem involving the use of two scarce resources: time and wealth. The citizen's objective is utility maximization, subject to budget constraints on wealth and time. Among the arguments of the utility function are goods provided by government, whether public or private. Entering the budget constraint are factor prices that depend on government actions, taxes and subsidies, and contributions to political organizations. The time constraint also incorporates allocations to political activities.

Regulation enters the optimization problem in several ways. First, regulatory actions affect the arguments of the utility function by changing the quality of private goods and the consumption of externalities. Second, regulatory actions enter the budget constraint by changing factor and product prices. Third, because regulatory actions are affected by political participation, the benefits and costs of participation in regulatory policy making must be taken into account. This requires making regulatory actions a function of a citizen's political participation, and including participation costs in the budget and time constraints. Of course, other policy instruments are incorporated into the optimization problem in the same way.

Although forms of political participation are numerous, we will focus on four categories: voting, contributing to parties and candidates, taking

473

part in the policy making process (lobbying, participating in regulatory proceedings, appealing government decisions to the courts) and participating in organizations that engage in political activities. This list is not exhaustive; for example, it ignores policy research and articles or speeches intended to convince voters to favor a policy. For most citizens, however, the list includes the important relevant alternatives.

Voting behavior

The most important characteristics of voting are that it is cheap and that it is a low information process. Voting consists of sending a simple dichotomous signal to parties and/or candidates, each of which offers a complex combination of positions and other relevant characteristics such as integrity, administrative capability, and ideology. Each vote has little effect so voters have little incentive to allocate effort and resources in fine-tuning adjustments about ballot alternatives, other than to the extent that acquiring political knowledge is an enjoyable consumer good.

These features of voting have several important consequences. First, voters will pay attention to few issues in an election. Second, most issues will be expressed at high levels of generality, incorporating several related policies. Examples are the overall performance of the economy, the general state of international affairs, the leadership qualities of candidates and party leaders, and ideology. More specific issues (health care, education or regulation) can become salient issues – but few will achieve this status. Third, because information is sparse, campaign strategies involve providing selective free information and establishing the agenda of the debate.

In this milieu, the rational voter first asks what policies are most important to his or her welfare, and then examines historical records and information from mass media, interest groups, candidates and parties to decide how to vote. One element of the calculation is the provision of government goods – defense, health care, education. Another element is particularistic government activities. Government employment and procurement is the direct source of a substantial fraction of income. Government also affects income through taxation and regulation. Expenditure programs may supply public goods that enter many utility functions, but they do so by awarding contracts and employing workers. The latter characteristics are more concentrated than the former, so that winners and losers on the expenditure side have more per capita welfare at stake in a program than do consumers of the public good.

Regulation also has a diffuse impact on the users of regulated products, and a concentrated impact on people who earn income in the regulated industry. Regulatory cases can be highly particularistic, like procurement, if they apply to a specific firm; however, much regulation is more general, consisting of rules to guide case-by-case decisions. Rules are in part a public good with exclusion. Part of the effect is shared by people whose income is collectively and simultaneously affected by them.

Rational voting decisions must be based on both aspects of government. For each person, government will have a shared, diffuse effect through general taxation, public goods, and prices of widely-purchased goods, and particularistic effects, entering primarily through the budget constraint. If voters believe that elections are equally important in deciding both generic and particularistic effects, and posses equal information about both, they will weigh each equally in evaluating competing candidates and parties. But the likely case is that votes give greater weight to particularistic effects.

One reason is that voters are unlikely to be equally well informed about all issues. Because voters will not bear much cost to become informed about an issue in which they have low personal stakes, they are likely to have uneven information across issues. In the aggregate, the importance of each category of public good may be very high; however, for a voter who is dependent on the state for contracts or through regulation, the importance of the latter is likely to be larger. Hence the incentive is greater to be informed about the implications of the election on a particularistic action. Political leaders respond to this situation by claiming credit for income-producing actions of government when communicating with the lucky winners.

Regulatory policy illustrates these general characteristics. If regulation attacks a market failure, it provides diffuse benefits to numerous voters. In some cases, such as environmental regulation, voters may easily perceive a great stake in the issue; however, most regulatory policies are narrow and have a small per capita impact on citizens. The per capita stakes of people in a regulated industry are much higher. Consequently, when the generic issue of regulatory policy is not salient, the income side of regulatory policies will have more electoral significance than the correction of market failures.

The relative importance of particularistic versus generic issues in voting decisions is likely to depend on the form of government system. Consider two extremes in the spectrum of organizing a representative democracy. One is separate legislative and executive branches, with legislators elected from single member constituencies, such as in the United States and France in the Fifth Republic. The other is a parliament elected by proportional representation from party lists which are selected and ordered by a central party authority. The former provides legislators with an opportunity to be autonomous from parties if they are popular with constituents. Collectively, these legislators have an incentive to

475

construct a legislative process that enables them to provide services to constituents so that they can claim credit for particularistic actions (contracts, construction projects, etc.). A rational voter will then see a representative as a relatively powerless single vote on generic policy issues, but a monopolistic supplier of particularistic favors, as explained in Fiorina and Noll (1979). If a legislator functions effectively in this role, challengers will face a great barrier in winning an election, for their ability to provide favors will be conjectural against the proven ability of the incumbent. Thus, legislators will downplay their role in generic (and especially controversial) public issues, and emphasize their role in obtaining particularistic favors.

In a parliamentary system with nationwide proportional representation, the close pairing of generic and particularistic issues is inescapable. Even here particularism is a potent political force: concentrated effects are more likely to have electoral consequences than are diffuse ones. Consequently, parties will behave like individual representatives in the other system: constructing a process for dealing directly with particularistic interests and communicating particularistic accomplishments. But all citizens will have access to alternative routes for particularistic favors (in some sense all parties can supply favors, not just a single incumbent). Moreover, parties, unlike specific legislators, can not argue simultaneously that they ought to be in power on particularistic grounds and that they are powerless in establishing generic policies.

In parliamentary systems, single-representation districts are more prone to particularism than proportional representation. Parties can solidify power by allowing members of parliament to become favorites with their districts. One way to achieve this is to make them ombudsmen. For example, Cain, Ferejohn and Fiorina (1983) show that British MPs actually spend more time doing constituency service than do members of the U.S. House of Representatives.

The effect of an independent executive is more conjectural. Independence makes legislators more prone to particularism, even under proportional representation, because they are not as accountable for generic policies. But an independent President can not rely as much on favors for specific constituents, owing to the legislature's function in writing laws and making appropriations. The exception is a very powerful presidency, such as in the Fifth Republic, that controls the agenda of the legislature and, therefore, can claim credit for every legislative action.

From the perspective of the voter, an independent executive offers the prospect of escaping from the prisoner's dilemma created by the legislature. Collectively, citizens can recognize that all are better off if particularism does not drive government policy. Individually, voters are better off voting for candidates and/or parties that supply favors to them. A candidate for chief executive, running separately from the legislature, can promise to implement the cooperative solution: to run against the behavior legislators are prone to pursue. Thus, an independent executive has two effects operating in opposite directions, with an uncertain qualitative resultant: it makes the legislature more particularistic, but the executive less so. The net result depends on the details of the separation of powers between the two branches.

The conclusion to be drawn from voting theory is that it is more sensitive to particularistic, distributive issues than to generic public policy questions. Exceptions occur when the performance in a specific area of policy becomes sufficiently poor that, as a generic issue, it becomes salient. This requires one of two eventualities. First, the diffuse generic effects become high enough, per capita, to become an important element in voting behavior. Second, an entrepreneurial party or candidate pays the informational costs of bringing an issue of lesser (but significant) import to the attention of voters. These routes are not totally independent: *ceteris paribus*, a rational political actor will pick up a new issue according to its per capita impact. But they are not the same, either. Elections being relatively low information processes, the attractiveness of a new issue to a political entrepreneur depends on its amenability to presentation to voters in a simple yet dramatic form. Favorites are dollars of gross waste in a program, and horror stories about how some group profits at the public's expense.

Voting and regulation

The implications for regulatory policy are as follows. Recall that regulatory legislation need not create identifiable winners and losers. The law can be specific, imposing a cost on one group or legalizing a monopoly for another, or it can be vague, moving into the regulatory forum and later the courts the ultimate decision as to who wins and who loses. The political context in which regulatory policy arises should play a role in determining this choice.

When regulatory legislation creates identifiable winners at the expense of diffuse losers, such as when it creates a monopoly, the corresponding electoral state should be that the regulatory policy in question has not achieved generic political salience. Thus, legislation creating occupational licensing or agriculture marketing orders should be the result of pressures from a particularistic constituency in the face of ennui in the general electorate.

When regulation creates diffuse winners at the expense of identifiable losers, the electoral foundation should be a salient generic issue, probably

477

placed on the political agenda by a political entrepreneur attempting to enhance his or her power by creating a new public issue with which he or she can be identified. The opposition should be relatively weak, disorganized particularistic groups.

When regulation delegates decisions to a regulatory authority and the courts, shifting to another forum, a case examined by Fiorina (1984), a pivotal number of legislators should face unavoidable controversy. If the issue is not generic, particularistic interests are in conflict. If it is generic, it threatens enough powerful particulartistic interests so that the issue creates an electoral dilemma for politicians. Conceivably, the generic, diffuse issue could be inherently controversial (abortion, monarchy, or the independence of church and state); however, market failures usually lead to consensus on the desirable direction of regulatory policy.

Political contributions

In many ways, voting and contributing have the same motive, so require little separate analysis. But unlike voting, direct contributions to parties and candidates can register intensities of preferences by the amount of resources given. They are also more likely than voting to relate to particularistic rather than generic issues. One reason is that contributions have a higher threshold level of importance that must be crossed to motivate action. Moreover, generic issues pose a more difficult free-rider problem for contributors than do particularistic issues. The former require smaller contributions from a larger number of people because small contributions are consistent with the diffuse stake citizens have in generic issues. The latter may pose no free-rider problem: a regulated monopoly or a firm with government contracts views contributions as essentially private arrangements with no free-riding beneficiaries.

The role of contributions varies enormously among countries. It is determined by the rules regarding campaign expenditures, the duration of campaigns, and the relative importance of parties in relation to individual candidates. In countries in which campaign expenditures are important and individual contributions are loosely controlled, the force of particularistic issues is enhanced. Making the government the source of campaign resources is not obviously an improvement. If expenditures are important in campaigns, elected leaders have an incentive to control public resources to their benefit, and so to stack the deck against potential political competitors, whether ambitious politicians within a party or new parties. Because political entrepreneurs bring generic issues onto the political agenda, denying them resources can prolong, if not perpetuate, particularistic control of an area of policy, including regulation.

Participation in policy processes

A third form of participation is to enter forums for making policy decisions: lobbying political leaders, taking part in an administrative proceeding, or appealing legislative or regulatory outcomes to courts. Like contributions, these forms of participation provide a means for reflecting intensities of preferences, for they can be pursued with varying cost and effectiveness. Like contributions, they overrepresent particularistic interests, in part because of a higher threshold of stakes and in part because private actions to alter public policies benefit other, similarly situated people and so face the free-rider problem.

Lobbying is most like contributing; indeed the two are closely associated. People may contribute to candidates to gain access if the need arises, or may promise future resources while lobbying for current support. Moreover, lobbying has few rules and no evidentiary standards.

Regulatory and legal proceedings have a strong element of substance. Effective participation in these forums requires marshalling facts and logic in defense of a favored position. Consequently, effective participation has a minimum of fixed costs, depending upon the technical content of the issue and the number of opposing positions that are represented. The fixed costs correspond to the minimum effort required to marshall relevant facts and an effective presence during a proceeding. Thus, the threshold of stakes for an issue to motivate participation in these proceedings is higher than for other forms of participation. Moreover, the free-rider problem is also more severe. Preparation for participation in a formal proceeding requires generating relevant information for presentation to decision makers. This information is a public good for all who are on the same side of the issue. Hence, participation in these forums faces free-rider problems on both the cost and the benefit side.

All of these phenomena contribute to enhancing particularistic influence in regulatory policy. Regulatory processes, because they stand at the extreme in the number of steps in decision making and in formal evidentiary requirements, present the most formidable fixed cost barriers to effective participation. But one factor working in the opposite direction is that decisions must satisfy higher standards for rationality than in other political or bureaucratic processes – assuming that regulatory officials actually satisfy them, either for some fundamental reason or because a disgruntled loser may challenge their decisions in court.

The relative importance of this feature of regulation varies according to how the regulatory process is constructed. One dimension of choice is case-by-case versus general rules. If a regulatory authority adopts only vague general policies, leaving most of the action to specific cases,

479

particularistic forces are enhanced. The objects of regulation – say, firms engaging in pollution – have had their side of the free-rider problem ameliorated, for each will face a narrow case in which its welfare is on the line. The generic interest, however, will be diffused over cases, much as pollution results from the combined effects of several independent sources. Case-by-case decisions will have no effect on the incentive of a polluter to participate on the specific issue applying to it, but will substantially reduce the incentive of environmentalists to participate because victory in one case contributes little to environmentalists' overall objective.

The case-by-case method also makes it easier for regulatory authorities to discriminate among parties. Proceedings that produce general rules require the agency to make specific exceptions if it seeks to favor a special friend. This places a red flag on aspects of the decision that are unequal or exceptional. Because more participants are likely to emerge in a general proceeding, those who seek a special favor are more likely to find opposition. Hence, to the extent outcomes depend on participation and evidence, the agency will be less able to provide particularistic favors.

Another aspect of agency process is the details of procedural requirements and court review, an issue explored by McCubbins (1983). Agencies vary according to number of stages in the decision process, formal legal requirements, and grounds on which reviews by courts are possible by appeal – or even required. Procedural complexity increases the costs of participation in ways unrelated to substance. They protract proceedings (increasing the opportunity cost of participation and delaying its benefits) and increase expenditures on purely representational functions, as contrasted to generating new information for regulators. Procedural complexity, then, filters out some potential participants whose lower stakes do not justify the higher participation costs of a more complex process.

Still another structural dimension is the availability of resources to the agency in relation to the caseload it faces and the technical content of its responsibility. Examples of resources an agency can possess are a technical bureaucracy for independent research and analysis that participates in the agency's proceedings; a communications bureaucracy for disseminating information about agency rules, cases in progress, and technical issues; and a budget for subsidizing participants in its proceedings. An agency that has these resources is obviously more likely to generate evidence opposed to particularistic interests.

All of these structural features can be controlled by political leaders. Thus, they should reflect the political environment that gives rise to regulation. An agency that has cumbersome procedures and few internal resources should reflect a political intent to benefit regulated firms, or at least to minimize the number of competing interests with which the agency must contend. The corresponding political situation should include a strong particularistic interest and only generic interests that are too diffuse to be represented in the detailed design of the regulatory bureaucracy. Generic interests organized by political entrepreneurs are prone to this problem, for obtaining a change in regulation, not designing its implementation, is the simple, dramatic political opportunity.

The old idea of regulatory capture corresponds to this situation. Both particularistic and generic elements are present in establishing the agency, but the agency is organized to be oriented toward the particularistic. By contrast, regulation to form a cartel – say, occupational licensing – requires no staff, but neither does it require cumbersome procedures. Generic interests play no role in its formation, and are unlikely to participate even in an inexpensive regulatory process. Politicians have no reason to impose unnecessary costs on the cartel, and so make the process as cheap as possible, focusing resources on enforcing, rather than writing cartel rules. In the extreme, the regulatory authority need not be governmental. For example, as discussed in Berger (1980), some governments, notably Sweden, pursue corporatism, endowing peak associations (labor unions, trade associations) with regulatory powers that escape bureaucratic process altogether. In the United States, the cartel-like Interstate Commerce Commission (ICC), which regulates surface transportation, gave substantial rate-making power to regional trade associations.

A second situation giving rise to cumbersome procedures and few resources is conflict among strong particularistic interests which will participate effectively in regulatory processes. Elaborate procedures distance political leaders from outcomes that are offensive to strong interests, and sparse resources avoid appropriating funds to produce offensive studies. Cumbersome procedures mitigate against participation motivated by diffuse or weak particularistic interests. An example in the United States is the National Labor Relations Board, which regulates collective bargaining. In labor disputes, unions and management are active participants; cumbersome procedures keep out people experiencing secondary effects (consumers, unorganized workers); the structure allows politicians to escape blame from losers.

A process that is rich in resources and procedurally simple invites maximal participation, and hence is minimally particularistic. It should occur when the political environment finds multiple interests that are conflicting, have varying stakes in the issue that make participation sensitive to costs, and are each a political threat. The rich resources are a response to a salient generic political issue or a weak particularistic one. The agency can then provide information that otherwise would not be presented.

The combination of resources with procedural complexity represents a response to still another situation. It limits participation, and gives the agency more independence of action. Thus, it should be a response to conflict between a highly salient generic issue and powerful particularistic forces in a situation in which only the latter is likely to participate, regardless of representation costs.

The magnitude of the effect of resources depends in part on what motivates bureaucrats. The nature of civil service is one in which opportunities for advancement and, especially, financial reward are relatively limited compared to private sector organizations. One can imagine three reasons for pursuing such a career: risk aversion, leading to a strategy to avoid being noticed and hence penalized; power or professionalism, rather than personal advancement, implying independence (perhaps arbitrariness, perhaps pursuit of professional norms); or subsequent opportunities, in politics or the private sector. An agency satisfying the capture or cartel characteristics would be attractive to two types: the risk averse, who seek a quiet, noncontroversial arena, and the power seeker who wants to serve the particularistic purpose of whatever interest controls the agency. The other goals, whether entrepreneurial or professional, require an environment in which one can show independence and demonstrate proficiency at solving problems. The size of the agency also will play some role. An agency that is rich in resources will be more hierarchical to maintain internal control, and hence will offer more opportunities for career advancement, within the limitations of government service. Moreover, it will have the potential to be a mobilizable support group for an internal entrepreneur.

To a political leader, granting substantial resources to a supposedly captured agency is a needless risk. The particularistic interest can supply the information necessary to support its position in court; any attempt to subsidize the cartel by transferring analytic capability to the public budget runs the risk of losing policy control to an entrepreneur or a group with a professional norm of public service, however defined (for economists, surplus maximization; for engineers, technical advancement; for lawyers, preservation of equities and procedural fairness). Because a strong analytical capability invites mischief, rationality requires that it be, for the purpose of countervailing, the force of those most likely to be represented in the process.

Participation in interest groups

Thus far, the analysis has proceeded under the maintained assumption that political participation of all forms is purely individualistic rather than collective through an organization. This method of argument is intentional – to demonstrate that particularistic tendencies are a natural part of individualistic political processes even in the absence of organized interest groups. Most of the literature on the political economy of regulation begins with the role of interest groups, creating the impression that somehow interest groups cause the problem of particularism. This conclusion is incorrect; democratic processes create genuine prisoner's dilemmas for citizens that political leaders can exploit to their advantage. Nevertheless, interest groups play an important role, especially in regulatory politics, so to ignore them completely would be as misleading as to focus sole attention on them.

Interest groups represent a means for collective acquisition of public goods – the political outcome itself, which is simultaneously acquired by the members, and the information and representation that are required to affect the process. Group cooperation allows members to avoid duplication in acquiring, say, a competent demand analysis for submission into a regulatory proceeding. Pooling of resources also makes groups a greater threat to decision makers, and hence more worthy of their scarce attention.

From the perspective of participants, groups also have costs. First, they must become organized and reach decisions on what position to take and how to share costs. Second, if preferences of members differ, the positions advocated by the collectivity will be at variance with at least some members' most desired position, so that the latter will be less exactly represented by the group than if they each remained fully independent.

In addition, interest groups, like all collectivities, need to overcome free-riding incentives. Some members will seek to avoid joining if they perceive the success of the group to be largely independent of their participation and if the group can not exclude nonmembers from its benefits. Members who join have an incentive to play strategic games in internal decision processes regarding cost-sharing and position-taking so as to maximize their net gains from membership.

These characteristics of interest groups have important implications about the kinds of groups that will be represented in political processes. This issue has been extensively analyzed by Olson (1965) and, for groups in regulatory policies, by Noll and Owen (1983). The effect of groups on regulatory outcomes constitutes the heart of the theory of regulation developed by Stigler (1971), Posner (1974) and Peltzman (1976). Hence, this discussion will state only the most important conclusions of this work.

1. If two collectivities have the same total stake in an issue, the smaller one will be more likely to be organized into an interest group, all other

things being equal, because it will have lower organization costs and less incentive to free ride.

2. If two collectivities are otherwise the same, the one having greater heterogeneity of tastes will be less likely to be effectively organized because it will face higher organization costs and, on average, lower expected payoff.

3. If two collectivities are otherwise the same, the one that can exclude nonmembers from some benefits of the organization will be more likely to become organized and, if both are organized, will devote more resources to political participation, because it will have lower organization costs and fewer free riders. A corollary is that groups already organized for another purpose, such as club-like organizations providing private services to members, have an advantage over people whose only common interest is a shared political objective.

4. All other things being equal, a collectivity will be more likely to organize effectively if the stakes of each member of the group are known with certainty than if they are uncertain. Uncertainty enhances the opportunity for strategic behavior in group decision making and, assuming risk aversion, reduces the expected utility from participation. A corollary is that it is easier to organize to defend the status quo than to change it, assuming the expected stakes of proponents and opponents of change are equal and the groups are otherwise identical.

5. Citizens are more likely to support organizations representing particularistic (income-generating) interests or issues in which public policy is perceived to be most distant from their ideal points (e.g. single issue mass groups) than to groups representing more generic interests because the former groups are likely to be smaller, are likely to involve a higher personal stake, are likely to be more homogeneous, are likely to be organized for another purpose, and are likely to present a relatively certain personal outcome if successful.

All of the analytical points regarding the identity of represented groups bear close similarity to the reasons why democratic processes have a strong particularistic flavor. This is not surprising, because interest groups are collectivities within the national collectivity, and so have similar participation incentives, and exist as a vehicle for undertaking more cost-effective political participation in that same national process. Less obvious is that their relative importance depends on political institutions, and varies according to the kind of public policy in question.

Consider first the most general issue, the effect of electoral institutions. Nationwide proportional representation, as opposed to single-representative constituencies, enhances the attractiveness of particularistic interests that are rich in electoral resources but poor in financial ones; that is, citizens' groups engaged in single-issue politics and containing a small fraction (but large number) of people that are very disgruntled by a specific policy. Such groups have little chance of gaining influence if they vote in winner-take-all constituencies and make no contributions to major parties or candidates, but have a chance if they are awarded seats on the basis of total national votes. If the number of splinter groups becomes large, they can become influential because no party appealing to a more hetergeneous constituency can achieve power on its own. An example of such a situation is the role of the religious fundamentalists in the Likud coalition in Israel.

The implications for regulation are certainly not obvious to me, but they are unlikely to be nonexistent. It seems to me that fragmentation of parties makes a generic movement relating to regulatory policy (or any other policy) less likely to succeed, but it also increases the number of particularistic interests that have power, some of which can represent more diffuse opponents of groups that might otherwise capture regulation. For example, the Greens in West Germany probably owe their political significance to the German system of legislative representation. They act as a radical counterforce in environmental policy to particularistic interests that might use environmental regulation as a device for enhancing their wealth by becoming protectionist of established interests. This could motivate the parties in power to undertake a more balanced and efficient environmental policy; but it also reduces the possibility that a centrist political entrepreneur might adopt the generic of efficient regulation as a means for attracting political support. The reason is that without the Greens, the generic issue of regulatory reform would attract some of the Greens' supporters who would see this position as closer than the status quo to their extreme environmentalist interests. Thus, the presence of the Greens could improve the efficiency of environmental policy, but make less likely a more efficient policy, say, regarding prices and entry in telecommunications.

More obvious is the difference in regulation and other kinds of policies in their sensitivity to particularistic interest groups. Weingast, Shepsle and Johnson (1981) have provided a useful model for analyzing the relationships between economic efficiency and particularism in the standard areas of public policy: expenditure programs and the structure of the tax system. The principal insight is that political calculations by parties and candidates count some of the costs of a program as benefits – namely, the income-creating actions that help a loyal constituency at the expense of a constituency one would not have anyway. Particularistic political benefits are essentially linear in dollar payoffs, and are awarded in proportion to votes and contributions from particularistic interests.

485

This is the process that members of the Chicago School are modeling: regulatory benefits, like other government goods, are sold in relation to the amount contributed, as explicitly analyzed by Peltzman (1976). This seems to make regulation no different than other forms of policy.

But the straightforward interest-group, supply-demand analysis overlooks two important differences between regulation and more prosaic forms of government means to supply particularistic benefits. One is that the process consumes resources of interest groups that could otherwise be spent on parties and candidates. The other is that the decisions are constrained by process and evidence, simultaneously limiting the maximum effect of participation and attenuating the connection between politics and decisions.

These aspects of regulation are necessary even if it is purely particularistic. Stigler (1971) correctly notes that cartels need regulation to prevent entry. But this can be accomplished quite cheaply, as with occupational licensing or corporatism. It does not explain why regulators and regulated firms are required to devote resources to any activity other than licensing and enforcement.

Compared to other areas of public policy, regulation has a high fixed cost of participation, but beyond the expenditure necessary to present one's case, decreasing marginal returns to further information. Thus, if other interests find it worthwhile to pay the fixed costs against a very well endowed participant, the result will not necessarily be very closely related to the actual or potential amount any group did or could spend in the process.

This leads to the conclusion that regulation can be either more or less particularistic than other programs, depending on the underlying politics and representation. The payoff function to participation has a minimum efficient scale that depends on how cumbersome regulation is. Hence, regulation can be made highly particularistic – freezing out all but one interest. Cumbersome agencies with no significant resources can be used to weaken already weak groups that might have more influence in, say, tax or subsidy policies. Nevertheless, we should expect subsidies to accompany regulatory cartels and capture: if an interest can buy an agency, it can also procure subsidies. In the United States, this seems to be borne out. The high point of airlines cartelization through regulation was during a period of general subsidization; the ICC was created in the same era that granted the railroads extensive rights-of-way from the public lands; price and acreage controls in agriculture are accompanied by massive subsidies; and the period when the ICC cartelized trucks also witnessed governmental subsidization of a national highways system.

By the same argument, regulatory processes that are battlegrounds among contending interests should not be associated with subsidies or other forms of particularism. One does not see, for example, a pattern of subsidies and special tax credits for polluters in parallel with environmental standard setting.

A final aspect of regulation that seems to set it apart is that cause and effect between policy and the formation of interest groups is partly reversed for regulation. Regulation provides a means and incentive for creating interest groups.

After regulation has been in place for a long enough period to affect the structure of an industry, two phenomena emerge. First, expertise at dealing with regulatory, legal and political processes becomes important to a firm's financial performance. People who manage regulated firms will have a strong interest in preserving the regulated status of the industry, even if regulation is not serving the industry's interest, because it enhances their productivity. Prior to regulation, these people will not know who they are; however, once regulation is in place, they will be a well-defined group that can easily organize to lobby for continued regulation.

Second, because regulation creates inefficiencies – high-cost firms are protected, some customer groups are charged favorable prices, product quality shifts away from the competitive equilibrium – firms will have an interest in preventing a disruption of the regulated equilibrium. Suppliers may not benefit from the regulatory perturbation, but they will have investments in place that are predicated on serving the market in the way regulation drives the system. In seeking to protect these investments, they will support the status quo because reforms to improve efficiency would cause a short-term capital loss. Thus, regulatory politics can have the peculiar history that firms fight the imposition of regulation when it is proposed, but then later fight to prevent deregulation or a more efficient form of regulation. In the United States, truckers fought the adoption of the 55 miles per hour speed limit during the energy crisis of 1973–74, and are now fighting repeal of the same law. In the intervening years, lower speeds (and the implicit capacity reduction they caused) induced entry, which would become excess capacity (and would lower incomes to truckers) if speeds were raised.

Like subsidies, tax benefits and general expenditure programs, regulation provides particularistic benefits, but more than other programs it creates interests that are unidentified when regulatory policy is enacted. One person's inefficiency, whether a regulation induced cost or a corporate vice presidency for government affairs, is another person's income – and a competitively-determined income at that, not a scarcity rent created by an artificial entry barrier.

Also like other programs, the force that threatens particularism in regulation is a political entrepreneur who uses inefficiency as an element

487

in raising a generic political issue. Regulation is more vulnerable than other policies to this kind of attack. In addition to the distributional aspects of particularism that it shares with other programs, it creates other inefficiencies as well: higher production costs, dead-weight losses, and procedural costs for participants in its processes. Consequently, among particularistic policies, regulation stands near the extreme in the difference between the losses imposed on losers and the benefits conferred to winners. Of the relevant alternatives to regulation, civil litigation is arguably the only one that is a less efficient method for allocating wealth.

This has several consequences. If an important subset of losers is relatively easy to organize, the difference in impact provides an extra incentive to do so that may make the difference – and thereby create the counterforce against particularism. It also makes regulation a good target for a political entrepreneur looking for mismanagement, inefficiency and favoritism to raise as a generic issue among the more diffuse, heterogeneous groups of losers. The subset of losers that is organized may help the cause by contributing.

Hence, regulation that becomes protectionist creates the conditions for its own reform; at some critical point, the redistributional effects plus the inefficiencies become sufficient to cause a backlash. The location of this critical point depends on the specifics of the program: the size of the losses of the losers, the distribution of losses among them, and the ease with which the problem can be simply and dramatically expressed by a political entrepreneur. Whether regulation can make the list of salient issues also depends on what else is happening in the society. Regulatory reform is an unlikely issue during a war or period of extreme international tension, but it has a good chance if the international scene is relatively placid and the domestic economy is performing poorly.

A common objection against the self-correcting argument described in the preceding paragraph is that it seems inconsistent with economic equilibrium analysis. Why would a rational set of political actors institute a policy that was so inefficient that it caused a reaction against itself? Presumably an equilibrium point exists, goes the argument, whereby regulatory policy supplies exactly the amount of particularistic favors that is just below the threshold necessary to induce the reaction against the program.

The reasons that this argument does not hold are as follows. First, at the most fundamental level, elections and legislatures are majority-rule institutions, and these do not necessarily have an equilibrium. To be sure, as Shepsle's (1979) analysis shows, legislators have means available to protect against the instability of electoral institutions, whether the internal structure of the legislature in countries in which representatives are autonomous or the party system that predominates in parliamentary democracies. But these mechanisms delay more than permanently suppress disequilibrium. As Riker (1982) has cogently argued, the job of the political entrepreneur in the face of electoral instability is to identify new issues that will upset the status quo.

Second, random, exogenous events determine which issues achieve general political salience. Only in an expected value sense could political leaders calculate the regulatory policy that was optimally particularistic. Unless political leaders are extremely risk averse (and hence create regulatory policies that are not very particularistic), at some point external events would conspire to make particularistic regulation a generic political issue.

Third, a policy reversal in a particularistic program does not necessarily disadvantage the political leaders who created it. Recall that elections are low-information processes. Candidates do not make particularistic favors part of the public rhetoric of a campaign; generic issues occupy speech writers. Hence it is entirely possible for a politician who created a particularistic program to run against it later when its effects become a generic issue. This is especially likely to be the case in nations having independent legislative and executive branches, for then generic issues are likely to be fought out in presidential elections.

For these reasons, regulatory policy can have variable characteristics over time. It is unlikely permanently to facilitate a cartel; however, it is unlikely to be insensitive to organized, supply-side interests. It is also not likely to be consistently an important item on the national political agenda or an invisible political backwater.

III. SUMMARY AND CONCLUSIONS

Regulations was the source of a great deal of cynicism by academics during the 1960s and 1970s. The standard view was that regulatory policy was an evil conspiracy among politicians and select industries to construct an enforceable cartel. But at the peak of this cynicism, two developments took place that were inconsistent with it. One was the rise of environmental, health and safety regulation, which target industries almost universally opposed. The other was extensive reform and rationalization of regulation: deregulation in workably competitive industries that were subject to economic regulation and mandatory economic impact analysis for cases in which market failure is more plausible.

The political foundations of these changes are built of the same bricks that formed the foundations for the protectionism that caused the wave of academic cynicism. The same polity that gave the U.S. airline deregulation in the 1970s produced airline regulation in the 1930s, and a new economic regulatory agency – for commodity futures trading – simultaneously with the beginning of airline deregulation.

The key to understanding regulation is only partly in the heavy participation of organized, supply-side interests in the regulatory policy process. This can produce cartelization if others are asleep. But the rest of the story is that regulation is an extraordinarily cumbersome way to provide particularistic favors. Indeed, because its fact-finding and decision-making processes exhibit decreasing returns and make decision depend on evidence, they give other interests as good a chance as one can imagine in a political process. If the agency is given policy-making discretion, a simple process, and resources adequate to sift through the self-serving material submitted by represented interests, regulation is probably as removed from straightforward pluralist, interest-group politics as is possible.

Moreover, regulation has the potential for attracting general public attention when it goes stale. People genuinely believe the rhetoric that regulation is supposed to protect society from market failures. This means that they expect regulation to confer net social benefits: winners ought to gain more than is lost by losers. Regulation is also a sloppy form of cartel; if it becomes one, the inefficiencies tend to dissipate the gains of cartel members. This means that the losses of the losers are large compared to the gains of the victors, a situation that attracts political entrepreneurs.

In the economic regulatory sphere, most nations do not engage in extensive regulation of the narrow, technical form that is practiced in the United States. Among the alternatives is a nationalized entity, which suggests parallels to the American postal service: should the public enterprise be a ministerial office, directly run by the political process, or a quasi-independent authority that is regulated by a government bureau? Another possibility is corporatism, which lets industry regulate itself with loose ties to government.

The thrust of the argument in this paper is to favor approaches involving an intermediating, resource-rich agency. The reason is that the regulatory process provides some opportunity for checking the particularistic pressures that are missing in public expenditure programs or administrative methods lacking procedural safeguards. The argument of this paper is that, indeed, such a change will take place when the performance of ministerial public enterprise or corporatism gets bad enough, for some political entrepreneur will eventually sense the opportunities in raising the issue. In countries with parliamentary systems and with single-representative constituencies, like Britain, however, one can wait a long time before observing this event.

Political foundations of regulatory policy

With respect to social regulation, the conclusions from political economic analysis are as follows. Economic incentives – taxes and subsidies – are less attractive than economic theory implies. Both are more susceptible than regulation to particularism, whether implemented through case-by-case bureaucratic decisions or legislation. To be efficient, they must be applied differentially among industries and even firms, which opens the door to political determination of differences. A similar argument applies to greater reliance on civil litigation. It has high participation costs and requires case-by-case decisions.

Among the alternatives, the most promising is artificial markets for property rights in exposing society to risks, as examined in Noll (1983). This requires a process to define acceptable risk and to establish and enforce the property rights; however, markets allocate rights among producers of risks. The regulatory component is general rule-making; the decisions about how each firm will respond to rules are decentralized through a market. The first invites maximal participation; the latter avoids the step in which particularistic forces are most likely to be controlling. Normatively, this approach should be superior to current methods of regulation; positively, whether they will be adopted depends on how badly social regulation performs and how long it takes for the political environment to ripen so that reform becomes salient.

REFERENCES

Berger, S., (ed.) 1980. *Organizing Interests in Western Europe: Pluralism, Corporatism, and the Transformation of Politics*, New York.
Breyer, S. 1981. *Regulation and Its Reform*, Cambridge, MA.
Cain, B. E., Ferejohn, J. A. and Fiorina, M. P. 1983. "The Constituency Component: A Comparison of Service in Great Britain and the United States," *Comparative Political Studies*, 16, 67–91.
Edelman, M. 1964. *The Symbolic Use of Politics*, Champaign, IL.
Fiorina, M. P. 1984. "Group Concentration and the Delegation of Legislative Authority," in: R. Noll (ed.), *Regulatory Policy and the Social Sciences*, Berkeley, CA.
and Noll, R. G. 1979. "Majority Rule Models and Legislative Elections," *Journal of Politics*, 41, 1081–1104.
Kolko, G. 1963. *Railroads and Regulation 1877–1916*, New York.
McCubbins, M. 1983. *A Formal Model of the Form of Regulatory Intervention* (Paper presented at the Annual Meeting of the Public Choice Society), Savannah, GA.
Niskanen, W. 1971. *Bureaucracy and Representative Government*, Chicago, IL.
Noll, R. G. 1983. "The Feasibility of Marketable Emissions Permits in the United States," pp. 189–225, in: J. Finsinger (ed.), *Public Sector Economics*, London.
and Owen, B. M. 1983. *The Political Economy of Deregulation*, Washington, D.C.
Olson, M. 1965. *The Logic of Collective Action*, Cambridge, MA.

Owen, B. M. and Braeutigam, R. R. 1978. *The Regulation Game*, Cambridge, MA.

Peltzman, S. 1976. "Toward a More General Theory of Regulation," *Journal of Law and Economics*, 14, 109–148.

Posner, R. 1974. "Theories of Economic Regulation," *Bell Journal of Economics*, 5, 335–358.

Riker, W. H. 1982. *Liberalism Against Populism*, San Francisco, CA.

Shepsle, K. 1979. "Institutional Arrangements and Equilibrium in Multidimensional Voting Models," *American Journal of Political Science*, 23, 27–59.

Stigler, G. 1971. "The Theory of Economic Regulation," *Bell Journal of Economics*, 2, 3–21.

Weingast, B., Shepsle, K. and Johnson, C. 1981. "The Political Economy of Benefits and Costs," *Journal of Political Economy*, 89, 642–664.

Wilson, J. Q. 1980. *The Politics of Regulation*, New York.

19

Congressional influence over policy making: the case of the FTC

RANDALL L. CALVERT, MARK J. MORAN, AND
BARRY R. WEINGAST

Inevitably, much of the "making" of public policy takes place in the process of its administration. There is considerable disagreement, however, over whose influence lies behind policy decisions. Since the bureaucracy is the agent of that process, some analysts agree with Lindblom (1980, p. 68) that

policy making rests overwhelmingly in the hands of the bureaucracy, leaving relatively few policies to be determined elsewhere. Although the executive, the legislature, and the judiciary set some of the most important policies, the bureaucracy sets most, including those of the highest importance. Policy emerges specifically in the mutual interactions of bureaucratic politics.

Two implications follow from this conclusion: First, to understand and explain policy and policy failures, one must study the bureaucracy; and second, to improve policy outcomes in general, it is necessary (and perhaps sufficient) to impose new controls and institutional innovations upon the bureaucracy.

In contrast to Lindblom, many students of Congress attribute patterns of government policy outcomes to legislative politics. The major works on Congress of the last decade, such as Fenno (1973), Mayhew (1974), and Fiorina (1977), incorporate the view that both congressional institutions and government policy making serve the purposes of members of Congress. Fiorina (1981, p. 333) puts this in stark terms:

The bureaucracy is not out of control because the Congress controls the bureaucracy, and the Congress gives us the kind of bureaucracy it wants. If some modern day James Madison were to conceive a plan that would guarantee an efficient, effective, centrally directed bureaucracy, Congress would react with fear and loathing.

We are grateful to Morris Fiorina, Thomas Hammond, Mathew McCubbins, Forrest Nelson, Robert Parks, and Kenneth Shepsle for their advice and comments.

Though the possibility of congressional control sometimes gets support from casual observation or case studies,[1] attempts to detect and measure it systematically have not been uniformly convincing. Even the famous pork barrel has proven elusive. If congressional politics is an important determinant of policy implementation, one must consider quite different kinds of reform than those prescribed by the bureaucratic focus.

In this paper, we argue that there is much confusion in the literature on congressional-bureaucratic relations. We show that much of the evidence taken to indicate bureaucratic independence is also perfectly consistent with congressional dominance. This implies that the case for bureaucratic independence has to yet be made. Our approach provides theoretical and empirical reasons to believe that congressional influence over policy making is extensive. This is not to deny that either bureaucratic politics or executive influence is important; rather, it is to say that previous methods of studying policy making have not successfully disentangled the subtle forms of influence by various actors. Though we believe that Congress and the congressional committee system play an important and underappreciated role in bureaucratic policy making, neither this study nor previous studies are able to draw the line between bureaucratic autonomy and congressional influence or between congressional and presidential influence. Our goal here is to push the congressional explanation as far as it will plausibly go, to see how much of observed bureaucratic choice can potentially be explained by appealing only to the forces of congressional politics.

To achieve our goal we must first develop a more realistic and comprehensive perspective on Congress. Relying on an insight drawn by students of congressional oversight (see, for example, Fiorina 1981; McCubbins and Schwartz 1984; Ogul 1981), namely, that much congressional influence takes place through informal and "latent" means, we address this issue in three ways. First, we review how features of congressional politics such as interest groups and the committee system provide Congress with powerful but subtle means to insure that agencies administer programs so as to meet congressional goals. This influence may extend down to some of the most arcane details of policy. As we show, the exercise of this influence is sufficiently subtle that it can easily appear on the surface to be bureaucratic autonomy. Second, we examine how congressional influence can remain invisible if analysts observe only the *processes* of policy administration and oversight. Third, because observing the process of administration is insufficient, we suggest how congressional influence can be distinguished in practice.

As a second step toward applying the congressional explanation, we then illustrate these points using the Federal Trade Commission (FTC) as

494

an example. The FTC provides an opportunity to test empirically for indirect congressional influence in policy implementation. The methodology developed below allows us to sidestep the issue of the mechanics of influence and control by directly testing for FTC response to congressional preferences. By analyzing data on FTC case selection and congressional committee characteristics, we demonstrate a surprising connection between congressional goals and the ultimate administrative choices of the agency. This method bears a close relation to the literature on measurement of congressional pork-barreling, as we will show.

The paper proceeds as follows. First, we review some of the findings of the various studies of congressional influence on policy making. Second, we develop a theory of indirect congressional influence, suggesting some reasons for the mixed findings on congressional influence summarized earlier. Third, we turn to the study of the FTC and review its recent history and attending academic literature. We then develop our methodology for detecting indirect congressional influence and then report the results. Finally, we elaborate some implications of our approach and findings in the concluding discussion section.

FAITH AND EVIDENCE ON CONGRESSIONAL INFLUENCE

The idea that Congress strongly influences the administration of programs is widespread among Congress scholars. However, the empirical foundations of this notion are shaky, and many students of bureaucracy hold an altogether different view. We examine this disagreement by reviewing three areas of research in which scholars have sought evidence of congressional influence: (1) formal and informal "congressional oversight"; (2) pork barrel politics; and (3) the politics of regulation.

Congressional oversight

Traditionally, congressional influence over policy administration is viewed as taking place through the process of congressional oversight: that is, the public hearings and investigations of Congress concerning agency proceedings. In trying to assess the extent of congressional influence, then, several scholars have attempted to discover how prevalent such oversight is. Dodd and Schott (1979, chap. 5) counted occurrences of oversight hearings and related activities and concluded that Congress exercises little control in this fashion.[2] Ogul's (1976) case study of oversight by the Post Office and Civil Service committees also drew negative conclusions. He pointed out that under most circumstances the incentives for members of Congress to engage in oversight activities is limited. Scher (1963) reached a similar general conclusion, although his classic case study of oversight of the National Labor Relations Board illustrates an instance of extensive oversight activity. There seems little doubt that formal congressional oversight and monitoring are infrequent and ad hoc.

In a later work, however, Ogul (1981) suggests that much important communication and influence might take place through informal channels and that bureaucrats might actually anticipate congressional reactions. As we argue later, there are considerable a priori grounds for taking this view seriously despite the fact that, until recently, it has received only scant attention.

Pork barrel politics

Other scholars have sought evidence of congressional influence by trying to identify its results. The most fertile ground for such measurement ought to be in policy areas that lend themselves to classic pork barrel politics. Ferejohn (1974) found some evidence that members of the relevant congressional committees and appropriations subcommittees received more than their share of federal rivers and harbors money; however, his results have been questioned on methodological grounds by Arnold (1979). Plott (1968) found prima facie evidence of pork-barreling by House Banking and Currency Committee members in urban renewal policy, but Rundquist (1973) could find none in the allocation of military contracts. In related areas, using a methodology similar to that of Ferejohn (1974), Faith, Leavens, and Tollison (1982) detected a significant relation between the location of firms targeted for FTC antitrust cases and membership on the FTC oversight committees.

Arnold's study represents the current state of the art. His study of several programs (model cities, sewage treatment grants, and military base closings) improved upon previous studies methodologically (see his review and critique, 1979, pp. 81–91 and 217–24). In each policy area, he discerned some ability of key members of Congress, especially appropriations subcommittee members, to acquire and protect federal funds for their districts. From the evidence, Arnold concluded that bureaucrats administer programs strategically, so as to further their goals in Congress. Thus, although the common wisdom is that pork-barreling is rampant, the evidence has been inconsistent, and interpretable either as congressional influence *or* bureaucratic control.

Regulatory politics

Outside the distributive arena, some scholars maintain the same assumption about congressional influence as is common in pork barrel politics. Mayhew (1974, p. 135) says of regulatory policy that

Congressional influence over policy making

What happens in enforcement is largely a result of congressional credit-claiming activities on behalf of the regulated; there is every reason to believe that the regulatory agencies do exactly what Congress wants them to do.

In a similar vein, Noll disputed the antibureaucratic thrust of the 1971 Ash Council proposals for regulatory reform, saying that the extensive influence of Congress is the source of much bad regulatory policy (1971, especially chap. 4). Gellhorn (1980) attributes the rise and fall of the FTC in the 1970s partly to changing congressional interests. Weingast (1981, 1984) argues that Congress exercises systematic influence in several regulatory contexts, including airlines, communications, and securities regulation. Moreover, Fiorina (1981, 1982), Barke and Riker (1982), and McCubbins (1985) elaborated models that show how congressional delegation to bureaucrats may nonetheless serve congressional purposes. Finally, a host of case studies provide evidence of a congressional role in many regulatory agency decisions (see, e.g., Cary 1967; Kohlmeier 1969; Krasnow, Longley, and Terry 1982).

Nonetheless, the difficulty of detecting any systematic pattern of even traditional pork-barreling activities questions whether this emphasis on congressional interference is justified anywhere, outside of a few special cases. Many who have closely observed the regulatory agencies express such doubts. Levine (1980), drawing conclusions from his own participation on the Civil Aeronautics Board after years as an outside critic, opines that regulatory reform and perhaps the general direction of regulatory policy are to be understood simply as the result of reasonably well-intentioned public servants doing the best they can with what limited ability and expertise they possess. In other words, regulatory policy is explained largely by the background and training of agency personnel. Katzmann (1980, chaps. 2–6) concurs at least in part, concluding that many features of FTC antitrust policy can be explained by the (not always altruistic) professional and career orientations of agency lawyers and economists. Bernstein (1955) emphasizes the "revolving door" through which people move between jobs with the regulatory agencies and employment in regulated firms (or with the regulation bar). The thrust of these studies is well summarized by Wilson (1980, pp. 388, 391) in his edited collection of regulatory agency analyses, where he concludes that

By and large, the policies of regulatory commissions are not under the close scrutiny or careful control of either the White House or of Congress simply because what these agencies do has little or no political significance for either of these institutions. . . . The organizations studied for this book operate with substantial autonomy. . . . There is supposed to be an "iron triangle" of influence linking each agency, congressional committee, and interest group. . ., but we have not seen many of these triangles.

497

INDIRECT CONGRESSIONAL INFLUENCE

Whether the faith of the congressional influence believers is justified or not, it is clear that (1) Congress does not engage in very much formal oversight, nor does it seem equipped or inclined to do so: and (2) the federal bureaucracy gives at least the appearance of exercising considerable discretion in policy administration. How might extensive congressional influence nonetheless be possible? To answer this, let us focus on congressional authority, the institutions and norms of Congress, and the goals of members. We provide an approach to congressional-bureaucratic relations that shows how Congress may wield considerable influence without having to closely monitor or scrutinize agency proceedings at a detailed level.

Tools and incentives

The first component of our approach involves the principle of "anticipated reaction": bureaucrats anticipate and pursue congressional interests because Congress possesses positive rewards for service and negative sanctions for failure to serve. In theory at least, Congress has complete authority over many of the things bureaucrats value. It creates new programs and authorizes changes in old ones, even down to the level of very specific administrative decisions (as is often seen in riders to appropriations bills). It can feed or starve agencies through the appropriations process, altering actual program funding or bureaucratic perquisites. Though nearly all agencies seek budget increases, extensions in their authority, or statutory underpinnings for their pet projects and policy initiatives, Congress decides which agencies get the budget increases or desired legislation. It is only natural that these scarce resources will be devoted to those agencies serving congressional purposes and denied to those that are not. This targeting of congressional resources induces bureaucrats to anticipate the concerns of members of the relevant congressional committees and subcommittees and to take those wishes into account when making administrative decisions.[3]

A second important congressional tool is the Senate's power to approve or disapprove appointments to regulatory commissions. Some scholars minimize the importance of this power because it is little exercised; hearings for nominees are generally perfunctory, and nearly all nominations are approved. Katzmann (1980, pp. 140–45), for example, makes this argument with regard to the FTC. However, there is significant evidence that Congress manipulates the *selection of the nominee*,[4] and Katzmann himself reports three instances in the middle 1970s in which the Senate Commerce Committee virtually dictated

498

nominations to the commission. In such cases, it is no wonder that the confirmation hearings appear perfunctory. By exercising such control when necessary, interested members of Congress can assure that any regulatory agency is staffed with personnel sympathetic to their needs and viewpoints. In general, Congress possesses all the sanctions it might ever need to insure agency cooperation; however, many of these powers are used quite sparingly, and often inconspicuously.

Congressional institutions and norms determine in large measure the ways in which these formal powers can be employed. The decentralized system of semiautonomous committees and subcommittees, on which membership is largely self-selected, means that much of the available power over a given agency will be in the hands of a few members of Congress who care the most about it (see Fenno 1973; Shepsle 1978). This system is strengthened by what are often referred to as *norms* of reciprocity and universalism (Fenno 1966; Mayhew 1974), which encourage members to defer to one another's private political needs when possible. Further, individual members and committees maintain large staffs to assist them in achieving their political goals.[5] The availability of staff means that members can maintain extensive contacts in the bureaucracy; and, together with the long tenure of members on single committees, it enables members to develop at least a moderate degree of policy expertise. Taken together, these institutional features of Congress often allow members concerned with the administration of a particular program to do something about it, should they wish to.

Within this institutional structure, congressmen seek reelection and career advancement. Mayhew (1974) and Fenno (1973) discuss at length the pervasive effects of these goals upon congressional institutions and politics. In particular, members must act to further the interests of attentive and politically active groups in their constituencies. Because these interests are unevenly distributed among districts and states, and because of the opportunities presented by the committee system, many members are able to provide genuine policy benefits to those interests.

Indirect control

These institutional and behavioral components of congressional politics make possible two powerful but subtle methods through which Congress can exercise control over administration. First, Congress can demand changes in even the arcane details of many programs, despite its inability (even with the expertise of staff and committee specialization) to monitor those details. Lobbyists and the organized interests they represent play a crucial role in overcoming information barriers. Congressmen on the relevant committees do not learn how well a program is working through in-depth study, as an academic might. Rather, they judge a program's performance by listening to those affected constituents who have both the incentive and the resources to scrutinize bureaucratic decisions. Members need not be experts on agency affairs or conduct formal investigations to be able to pressure agencies effectively on behalf of their organized constituents, even at the level of detailed policy administration.

This practice of constituent monitoring has significant implications for the actual pattern of congressional oversight, as persuasively argued by McCubbins and Schwartz (Chapter 16). They suggest that in the face of a multitude of bureaucratic activities, it is inefficient and ineffective for congressmen to search systematically through agency actions looking for lack of compliance (surveillance or "police-patrol" oversight). Rather, it is effective for them to react to specific problems, brought to their attention by constituents, where bureaus fail to serve their interests (constituency-trigger or "fire-alarm" oversight). Viewed in this way, the lack of regular, public congressional hearings and investigations in no way implies a lack of congressional influence. Attention, which is all the more effective when it is focused through the more effective "fire-alarm" system, induces bureaucrats to anticipate and serve congressional interests.[6]

In the second method of indirect control, Congress can sometimes effectively constrain the ultimate actions of an agency by the way it initially authorizes a program. By setting the bureaucratic agenda, Congress may design the agency to perform like an automatic pilot, making precisely those decisions desired by Congress, but without the day-to-day involvement of congressmen. Arnold (1979) mentions this type of congressional influence but explicitly states that his methodology does not afford tests of its existence. But agenda setting by Congress with subsequent delegation to bureaus may be an effective, easily managed procedure. Barke and Riker (1982) illustrate how such agenda setting can work in regulatory policy, with Congress mandating hearings, notification, and similar processes to insure that special and local interests are heard. In distributive programs, representatives may encourage and assist local officials in their districts to produce grant applications. In fact, it has been suggested that congressmen create many programs with one eye, from the start, on the ombudsman and credit-claiming opportunities they will present later on (see Fiorina 1977, 1981; Fiorina and Noll 1978; Salisbury and Heinz 1970). Thus, members of Congress may determine the agenda for a program in such a way as to benefit their own constituencies, but the influence of Congress may be unobservable in what Arnold termed the "choice" stage. This is still properly "congressional" influence, because the patterns of policy implementation will reflect the political considerations of Congress, not independent forces of bureaucratic politics.

Appearances are deceiving

Let us summarize our view of the congressional-bureaucratic system. First, bureaucrats know what types of policies they need to pursue in order to survive and advance (the principle of anticipated reaction). Interest groups monitor congressmen because they, unlike congressmen, have the incentive to follow the day-to-day actions of agencies (constituency-trigger mechanism). And, finally, congressmen claim credit from their constituents for aggressively pursuing agencies that fail to provide benefits and otherwise insuring that the benefits continue to flow (fire-alarm oversight).

Notice what the politics of policy implementation will look like if Congress fully uses these kinds of effective tools. The rare thrashing of an agency by dissatisfied congressmen will serve as reminders to the rest. Aside from such episodes, however, Congress can leave the bureaucrats to make decisions yielding the appropriate patterns of benefits to please the interests represented on the relevant congressional committees. Meanwhile, relying on the constituency-trigger mechanism, members of Congress need not conduct formal oversight activities or even show much interest in the policy area. Any inquiries they do conduct are likely to be perfunctory, as long as the relevant groups are being satisfactorily served. After all, congressmen have many other demands on their time.

To any observer of the *process* of policy administration, this type of congressional influence will seldom be visible at all. Indeed, the process, when working smoothly, will have precisely the appearance of the classic autonomous bureaucracy serving its interest-group clientele (Rourke 1976, chap. 3, provides an extended description from this point of view). This fact leads to the following important methodological conclusion: *the process of policy administration by autonomous agencies is observationally equivalent to that under strict congressional control.* Both predict minimal public or "official" interactions between agencies and their overseers in Congress; both predict that those official interchanges that do take place (annual appropriations hearings, confirmation of regulatory heads) appear perfunctory. Thus, observing the process alone, even through an extensive case study, may not be sufficient to unearth even a pattern of pervasive congressional influence, simply because so much takes place through threat of action rather than through command and control. Unfortunately, the literature on public policy making is rich in studies using precisely this type of approach.

THE CASE OF THE FEDERAL TRADE COMMISSION

The conclusions of the previous section have considerable practical significance when we attempt to understand real-life relations between Congress and bureaucratic agencies. For example, when administrators of a program are accused of violating "congressional intent," it is, contrary to common political rhetoric, often not a matter of "runaway bureaucracy" but rather one of changed congressional intent. To illustrate this, we examine the tribulations of the Federal Trade Commission during the 1970s. Although much recent congressional influence over the FTC has been exercised through more direct means than those we have discussed, this episode reveals the kind of congressional demands that bureaucrats face and the kind of sanctions they fear. Following this discussion, we shall give, in section IV, evidence of *indirect* congressional influence on the commission as well.

Once called "the little old lady of Pennsylvania Avenue," the agency ended decades of quiescence after harsh criticism from public interest advocates in the late 1960s (American Bar Association 1969; Cox, Fellmeth, and Schultz 1969). It initiated a vigorous policy, during the 1970s, of innovative antitrust and unfair-practices cases. By the late 1970s, however, the commission's efforts to continue this course met with stiff resistance from the business community and certain members of Congress; and by 1982 the new policies had been largely reversed. Although the rhetoric surrounding this whole episode has emphasized "runaway bureaucracy," congressional action preceded FTC changes along every step of the way.

Bureaucratic features

The FTC possesses many of the features associated with an autonomous bureaucracy. The agency's vague mandates to prevent "deceptive practices," "unfair methods of competition," and so on, give it a broad jurisdiction, in which it must provide extensive interpretation of the law. At the same time, the agency's relatively small budget means that its selection of cases for investigation is necessarily spotty; to investigate all apparent violations of the law is out of the question. In addition to deciding individual cases, the FTC is empowered to promulgate general rules for whole industries or areas of economic activity, again based only on the commissioners' interpretation of agency mandates. Decisions on what matters to pursue, in both individual cases and rule making, often depend on the studies undertaken by the FTC staff, which is made up largely of lawyers and economists who follow their own ideas about appropriate professional behavior (see Katzmann 1980, chaps. 2, 4–6).

Clarkson summarizes the result of all this: "Even with its most effective tools, Congress can redirect resources into or away from specific programs only after detailed analysis at a level *beyond the institutional competence of Congress* except on an, at most, occasional project" (1981, p. 34; emphasis added). Thus, the FTC appears to some observers to be operating largely without congressional guidance.

Political rhetoric concerning the commission has often employed antibureaucratic themes as well. The American Bar Association report (1969) criticized the FTC especially harshly for pursuing trivial cases, blaming a "lack of adequate planning" (p. 39) and failure of the commission to set priorities, goals, and definitions of problems. In the late 1970s, with the FTC now pursuing some uncomfortably nontrivial activities, complaints from the business community also criticized the agency as an irresponsible bureaucracy. For example, in the Senate Commerce Subcommittee for Consumers 1979 FTC oversight hearings (U.S. Congress 1979), various aggrieved witnesses accused FTC "bureaucrats, insulated from responsibility to voters" (p. 264), of "obstruct[ing] legislative intent" (p. 178) and of having "exceeded its administrative authority" (p. 469) in pursuing several recent cases. Witnesses asked Congress to "regain control of the federal regulatory process" in order to "alleviate...problems resulting from a burgeoning bureaucracy" (p. 323). When Congress began in earnest its attack on the FTC in late 1979, Sen. John Durkin termed the legislative actions "shock therapy for bureaucrats," and Rep. Elliott Levitas, sponsor of a legislative veto provision, proclaimed "an end to government by bureaucratic fiat" (*Wall Street Journal* 1979). Such opinions were widely repeated during the legislative sessions that followed. Thus, FTC procedures, surface appearances, and the public rhetoric of lobbyists and politicians all point to bureaucratic discretion as the explanation of the policies pursued by the commission.

Congressional actions

In our view, the above interpretation is misleading. During the 1970s, Congress gave the FTC considerable attention through formal oversight hearings and statutory changes,[7] twice bringing about large-scale reversals in the commission's approach. Prior to the early 1970s, "the FTC...tended to select relatively trivial goals for staunch enforcement measures," displaying "a preoccupation with projects of marginal importance" (American Bar Association 1969, p. 39). By 1970, the issue of consumer protection was popular among members of Congress, who often pursued their newly found interest by recommending a strengthened FTC and specific investigations that the agency ought to undertake. Action was especially heavy in the Senate Commerce Committee,[8] which held hearings in 1970 leading to pressure on the FTC to investigate advertising aimed at children, particularly advertising practices of the cereal industry. Also in that year, the committee first reported a bill seeking to clarify and strengthen the FTC's power to issue trade regulations. They held the first hearings on product warranties in 1971. These efforts culminated in the passage of the Magnuson–Moss Warranties Act and the FTC Improvements Act in 1975, considerably expanding FTC rulemaking powers. The appointments to the commission of consumer advocates Elizabeth Hanford in 1973 and David Clanton in 1976, and the institution of Michael Pertschuk as commission chairman in 1977 further strengthened the consumerism of the agency.[9] The Subcommittee for Consumers interfered in the FTC's administration of its powers only by spurring the agency on, encouraging it to undertake new and sweeping initiatives in the name of consumer protection. The main concern expressed in the 1974 Senate Commerce Committee hearings on FTC oversight (U.S. Congress 1974) was that the commission *was proceeding too slowly* in its investigations of high food and energy prices, children's advertising, and monopolistic practices. Gellhorn (1980) reports the same complaint was made in the appropriation hearings as late as 1976.

In sum, the policy initiatives of the 1970s can be interpreted as a concerted action by the FTC and its congressional supporters on the Senate Commerce Subcommittee for Consumers. Through at least 1977, relevant congressmen actively pushed the commission further.

The seeds of change in Congress's treatment of the FTC were sown in 1977, when there was an almost complete turnover in the membership of the Senate Commerce Subcommittee for Consumers. As Table 19.1 shows, 12 of the subcommittee's 14 members in 1976 left after that year; they include such consumerism proponents as Frank Moss, Gary Hart, John Pastore, and Vance Hartke, each of whom had earlier pushed for various new investigations by the FTC. They were replaced by only three new members. The new chairman of the subcommittee was Sen. Wendell Ford, who had served on the panel only since 1975. Up to this time Ford had been a typical subcommittee consumerist and FTC activism advocate, if only in a minor role. Ford's attitude seemed quite different after 1977.[10] The FTC's popularity among members of the committee continued downhill as increasing complaints were heard from members of the business community dissatisfied with the FTC's recent actions. In 1978 hearings before its Appropriations Subcommittee (U.S. Congress 1978), the agency took a pounding over its children's advertising investigation, its attempts to supersede state laws concerning self-

Congressional influence over policy making

Table 19.1. *Subcommittee turnover, 1976–1977 (Subcommittee for Consumers, Senate Commerce Committee)*

Member	1976 (years of subcommittee service)	1977 (years of subcommittee service)
Moss	10*	
Hart	9	
Pastore	12	
Hartke	12	
Inouye	8	
Beall	5	
Cannon	4	
Tunney	4	
Stevenson	4	
Weicker	2	
Buckley	2	
Baker	2	
Durkin	2	3
Ford	2	3*
Melcher		1
Packwood		1
Danforth		1
Average years continuous service	5.3	1.8

* Chairman.
Source: *Congressional Quarterly Almanac*, 1976, 1977.

regulating occupations, and the reports that it required from large businesses.

Back before the Subcommittee for Consumers in 1979, the commission was completely on the defensive (U.S. Congress 1979). Sen. Jack Schmitt had proposed a legislative veto to apply to FTC decisions, and Sen. John Danforth was looking critically at FTC funding for public interest testimony in its proceedings. The commission came in for general criticism of its procedures, including alleged prejudging of cases by the commissioners and the use of rule making instead of the case-by-case approach. Senators questioned several then-current investigations, including those of standards and certification, used cars, children's television, the cereal industry, and funeral homes. Although both pro- and anti-FTC positions were represented among witnesses, the senators seemed to be in substantial agreement that the FTC had, in several areas, gone too far.

Finally, in 1980 Congress passed an FTC funding authorization, after considerable delay, that included a two-house legislative veto provision and restricted several proposed or ongoing regulations: (1) The agency was barred from conducting any study of the insurance industry except at the specific request of either the Senate or House Commerce Committee; (2) the 1974 Magnuson–Moss bill was interpreted as *not* giving FTC any authority to regulate trade groups that set industry standards; (3) the "unfairness" standard for determining improper advertising was suspended for three years (this was the basis of the children's TV investigation); and (4) the agency was prohibited from pursuing its efforts to cancel trademarks that had become generic words, such as in the Formica case (see *Congressional Quarterly Weekly Report* 1980, pp. 1407–8. The legislative veto was exercised in 1981 to kill the agency's long-awaited used-car ruling.[11]

Thus, relevant congressional oversight committees reversed the FTC's activist regulatory activities when these policies were out of harmony with the new interests represented on the committees. Ironically, it was members of these very committees (though with different policy views) who earlier had instigated many of the activities receiving strong criticism in 1979 and 1980.

Control over policy details?

In recent years, then, Congress, and especially certain subcommittees, have aggressively directed the commission to change its approach in various ways. In some instances, individual FTC rule-making cases have been modified by statute. Moreover, the commission has gone beyond statutory requirements in several instances to meet new congressional demands. For example, controversial investigations against cereal manufacturers, big oil companies, the auto manufacturers, and television advertising aimed at children – all originally undertaken at congressional behest – were dropped by the agency. The commission has resumed the pursuit of Robinson–Patman cases, an area favored by small business and its representatives but from which the agency had all but withdrawn during its activist period (*National Journal* 1981, p. 577). At the level of overall policy direction, congressional influence was considerable throughout the 1970s. Along the way, the public was treated to a clear view of (1) the very specific constituent demands upon executive agencies that are typically transmitted (directly or indirectly) through members of Congress; and (2) the strong sanctions that Congress can and will apply to agencies when necessary.

Yet the statutory and other direct, congressionally inspired changes of the last 15 years have affected only a fraction of the FTC's total jurisdiction and acted directly on only the biggest issues in commission policy. In the previous section, we also claimed that Congress could influence, through indirect means, even the finer details of agency policy. In the next section, we demonstrate one way in which this, too, has been true in the case of the FTC. Specifically, the commission appears to have fine-tuned its allocation of resources to various areas of its jurisdiction in response to the general policy preferences of members of relevant congressional subcommittees.

MEASURING CONGRESSIONAL INFLUENCE: AN APPLICATION

In order to detect indirect congressional influence, we must demonstrate a connection between the interests of members of Congress and the policy decisions made by an agency. The studies of pork barrel politics take this approach, using characteristics of members' districts as indicators of the districts' need for a particular type of project and, more generally, using a congressman's membership on the committee or subcommittee with jurisdiction over a particular distributive program as evidence that he regards the goods offered by that program as helpful to him in being reelected. Our approach to FTC decisions is analogous: membership on the relevant authorizing committees is evidence that a legislator sees FTC-related policy (or some other policy overseen by the committee) as a reelection tool. We must go one step further, however, and ascertain exactly what *kind* of FTC decisions are valued by members, since, outside the distributive policy arena, policy goods are not one-dimensional quantities in which "more" is generally regarded as better. Specifically, then, we need to (1) determine the kinds of cases committee members want the FTC to pursue, and (2) test whether FTC case selection reflects these preferences.

The FTC has jurisdiction over numerous areas of economic activity, through a variety of statutes. The FTC actions of concern here are those having clear connotations as either old-style (before the late 1960s), protecting small business and pursuing cases with little economic impact; or new style, for example, innovative antitrust actions and broad consumer protection rule making (as seen in the 1970s). On the assumption that an activist FTC oriented toward consumer protection was the goal of certain political entrepreneurs in Congress beginning in the late 1960s, we seek evidence that FTC selection of cases in such areas has reflected the strength of this congressional sentiment. Ideally, then, an appropriate empirical technique should measure congressional preferences for FTC activism, taking into account the privileged positions of certain committee and subcommittee members; and should determine the effect of these preferences on the mix of "old-style" and "new-style" cases pursued by the commission.

507

Congressional preferences

As a measure of congressional preferences, we have used the voting scores of members as compiled by the Americans for Democratic Action (ADA) to assess general support for an activist FTC. Though use of these scores has received considerable criticism (Are they a measure of "ideology"? Are they subject to strategic manipulation?), our use avoids the usual problems. Our argument is entirely empirical: these scores are good predictors of members' votes on bills related to FTC activism during the period we are studying,[12] correctly forecasting 82 percent of such individual votes (see Weingast and Moran 1983, App. 1).[13] Thus, no matter what the underlying meaning of these scores, they serve as an excellent proxy measure for a member's apparent preference that the FTC pursue a more active, consumerist-oriented course. The higher a member's ADA score, the more he votes in favor of an activist FTC.

Rather than use the ADA score for each individual member of Congress in each year, we summarize them in three different yearly values for each house of Congress. These measures are: (1) the ADA score of the chairman of the subcommittee having the most direct jurisdiction over FTC activities (the Senate Commerce Committee's Subcommittee for Consumers and the House Commerce Committee's Consumer Protection Subcommittee, whose name varied during the period); (2) the average ADA score of members of the two subcommittees other that the chairmen; and (3) the average scores for the whole House and whole Senate, exclusive of the subcommittee's members.[14]

FTC decisions

Our data on FTC decisions consist of the entire set of cases considered by the commission between 1964 and 1976 (from FTC decisions, yearly). For our purposes, each case "occurs" in the calendar year in which it came before the five commissioners for final disposition. This final review by the commissioners represents the last in a series of steps in which the commission staff has chosen to pursue an investigation. Thus, the cases here reveal the FTC's collective decisions about the kinds of activities the agency should be spending its resources on.

The cases are classified by the statutes under which the action has been undertaken by the agency. Some of these categories are quited broad, in fact too broad for our purposes. For example, section 5 of the FTC Act, dealing with "deceptive practices," covers both trivial cases typical of the early FTC and some more innovative and important recent cases. Other categories are too small to be of use. Therefore, we restrict our attention to four kinds of cases. The activist FTC of the 1970s is represented by cases brought under the Truth-in-Lending Act or the Fair Credit Reporting Act (called *credit cases* henceforth). These are two recent (1967 and 1968) statutes which, though not inherently different from some older statutes dealing with unfair business practices, were created by congressional consumerists and have been viewed as significant new consumer protection policies.[15] In its role as protector of small business, the FTC acts through the Robinson–Patman Act, which amended section 2 of the old Clayton Act, prohibiting various "unfair" strategies of business competition (henceforth *Robinson–Patman* cases). The Fur Act, Wool Act, and Textile Act (*textile* cases) deal with accurate labeling of those products, and have generally been the basis of nitpicking cases having little impact on the economy or on consumer welfare. Finally, corporate mergers reviewed by the FTC under section 7 of the Clayton Act (*merger* cases) have provided fairly constant numbers of cases despite other changes in emphasis at the agency. This category provides a convenient base against which to measure the other three types of cases. Altogether, the four categories include 1,316 out of a total of 2,781 cases reviewed by the commission between 1964 and 1976.

Budget effects

One further independent variable is necessary for a well-specified model of FTC choices: the budget appropriated for the agency. This variable may affect FTC policy in two ways. First, matters of budgetary politics unrelated to FTC activism affect the overall budget and thus the FTC budget; the budget changes may cause the agency to alter its mix of activities. Such effects are not relevant to our assessment of substantive congressional influence over policy details but ought to be included in our statistical model to insure that the more relevant parameters are estimated correctly. Second, members of the relevant authorization or appropriation subcommittees can influence commission policies through the appropriations process, by increasing or reducing the agency's budget. Appropriations members, of course, can do this directly, subject to full committee and floor approval. But it would be inappropriate to use appropriations as a measure of this influence because members of the authorizing subcommittee can ask the appropriations subcommittee to act on their behalf. In fact, during the period under study, several senators held simultaneous memberships on both subcommittees.

In our statistical analysis, therefore, we want to be careful not to confuse any of the influence exercised by the authorizing subcommittee with either the independent influence of the appropriations subcommittee or the overall effects of federal budget changes. To do this, we introduce the FTC budget as an explanatory variable, but only after cleansing it of any direct influence of the authorizing subcommittee.[16] Thus, all influence by the authorizing subcommittees should be captured by our estimates of the effect of subcommittee ADA scores. General fiscal effects, along with any substantive influence by the appropriations subcommittees that is exerted through budgetary changes, will appear as an effect of the budget residual.[17]

The model

These variables provide the basis for an empirical test for congressional influence. To the extent that Congress plays little role in bureaucratic choice, changes in congressional preferences should not have important effects on FTC policy choice. However, if Congress plays an important role, then changes in congressional preferences should lead to changes in policy choice. Moreover, our model specifies that it is not simply changes in the overall Congress that are important but changes *on the relevant committees*. We will use the model to assess the existence of this pattern of congressional influence and to measure its strength.

For our purposes, each case in one of the four categories (credit, textile, Robinson–Patman, merger) is assumed to be independent of decisions made outside those four categories of FTC activity. No potential type of case can be declined altogether. In this abstract form, the basic model of agency decision making gives the outcome of any potential case as a function of budget residual, House average ADA score, House subcommittee ADA, House subcommittee chairman ADA, Senate ADA, Senate subcommittee ADA, and Senate subcommittee chairman ADA.

We can estimate the form of this relationship using polytomous logit analysis. This technique assumes a linear relationship between the independent variables and the logarithm of the odds of bringing a credit, textile, or Robinson–Patman case versus bringing a merger case. It yields a set of coefficients for each of the first three categories of cases, describing the effects of the independent variables on the probability of bringing the given type of case relative to the probability of bringing a merger case.[18]

Results

The estimated coefficients are shown in Table 19.2. Due to a high correlation between full House and full Senate ADA scores, it was necessary to omit one of them from the analysis. We chose to omit the House for two reasons. First, we could compare full Senate effects with

Table 19.2. *Coefficients from 4-category logit analysis (t-values in parentheses)*

Independent variable	Credit	Textile	Robinson-Patman
Constant	−27.4** (−5.14)	5.35* (2.38)	.0643 (.0233)
Budget residual	−1.67** (−6.52)	−.276* (−2.26)	.386** (2.63)
House subcommittee	.0362 (.507)	−.126** (−5.43)	−.146** (4.88)
House subcommittee chairman	−.0252 (−1.01)	−.0314* (−2.09)	−.0823** (−3.82)
Senate	.639** (4.43)	.190** (3.78)	.461** (6.53)
Senate subcommittee	−.258** (−4.07)	−.0556** (−2.90)	−.0520* (−2.33)
Senate subcommittee chairman	.108* (2.19)	−.0287** (−3.02)	−.0801** (−5.22)

Note: Base category = merger cases.
 * Significant at .05-level.
 ** Significant at .01-level.

the effects of the Senate subcommittee that has played such an important public role; and second, the correlation between the House and the House subcommittee was .95, leading again to problems of multicolinearty. For textile cases and Robinson–Patman cases, all coefficients are significant at the .05 level, and all subcommittee ADA and subcommittee chairman ADA coefficients have the expected signs: a higher apparent preference for FTC activism among those congressmen and senators results in less FTC emphasis on their more traditional types of cases. The coefficients for the full Senate, however, are of the opposite sign and apparently larger, although the magnitudes of these raw coefficients must be carefully interpreted, as we show below. For now, it suffices to note that, aside from the FTC subcommittee, liberalism among senators seems to mean an increase in both textile and Robinson–Patman activity. Since full House ADA scores tend to mirror those of the Senate, presumably a liberal House has the same effect as a liberal Senate on FTC choices.

The coefficients for credit cases do not appear as expected. Neither House variable has any significant effect, and the sign for the Senate subcommittee is the opposite of what it should be if in fact members perceive credit cases as the mark of an activist FTC. However, the coefficient is solidly significant, statistically. This could be an indication that, aside from the chairmen, subcommittee members saw credit cases as rather small potatoes, given the other activities in which the FTC could have been engaging – large antitrust cases and the like. That the chairmen would see differently is not unlikely, since for all but the first year of the period under study the subcommittee was chaired by either Senator Magnuson or Senator Moss, who sponsored this FTC consumer protection legislation in the late 1960s. In any event, the results from the other two categories fit very well with the original hypotheses, whereas those on credit cases must reflect a violation either of our assumption that these "potential cases" are independent of other FTC activities (due to trade-offs between credit and more important activities) or of our identification of credit cases with FTC activism and congressional liberalism.

The liberalism – activism connection does not seem to hold for the full Senate either, but, contrary to appearances, the full Senate effects are *less* important than the subcommittee effects. To understand this point, as well as to analyze generally the *sizes* of the effects represented by the logit coefficients, we turn to Table 19.3. There the coefficients have been translated into their actual effects on the *probabilities* of bringing each kind of case.[19] They may be interpreted as follows: Suppose all variables are at their means and that, say, the full Senate ADA is increased by one point. Then the predicted probability of a credit case will increase by about .14, that of a textile case by .041, and that of a Robinson–Patman case by .074. (The predicted probability of a merger case will increase by the negative of the sum of all three, that is, decrease by .255, since the probabilities must always sum to 1.0.)

Although the absolute values of the Senate effects in Table 19.3 are larger than those of the subcommittee or chairman, this does not reflect the relative influence of the subcommittee versus the full Senate. There are several ways to see this. Since the Senate is large and the subcommittee is small, year-to-year changes in the full Senate's average ADA scores are small in comparison with those of the subcommittee or its chairman. During the period under study, the Senate had an average of 89.77 members *not* on the subcommittee and an average of 9.23 subcommittee members besides the chairman. Dividing the partial derivatives in Table 19.3 by these figures provides a measure of the average effectiveness of individual senators in influencing the FTC. These results are shown on the table as well, in the rows labeled "per member." Thus, for example, in the area of textile cases, an increase of the point in the ADA score of one senator would, on average, change the probability of a textile case by −.006 if that senator were chairman of the subcommittee for consumers, by −.0013 if he were another member of the

512

Table 19.3. *Partial derivative of probability of a given case type measured at means of all independent variables*

Partial derivative with respect to:	Credit	Textile	Robinson-Patman
Budget residual	−.365	−.060	.062
House subcommittee	.008	−.027	−.023
House subcommittee chairman	−.006	−.007	−.013
Senate (per member)	.140	.041	.074
	(.0016)	(.0005)	(.0008)
Senate subcommittee (per member)	−.057	−.012	−.008
	(−.0061)	(−.0013)	(−.0009)
Senate subcommittee chairman	.024	−.006	−.013

subcommittee, and by only +.0005 if he were not a member of the subcommittee. Thus, for textile cases, a subcommittee member has over two-and-a-half times the influence and the subcommittee chairman 12 times the influence of a senator not on the subcommittee. Similar comparisons hold for credit and Robinson–Patman cases (and, therefore, for merger cases). Inasmuch as the measured Senate effect also captures the full House effect, the actual independent influence of an individual senator may be even smaller than indicated.

Finally, we can perform a related exercise to demonstrate that the changes in the Senate from 1976 to 1979 (the latest year for which figures are available), the years immediately following those used in the statistical estimation above, should have been expected to yield drastic changes at the FTC. Table 19.4 shows the changes in ADA scores for that period, and Table 19.5 indicates the total effect on FTC case selection. The results are dramatic: the large predicted increases in textile and Robinson–Patman activity and decrease in credit cases could signal the return of "the little old lady of Pennsylvania Avenue." This change is due largely to Senate changes, since ADA scores decreased markedly in that body and especially on the subcommittee, whereas changes on the House side were mixed and smaller (see Table 19.4). The last rows in Table 19.5 indicate the separate contributions of the subcommittee (chairman included) and the rest of the Senate to this predicted change, showing the importance of subcommittee influence change.

These results do not prove that our comprehensive perspective is correct. But they do have direct bearing on crucial parts of the argument. Overall, the results indicate (1) that the preferences of congressmen have considerable effect on agency policy choices and that this influence need not take the form of new legislation; and (2) that the structure and politics of Congress give some members much more influence than

Table 19.4. *Changes in ADA scores from 1976 to 1979*

Full House	0.25
House subcommittee	−11.31
House subcommittee chairman	4.0
Full Senate	−5.0
Senate subcommittee	−24.75
Senate subcommittee chairman	−28.0

Note: Negative sign indicates a decrease in ADA.

Table 19.5. *Changes in predicted probabilities due to 1976–1979 ADA changes*

	Credit	Textile	Robinson-Patman
Predicted probabilities, 1976	.3282	.3447	.1428
Predicted probabilities, 1979	.0355	.6587	.2778
Total predicted change	−.2927	+.3140	+.1350
Ratio of absolute subcommittee effect to other senators' effects*	2.94**	2.27	1.52

Note: Budget residual for 1979 assumed equal to that in 1976.
  * Computed as linear approximations, using the partial derivatives in Table 19.3. Chairman included in subcommittee.
** However, opposite signs of subcommittee effect and chairman effect almost cancel each other out.

others. In this case, due to the effects of the committee system in both houses, and due to the ability of some senators to gain electoral advantages from such issues as consumerism and "runaway bureaucracy" (thanks perhaps to their large constituencies and high visibility), the Senate Commerce Subcommittee for Consumers appears to have been the seat of power on FTC policy during the late 1960s and 1970s.

DISCUSSION

In this paper, we have argued that Congress influences bureaucratic decision making through means that are powerful but indirect and that are often unobservable on the surface. The nature of the congressional committee system insures that members most interested in a given program have disproportionate influence in legislative action on that program (self-selection of committee members). Bureaucrats know what types of policies they need to pursue in order to survive and advance (the principle of anticipated reactions). Interest groups monitor agencies because they, unlike members of Congress, have the incentive and expertise to follow the agencies' operations in their area of concern (the constituency trigger). Finally, members of Congress protect the interests of their important supporters (through fire-alarm oversight).

Our statistical results do not provide definitive evidence for our case; indeed, even much more spectacular results would still cover only one agency for one period. They alone do not entirely disentangle congressional influence from that of bureaucrats or presidents. But they have taken us farther down the path toward our goal by showing that our perspective of subtle but extensive congressional control is plausible. Our purpose in articulating this view is, in part, to urge scholars to consider indirect forms of influence, rather than only the simpler and more direct sources commonly assumed but commonly found lacking. Decision making of this sort will surely not be uncovered by scholars who fail to look for it. Regardless of whether our logical perspective is an accurate model of regulatory policy making, it clearly demonstrates that the existing literature has not yet distinguished the influence of different actors. New methods and further studies are required.

It is reasonable to ask whether the kind of oversight we posit is really "congressional" influence in any meaningful sense. Certainly, our description accords well with the concept of subsystem or subgovernment politics used by many analysts to describe policy making (for a general account with illustrations, see Ripley and Franklin 1984). However, the congressional role is played by individual members or small groups of members, rather than by Congress as a body. The ultimate interests being served are those of organized interest groups, regardless of whether we think of them as acting through agencies, as clienteles; or through committees, as contituency groups. We claim that Congress as an institution is central to this pattern of policy benefits because congressional structure and politics determine which groups get access to the policy process and what kinds of policy goods they are able to obtain and protect. For example, Magnuson's entrepreneurial "discovery" of consumerism as a political image for himself led eventually to the FTC's pursuit of many of the goals of the consumer movement; when the committee's membership changed in the late 1970s, the influence of this constituency waned. Institutional changes can likewise yield changes in patterns of interest group and agency politics. For example, the strengthening of House subcommittees in the early 1970s has led to an increased emphasis on agency service to special interests of all types at the expense of broader policy concerns. Our point, then, is that subsystem politics is structured by congressional politics; in that sense, what we have described in this paper truly is congressional influence.

We have said nothing thus far about presidential influence over the bureaucracy or about competition between the president and the legislature over policy goals. We do not doubt that a president who takes an active and sustained interest in a given agency's activity brings to bear powerful tools of influence.[20] In such cases, presidents can potentially frustrate congressional preferences and sometimes even ignore formal congressional actions. But the problem for the president is that his time and political resources are scarce; maximum attention focused in one place means minimum attention elsewhere. Put simply, the president can given sustained attention only to a very limited number of areas. Outside these areas, although presidents are key players, congressional-bureaucratic politics is the game being played. Simply expressing a preference, and often even putting top aides to work, is not sufficient to achieve presidential goals. Our perspective indicates, in part, the kinds of tactics presidents ought to use: they must concentrate on congressional committee politics and the interests represented there.

A major implication of our approach is methodological. We have argued that, in a system of smoothly functioning incentives, congressional control is observationally equivalent to bureaucratic autonomy. Therefore, one cannot distinguish between these two views through the typical case-study technique of simply observing the process of policy making. Analysts looking for subtle congressional influence can usually find it, whereas others, looking at the same agencies, miss it entirely and conclude that real policy making is under the control of the bureaucracy. Numerous case studies bear this out, giving contradictory interpretations of identical programs. The substantive evidence given in Section III and in Gellhorn (1980) stands in marked contrast to the conclusions of Katzmann (1980) and especially Clarkson (1981). Elsewhere, Krasnow, Longley, and Terry (1982) see Congress as the driving force behind the actions of the Federal Communications Commission, whereas Cole and Oettinger (1978) view Congress as, at best, a peripheral player. Weingast (1984) describes significant influence by Congress over the Securities and Exchange Commission's major policy initiatives in the 1960s and 1970s, but Seligman (1982) reports little such influence.

Because of this ambiguity in the surface appearance of the policy-making process, a better place to look for congressional influence is in patterns or episodes of policy change. Our analysis suggests one important sufficient condition for such shifts: when the interests represented on the relevant congressional committees change, so will policy. If regulatory agencies were substantially independent of Congress, such changes in Congress would have little connection with agency decisions. But, in the case of the FTC, we showed that year-to-year variations in the policy preferences of committee members were reflected in the FTC's allocation of effort to its several jurisdictions and that wholesale change on the most important subcommittee presaged wholesale change in commission activity.

As a method of predicting policy changes, this attention to congressional committees compares favorably with other methods. Models of policy incrementalism, such as that of Davis, Dempster, and Wildavsky (1966), do not predict shifts in emphasis between ongoing programs, or large, discontinuous changes. Examination of agency–clientele relations only "explains" policy change after the fact. Public opinion measurements do not indicate whose opinion counts in the policy process or how well strategically placed actors can delay and deflect pressures for change. Our focus on congressional committees suffers none of these weaknesses. Although there are also noncongressional sources of policy change (such as in the relatively few areas upon which close presidential attention is brought to bear), the congressional side is often the first mover when subgovernments change shape and agencies take new approaches. Congressional influence over the administration of policy is probably just as extensive as Congress scholars have tended to assume.

NOTES

1 See, for example, Cary 1967; Kolhmeier 1969; Krasnow, Longley, and Terry 1982.

2 Though they repeatedly show instances of indirect and covert congressional influence over administration, they sum up their general interpretation as follows: The federal bureaucracy is, "in many respects, a prodigal child. Although born of congressional intent, it has taken on a life of its own and has matured to a point where its muscle and brawn can be turned against its creator" (Dodd and Schott 1979, p. 2)

3 Fenno (1966) and Wildavsky (1978) give some illustrations of the deference that agency decision makers show toward congressional interests.

4 Students of regulation have long observed the veto power over appointees exercised by Congress. Noll, studying industry-specific regulation prior to any deregulation, concludes that, "while the appointment process does not necessarily produce commissioners who are consciously controlled by the industry they regulate, it nearly always succeeds in excluding persons who are regarded as opposed to the interests of the regulated" (Noll 1971, p. 43). Cary (1967) and Kohlmeier (1969) make similar observations. Systematic evidence for the influence of Congress over appointments is provided in U.S. Congress 1976.

5 Staffs are often accused of being autonomous, "unelected representatives" (see Malbin 1980); but there is every reason to believe that the incentives for staffers are such that they act as extensions of the elected legislators for whom they work (Salisbury and Shepsle 1981). Although legislators may not be able to follow every detail or exercise ex ante judgment over choices made by staff members, congressmen can certainly tell ex post whether the action gets a positive, a negative, or no reaction back in the district. Staff members know that ex post sanctions will occur if they violate their authority; and therefore

517

these sanctions provide ex ante incentives to exercise appropriate judgment. In sum, the actions of personal and committee staff members are motivated, ultimately, by the same political factors that underlie the actions of congressmen.

6 Cole and Oettinger (1978, pp. 161–63) give a fine example: when the FCC threatened to start enforcing its radio commercial time standards in 1964 (hurting the congressional clientele, broadcasters), Congress almost took away their jurisdiction over the issue. Ten years later, FCC was still unwilling to touch the issue. Herring (1936, pp. 110–124) reports that the FTC had similar experiences from its very beginning. In 1921, after it recommended further antitrust action against the meat packers, jurisdiction over this industry was transferred to the Department of Agriculture. Finally, the recent removal of Anne Burford as head of the Environmental Protection Agency showed all other Reagan appointees that they could not ignore the interests of Congress in their decisions.

7 See, for example, Kovacic's (1982) extensive discussion of the seemingly endless set of hearings undertaken on antitrust issues alone during this period.

8 Nadel (1971) details Warren Magnuson's role in consumer issues. Through his role as chairman of the FTC oversight committee and then the full Commerce Committee, he played a leading role in establishing the congressional underpinning of FTC activism. Nadel further suggests how the views represented on Magnuson's subcommittee and those within the FTC were in harmony during this period. See also Gellhorn 1980.

9 The Commerce Committee's pivotal role in securing these appointments is described in Katzmann 1980, pp. 143–45.

10 In 1977, Ford introduced a new "FTC Improvement Act" to further strengthen the agency. A change in congressional attitudes was apparent, however, when the hearings on the bill (U.S. Congress 1977) were held. Several potentially aggrieved parties, including a delegation from nonprofit organizations (potentially regulated under the new act) from Ford's home state of Kentucky, had the opportunity to register their objections to the proposed legislation. Ford's attitude toward the opponents of his bill seemed, from his statements and questions in the hearing, to be sympathetic. In short, he heard his constituents' clamor and changed his position.

11 Much stronger provisions had surfaced on the House and Senate floors before the authorization passed in its final form, and such proposals continued thereafter: in May 1982, for example, the Senate Commerce Committee reported a measure that would prohibit any FTC action against professional organizations already regulated by the states, narrow the definition of "unfair business practices," and cancel the agency's authority to act against agricultural cooperatives (Congressional Quarterly Weekly Report 1982, p. 1131).

12 Naturally, we controlled for any inclusions of FTC votes themselves in the ADA index.

13 ADA scores, unlike the CFA scores which might otherwise be more appropriate for our purposes, are available for the full period we consider. This substitution seems quite appropriate since ADA and CFA scores are highly correlated in years when both were available; Poole (1981, pp. 56–57) shows that ADA correlates at about .92 with an underlying explanatory

dimension of interest group ratings during 1969–76, whereas CFA correlates at about .84 with the same dimension from 1971 to 1976.

14 We originally included the full Commerce Committees in this scheme as well, but their scores were so highly correlated with those of the full House and Senate that their effects could not be distinguished. They have therefore been deleted. We have used mean rather than median ADA scores because the series of median scores closely resembles that of the means, and the means are computationally simpler.

15 Upon passage, for example, the Truth-in-Lending Act was hailed as a new "Bill of Rights for the Consumer" by activist members of the Senate subcommittee.

16 Specifically, we performed an ordinary least squares regression of yearly FTC budget upon total federal budget and the ADA variables. The budgets are fiscal-year figures, whereas the ADA scores come from the calendar year in which the corresponding fiscal year ended. The result is an OLS residual that will serve as our budget variable in the main model. With each FTC case, then, we associate the corresponding budget residual from the fiscal year during which the case "occurred."

17 For the purposes of this analysis, we have omitted any consideration of separate, indirect influences of the appropriations subcommittees, such as might be captured by including their ADA scores as well. We are presently undertaking such a study. At present, there are two reasons for considering the results here as they stand. First, because of its wider jurisdiction, it is probably the case that relatively few members of the appropriations subcommittee in either house are unusually concerned with FTC, in contrast at least with the apparent situation on the Senate Commerce Subcommittee for Consumers. Thus, we do not expect to find a strong effect of the ADA scores for members of the appropriations committees. Second, overlapping memberships on the Senate subcommittees make the situation complicated. What influence should be attributed to the authorizing subcommittee, and what influence to appropriations? The simpler approach taken here, though perhaps not revealing the full story, seems a reasonable way to begin. One would expect any influence that shows up here to show up also in a more complicated model.

18 The categorical (that is, nonordinal) nature of the dependent variable, as well as the availability of credit cases only for potential cases occurring after 1969, can be directly provided for in a logit framework (see McFadden 1974). Computational feasibility dictates our use of logit, as opposed to the equally reasonable probit specification. The coefficients were estimated by using a numerical approximation technique to maximize the likelihood function corresponding to our model under the assumptions of logit analysis.

19 Since the logit specification makes probability a nonlinear function of the independent variables, these partial derivatives (slopes) change as the variables' values change. Table 19.3 shows these slopes evaluated at the means (across all cases) of the independent variables.

20 For further discussion of presidential influence, its sources of power, and the subtle forms it may take, see Moe 1982, 1984. He, too, emphasizes the point made above, namely that disentangling the influence of various actors requires subtle and sophisticated methodologies yet to be employed systematically in the study of regulatory policy making.

REFERENCES

American Bar Association. 1969. *Report of the ABA Commission to Study the Federal Trade Commission*. New York: American Bar Association.

Arnold, R. Douglas. 1979. *Congress and the Bureaucracy*. New Haven: Yale University Press.

Barke, Richard P., and William H. Riker. 1982. "A Political Theory of Regulation with Some Observations on Railway Abandonments." *Public Choice* 39: 73–106

Bernstein, Marver H. 1955. *Regulating Business by Independent Commission*. Princeton, N.J.: Princeton University Press.

Cary, William. 1967. *Politics and the Regulatory Commission*. New York: McGraw-Hill.

Clarkson, Kenneth W. 1981. "Legislative Constraints." In *The Federal Trade Commission since 1970*, ed. K. W. Clarkson and T. J. Muris. Cambridge: Cambridge University Press.

Cole, Barry, and Mel Oettinger. 1978. *Reluctant Regulators: The FCC and the Broadcast Audience*. Reading, Mass.: Addison-Wesley.

Congressional Quarterly Almanac. Washington, D.C.: Congressional Quarterly, Inc., various years (1964–79).

Congressional Quarterly Weekly Report 38. "FTC Fund Bill with Legislative Veto Clears." May 24, 1980: 1407–8.

Congressional Quarterly Weekly Report 40. "Panel's Vote Squeezing FTC May Threaten Authorization." May 15, 1982: 1131–32.

Cox, E. F., R. C. Fellmeth, and J. E. Schultz. 1969. *The Nader Report on the Federal Trade Commission*. New York: Baron.

Davis, Otto A., M. A. H. Dempster, and Aaron Wildavsky. 1966. "A Theory of the Budgetary Process." *American Political Science Review* 60:529–47.

Dodd, L., and R. Schott. 1979. *Congress and the Administrative State*. New York: Wiley.

Faith, R., D. Leavens, and R. Tollison. 1982. "Antitrust Pork Barrel." *Journal of Law and Economics* 25:329.

Fenno, Richard F., Jr. 1966. *The Power of the Purse: Appropriations Politics in Congress*. Boston: Little, Brown.

1973. *Congressmen in Committees*. Boston: Little, Brown.

Ferejohn, John A. 1974. *Pork Barrel Politics*. Stanford, Calif.: Stanford University Press.

Fiorina, M. 1977. *Congress: Keystone of the Washington Establishment*. New Haven: Yale University Press.

1981. "Control of the Bureaucracy: A Mismatch of Incentives and Capabilities." In *Congress Reconsidered*, ed. L. C. Dodd and B. I. Oppenheimer, 2nd ed. Washington, D.C.: Congressional Quarterly.

1982. "Legislative Choice of Regulatory Forms." Carnegie Papers on Political Economy. *Public Choice* 39:33–66.

Fiorina, M. P., and R. G. Noll. 1978. "Voters, Bureaucrats, and Legislators: A Rational Choice Perspective on the Growth of Bureaucracy." *Journal of Public Economics* 9:239–53.

FTC Decisions. Washington, D.C.: U.S. Government Printing Office, various years.

Gellhorn, Ernest. 1980. "The Wages of Zealotry: The FTC under Siege." *Regulation*, January, pp. 33–40.

Herring, E. Pendleton. 1936. *Public Administration and the Public Interest.* New York: McGraw-Hill.

Katzmann, Robert A. 1980. *Regulatory Bureaucracy: The Federal Trade Commission and Antitrust Policy.* Cambridge, Mass.: MIT Press.

Kovacic, William. 1982. "The Federal Trade Commission and Congressional Oversight of Antitrust Enforcement." *Tulsa Law Journal* 17:587–671.

Kohlmeier, Louis M. 1969. *The Regulators.* New York: Harper & Row.

Krasnow, E., L. Longley, and H. Terry. 1982. *The Politics of Broadcast Regulation.* New York: St. Martin's Press.

Levine, Michael E. 1980. "Revisionism Revised? Airline Deregulation and the Public Interest." *Law and Contemporary Problems* 44:179–95.

Lindblom, Charles E. 1980. *The Policy-Making Process.* 2d ed. Englewood Cliffs, N.J.: Prentice-Hall.

Malbin, Michael J. 1980. *Unelected Representatives.* New York: Basic Books.

Mayhew, David R. 1974. *Congress: The Electoral Connection.* New Haven: Yale University Press.

McCubbins, Mathew. 1985. "The Legislative Design of Regulatory Structure." *American Journal of Political Science* 29:721–48.

McCubbins, Mathew, and Thomas Schwartz. 1984. "Police Patrols vs. Fire Alarms." *American Journal of Political Science* 28:165–79.

McFadden, Daniel. 1974. "Conditional Logit Analysis of Qualitative Choice Behavior." In *Frontiers in Econometrics,* ed. P. Zarembka. New York: Academic Press.

Moe, T. 1982. "Regulatory Performance and Presidential Administration." *American Journal of Political Science* 26:197–224.

1984. "Control and Feedback in Economic Regulation: The Case of the NLRB." Paper delivered at the Conference on the Politics of Economic Policy, Stanford University, May 10–11.

Nadel, Mark V. 1971. *Politics of Consumer Protection.* Indianspolis: Bobbs–Merrill.

National Journal. 1981. "Big Is Back in Favor – but Only If It Promotes Efficiency." April 4, pp. 573–77.

Noll, Roger G. 1971. *Reforming Regulation.* Washington, D.C.: Brookings Institution.

Ogul, Morris S. 1976. *Congress Oversees the Bureaucracy: Studies in Legislative Supervision.* Pittsburgh: University of Pittsburgh Press.

1981. "Congressional Oversight: Structures and Incentives." In *Congress Reconsidered,* ed. L. C. Dodd and B. I. Oppenheimer, 2nd ed. Washington, D.C.: Congressional Quarterly.

Plott, Charles R. 1968. "Some Organizational Influences on Urban Renewal Decisions." *American Economic Review* 58:306–21.

Poole, K. 1981. "Dimensions of Interest Group Evaluation of the U.S. Senate, 1969–1978." *American Journal of Political Sciences* 25:49–67.

Ripley, Randall, and Grace A. Franklin. 1984. *Congress, the Bureaucracy, and Public Policy.* Homewood, Ill.: Dorsey Press.

Romer, Thomas, and Howard Rosenthal. 1978. "Political Resource Allocation, Controlled Agendas, and the Status Quo." *Public Choice* 33:27–43.

Rourke, Francis E. 1976. *Bureaucracy, Politics, and Public Policy.* Rev. ed. Boston: Little, Brown.

Rundquist, Barry S. 1973. "Congressional Influences on the Distribution of Prime Military Contracts." Ph.D. dissertation, Stanford University.

Salisbury, Robert, and John Heinz. 1970. "A Theory of Policy Analysis and Some Preliminary Applications." In *Policy Analysis in Political Science*, ed. Ira Sharkansky. Chicago: Markham.

Salisbury, Robert H., and Kenneth A. Shepsle. 1981. "Congressional Staff Turnover and the Ties-that-Bind." *American Political Science Review* 75: 381–96.

Scher, Seymour. 1960. "Congressional Committee Members as Independent Agency Overseers: A Case Study." *American Political Science Review* 54:911–20.

1963. "Conditions for Legislative Control." *Journal of Politics* 25:526–51.

Seligman, Joel. 1982. *The Transformation of Wall Street.* Boston: Houghton Mifflin.

Shepsle, Kenneth A. 1978. *The Giant Jigsaw Puzzle.* Chicago: University of Chicago Press.

U.S. Congress, Senate, Committee on Appropriations. 1978. *Hearings on State, Justice, Commerce, the Judiciary, and Related Agencies Appropriations*, part 5. 95th Congress, 2nd session.

U.S. Congress, Senate, Committee on Commerce. 1974. *Hearings on Federal Trade Commission Oversight.* 93rd Congress, 2nd session, March 1, 7, 14; May 9.

1976. *Appointments to the Regulatory Agencies*, 94–2, Committee Print. Washington, D.C.: GPO.

U.S. Congress, Senate, Subcommittee for Consumers of the Committee on Commerce, Science, and Transportation. *Hearings on S1288, the Federal Trade Commission Improvements Act of 1977.* 95th Congress, 1st session, May 3, 4.

1979. *Hearings on Oversight of the Federal Trade Commission.* 96th Congress, 1st session, Sept 18, 19, 27, 28; Oct. 4, 5, 10.

Wall Street Journal. 1979. "FTC Stirs Up a Vast Array of Opponents, and Congress Weighs Curbs on Its Power," by Stan Crock and Burt Schorr. October 18, p. 40.

Weingast, Barry R. 1981. "Regulation, Reregulation, and Deregulation: The Political Foundations of Agency-Clientele Relations." *Law and Contemporary Problems* 44:147–77.

1984. "The Congressional Bureaucratic System: A Principal-Agent Perspective (with Applications to the SEC)." Carnegie Papers on Political Economy. *Public Choice* 44:147–91.

Weingast, Barry R., and Mark J. Moran. 1984. "Bureaucratic Discretion or Congressional Control: Regulatory Policymaking by the FTC." *Journal of Political Economy* 91:765–800.

Wildavsky, Aaron. 1978. *The Politics of the Budgetary Process.* 3rd ed. Boston: Little, Brown.

Wilson, James Q., ed. 1980. *The Politics of Regulation.* New York: Basic Books.

20

Legislators, bureaucrats, and locational decisions

R. DOUGLAS ARNOLD

INTRODUCTION

Geography and governmental spending

Our government allocates an ever increasing proportion of the national output. National, state, and local government appropriate directly over one third of the Gross National Product. Indirectly, they affect how a considerable proportion of the rest is allocated, by means of extensive regulations and prohibitions and through positive inducements offered in the tax code. The expanding size and scope of governmental activities impel social scientists to develop better explanatory models of government behavior. Understanding how and why governments make the choices they do is increasingly important for understanding everything from the performance of the national economy to the changing fortunes of businesses, cities, and regions.

This paper investigates the world of government spending. Specifically, it explores how the federal government makes decisions about the geographic allocation of expenditures. The central questions are: Does it make any difference *how* such decisions are made? Do legislators make significantly different decisions from bureaucrats? Does it matter whether one employs allocational formulas rather than making individual case-by-case decisions?

Decisions about geographic allocation may appear peripheral and insignificant compared to obviously central decisions, such as the proper ends of government, appropriate means to those ends, priorities among competing programs, and the relative sizes of the public and private sectors. This view is mistaken. First, geographic decisions are important in their own right. Federal expenditures have an enormous impact on the

Reprinted from *Public Choice* 37 (1981):107–132. (Martinus Nijhoff, publishers.)

fortunes of localities and regions, on the health of their economies, and on the quality of life for their inhabitants. Since the federal government spends nearly a quarter of national output, the differential geographic effects of that spending cannot be ignored any more than one could ignore its differential effects by income or race. Second, decisions about ends, means, priorities, and governmental size are not made independently from decisions about geographic allocation. In fact, choices about the former are often impossible without simultaneously resolving issues about the geographic allocation of benefits. Some have argued that difficulties in resolving these allocational issues contribute to the adoption of inefficient or inappropriate means, distort priorities among programs, or foster governmental growth.

Thus, geographic allocation is important both because it is a significant policy issue itself and because it affects how other policy conflicts are resolved. Unfortunately, there is rather meager literature on the subject. Part of the literature explores how a legislature with geographic representation would handle the problem of allocation.[1] These works reach for broad generalizations, but ignore all the complexities of the real world where the differences between programs frequently outweigh their similarities. The others are case study literature that investigate the politics of geographic allocation for individual programs.[2] They demonstrate the importance that differences in process and policy can make, though not in any systematic fashion.

This essay is the fourth in a series on the politics of geographic allocation. My previous works developed a comparative framework for understanding allocational politics for various policy types, investigated the extent of congressional influence over bureaucrats' allocational decisions, explored how Congress shapes various programs of formula and project grants, and examined the logic of explanations for governmental growth that are based on models of legislative competition for local benefits.[3] This paper builds on this empirical base and on the works of others, in an attempt to evaluate what difference it makes *how* allocational decisions are made.

Allocational processes

Four alternative methods are available for making decisions about the geographic allocation of expenditures. Decisions can be made either by legislators or by bureaucrats, in the form of individual case-by-case decisions or by writing a general allocational formula. Currently, all four methods are being used for various federal expenditures. For some programs, Congress allocates funds geographically with either formulas or individual project decisions. For others, Congress delegates allocational authority to bureaucrats, who then either make individual decisions or write general formulas. Hybrid programs that combine elements from two or more methods exist, but they are not very common.

Most forms of federal spending could be allocated by any of the four methods. The question then arises: How ought one choose a method for allocating benefits in a specific program? Two approaches seem evident. The first consists of a detached analysis of process itself, in which one evaluates the internal logic and rationale of each method in an attempt to match one's principal policy aims with a compatible allocational method. The second deals less with process and more with outputs. Here, one estimates how benefits will actually be allocated under the various methods, taking into account the inevitable political pressures associated with geographic allocation. One then compares the estimated patterns of allocation with how one believes benefits should be allocated. This essay, after a brief discussion of the rationale of each method, concentrates on an analysis of outputs, particularly on how political pressures distort actual allocations from that which advocates first envisioned when designing programs and choosing allocational methods.

Allocation by formula rests on several assumptions: that differences between the needs and capabilities of rival claimants for benefits can be anticipated; that these differences are relatively simple and few in number; that they can be reliably measured; and that there are sensible ways to aggregate claimants' scores along various evaluative dimensions. Clearly, these criteria cannot be met for such complex decisions as the award of defense contracts, though they are met easily for the procurement of standardized commodities such as fuel. Formulas are used most commonly to allocate intergovernmental grants such as highway assistance, educational aid for federally impacted areas, and revenue sharing. These formulas typically include such factors as population, per capita income, land area, and the like.

The allocation of benefits on the basis of individual case-by-case decisions reflects a contrary philosophy. There is no presumption that the relevant differences between rival claimants can be anticipated, categorized, or measured with any precision. Complexity is openly acknowledged. Elaborate procedures for application, review, and negotiation over terms are designed to break down that complexity and expose claimants' individual strengths and weaknesses. There is also no presumption that all claimants deserve a share of benefits. The concentration of benefits in some areas and the denial of shares for other areas is perfectly legitimate. Individual case-by-case decisions are used for the procurement of complex items for the defense establishment, the location of military bases and other federal installations, and certain types of intergovernmental grants. They are particularly valuable for grant programs which are designed either to encourage innovation or to target benefits according to extreme need or distress.

Thus, allocation by formula and allocation by individual project decisions rest on different rationales. The choice as to whether legislators or bureaucrats should make these decisions is less clear. Bureaucrats are clear favorites when technical expertise is required, such as the allocation of research grants. But technical expertise itself frequently can be codified for legislators in a way that allows them to make informed value choices. Bureaucrats are often thought to make fewer "political" allocations than legislators, and some see this as a great virtue. Later I examine just how extensively congressional politics – i.e., the competition among legislators for shares of local benefits – affects both legislative and bureaucratic choices.

Abstract arguments about process can be made for or against each of the other allocational methods. In fact, the federal government has passed through various phases where one or another method was thought superior for entire collections of new programs.[4] Intergovernmental grants have gone through at least three phases. Early grants were predominantly of the formula type. Their aim was to help state governments perform their traditional functions in areas such as highway construction, agricultural development, and vocational education. Simple formulas based on population and a few other factors were adequate for this task. Great Society legislation in the early 1960's sought to shift the emphasis towards local governments, and to target funds in areas of most extreme need. The obvious choice, given these objectives, was to have bureaucrats allocate funds on a project-by-project basis. Some of the programs established during this period include model cities, air pollution control, community action, and aid for educationally disadvantaged children. The "New Federalism" in the early 1970's sought to give local governments greater control over how money is spent and to diminish (national) bureaucratic power. Therefore, the federal government shifted to allocation by congressional formula for initiatives such as revenue sharing, and the series of block grant programs such as community development block grants. Here, local governments may determine exactly how money is to be spent once it arrives.

The politics in allocation

Evaluating alternative allocation processes in a detached fashion has its uses, particularly when one is concerned with broad issues such as bureaucratic versus local control. But there is also value in assessing how decisions are actually made under various allocational methods. Here, the question is not merely how methods look on paper, but how they operate in a very political environment. And the world of geographic allocation is *very* political.

It is a world where legislators compete vigorously to acquire benefits for their districts. Congressmen care intensely about where benefits are allocated because they believe that playing this game well yields important electoral dividends. The wisdom on Capitol Hill is that voters are impressed by congressmen who bring home the bacon. It provides legislators with many opportunities to generate self-serving publicity. In addition, the direct beneficiaries of federal largess are excellent prospects for campaign contributions, organizational support, and public endorsements. In fact, whether the acquisition of shares of federal spending pays any electoral dividends is not known. But congressmen *think* it does, and it is this perception that impels them to compete vigorously for local shares of spending.[5]

None of the four allocational methods is immune from the effects of congressmen's quest for local benefits. Congressional conflict over funds can leave its imprint on policy regardless of whether allocational decisions are made in Congress or in the bureaucracy, individually or with formulas. The nature and extent of those policy effects, however, can vary widely depending on how decisions are made and by whom.

Here I assess the impact of congressman's quest for local benefits on the shape of public policy according to two evaluative dimensions: political allocations and political repercussions. The former is meant to be a descriptive, value-neutral dimension. The latter is a value-laden dimension that focuses on the negative policy effects of various allocational mechanisms. As used here, it necessarily represents my own values.

Political allocations refer to actual geographic distributions of benefits that reflect congressmen's struggle for shares of spending. They can be contrasted with nonpolitical allocations, which are what would be expected from decision makers who share the same basic policy preferences as congressmen but who are unencumbered by any personal interest in geographic allocation. Conceptually, it is easy to distinguish between political and nonpolitical allocations. Empirically, it is more difficult, for one must compare known political allocations with estimated nonpolitical ones.

Political repercussions refer to the negative policy effects that flow from a system where legislators actively compete for local benefits. One such repercussion is that government may choose inefficient or inappropriate means towards agreed-upon ends. Congressional preference for solutions involving vast and politically visible public works (e.g., sewage treatment plants) rather than more indirect and invisible methods

527

(effluent charges) is an example. A second repercussion is that government may overspend in a given functional area. This occurs when congressional politics dictate that unjustifiable projects in some geographic areas must be funded along with exemplary ones in other areas. A third is that government may become unable to terminate a program after benefits begin to flow into every legislator's district. New programs are added, but old ones can never be displaced. A fourth possible repercussion, an outgrowth of the first three, is that governmental spending grows continuously.

Political allocations and political repercussions often occur jointly, but they need not. Benefits can be allocated politically without necessarily producing any of the above undesirable consequences. For example, NASA's choice of Houston as the center for manned space flight was almost certainly a political decision.[6] But there were no obvious political repercussions associated with that decision or with the other political allocations of NASA facilities.

Political allocations and political repercussions may emerge no matter what policy or which allocational method is eventually adopted. But this emergence is not equally likely for all types of policies. It is easy to assume that the attractiveness of a policy depends *solely* on the allocation of local benefits. For some programs this may well be true. But most programs produce something of value other than shares of local benefits for congressmen.

One can imagine that policies offer (and congressmen evaluate) three classes of benefits. *General* benefits, such as national security, economic prosperity, and improved public health, are goods that people value because they believe that everyone profits, including themselves. *Group* benefits are those that accrue to one segment of society, for example teachers, oil companies, or airplane manufacturers. *Local* benefits are those which flow to specific geographic areas. Most policies include some combination of all three classes.

The importance of local benefits in the policy-making process depends on how citizens and congressmen evaluate whatever general or group benefits there might be.[7] When general benefits are substantial and the support for them is widespread, programs survive and prosper without having to allocate local benefits carefully to maintain a congressional coalition. National defense, medical research, and the national park system are examples of programs where the importance of general benefits diminishes the role of local benefits. Other programs deliver relatively few general or group benefits. They survive only when local benefits are carefully allocated among legislators' districts. Many public works and intergovernmental grant programs are of this type.

Legislators, bureaucrats, and decisions

Five propositions

This essay advances the following five propositions about the effects of alternative allocational mechanisms on public policy:

1. Political allocations tend to be greater when legislators, rather than bureaucrats, make allocational decisions.

2. Political allocations in the form of broadened distributions of benefits tend to be greater when formulas, rather than individual project decisions, are used to allocate benefits.

3. Political allocations in the form of larger shares for specific legislators tend to be greater when individual project decisions, rather than formulas, are used to allocate benefits.

4. Political allocations tend to be greater when programs supply relatively few general benefits and relatively few group benefits.

5. The extent of political repercussions tends to be directly related to the extent of political allocations.

The remaining sections advance these five propositions, both with arguments and with limited empirical evidence. In principle, it should be possible to test each of these propositions with systematic evidence. In practice, however, such an undertaking would require enormous resources. The major task is to identify and measure the extent of political allocations and political repercussions. This requires careful, painstaking work for even a single program; yet many such studies, spanning a broad range of programs, would be required before one could assess with confidence the validity of the propositions. At present, there are only a handful of empirical studies that are relevant to the problem.

THE EFFECTS OF ALLOCATIONAL MECHANISMS

Congress and federal projects

Before the rise of intergovernmental grants, geographic allocations were inevitably made by individual decisions about individual projects. Typical decisions included: where to build military installations, station troops, and harbor the navy; where to procure weapons and supplies; where to build public waterways improvements for irrigation, navigation, and flood control; and where and how to acquire, develop, and dispose of federal lands. These programs once constituted most of federal spending. Their size is still considerable, although they are now overshadowed by transfer payments to individuals (decisions lacking any geographic component), and by intergovernmental grants. Congress once directly allocated all of these benefits. Bureaucrats now handle all procurement contracts, and they dominate the early stages of decision making about the location of military installations and other federal facilities. Congress continues to dominate locational decisions for water projects and issues related to federal lands.

Most of what we know about how Congress makes project decisions concerns the selection of water projects. The literature in this area is extensive, considering that less than one percent of the federal budget goes to water projects, and relatively consistent in its explanations and evaluations.[8] Congress is thought to make relatively poor decisions about water policy, because everyone is looking out for local interests and no one is protecting the national interest.

The decision-making process is well known. Localities initially assemble proposals for developing harbors, deepening channels, connecting rivers, or building dams. Working through their congressmen, they petition Congress to authorize a feasibility study. For any congressman who does his homework, this is easily accomplished. The Army Corps of Engineers then performs studies which include cost-benefit analyses. Not all proposals are discovered to be worthy of investment, but many are. Disinterested observers have long noted that the Corps is remarkably generous when estimating benefits, and equally adept at underestimating the true costs. Such creative accounting is hardly surprising to students of bureaucratic politics, for it is the Corps itself that will eventually construct these works. Congress retains final control over the actual choice of projects, first at the authorization stage, where each project must be individually approved, and then at the appropriations stage, where mention in the committee report is essential.

The politics in this decision-making process follows naturally from the composition of benefits. Most projects produce concentrated benefits for groups and localities, and impose only diffuse costs on the general taxpayer. Group benefits accrue both to the common carriers who use waterways without fee and to those industries who enjoy lower transportation costs. Local benefits accrue to the areas where projects are built, both from the infusion of funds for construction and from the economic development that frequently follows improvements in transportation. Costs are borne by the general taxpayer across the country. For any given project, then, the benefits are concentrated and visible, the potential beneficiaries have good reason to organize for action, and their representatives have powerful incentives to work with them. The costs, on the other hand, are diffuse and practically invisible. Those who pay have no incentive to organize, and few congressmen see profit for themselves in leading the opposition. Any given project could easily be defeated if it were considered alone, for even two or three enthusiastic supporters would be no match for four hundred weak opponents. This problem is overcome by placing all projects in a single omnibus bill, so that the supporters of individual projects must stand together. It is the classic American logroll; it is unbeatable.

Political allocations are inevitable, for they provide the glue that holds these coalitions so firmly together. They emerge in two forms. First, distributions of projects across as many congressional districts as possible are common. If meritorious proposals happen to be concentrated in a handful of districts, then less worthy projects from other districts must be included. Politics dictates that benefits must be widely dispersed if large supporting coalitions are to be maintained. Second, some congressmen garner more benefits for their districts than either merit or the political requirement for wide distributions would seem to allow. Typically, these congressmen sit on either the Public Works Committee or the Appropriations subcommittee that together pass upon all rivers and harbors projects.[9] They use their committee positions to obtain disproportionate benefits for their own districts, either as more or larger projects. The huge, multi-billion dollar extravaganzas that capture journalists' attention, such as the Arkansas River project that made Tulsa, Oklahoma, a seaport, or the current attempt to connect the Tennesee River with the Gulf of Mexico through Alabama, invariably benefit committee members. Political allocations, then, reflect both forces of concentration and forces of dispersion.

Satisfying both forces produces political repercussions. The substitution of political criteria where acceptable merit-related criteria exist necessarily results in an inefficient allocation of resources. Cost-benefit analyses performed by disinterested observers have shown that some projects do not return benefits commensurate with their costs. For example, two economists who have examined the aforementioned 1.7 billion dollar project to provide a second route from the Tennessee River to the Gulf of Mexico estimate a return of only 39 cents on the dollar, while the more optimistic Army Corps of Engineers estimates a return of $1.20.[10] A second consequence is that the nation overspends on water projects. The problem is not simply that the system selects the wrong projects, for there is no long list of meritorious projects passed over in favor of politically more important ones. The problem is that the nation has already built most of the high-quality projects, and each year it must dip lower and lower into the barrel. Thus, it overspends on water projects, relative to competing needs. One ill that cannot be traced to the congressional system for allocating water projects is the growth of governmental spending. If anything, water projects have been a drag on such growth, not the engine behind it, since they have declined from 2.4

percent of federal expenditures in 1927, to .9 percent in 1957, to less than .5 percent today.[11]

Knowledge about the allocational system for water projects is probably more complete and extensive than it is for any other allocational decisions. Most observers agree that the system produces substantial political allocations and political repercussions. Why is this so? Is it simply a necessary consequence of having the legislature itself make decisions about individual projects? Or is the source of the problem more related to the nature of the policy itself, where concentrated local and group benefits overpower distributed general costs? Most likely, both are contributing causes. But at this point it is difficult to say with confidence which is the greater villain, largely because water projects are the only major project decisions that today's Congress makes. One gains some perspective by examining how bureaucrats make project decisions.

Bureaucrats and federal projects

Congress has delegated to bureaucrats the primary responsibility for allocating most other direct federal spending, except for intergovernmental grants and transfer payments. Included are: locational decisions for new federal facilities, office buildings, and military installations; decisions about where federal employees will work; the awarding of procurement contracts for both defense and non-defense items; and the allocation of research money among firms and universities. The fact that Congress has delegated much of the responsibility for these decisions to bureaucrats does not necessarily mean that congressional influence is less, nor that political allocations and political repercussions are less pronounced. Just as the Army Corps of Engineers accommodates congressmen's wishes when it studies the feasibility of water projects, so, too, can bureaucrats in other agencies be very accommodating when they make actual allocational decisions. After all, Congress can easily take back allocational authority if it does not like the way it is exercised.

Cooperation among congressmen and bureaucrats can be mutually satisfying. Congressmen want bureaucrats' help in channeling funds into their districts at appropriate times and with appropriate opportunities for congressional credit. Bureaucrats want congressmen to approve their budgetary requests, to give them wide latitude in areas unrelated to constituency benefits, and to avoid undue criticism at public hearings. As long as congressmen care more about constituency benefits than about bureaucrats' principal aims (and bureaucrats care less), there is ample room for mutual accommodations. Bureaucrats can defer to congressmen's allocational perferences in exchange for congressional deference to their goals.[12]

How much do bureaucrats accommodate congressmen's preferences? There is good reason to believe it varies from policy to policy. Unfortunately, the requisite empirical studies to assess accurately how allocational decisions are made across all policies have not yet been done. The best one can do is to make inferences from the few existing studies.

Defense benefits

One can probably speak most confidently about locational decisions related to military installations and defense contracts. These basic choices account for the eventual geographic distribution of 130 billion dollars annually, or one quarter of federal spending. For military installations, there are three locational decisions of consequence: where to build new bases (historically important, but now trivial because few are constructed), which bases should be closed, and how to allocate military personnel among existing installations. Congressmen apparently take greatest interest in closing decisions, for their constituencies have already acquired a large, visible stake in the outcome. Virtually all congressmen endeavor to keep bases in their districts open. All have not been equally successful, however, as more than a hundred major installations have been closed during the past two decades.

The question arises: Does congressional politics affect in any way bureaucrats' selection of bases to be closed? The presumption has always been that members of the military committees were able to protect military installations in their districts, but there has been little systematic evidence to support this hypothesis. Recently, I assembled appropriate data from Pentagon files on the closing of 58 Army and 67 Air Force installations between 1952 and 1974, and used it to test a multivariate model of how installations were selected for closing during this period. The evidence is compelling that bureaucrats avoided closing bases in districts with representatives on the military committees in the House – i.e., the Armed Services Committee and the two military subcommittees of the Appropriations Committee. Separate probit estimates for Army and Air Forces bases suggest that installations represented on military committees faced probabilities of closure that were less than half as great as those without such representation. This occurred during a period in which 41 percent of all installations were actually closed. These differences persist even when other effects related to installations' quality are controlled.[13] The evidence is strong that bureaucrats defer to the locational preferences of those congressmen who are in the best position to affect bureaucrats' futures. Members of these committees must pass on all funds for the Pentagon and, thus, their good will and active support is crucial to bureaucrats' well being.

There is also evidence that locational decisions for new bases are affected by congressional politics. In a study of site selection for the 38 new Army and Air Force installations built between 1952 and 1974, I discovered that a disproportionate number of sites were chosen from districts represented on the military committees, and particularly the House Armed Services Committee. Again, this is evidence of bureaucrats bending their allocational decisions to suit their congressional overseers, though the extent of influence is somewhat smaller for site selection than it is for base closings.[14] Thus far, I have not been able to model satisfactorily decisions about the allocation of military personnel among installations, nor to uncover any patterns of congressional influence over these decisions. Committee members appear to enjoy no special advantage here.[15]

The existence and extent of political allocations in the vast field of defense contracting is still an open question. Impressionistic, anecdotal, and largely circumstantial accounts see much smoke; but the best systematic studies have yet to uncover any fire.[16] Immense data problems, relating to subcontracting and bureaucrats' limited range of alternatives when placing contracts, suggest that we are still a long way from accurate identification and measurement of whatever political allocations may exist here. Most likely, they are relatively slight, which is why they have been so elusive.

For military benefits, then, political allocations do exist, but their extent varies according to the particular type of benefit. In any event, these political allocations are substantially less extensive than for water projects and largely confined to members of military committees. Elsewhere, I have estimated from the appropriate probit equations that bureaucrats at the Pentagon have adjusted no more than 15 percent of all their closing and site selection decisions to conform wth congressmen's allocational preferences.[17] This contrasts with the case of water projects where many, perhaps most, such allocational decisions are largely political.

One explanation for this difference is that congressmen perceive defense policy and water policy in fundamentally different terms. Defense policy delivers substantial general benefits, as well as significant local and group benefits. Consequently, most congressmen support relatively high levels of defense spending regardless of whether their districts receive shares of local benefits. They support it for the general benefit of national security. This gives bureaucrats considerable freedom in allocating local benefits, for proper allocation is not the key to a winning coalition. Careful attention to committee members' districts still has value because their strong and enthusiastic support helps to grease the congressional wheels and ease the approval of requests from the military. However, it is not the key to survival. This contrasts with water policy, where there are few general benefits of consequence. Congressmen who are denied shares of local benefits have little reason to support rivers and harbors projects for everyone else. For water policy, then, local benefits are the key to a winning coalition.

Thus, differences in policy are important. But is it also important that Congress allocates water projects whereas bureaucrats allocate defense benefits? I think it is. Consider the case of closing military installations. During the past two decades, the Pentagon has closed well over a hundred military installations, in response to a decline in total military personnel and in an effort to economize by consolidating personnel at larger bases. Such decisions are clearly in bureaucrats' interests, for they conserve resources for new weapons and other priority items. They are not in congressmen's interests, however, and congressmen have fought them for years. Congressmen have never been sympathetic to imposing substantial local costs on their districts in return for modest economies. Even the most fiscally conservative legislator can instantly give an impassioned speech on "false economy" when his district's interests are at stake. Congressmen's efforts to stop the closing of military installations have been hampered by the fact that committee members seldom suffer this pain. Bureaucrats have been careful to spare congressmen who are best in a position to stop them. Imagine, however, that Congress itself were to make closing decisions. The most likely consequence would be that economy would take the back seat, and most bases would remain open. It is far easier for affected rank-and-file congressmen to defend their local turf when Congress makes the decisions than it is when they must somehow coalesce to reverse bureaucrats' decisions.

Other federal projects

Political allocations may also arise in other areas where bureaucrats make project decisions. Most decisions about where research and development funds are to be spent are relatively nonpolitical. Congressmen seldom meddle with the National Science Foundation in an attempt to channel more grants to universities in their districts. The existing distribution of universities and firms capable of high-quality research is the constraint on allocational politics, not the activities of congressmen. Likewise, medical, defense, and scientific research survive on the basis of their general benefits, not in response to carefully devised allocational strategies. Although political considerations seldom override merit criteria in these areas, they do enter when the latter are inconclusive. This happens particularly when the federal government seeks to construct from scratch some totally new research installations. There may be acceptable criteria for separating good and bad locations, but seldom can one define objective criteria that lead to a single, best location. Political criteria are frequently used to choose among the most acceptable locations. Surely, it made little difference to NASA exactly where astronauts were to be trained. It did make a difference to Representative Thomas of Houston, chairman of the Appropriations subcommittee with jurisdiction over NASA. And so a Manned Spacecraft Center was born – in Houston.[18] The political logic was compelling. Similarly, it made little difference whether a new proton accelerator was located in New York, California, or Illinois. Organized pressure from midwestern congressmen made Weston, Illinois the choice.[19] So, political allocations are not uncommon in areas related to research and development. But they arise principally when other criteria fail to produce a single choice, or when the differences between top-ranked choices are minor.

The logic is similar for locational decisions concerning other federal facilities such as office buildings. Initially, Congress battles over program-related questions about general and group benefits and costs. Later, the question arises of where all those workers who administer these programs will be located. Political allocations are possible here, too, but they usually occur peripherally. Battles over where new federal facilities should be located are sometimes intense, but they make little difference to anyone but the congressmen involved in the conflict (and their constituents).

Political allocations exist across the whole range of locational decisions that bureaucrats make. But these political allocations usually do not produce the serious political repercussions that they do when Congress selects water projects. It is difficult to find examples of programs within this class that can survive only by the strategic allocation of local benefits, as was the case for water projects. Similarly, it is difficult to find programs that were originally passed only as a way to create barrels full of pork for congressmen.

The most serious political repercussions generally occur for programs that should be terminated or curtailed. If some congressmen are able to protect military installations in their districts from closure, then bases in other districts must suffer that fate. Such decisions are inefficient when the latter installations are actually superior to the former. More seriously, congressmen often band together to prevent termination of defense contracts. They keep production lines open for certain weapons systems long after the Pentagon's requirements have been met. One example is the F-111, which the Texas delegation was able to keep in production for four years after the administration recommended closure.[20] Politically, it is easier to keep a weapons system in production than to keep a single base open, because a single defense contract usually includes scores of major subcontracts distributed around the country.

It is instructive to compare water projects with other federal projects. One finds substantial political allocations when Congress handles water projects. These allocations are essential to the survival of the program, and they inevitably lead to significant political repercussions. Much smaller political allocations associated with most programs are found when bureaucrats make individual locational decisions. Ordinarily, these allocations are helpful, but not essential, to a program's survival. Since they are less central to a program's existence, they tend to produce less severe political repercussions.

The source of this difference between water projects and other forms of direct federal spending is the existence of general benefits for the latter, which provide a firm basis for congressional support, and their nonexistence for water projects, which makes allocational politics the center of the entire game. But there are also important differences hinging upon who makes the allocational decisions, congressmen or bureaucrats. For congressmen, the allocation of local benefits is central to their political lives. For bureaucrats, allocating benefits is more a means to the end of satisfying their budgetary and other goals. Bureaucrats do defer to congressmen's allocational preferences, but only as it serves these other goals. Thus, by giving bureaucrats allocational authority, the extent of political allocations is diminished.

Intergovernmental grants

In principle, intergovernmental grants can be allocated among states and localities according to any of the four allocational methods. In practice, two methods predominate: congressional allocation by formula, and bureaucratic allocation with individual project decisions. The questions here are: Does it make any difference which method is chosen? Are political allocations more common under one method? Are political repercussions more likely or more serious?

The world of intergovernmental grants is considerably different from that of direct federal spending. Most direct programs deliver substantial general benefits that both voters and congressmen value. They also deliver valuable local benefits, but these usually are of secondary importance when a program is first adopted. Congressmen compete vigorously for shares of local benefits, but their support is not contingent upon receiving them. Water projects, as I have noted, are the principal exception, for here general benefits are few, and local benefits predominate. Grant programs resemble water programs more than they do other forms of federal spending. Local benefits abound while general benefits are relatively scarce. Consequently, few congressmen support

537

particular grant programs without first calculating how their own districts will benefit. The question of how local benefits are to be allocated is not a peripheral issue for grant programs. It is often the central issue.

Estimating just how political are the actual geographic allocations for various grant programs presumes that one has some standard for comparison – a sense of how benefits would be allocated in the absence of congressional competition for funds. Unfortunately, there is no single standard of comparison. Such standards reflect conceptions of what ends these programs should serve, and there is little consensus on these ends. Should they be redistributional schemes that concentrate funds on poor areas? Should they reward those local governments that already tax themselves heavily? Or perhaps those with high taxes should be punished. Should they target funds according to local needs for services? Should equalization of services across localities be the principal aim? Should the federal government use its funds to encourage the development of innovative solutions to problems? Or should it merely subsidize traditional approaches? These questions, related to the fundamental purposes of particular programs, have obvious implications for how benefits are eventually allocated geographically.

Three types of decisions must be made for any grant program: decisions about the *broad purpose* of federal assistance (e.g., rejuvenate cities, train the unemployed), decisions about the *specific means* toward those ends (e.g., subsidize development, subsidize employers), and decisions about *geographic location*. These decisions are separable, and each, except the last, could be made by the legislature, the bureaucracy, or localities themselves. (Localities cannot allocate funds geographically.) As Table 20.1 shows, no institution has a monopoly on any of these decisions.

Project grants

The majority of grant programs dispense project grants, although together they account for only about one third of the total funds for intergovernmental assistance. Typically, these programs distribute funds to localities for specific, narrow purposes, in response to applications that detail exactly how localities propose to spend the funds. Congress defines the broad purposes for these categorical programs, and outlines what means are to be encouraged. Bureaucrats define more narrowly what means are acceptable, both through detailed regulations and through their actual acceptance of various types of local proposals. Bureaucrats also have authority to make all locational decisions. These are truly discretionary programs, with most authority vested in bureau-

Table 20.1. *Decision making for intergovernmental grants*

Types of programs	Broad purpose	Specific means	Geographic location
	Decisions about		
Categorical-project	Congress	Congress and bureaucracy	Bureaucracy
Categorical-formula	Congress	Congress	Congress
Block-grant-formula	Congress	Localities	Congress
Revenue sharing	Localities	Localities	Congress

crats. Laws that authorize these programs may be only a few paragraphs long.

Project grants are usually the choice when program designers seek either to concentrate funds in areas of greatest need or to encourage localities to develop innovative solutions through competition for limited funds. They, alone, among the alternative mechanisms for delivering assistance, allow precise targeting of funds – at least in theory. But how close do real-world programs come to this ideal? It all depends on what that ideal is. If the aim is to concentrate funds so much that only a handful of congressional districts eventually benefit, then the ideal is never approached. Programs that promise benefits only for decaying inner cities have little chance of emerging from Congress intact. Most congressmen know from the beginning that their districts will not be included, and they react accordingly. On the other hand, if the aim is to concentrate funds in needy areas, but need is defined so that most districts have a few qualifying areas, then the ideal is often reached. Project grants permit concentration of funds, but congressional politics place limits on the degree of concentration.

Political allocations of project grants usually have their roots in the initial congressional consideration of a program. Those who design such programs occasionally try to enact ones that would truly concentrate benefits in areas of greatest need. The usual congressional reaction is to broaden the eligibility criteria so that benefits will flow into many more congressional districts. The classic case was the model cities program, which was initially designed to pour massive federal funds into a few urban communities to demonstrate how saturation spending could transform decaying areas into new cities. It was to be an experimental program with, at most, a dozen cities participating. By the time it emerged from Congress in late 1966, it spread the same funds among 150 cities. Congress even redefined "city" so that rural hamlets were included.[21] The model cities example is typical of what happens when proposals for concentrated benefits move through Congress. A water and sewer program, intended for rapidly growing communities, is transformed into one that spreads funds thinly across all communities.[22] Economic development programs are reshaped so that less distressed areas are included. Poverty programs suddenly encompass those 'pockets of poverty' that even economically healthy areas contain.

Political allocations, then, have their beginnings when Congress first considers these programs. It is here that they are broadened so that most congressional districts become eligible for shares of benefits. By examining actual allocational decisions, one sees that bureaucrats take excellent advantage of these broadened criteria. They tend to accept applications from as many districts as possible, thus satisfying as many congressmen as possible. The 150 model cities, for example, were chosen so that 226 congressional districts were included (some cities had multiple districts); only five districts received more than one district.[23] Similarly, bureaucrats at HUD managed to place at least one water and sewer grant in each congressional district within a few years of that program's beginning.[24] The urban renewal program was originally passed in 1949 as a slum-clearance program for larger cities. As bureaucrats sought to build a broader coalition of support, it evolved into a program with benefits for communities of all sizes.[25]

Political allocations may also take the form of extra shares of benefits for specific legislators who are important to a program's prosperity. Typically, these are members of the relevant legislative committees and appropriations subcommittees, but others who have provided crucial support may also be rewarded. Again, the model cities program illustrates both tactics. Bureaucrats clearly gave special preference to members of those committees with authority over the program. They also accepted a disproportionate number of applications from rank-and-file congressmen who provided crucial support when model cities was first funded.[26] Evidence from other grant programs; such as water and sewer grants, urban renewal, and economic development grants, reveals similar rewards for specific legislators.[27] From the perspective of bureaucrats, such political allocations are rational, for they help protect their programs and budgets from congressional interference. The two forms of political allocations – broadened distribution of benefits and extra shares for specific legislators – are not mutually exclusive. One can, without contradiction, spread benefits more widely than originally intended while still providing extra shares for committee members. What inevitably suffers when these twin tactics are used is the concentration of benefits according to criteria of merit or need.

These political allocations have obvious political repercussions. Federal funds are not allocated strictly on the basis of merit or concentrated solely in areas of greatest need. Experimental programs such as the original model cities programs, designed to create a handful of demonstration cities, are virtually impossible, given the political constraints. If experimentation is the aim of policy makers, then political repercussions are practically guaranteed and of considerable magnitude, for a substantial proportion of funds are drained from the original purpose and spent politically to maintain a broad coalition of support. For programs with less ambitious aims, however, the repercussions are much less serious. Bureaucrats who allocated funds for the urban renewal program needed to spread funds across many congressional districts for political reasons. But they were still able to concentrate funds *within* districts, according to their perceptions of need. Similarly, they were able to adjust the amounts of the grants in any way they pleased so that political allocations would consume a relatively small share of funds.

The extent of political repercussions varies for different types of project grants. In general, they appear less severe than in the case of water projects, and somewhat greater for the other forms of direct federal spending. But much depends on whether or not designers have envisioned politically realistic programs from the start. Those that are not may become severely distorted and yield substantial political repercussions.

Formula grants

Formula programs come in three varieties: categorical grants, block grants, and revenue sharing. They differ principally in how and by whom decisions are made about each program's spending (Table 20.1). For categorical programs, Congress defines their broad purposes, selects specific means to achieve those ends, and writes formulas for allocating funds among states and localities. For block-grant programs, Congress defines the broad purposes and writes the allocational formulas, but it is up to the localities to decide exactly how funds are to be spent within the congressionally defined purposes. Revenue sharing gives localities almost complete freedom in defining the purposes of spending and the means towards those ends. Congress merely writes the allocational formula. These programs differ, then, in how much discretion is given to states and localities. Bureaucrats administer all programs, but their role is relatively minor; they have no exclusive authority over any of the three decisions.

Formula programs emphasize all-inclusive criteria. Unlike project grants, the question is not who should receive benefits and who should not. The question is simply how much each recipient should receive.

Ordinarily, all governmental units at a certain level, i.e., state, county, city, village, are entitled to shares. Although formula programs tend to spread funds thinly across the nation rather than to concentrate them in limited areas, there is nothing inherent in the formula approach that leads to this outcome. Formulas *could* be written with thresholds: those scoring below a certain level would receive nothing, while those scoring above it would receive varying amounts according to the formula. However, they usually are not written this way.

In principle, one should be able to write a formula that reflects any combination of merit-related criteria that one wished to reward. Criteria related to need, competence, capacity, past accomplishment, or demand for governmental services can all be approximated with some measuring device that yields quantitative estimates that can be incorporated into a formula. In practice, formula writers usually adopt criteria for which data already exist for all possible recipients. For states, there are many indicators from which to choose. For localities, there are relatively few, chiefly those collected by the census, by other governmental agencies, or by the localities themselves, such as school enrollments. These statistics are far from ideal. Reliance upon them alone makes it difficult to write good formulas that accurately reflect underlying needs and abilities.

It is not an easy task to estimate just how political the actual allocations are under the 150 or so formulas presently in use, for as yet there is no systematic literature on the subject. In a previous essay, I examined most of the current formulas, but this can only be the beginning. For now, however, it is all that is available. On this base, the following judgments rest.[28]

Looking first at categorical formulas, one finds how infrequently formulas are constructed around even a modest collection of merit-related criteria. Many formulas completely ignore legitimate differences in demand for governmental services, even when rudimentary data do exist. For example, urban mass transit grants include factors of urban population and density, but not the actual use of mass transit. As a consequence, New York, a city built around mass transit, receives a subsidy of 2 cents per passenger, while Grand Rapids receives 45 cents per passenger.[29]

Formulas rely most heavily on population data, with occasional data for various subpopulations such as school-age children. Such factors, in the absence of strong, countervailing merit-related factors, create relatively even distributions of funds among localities. These formulas reflect fundamental congressional forces toward political equity rather than the contrary forces toward concentration of funds by need, demand, or capacity.

Allocational rules that stress population are usually well received in the House. Such rules guarantee all congressmen relatively equal shares so that no congressman must face his electorate with less than others. The Senate, built on a different concept of political equity, frequently tinkers with these formulas. A favorite technique is to add a minimum and maximum allocation. This guarantees small states far more than their due while denying the largest two or three states their entitled allotment.

The reliance on population and the adoption of minimum floors and maximum ceilings are forms of political allocation, especially when they displace the search for good merit-related criteria. All this is done in a gentlemanly fashion. There is an easy acceptance of this political equity. Congressmen do not fight to obtain maximum shares for their districts or have a long debate about what allocations would best serve the public interest.

Recent block-grant programs, e.g., Community Development Block Grants, are larger and more broad based than most of their categorical predecessors. One sees similar outcomes, but with some fascinating twists. Congress does not write these formulas in the nonconflictual environment just described for categorical grants, where political equity triumphs easily. Instead, there are endless quarrels, in subcommittee, in committee, on the floors of both House and Senate, and in conference, over exactly what 'merit' criteria belong in these formulas. Many of these conflicts have politics at the heart. Congressmen show a remarkable ability to vote for the formula factors that treat their districts best. Consider, for example, the recent fight over the allocational formula for a program of block grants to states, designed to help the poor pay their heating bills. The dispute evolved into a contest between North and South over the division of funds between them. On a roll call vote, congressmen from 35 frostbelt states were practically unanimous (93%) in support of a formula weighted towards colder states, while those from the remaining sunbelt states were equally united (96%) in opposition.[30] The rhetoric in such debates emphasizes differing conceptions of merit, but the actual votes reveal the conflicting interests of congressmen, each determined to improve his district's share.

It is not completely clear why formula writing is more political for the new block grants than it was for categorical programs. One explanation is that Congress now has its own computers, so that each congressman can know precisely how each minor change in a formula will affect his district.[31] Thus, it is now considerably easier to fine tune formulas. Second, the new programs are much larger. Investing energy in long battles over each formula is potentially more worthwhile when many millions are at stake.

For whatever reasons, the formulas for these new programs are increasingly political. Their foundation is still one of political equity – large, relatively uniform shares for everyone. Unlike project grants, no one goes without a share. But at the margins, there is intense conflict over what localities will do best. The outcomes depend on the shifting coalitions of the time. Formulas are written not for the ages, but until a new coalition forms to write a better formula for its members.

Political allocations under formula programs appear far greater than under project grants. For project grants, political allocations appear in the form of broader distributions of benefits than program designers usually intend, and include relatively small extra allocations for members of important congressional committees. For categorical formula grants, they appear in the form of political equity and relatively uniform distributions of benefits, with arbitrary floors and ceilings that reward the smallest states and punish the largest. For broad-based programs, competition among congressmen becomes intense. Political allocations here reflect most forcefully the interests of those congressmen in the winning coalition of the moment.

Political repercussions appear least under project grants. The proportion of benefits diverted for political purposes is usually relatively small, except in cases where benefits properly belong to but a small fraction of congressional districts. Ordinarily, bureaucrats can spread benefits across a wide range of congressional districts and award extra shares to important committee members *without* distorting a program's fundamental purpose. Benefits can be awarded largely according to bureaucrats' perceptions of recipients' needs, while still meeting these simple political constraints. This follows because, although bureaucrats may be forced to distribute benefits widely *across* districts, they can still concentrate them *within* districts according to whatever merit-related criteria they choose.

The repercussions appear somewhat greater under categorical formula grants. Attempts to concentrate funds according to need inevitably become watered down in Congress. The tendency to adopt formulas that spread benefits relatively evenly means that only a small proportion of all federal funds actually flow into areas of greatest need. Although the administrative neatness of formulas cannot be denied, the policy outcomes often depart considerably from the merit-related criteria upon which they supposedly rest. Political repercussions appear even greater for the new block grant programs. The competition over which factors will appear in these formulas seems to have moved them even further away from conceptions of merit. The principal limitation of formula programs as actually implemented is that they tend to distribute benefits broadly both *across* districts and *within* them.

THE CHOICE OF ALLOCATIONAL MECHANISMS

Returning to the original question: Does it make a difference how allocational decisions are made, whether by legislators or bureaucrats, and whether with formulas or project decisions? As I hope to have shown, it makes a considerable difference. The choice of allocational mechanism is not a neutral decision.

The evidence needed for this judgment is far from complete. My inferences are drawn from a very limited literature. There are no studies of the politics of formulas when bureaucrats design them, and only one related to congressional design of formulas. Studies related to project decisions, either by congressmen or bureaucrats, are more numerous, but hardly extensive enough to create a firm foundation for confident judgment.

Also, remember that the allocational mechanism is only one factor that affects the nature of political allocations and repercussions. The relative composition of general, group, and local benefits is more important. Political allocations and repercussions are invariably greater when general and group benefits are slight relative to local benefits, as in water projects and most intergovernmental grants. Tinkering with allocational mechanisms may reduce political allocations and repercussions in such cases, but the predominance of local benefits places real limits on how much they can be reduced.

Political allocations and repercussions appear to be less when bureaucrats rather than legislators make decisions, and when individual project decisions rather than formulas are used. To be sure, bureaucrats are capable of using local benefits to their advantage, and there is evidence that they make many shrewd political allocations. They make such allocations not out of habit, but rather as a means of advancing their principal goals and securing adequate support in Congress. Thus, one expects that bureaucrats allocate benefits strategically only to the extent necessary to maintain a supporting coalition. Congressmen, on the other hand, have every incentive to play the allocation game fully, even when further political allocations are unnecessary to maintain a coalition.

The argument that project decisions produce *fewer* political allocations than formula decisions runs contrary to first impressions. One might argue that project decisions are inherently more political because they can be allocated individually to reward committee members or other individual congressmen, whereas formula decisions cannot be targeted politically in the same way. The argument is true only if one's conception of political allocations is limited to those benefits that are traded individually for political support. Political allocations, however, should

545

also include the congressional tendency to broaden programs and spread benefits relatively uniformly across the country. Although programs of project grants often end up spreading benefits more widely than early advocates might have hoped, this tendency is far greater and the actual allocations far more uniform for formula programs. The essential difference, then, is between project grants, which distribute benefits broadly across districts but which still allow concentration within districts, and formula grants, which spread benefits more evenly both across districts and within them.

Advocates of the "New Federalism" usually prefer formula grants, and especially block grants, to project grants because they believe such programs will redistribute power away from bureaucrats and toward local officials. Indeed they do. But the federal government must still allocate each program's funds geographically. One implication of this essay is that this diminution of bureaucratic control has come at the price of increased politicization of the allocational system. Whether this represents a gain or a loss, is not at issue here. But the case for the "New Federalism" is not as clearcut at those who focus solely on the issue of bureaucratic control might believe.

NOTES

1 See, for example, James M. Buchanan and Gordon Tullock, *The Calculus of Consent* (Ann Arbor: University of Michigan Press, 1962), pp. 135–145; Brian Barry, *Political Argument* (London: Routledge and Kegan Paul, 1965), pp. 250–256; and Theodore J. Lowi, "American Business, Public Policy, Case Studies, and Political Theory," *World Politics* 16 (1964), pp. 677–715.

2 Carol F. Goss, "Military Committee Membership and Defense-Related Benefits in the House of Representatives," in *Western Political Quarterly* 25 (1972), pp. 215–233; Charles R. Plott, "Some Organizational Influences on Urban Renewal Decisions," *American Economic Review* 58 (May 1968), pp. 306–321; Barry S. Rundquist, "Congressional Influences on the Distribution of Prime Military Contracts" (Ph.D. dissertation, Stanford University, 1973); Rundquist, "On Testing a Military Industrial Complex Theory," *American Politics Quarterly* 6 (1978), pp. 29–53; J. Theodore Anagnoson, "Politics in the Distribution of Federal Grants: The Case of the Economic Development Administration" (unpublished paper, University of California, Santa Barbara, October 1978); John A. Ferejohn, *Pork Barrel Politics* (Stanford: Stanford University Press, 1973).

3 R. Douglas Arnold, *Congress and the Bureaucracy: A Theory of Influence* (New Haven: Yale University Press, 1979); "The Local Roots of Domestic Policy," in Thomas E. Mann and Norman J. Ornstein (eds.), *The New Congress* (Washington: American Enterprise Institute, 1981); and "Legislatures, Overspending, and Government Growth," Conference on the Causes and Consequences of Public Sector Growth (Dorado Beach, Puerto Rico, November 1978).

4 For a discussion of the development of the federal grant system, see James L.

Sundquist, *Making Federalism Work* (Washington: Brookings, 1969), pp. 1–13; Donald M. Haider, *When Governments Come to Washington* (New York: Free Press, 1974), pp. 54–57; and Advisory Commission on Intergovernmental Relations, *Categorical Grants: Their Role and Design* (Washington: Government Printing Office, 1978), pp. 15–47.

5 David R. Mayhew, *Congress: The Electoral Connection* (New Haven: Yale University Press, 1974).

6 Thomas P. Murphy, *Science, Geopolitics, and Federal Spending* (Lexington, Mass: Health Lexington Books, 1971), pp. 210–218.

7 Arnold (1979), pp. 37–71; (1981), pp. 4–6.

8 Arthur Maass, *Muddy Waters* (Cambridge: Harvard University Press, 1951); James T. Murphy, "The House Public Works Committee: Determinants and Consequences of Committee Behavior" (Ph.D. dissertation, University of Rochester, 1969); Ferejohn (1973).

9 Ferejohn (1973), pp. 129–232.

10 Alvin M. Josephy, Jr., "The South's Unstoppable Waterway," *Fortune* (August 27, 1979), p. 81.

11 U.S. Bureau of the Budget, *The Budget of the U.S. Government* (1928, 1958, 1979).

12 Arnold (1979), pp. 19–71.

13 Ibid., pp. 107–115.

14 Ibid., pp. 115–119.

15 Ibid., pp. 119–120.

16 Rundquist (1973, 1978).

17 Arnold (1979), pp. 115, 118.

18 Murphy (1971), pp. 210–218.

19 Murphy (1971), pp. 291–326; Theodore J. Lowi and Benjamin Ginsberg, *Poiliscide* (New York: Macmillan, 1976), pp. 87–107.

20 Peter Ognibene, "Grounding the Texas Air Force," *New York Times* (May 10, 1975), p. 29.

21 Arnold (1979), pp. 165–169.

22 Ibid., pp. 129–133.

23 Ibid., pp. 165–206.

24 Ibid., pp. 129–164.

25 Plott (1968); Arnold (1979), p. 211–212.

26 Arnold (1979), pp. 165–206.

27 Arnold (1979), pp. 129–164; Plott (1968); and Anagnoson (1978).

28 Arnold (1981).

29 William C. Freund, "Can Quotas, Tariffs, and Subsidies Save the Northeast?" in George Sternlieb and James W. Hughes (eds.), *Revitalizing the Northeast* (New Brunswick: Center for Urban Policy Research, 1978), p. 204.

30 Arnold (1981).

31 Stephen E. Frantzich, "Computerized Information Technology in the U.S. House of Representatives," *Legislative Studies Quarterly* 4 (1979), p. 266.

REFERENCES

Advisory Commission on Intergovernmental Relations 1978. *Categorical Grants: Their Role and Design.* Washington: Government Printing Office.

R. Douglas Arnold

Anagnoson, J. T. 1978. Politics in the Distribution of Federal Grants: The Case of the Economic Development Administration. University of California, Santa Barbara, unpublished paper.

Arnold, R. D. 1978. Legislatures, Overspending, and Government Growth. Conference on the Causes and Consequences of Public Sector Growth. Dorado Beach, Puerto Rico.

1979. *Congress and the Bureaucracy: A Theory of Influence.* New Haven: Yale University Press.

1981. The Local Roots of Domestic Policy. *The New Congress,* eds. T. E. Mann and N. J. Ornstein. Washington: American Enterprise Institute.

Barry, B. 1965. *Political Argument.* London: Routledge and Kegan Paul.

Buchanan, J. M. and Tullock, G. 1962. *The Calculus of Consent.* Ann Arbor: University of Michigan Press.

Ferejohn, J. A. 1973. *Pork Barrel Politics.* Stanford: Stanford University Press.

Frantzich, S. E. 1979. Computerized Information Technology in the U.S. House of Representatives. *Legislative Studies Quarterly,* 4:266.

Freund, W. C. 1978. Can Quotas, Tarriffs, and Subsidies Save the Northeast? *Revitalizing the Northeast.* eds. G. Sternlieb and J. W. Hughes. New Brunswick: Center for Urban Policy Research.

Goss, C. F. 1972. Military Committee Membership and Defense Related Benefits in the House of Representatives. *Western Political Quarterly,* 25:215–233.

Haider, D. M. 1974. *When Governments Come To Washington.* New York: Free Press.

Josephy, A. M. 1979. The South's Unstoppable Waterway. *Fortune,* August 27:81.

Lowi, T. J. 1964. American Business, Public Policy, Case Studies, and Political Theory. *World Politics,* 16:677–715.

Lowi, T. J. and Ginsberg, B. 1976. *Poiliscide.* New York: Macmillan.

Maass, A. 1951. *Muddy Waters.* Cambridge: Harvard University Press.

Mayhew, D. R. 1974. *Congress: The Electoral Connection.* New Haven: Yale University Press.

Murphy, T. P. 1969. The House Public Works Committee: Determinants and Consequences of Committee Behavior. Ph.D. dissertation, University of Rochester.

1971. *Science, Geopolitics, and Federal Spending.* Lexington, Mass.: Heath Lexington Books.

Ognibene, P. 1975. Grounding the Texas Air Force. *New York Times,* May 10, 1975:29.

Plott, C. R. 1968. Some Organizational Influences on Urban Renewal Decisions. *American Economic Review,* 58:306–321.

Rundquist, B. S. 1973. Congressional Influences on the Distribution of Prime Military Contacts. Ph.D. dissertation, Stanford University.

1978. On Testing a Military Industrial Complex Theory. *American Political Quarterly,* 6:29–53.

Sundquist, J. L. 1969. *Making Federalism Work.* Washington: Brookings.

U.S. Bureau of the Budget. 1928, 1958, 1979. *The Budget of the U.S. Government.* Washington: U.S. Government Printing Office.

Index

Index

Index

Index

Index

Index

representation (cont.)
  and institutional structure, 7
  proportional, 475–6, 484
  single-member, 476, 484
republican government, 3, 13
republican monarchy, 2
republican politics, 1
Resoluteness condition, 326, 336–8
Resource Conservation and Recovery Act
  (RCRA), 412, 420
responsibility, 73, 76
responsiveness, 73, 431, 455–8
restrained partisanship, 153–5, 161
retirement, 74
Reuss, Henry, 35
revenue sharing, 541
Rice, Stuart A., 94, 236
  and index of cohesion, 236–7
riders, 353
Rieselbach, Leroy N., 11
Riker, William H., 11, 131–4, 311–13,
  316, 344, 489, 497, 500
Ripley, Randall B., 90, 131, 235, 414, 430,
  434–5, 515
risk aversion, 470, 482, 489
rivers and harbors, 86, 209, 212–16,
  219–29, 531–7, 540
Rivers and Harbors, House Committee on,
  228–30
Robinson, Glen, 409, 413
Robinson, James A., 274–5
Robinson–Patman Act, 506, 510–13
Rodney, Caesar A., 106, 125
Rohde, David W., 8, 86–7, 371
roll call voting, 19, 24, 28
  and marginality, 303
  and position taking, 23–4
Romer, Thomas, 352, 371
Roosevelt, Franklin, 93, 254
Roosevelt, Theodore, 267
Rosenbaum, David E., 28
Rosenthal, Howard, 352, 371
Rourke, Francis E., 501
Rudder, Catherine, 398
rule-making decisions, 443–5, 450–3,
  459, 468, 491, 502, 506–7
rule of thumb, 30–1
Rules, House Committee on, 262–8,
  273–80
rules and procedures, 3–4, 25, 274–5,
  347, 384–5, 406, 416, 427, 488
  administrative, 409, 412–22, 435,
  441–5, 450, 453–8, 466–8,
  471–4, 479–81, 500
  of committee assignments, 180–1
  on committees, 86, 148–50, 158, 165,
  173, 175

as constraints, 150
and credit claiming, 25
institutional structure, 309–12, 315
as reform, 261, 266–70, 276–80,
  369–71
see also institutional structure;
  universalism
runaway bureaucracy, 502, 514
Rundquist, Barry S., 496

Sabath, Adolph, 274
safe seat, 15, 29, 41, 44, 55
  see also marginal districts
Salisbury, Robert, 500, 517
Satterwaite, Mark A., 338
Saylor, John, 159
Schattschneider, Elmo E., 29, 131, 232, 235
Scher, Seymour, 495
Schick, Allan, 212, 226, 407
Schmitt, Harrison, 505
Schneier, Edward V., Jr., 235–7
Schofield, Norman J., 331, 371, 416
school board, 352
Schott, Richard, 407, 427, 431, 435, 495
Schultz, J.E., 421, 502
Schultze, Charles, 436
Schwartz, Thomas, 7–8, 10, 309–11,
  328–33, 338–9, 404–5, 414, 417,
  432, 494, 500
  impossibility theorem of, 324–7
scope of government, 35, 40
Scott, Hugh, 263
Security and Exchange Commission (SEC),
  516
Sedgwick, Theodore, 113
Seidman, Harold, 407, 430
self-interest, 468, 473
  see also motivations
Sen, Amartya K., 329, 346
seniority, 25, 36, 86, 99, 106–11, 125,
  150, 166, 169, 192–3, 274, 291, 294
Separability condition, 332, 363–4, 368
separation of powers, 2, 88, 288, 309, 349,
  462, 477
Shannon, W. Wayne, 235
Shapiro, Michael, 16, 89
Shepsle, Kenneth A., 10, 86–7, 133,
  211–16, 221, 224, 231–2, 311–16,
  343, 371–2, 376–7, 381, 384–96,
  399, 403–4, 416, 485, 488, 499, 517
Sherill, Robert, 27
Sherman, James S., 262
simple institutional arrangement (SIA), 382
simple majority rule, 318–20, 328, 355,
  358
  see also majority rule
sincere voting, see strategies

560

Index

Index